Magus of the Library
Mitsu Izumi

Based on *Kafna of the Wind*
Written by Sophie Schwimm • Translated by Hiroto Hamada

3

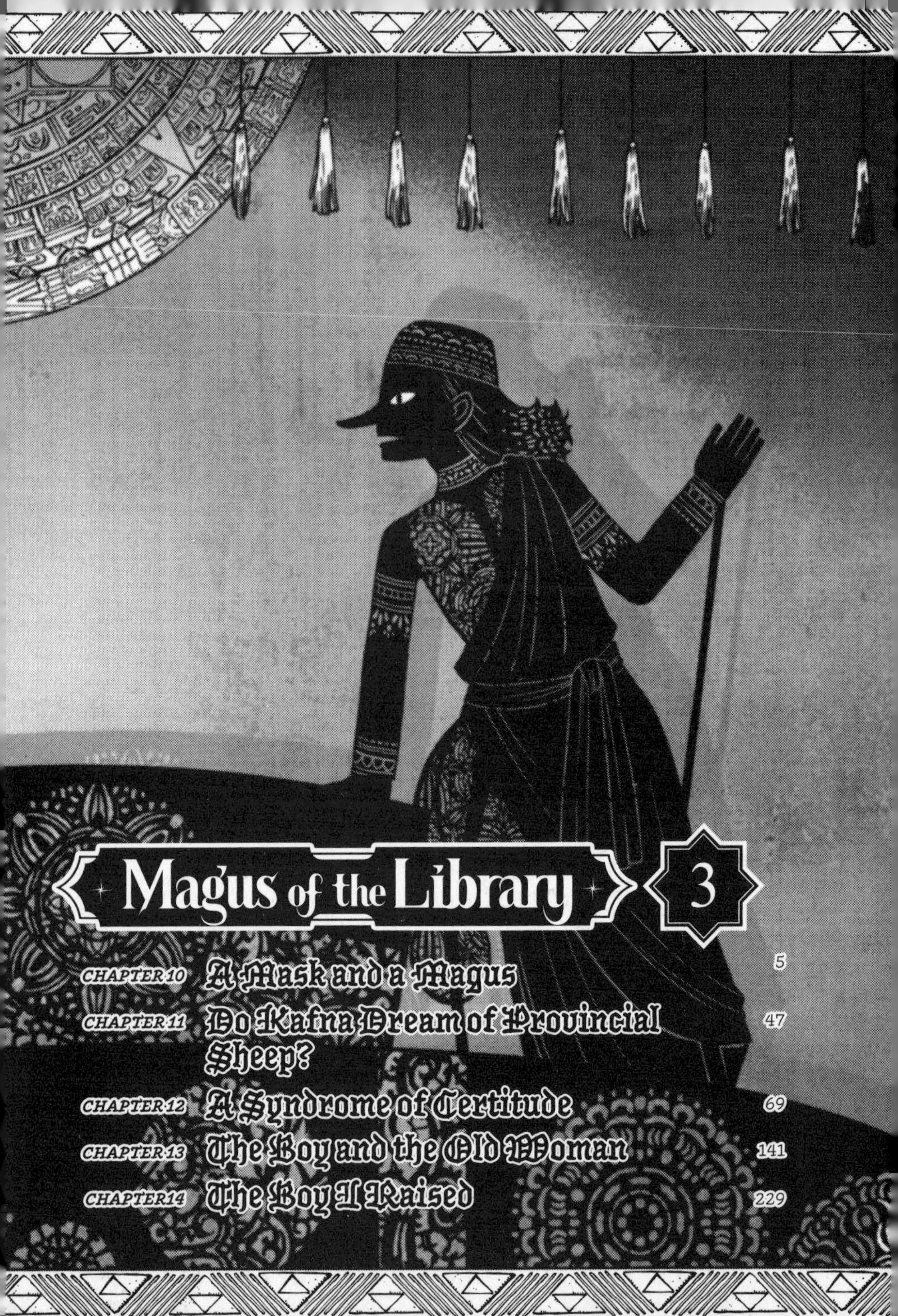

Magus of the Library 3

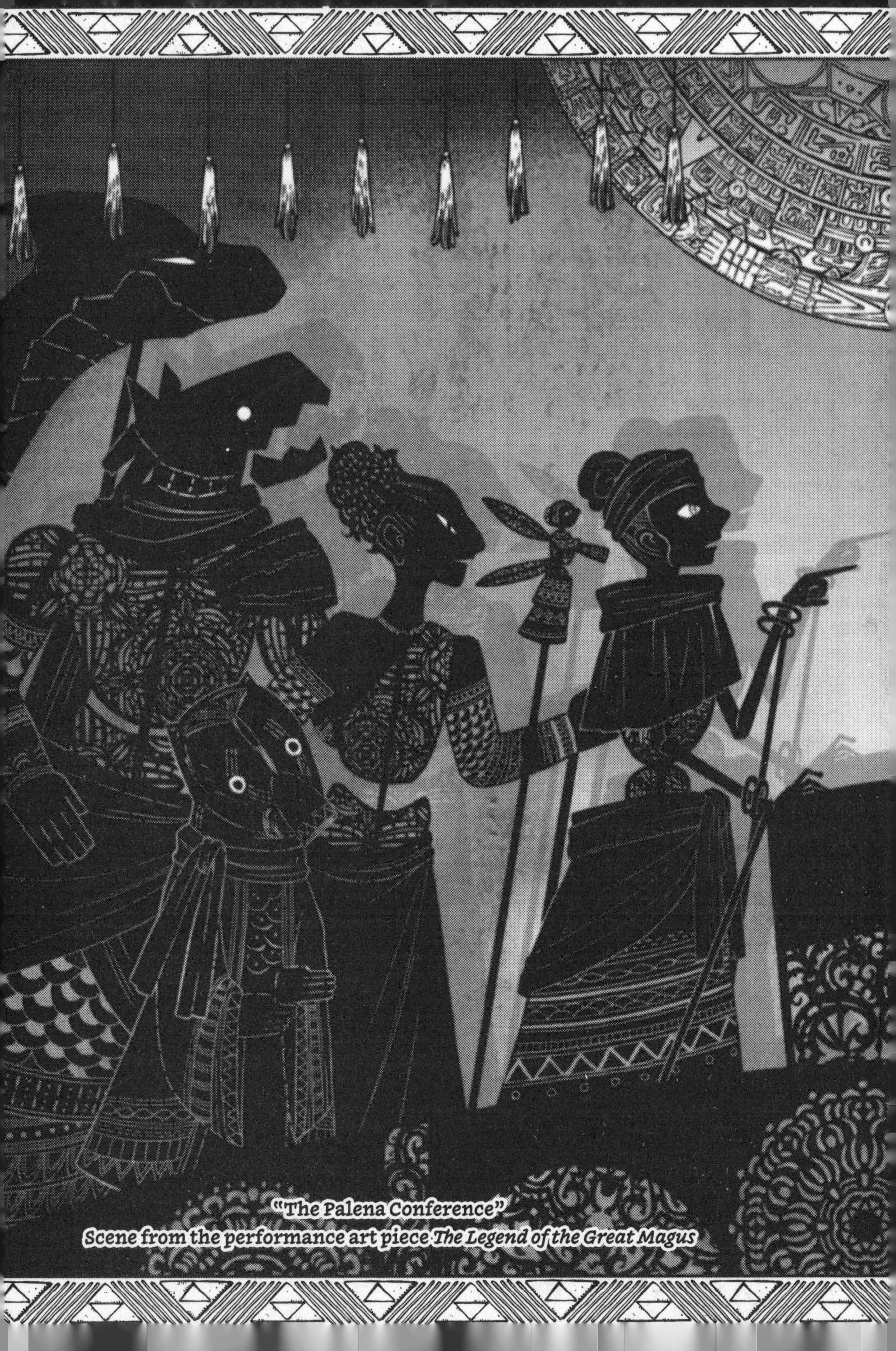

"The Palena Conference"
Scene from the performance art piece *The Legend of the Great Magus*

"To protect a text is to protect the world itself."

—Words of the One Who Did Not Return

From ***The Book with No Name***

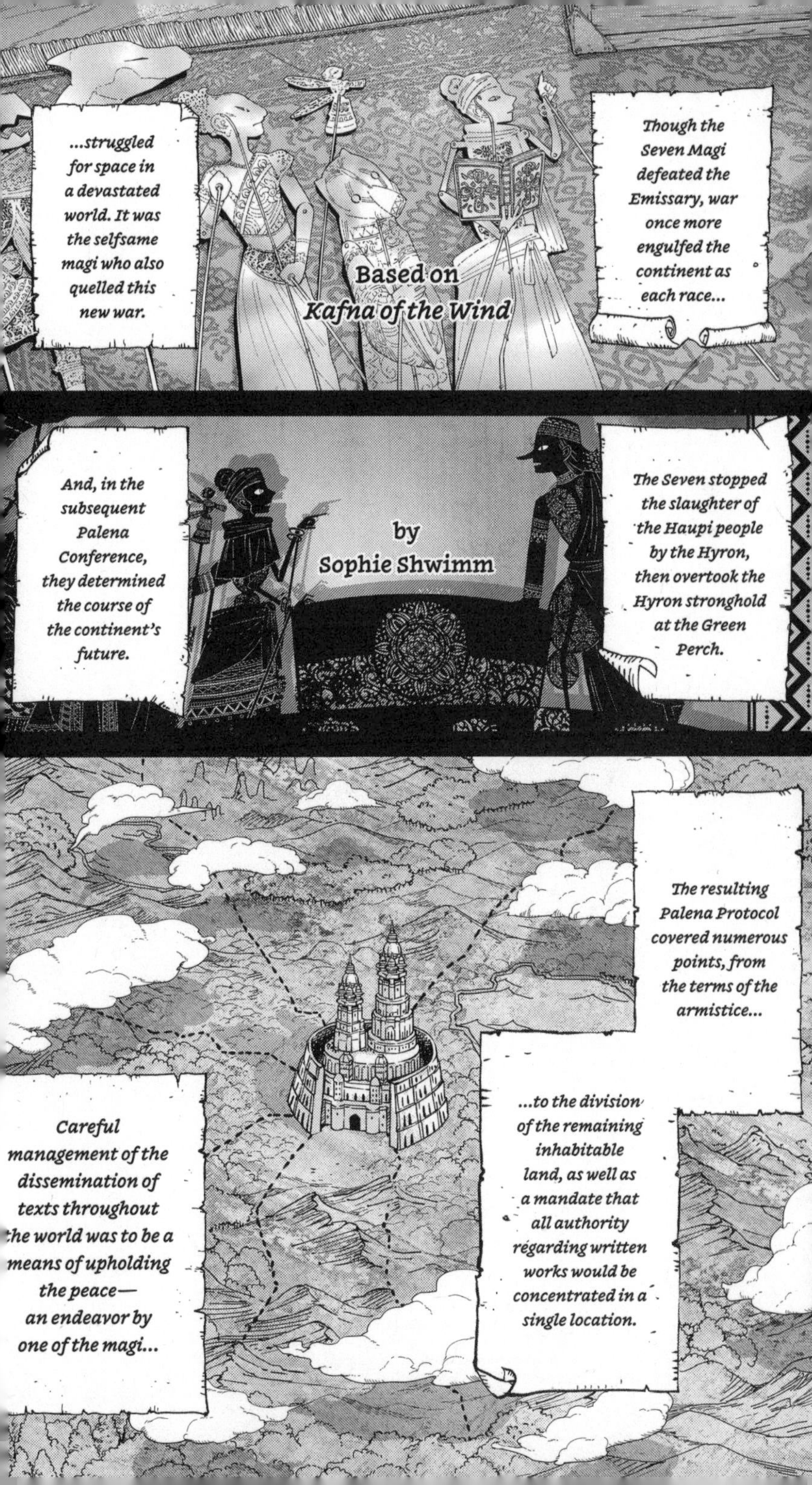
Though the Seven Magi defeated the Emissary, war once more engulfed the continent as each race...
...struggled for space in a devastated world. It was the selfsame magi who also quelled this new war.
Based on
Kafna of the Wind
The Seven stopped the slaughter of the Haupi people by the Hyron, then overtook the Hyron stronghold at the Green Perch.
by
Sophie Shwimm
And, in the subsequent Palena Conference, they determined the course of the continent's future.
The resulting Palena Protocol covered numerous points, from the terms of the armistice...
...to the division of the remaining inhabitable land, as well as a mandate that all authority regarding written works would be concentrated in a single location.
Careful management of the dissemination of texts throughout the world was to be a means of upholding the peace—an endeavor by one of the magi...

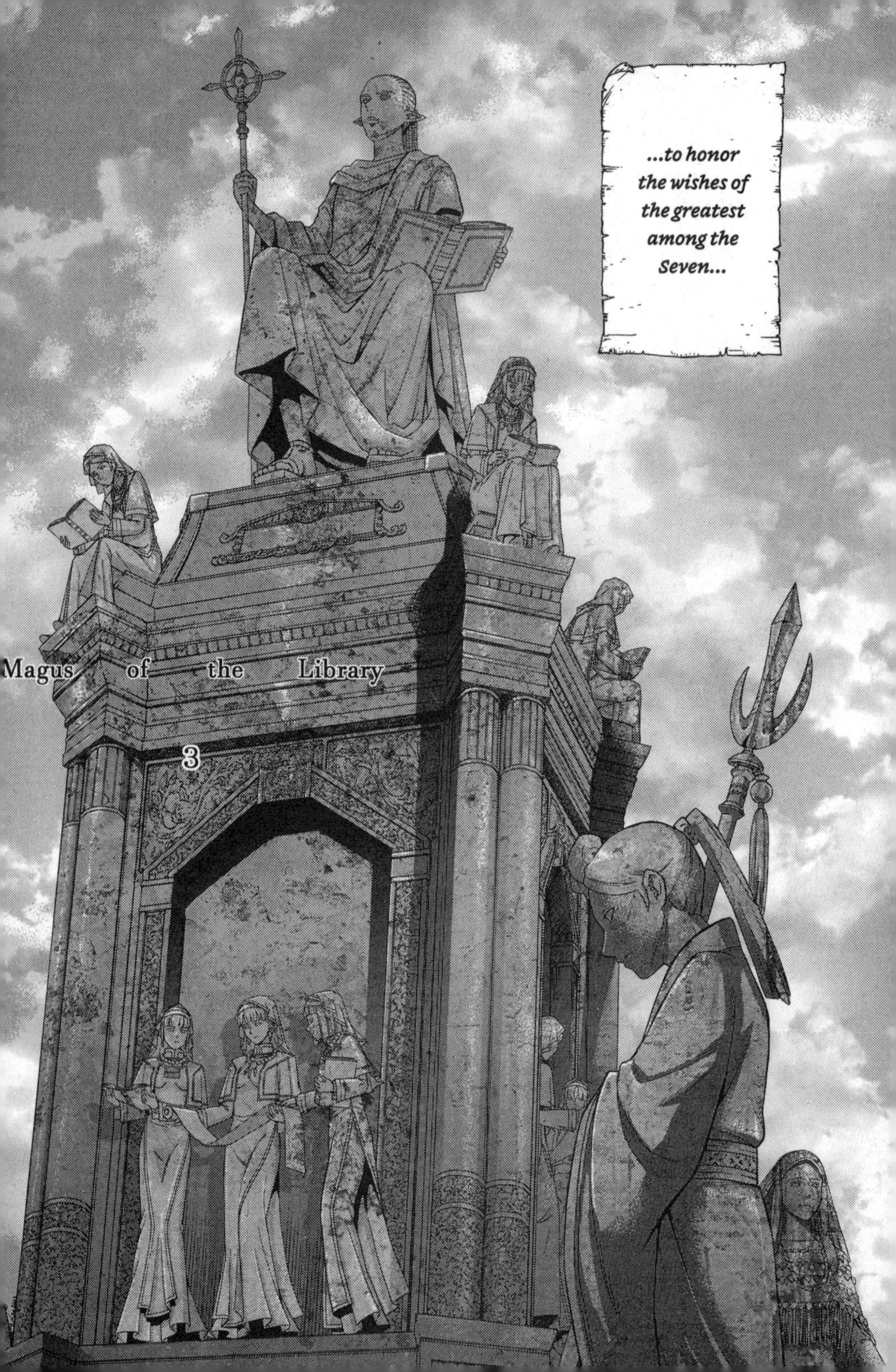

...to honor the wishes of the greatest among the Seven...
Magus of the Library
3

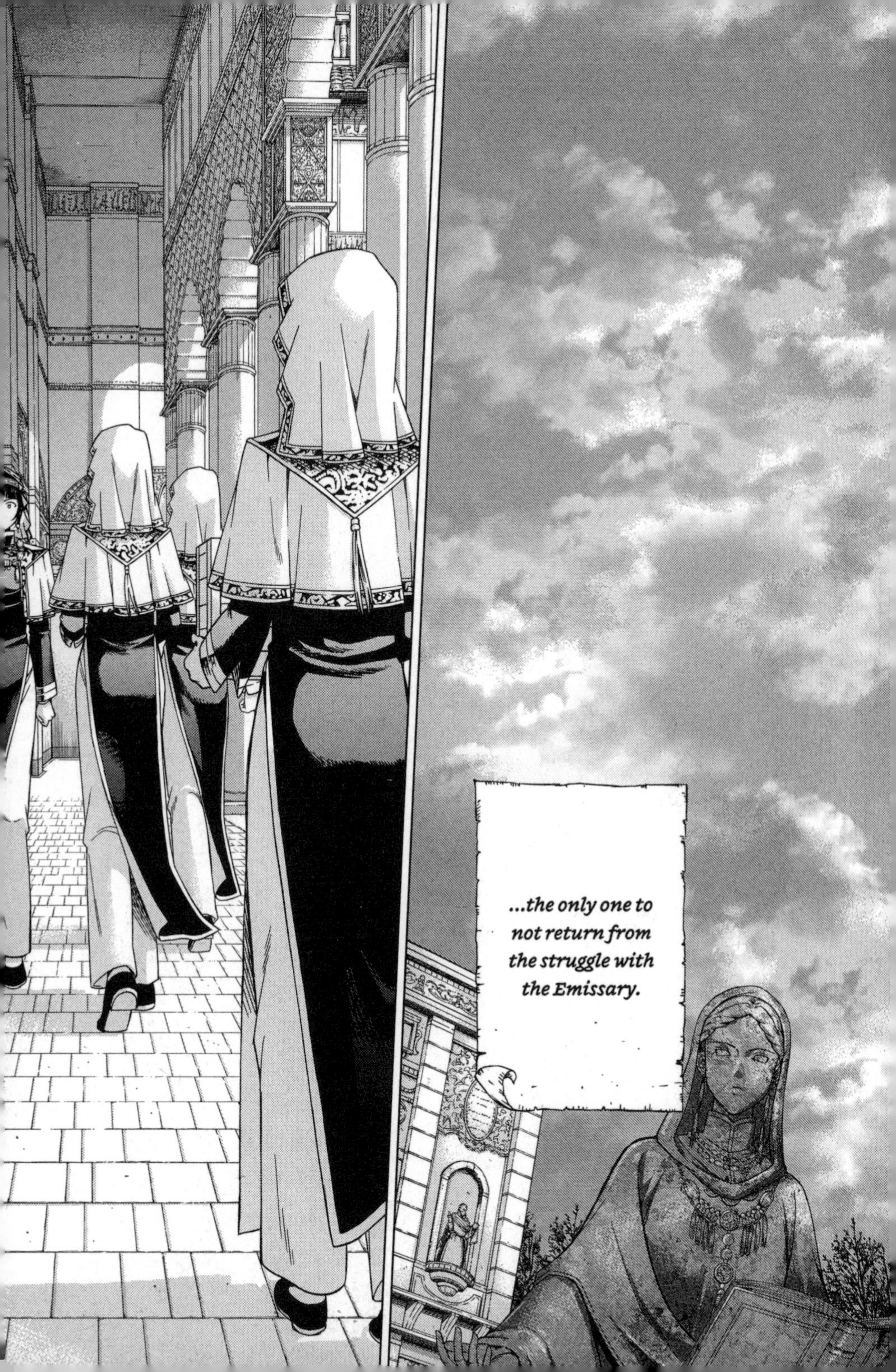
...the only one to not return from the struggle with the Emissary.

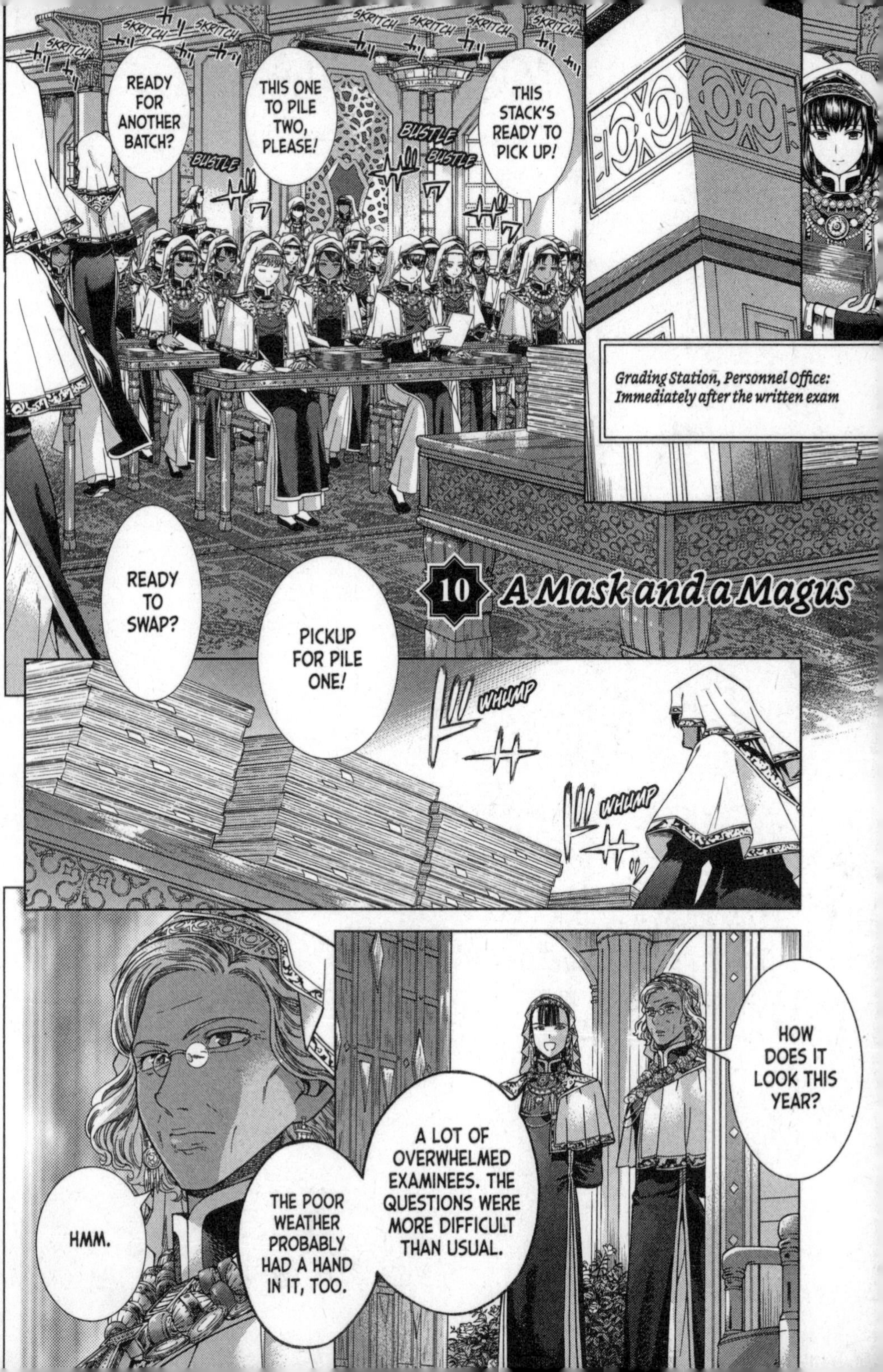
Grading Station, Personnel Office: Immediately after the written exam
10 A Mask and a Magus
SKRITCH SKRITCH SKRITCH SKRITCH SKRITCH
THIS STACK'S READY TO PICK UP!
BUSTLE BUSTLE
THIS ONE TO PILE TWO, PLEASE!
BUSTLE
READY FOR ANOTHER BATCH?
PICKUP FOR PILE ONE!
READY TO SWAP?
WHUMP
WHUMP
HOW DOES IT LOOK THIS YEAR?
A LOT OF OVERWHELMED EXAMINEES. THE QUESTIONS WERE MORE DIFFICULT THAN USUAL.
THE POOR WEATHER PROBABLY HAD A HAND IN IT, TOO.
HMM.

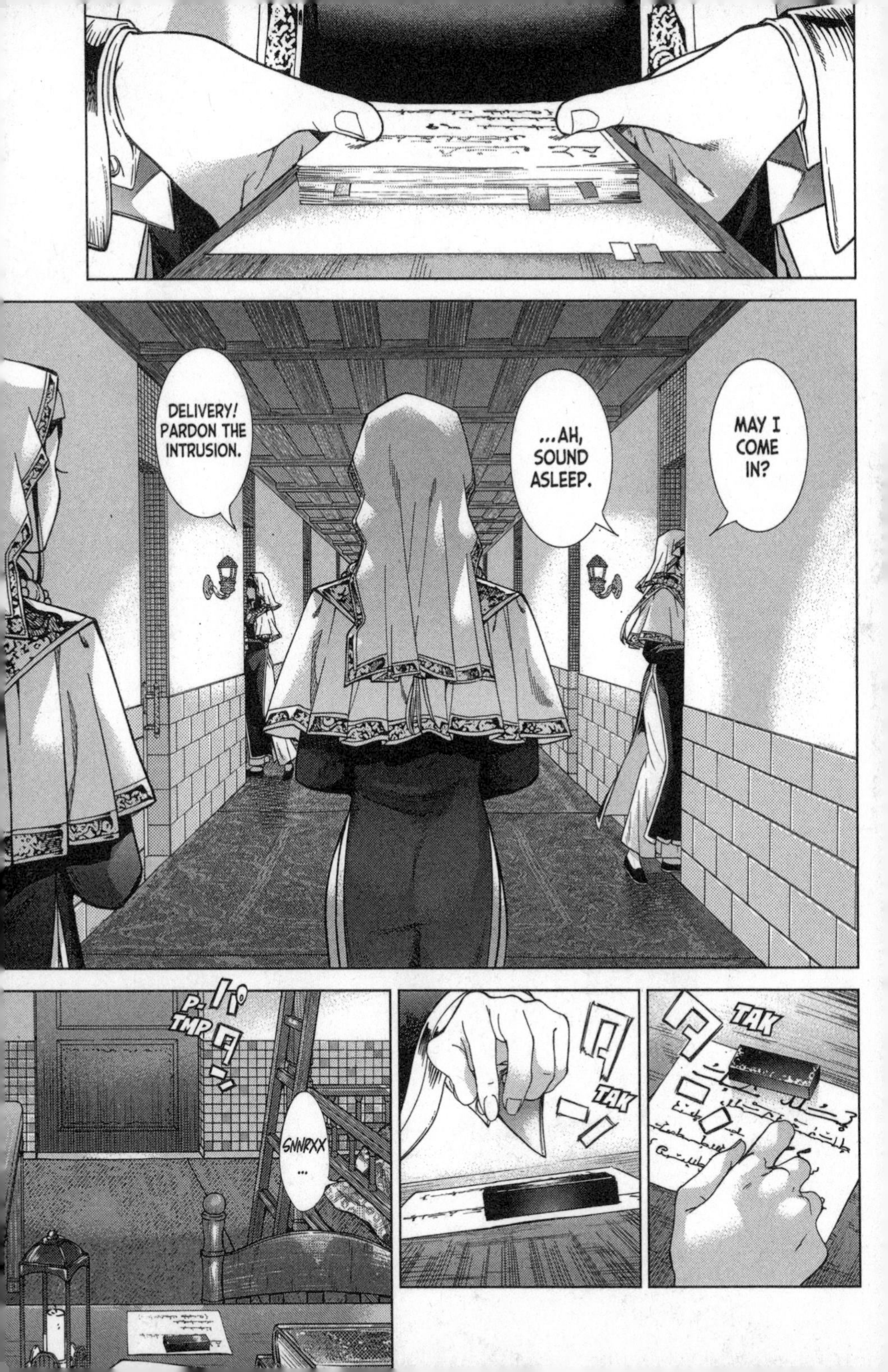
MAY I COME IN?
...AH, SOUND ASLEEP.
DELIVERY! PARDON THE INTRUSION.
TAK
TAK
P-TMP
SNNRXX ...

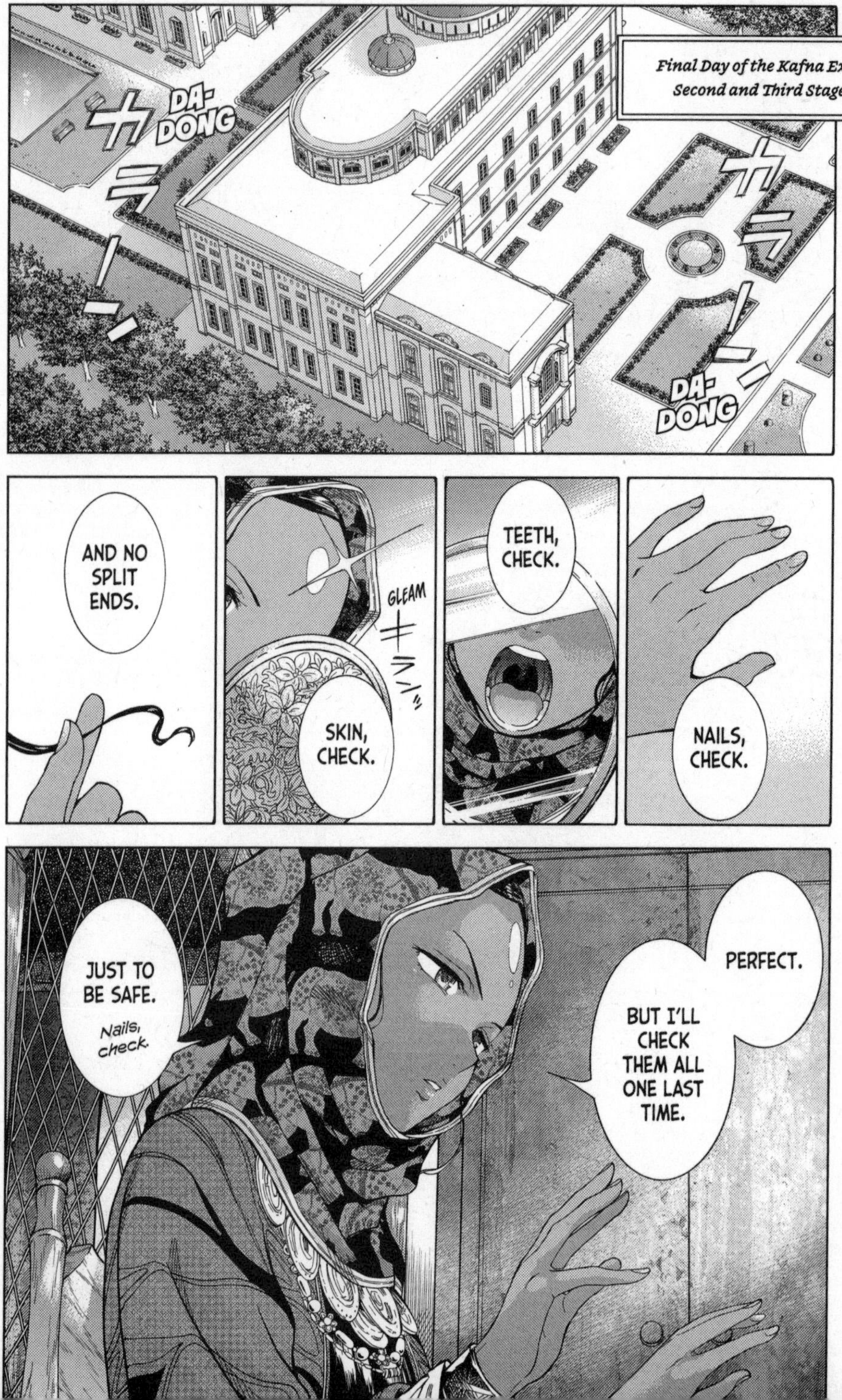
Final Day of the Kafna Exam
Second and Third Stages
DA-DONG
DA-DONG
NAILS, CHECK.
TEETH, CHECK.
GLEAM
SKIN, CHECK.
AND NO SPLIT ENDS.
PERFECT.
BUT I'LL CHECK THEM ALL ONE LAST TIME.
JUST TO BE SAFE.
Nails, check.

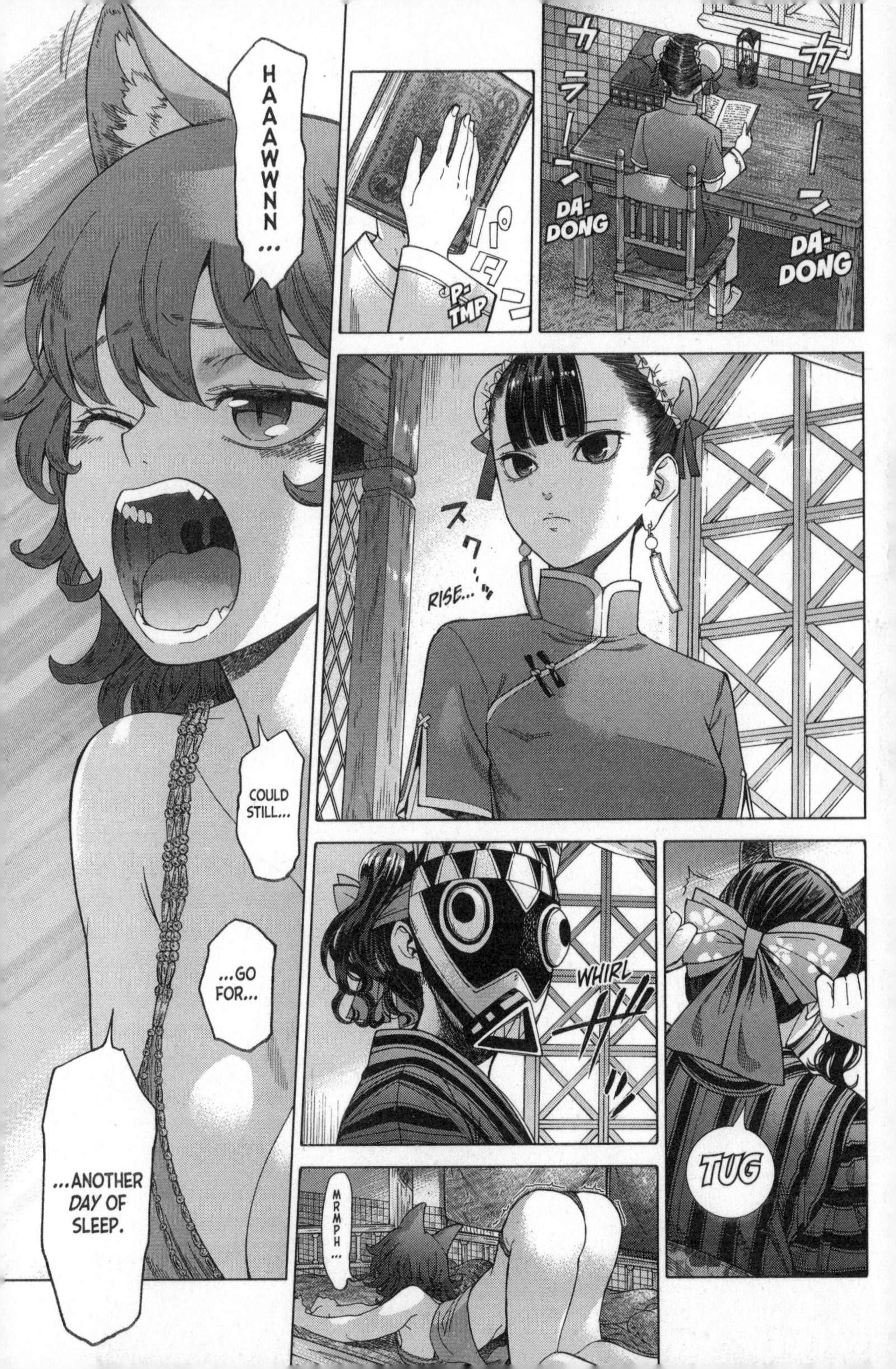

カラーン
DA-DONG
カラーン
DA-DONG
パタン
P-TMP
スク…
RISE...
TUG
WHIRL
MRMPH...
HAAAAWWNN...
COULD STILL...
...GO FOR...
...ANOTHER DAY OF SLEEP.

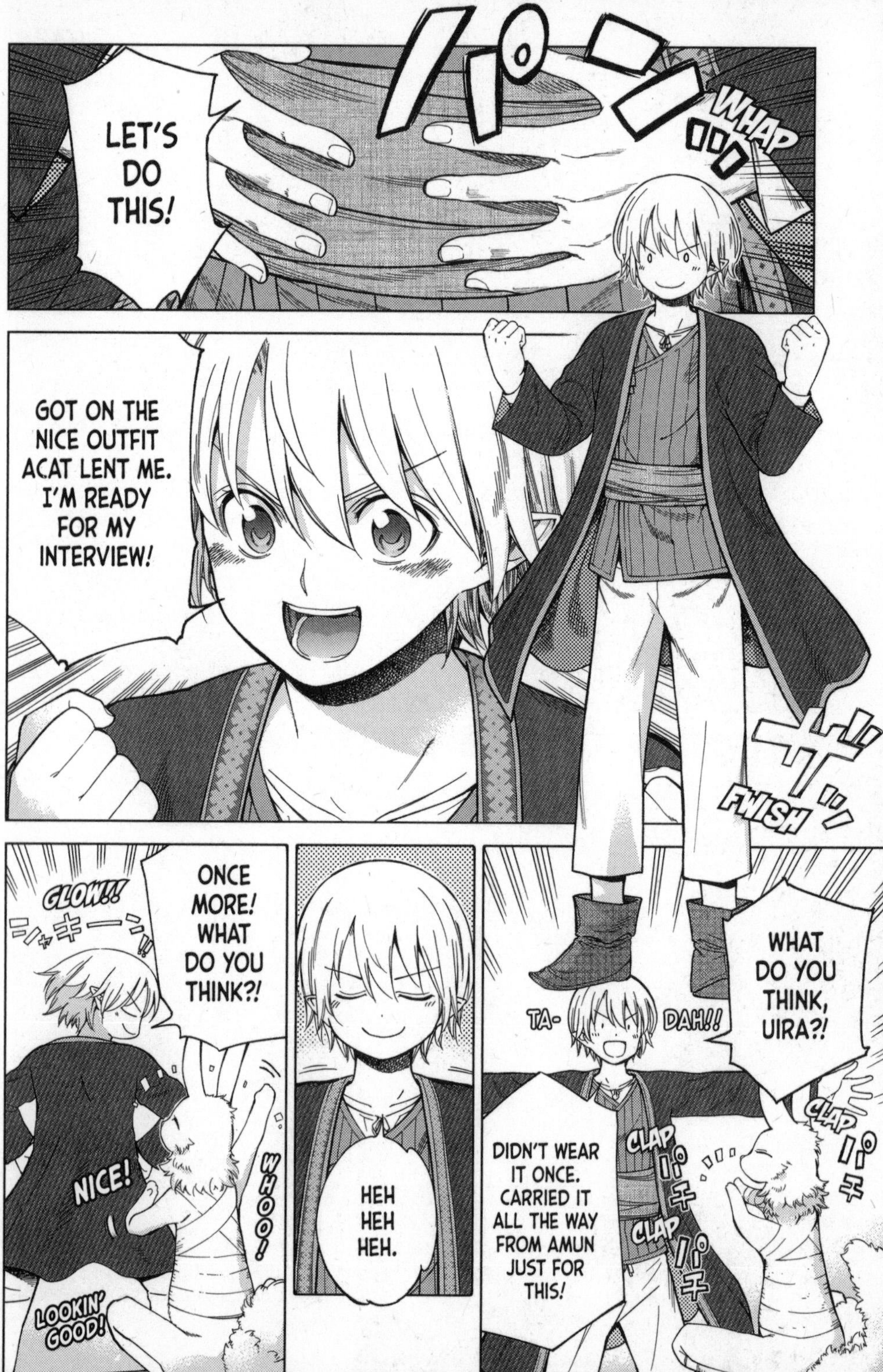
LET'S DO THIS!
パーン
WHAP
ザッ
FWISH
GOT ON THE NICE OUTFIT ACAT LENT ME. I'M READY FOR MY INTERVIEW!
WHAT DO YOU THINK, UIRA?!
TA- DAH!!
DIDN'T WEAR IT ONCE. CARRIED IT ALL THE WAY FROM AMUN JUST FOR THIS!
CLAP
CLAP
CLAP
HEH HEH HEH.
ONCE MORE! WHAT DO YOU THINK?!
GLOW!!
シャキーン!!
NICE!
WHOOO!
LOOKIN' GOOD!

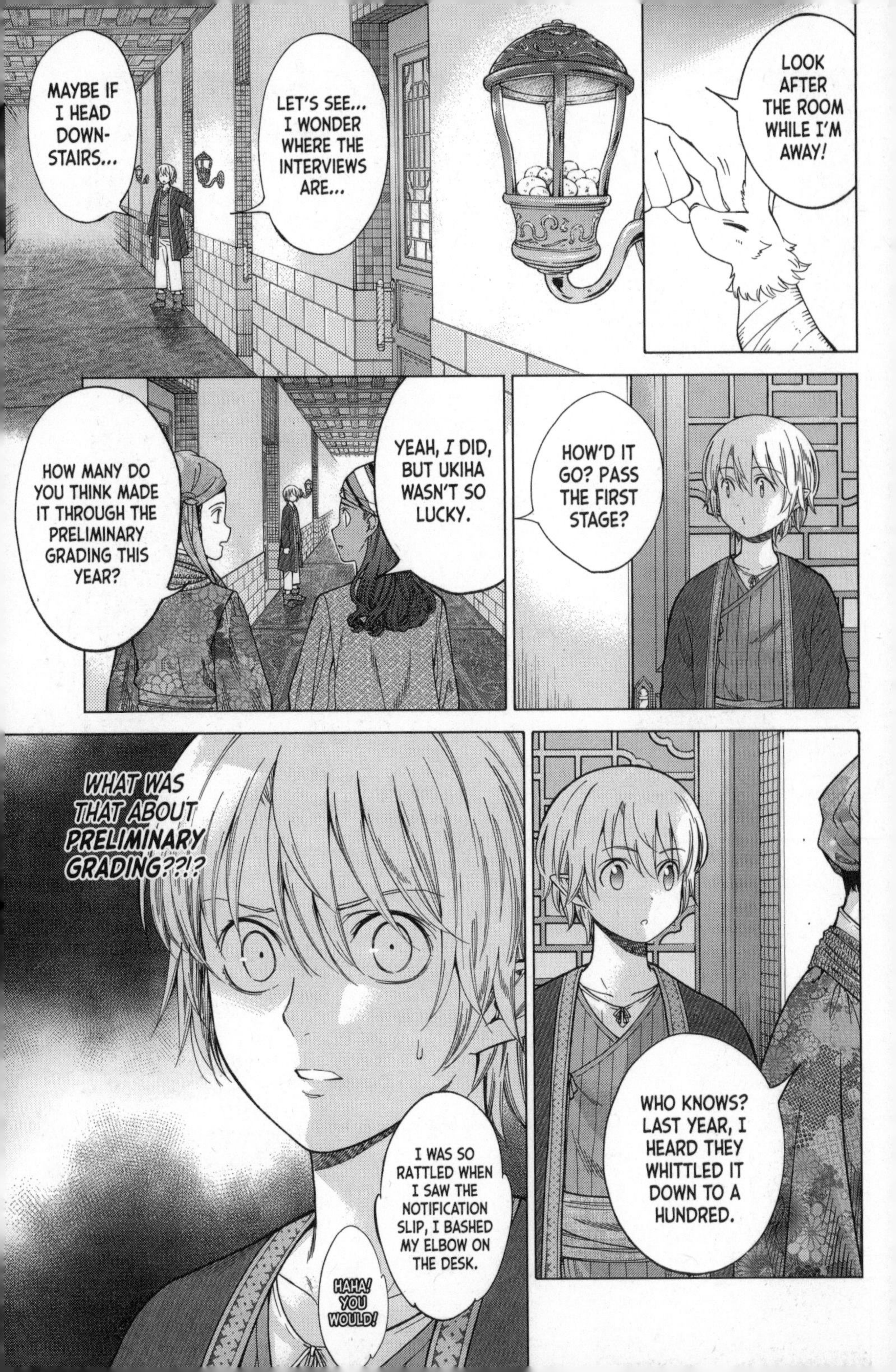
LOOK AFTER THE ROOM WHILE I'M AWAY!
LET'S SEE... I WONDER WHERE THE INTERVIEWS ARE...
MAYBE IF I HEAD DOWN-STAIRS...
HOW'D IT GO? PASS THE FIRST STAGE?
YEAH, *I* DID, BUT UKIHA WASN'T SO LUCKY.
HOW MANY DO YOU THINK MADE IT THROUGH THE PRELIMINARY GRADING THIS YEAR?
WHO KNOWS? LAST YEAR, I HEARD THEY WHITTLED IT DOWN TO A HUNDRED.
WHAT WAS THAT ABOUT PRELIMINARY GRADING??!?
I WAS SO RATTLED WHEN I SAW THE NOTIFICATION SLIP, I BASHED MY ELBOW ON THE DESK.
HAHA! YOU WOULD!

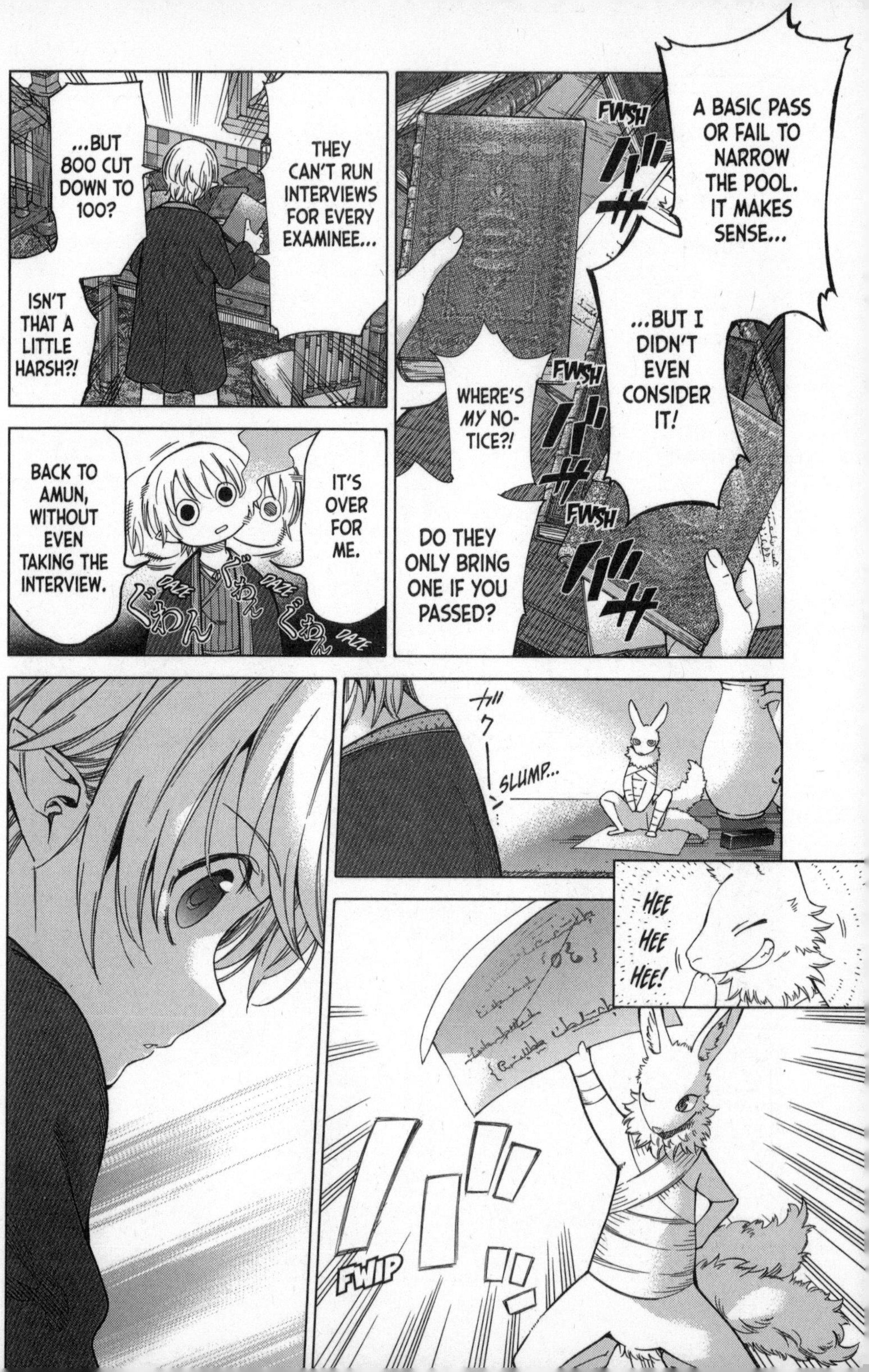

A BASIC PASS OR FAIL TO NARROW THE POOL. IT MAKES SENSE...
FWSH
...BUT I DIDN'T EVEN CONSIDER IT!
WHERE'S MY NO-TICE?!
FWSH
FWSH
DO THEY ONLY BRING ONE IF YOU PASSED?
THEY CAN'T RUN INTERVIEWS FOR EVERY EXAMINEE...
...BUT 800 CUT DOWN TO 100?
ISN'T THAT A LITTLE HARSH?!
IT'S OVER FOR ME.
BACK TO AMUN, WITHOUT EVEN TAKING THE INTERVIEW.
DAZE
DAZE
DAZE
SLUMP...
HEE HEE HEE!
FWIP

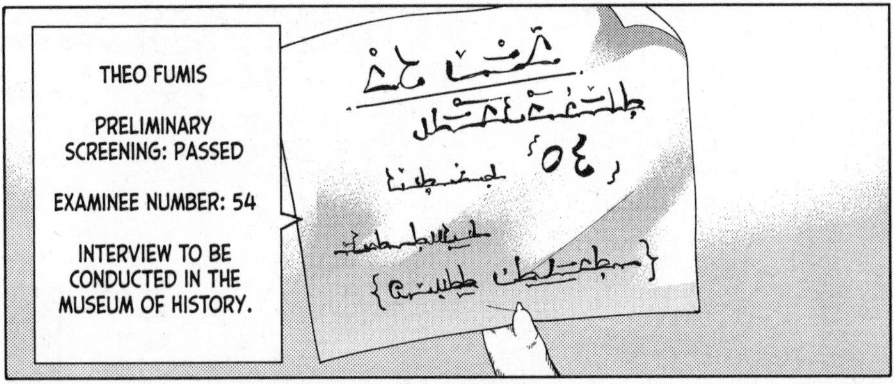
THEO FUMIS
PRELIMINARY SCREENING: PASSED
EXAMINEE NUMBER: 54
INTERVIEW TO BE CONDUCTED IN THE MUSEUM OF HISTORY.

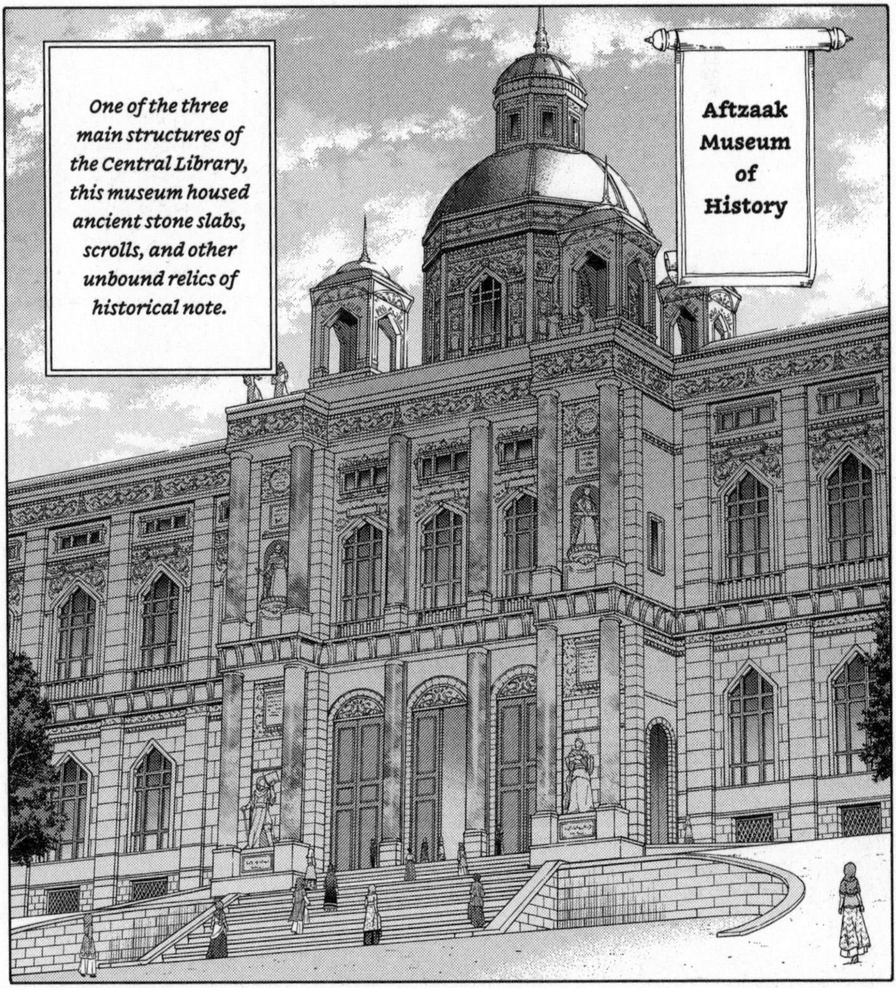
Aftzaak Museum of History
One of the three main structures of the Central Library, this museum housed ancient stone slabs, scrolls, and other unbound relics of historical note.

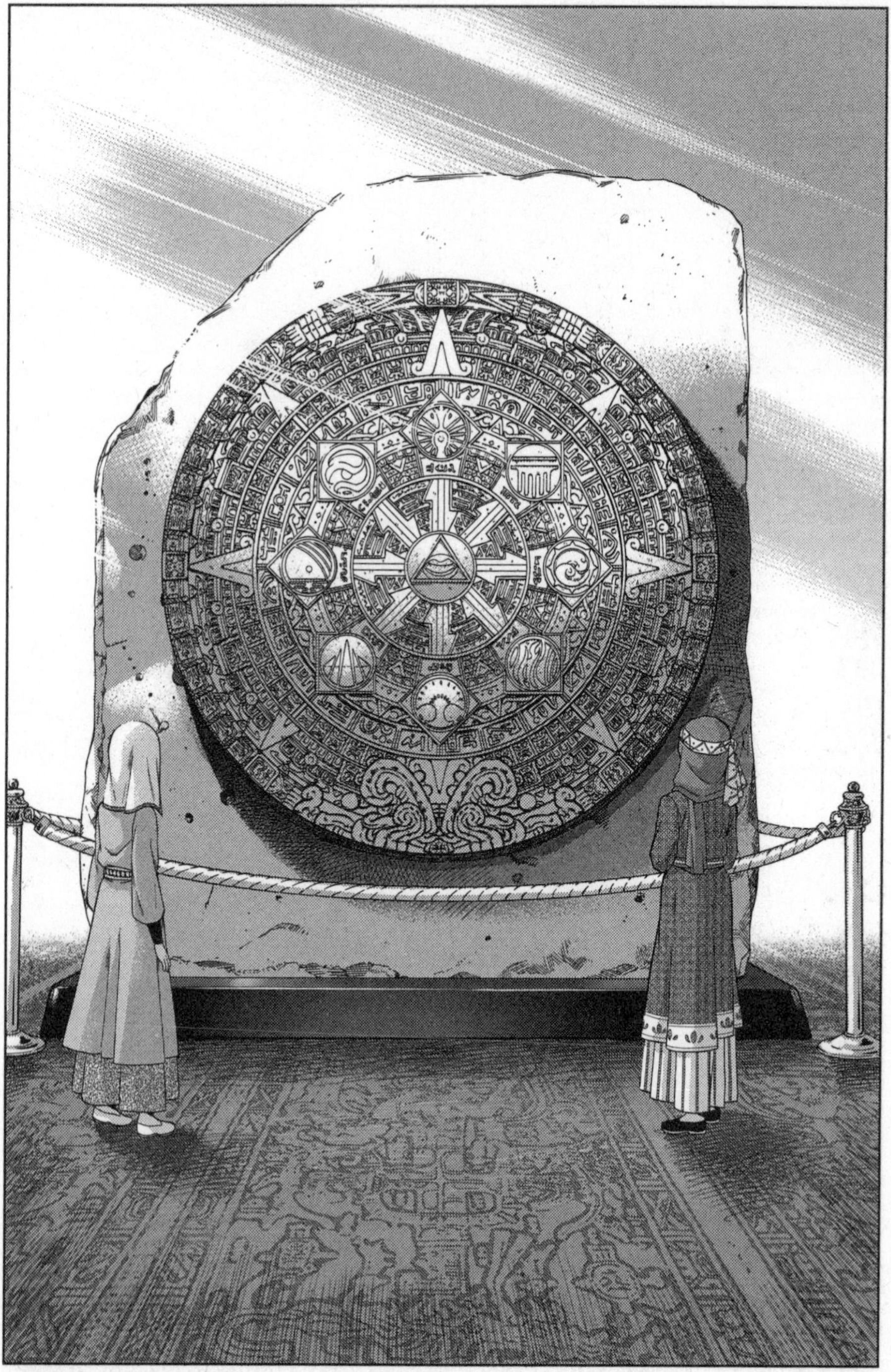

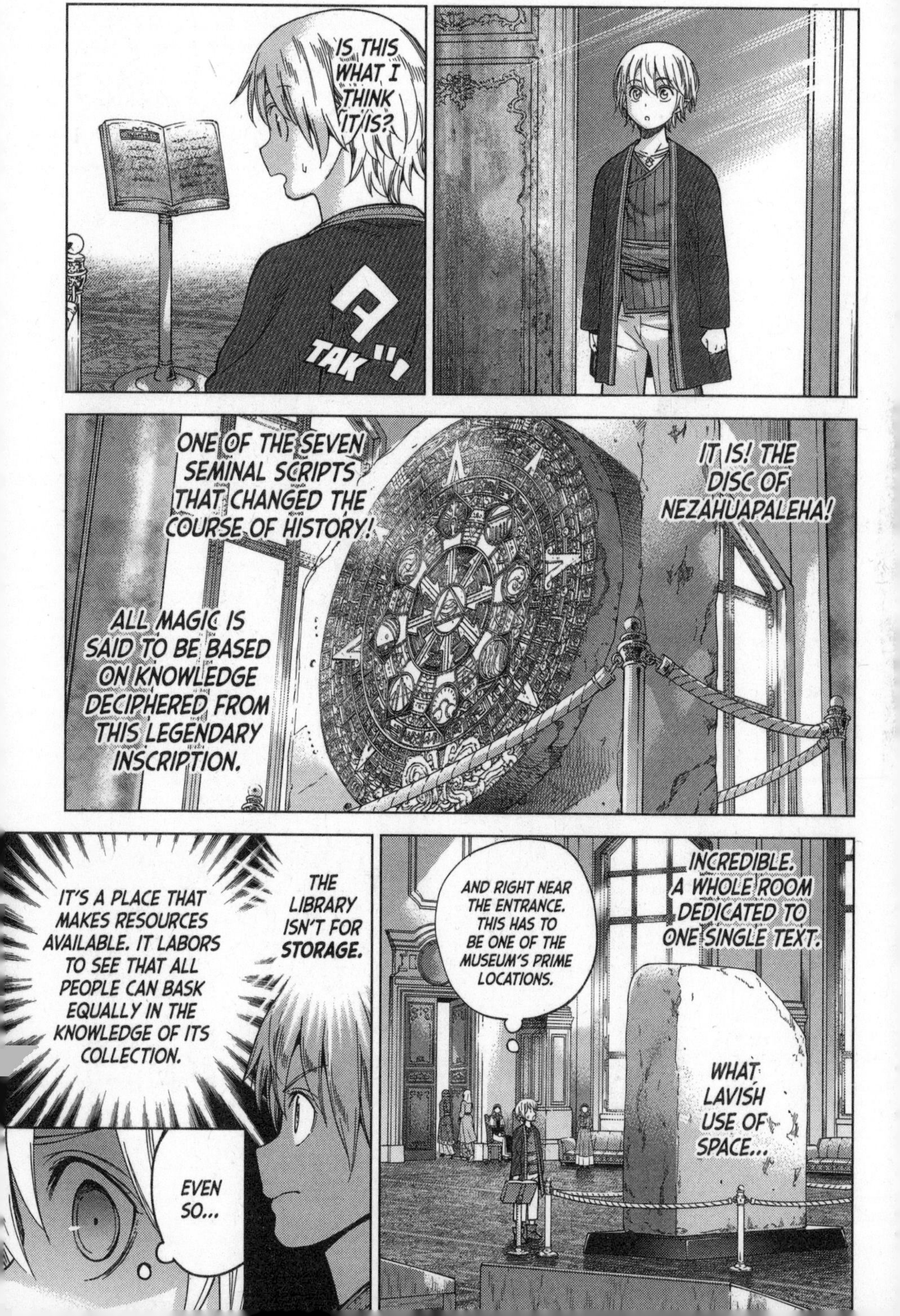
IS THIS WHAT I THINK IT IS?
TAK
IT IS! THE DISC OF NEZAHUAPALEHA!
ONE OF THE SEVEN SEMINAL SCRIPTS THAT CHANGED THE COURSE OF HISTORY!
ALL MAGIC IS SAID TO BE BASED ON KNOWLEDGE DECIPHERED FROM THIS LEGENDARY INSCRIPTION.
INCREDIBLE. A WHOLE ROOM DEDICATED TO ONE SINGLE TEXT.
AND RIGHT NEAR THE ENTRANCE. THIS HAS TO BE ONE OF THE MUSEUM'S PRIME LOCATIONS.
WHAT LAVISH USE OF SPACE...
THE LIBRARY ISN'T FOR STORAGE.
IT'S A PLACE THAT MAKES RESOURCES AVAILABLE. IT LABORS TO SEE THAT ALL PEOPLE CAN BASK EQUALLY IN THE KNOWLEDGE OF ITS COLLECTION.
EVEN SO...

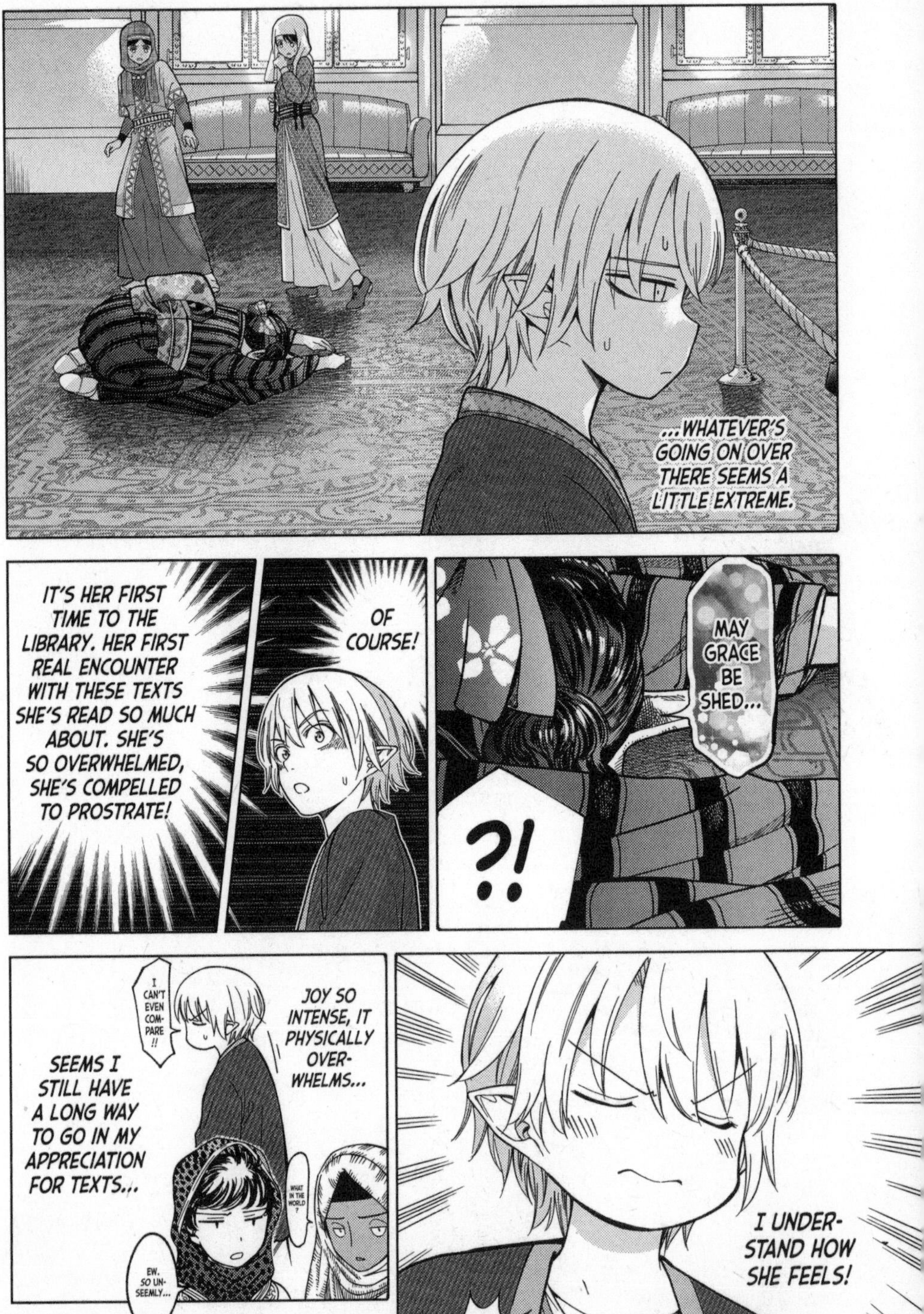
...WHATEVER'S GOING ON OVER THERE SEEMS A LITTLE EXTREME.
MAY GRACE BE SHED...
?!
OF COURSE!
IT'S HER FIRST TIME TO THE LIBRARY. HER FIRST REAL ENCOUNTER WITH THESE TEXTS SHE'S READ SO MUCH ABOUT. SHE'S SO OVERWHELMED, SHE'S COMPELLED TO PROSTRATE!
I UNDER-STAND HOW SHE FEELS!
JOY SO INTENSE, IT PHYSICALLY OVER-WHELMS...
I CAN'T EVEN COMPARE !!
SEEMS I STILL HAVE A LONG WAY TO GO IN MY APPRECIATION FOR TEXTS...
WHAT IN THE WORLD?
EW. SO UNSEEMLY...

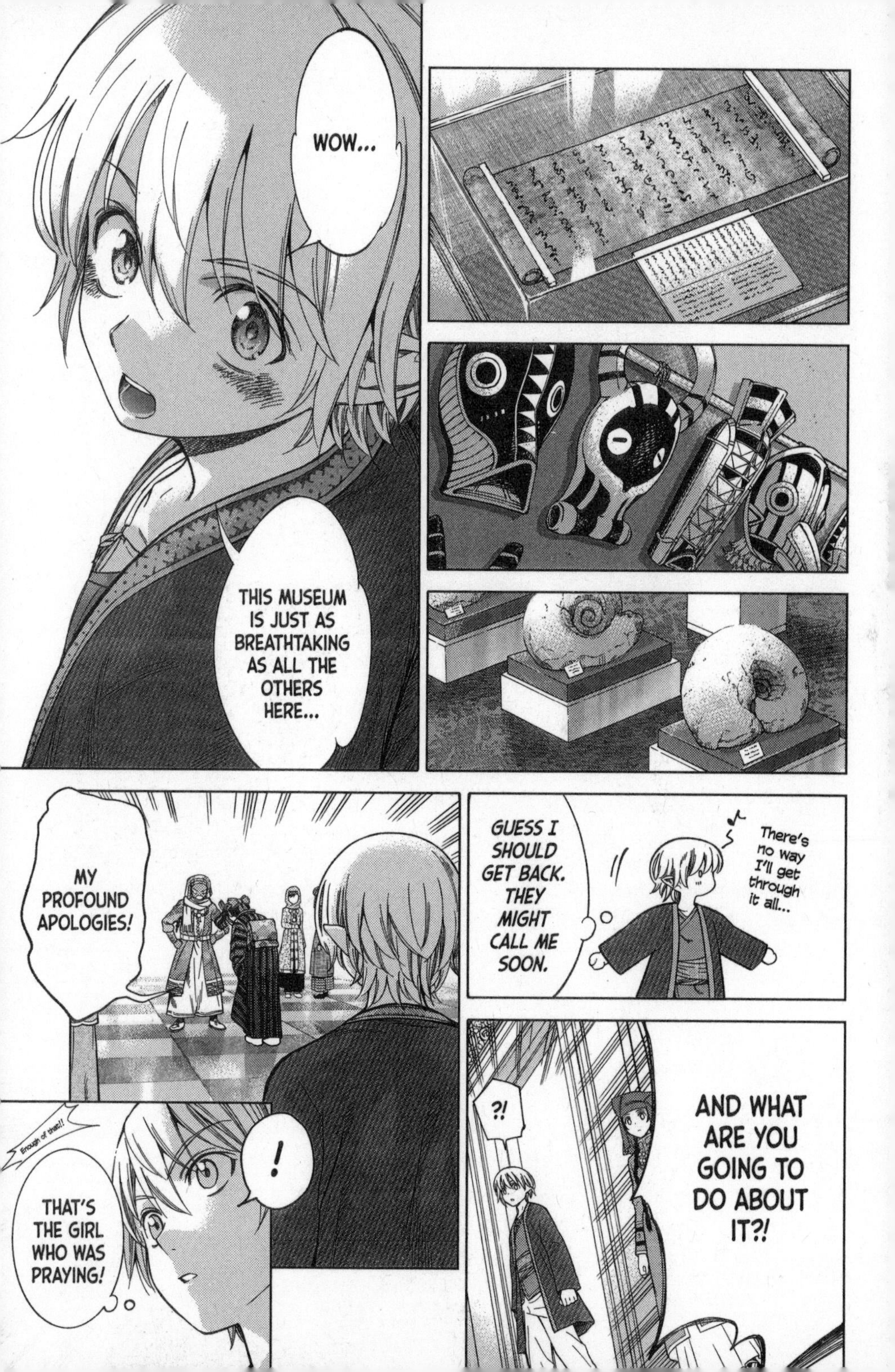
WOW...
THIS MUSEUM IS JUST AS BREATHTAKING AS ALL THE OTHERS HERE...
There's no way I'll get through it all...
GUESS I SHOULD GET BACK. THEY MIGHT CALL ME SOON.
MY PROFOUND APOLOGIES!
AND WHAT ARE YOU GOING TO DO ABOUT IT?!
?!
!
Enough of that!!
THAT'S THE GIRL WHO WAS PRAYING!

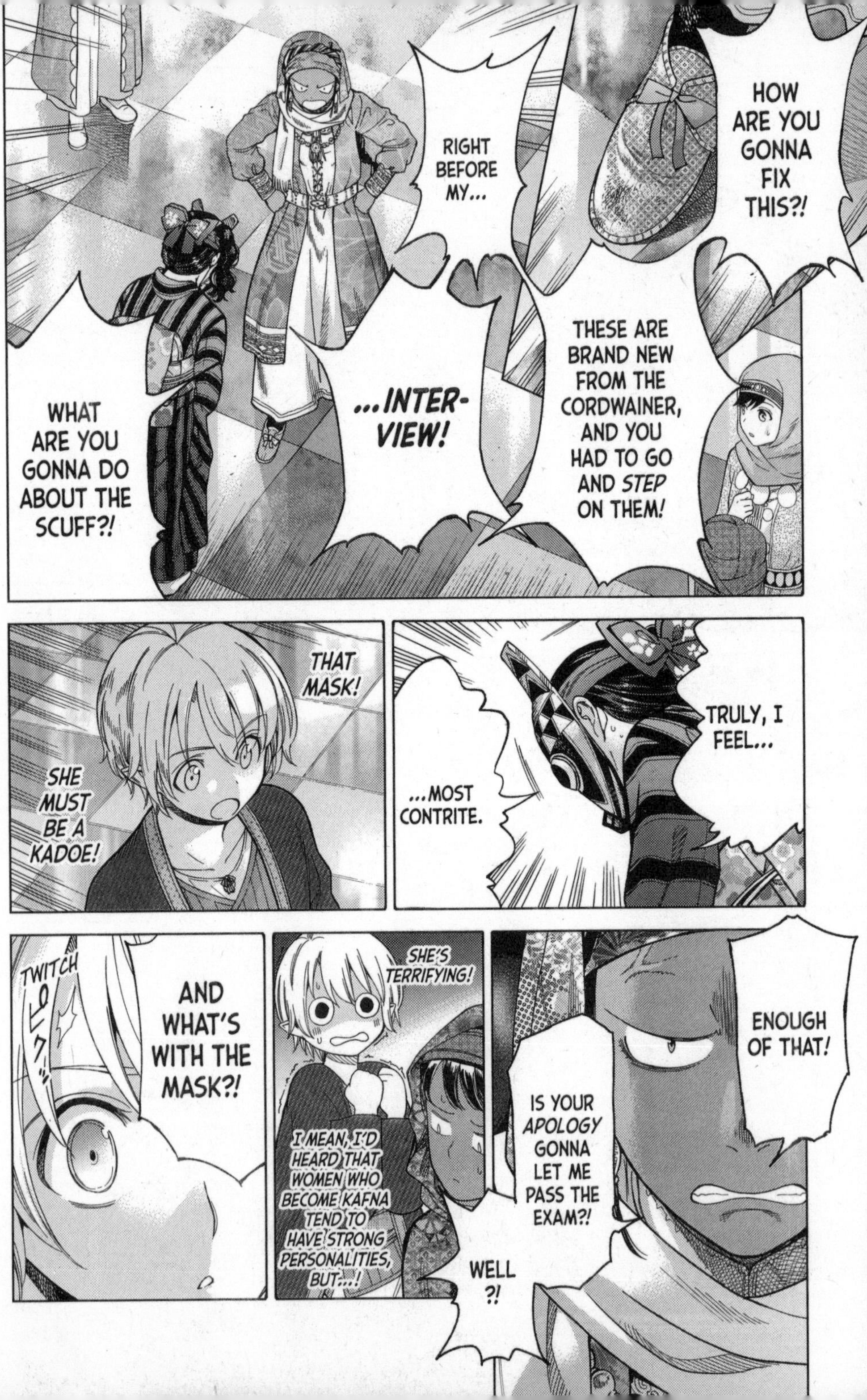
HOW ARE YOU GONNA FIX THIS?!
RIGHT BEFORE MY...
...INTER-VIEW!
THESE ARE BRAND NEW FROM THE CORDWAINER, AND YOU HAD TO GO AND *STEP* ON THEM!
WHAT ARE YOU GONNA DO ABOUT THE SCUFF?!
TRULY, I FEEL...
...MOST CONTRITE.
THAT MASK!
SHE MUST BE A KADOE!
ENOUGH OF THAT!
IS YOUR *APOLOGY* GONNA LET ME PASS THE EXAM?!
WELL ?!
SHE'S TERRIFYING!
I MEAN, I'D HEARD THAT WOMEN WHO BECOME KAFNA TEND TO HAVE STRONG PERSONALITIES, BUT...!
AND WHAT'S WITH THE MASK?!
TWITCH

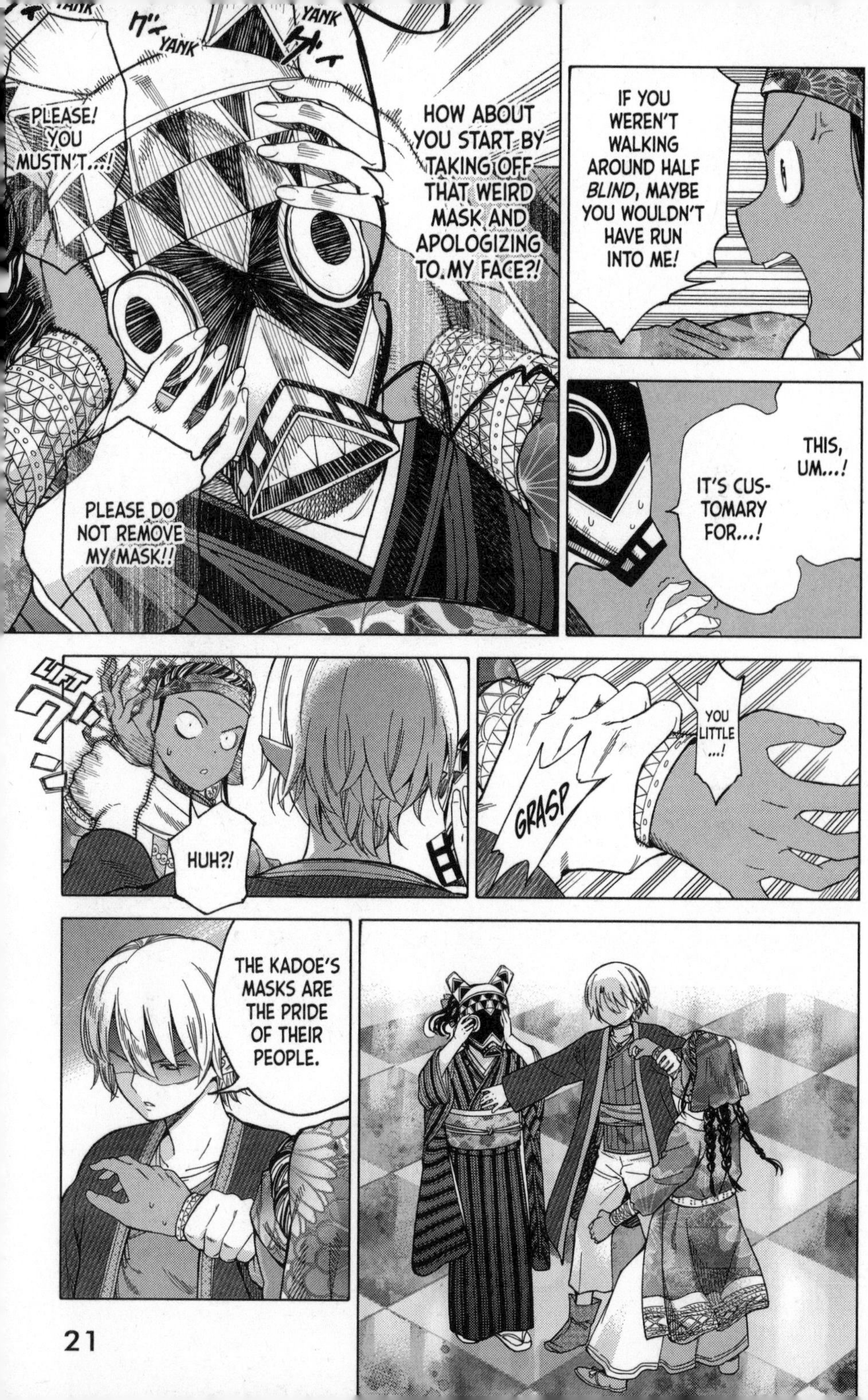
IF YOU WEREN'T WALKING AROUND HALF *BLIND*, MAYBE YOU WOULDN'T HAVE RUN INTO ME!
THIS, UM...!
IT'S CUS-TOMARY FOR...!
YANK
YANK
YANK
HOW ABOUT YOU START BY TAKING OFF THAT WEIRD MASK AND APOLOGIZING TO MY FACE?!
PLEASE! YOU MUSTN'T...!
PLEASE DO NOT REMOVE MY MASK!!
YOU LITTLE ...!
GRASP
LIFT
HUH?!
THE KADOE'S MASKS ARE THE PRIDE OF THEIR PEOPLE.

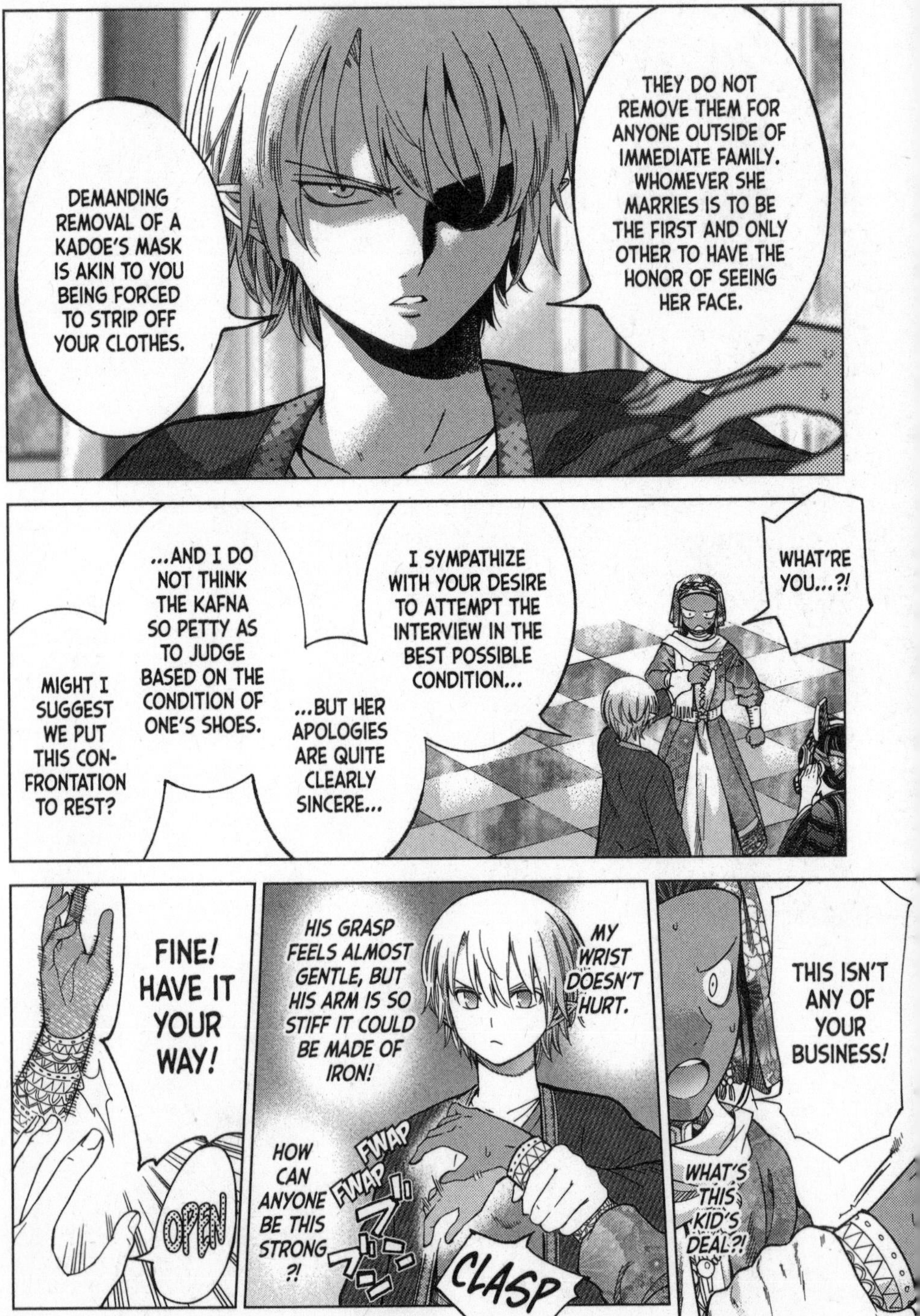
THEY DO NOT REMOVE THEM FOR ANYONE OUTSIDE OF IMMEDIATE FAMILY. WHOMEVER SHE MARRIES IS TO BE THE FIRST AND ONLY OTHER TO HAVE THE HONOR OF SEEING HER FACE.
DEMANDING REMOVAL OF A KADOE'S MASK IS AKIN TO YOU BEING FORCED TO STRIP OFF YOUR CLOTHES.
WHAT'RE YOU...?!
I SYMPATHIZE WITH YOUR DESIRE TO ATTEMPT THE INTERVIEW IN THE BEST POSSIBLE CONDITION...
...BUT HER APOLOGIES ARE QUITE CLEARLY SINCERE...
...AND I DO NOT THINK THE KAFNA SO PETTY AS TO JUDGE BASED ON THE CONDITION OF ONE'S SHOES.
MIGHT I SUGGEST WE PUT THIS CON-FRONTATION TO REST?
THIS ISN'T ANY OF YOUR BUSINESS!
WHAT'S THIS KID'S DEAL?!
MY WRIST DOESN'T HURT.
HIS GRASP FEELS ALMOST GENTLE, BUT HIS ARM IS SO STIFF IT COULD BE MADE OF IRON!
FWAP FWAP
HOW CAN ANYONE BE THIS STRONG?!
CLASP
FINE! HAVE IT YOUR WAY!
OPEN

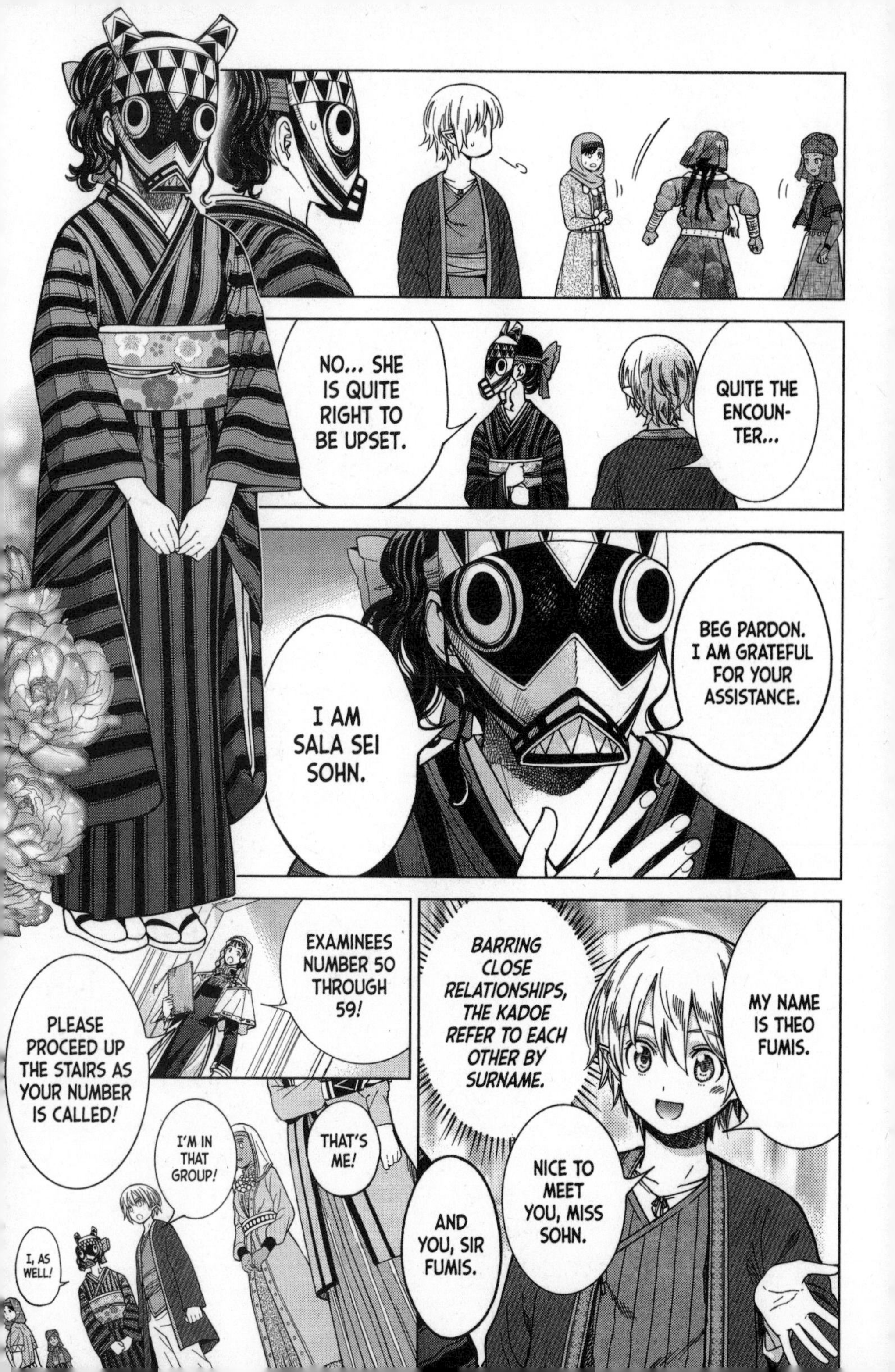
QUITE THE ENCOUN-TER...
NO... SHE IS QUITE RIGHT TO BE UPSET.
BEG PARDON. I AM GRATEFUL FOR YOUR ASSISTANCE.
I AM SALA SEI SOHN.
MY NAME IS THEO FUMIS.
BARRING CLOSE RELATIONSHIPS, THE KADOE REFER TO EACH OTHER BY SURNAME.
NICE TO MEET YOU, MISS SOHN.
AND YOU, SIR FUMIS.
EXAMINEES NUMBER 50 THROUGH 59!
PLEASE PROCEED UP THE STAIRS AS YOUR NUMBER IS CALLED!
THAT'S ME!
I'M IN THAT GROUP!
I, AS WELL!

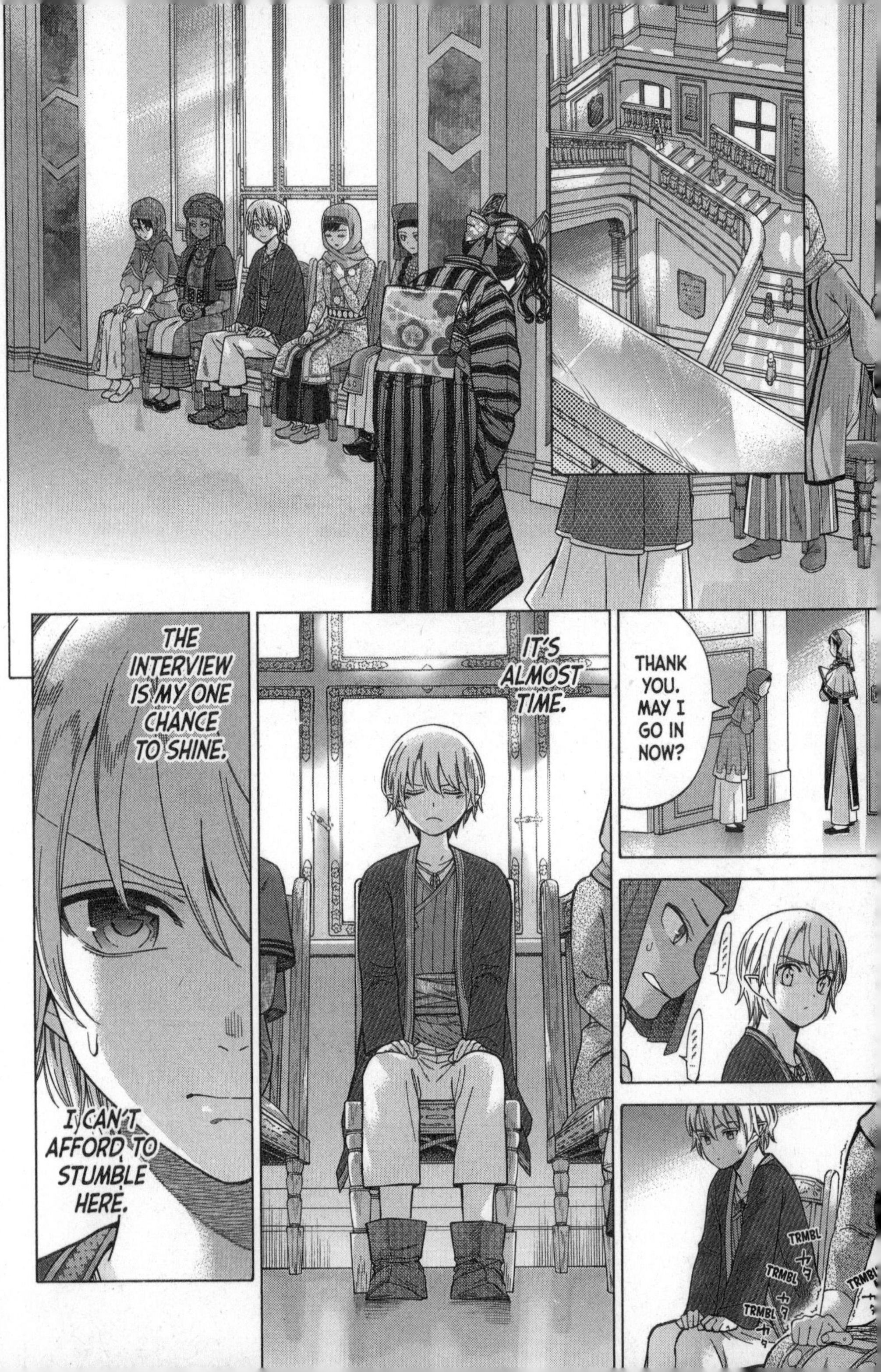
THANK YOU. MAY I GO IN NOW?
...
...
TRMBL
TRMBL
TRMBL
TRMBL
IT'S ALMOST TIME.
THE INTERVIEW IS MY ONE CHANCE TO SHINE.
I CAN'T AFFORD TO STUMBLE HERE.

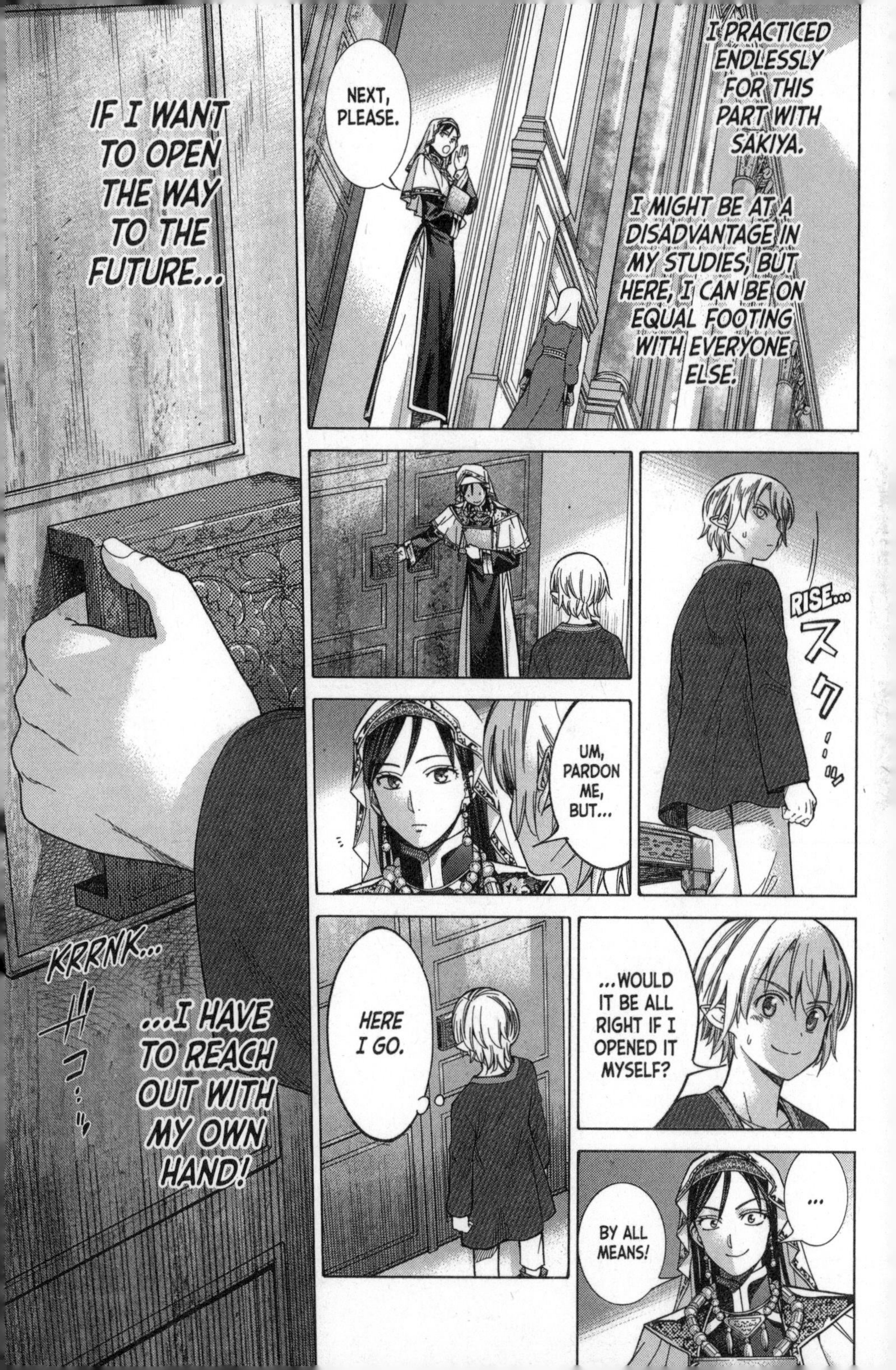
I PRACTICED ENDLESSLY FOR THIS PART WITH SAKIYA.
I MIGHT BE AT A DISADVANTAGE IN MY STUDIES, BUT HERE, I CAN BE ON EQUAL FOOTING WITH EVERYONE ELSE.
NEXT, PLEASE.
RISE...
スク…
UM, PARDON ME, BUT...
...WOULD IT BE ALL RIGHT IF I OPENED IT MYSELF?
...
BY ALL MEANS!
HERE I GO.
IF I WANT TO OPEN THE WAY TO THE FUTURE...
KRRNK...
ガコ…
...I HAVE TO REACH OUT WITH MY OWN HAND!

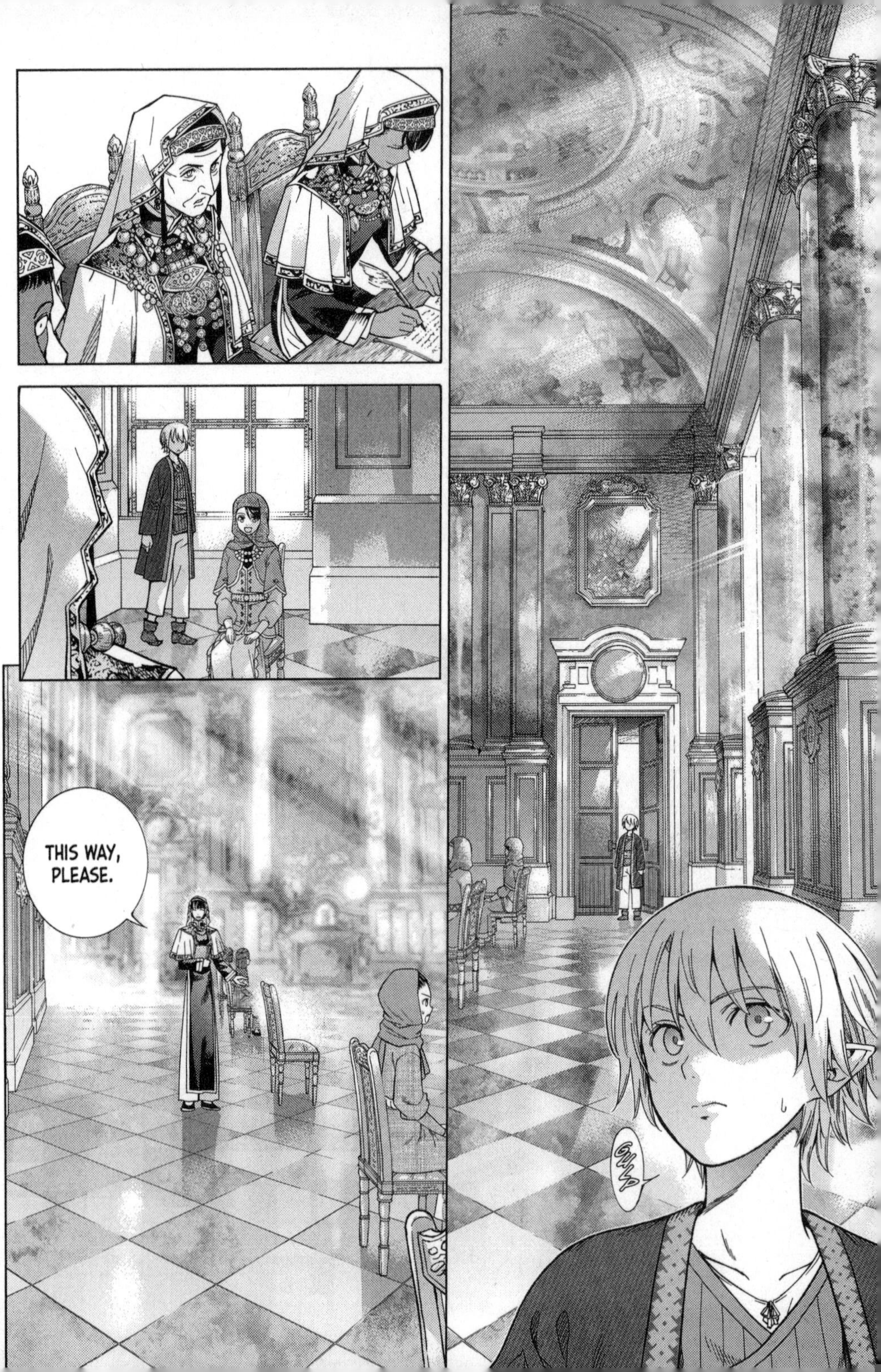
GULP
THIS WAY, PLEASE.

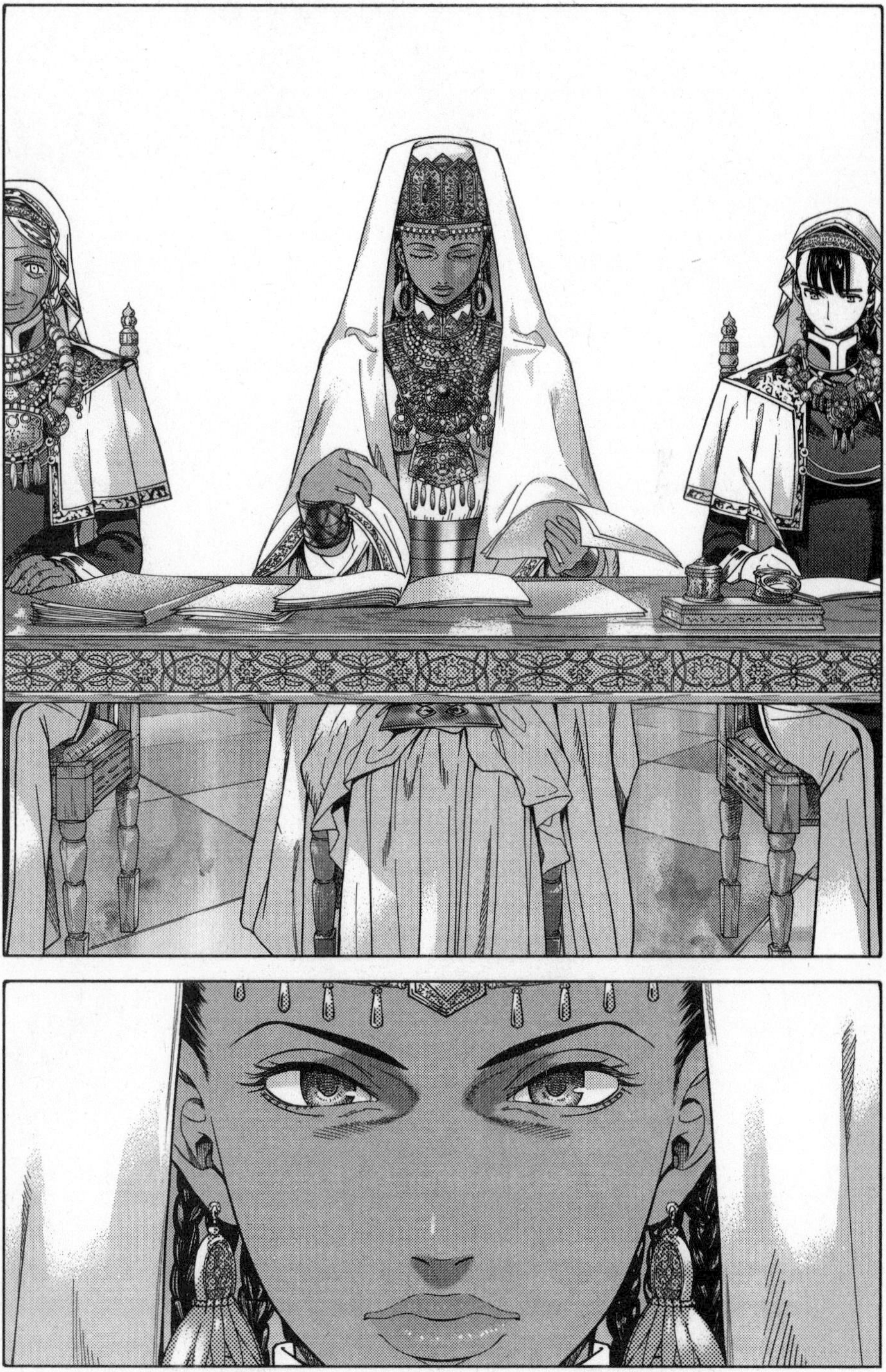

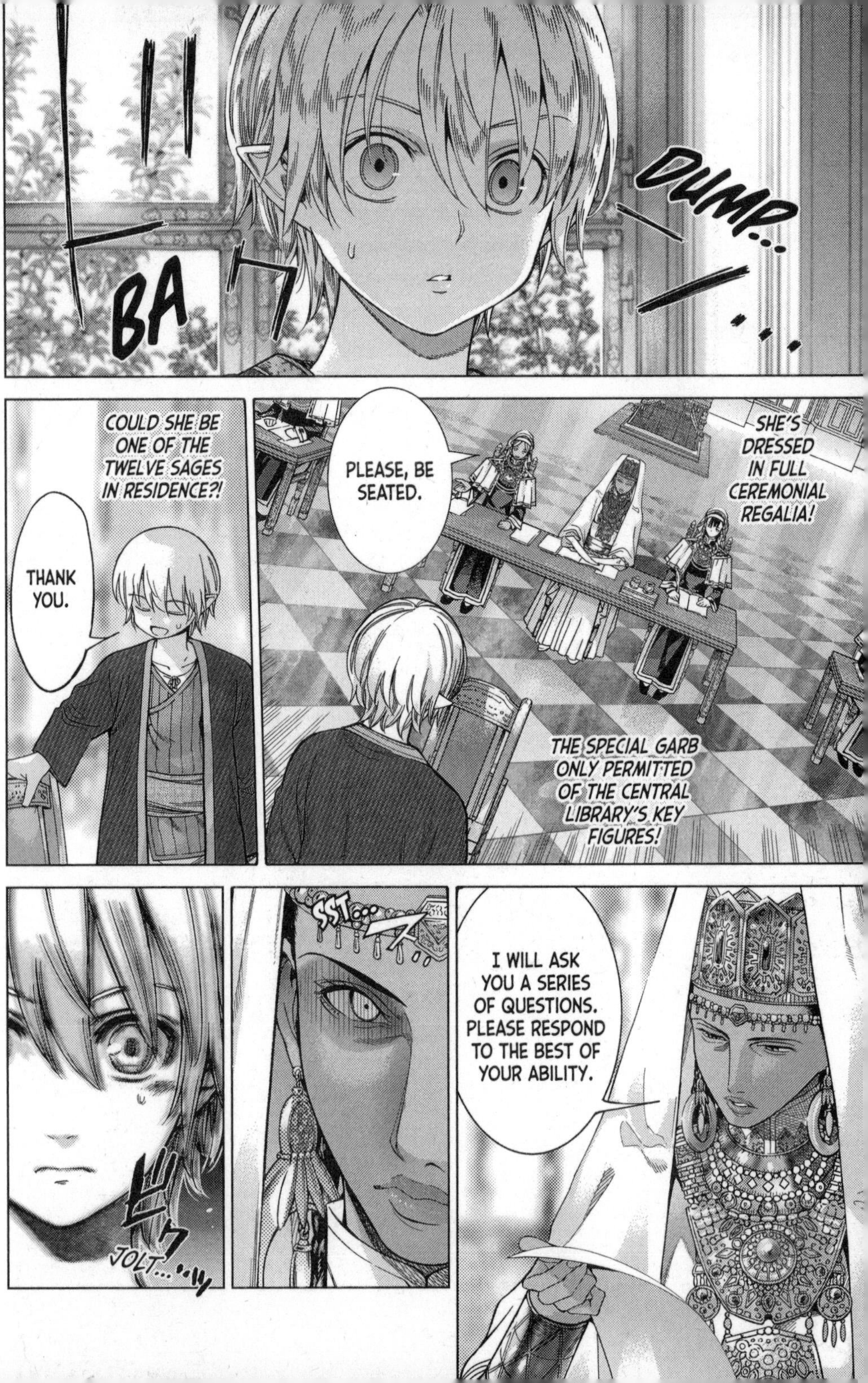
DUMP...
BA
SHE'S DRESSED IN FULL CEREMONIAL REGALIA!
PLEASE, BE SEATED.
THE SPECIAL GARB ONLY PERMITTED OF THE CENTRAL LIBRARY'S KEY FIGURES!
COULD SHE BE ONE OF THE TWELVE SAGES IN RESIDENCE?!
THANK YOU.
I WILL ASK YOU A SERIES OF QUESTIONS. PLEASE RESPOND TO THE BEST OF YOUR ABILITY.
SST...
JOLT...

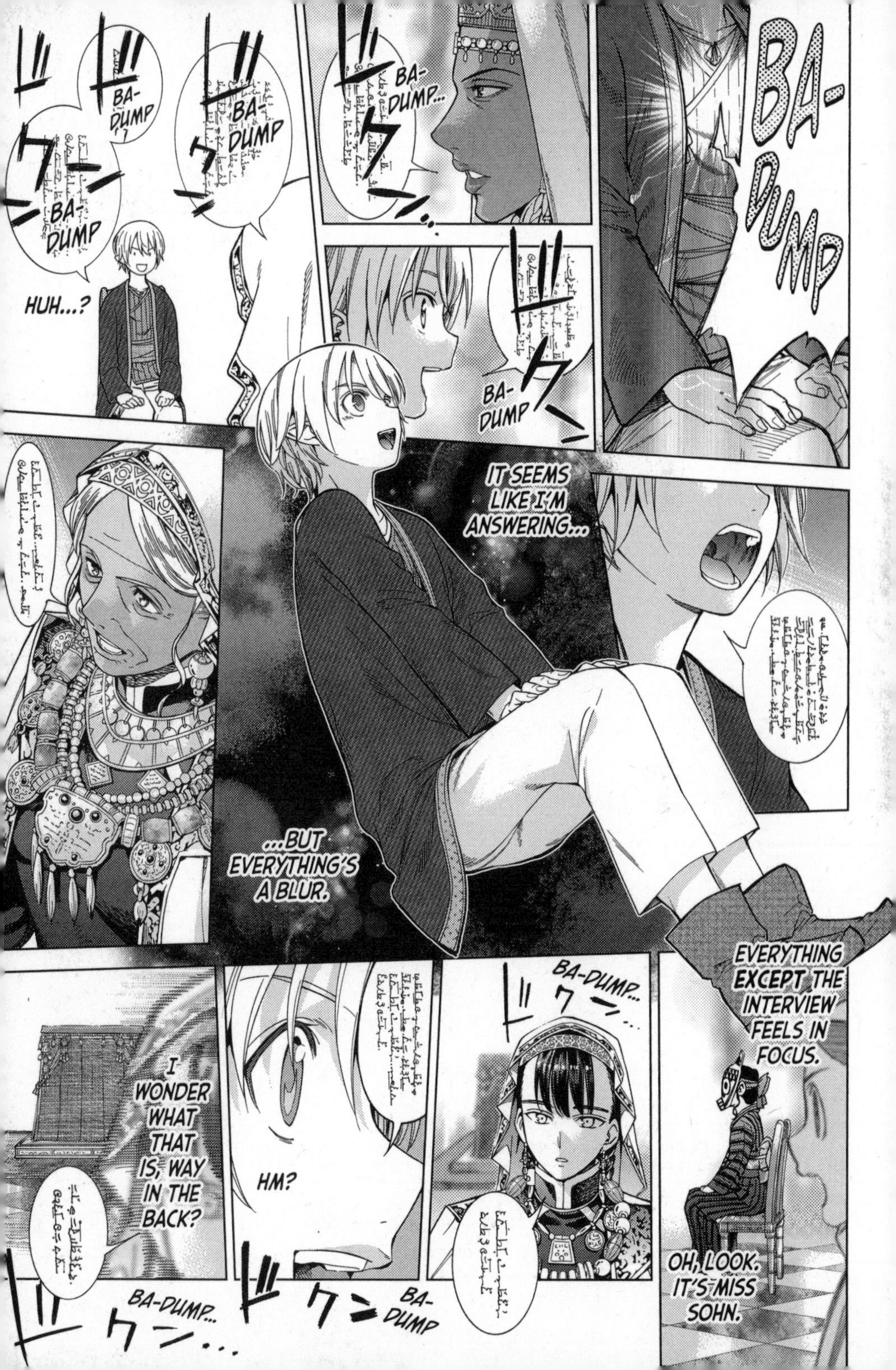
BA-DUMP
ドクン…
BA-DUMP…
ドクン
BA-DUMP
ドクン
BA-DUMP
ドクン
BA-DUMP
ドクン
BA-DUMP
HUH…?
IT SEEMS LIKE I'M ANSWERING…
…BUT EVERYTHING'S A BLUR.
EVERYTHING EXCEPT THE INTERVIEW FEELS IN FOCUS.
OH, LOOK. IT'S MISS SOHN.
ドクン…
BA-DUMP…
HM?
I WONDER WHAT THAT IS, WAY IN THE BACK?
ドクン
BA-DUMP
ドクン…
BA-DUMP…

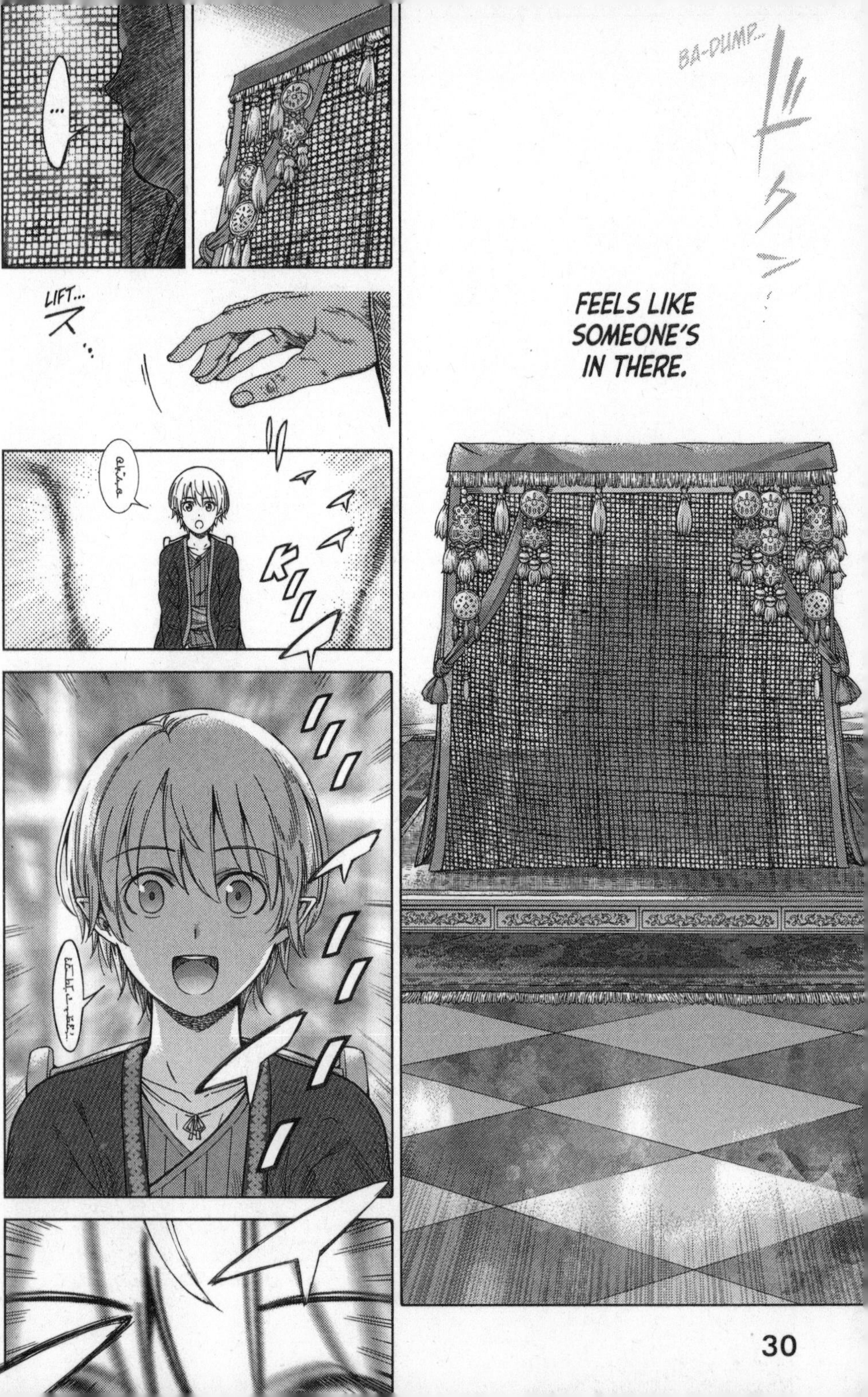

BA-DUMP...
FEELS LIKE SOMEONE'S IN THERE.
...
LIFT...
KIII

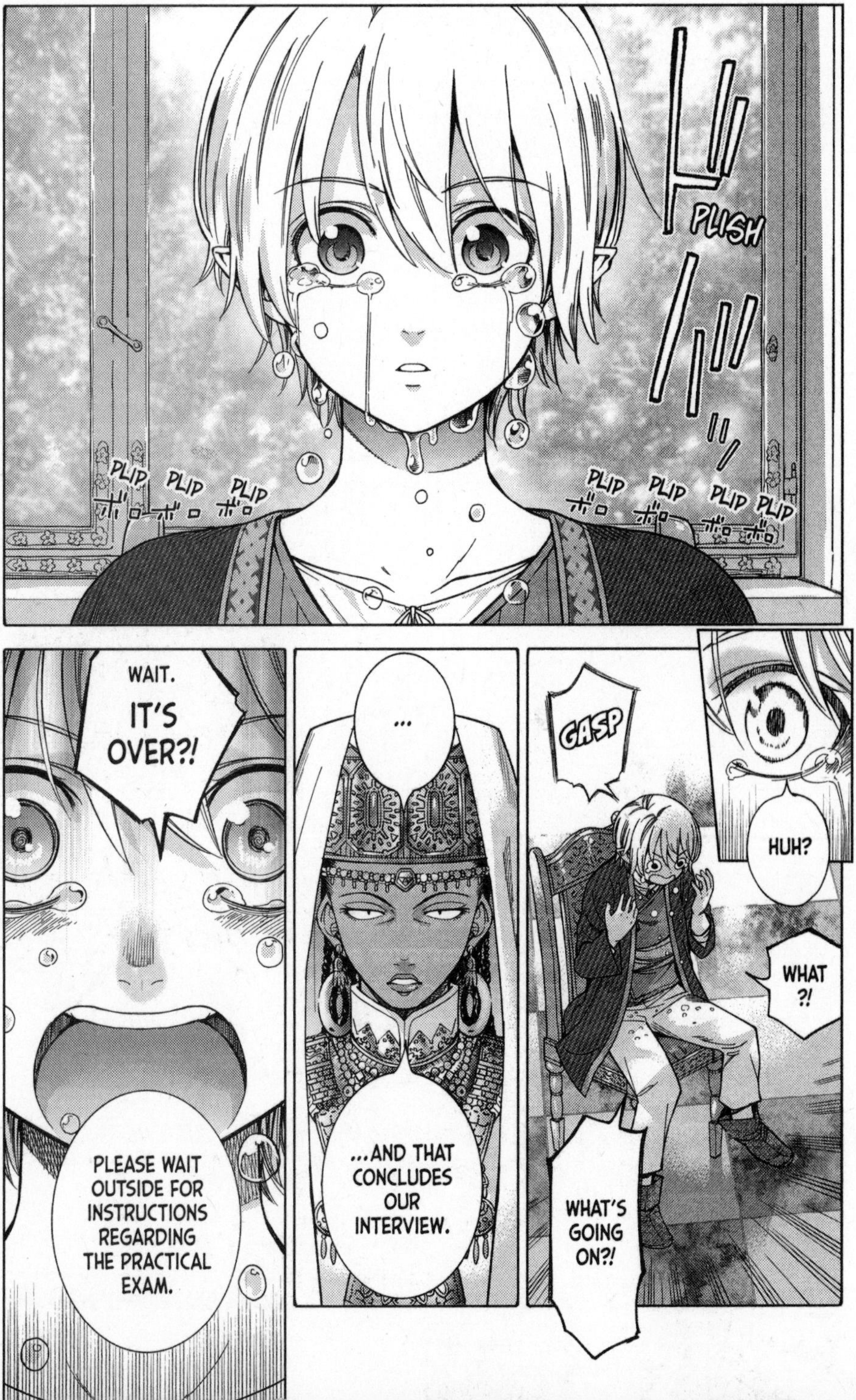
PLISH
PLIP
PLIP
PLIP
PLIP
PLIP
PLIP
PLIP
HUH?
GASP
WHAT?!
WHAT'S GOING ON?!
...
...AND THAT CONCLUDES OUR INTERVIEW.
WAIT. IT'S OVER?!
PLEASE WAIT OUTSIDE FOR INSTRUCTIONS REGARDING THE PRACTICAL EXAM.

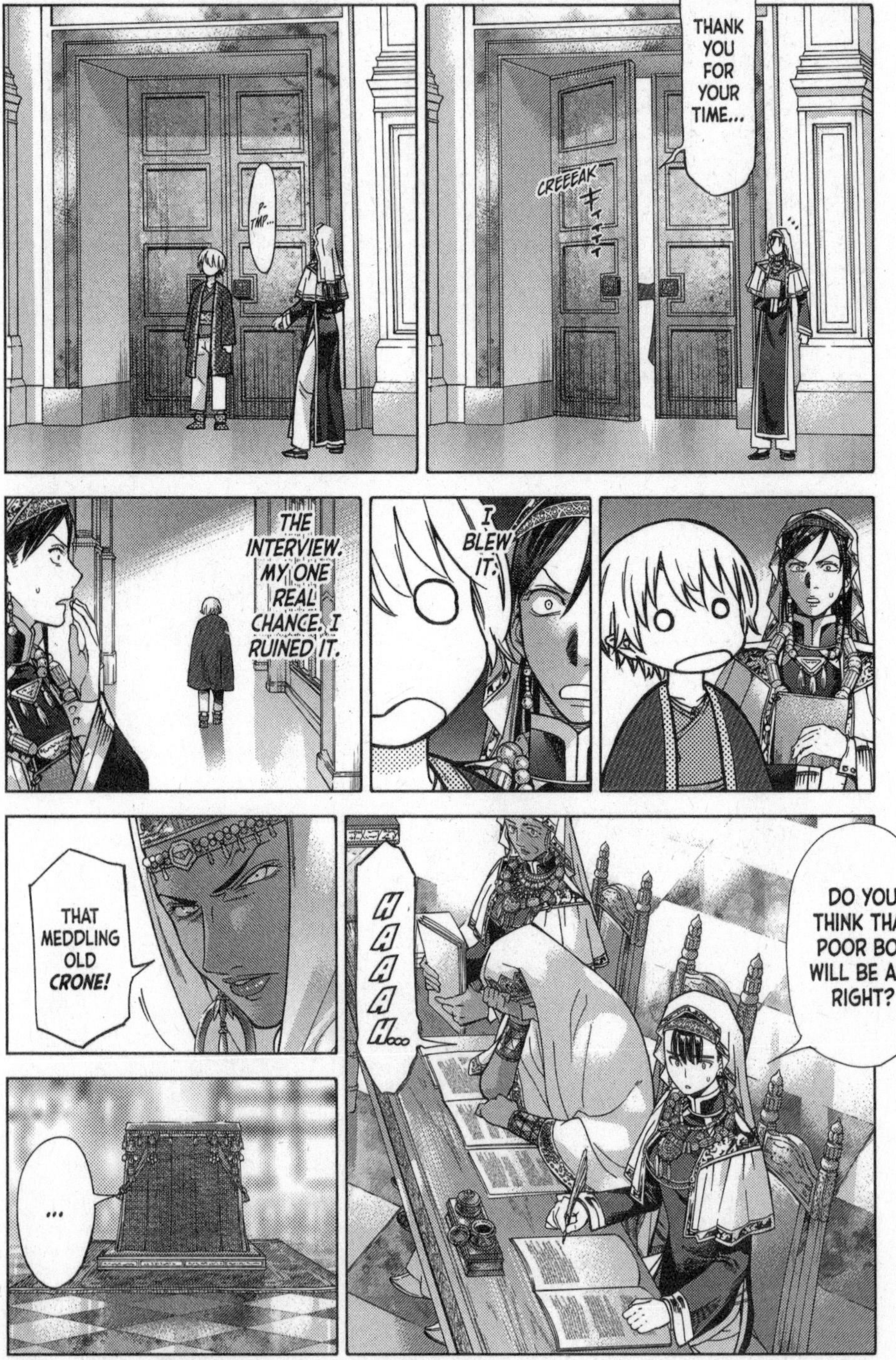
THANK YOU FOR YOUR TIME...
CREEEAK
P-TMP...
I BLEW IT;
THE INTERVIEW. MY ONE REAL CHANCE. I RUINED IT.
DO YOU THINK THAT POOR BOY WILL BE ALL RIGHT?
HAAAAH...
THAT MEDDLING OLD CRONE!
...

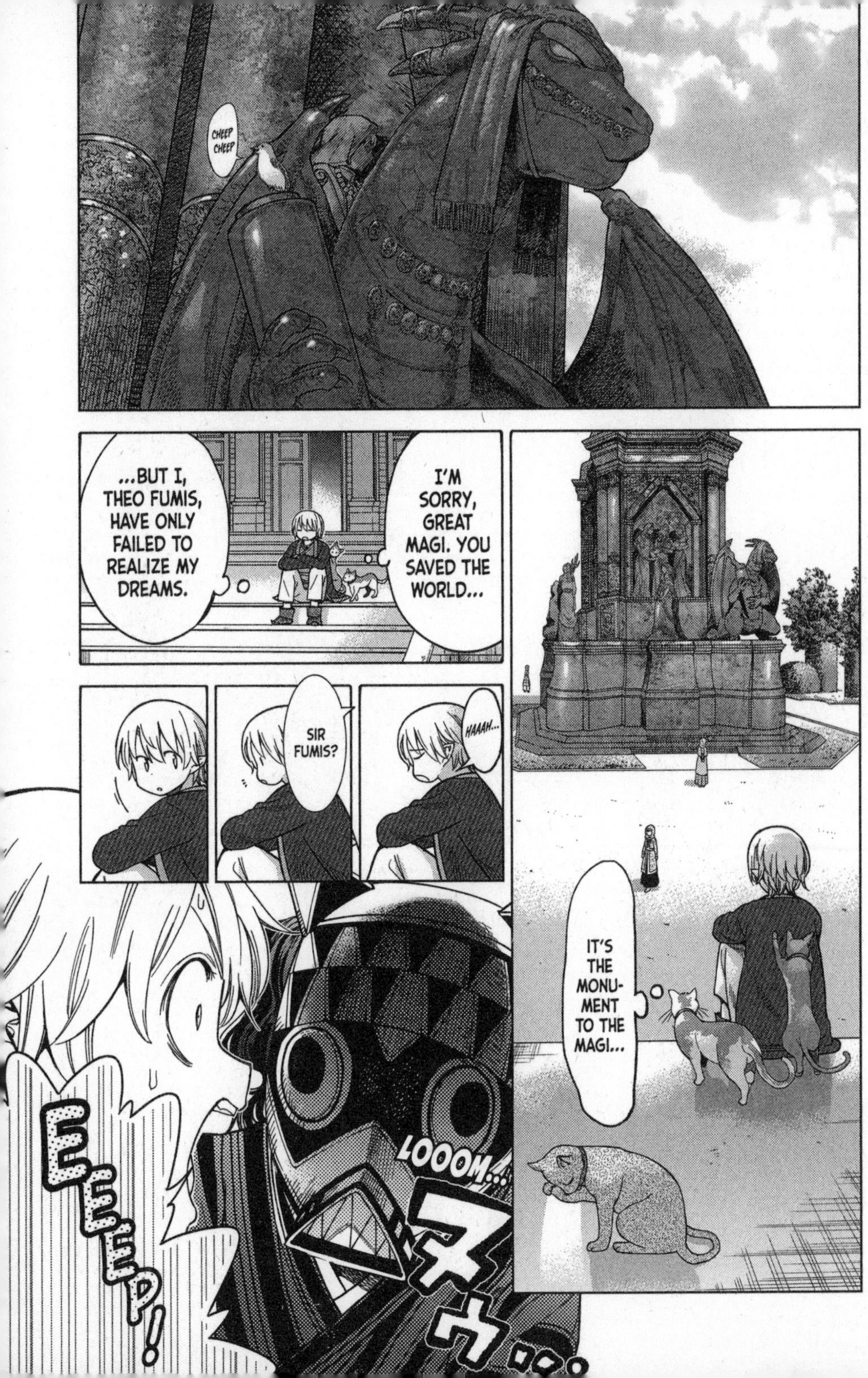
CHEEP CHEEP
IT'S THE MONUMENT TO THE MAGI...
I'M SORRY, GREAT MAGI. YOU SAVED THE WORLD...
...BUT I, THEO FUMIS, HAVE ONLY FAILED TO REALIZE MY DREAMS.
HAAAH...
SIR FUMIS?
LOOOM...
EEEEP!

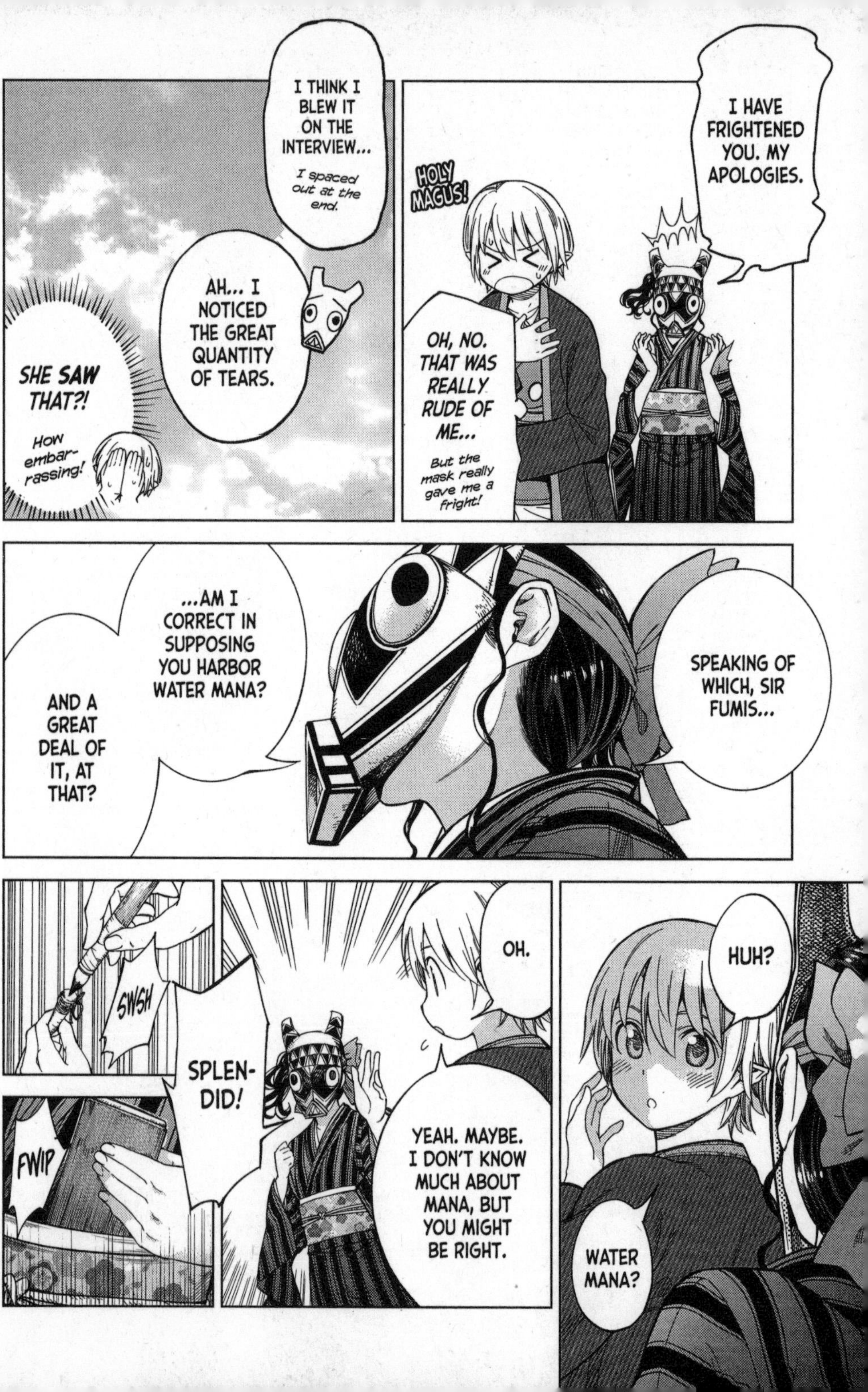
I HAVE FRIGHTENED YOU. MY APOLOGIES.
HOLY MAGUS!
OH, NO. THAT WAS REALLY RUDE OF ME...
But the mask really gave me a fright!
I THINK I BLEW IT ON THE INTERVIEW...
I spaced out at the end.
AH... I NOTICED THE GREAT QUANTITY OF TEARS.
SHE SAW THAT?!
How embar-rassing!
SPEAKING OF WHICH, SIR FUMIS...
...AM I CORRECT IN SUPPOSING YOU HARBOR WATER MANA?
AND A GREAT DEAL OF IT, AT THAT?
HUH?
WATER MANA?
OH.
YEAH. MAYBE. I DON'T KNOW MUCH ABOUT MANA, BUT YOU MIGHT BE RIGHT.
SPLEN-DID!
SWSH
FWIP

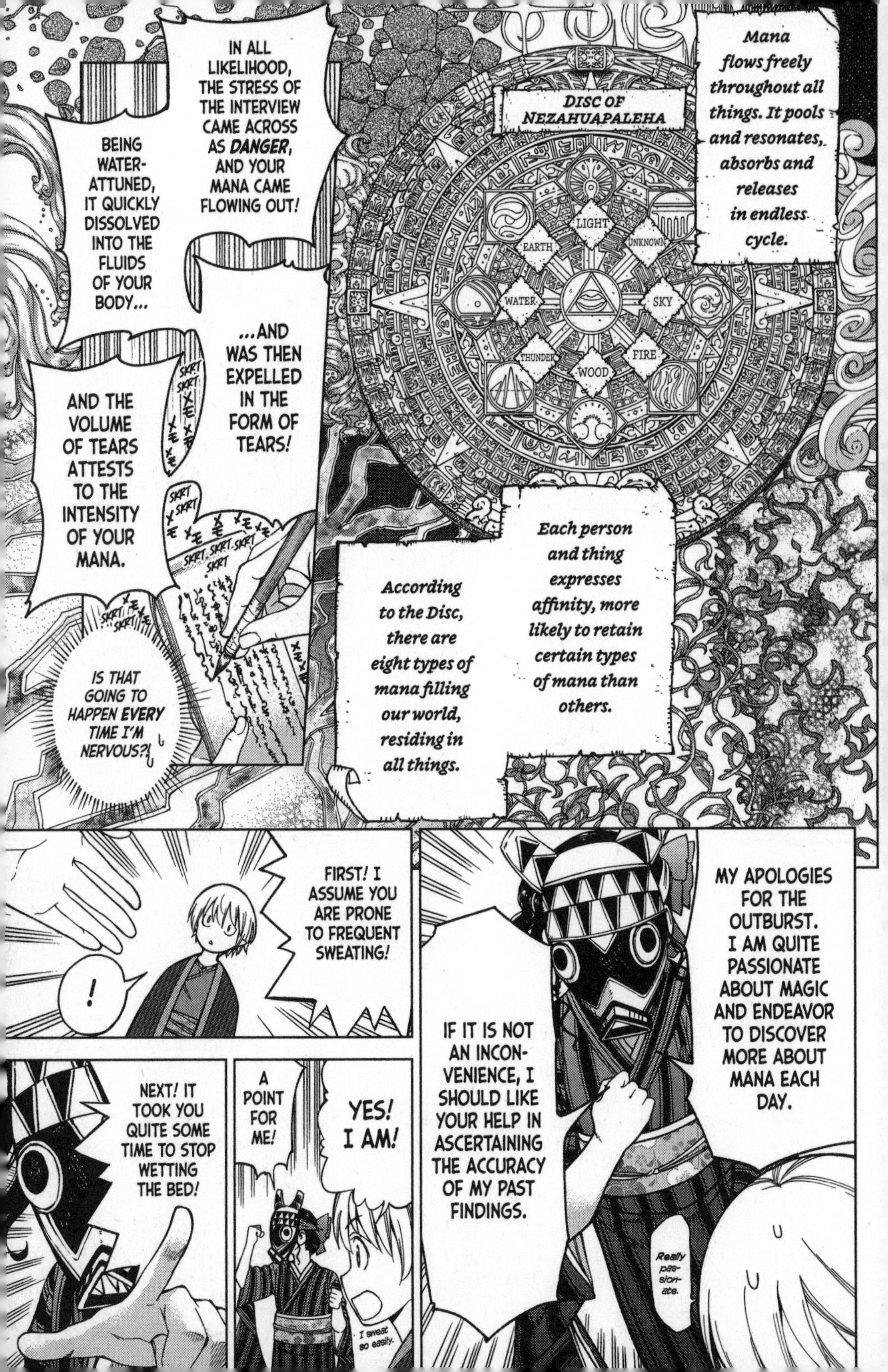

Mana flows freely throughout all things. It pools and resonates, absorbs and releases in endless cycle.
DISC OF NEZAHUAPALEHA
LIGHT
UNKNOWN
EARTH
SKY
WATER
FIRE
THUNDER
WOOD
Each person and thing expresses affinity, more likely to retain certain types of mana than others.
According to the Disc, there are eight types of mana filling our world, residing in all things.
IN ALL LIKELIHOOD, THE STRESS OF THE INTERVIEW CAME ACROSS AS DANGER, AND YOUR MANA CAME FLOWING OUT!
BEING WATER-ATTUNED, IT QUICKLY DISSOLVED INTO THE FLUIDS OF YOUR BODY...
...AND WAS THEN EXPELLED IN THE FORM OF TEARS!
AND THE VOLUME OF TEARS ATTESTS TO THE INTENSITY OF YOUR MANA.
SKRT SKRT
SKRT SKRT
SKRT SKRT SKRT
SKRT
SKRT SKRT
IS THAT GOING TO HAPPEN EVERY TIME I'M NERVOUS?!
MY APOLOGIES FOR THE OUTBURST. I AM QUITE PASSIONATE ABOUT MAGIC AND ENDEAVOR TO DISCOVER MORE ABOUT MANA EACH DAY.
IF IT IS NOT AN INCON-VENIENCE, I SHOULD LIKE YOUR HELP IN ASCERTAINING THE ACCURACY OF MY PAST FINDINGS.
Really pas-sion-ate.
FIRST! I ASSUME YOU ARE PRONE TO FREQUENT SWEATING!
!
YES! I AM!
A POINT FOR ME!
I sweat so easily.
NEXT! IT TOOK YOU QUITE SOME TIME TO STOP WETTING THE BED!

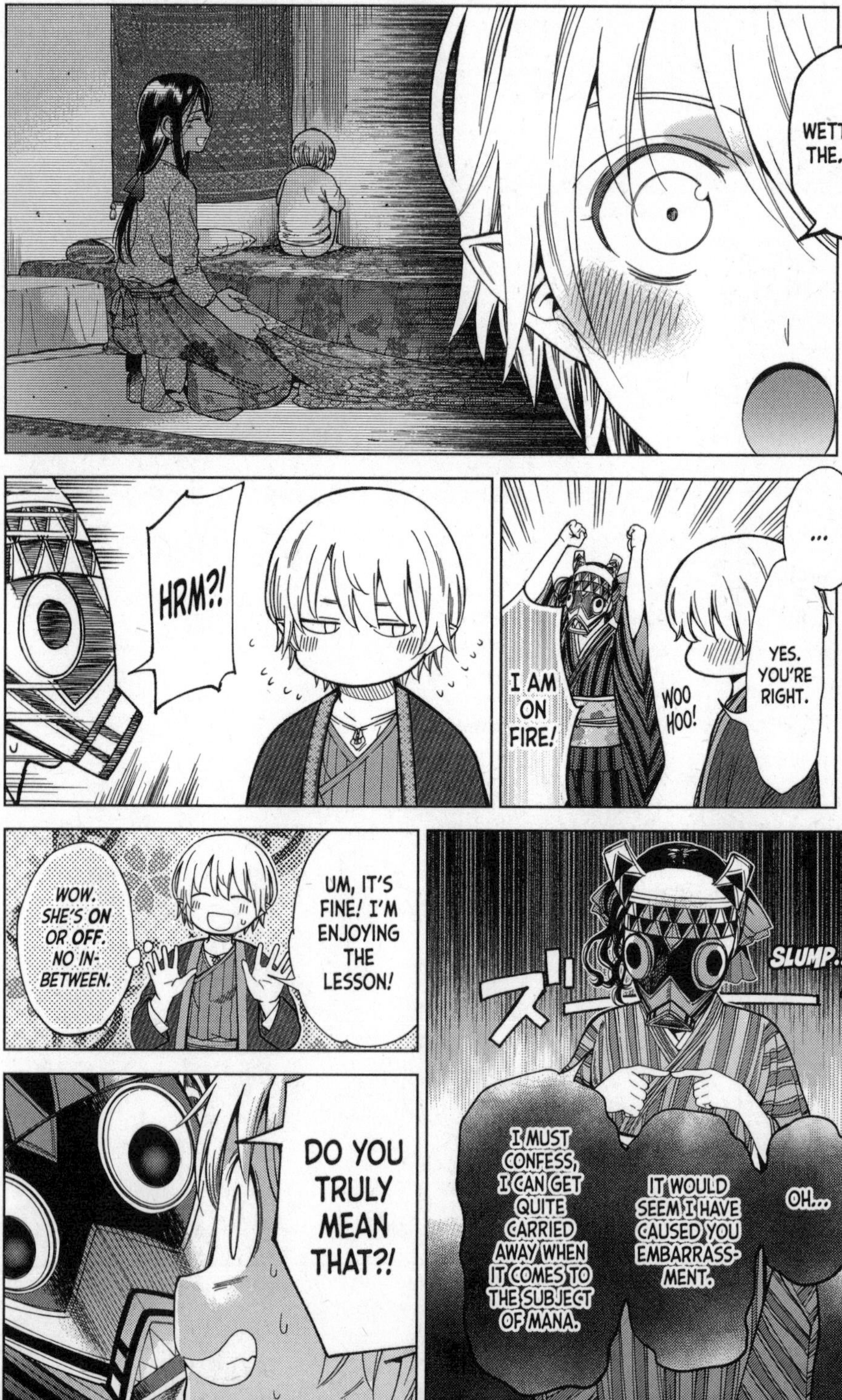
WETTING THE...?!
...
YES. YOU'RE RIGHT.
WOO HOO!
I AM ON FIRE!
HRM?!
SLUMP...
...
OH...
IT WOULD SEEM I HAVE CAUSED YOU EMBARRASSMENT.
I MUST CONFESS, I CAN GET QUITE CARRIED AWAY WHEN IT COMES TO THE SUBJECT OF MANA.
UM, IT'S FINE! I'M ENJOYING THE LESSON!
WOW. SHE'S ON OR OFF. NO IN-BETWEEN.
DO YOU TRULY MEAN THAT?!

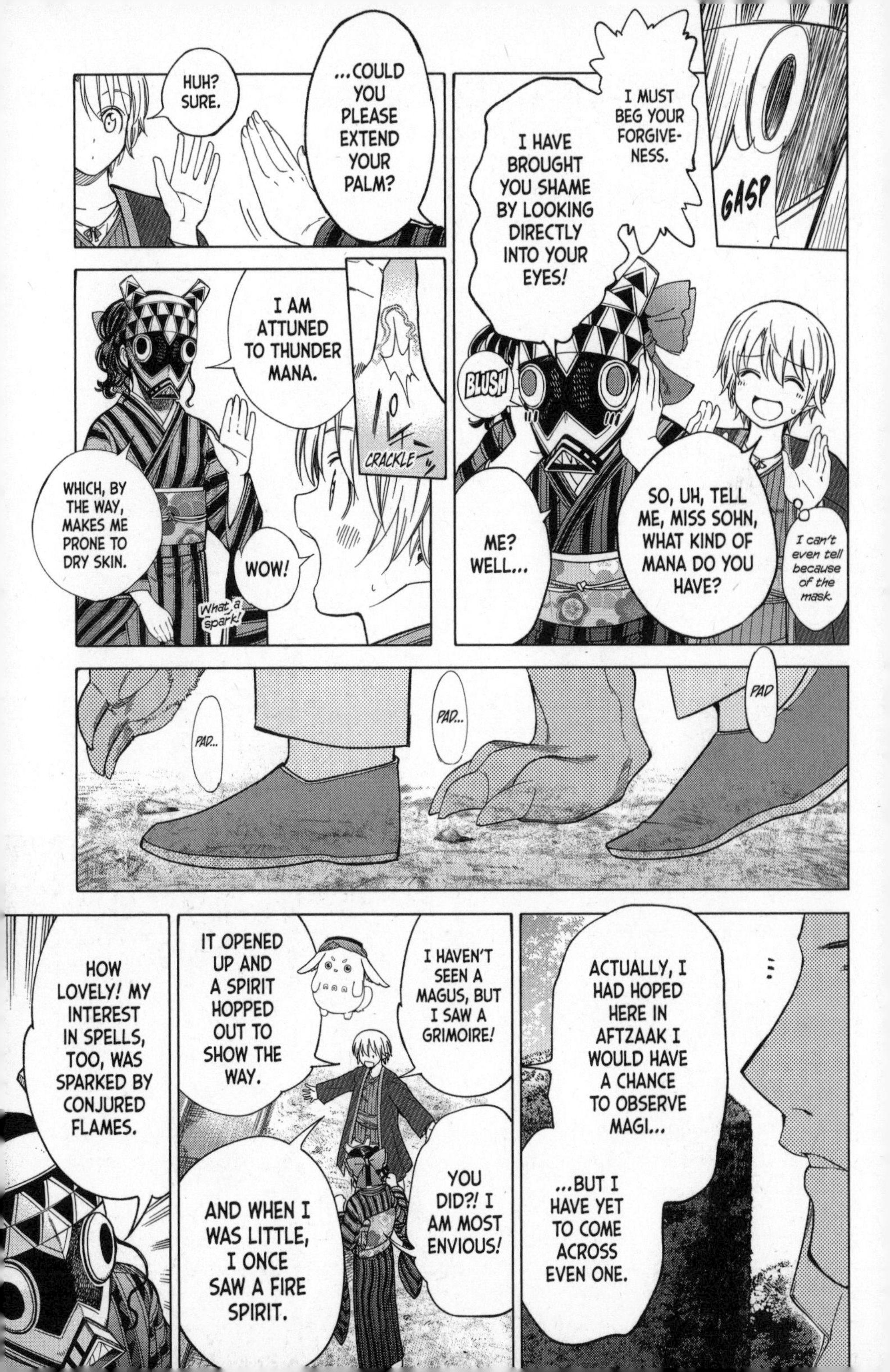
GASP
I MUST BEG YOUR FORGIVE-NESS.
I HAVE BROUGHT YOU SHAME BY LOOKING DIRECTLY INTO YOUR EYES!
BLUSH
SO, UH, TELL ME, MISS SOHN, WHAT KIND OF MANA DO YOU HAVE?
I can't even tell because of the mask.
ME? WELL...
...COULD YOU PLEASE EXTEND YOUR PALM?
HUH? SURE.
CRACKLE
I AM ATTUNED TO THUNDER MANA.
WOW!
What a spark!
WHICH, BY THE WAY, MAKES ME PRONE TO DRY SKIN.
PAD
PAD...
PAD...
...
ACTUALLY, I HAD HOPED HERE IN AFTZAAK I WOULD HAVE A CHANCE TO OBSERVE MAGI...
...BUT I HAVE YET TO COME ACROSS EVEN ONE.
I HAVEN'T SEEN A MAGUS, BUT I SAW A GRIMOIRE!
IT OPENED UP AND A SPIRIT HOPPED OUT TO SHOW THE WAY.
YOU DID?! I AM MOST ENVIOUS!
AND WHEN I WAS LITTLE, I ONCE SAW A FIRE SPIRIT.
HOW LOVELY! MY INTEREST IN SPELLS, TOO, WAS SPARKED BY CONJURED FLAMES.

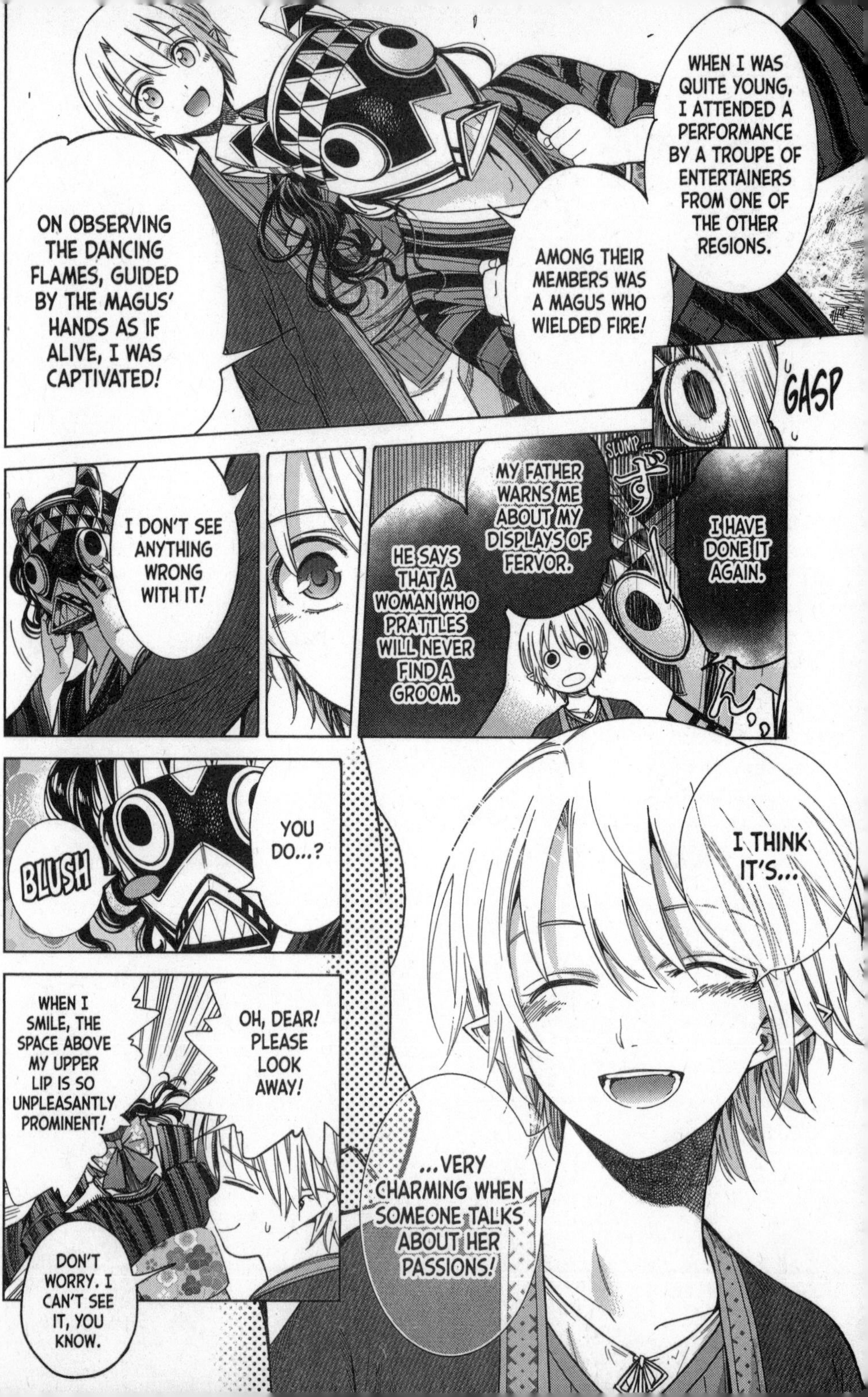
WHEN I WAS QUITE YOUNG, I ATTENDED A PERFORMANCE BY A TROUPE OF ENTERTAINERS FROM ONE OF THE OTHER REGIONS.
AMONG THEIR MEMBERS WAS A MAGUS WHO WIELDED FIRE!
ON OBSERVING THE DANCING FLAMES, GUIDED BY THE MAGUS' HANDS AS IF ALIVE, I WAS CAPTIVATED!
GASP
SLUMP...
I HAVE DONE IT AGAIN.
MY FATHER WARNS ME ABOUT MY DISPLAYS OF FERVOR.
HE SAYS THAT A WOMAN WHO PRATTLES WILL NEVER FIND A GROOM.
I DON'T SEE ANYTHING WRONG WITH IT!
I THINK IT'S...
...VERY CHARMING WHEN SOMEONE TALKS ABOUT HER PASSIONS!
YOU DO...?
BLUSH
OH, DEAR! PLEASE LOOK AWAY!
WHEN I SMILE, THE SPACE ABOVE MY UPPER LIP IS SO UNPLEASANTLY PROMINENT!
DON'T WORRY. I CAN'T SEE IT, YOU KNOW.

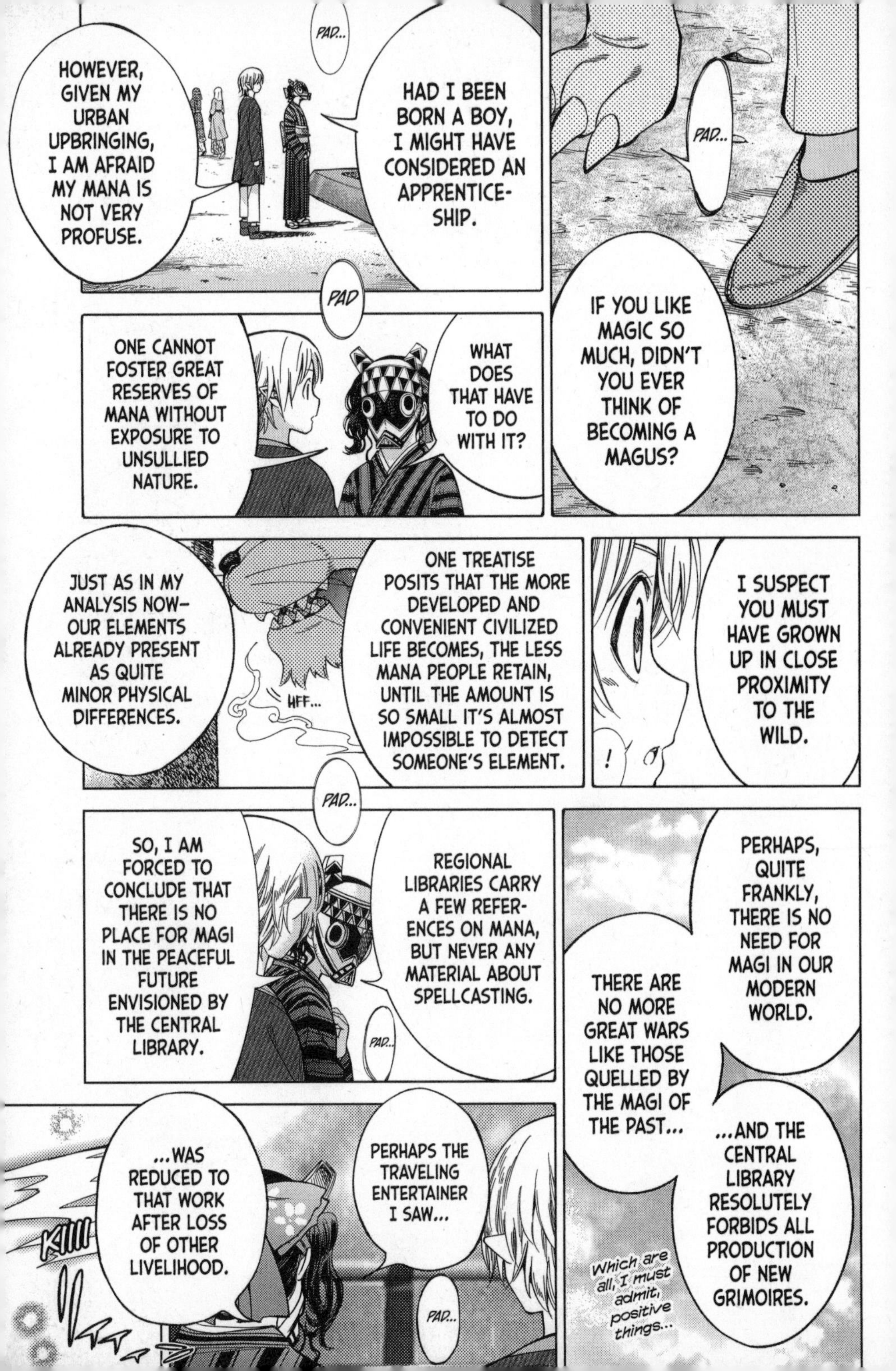
PAD...
IF YOU LIKE MAGIC SO MUCH, DIDN'T YOU EVER THINK OF BECOMING A MAGUS?
PAD...
HAD I BEEN BORN A BOY, I MIGHT HAVE CONSIDERED AN APPRENTICE-SHIP.
HOWEVER, GIVEN MY URBAN UPBRINGING, I AM AFRAID MY MANA IS NOT VERY PROFUSE.
PAD
WHAT DOES THAT HAVE TO DO WITH IT?
ONE CANNOT FOSTER GREAT RESERVES OF MANA WITHOUT EXPOSURE TO UNSULLIED NATURE.
I SUSPECT YOU MUST HAVE GROWN UP IN CLOSE PROXIMITY TO THE WILD.
!
ONE TREATISE POSITS THAT THE MORE DEVELOPED AND CONVENIENT CIVILIZED LIFE BECOMES, THE LESS MANA PEOPLE RETAIN, UNTIL THE AMOUNT IS SO SMALL IT'S ALMOST IMPOSSIBLE TO DETECT SOMEONE'S ELEMENT.
HFF...
JUST AS IN MY ANALYSIS NOW— OUR ELEMENTS ALREADY PRESENT AS QUITE MINOR PHYSICAL DIFFERENCES.
PERHAPS, QUITE FRANKLY, THERE IS NO NEED FOR MAGI IN OUR MODERN WORLD.
THERE ARE NO MORE GREAT WARS LIKE THOSE QUELLED BY THE MAGI OF THE PAST...
...AND THE CENTRAL LIBRARY RESOLUTELY FORBIDS ALL PRODUCTION OF NEW GRIMOIRES.
Which are all, I must admit, positive things...
PAD...
REGIONAL LIBRARIES CARRY A FEW REFER-ENCES ON MANA, BUT NEVER ANY MATERIAL ABOUT SPELLCASTING.
PAD...
SO, I AM FORCED TO CONCLUDE THAT THERE IS NO PLACE FOR MAGI IN THE PEACEFUL FUTURE ENVISIONED BY THE CENTRAL LIBRARY.
PERHAPS THE TRAVELING ENTERTAINER I SAW...
...WAS REDUCED TO THAT WORK AFTER LOSS OF OTHER LIVELIHOOD.
PAD...
KIIII

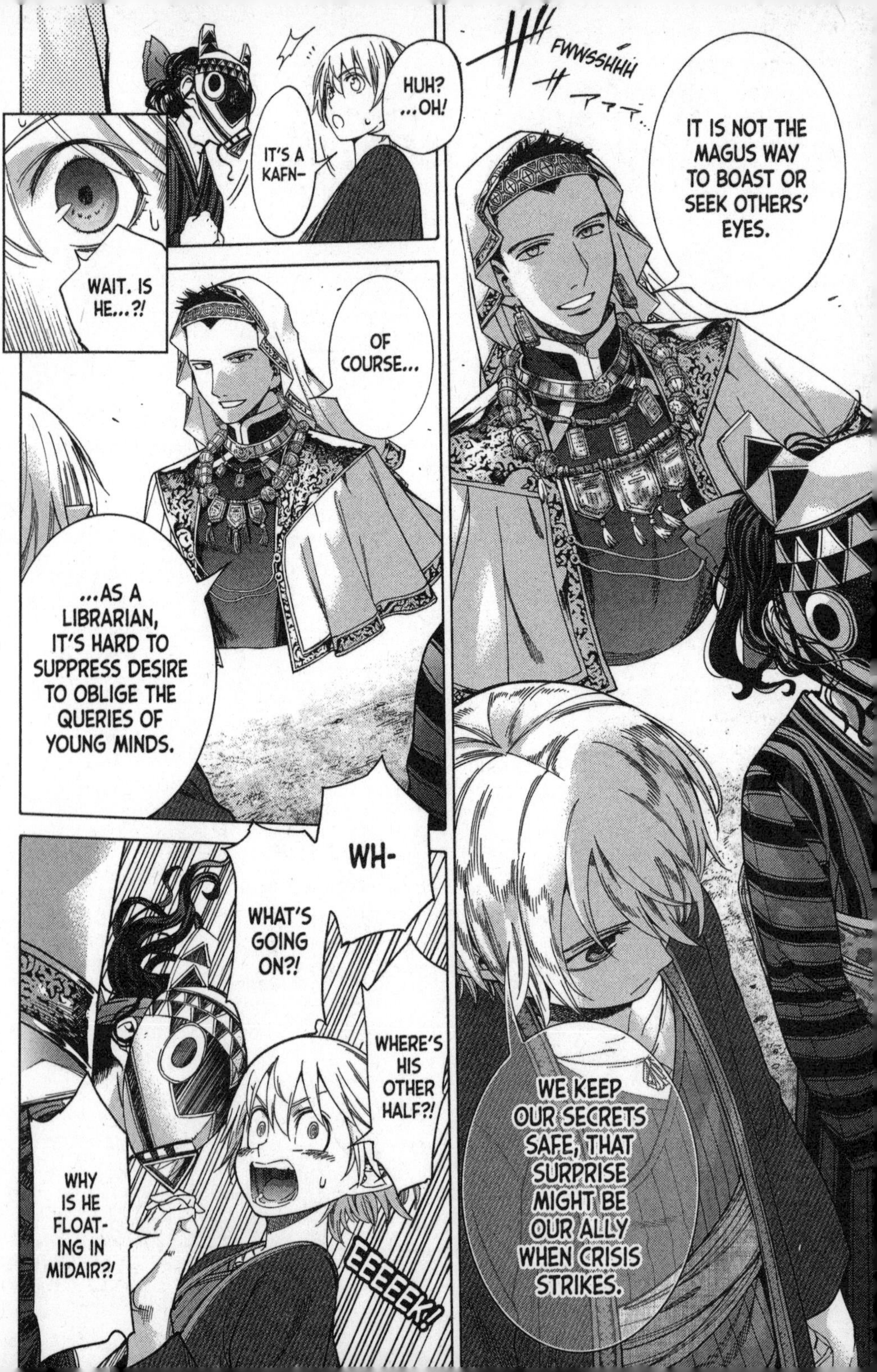
FWWSSHHH
アァァ…
IT IS NOT THE MAGUS WAY TO BOAST OR SEEK OTHERS' EYES.
WE KEEP OUR SECRETS SAFE, THAT SURPRISE MIGHT BE OUR ALLY WHEN CRISIS STRIKES.
HUH? ...OH!
IT'S A KAFN-
WAIT. IS HE...?!
OF COURSE...
...AS A LIBRARIAN, IT'S HARD TO SUPPRESS DESIRE TO OBLIGE THE QUERIES OF YOUNG MINDS.
WH-
WHAT'S GOING ON?!
WHERE'S HIS OTHER HALF?!
WHY IS HE FLOATING IN MIDAIR?!
EEEEEK!

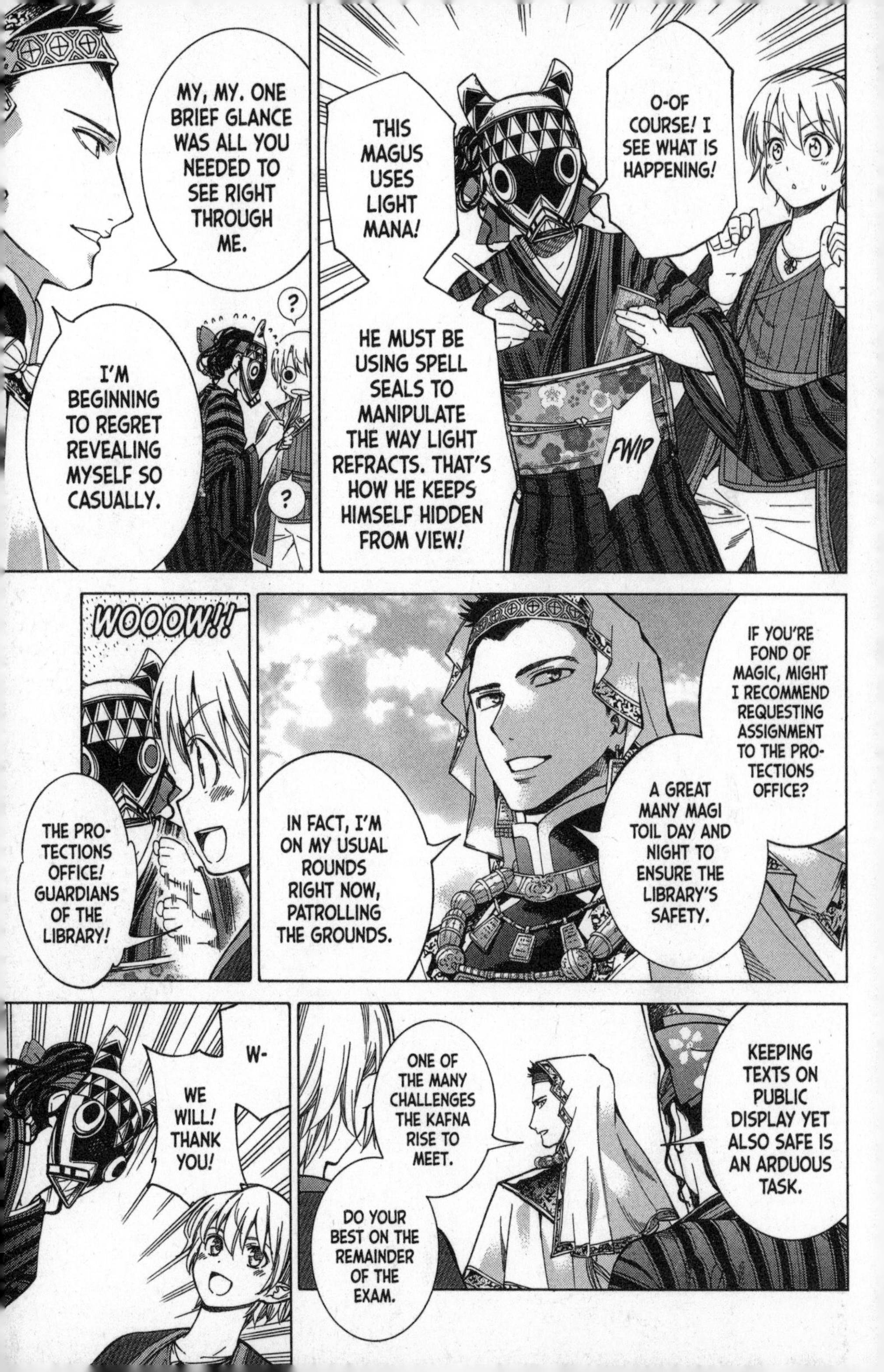
O-OF COURSE! I SEE WHAT IS HAPPENING!
THIS MAGUS USES LIGHT MANA!
HE MUST BE USING SPELL SEALS TO MANIPULATE THE WAY LIGHT REFRACTS. THAT'S HOW HE KEEPS HIMSELF HIDDEN FROM VIEW!
FWIP
MY, MY. ONE BRIEF GLANCE WAS ALL YOU NEEDED TO SEE RIGHT THROUGH ME.
?
?
I'M BEGINNING TO REGRET REVEALING MYSELF SO CASUALLY.
IF YOU'RE FOND OF MAGIC, MIGHT I RECOMMEND REQUESTING ASSIGNMENT TO THE PRO-TECTIONS OFFICE?
A GREAT MANY MAGI TOIL DAY AND NIGHT TO ENSURE THE LIBRARY'S SAFETY.
IN FACT, I'M ON MY USUAL ROUNDS RIGHT NOW, PATROLLING THE GROUNDS.
WOOOW!!
THE PRO-TECTIONS OFFICE! GUARDIANS OF THE LIBRARY!
KEEPING TEXTS ON PUBLIC DISPLAY YET ALSO SAFE IS AN ARDUOUS TASK.
ONE OF THE MANY CHALLENGES THE KAFNA RISE TO MEET.
DO YOUR BEST ON THE REMAINDER OF THE EXAM.
W-
WE WILL! THANK YOU!

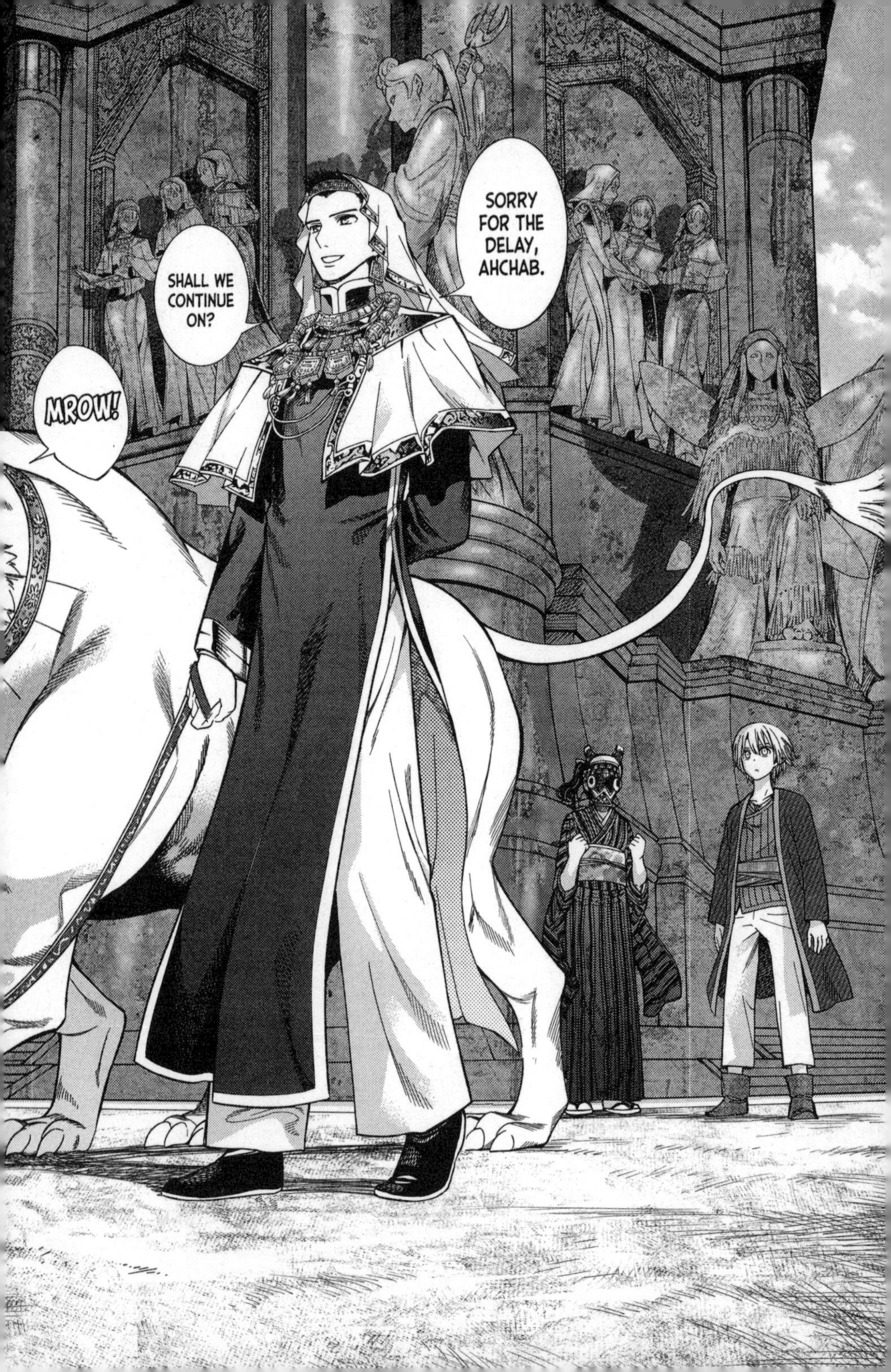
SORRY FOR THE DELAY, AHCHAB.
SHALL WE CONTINUE ON?
MROW!

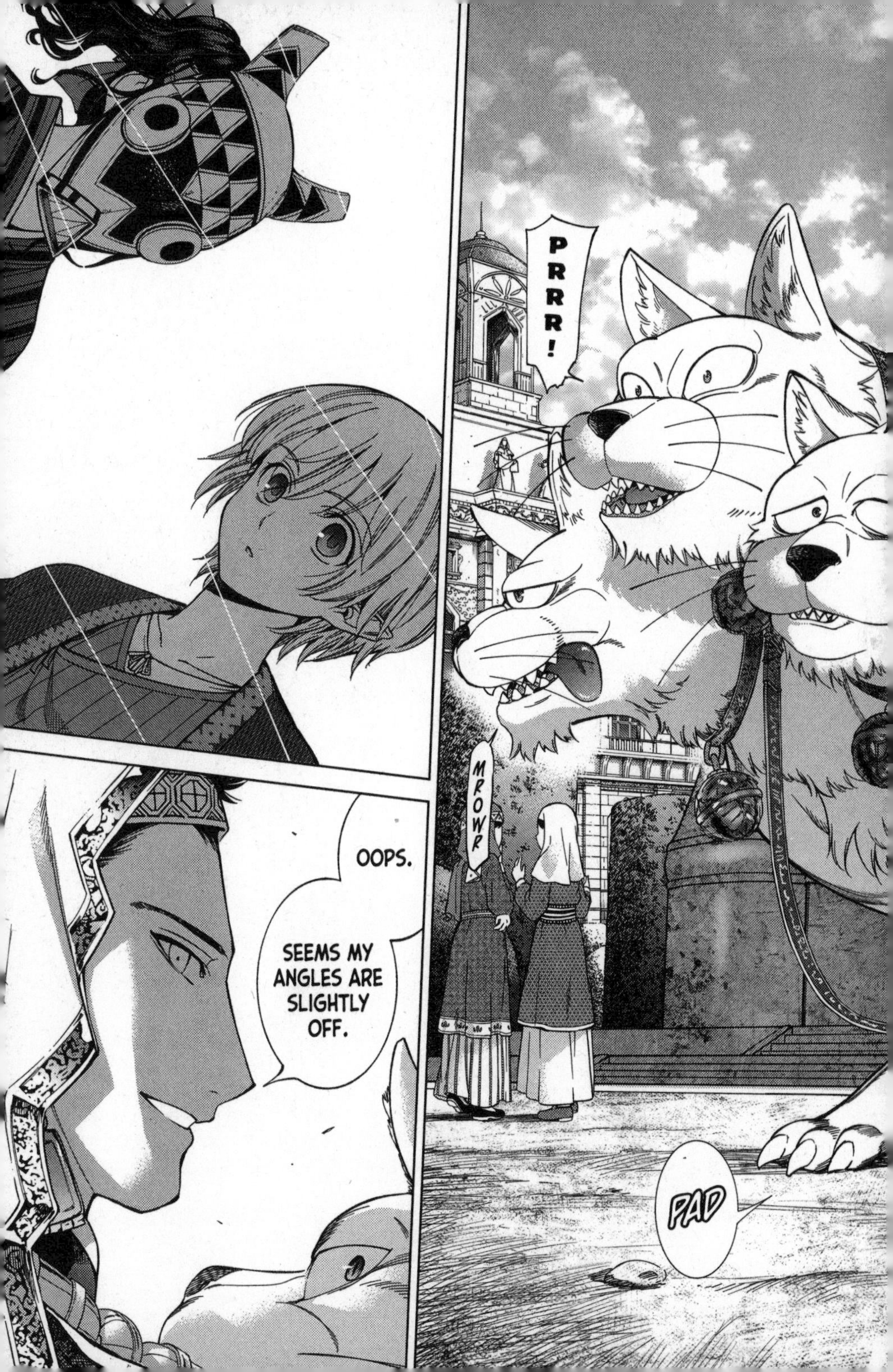
PRRR!
MROWR
PAD
OOPS.
SEEMS MY ANGLES ARE SLIGHTLY OFF.

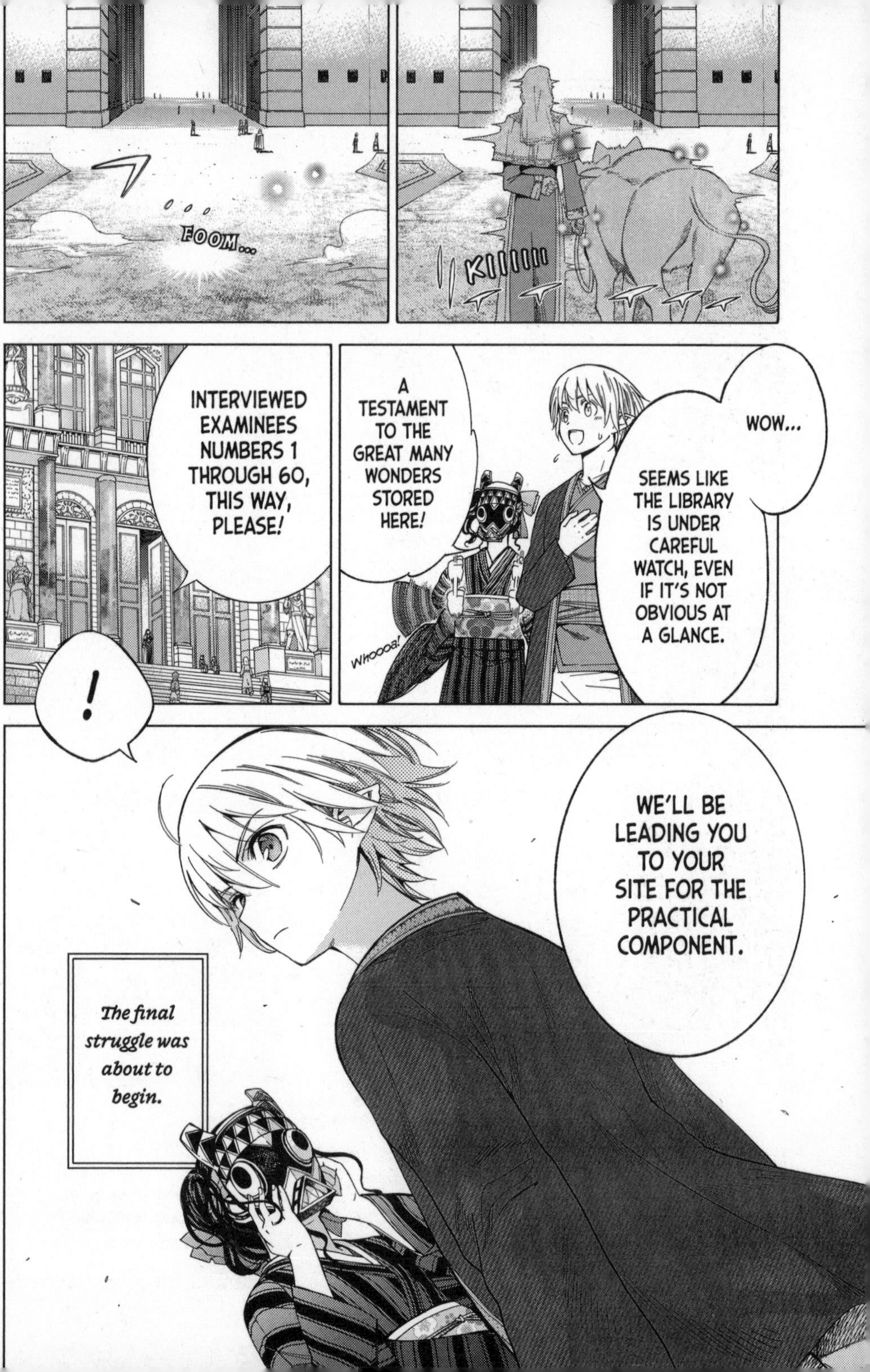
KIIIIII
FOOM...
WOW...
SEEMS LIKE THE LIBRARY IS UNDER CAREFUL WATCH, EVEN IF IT'S NOT OBVIOUS AT A GLANCE.
A TESTAMENT TO THE GREAT MANY WONDERS STORED HERE!
Whoooa!
INTERVIEWED EXAMINEES NUMBERS 1 THROUGH 60, THIS WAY, PLEASE!
WE'LL BE LEADING YOU TO YOUR SITE FOR THE PRACTICAL COMPONENT.
!
The final struggle was about to begin.

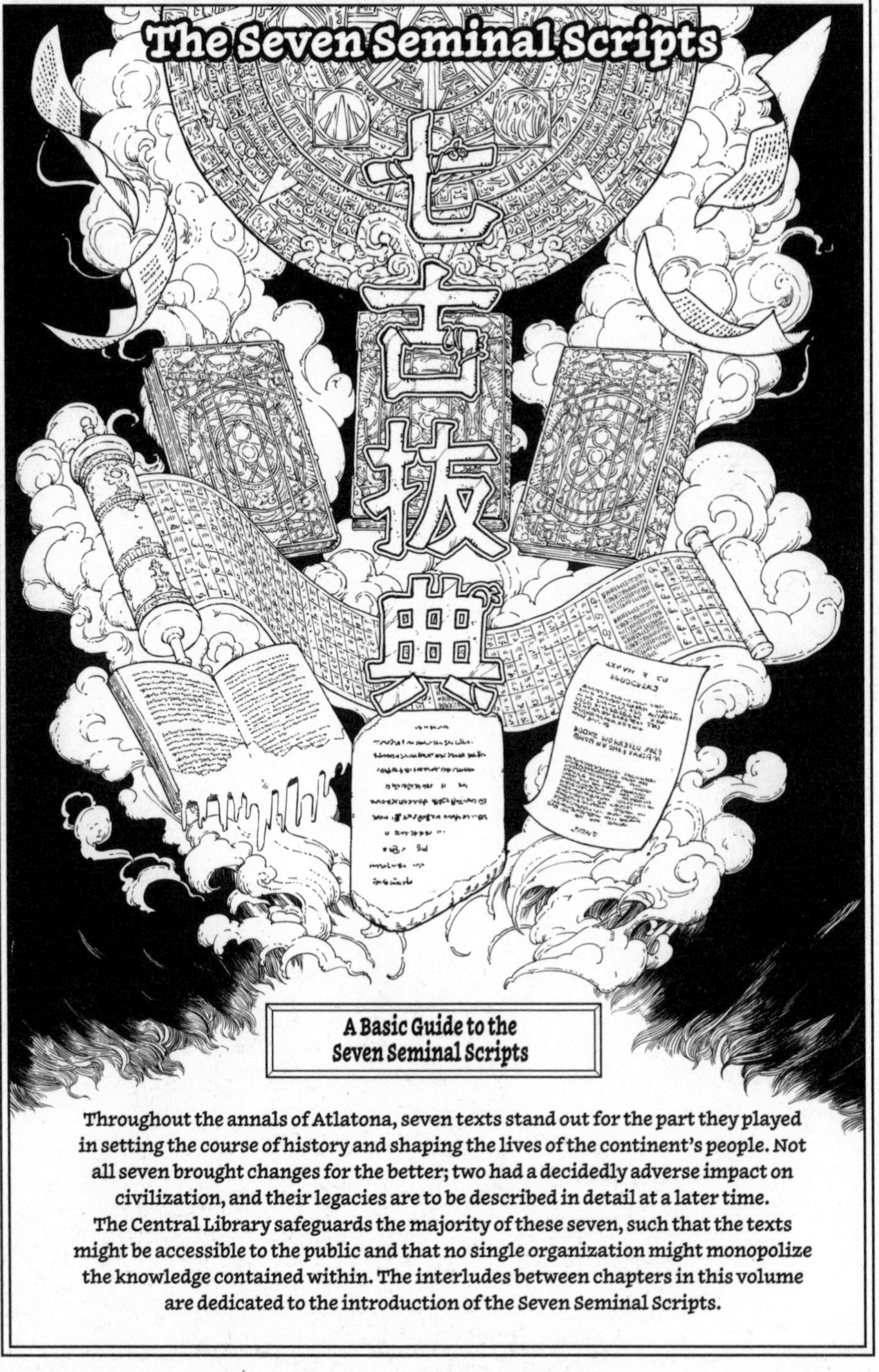
The Seven Seminal Scripts
七古抜典

A Basic Guide to the Seven Seminal Scripts

Throughout the annals of Atlatona, seven texts stand out for the part they played in setting the course of history and shaping the lives of the continent's people. Not all seven brought changes for the better; two had a decidedly adverse impact on civilization, and their legacies are to be described in detail at a later time. The Central Library safeguards the majority of these seven, such that the texts might be accessible to the public and that no single organization might monopolize the knowledge contained within. The interludes between chapters in this volume are dedicated to the introduction of the Seven Seminal Scripts.

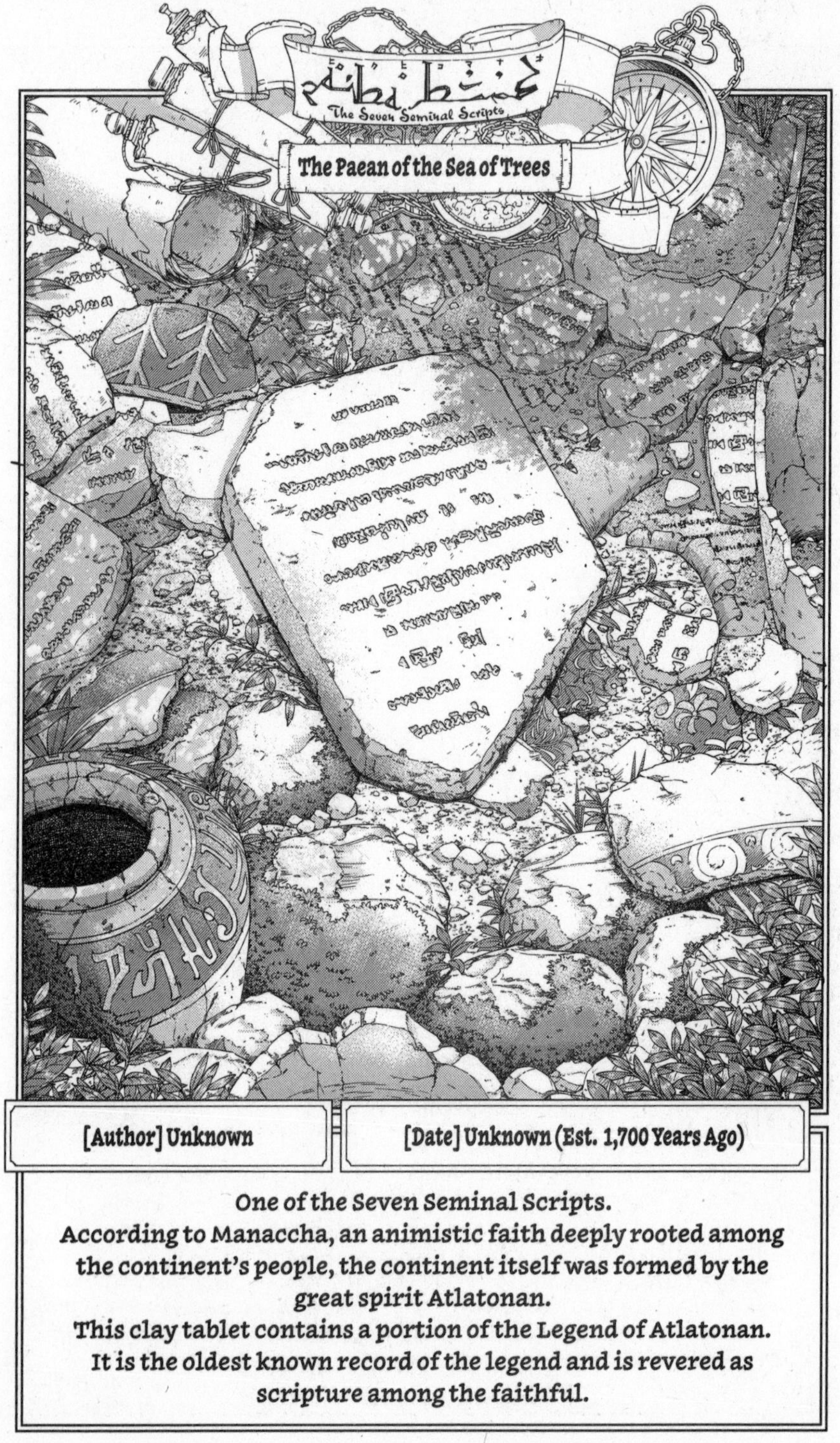
The Seven Seminal Scripts
The Paean of the Sea of Trees

[Author] Unknown

[Date] Unknown (Est. 1,700 Years Ago)

One of the Seven Seminal Scripts.
According to Manaccha, an animistic faith deeply rooted among the continent's people, the continent itself was formed by the great spirit Atlatonan.
This clay tablet contains a portion of the Legend of Atlatonan.
It is the oldest known record of the legend and is revered as scripture among the faithful.

11 Do Kafna Dream of Provincial Sheep?

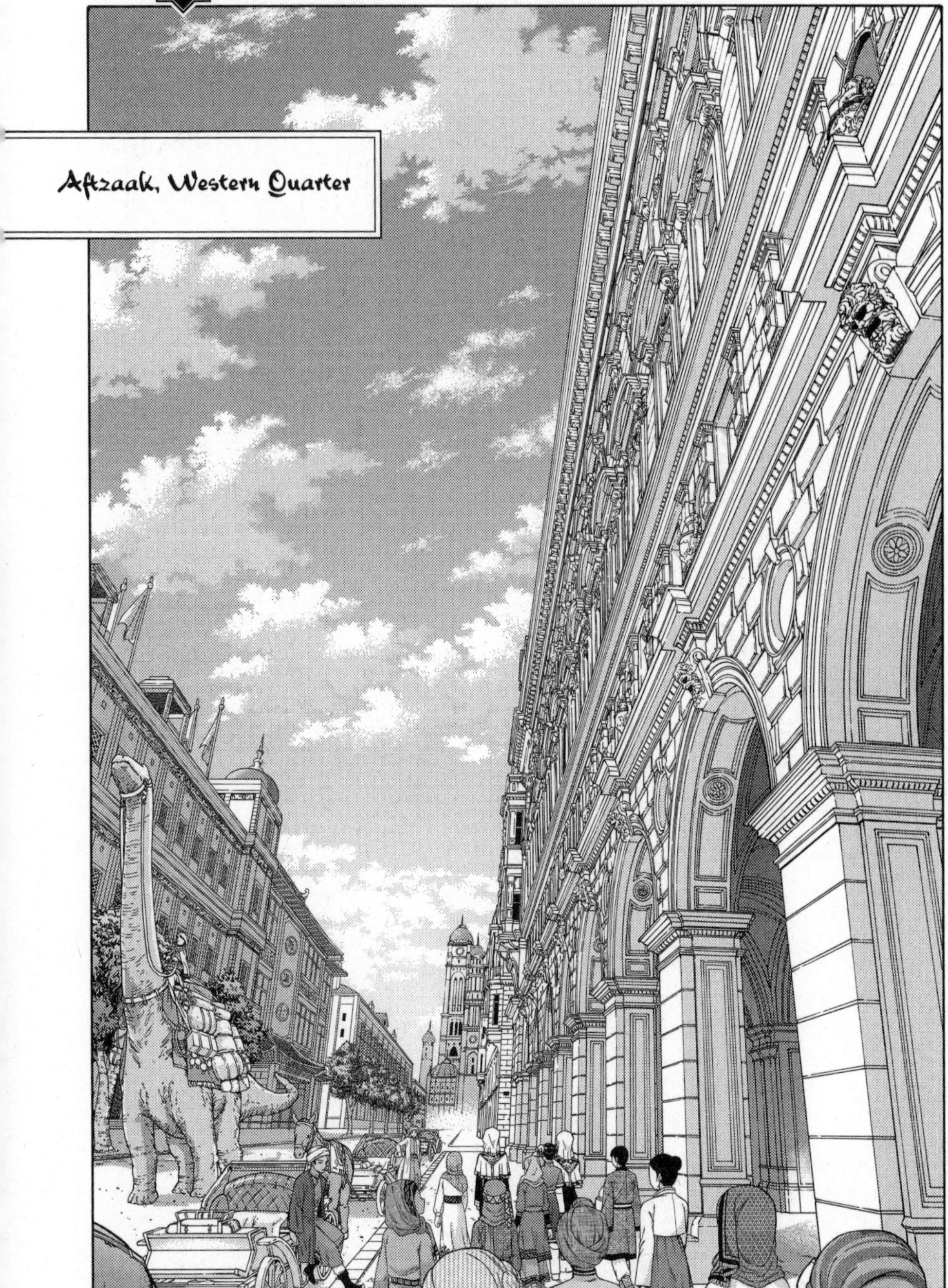
Aftzaak, Western Quarter

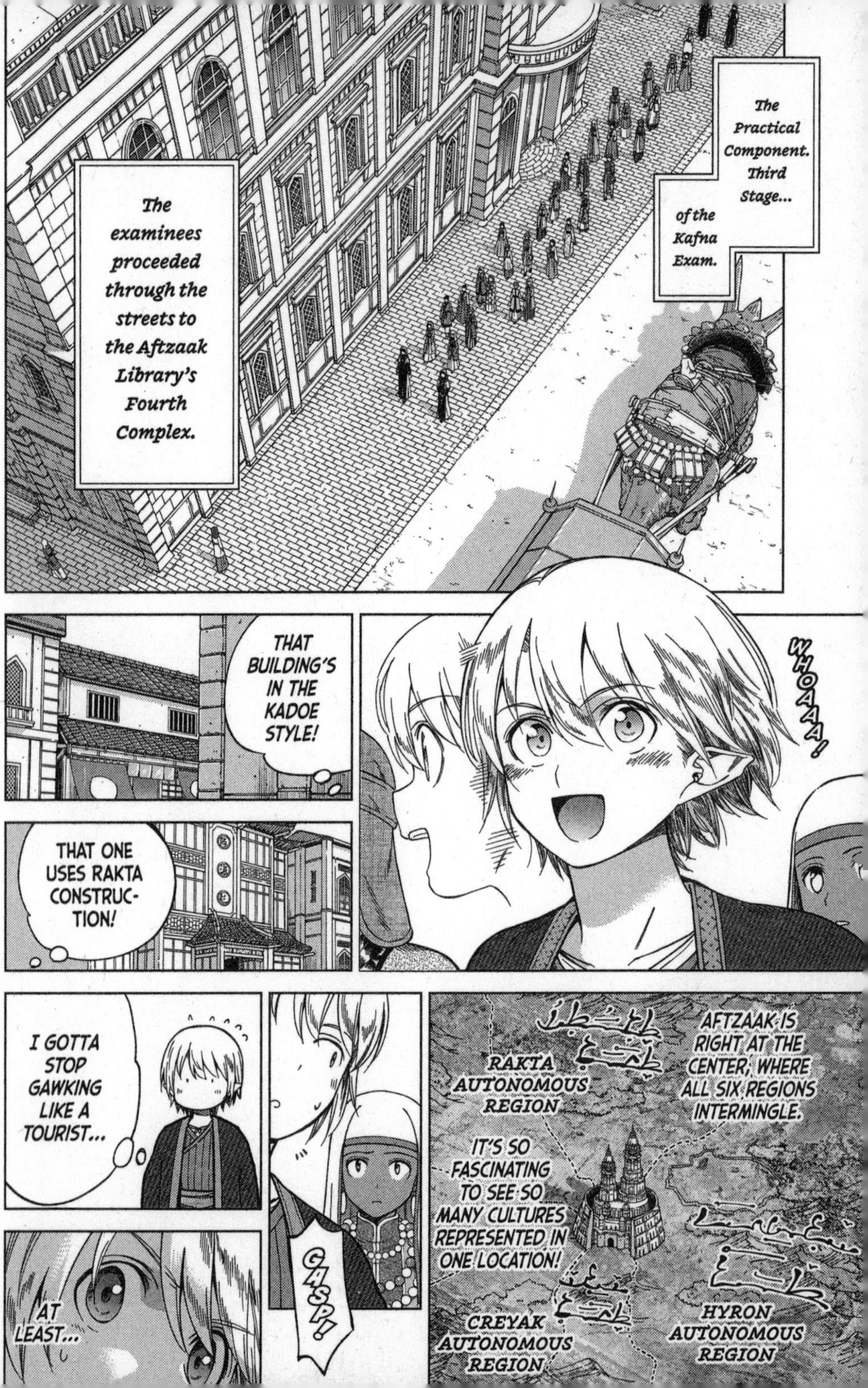
The Practical Component. Third Stage... of the Kafna Exam.
The examinees proceeded through the streets to the Aftzaak Library's Fourth Complex.
WHOAAA!
THAT BUILDING'S IN THE KADOE STYLE!
THAT ONE USES RAKTA CONSTRUCTION!
AFTZAAK IS RIGHT AT THE CENTER, WHERE ALL SIX REGIONS INTERMINGLE.
RAKTA AUTONOMOUS REGION
IT'S SO FASCINATING TO SEE SO MANY CULTURES REPRESENTED IN ONE LOCATION!
HYRON AUTONOMOUS REGION
CREYAK AUTONOMOUS REGION
GASP!
I GOTTA STOP GAWKING LIKE A TOURIST...
AT LEAST...

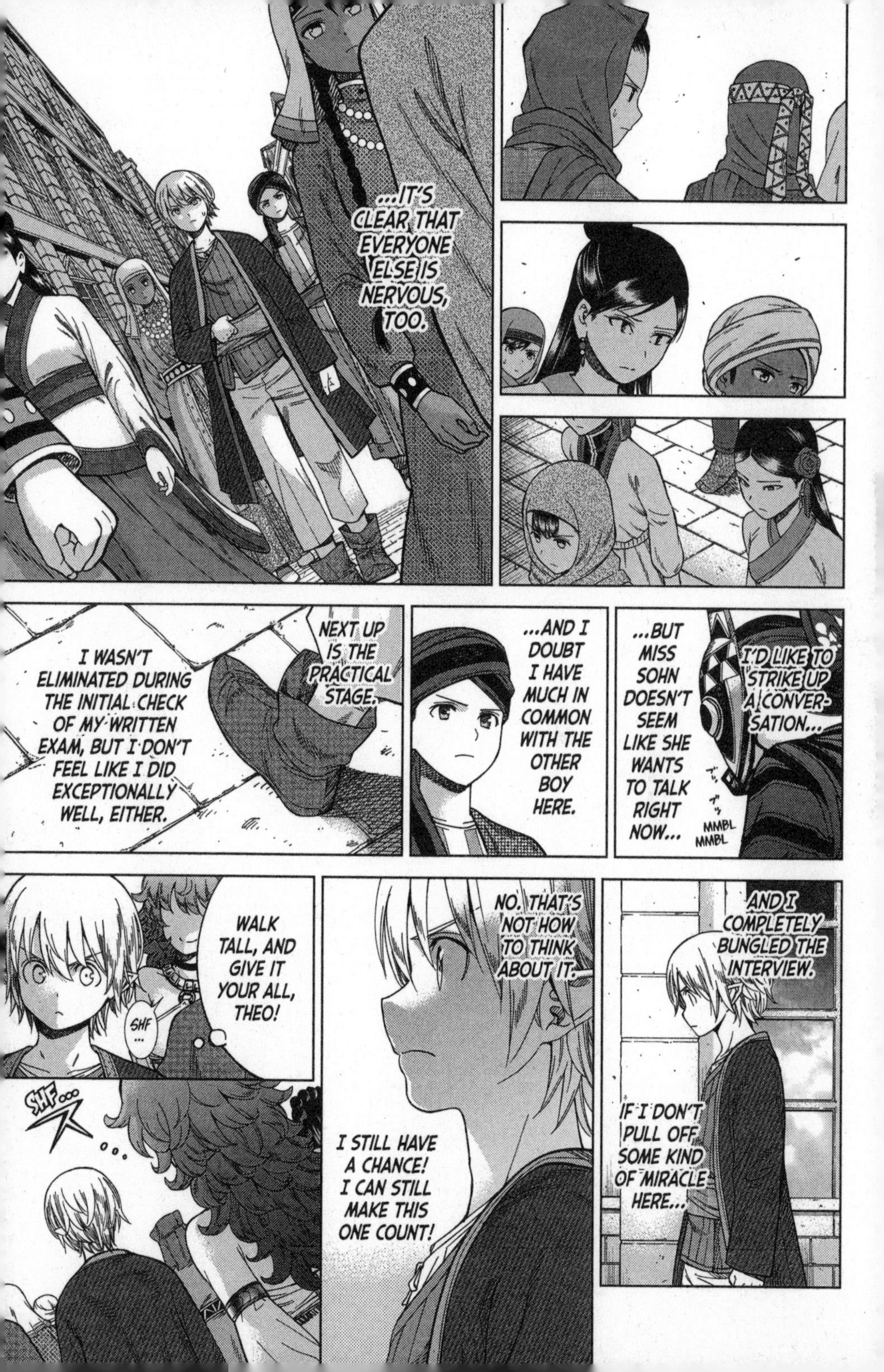
...IT'S CLEAR THAT EVERYONE ELSE IS NERVOUS, TOO.
I'D LIKE TO STRIKE UP A CONVERSATION...
...BUT MISS SOHN DOESN'T SEEM LIKE SHE WANTS TO TALK RIGHT NOW...
MMBL MMBL
...AND I DOUBT I HAVE MUCH IN COMMON WITH THE OTHER BOY HERE.
NEXT UP IS THE PRACTICAL STAGE.
I WASN'T ELIMINATED DURING THE INITIAL CHECK OF MY WRITTEN EXAM, BUT I DON'T FEEL LIKE I DID EXCEPTIONALLY WELL, EITHER.
AND I COMPLETELY BUNGLED THE INTERVIEW.
IF I DON'T PULL OFF SOME KIND OF MIRACLE HERE...
NO. THAT'S NOT HOW TO THINK ABOUT IT.
I STILL HAVE A CHANCE! I CAN STILL MAKE THIS ONE COUNT!
WALK TALL, AND GIVE IT YOUR ALL, THEO!
SHF...
SHF...
...

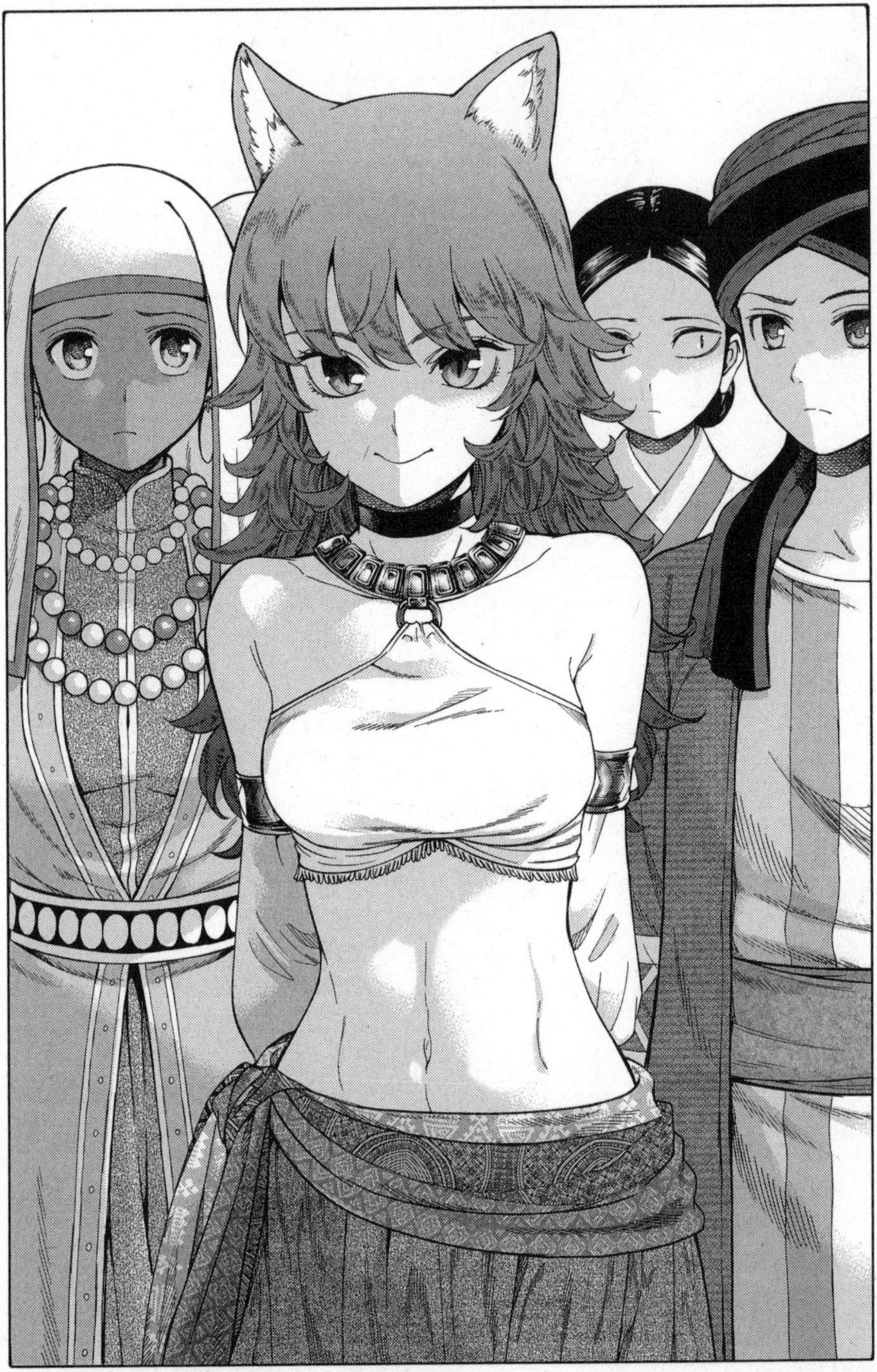

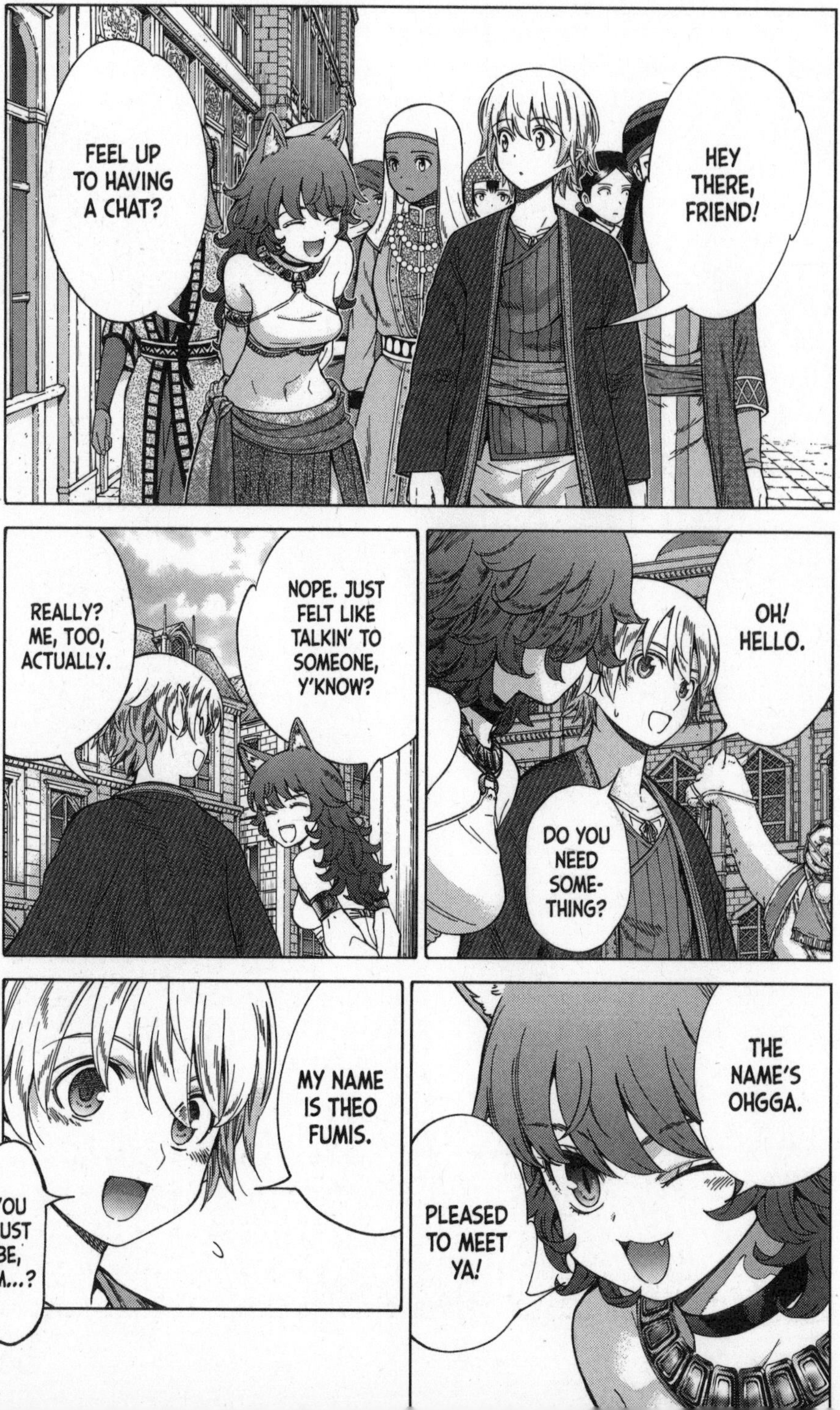
HEY THERE, FRIEND!
FEEL UP TO HAVING A CHAT?
OH! HELLO.
DO YOU NEED SOME-THING?
NOPE. JUST FELT LIKE TALKIN' TO SOMEONE, Y'KNOW?
REALLY? ME, TOO, ACTUALLY.
THE NAME'S OHGGA.
PLEASED TO MEET YA!
MY NAME IS THEO FUMIS.
YOU MUST BE, UM...?

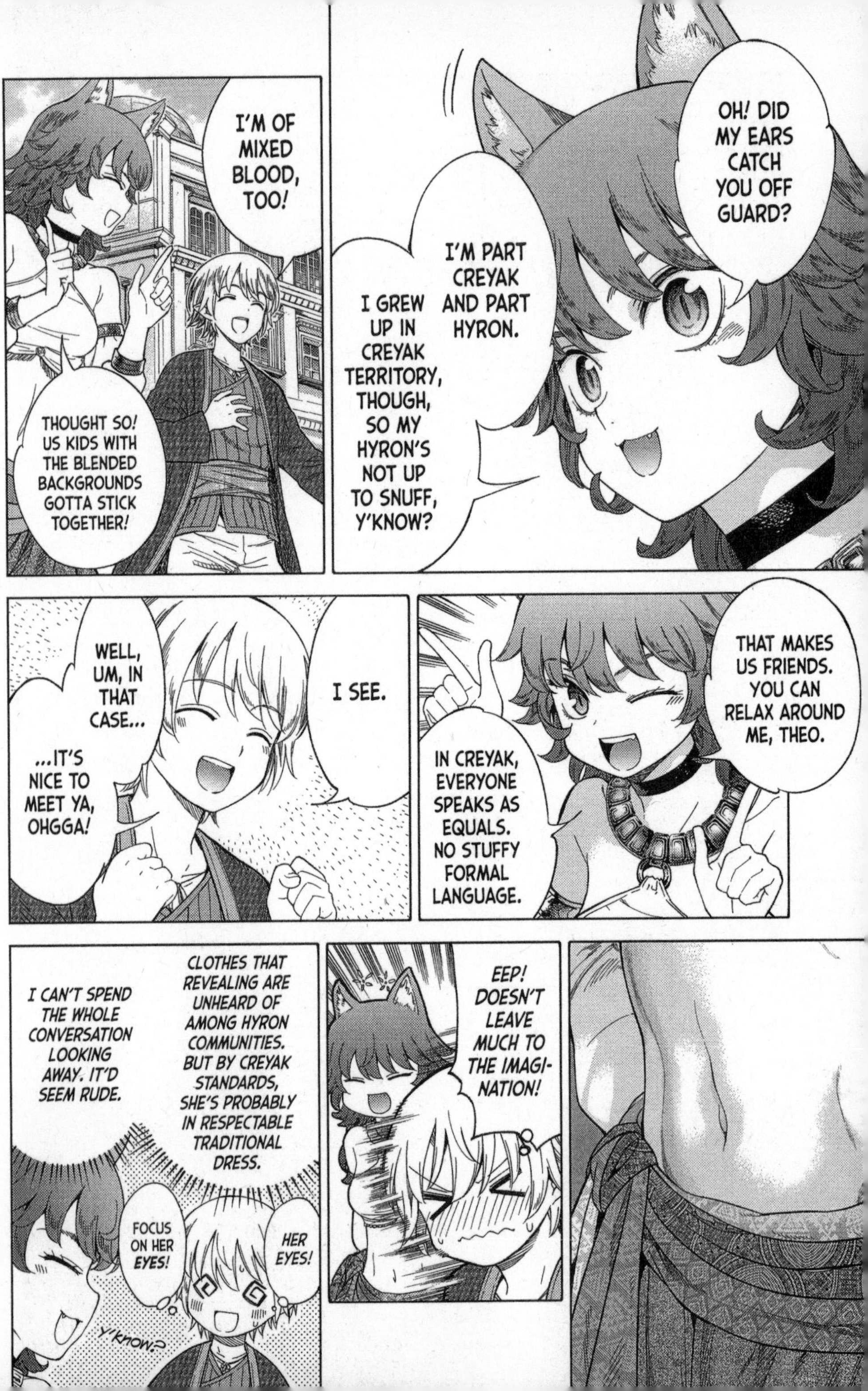
OH! DID MY EARS CATCH YOU OFF GUARD?
I'M PART CREYAK AND PART HYRON.
I GREW UP IN CREYAK TERRITORY, THOUGH, SO MY HYRON'S NOT UP TO SNUFF, Y'KNOW?
I'M OF MIXED BLOOD, TOO!
THOUGHT SO! US KIDS WITH THE BLENDED BACKGROUNDS GOTTA STICK TOGETHER!
THAT MAKES US FRIENDS. YOU CAN RELAX AROUND ME, THEO.
IN CREYAK, EVERYONE SPEAKS AS EQUALS. NO STUFFY FORMAL LANGUAGE.
I SEE.
WELL, UM, IN THAT CASE...
...IT'S NICE TO MEET YA, OHGGA!
EEP! DOESN'T LEAVE MUCH TO THE IMAGI-NATION!
CLOTHES THAT REVEALING ARE UNHEARD OF AMONG HYRON COMMUNITIES. BUT BY CREYAK STANDARDS, SHE'S PROBABLY IN RESPECTABLE TRADITIONAL DRESS.
I CAN'T SPEND THE WHOLE CONVERSATION LOOKING AWAY. IT'D SEEM RUDE.
HER EYES!
FOCUS ON HER EYES!
Y'KNOW?

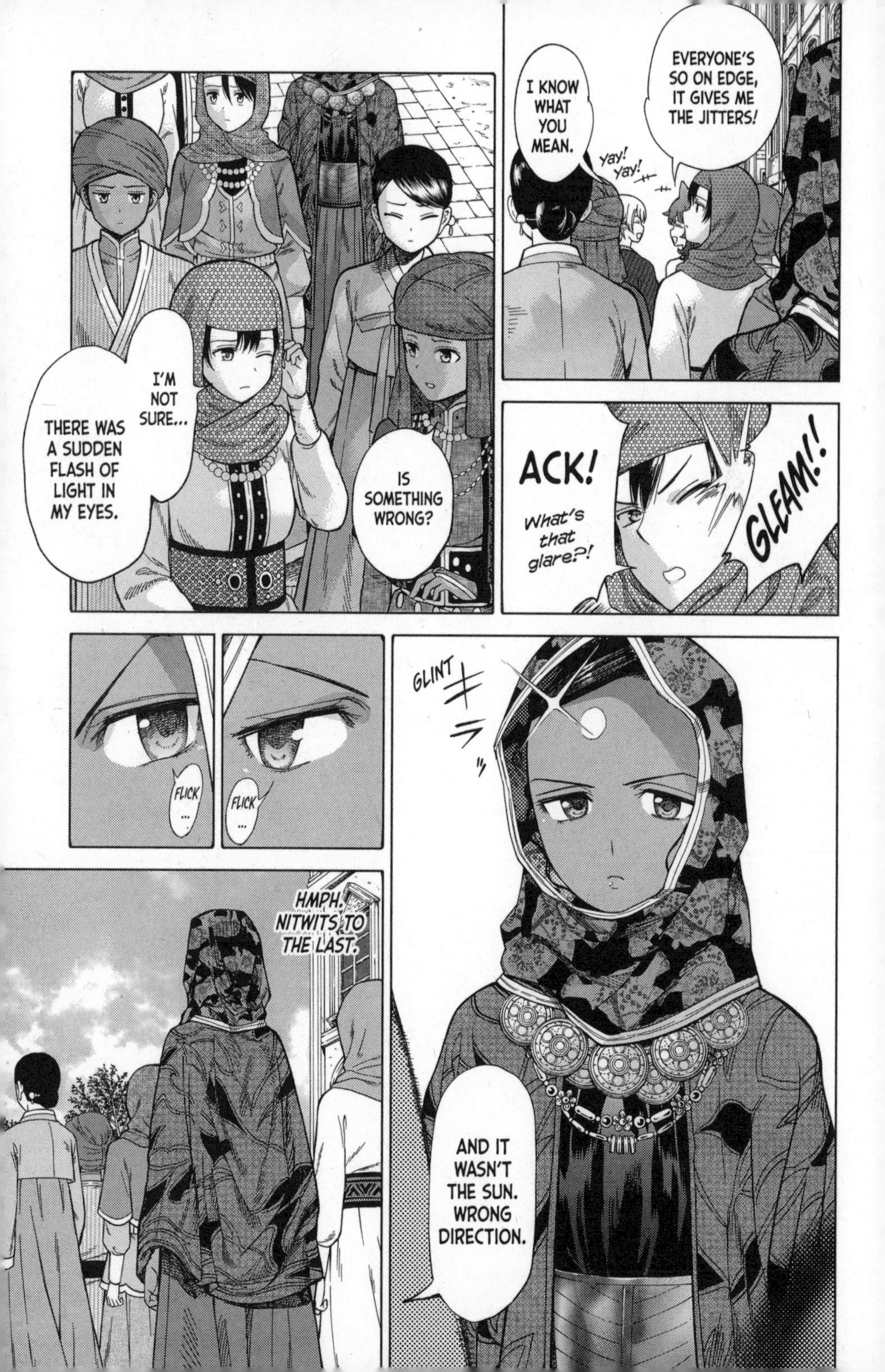
EVERYONE'S SO ON EDGE, IT GIVES ME THE JITTERS!
Yay! Yay!
I KNOW WHAT YOU MEAN.
GLEAM!!
ACK!
What's that glare?!
IS SOMETHING WRONG?
I'M NOT SURE...
THERE WAS A SUDDEN FLASH OF LIGHT IN MY EYES.
GLINT
AND IT WASN'T THE SUN. WRONG DIRECTION.
FLICK ...
FLICK ...
HMPH. NITWITS TO THE LAST.

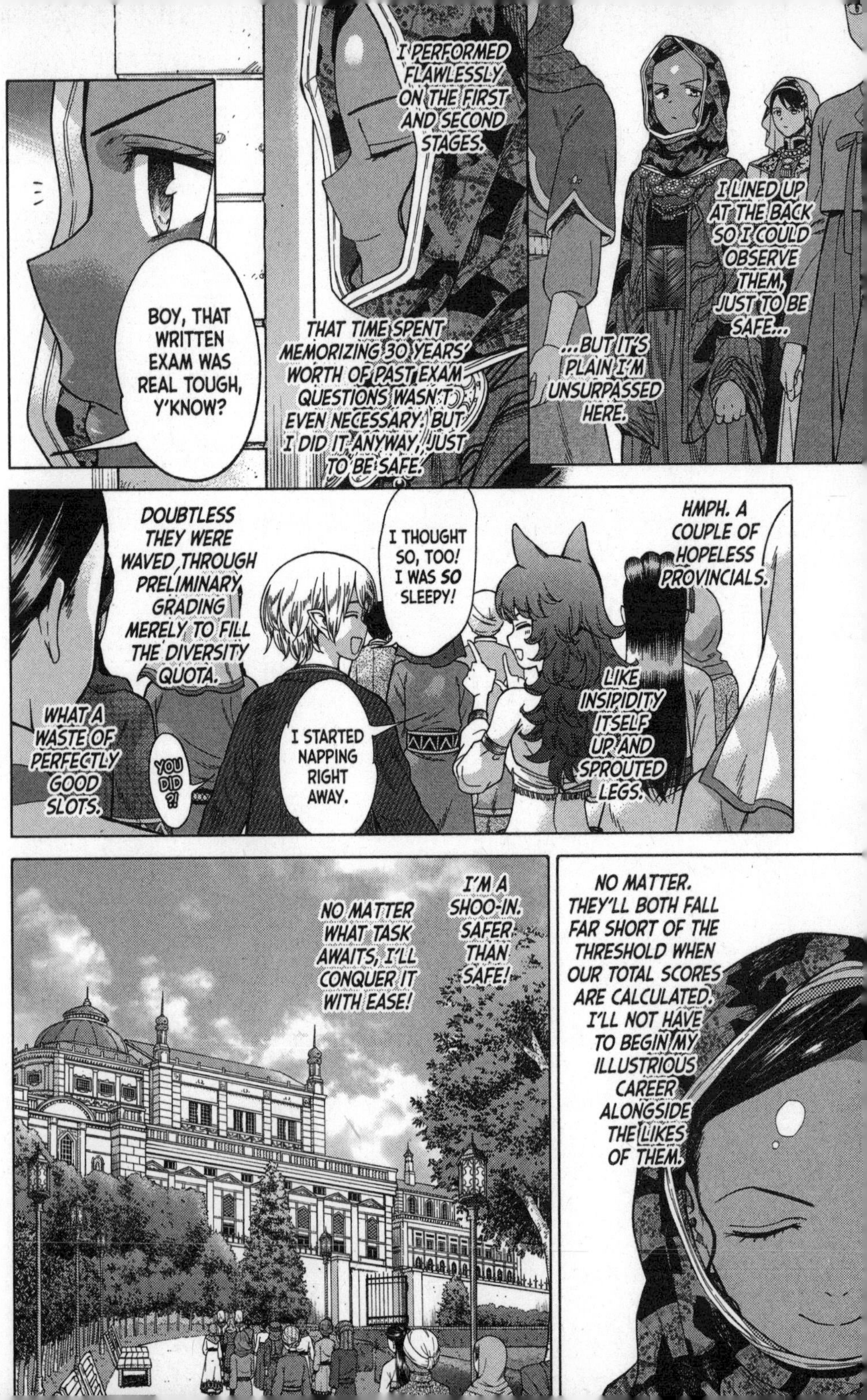
I LINED UP AT THE BACK SO I COULD OBSERVE THEM, JUST TO BE SAFE...
...BUT IT'S PLAIN I'M UNSURPASSED HERE.
I PERFORMED FLAWLESSLY ON THE FIRST AND SECOND STAGES.
THAT TIME SPENT MEMORIZING 30 YEARS' WORTH OF PAST EXAM QUESTIONS WASN'T EVEN NECESSARY, BUT I DID IT ANYWAY, JUST TO BE SAFE.
BOY, THAT WRITTEN EXAM WAS REAL TOUGH, Y'KNOW?
HMPH. A COUPLE OF HOPELESS PROVINCIALS.
I THOUGHT SO, TOO! I WAS SO SLEEPY!
LIKE INSIPIDITY ITSELF UP AND SPROUTED LEGS.
DOUBTLESS THEY WERE WAVED THROUGH PRELIMINARY GRADING MERELY TO FILL THE DIVERSITY QUOTA.
I STARTED NAPPING RIGHT AWAY.
YOU DID?!
WHAT A WASTE OF PERFECTLY GOOD SLOTS.
NO MATTER. THEY'LL BOTH FALL FAR SHORT OF THE THRESHOLD WHEN OUR TOTAL SCORES ARE CALCULATED. I'LL NOT HAVE TO BEGIN MY ILLUSTRIOUS CAREER ALONGSIDE THE LIKES OF THEM.
I'M A SHOO-IN. SAFER THAN SAFE!
NO MATTER WHAT TASK AWAITS, I'LL CONQUER IT WITH EASE!

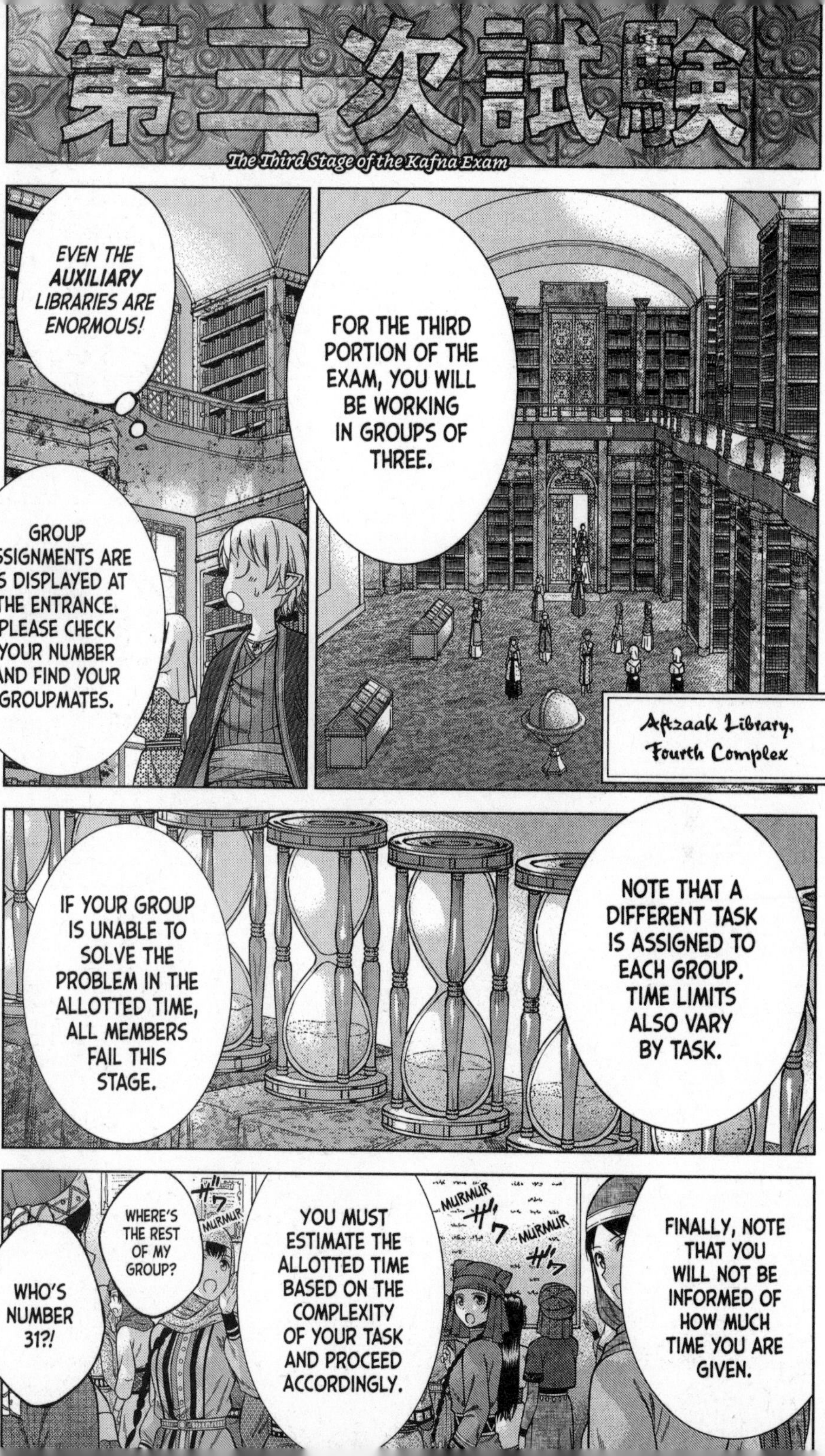
第三次試験
The Third Stage of the Kafna Exam
FOR THE THIRD PORTION OF THE EXAM, YOU WILL BE WORKING IN GROUPS OF THREE.
Aftzaak Library, Fourth Complex
EVEN THE AUXILIARY LIBRARIES ARE ENORMOUS!
GROUP ASSIGNMENTS ARE AS DISPLAYED AT THE ENTRANCE. PLEASE CHECK YOUR NUMBER AND FIND YOUR GROUPMATES.
NOTE THAT A DIFFERENT TASK IS ASSIGNED TO EACH GROUP. TIME LIMITS ALSO VARY BY TASK.
IF YOUR GROUP IS UNABLE TO SOLVE THE PROBLEM IN THE ALLOTTED TIME, ALL MEMBERS FAIL THIS STAGE.
FINALLY, NOTE THAT YOU WILL NOT BE INFORMED OF HOW MUCH TIME YOU ARE GIVEN.
MURMUR
ザワ
MURMUR
ザワ
YOU MUST ESTIMATE THE ALLOTTED TIME BASED ON THE COMPLEXITY OF YOUR TASK AND PROCEED ACCORDINGLY.
ザワ
MURMUR
WHERE'S THE REST OF MY GROUP?
WHO'S NUMBER 31?!

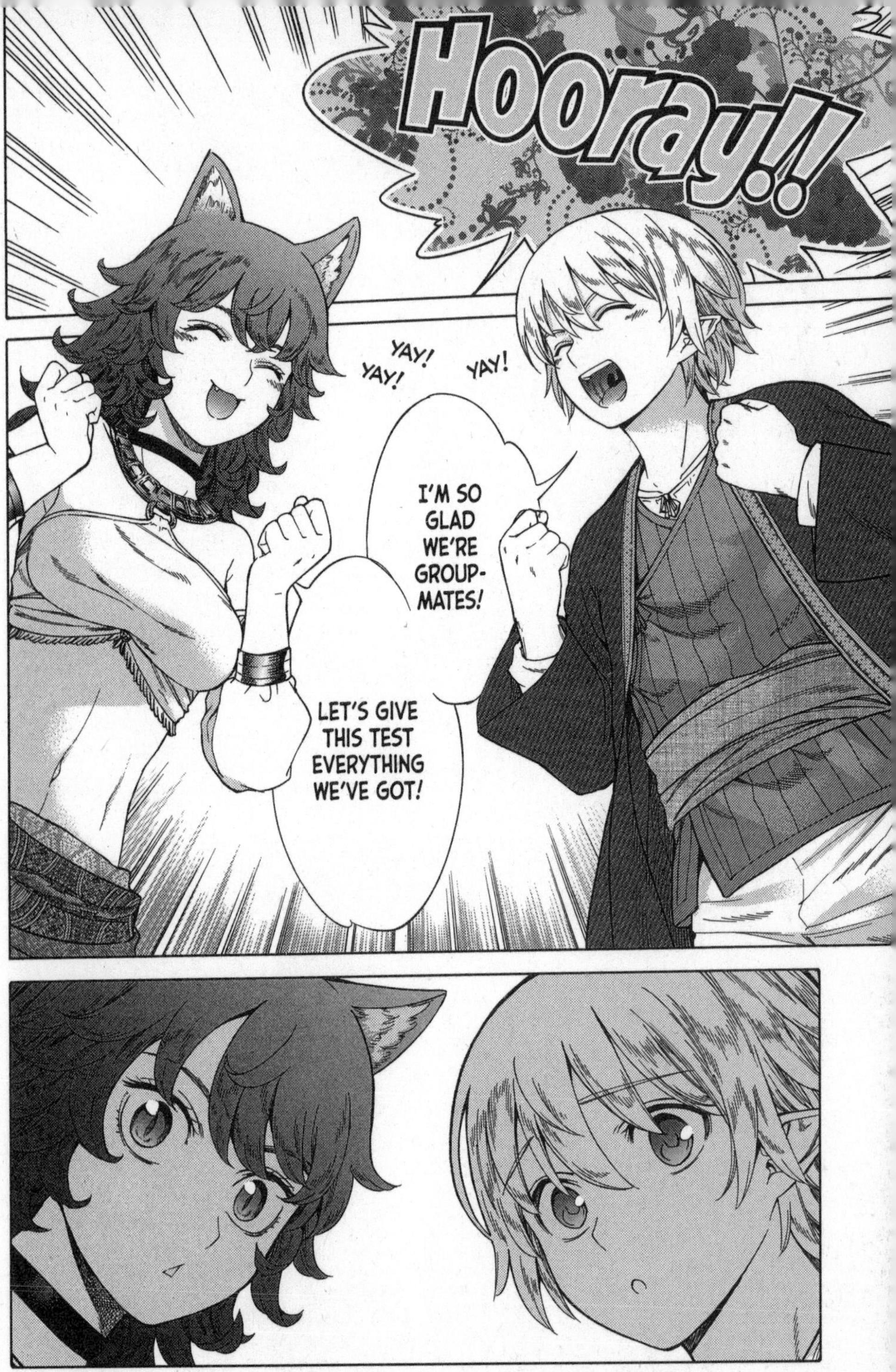
HOORAY!!
YAY! YAY! YAY!
I'M SO GLAD WE'RE GROUP-MATES!
LET'S GIVE THIS TEST EVERYTHING WE'VE GOT!

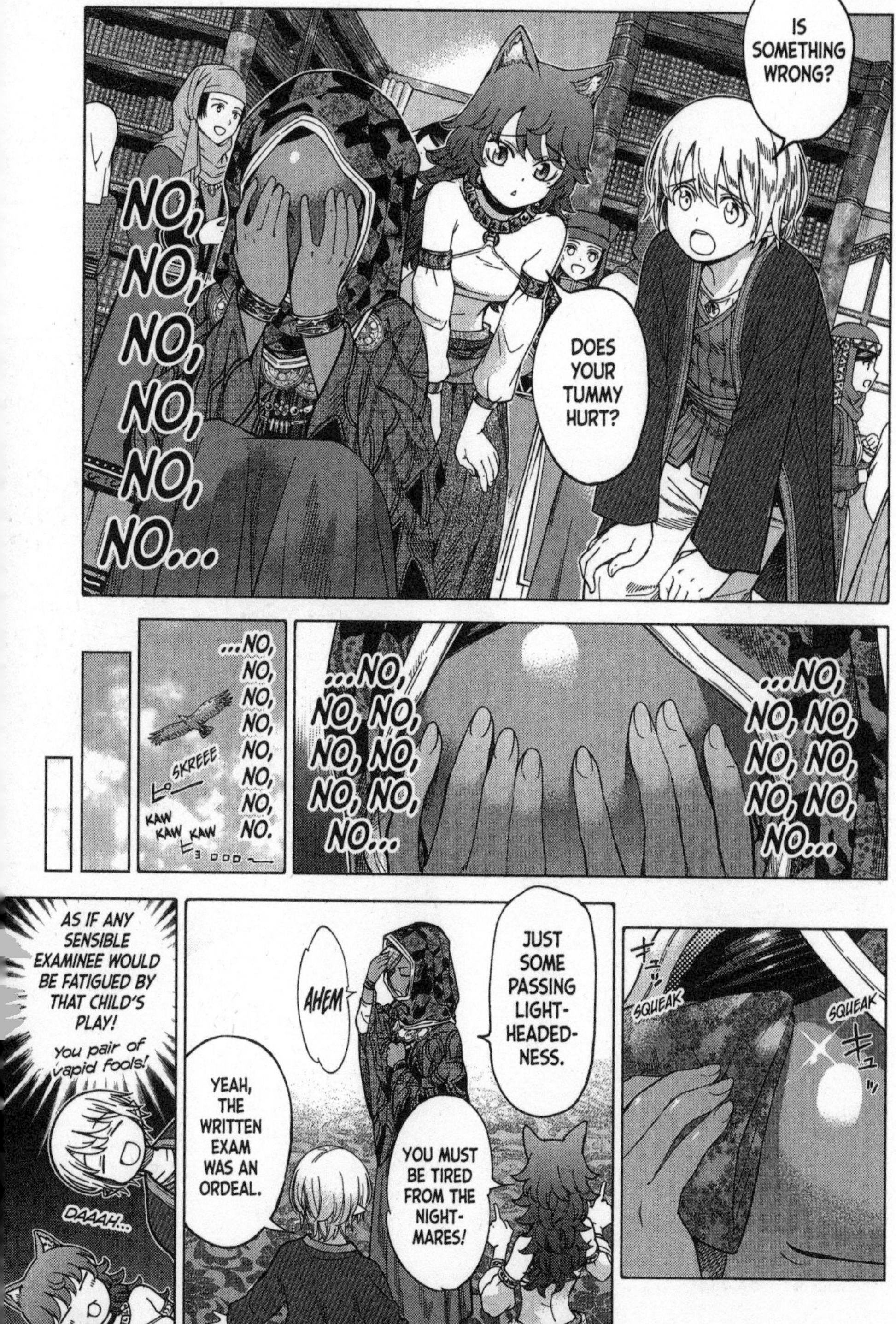
IS SOMETHING WRONG?
DOES YOUR TUMMY HURT?
NO, NO, NO, NO, NO, NO...
...NO, NO, NO, NO, NO, NO, NO, NO...
...NO, NO, NO, NO, NO, NO, NO, NO...
...NO, NO, NO, NO, NO, NO, NO, NO.
SKREEE
KAW KAW KAW
SQUEAK
SQUEAK
JUST SOME PASSING LIGHT-HEADED-NESS.
AHEM
YOU MUST BE TIRED FROM THE NIGHT-MARES!
YEAH, THE WRITTEN EXAM WAS AN ORDEAL.
AS IF ANY SENSIBLE EXAMINEE WOULD BE FATIGUED BY THAT CHILD'S PLAY!
You pair of vapid fools!
DAAAH...

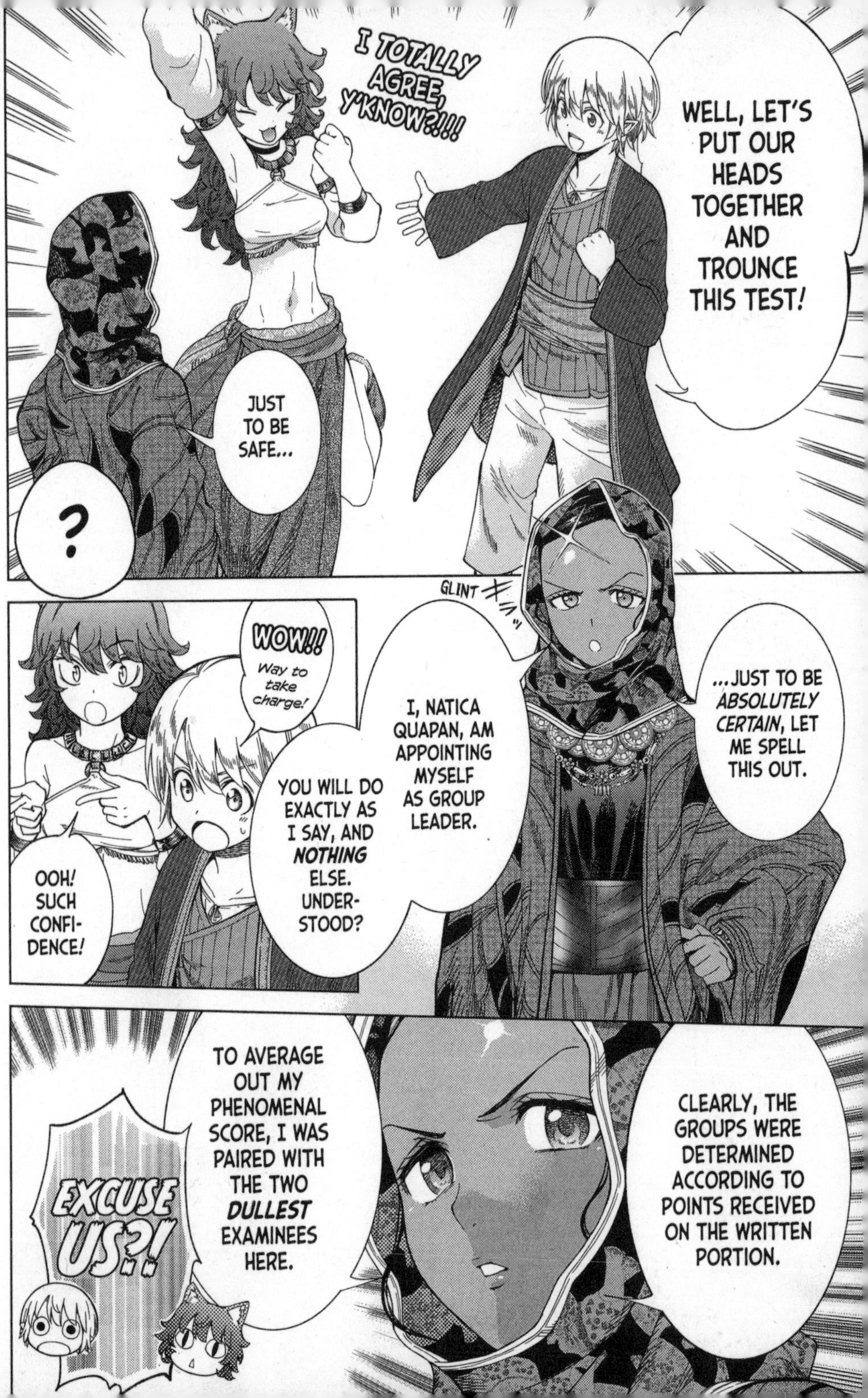
WELL, LET'S PUT OUR HEADS TOGETHER AND TROUNCE THIS TEST!
I TOTALLY AGREE, Y'KNOW?!!!
JUST TO BE SAFE...
?
GLINT
...JUST TO BE ABSOLUTELY CERTAIN, LET ME SPELL THIS OUT.
I, NATICA QUAPAN, AM APPOINTING MYSELF AS GROUP LEADER.
YOU WILL DO EXACTLY AS I SAY, AND NOTHING ELSE. UNDERSTOOD?
WOW!! Way to take charge!
OOH! SUCH CONFIDENCE!
CLEARLY, THE GROUPS WERE DETERMINED ACCORDING TO POINTS RECEIVED ON THE WRITTEN PORTION.
TO AVERAGE OUT MY PHENOMENAL SCORE, I WAS PAIRED WITH THE TWO DULLEST EXAMINEES HERE.
EXCUSE US?!

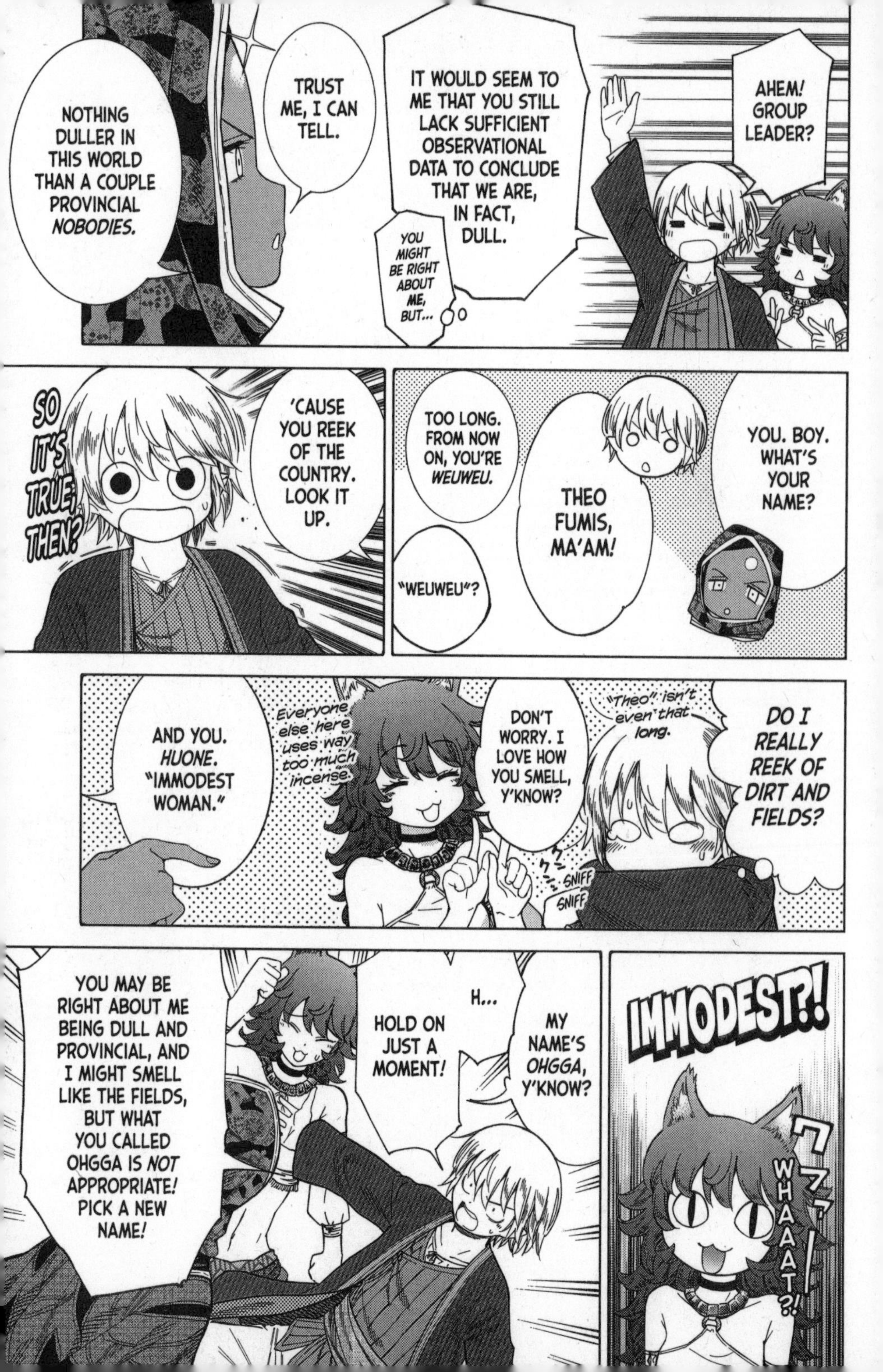

AHEM! GROUP LEADER?
IT WOULD SEEM TO ME THAT YOU STILL LACK SUFFICIENT OBSERVATIONAL DATA TO CONCLUDE THAT WE ARE, IN FACT, DULL.
YOU MIGHT BE RIGHT ABOUT ME, BUT...
TRUST ME, I CAN TELL.
NOTHING DULLER IN THIS WORLD THAN A COUPLE PROVINCIAL *NOBODIES.*
YOU. BOY. WHAT'S YOUR NAME?
THEO FUMIS, MA'AM!
TOO LONG. FROM NOW ON, YOU'RE *WEUWEU.*
"WEUWEU"?
'CAUSE YOU REEK OF THE COUNTRY. LOOK IT UP.
SO IT'S TRUE, THEN?
DO I REALLY REEK OF DIRT AND FIELDS?
"Theo" isn't even that long.
DON'T WORRY. I LOVE HOW YOU SMELL, Y'KNOW?
SNIFF SNIFF
Everyone else here uses way too much incense.
AND YOU. *HUONE.* "IMMODEST WOMAN."
IMMODEST?!
WHAAAT?!
MY NAME'S *OHGGA,* Y'KNOW?
H...
HOLD ON JUST A MOMENT!
YOU MAY BE RIGHT ABOUT ME BEING DULL AND PROVINCIAL, AND I MIGHT SMELL LIKE THE FIELDS, BUT WHAT YOU CALLED OHGGA IS *NOT* APPROPRIATE! PICK A NEW NAME!

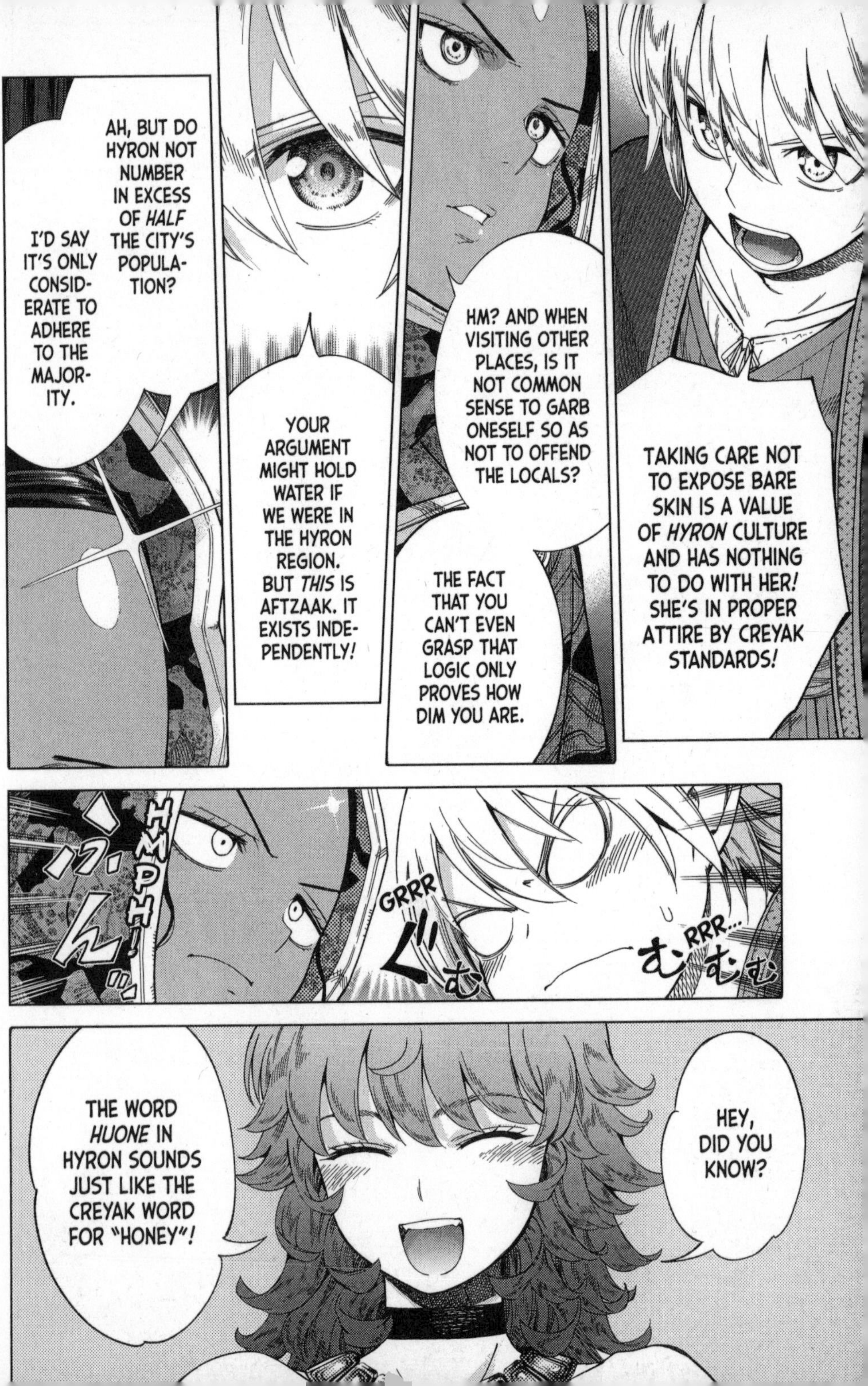
TAKING CARE NOT TO EXPOSE BARE SKIN IS A VALUE OF *HYRON* CULTURE AND HAS NOTHING TO DO WITH HER! SHE'S IN PROPER ATTIRE BY CREYAK STANDARDS!
HM? AND WHEN VISITING OTHER PLACES, IS IT NOT COMMON SENSE TO GARB ONESELF SO AS NOT TO OFFEND THE LOCALS?
THE FACT THAT YOU CAN'T EVEN GRASP THAT LOGIC ONLY PROVES HOW DIM YOU ARE.
YOUR ARGUMENT MIGHT HOLD WATER IF WE WERE IN THE HYRON REGION. BUT *THIS* IS AFTZAAK. IT EXISTS INDEPENDENTLY!
AH, BUT DO HYRON NOT NUMBER IN EXCESS OF *HALF* THE CITY'S POPULATION?
I'D SAY IT'S ONLY CONSIDERATE TO ADHERE TO THE MAJORITY.
むむむ RRR...
ぐむ GRRR
ふんっ HMPH!
HEY, DID YOU KNOW?
THE WORD *HUONE* IN HYRON SOUNDS JUST LIKE THE CREYAK WORD FOR "HONEY"!

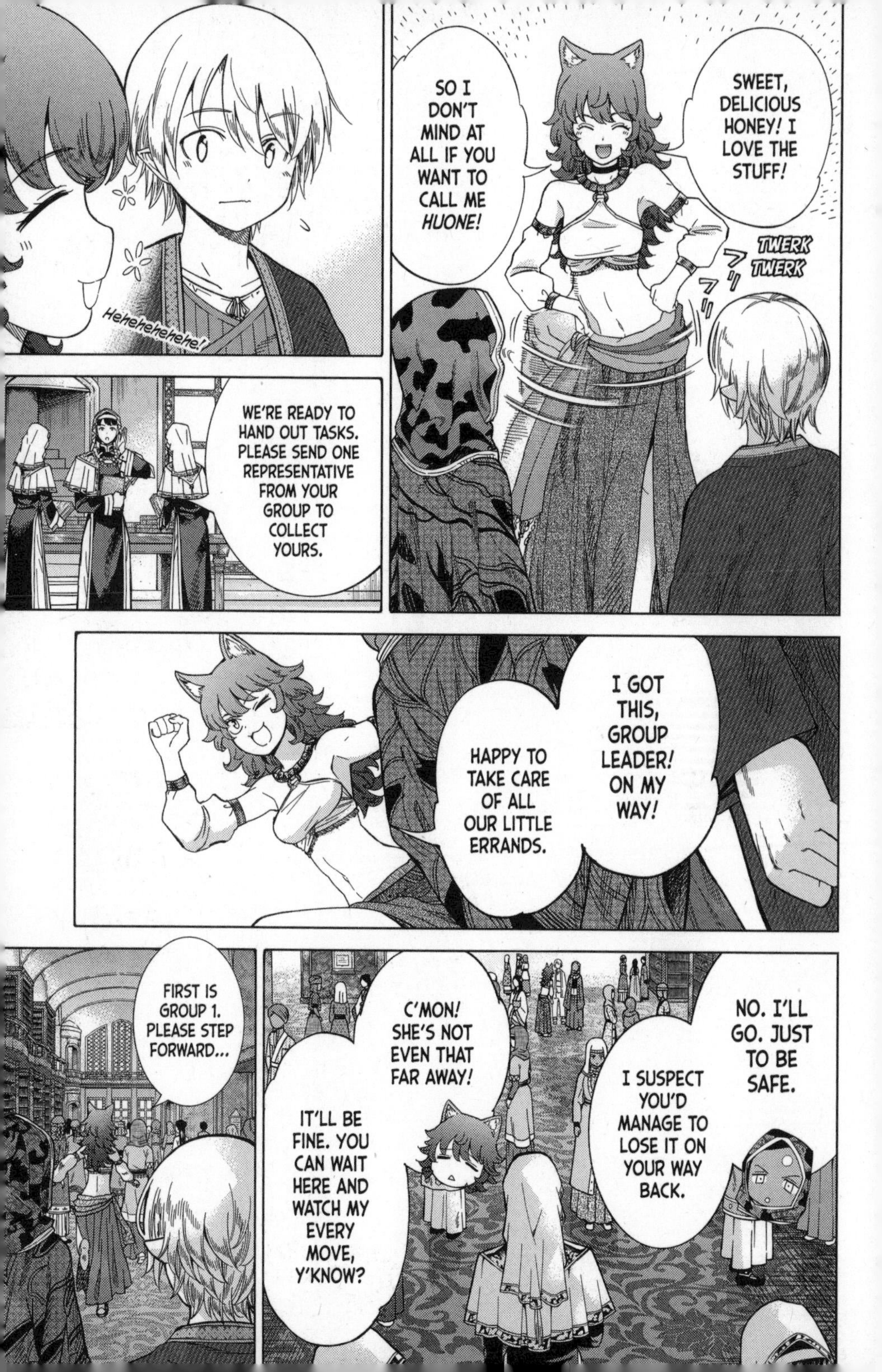
SWEET, DELICIOUS HONEY! I LOVE THE STUFF!
SO I DON'T MIND AT ALL IF YOU WANT TO CALL ME *HUONE!*
TWERK TWERK
Hehehehehehe!
WE'RE READY TO HAND OUT TASKS. PLEASE SEND ONE REPRESENTATIVE FROM YOUR GROUP TO COLLECT YOURS.
I GOT THIS, GROUP LEADER! ON MY WAY!
HAPPY TO TAKE CARE OF ALL OUR LITTLE ERRANDS.
NO. I'LL GO. JUST TO BE SAFE.
I SUSPECT YOU'D MANAGE TO LOSE IT ON YOUR WAY BACK.
C'MON! SHE'S NOT EVEN THAT FAR AWAY!
IT'LL BE FINE. YOU CAN WAIT HERE AND WATCH MY EVERY MOVE, Y'KNOW?
FIRST IS GROUP 1. PLEASE STEP FORWARD...

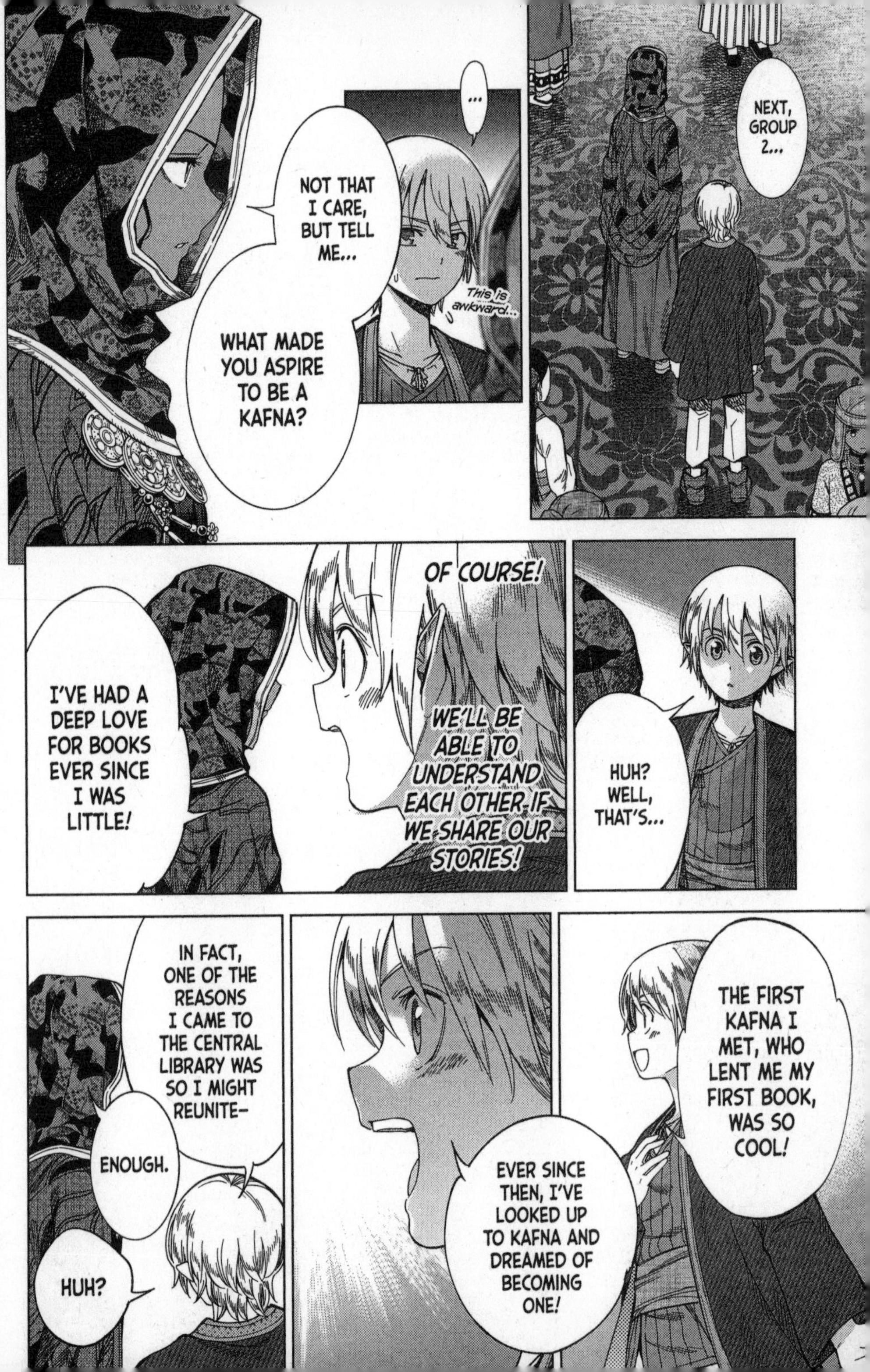
NEXT, GROUP 2...
...
This is awkward...
NOT THAT I CARE, BUT TELL ME...
WHAT MADE YOU ASPIRE TO BE A KAFNA?
HUH? WELL, THAT'S...
OF COURSE!
WE'LL BE ABLE TO UNDERSTAND EACH OTHER IF WE SHARE OUR STORIES!
I'VE HAD A DEEP LOVE FOR BOOKS EVER SINCE I WAS LITTLE!
THE FIRST KAFNA I MET, WHO LENT ME MY FIRST BOOK, WAS SO COOL!
EVER SINCE THEN, I'VE LOOKED UP TO KAFNA AND DREAMED OF BECOMING ONE!
IN FACT, ONE OF THE REASONS I CAME TO THE CENTRAL LIBRARY WAS SO I MIGHT REUNITE–
ENOUGH.
HUH?

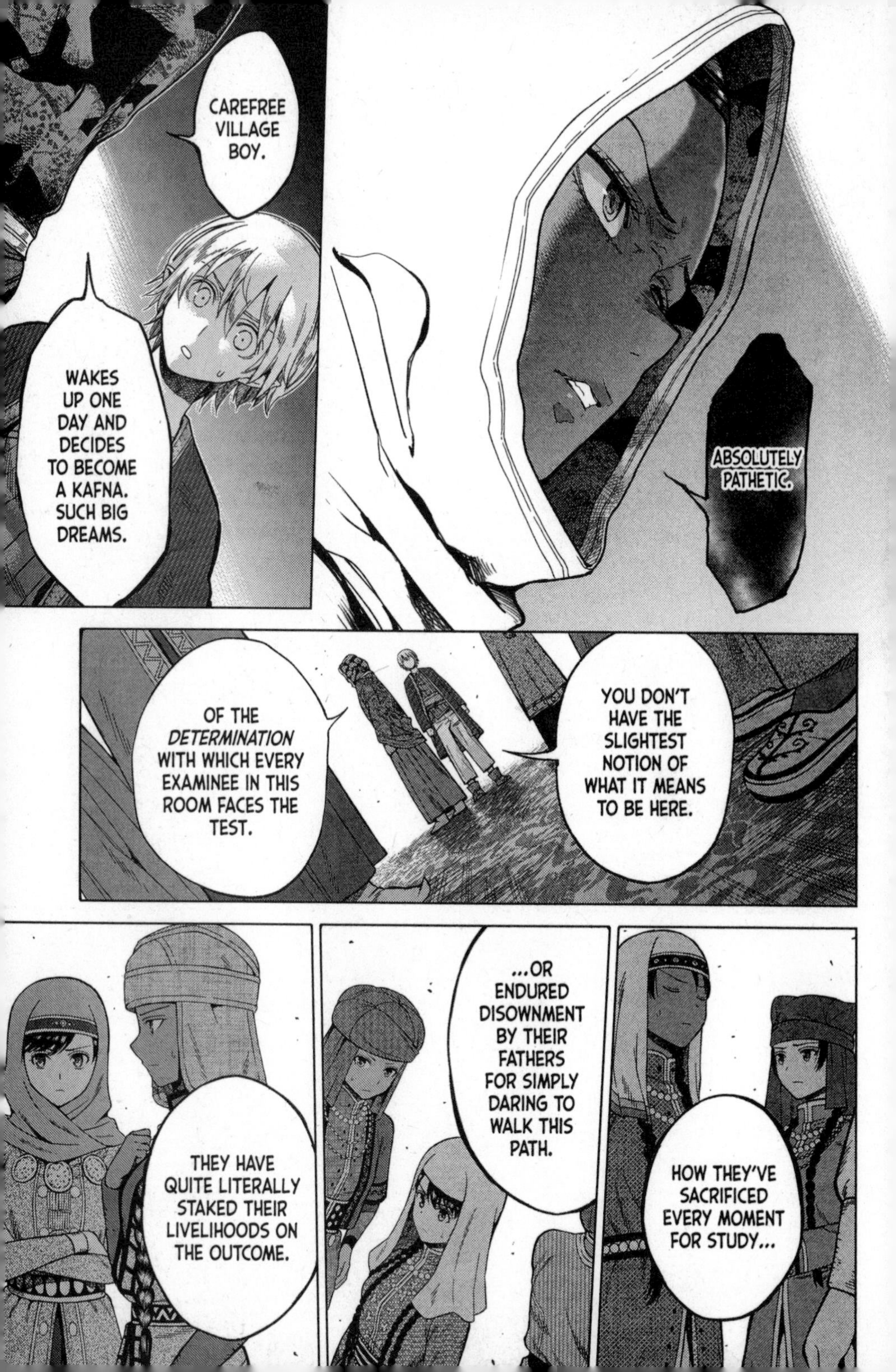
ABSOLUTELY PATHETIC.
CAREFREE VILLAGE BOY.
WAKES UP ONE DAY AND DECIDES TO BECOME A KAFNA. SUCH BIG DREAMS.
YOU DON'T HAVE THE SLIGHTEST NOTION OF WHAT IT MEANS TO BE HERE.
OF THE *DETERMINATION* WITH WHICH EVERY EXAMINEE IN THIS ROOM FACES THE TEST.
HOW THEY'VE SACRIFICED EVERY MOMENT FOR STUDY...
...OR ENDURED DISOWNMENT BY THEIR FATHERS FOR SIMPLY DARING TO WALK THIS PATH.
THEY HAVE QUITE LITERALLY STAKED THEIR LIVELIHOODS ON THE OUTCOME.

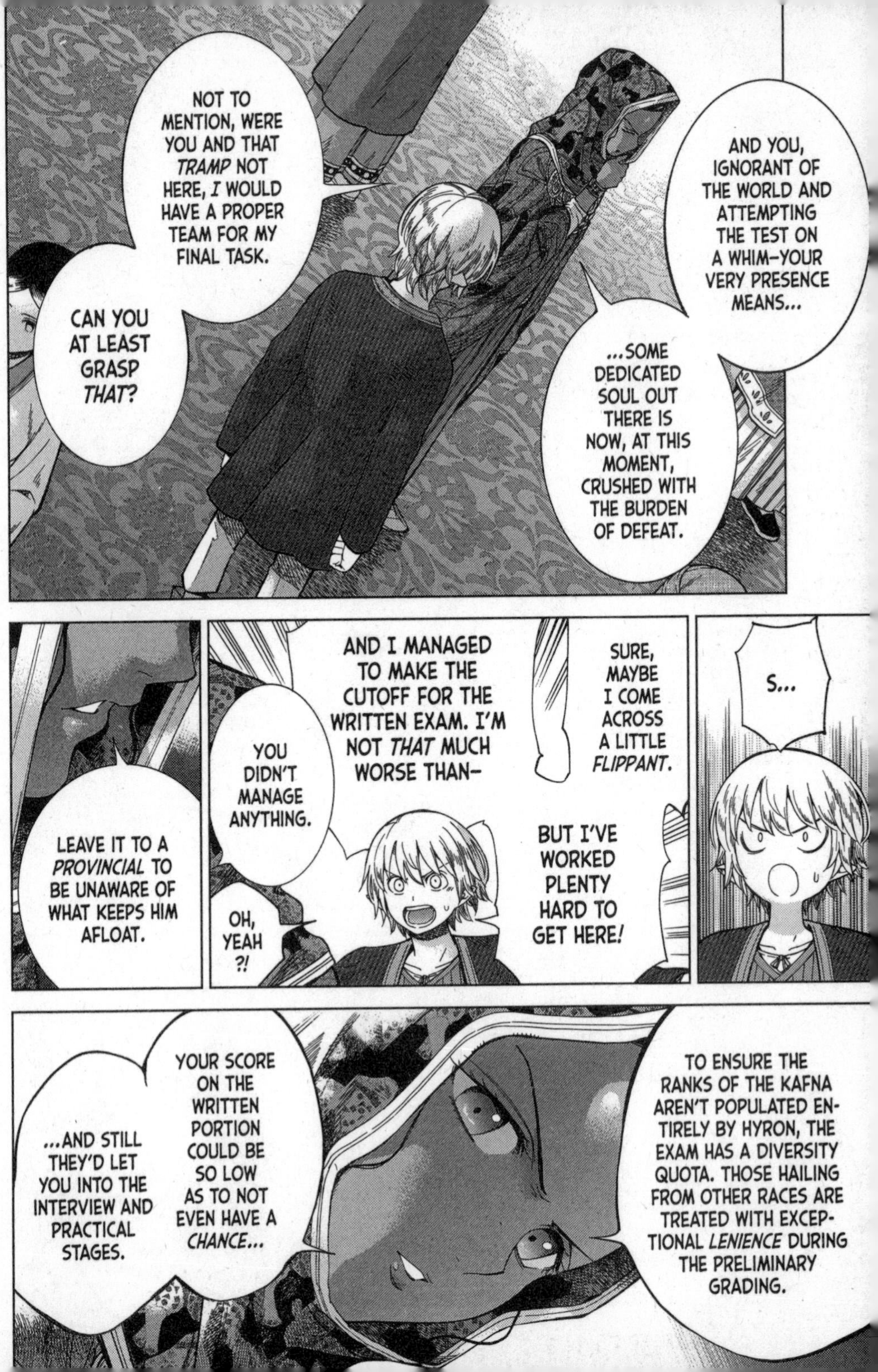
AND YOU, IGNORANT OF THE WORLD AND ATTEMPTING THE TEST ON A WHIM—YOUR VERY PRESENCE MEANS...
...SOME DEDICATED SOUL OUT THERE IS NOW, AT THIS MOMENT, CRUSHED WITH THE BURDEN OF DEFEAT.
NOT TO MENTION, WERE YOU AND THAT *TRAMP* NOT HERE, *I* WOULD HAVE A PROPER TEAM FOR MY FINAL TASK.
CAN YOU AT LEAST GRASP *THAT*?
S...
SURE, MAYBE I COME ACROSS A LITTLE *FLIPPANT*.
BUT I'VE WORKED PLENTY HARD TO GET HERE!
AND I MANAGED TO MAKE THE CUTOFF FOR THE WRITTEN EXAM. I'M NOT *THAT* MUCH WORSE THAN—
YOU DIDN'T MANAGE ANYTHING.
OH, YEAH?!
LEAVE IT TO A *PROVINCIAL* TO BE UNAWARE OF WHAT KEEPS HIM AFLOAT.
TO ENSURE THE RANKS OF THE KAFNA AREN'T POPULATED ENTIRELY BY HYRON, THE EXAM HAS A DIVERSITY QUOTA. THOSE HAILING FROM OTHER RACES ARE TREATED WITH EXCEPTIONAL *LENIENCE* DURING THE PRELIMINARY GRADING.
YOUR SCORE ON THE WRITTEN PORTION COULD BE SO LOW AS TO NOT EVEN HAVE A *CHANCE*...
...AND STILL THEY'D LET YOU INTO THE INTERVIEW AND PRACTICAL STAGES.

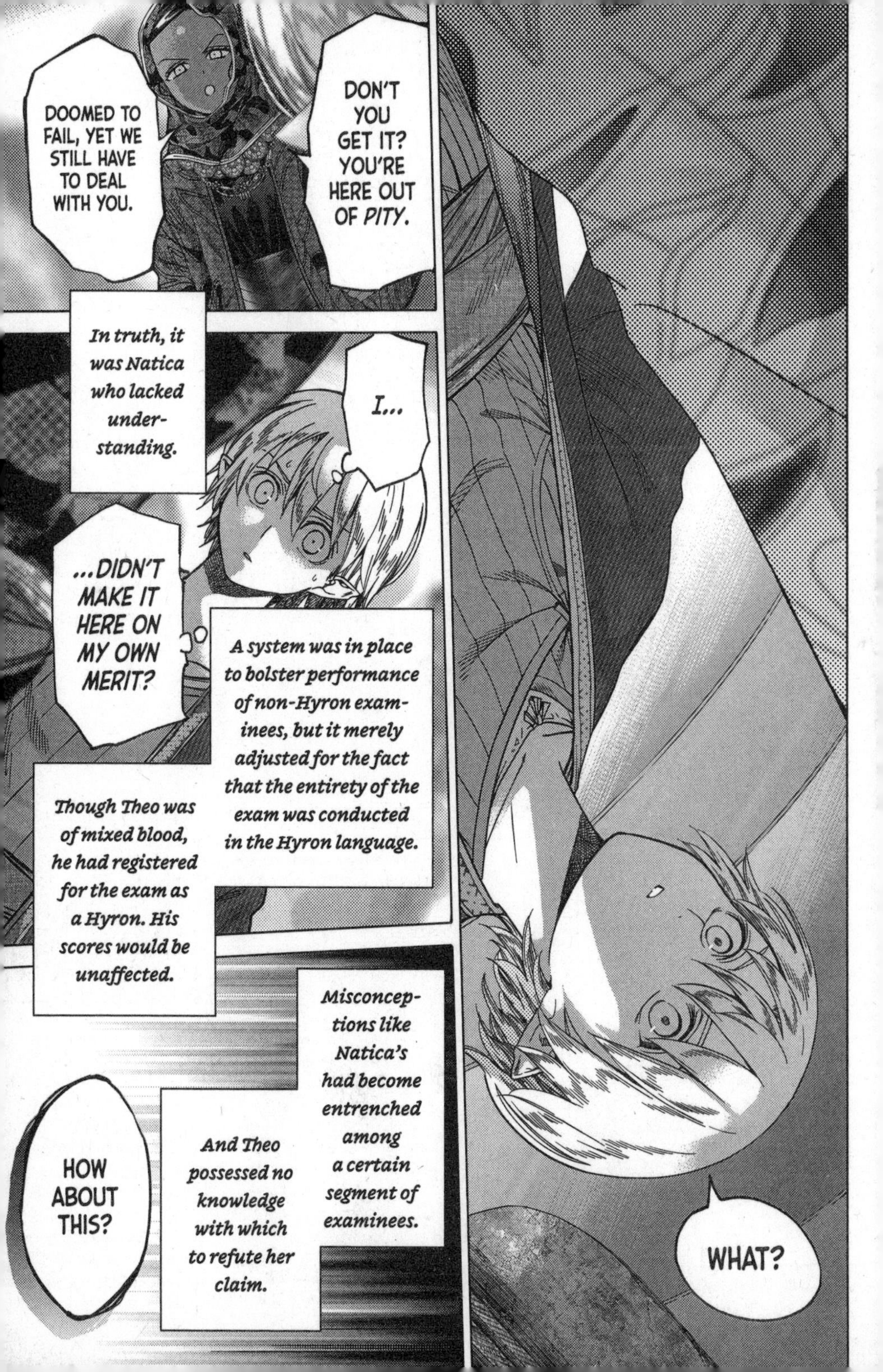
WHAT?
DON'T YOU GET IT? YOU'RE HERE OUT OF *PITY*.
DOOMED TO FAIL, YET WE STILL HAVE TO DEAL WITH YOU.
In truth, it was Natica who lacked under-standing.
I...
...DIDN'T MAKE IT HERE ON MY OWN MERIT?
A system was in place to bolster performance of non-Hyron exam-inees, but it merely adjusted for the fact that the entirety of the exam was conducted in the Hyron language.
Though Theo was of mixed blood, he had registered for the exam as a Hyron. His scores would be unaffected.
Misconcep-tions like Natica's had become entrenched among a certain segment of examinees.
And Theo possessed no knowledge with which to refute her claim.
HOW ABOUT THIS?

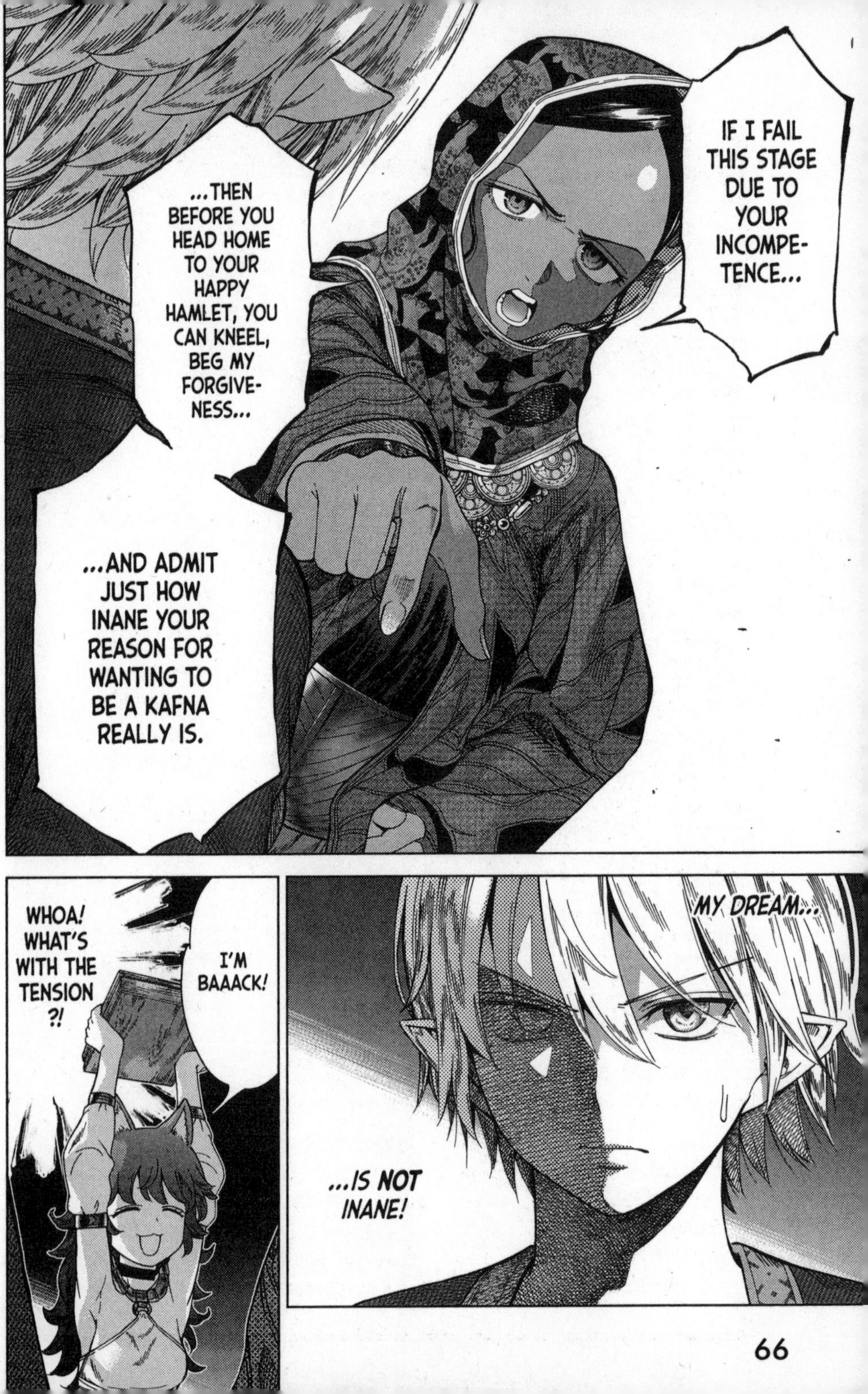
IF I FAIL THIS STAGE DUE TO YOUR INCOMPE-TENCE...
...THEN BEFORE YOU HEAD HOME TO YOUR HAPPY HAMLET, YOU CAN KNEEL, BEG MY FORGIVE-NESS...
...AND ADMIT JUST HOW INANE YOUR REASON FOR WANTING TO BE A KAFNA REALLY IS.
MY DREAM...
...IS NOT INANE!
I'M BAAACK!
WHOA! WHAT'S WITH THE TENSION ?!

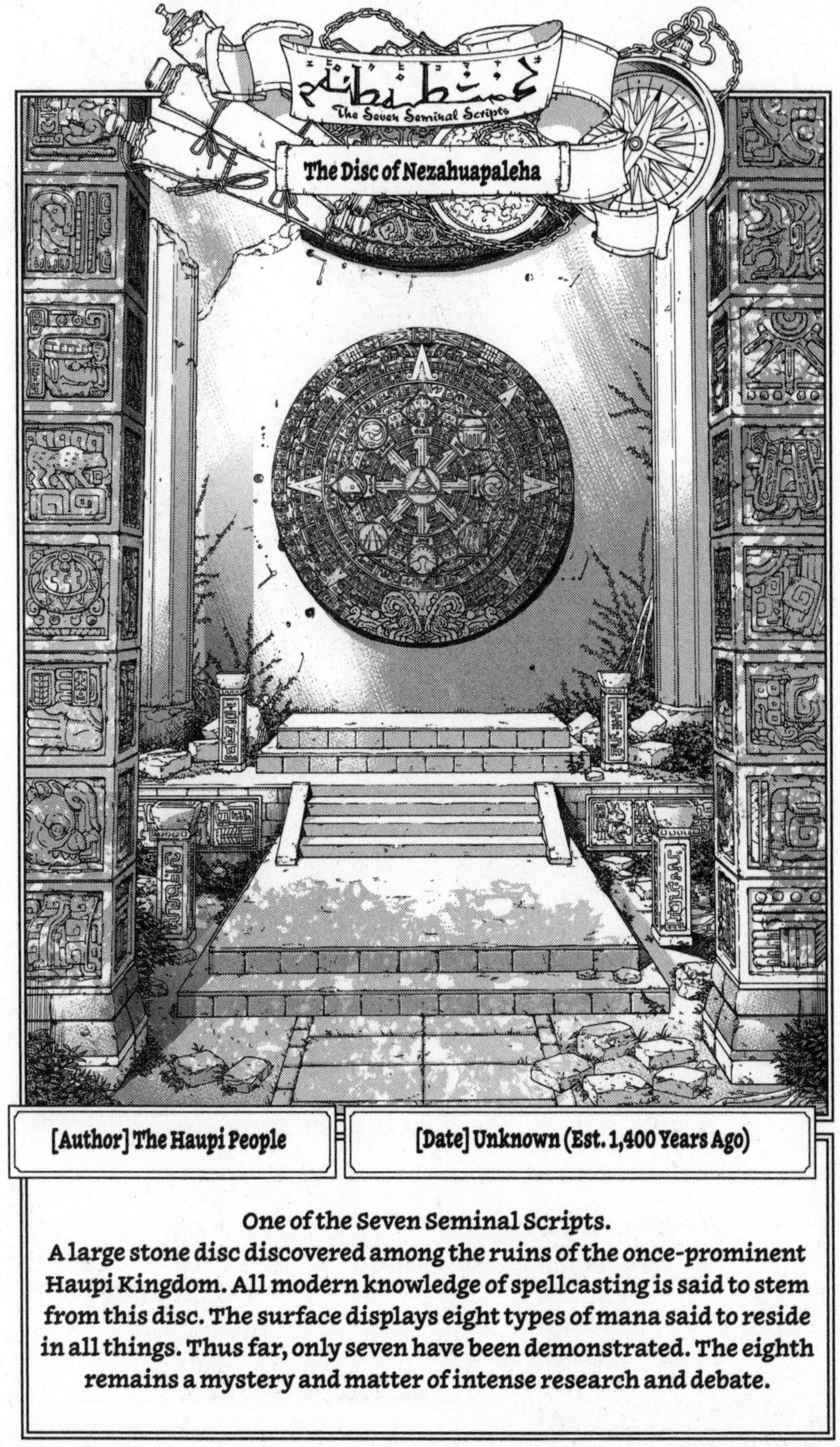
The Seven Seminal Scripts
The Disc of Nezahuapaleha

[Author] The Haupi People

[Date] Unknown (Est. 1,400 Years Ago)

One of the Seven Seminal Scripts.
A large stone disc discovered among the ruins of the once-prominent Haupi Kingdom. All modern knowledge of spellcasting is said to stem from this disc. The surface displays eight types of mana said to reside in all things. Thus far, only seven have been demonstrated. The eighth remains a mystery and matter of intense research and debate.

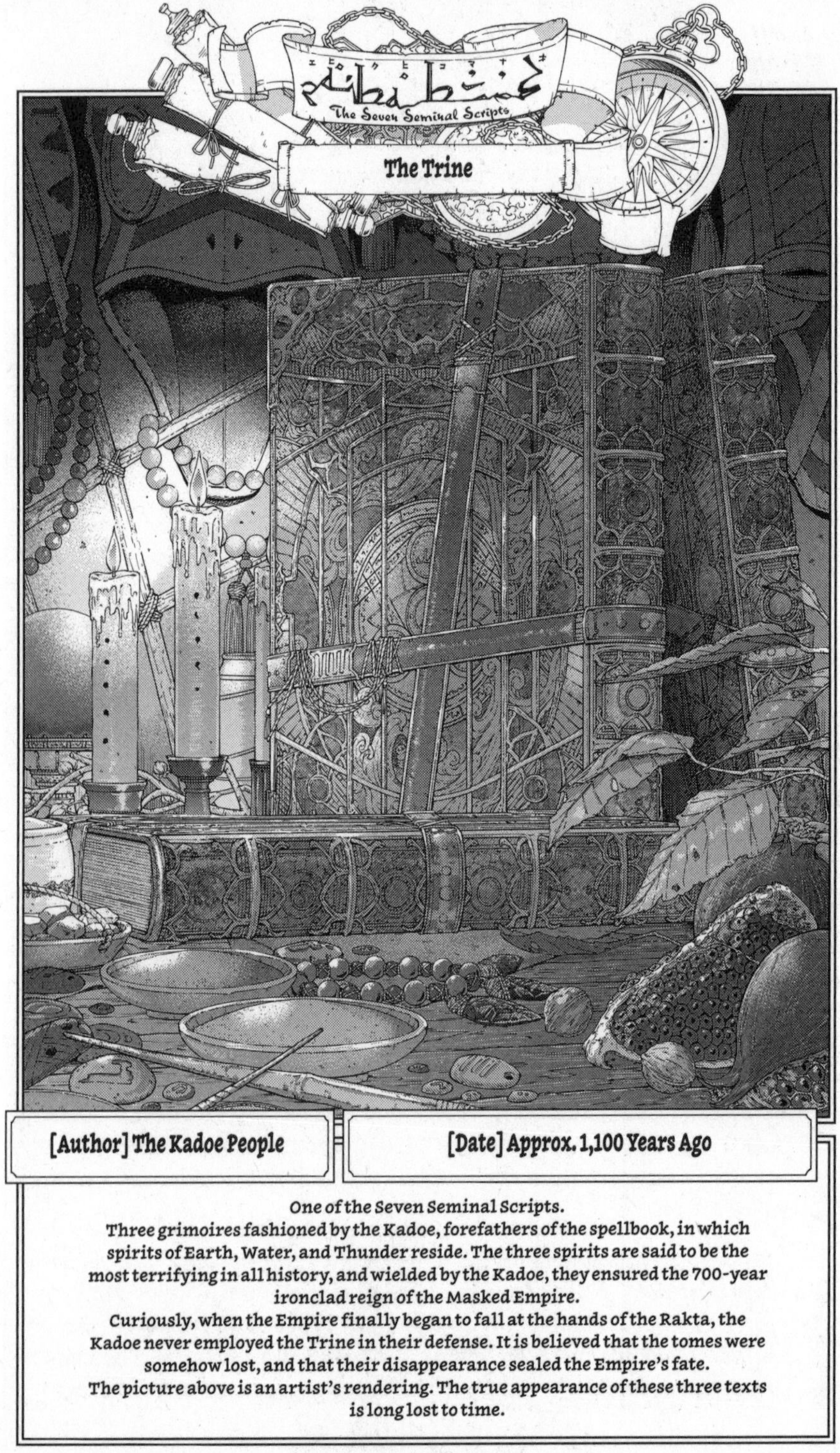
The Seven Seminal Scripts
The Trine

[Author] The Kadoe People

[Date] Approx. 1,100 Years Ago

One of the Seven Seminal Scripts.
Three grimoires fashioned by the Kadoe, forefathers of the spellbook, in which spirits of Earth, Water, and Thunder reside. The three spirits are said to be the most terrifying in all history, and wielded by the Kadoe, they ensured the 700-year ironclad reign of the Masked Empire.
Curiously, when the Empire finally began to fall at the hands of the Rakta, the Kadoe never employed the Trine in their defense. It is believed that the tomes were somehow lost, and that their disappearance sealed the Empire's fate.
The picture above is an artist's rendering. The true appearance of these three texts is long lost to time.

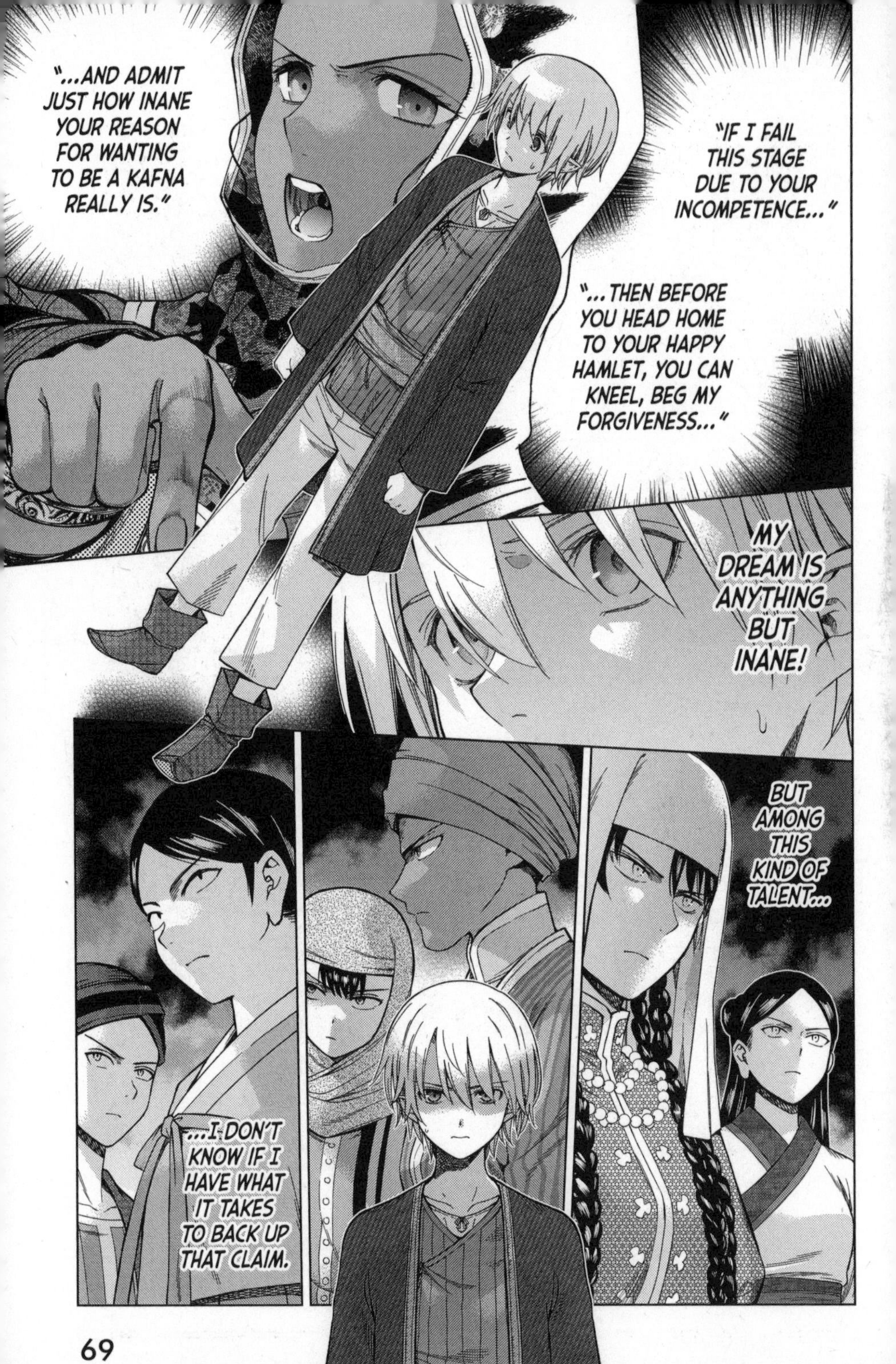
"IF I FAIL THIS STAGE DUE TO YOUR INCOMPETENCE..."
"...THEN BEFORE YOU HEAD HOME TO YOUR HAPPY HAMLET, YOU CAN KNEEL, BEG MY FORGIVENESS..."
"...AND ADMIT JUST HOW INANE YOUR REASON FOR WANTING TO BE A KAFNA REALLY IS."
MY DREAM IS ANYTHING BUT INANE!
BUT AMONG THIS KIND OF TALENT...
...I DON'T KNOW IF I HAVE WHAT IT TAKES TO BACK UP THAT CLAIM.

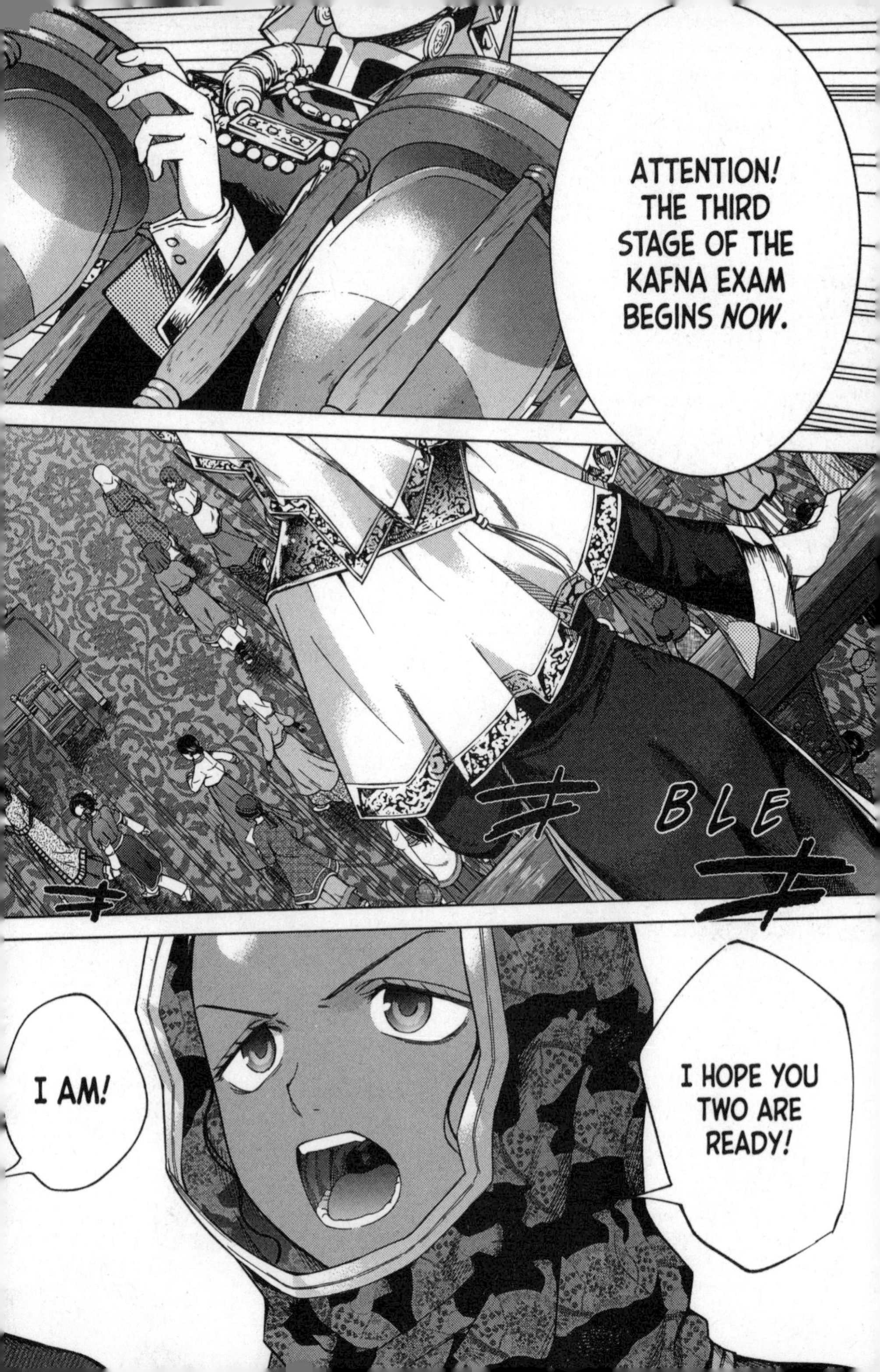
ATTENTION! THE THIRD STAGE OF THE KAFNA EXAM BEGINS *NOW*.
BLE
I HOPE YOU TWO ARE READY!
I AM!

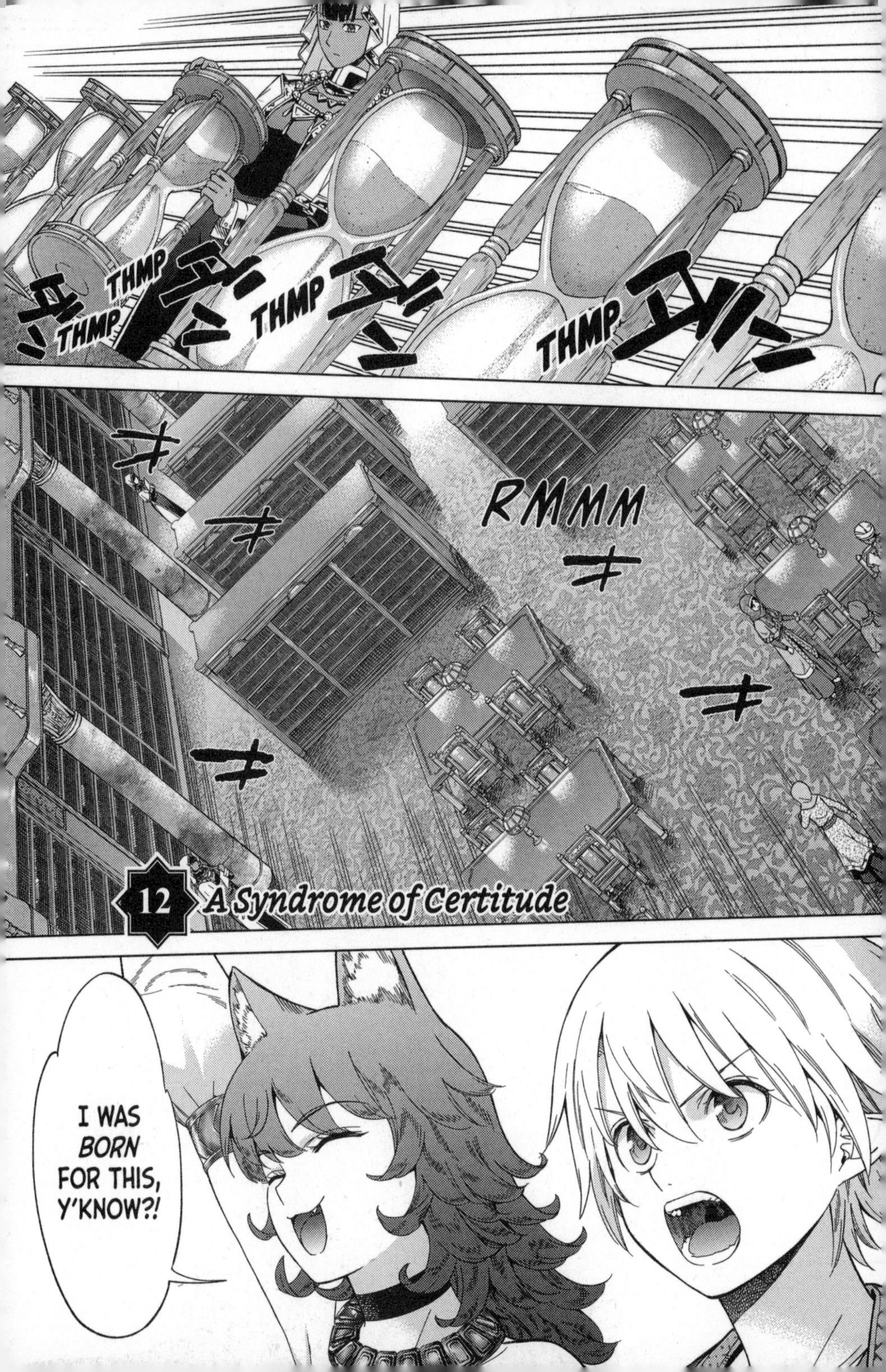
THMP
THMP
THMP
THMP
RMMM
12 A Syndrome of Certitude
I WAS *BORN* FOR THIS, Y'KNOW?!

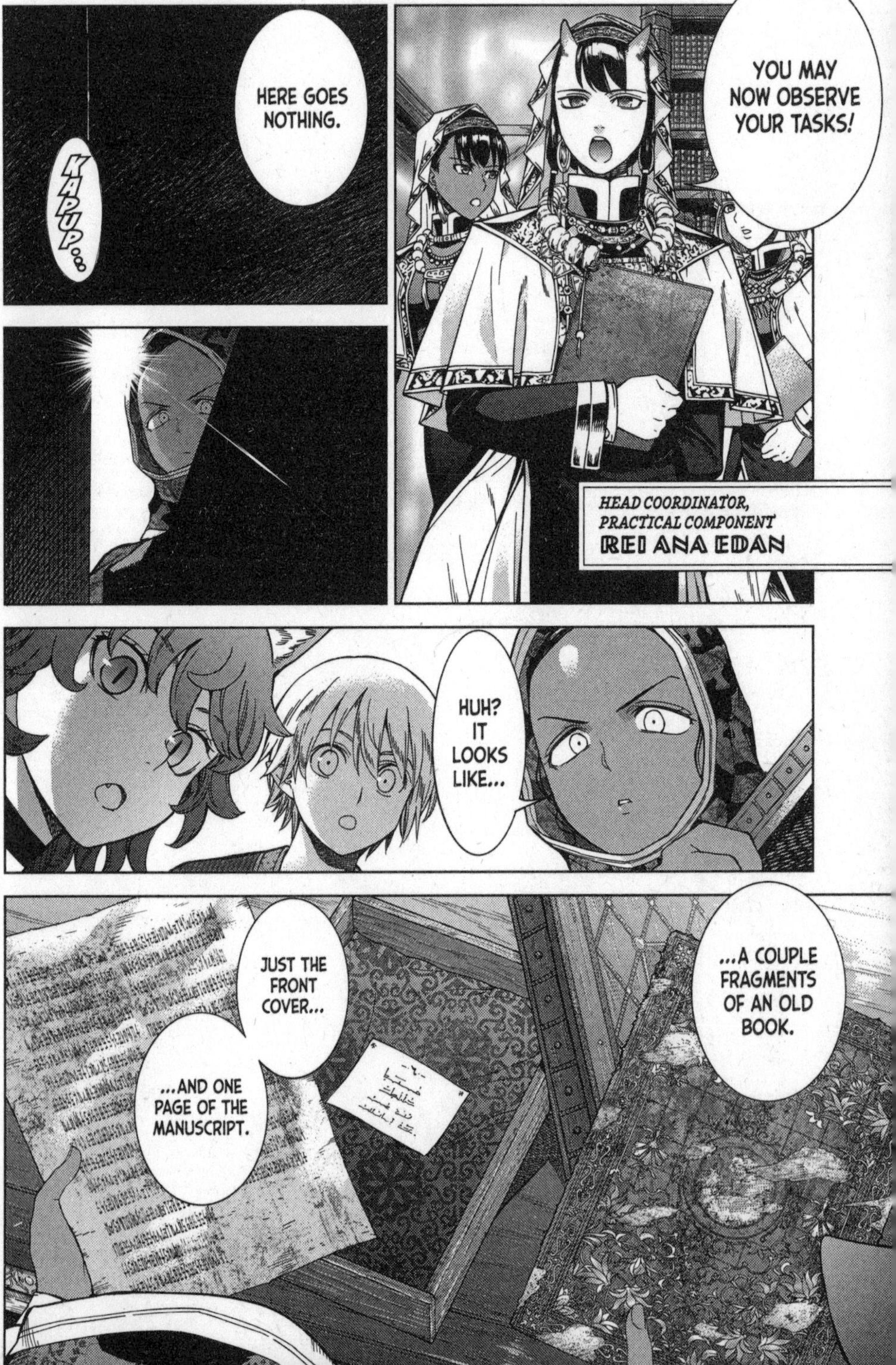
YOU MAY NOW OBSERVE YOUR TASKS!
HEAD COORDINATOR, PRACTICAL COMPONENT
REI ANA EDAN
HERE GOES NOTHING.
KAPUP...
HUH? IT LOOKS LIKE...
...A COUPLE FRAGMENTS OF AN OLD BOOK.
JUST THE FRONT COVER...
...AND ONE PAGE OF THE MANUSCRIPT.

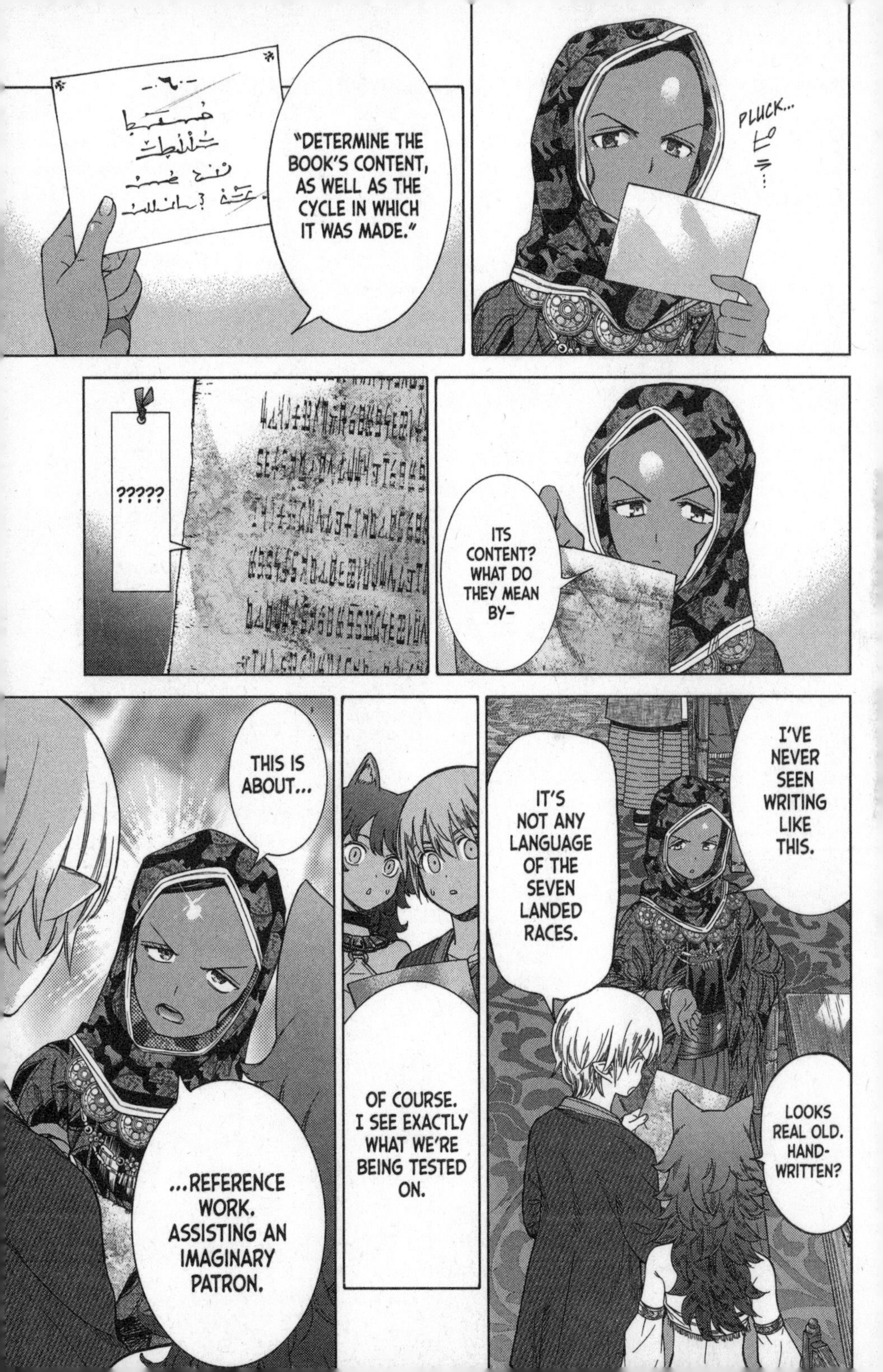

PLUCK...
"DETERMINE THE BOOK'S CONTENT, AS WELL AS THE CYCLE IN WHICH IT WAS MADE."
ITS CONTENT? WHAT DO THEY MEAN BY–
?????
I'VE NEVER SEEN WRITING LIKE THIS.
IT'S NOT ANY LANGUAGE OF THE SEVEN LANDED RACES.
LOOKS REAL OLD. HAND-WRITTEN?
OF COURSE. I SEE EXACTLY WHAT WE'RE BEING TESTED ON.
THIS IS ABOUT...
...REFERENCE WORK. ASSISTING AN IMAGINARY PATRON.

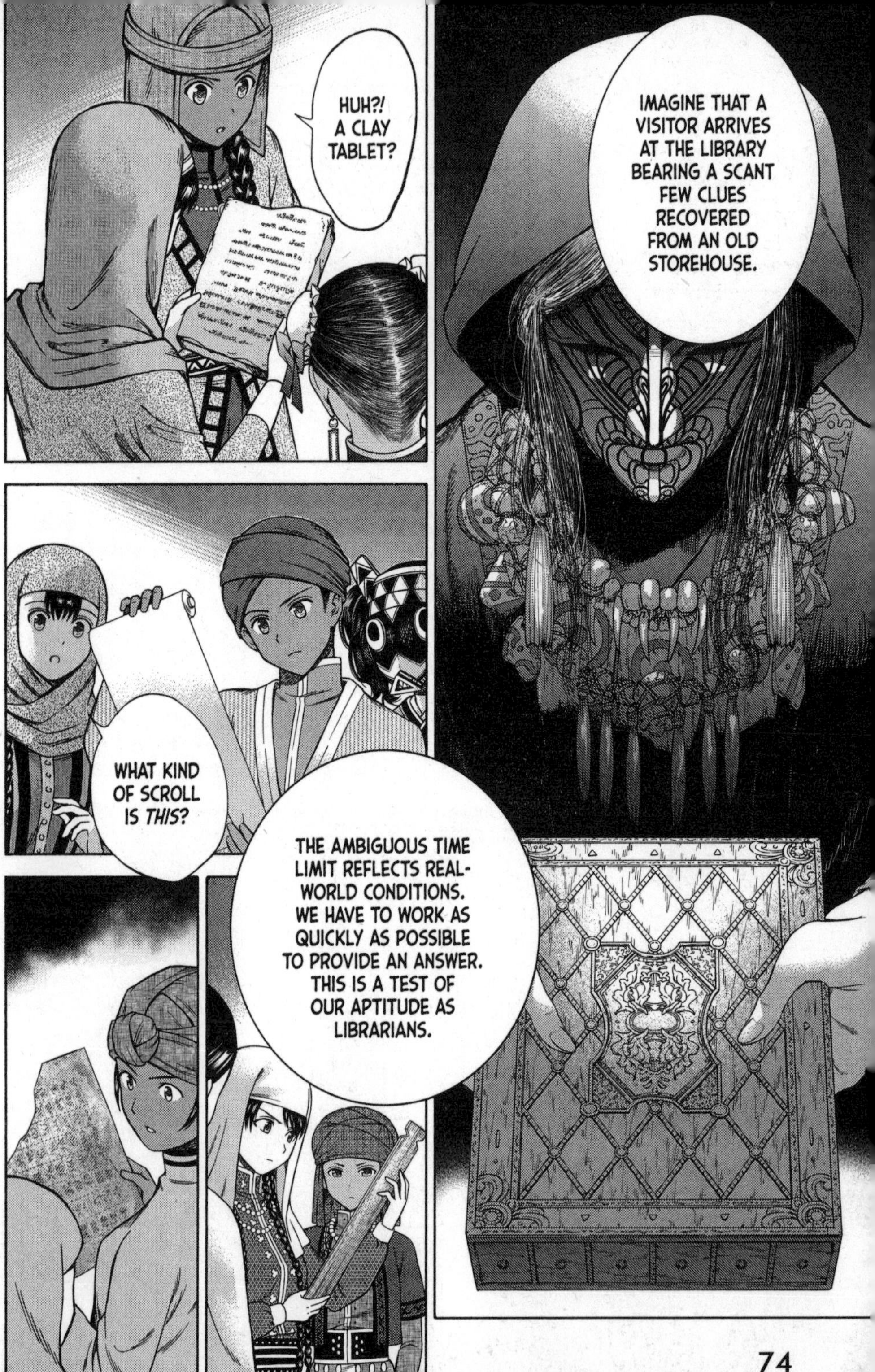
IMAGINE THAT A VISITOR ARRIVES AT THE LIBRARY BEARING A SCANT FEW CLUES RECOVERED FROM AN OLD STOREHOUSE.
HUH?! A CLAY TABLET?
WHAT KIND OF SCROLL IS *THIS*?
THE AMBIGUOUS TIME LIMIT REFLECTS REAL-WORLD CONDITIONS. WE HAVE TO WORK AS QUICKLY AS POSSIBLE TO PROVIDE AN ANSWER. THIS IS A TEST OF OUR APTITUDE AS LIBRARIANS.

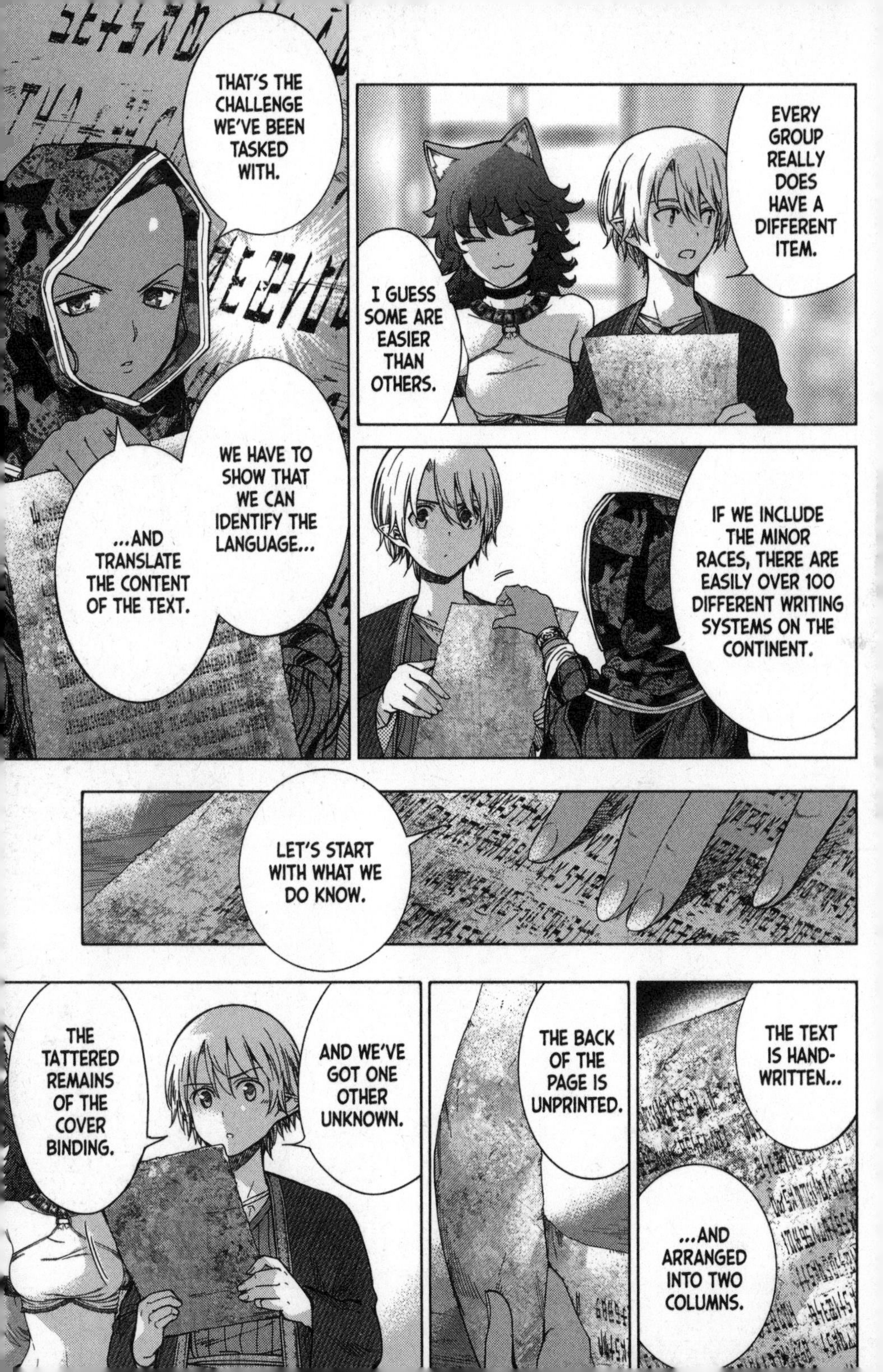
EVERY GROUP REALLY DOES HAVE A DIFFERENT ITEM.
I GUESS SOME ARE EASIER THAN OTHERS.
IF WE INCLUDE THE MINOR RACES, THERE ARE EASILY OVER 100 DIFFERENT WRITING SYSTEMS ON THE CONTINENT.
THAT'S THE CHALLENGE WE'VE BEEN TASKED WITH.
WE HAVE TO SHOW THAT WE CAN IDENTIFY THE LANGUAGE...
...AND TRANSLATE THE CONTENT OF THE TEXT.
LET'S START WITH WHAT WE DO KNOW.
THE TEXT IS HAND-WRITTEN...
...AND ARRANGED INTO TWO COLUMNS.
THE BACK OF THE PAGE IS UNPRINTED.
AND WE'VE GOT ONE OTHER UNKNOWN.
THE TATTERED REMAINS OF THE COVER BINDING.

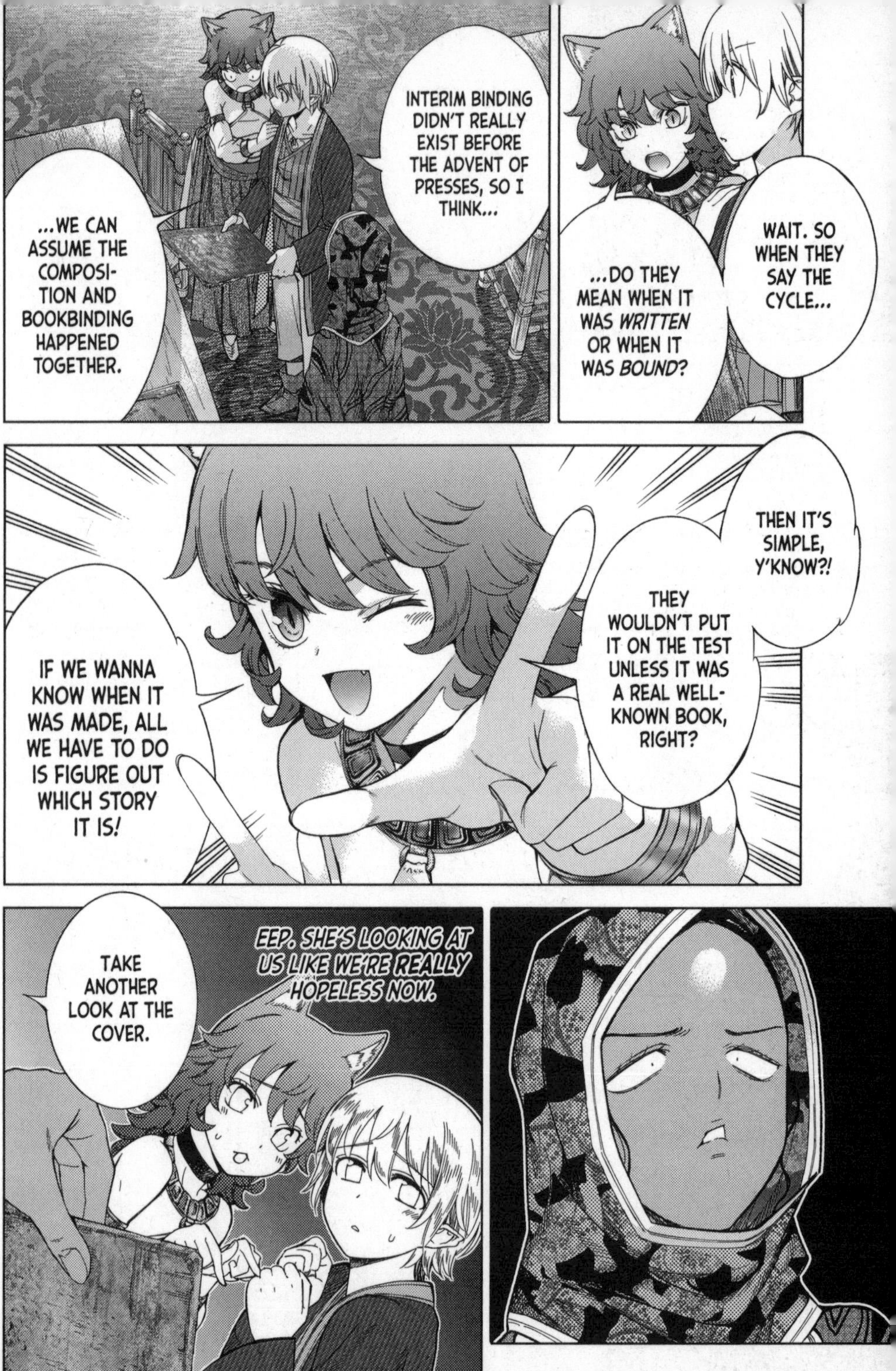
WAIT. SO WHEN THEY SAY THE CYCLE...
...DO THEY MEAN WHEN IT WAS *WRITTEN* OR WHEN IT WAS *BOUND*?
INTERIM BINDING DIDN'T REALLY EXIST BEFORE THE ADVENT OF PRESSES, SO I THINK...
...WE CAN ASSUME THE COMPOSITION AND BOOKBINDING HAPPENED TOGETHER.
THEN IT'S SIMPLE, Y'KNOW?!
THEY WOULDN'T PUT IT ON THE TEST UNLESS IT WAS A REAL WELL-KNOWN BOOK, RIGHT?
IF WE WANNA KNOW WHEN IT WAS MADE, ALL WE HAVE TO DO IS FIGURE OUT WHICH STORY IT IS!
EEP. SHE'S LOOKING AT US LIKE WE'RE REALLY HOPELESS NOW.
TAKE ANOTHER LOOK AT THE COVER.

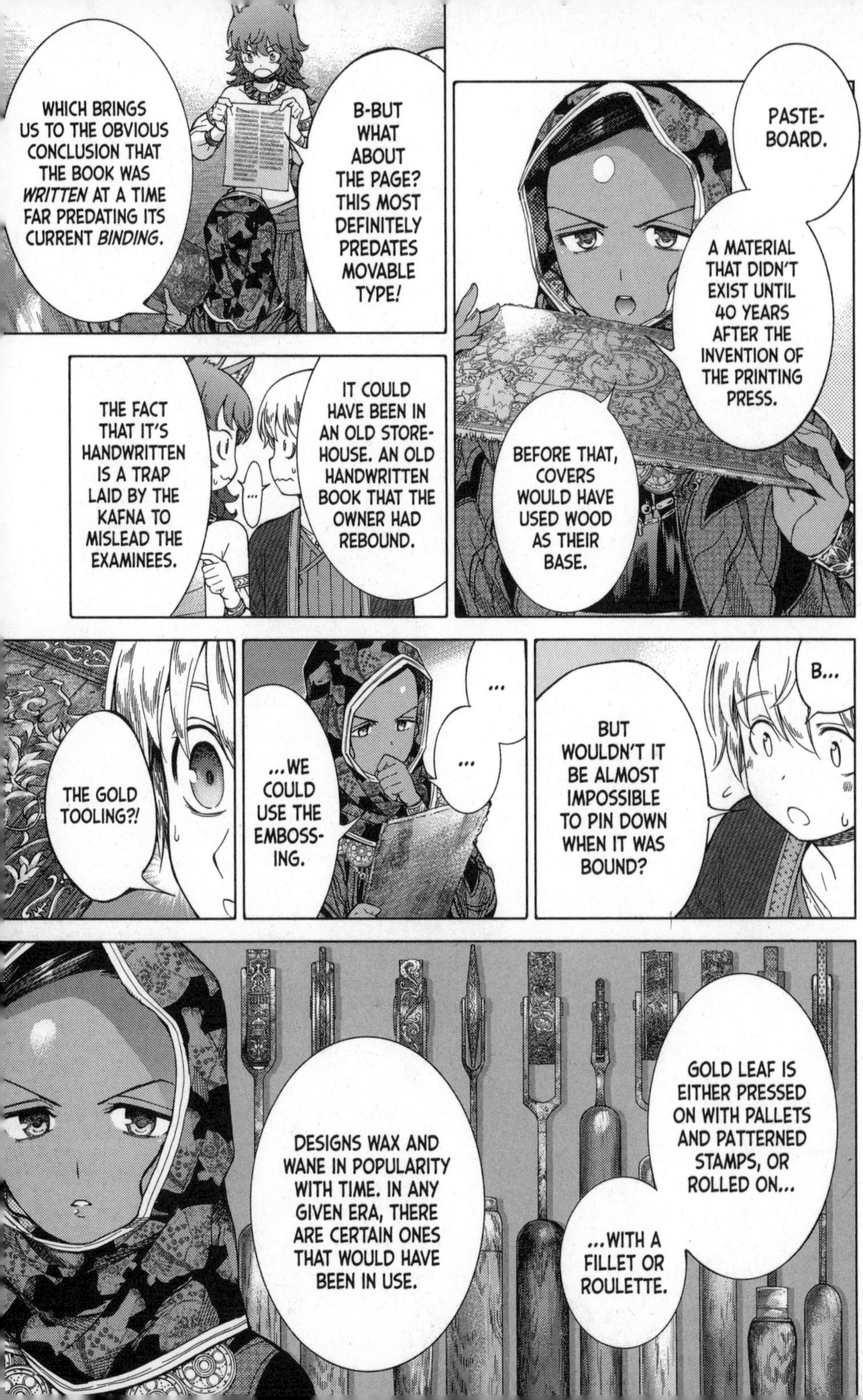
B-BUT WHAT ABOUT THE PAGE? THIS MOST DEFINITELY PREDATES MOVABLE TYPE!
WHICH BRINGS US TO THE OBVIOUS CONCLUSION THAT THE BOOK WAS *WRITTEN* AT A TIME FAR PREDATING ITS CURRENT *BINDING*.
IT COULD HAVE BEEN IN AN OLD STORE-HOUSE. AN OLD HANDWRITTEN BOOK THAT THE OWNER HAD REBOUND.
...
THE FACT THAT IT'S HANDWRITTEN IS A TRAP LAID BY THE KAFNA TO MISLEAD THE EXAMINEES.
PASTE-BOARD.
A MATERIAL THAT DIDN'T EXIST UNTIL 40 YEARS AFTER THE INVENTION OF THE PRINTING PRESS.
BEFORE THAT, COVERS WOULD HAVE USED WOOD AS THEIR BASE.
B...
BUT WOULDN'T IT BE ALMOST IMPOSSIBLE TO PIN DOWN WHEN IT WAS BOUND?
...
...
...WE COULD USE THE EMBOSS-ING.
THE GOLD TOOLING?!
GOLD LEAF IS EITHER PRESSED ON WITH PALLETS AND PATTERNED STAMPS, OR ROLLED ON...
...WITH A FILLET OR ROULETTE.
DESIGNS WAX AND WANE IN POPULARITY WITH TIME. IN ANY GIVEN ERA, THERE ARE CERTAIN ONES THAT WOULD HAVE BEEN IN USE.

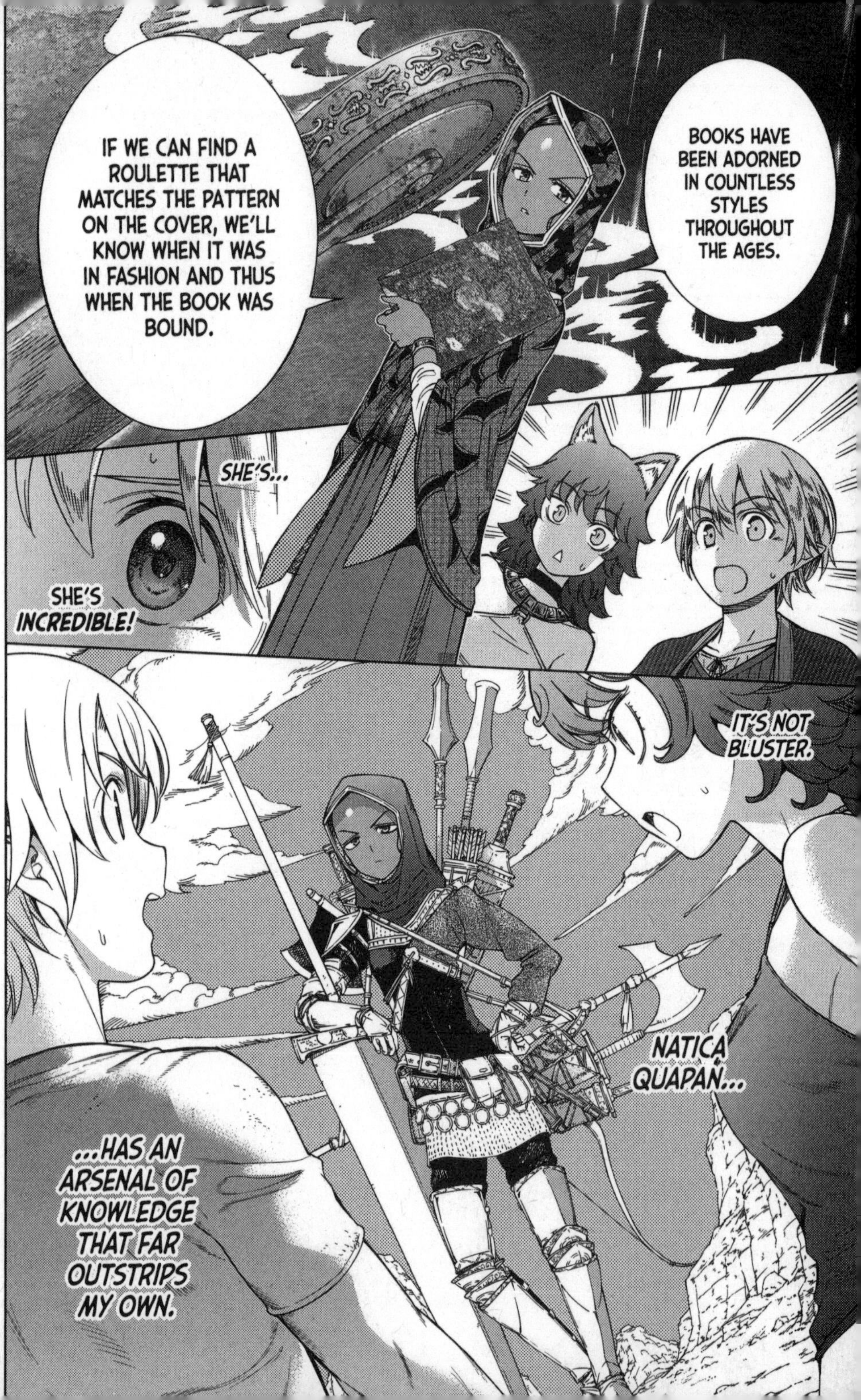
BOOKS HAVE BEEN ADORNED IN COUNTLESS STYLES THROUGHOUT THE AGES.
IF WE CAN FIND A ROULETTE THAT MATCHES THE PATTERN ON THE COVER, WE'LL KNOW WHEN IT WAS IN FASHION AND THUS WHEN THE BOOK WAS BOUND.
SHE'S...
SHE'S INCREDIBLE!
IT'S NOT BLUSTER.
NATICA QUAPAŃ...
...HAS AN ARSENAL OF KNOWLEDGE THAT FAR OUTSTRIPS MY OWN.

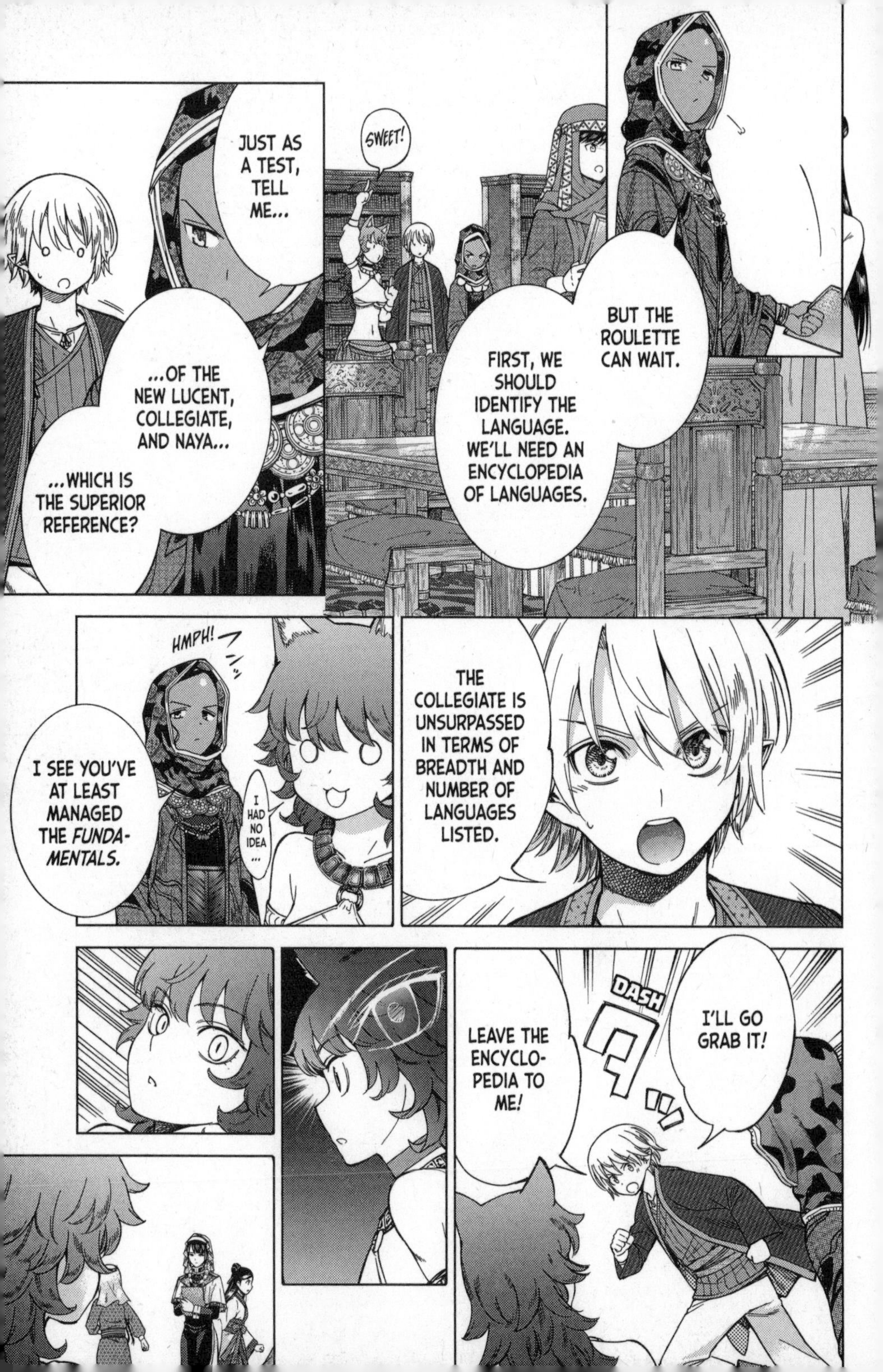
BUT THE ROULETTE CAN WAIT.
FIRST, WE SHOULD IDENTIFY THE LANGUAGE. WE'LL NEED AN ENCYCLOPEDIA OF LANGUAGES.
SWEET!
JUST AS A TEST, TELL ME...
...OF THE NEW LUCENT, COLLEGIATE, AND NAYA...
...WHICH IS THE SUPERIOR REFERENCE?
THE COLLEGIATE IS UNSURPASSED IN TERMS OF BREADTH AND NUMBER OF LANGUAGES LISTED.
HMPH!
I SEE YOU'VE AT LEAST MANAGED THE *FUNDAMENTALS.*
I HAD NO IDEA...
I'LL GO GRAB IT!
DASH
LEAVE THE ENCYCLOPEDIA TO ME!

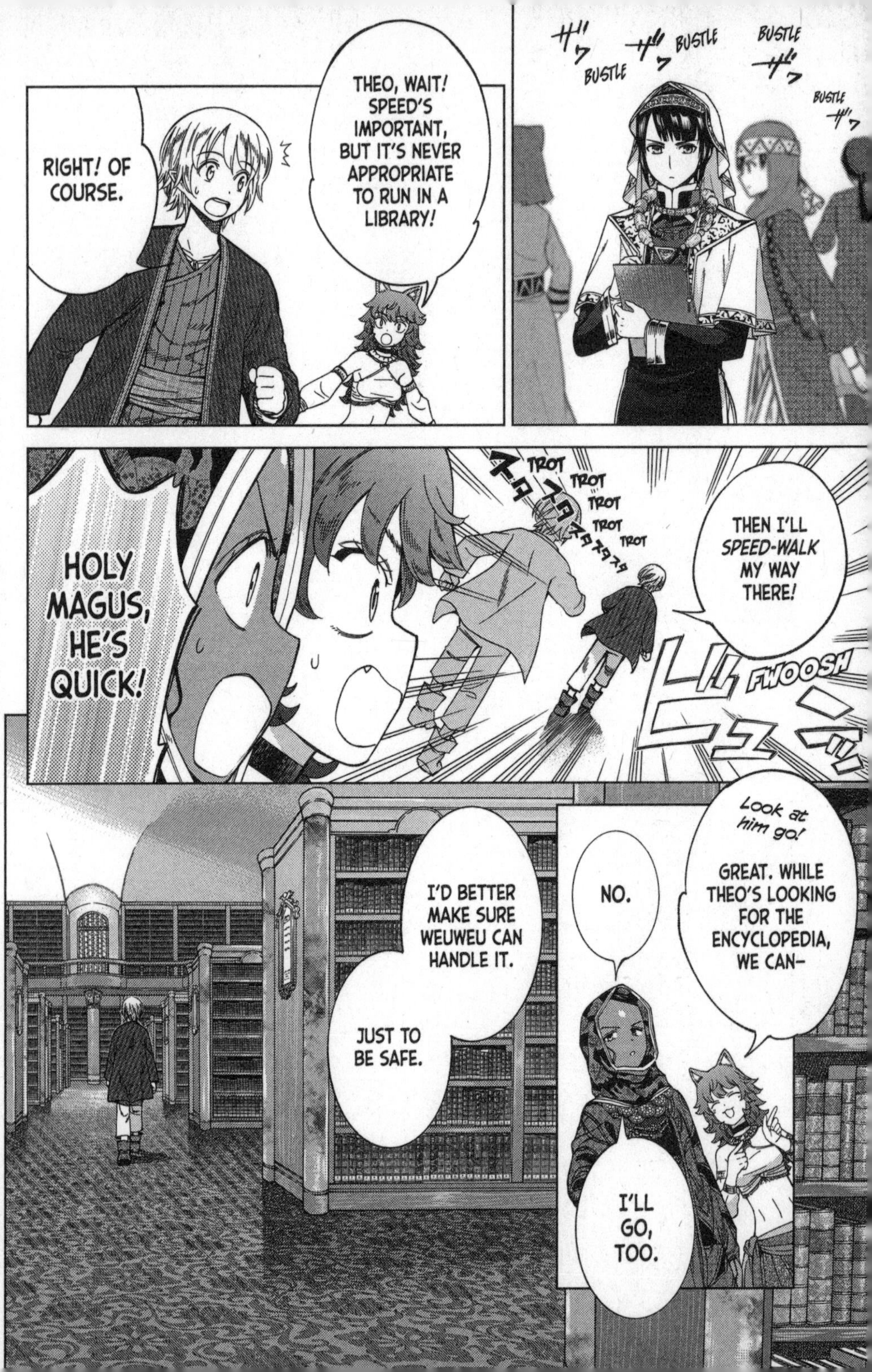
BUSTLE
BUSTLE
BUSTLE
BUSTLE
THEO, WAIT! SPEED'S IMPORTANT, BUT IT'S NEVER APPROPRIATE TO RUN IN A LIBRARY!
RIGHT! OF COURSE.
THEN I'LL SPEED-WALK MY WAY THERE!
FWOOSH
TROT TROT TROT TROT TROT
HOLY MAGUS, HE'S QUICK!
Look at him go!
GREAT. WHILE THEO'S LOOKING FOR THE ENCYCLOPEDIA, WE CAN–
NO.
I'LL GO, TOO.
I'D BETTER MAKE SURE WEUWEU CAN HANDLE IT.
JUST TO BE SAFE.

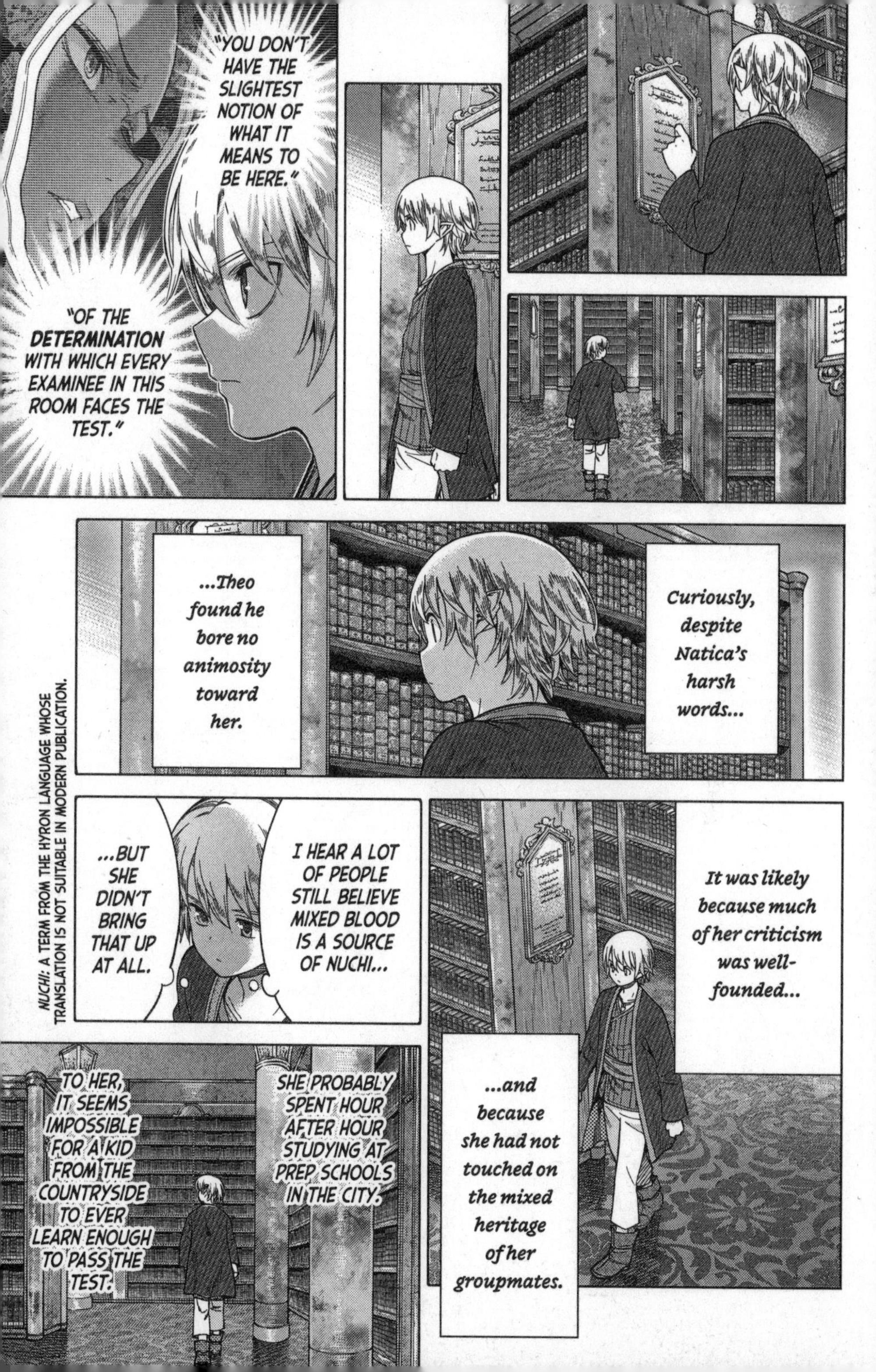
"YOU DON'T HAVE THE SLIGHTEST NOTION OF WHAT IT MEANS TO BE HERE."
"OF THE DETERMINATION WITH WHICH EVERY EXAMINEE IN THIS ROOM FACES THE TEST."
Curiously, despite Natica's harsh words...
...Theo found he bore no animosity toward her.
It was likely because much of her criticism was well-founded...
...and because she had not touched on the mixed heritage of her groupmates.
I HEAR A LOT OF PEOPLE STILL BELIEVE MIXED BLOOD IS A SOURCE OF NUCHI...
...BUT SHE DIDN'T BRING THAT UP AT ALL.
SHE PROBABLY SPENT HOUR AFTER HOUR STUDYING AT PREP SCHOOLS IN THE CITY.
TO HER, IT SEEMS IMPOSSIBLE FOR A KID FROM THE COUNTRYSIDE TO EVER LEARN ENOUGH TO PASS THE TEST.

NUCHI: A TERM FROM THE HYRON LANGUAGE WHOSE TRANSLATION IS NOT SUITABLE IN MODERN PUBLICATION.

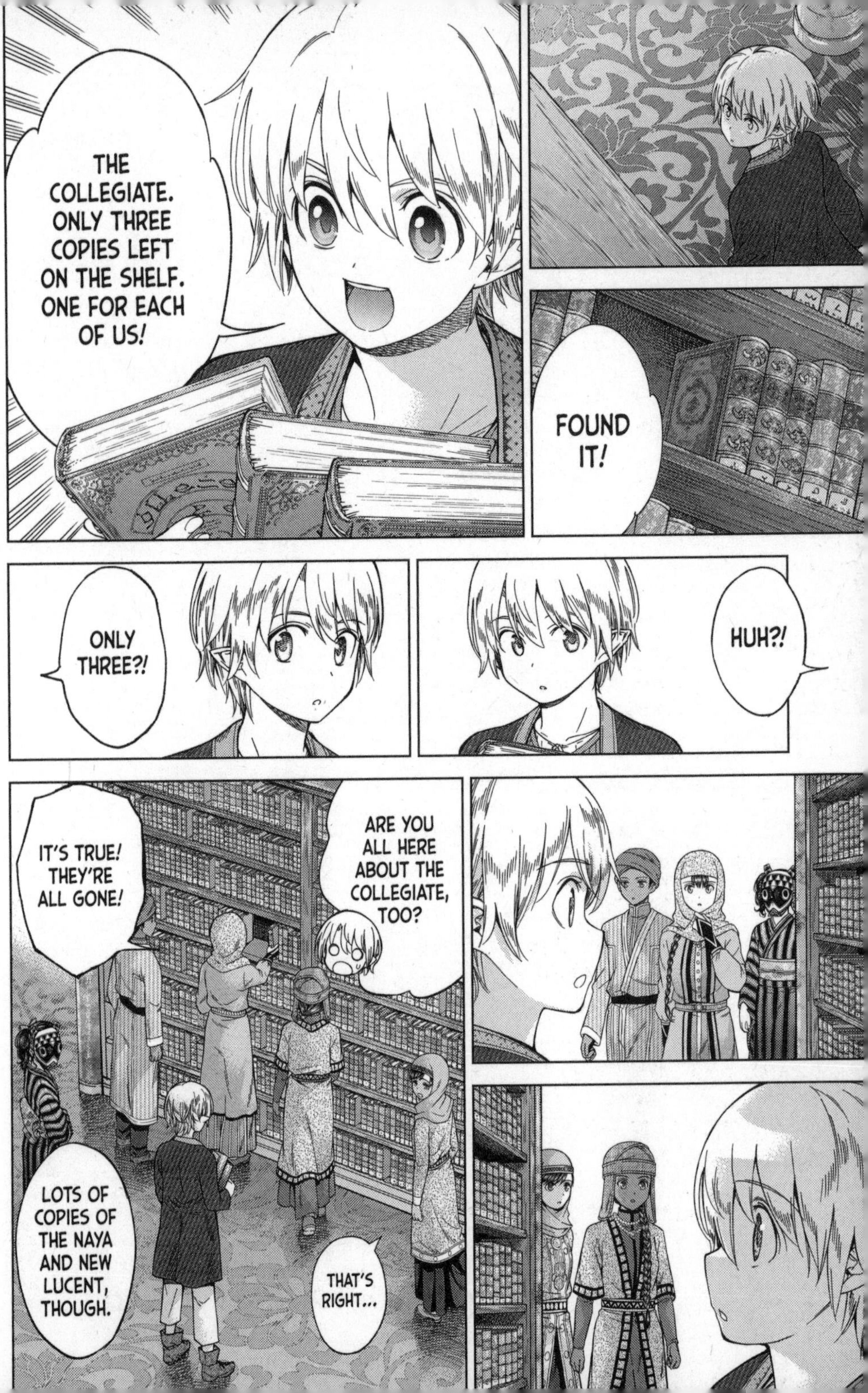
FOUND IT!
THE COLLEGIATE. ONLY THREE COPIES LEFT ON THE SHELF. ONE FOR EACH OF US!
HUH?!
ONLY THREE?!
ARE YOU ALL HERE ABOUT THE COLLEGIATE, TOO?
IT'S TRUE! THEY'RE ALL GONE!
THAT'S RIGHT...
LOTS OF COPIES OF THE NAYA AND NEW LUCENT, THOUGH.

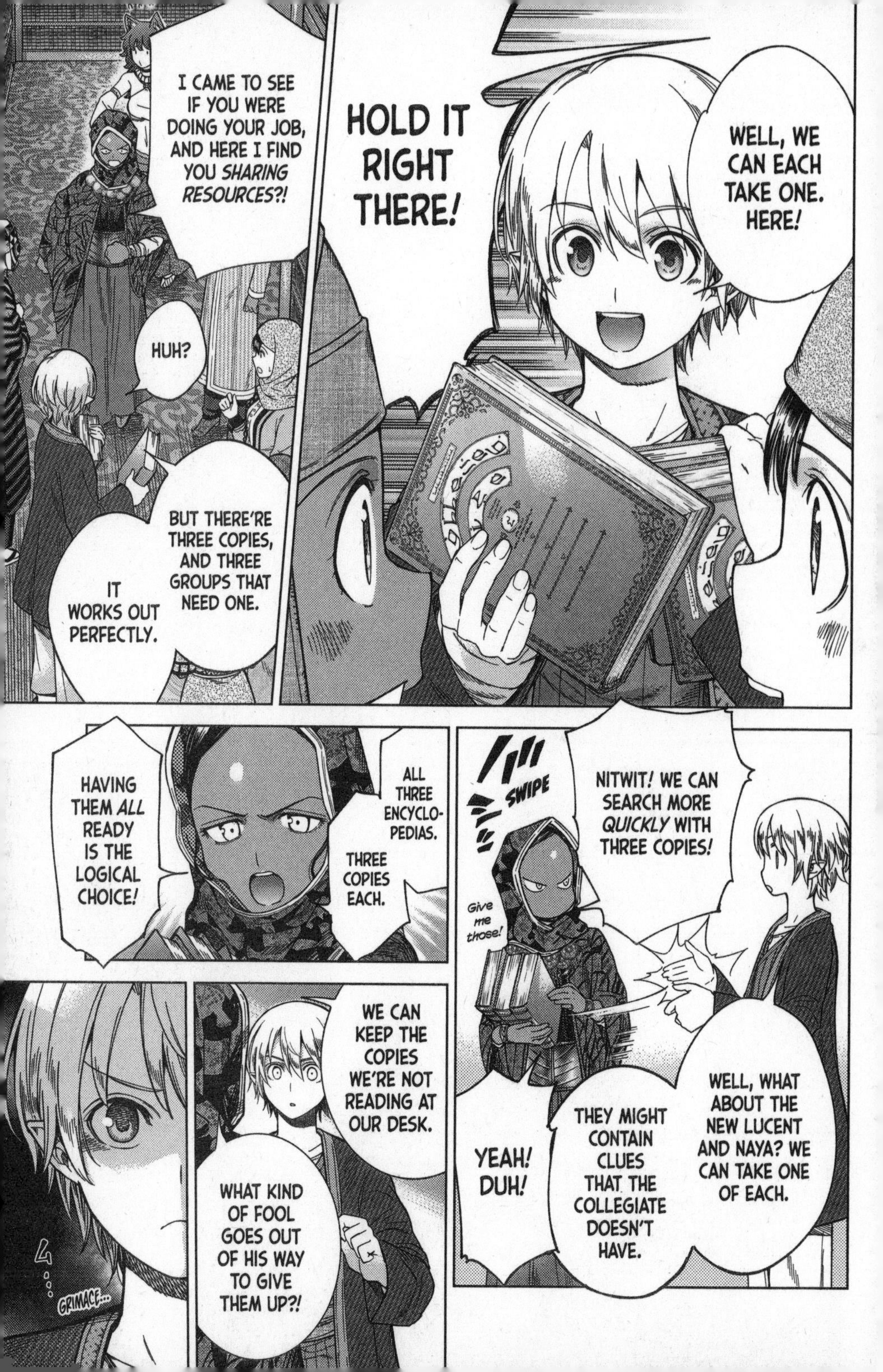
WELL, WE CAN EACH TAKE ONE. HERE!
HOLD IT RIGHT THERE!
I CAME TO SEE IF YOU WERE DOING YOUR JOB, AND HERE I FIND YOU *SHARING RESOURCES?!*
HUH?
BUT THERE'RE THREE COPIES, AND THREE GROUPS THAT NEED ONE.
IT WORKS OUT PERFECTLY.
NITWIT! WE CAN SEARCH MORE *QUICKLY* WITH THREE COPIES!
SWIPE
Give me those!
WELL, WHAT ABOUT THE NEW LUCENT AND NAYA? WE CAN TAKE ONE OF EACH.
THEY MIGHT CONTAIN CLUES THAT THE COLLEGIATE DOESN'T HAVE.
YEAH! DUH!
ALL THREE ENCYCLOPEDIAS.
THREE COPIES EACH.
HAVING THEM *ALL* READY IS THE LOGICAL CHOICE!
WE CAN KEEP THE COPIES WE'RE NOT READING AT OUR DESK.
WHAT KIND OF FOOL GOES OUT OF HIS WAY TO GIVE THEM UP?!
GRIMACE...

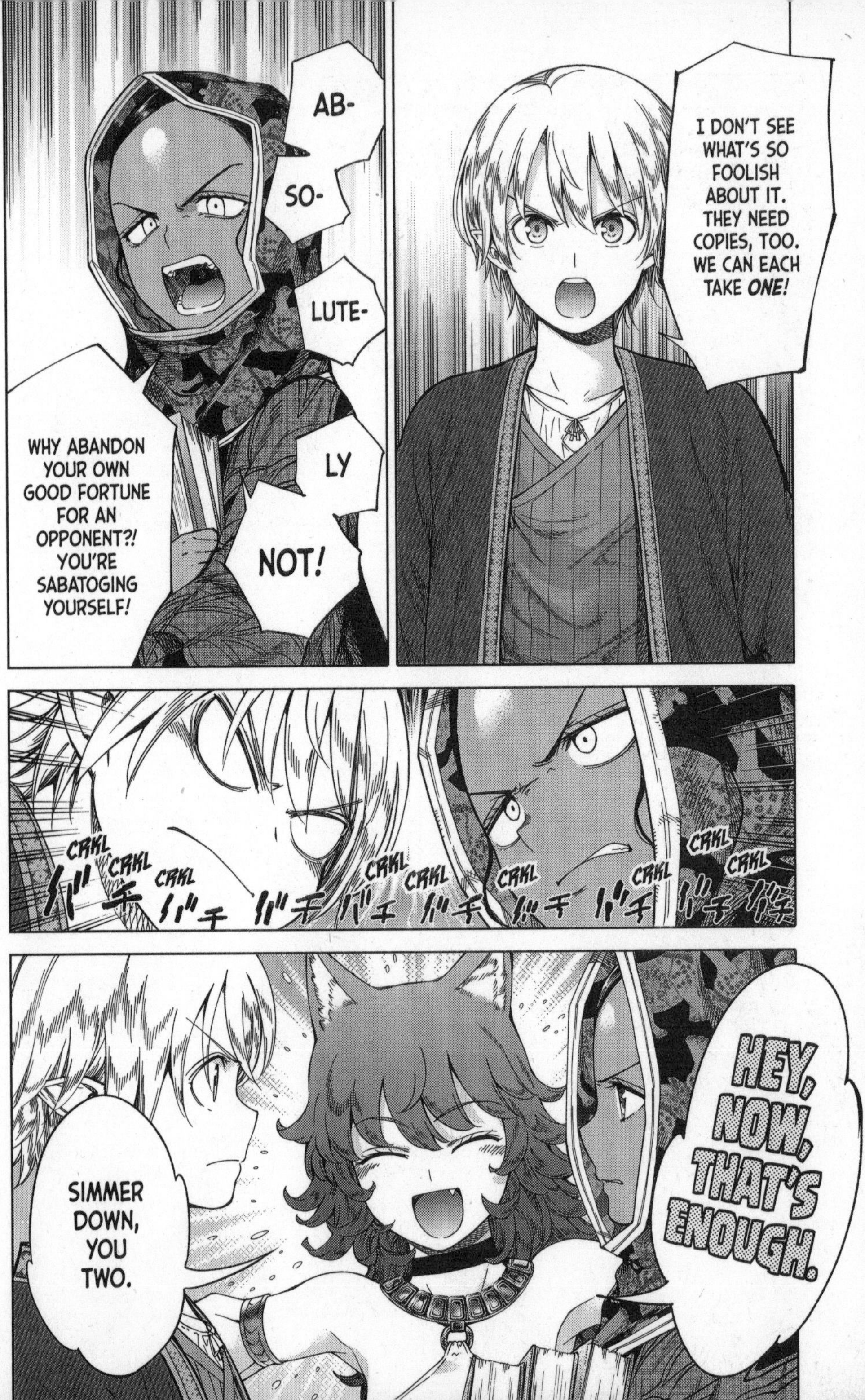
I DON'T SEE WHAT'S SO FOOLISH ABOUT IT. THEY NEED COPIES, TOO. WE CAN EACH TAKE *ONE!*
AB-
SO-
LUTE-
LY
NOT!
WHY ABANDON YOUR OWN GOOD FORTUNE FOR AN OPPONENT?! YOU'RE SABATOGING YOURSELF!
CRKL CRKL CRKL CRKL CRKL CRKL CRKL CRKL CRKL
HEY, NOW, THAT'S ENOUGH.
SIMMER DOWN, YOU TWO.

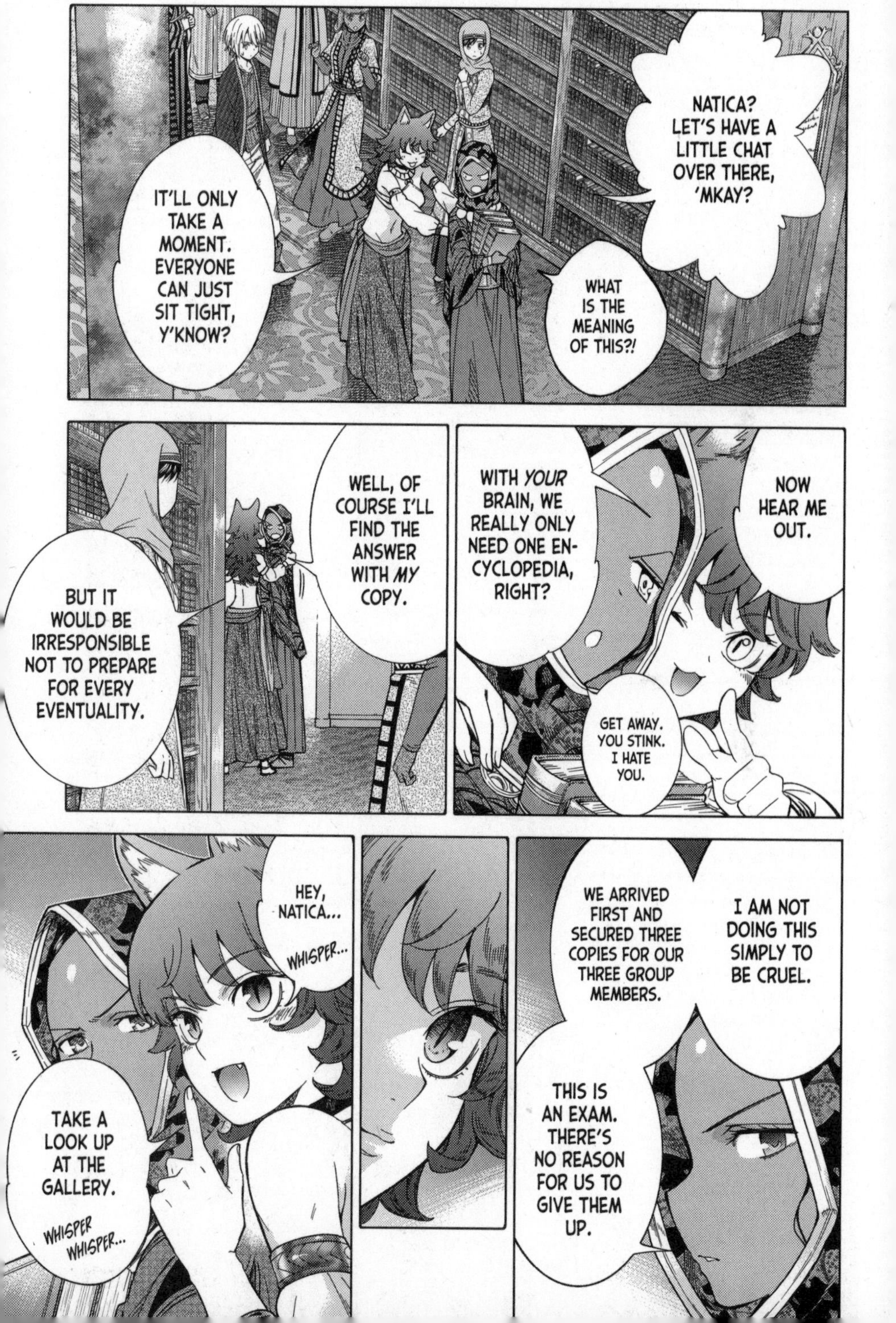
NATICA? LET'S HAVE A LITTLE CHAT OVER THERE, 'MKAY?
WHAT IS THE MEANING OF THIS?!
IT'LL ONLY TAKE A MOMENT. EVERYONE CAN JUST SIT TIGHT, Y'KNOW?
NOW HEAR ME OUT.
WITH *YOUR* BRAIN, WE REALLY ONLY NEED ONE EN-CYCLOPEDIA, RIGHT?
GET AWAY. YOU STINK. I HATE YOU.
WELL, OF COURSE I'LL FIND THE ANSWER WITH *MY* COPY.
BUT IT WOULD BE IRRESPONSIBLE NOT TO PREPARE FOR EVERY EVENTUALITY.
I AM NOT DOING THIS SIMPLY TO BE CRUEL.
WE ARRIVED FIRST AND SECURED THREE COPIES FOR OUR THREE GROUP MEMBERS.
THIS IS AN EXAM. THERE'S NO REASON FOR US TO GIVE THEM UP.
HEY, NATICA...
WHISPER...
TAKE A LOOK UP AT THE GALLERY.
WHISPER WHISPER...

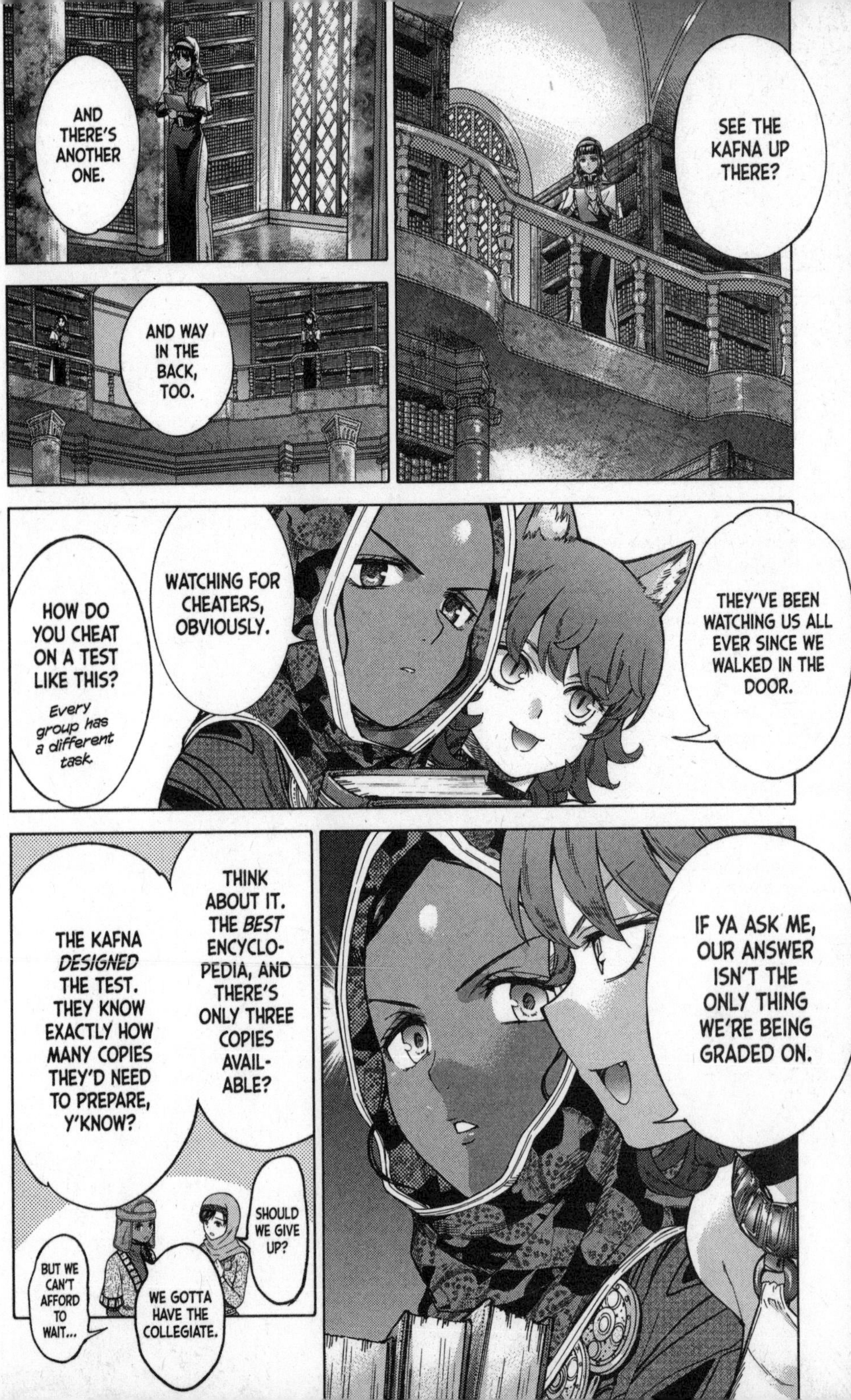
SEE THE KAFNA UP THERE?
AND THERE'S ANOTHER ONE.
AND WAY IN THE BACK, TOO.
THEY'VE BEEN WATCHING US ALL EVER SINCE WE WALKED IN THE DOOR.
WATCHING FOR CHEATERS, OBVIOUSLY.
HOW DO YOU CHEAT ON A TEST LIKE THIS?
Every group has a different task.
IF YA ASK ME, OUR ANSWER ISN'T THE ONLY THING WE'RE BEING GRADED ON.
THINK ABOUT IT. THE *BEST* ENCYCLO-PEDIA, AND THERE'S ONLY THREE COPIES AVAIL-ABLE?
THE KAFNA *DESIGNED* THE TEST. THEY KNOW EXACTLY HOW MANY COPIES THEY'D NEED TO PREPARE, Y'KNOW?
SHOULD WE GIVE UP?
WE GOTTA HAVE THE COLLEGIATE.
BUT WE CAN'T AFFORD TO WAIT...

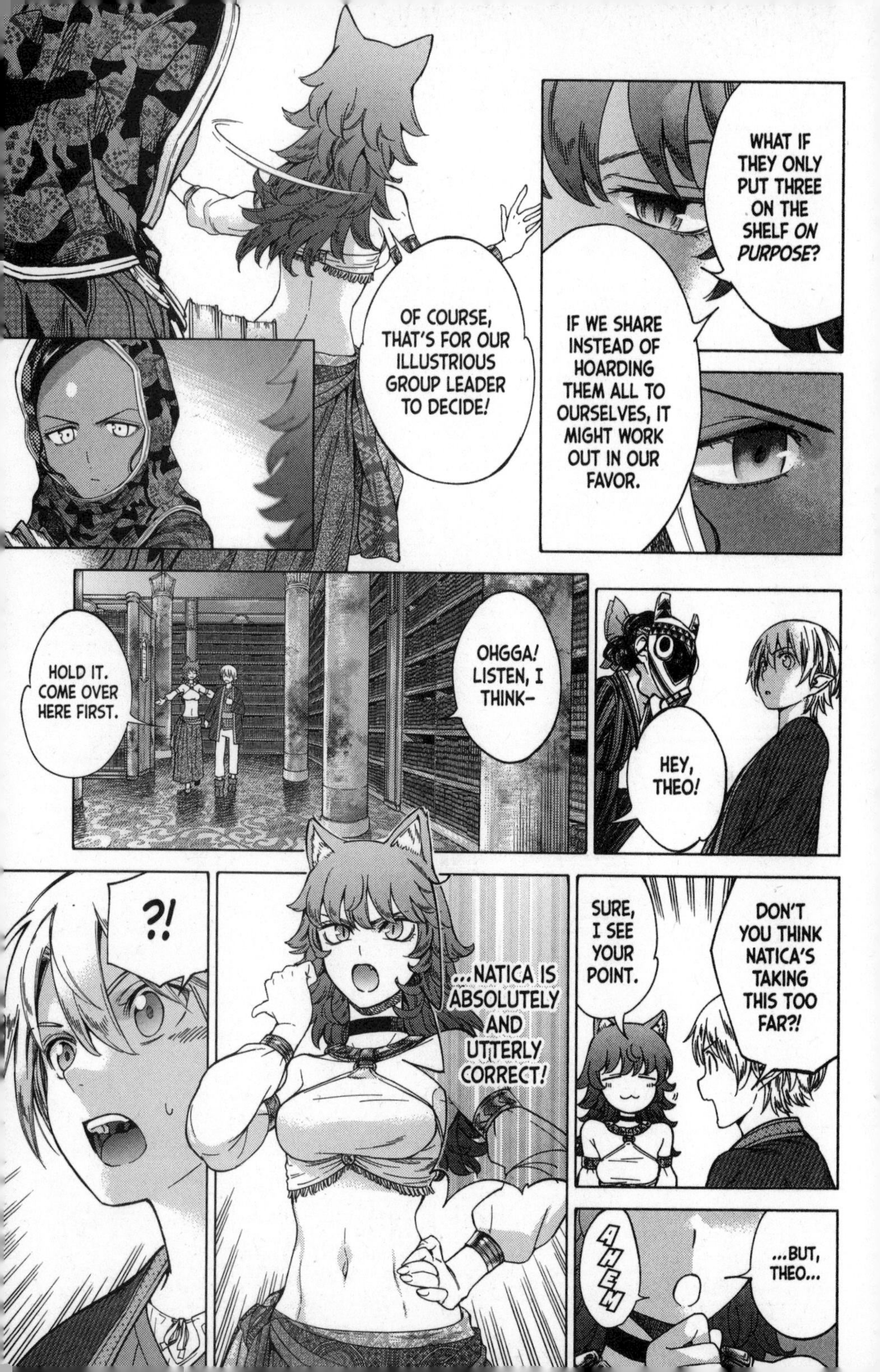
WHAT IF THEY ONLY PUT THREE ON THE SHELF *ON PURPOSE*?
IF WE SHARE INSTEAD OF HOARDING THEM ALL TO OURSELVES, IT MIGHT WORK OUT IN OUR FAVOR.
OF COURSE, THAT'S FOR OUR ILLUSTRIOUS GROUP LEADER TO DECIDE!
HEY, THEO!
OHGGA! LISTEN, I THINK–
HOLD IT. COME OVER HERE FIRST.
DON'T YOU THINK NATICA'S TAKING THIS TOO FAR?!
SURE, I SEE YOUR POINT.
...BUT, THEO...
AHEM
...NATICA IS ABSOLUTELY AND UTTERLY CORRECT!
?!

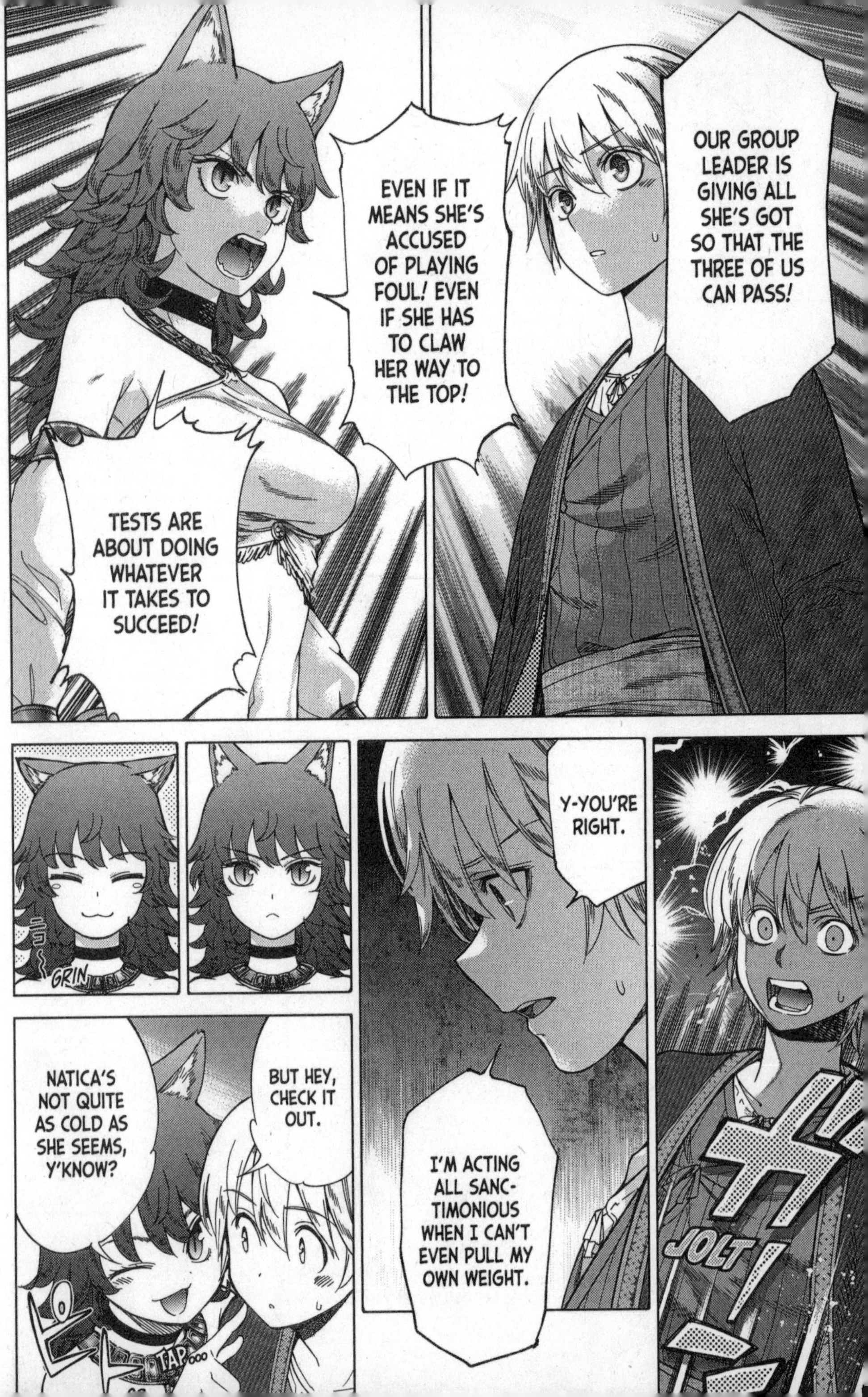
OUR GROUP LEADER IS GIVING ALL SHE'S GOT SO THAT THE THREE OF US CAN PASS!
EVEN IF IT MEANS SHE'S ACCUSED OF PLAYING FOUL! EVEN IF SHE HAS TO CLAW HER WAY TO THE TOP!
TESTS ARE ABOUT DOING WHATEVER IT TAKES TO SUCCEED!
JOLT
Y-YOU'RE RIGHT.
I'M ACTING ALL SANC-TIMONIOUS WHEN I CAN'T EVEN PULL MY OWN WEIGHT.
GRIN
BUT HEY, CHECK IT OUT.
NATICA'S NOT QUITE AS COLD AS SHE SEEMS, Y'KNOW?
TAP...

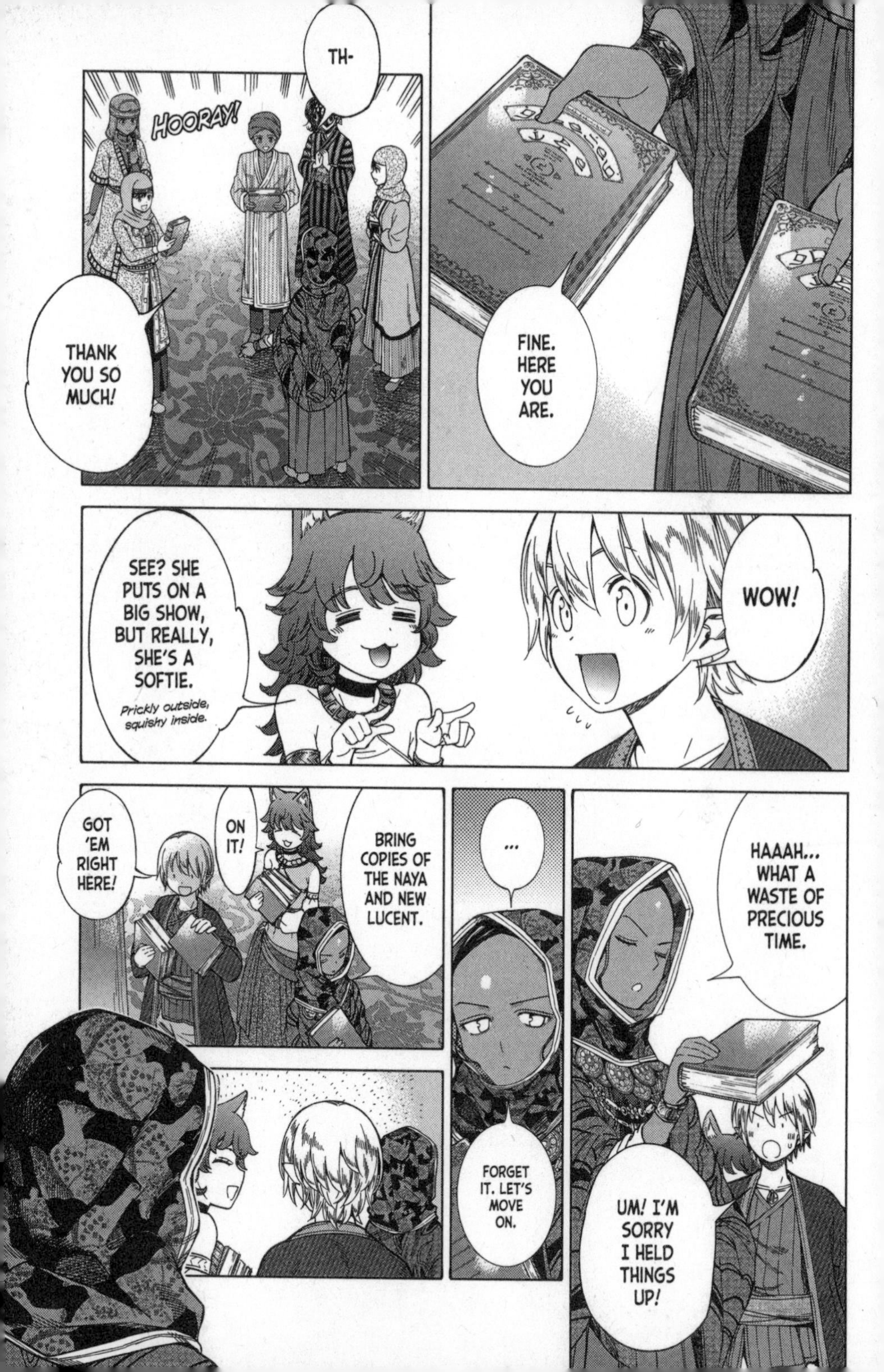
FINE. HERE YOU ARE.
TH-
HOORAY!
THANK YOU SO MUCH!
WOW!
SEE? SHE PUTS ON A BIG SHOW, BUT REALLY, SHE'S A SOFTIE.
Prickly outside, squishy inside.
HAAAH... WHAT A WASTE OF PRECIOUS TIME.
UM! I'M SORRY I HELD THINGS UP!
...
FORGET IT. LET'S MOVE ON.
BRING COPIES OF THE NAYA AND NEW LUCENT.
ON IT!
GOT 'EM RIGHT HERE!

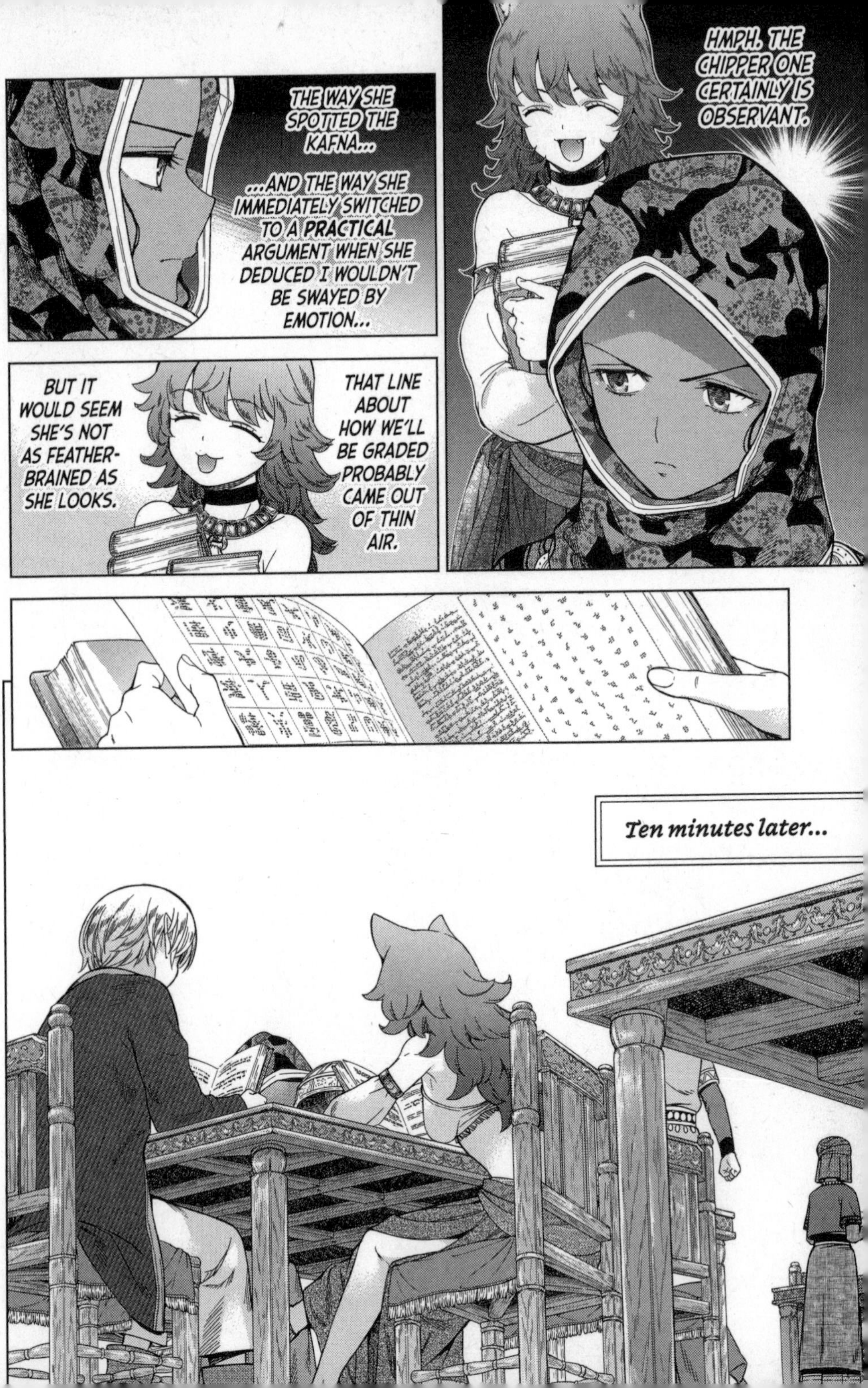
HMPH. THE CHIPPER ONE CERTAINLY IS OBSERVANT.
THE WAY SHE SPOTTED THE KAFNA...
...AND THE WAY SHE IMMEDIATELY SWITCHED TO A **PRACTICAL** ARGUMENT WHEN SHE DEDUCED I WOULDN'T BE SWAYED BY EMOTION...
THAT LINE ABOUT HOW WE'LL BE GRADED PROBABLY CAME OUT OF THIN AIR.
BUT IT WOULD SEEM SHE'S NOT AS FEATHER-BRAINED AS SHE LOOKS.
Ten minutes later...

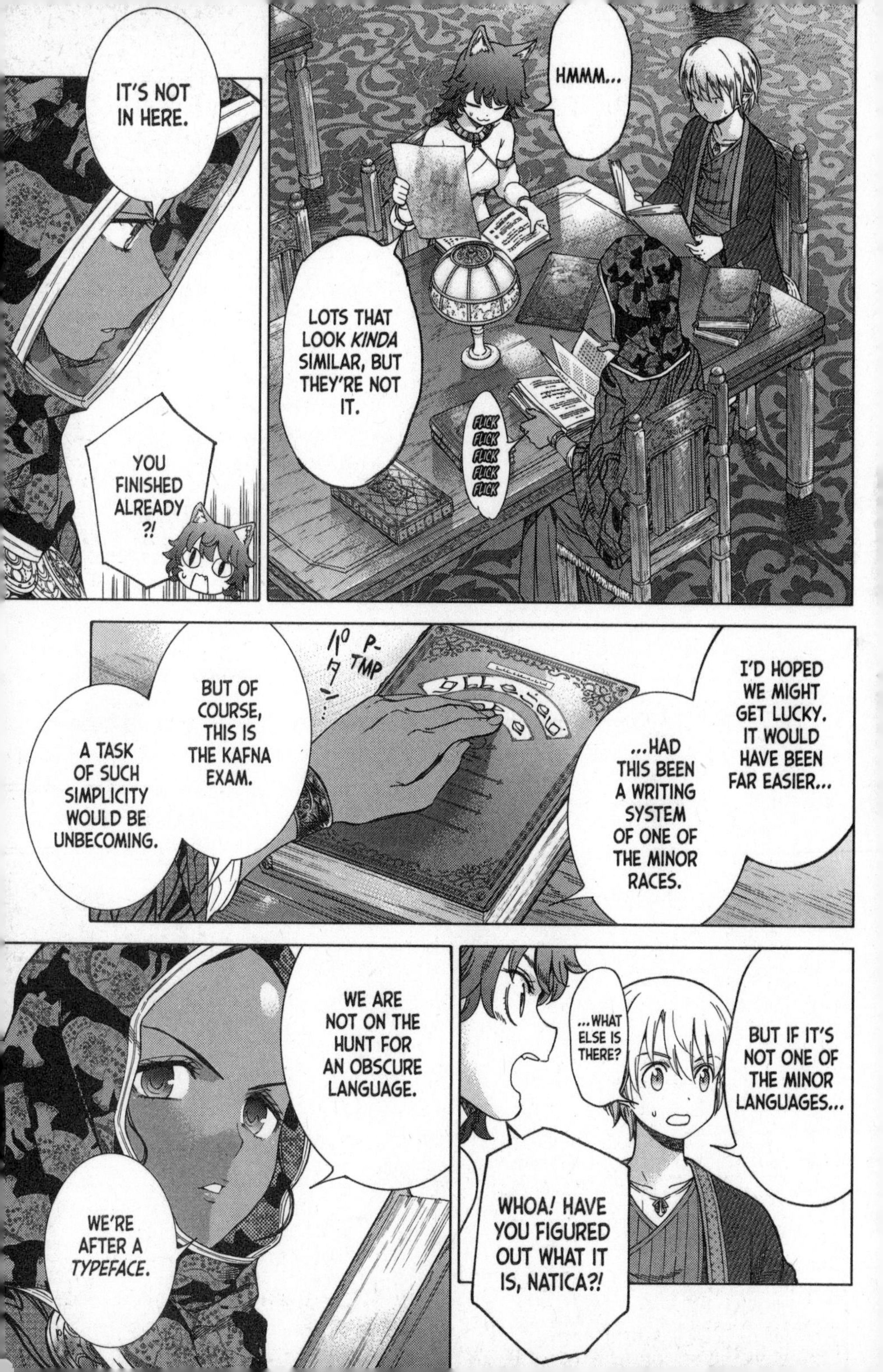
HMMM...
LOTS THAT LOOK *KINDA* SIMILAR, BUT THEY'RE NOT IT.
FLICK FLICK FLICK FLICK FLICK
IT'S NOT IN HERE.
YOU FINISHED ALREADY?!
I'D HOPED WE MIGHT GET LUCKY. IT WOULD HAVE BEEN FAR EASIER...
...HAD THIS BEEN A WRITING SYSTEM OF ONE OF THE MINOR RACES.
P-TMP
BUT OF COURSE, THIS IS THE KAFNA EXAM.
A TASK OF SUCH SIMPLICITY WOULD BE UNBECOMING.
BUT IF IT'S NOT ONE OF THE MINOR LANGUAGES...
...WHAT ELSE IS THERE?
WHOA! HAVE YOU FIGURED OUT WHAT IT IS, NATICA?!
WE ARE NOT ON THE HUNT FOR AN OBSCURE LANGUAGE.
WE'RE AFTER A *TYPEFACE*.

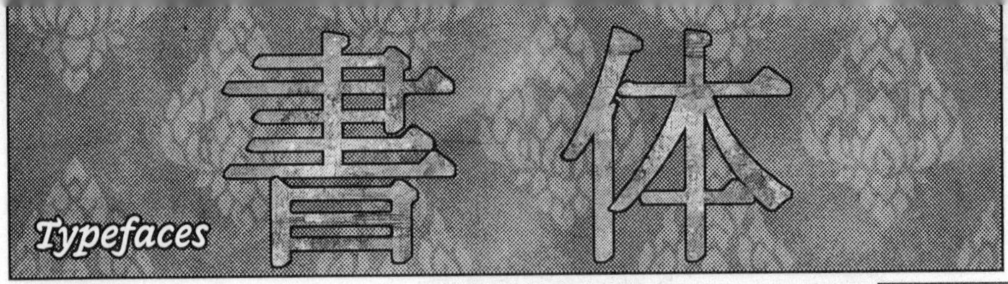
書体
Typefaces

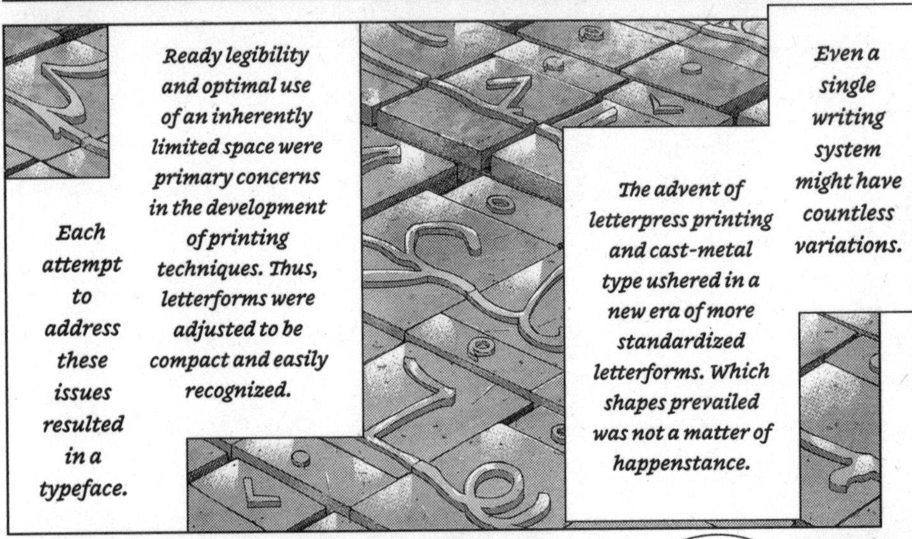
Even a single writing system might have countless variations.
The advent of letterpress printing and cast-metal type ushered in a new era of more standardized letterforms. Which shapes prevailed was not a matter of happenstance.
Ready legibility and optimal use of an inherently limited space were primary concerns in the development of printing techniques. Thus, letterforms were adjusted to be compact and easily recognized.
Each attempt to address these issues resulted in a typeface.

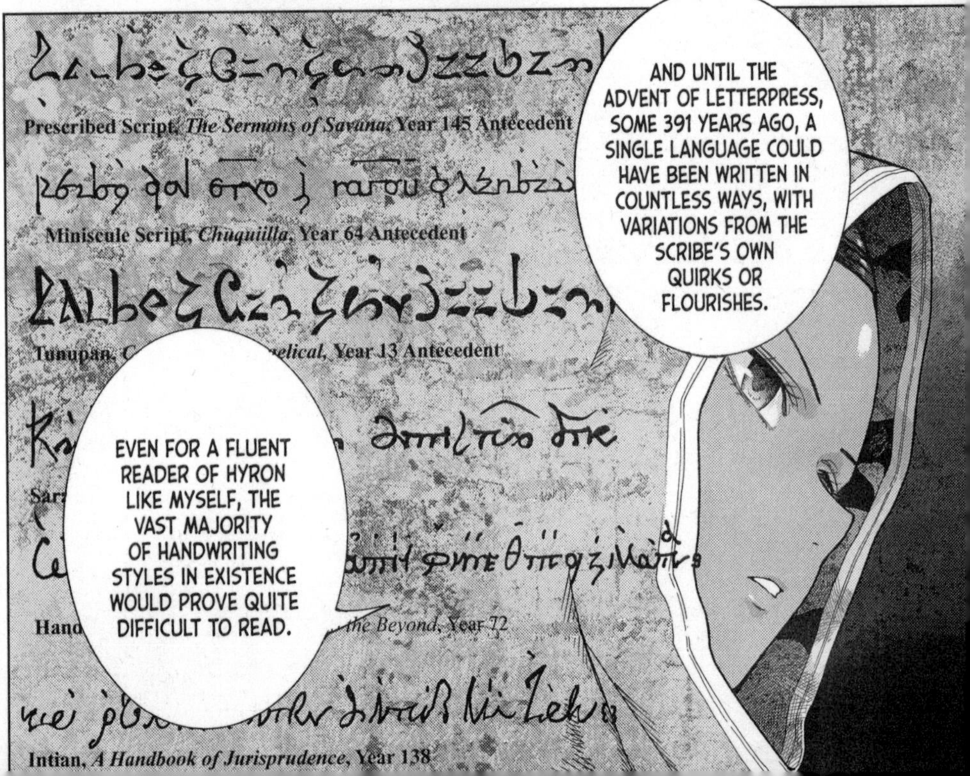
AND UNTIL THE ADVENT OF LETTERPRESS, SOME 391 YEARS AGO, A SINGLE LANGUAGE COULD HAVE BEEN WRITTEN IN COUNTLESS WAYS, WITH VARIATIONS FROM THE SCRIBE'S OWN QUIRKS OR FLOURISHES.
EVEN FOR A FLUENT READER OF HYRON LIKE MYSELF, THE VAST MAJORITY OF HANDWRITING STYLES IN EXISTENCE WOULD PROVE QUITE DIFFICULT TO READ.
Prescribed Script, *The Sermons of Savana*, Year 145 Antecedent
Miniscule Script, *Chuquiilla*, Year 64 Antecedent
Tunupan, C *elical*, Year 13 Antecedent
Hand *the Beyond*, Year 72
Intian, *A Handbook of Jurisprudence*, Year 138

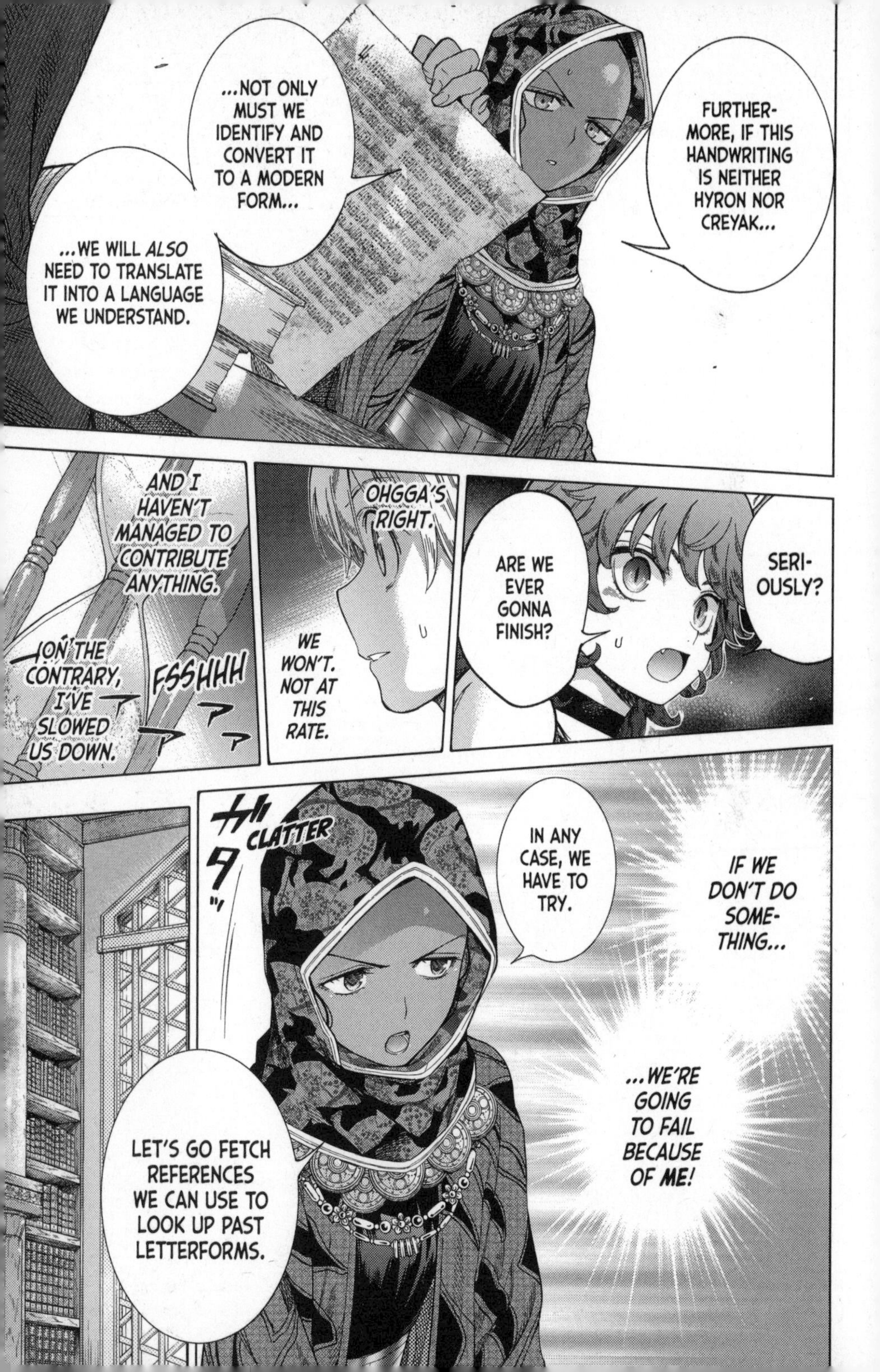
FURTHER-MORE, IF THIS HANDWRITING IS NEITHER HYRON NOR CREYAK...
...NOT ONLY MUST WE IDENTIFY AND CONVERT IT TO A MODERN FORM...
...WE WILL *ALSO* NEED TO TRANSLATE IT INTO A LANGUAGE WE UNDERSTAND.
SERI-OUSLY?
ARE WE EVER GONNA FINISH?
OHGGA'S RIGHT.
WE WON'T. NOT AT THIS RATE.
AND I HAVEN'T MANAGED TO CONTRIBUTE ANYTHING.
FSSHHH
ON THE CONTRARY, I'VE SLOWED US DOWN.
IF WE DON'T DO SOME-THING...
IN ANY CASE, WE HAVE TO TRY.
CLATTER
...WE'RE GOING TO FAIL BECAUSE OF *ME!*
LET'S GO FETCH REFERENCES WE CAN USE TO LOOK UP PAST LETTERFORMS.

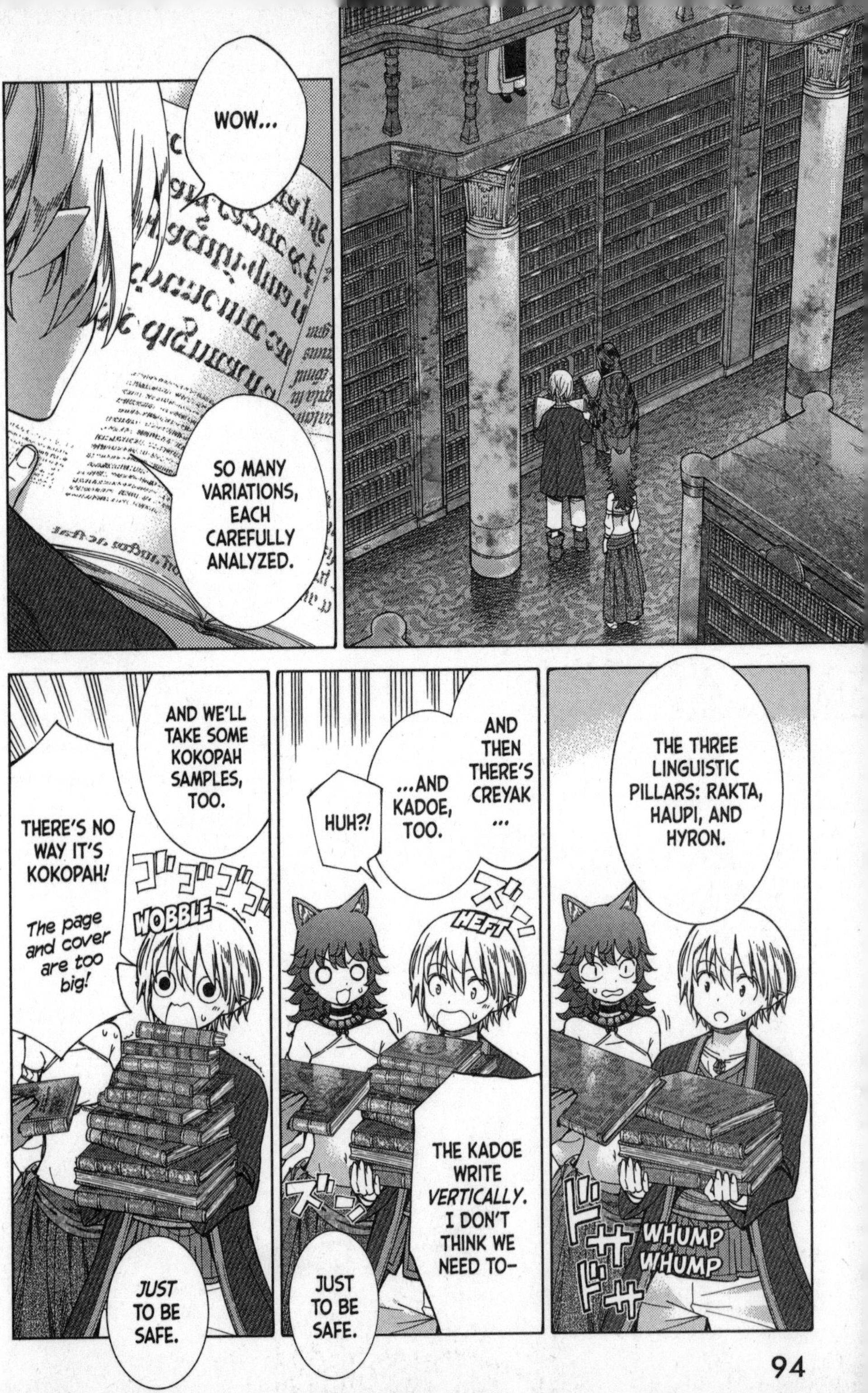
WOW...
SO MANY VARIATIONS, EACH CAREFULLY ANALYZED.
THE THREE LINGUISTIC PILLARS: RAKTA, HAUPI, AND HYRON.
WHUMP WHUMP
AND THEN THERE'S CREYAK ...
...AND KADOE, TOO.
HUH?!
HEFT
THE KADOE WRITE *VERTICALLY*. I DON'T THINK WE NEED TO–
JUST TO BE SAFE.
AND WE'LL TAKE SOME KOKOPAH SAMPLES, TOO.
THERE'S NO WAY IT'S KOKOPAH!
The page and cover are too big!
WOBBLE
JUST TO BE SAFE.

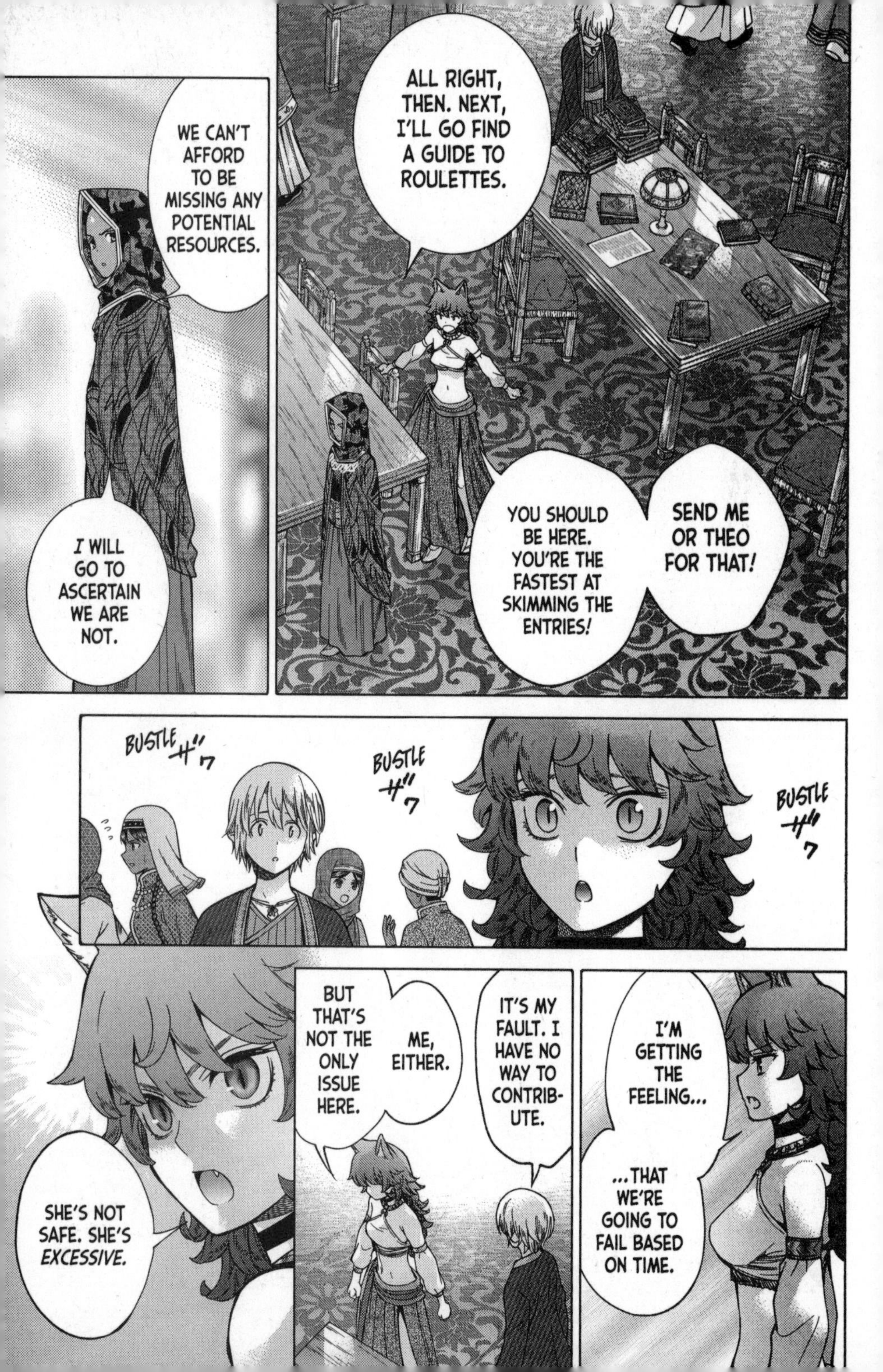
ALL RIGHT, THEN. NEXT, I'LL GO FIND A GUIDE TO ROULETTES.
SEND ME OR THEO FOR THAT!
YOU SHOULD BE HERE. YOU'RE THE FASTEST AT SKIMMING THE ENTRIES!
WE CAN'T AFFORD TO BE MISSING ANY POTENTIAL RESOURCES.
I WILL GO TO ASCERTAIN WE ARE NOT.
BUSTLE
BUSTLE
BUSTLE
I'M GETTING THE FEELING...
...THAT WE'RE GOING TO FAIL BASED ON TIME.
IT'S MY FAULT. I HAVE NO WAY TO CONTRIB-UTE.
ME, EITHER.
BUT THAT'S NOT THE ONLY ISSUE HERE.
SHE'S NOT SAFE. SHE'S *EXCESSIVE.*

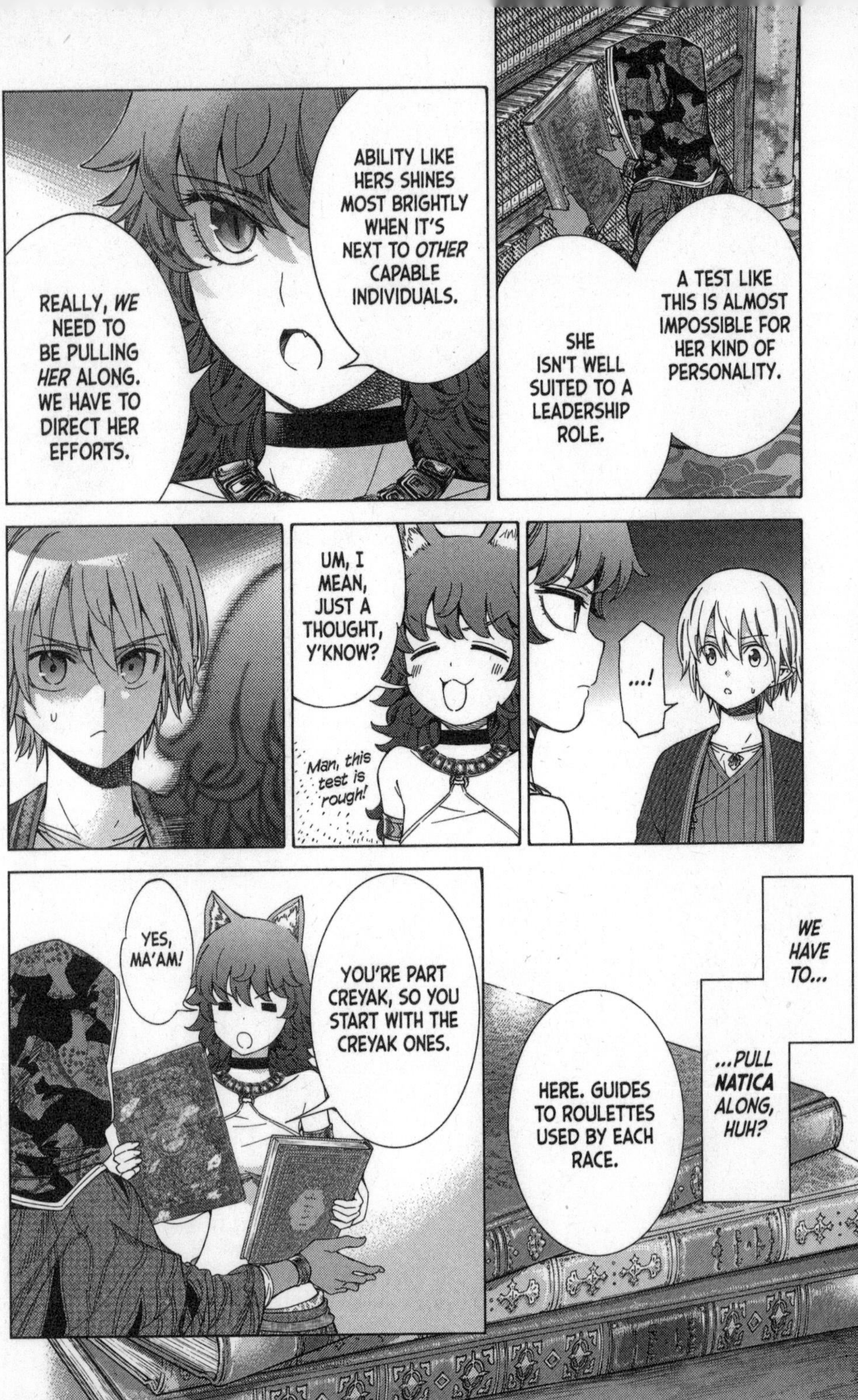
A TEST LIKE THIS IS ALMOST IMPOSSIBLE FOR HER KIND OF PERSONALITY.
SHE ISN'T WELL SUITED TO A LEADERSHIP ROLE.
ABILITY LIKE HERS SHINES MOST BRIGHTLY WHEN IT'S NEXT TO *OTHER* CAPABLE INDIVIDUALS.
REALLY, *WE* NEED TO BE PULLING *HER* ALONG. WE HAVE TO DIRECT HER EFFORTS.
...!
UM, I MEAN, JUST A THOUGHT, Y'KNOW?
Man, this test is rough!
WE HAVE TO...
...PULL NATICA ALONG, HUH?
HERE. GUIDES TO ROULETTES USED BY EACH RACE.
YOU'RE PART CREYAK, SO YOU START WITH THE CREYAK ONES.
YES, MA'AM!

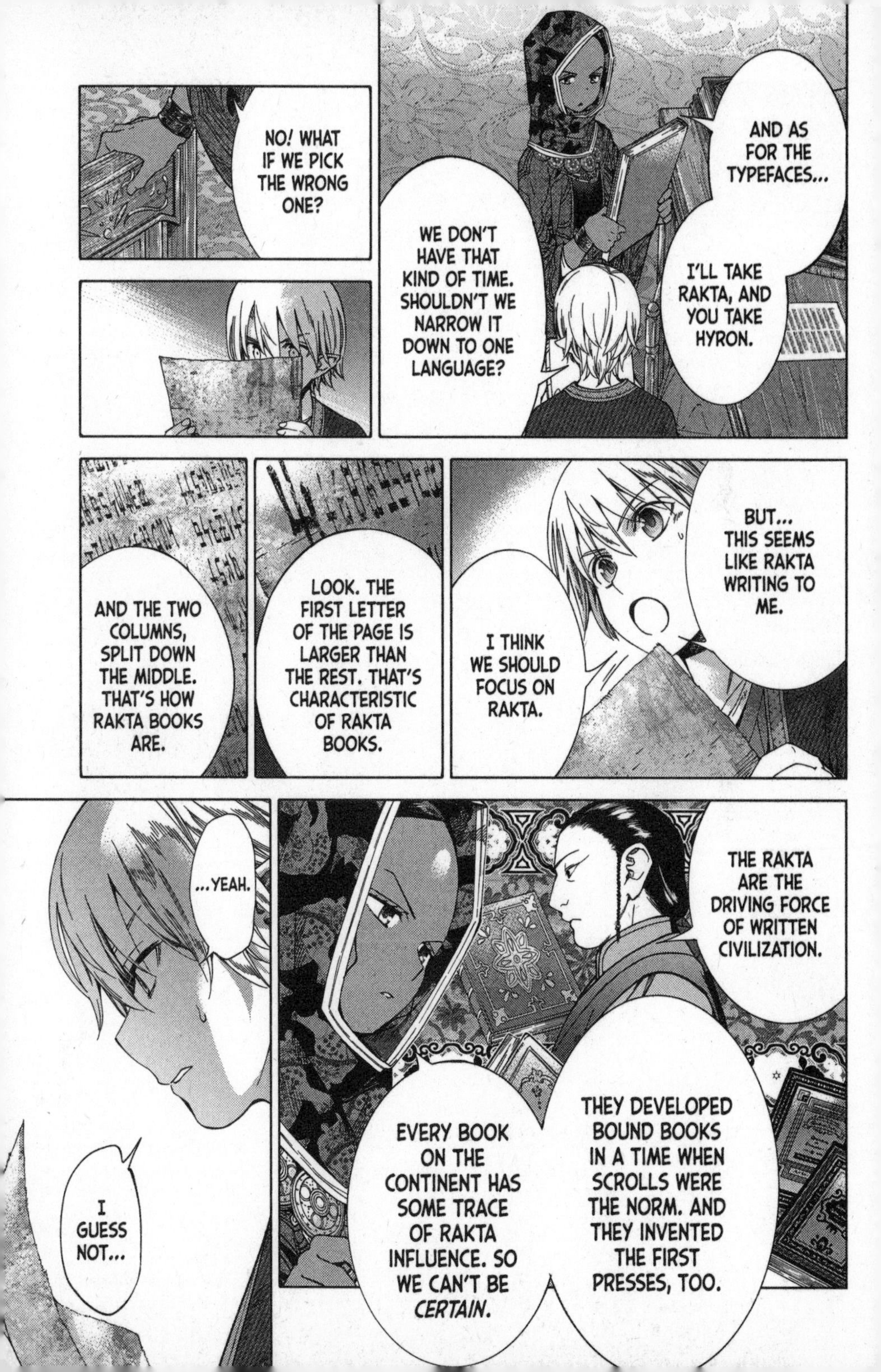
AND AS FOR THE TYPEFACES...
I'LL TAKE RAKTA, AND YOU TAKE HYRON.
WE DON'T HAVE THAT KIND OF TIME. SHOULDN'T WE NARROW IT DOWN TO ONE LANGUAGE?
NO! WHAT IF WE PICK THE WRONG ONE?
BUT... THIS SEEMS LIKE RAKTA WRITING TO ME.
I THINK WE SHOULD FOCUS ON RAKTA.
LOOK. THE FIRST LETTER OF THE PAGE IS LARGER THAN THE REST. THAT'S CHARACTERISTIC OF RAKTA BOOKS.
AND THE TWO COLUMNS, SPLIT DOWN THE MIDDLE. THAT'S HOW RAKTA BOOKS ARE.
THE RAKTA ARE THE DRIVING FORCE OF WRITTEN CIVILIZATION.
THEY DEVELOPED BOUND BOOKS IN A TIME WHEN SCROLLS WERE THE NORM. AND THEY INVENTED THE FIRST PRESSES, TOO.
EVERY BOOK ON THE CONTINENT HAS SOME TRACE OF RAKTA INFLUENCE. SO WE CAN'T BE *CERTAIN*.
...YEAH.
I GUESS NOT...

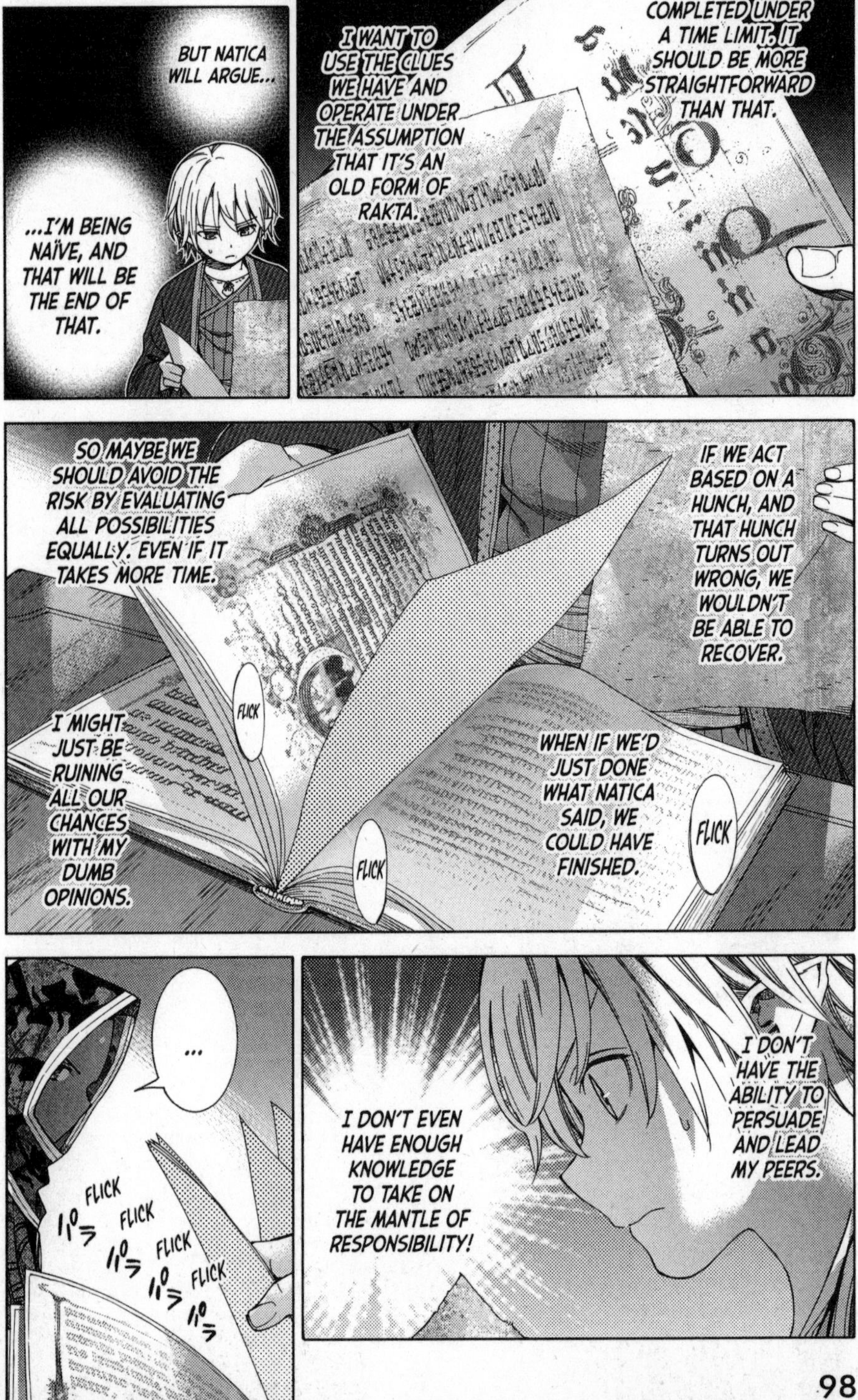
BUT IT'S A TEST DESIGNED TO BE COMPLETED UNDER A TIME LIMIT. IT SHOULD BE MORE STRAIGHTFORWARD THAN THAT.
I WANT TO USE THE CLUES WE HAVE AND OPERATE UNDER THE ASSUMPTION THAT IT'S AN OLD FORM OF RAKTA.
BUT NATICA WILL ARGUE...
...I'M BEING NAÏVE, AND THAT WILL BE THE END OF THAT.
IF WE ACT BASED ON A HUNCH, AND THAT HUNCH TURNS OUT WRONG, WE WOULDN'T BE ABLE TO RECOVER.
SO MAYBE WE SHOULD AVOID THE RISK BY EVALUATING ALL POSSIBILITIES EQUALLY. EVEN IF IT TAKES MORE TIME.
WHEN IF WE'D JUST DONE WHAT NATICA SAID, WE COULD HAVE FINISHED.
FLICK
FLICK
I MIGHT JUST BE RUINING ALL OUR CHANCES WITH MY DUMB OPINIONS.
FLICK
I DON'T HAVE THE ABILITY TO PERSUADE AND LEAD MY PEERS.
I DON'T EVEN HAVE ENOUGH KNOWLEDGE TO TAKE ON THE MANTLE OF RESPONSIBILITY!
...
FLICK
パラ
FLICK
パラ
FLICK
パラ
FLICK
パラ

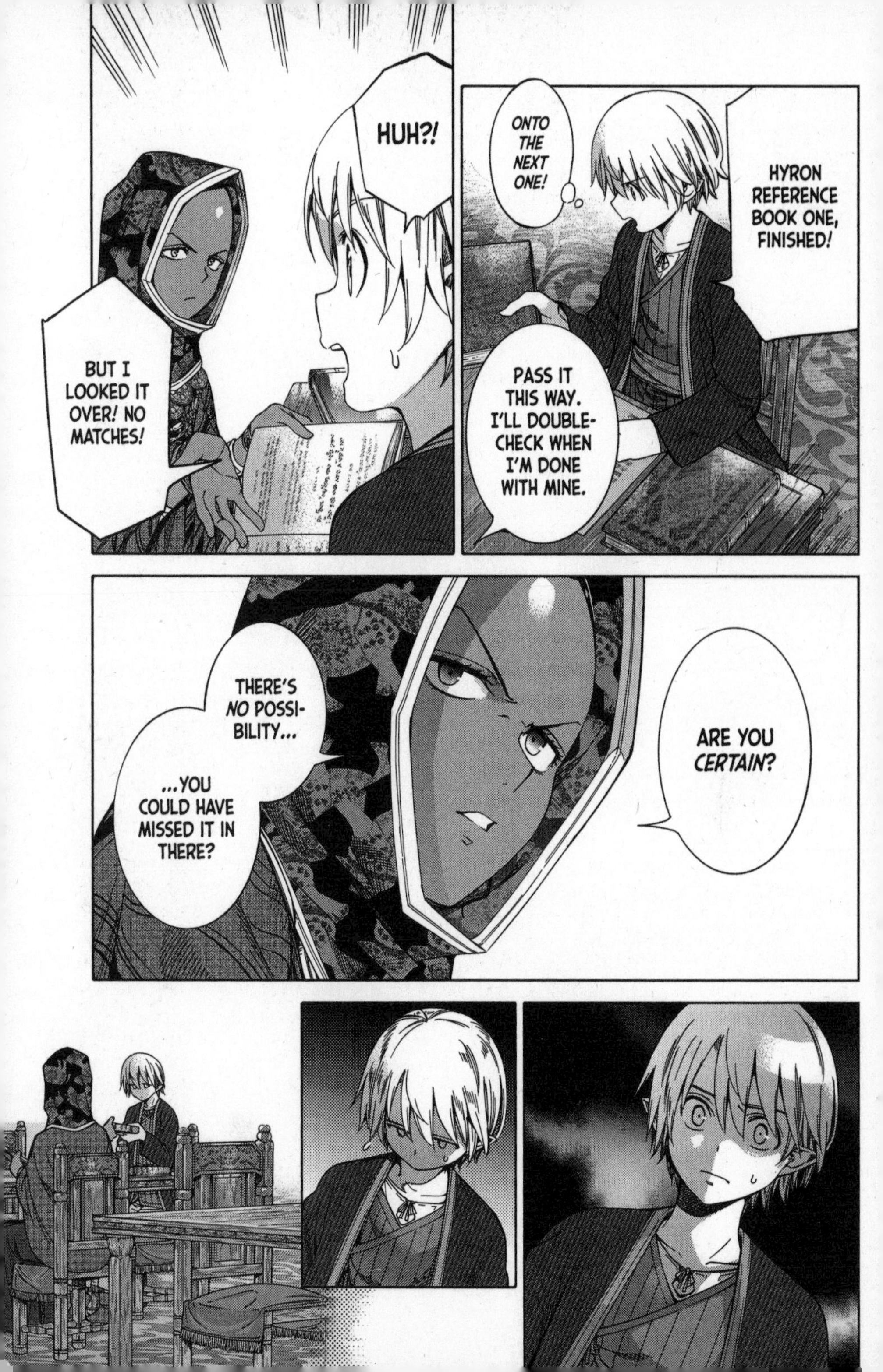
HYRON REFERENCE BOOK ONE, FINISHED!
ONTO THE NEXT ONE!
PASS IT THIS WAY. I'LL DOUBLE-CHECK WHEN I'M DONE WITH MINE.
HUH?!
BUT I LOOKED IT OVER! NO MATCHES!
ARE YOU *CERTAIN*?
THERE'S *NO* POSSIBILITY...
...YOU COULD HAVE MISSED IT IN THERE?

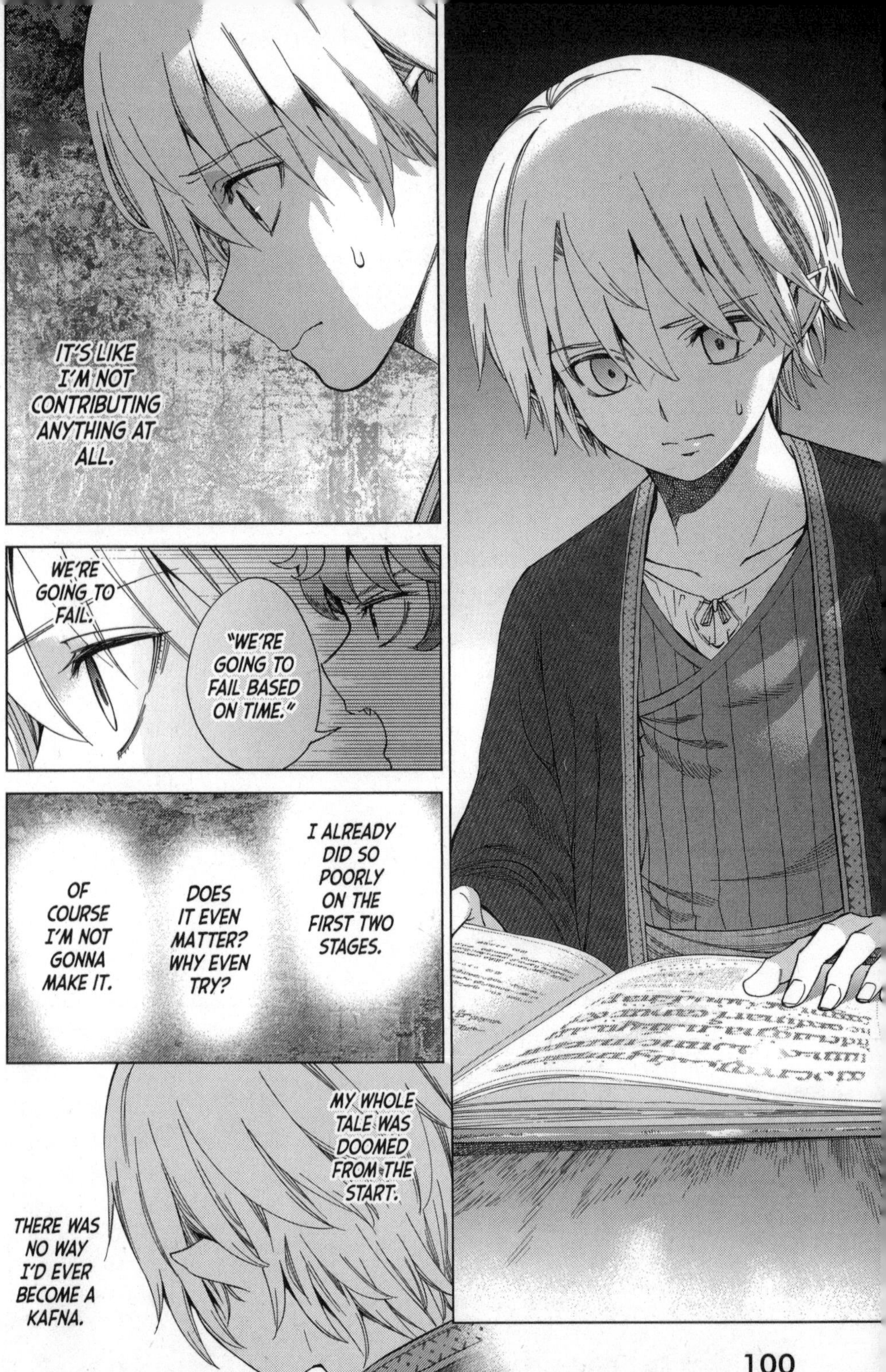
IT'S LIKE I'M NOT CONTRIBUTING ANYTHING AT ALL.
"WE'RE GOING TO FAIL BASED ON TIME."
WE'RE GOING TO FAIL.
I ALREADY DID SO POORLY ON THE FIRST TWO STAGES.
DOES IT EVEN MATTER? WHY EVEN TRY?
OF COURSE I'M NOT GONNA MAKE IT.
MY WHOLE TALE WAS DOOMED FROM THE START.
THERE WAS NO WAY I'D EVER BECOME A KAFNA.

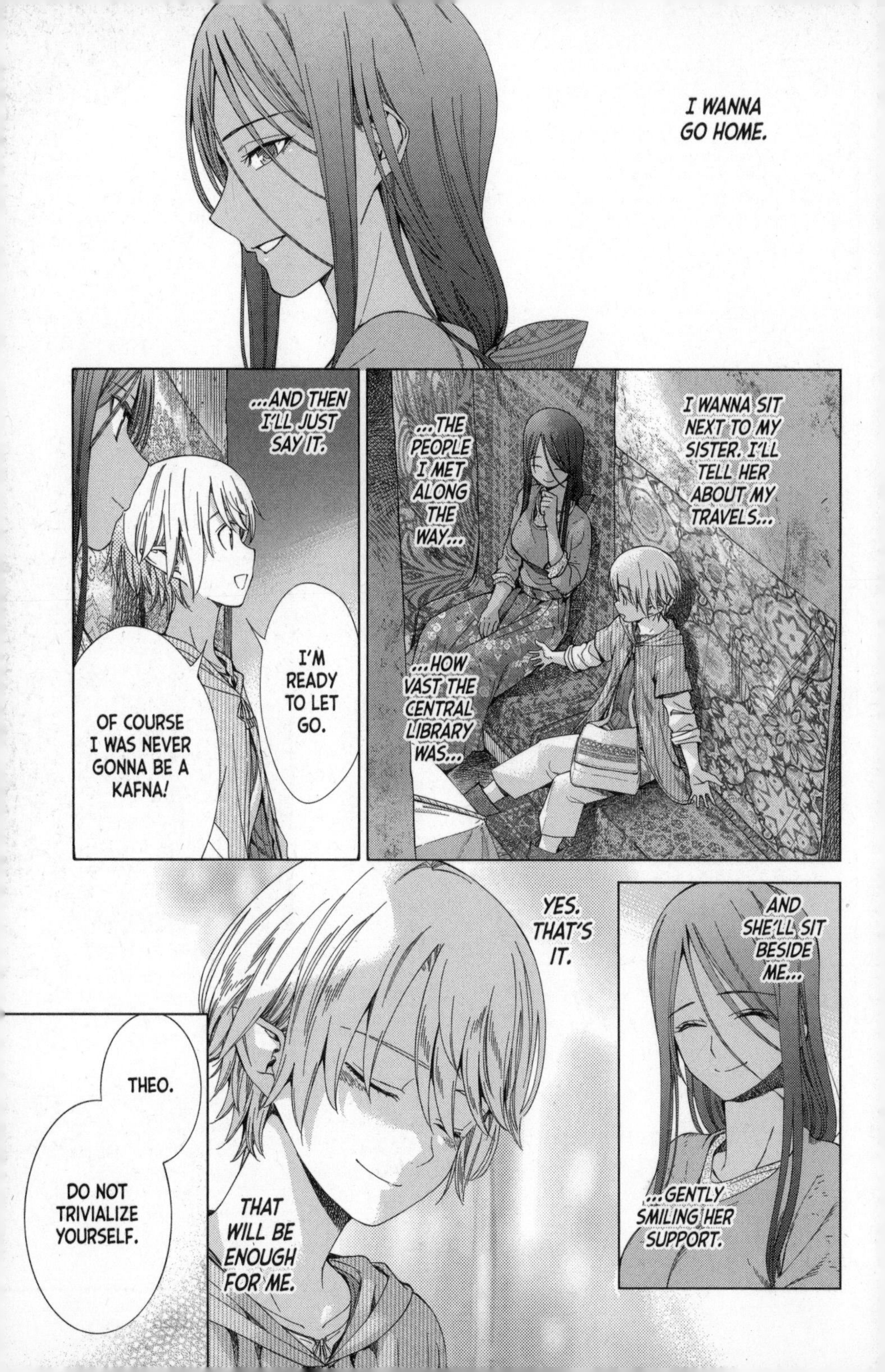
I WANNA GO HOME.
I WANNA SIT NEXT TO MY SISTER. I'LL TELL HER ABOUT MY TRAVELS...
...THE PEOPLE I MET ALONG THE WAY...
...HOW VAST THE CENTRAL LIBRARY WAS...
...AND THEN I'LL JUST SAY IT.
I'M READY TO LET GO.
OF COURSE I WAS NEVER GONNA BE A KAFNA!
AND SHE'LL SIT BESIDE ME...
...GENTLY SMILING HER SUPPORT.
YES. THAT'S IT.
THAT WILL BE ENOUGH FOR ME.
THEO.
DO NOT TRIVIALIZE YOURSELF.

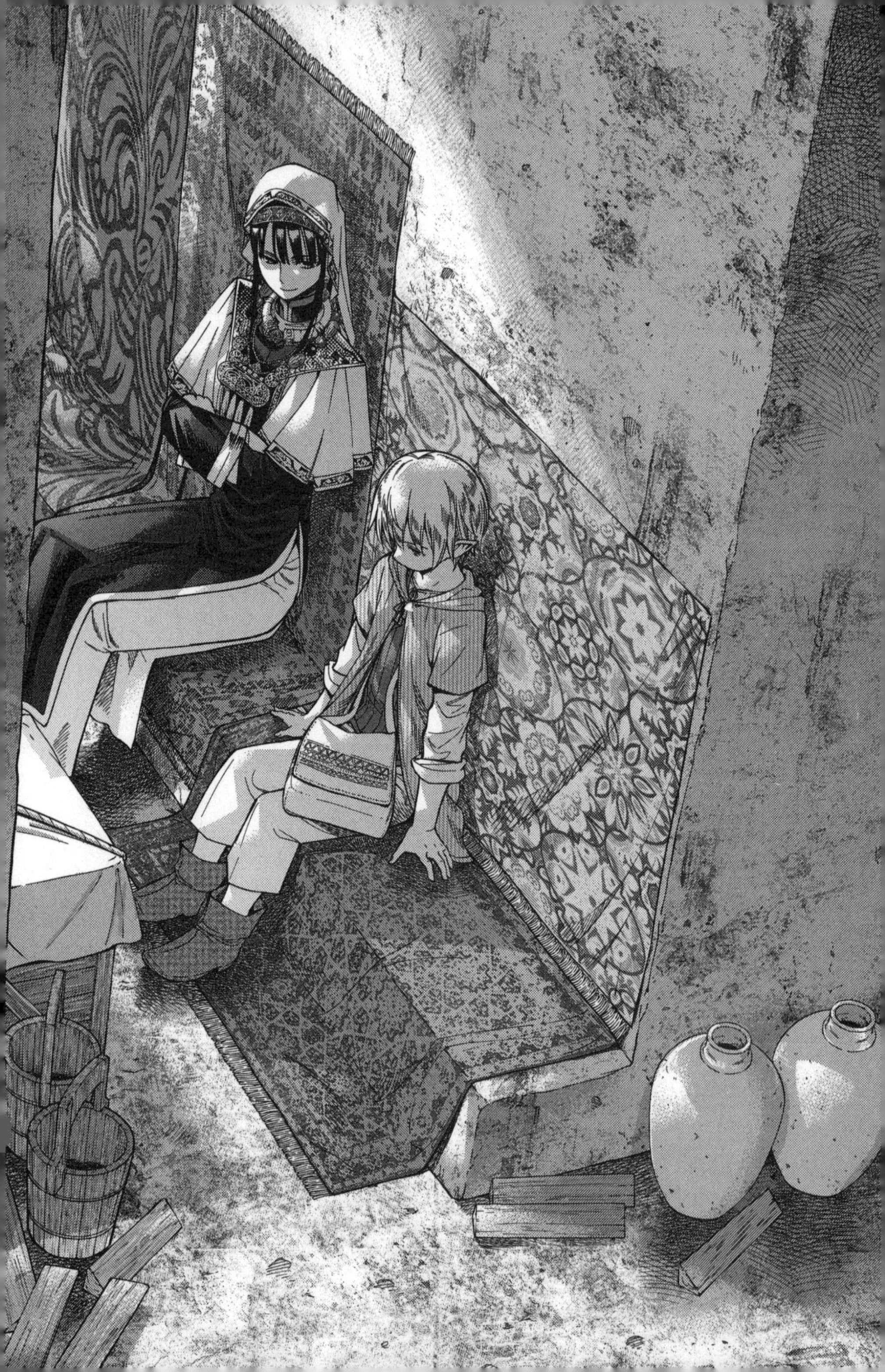

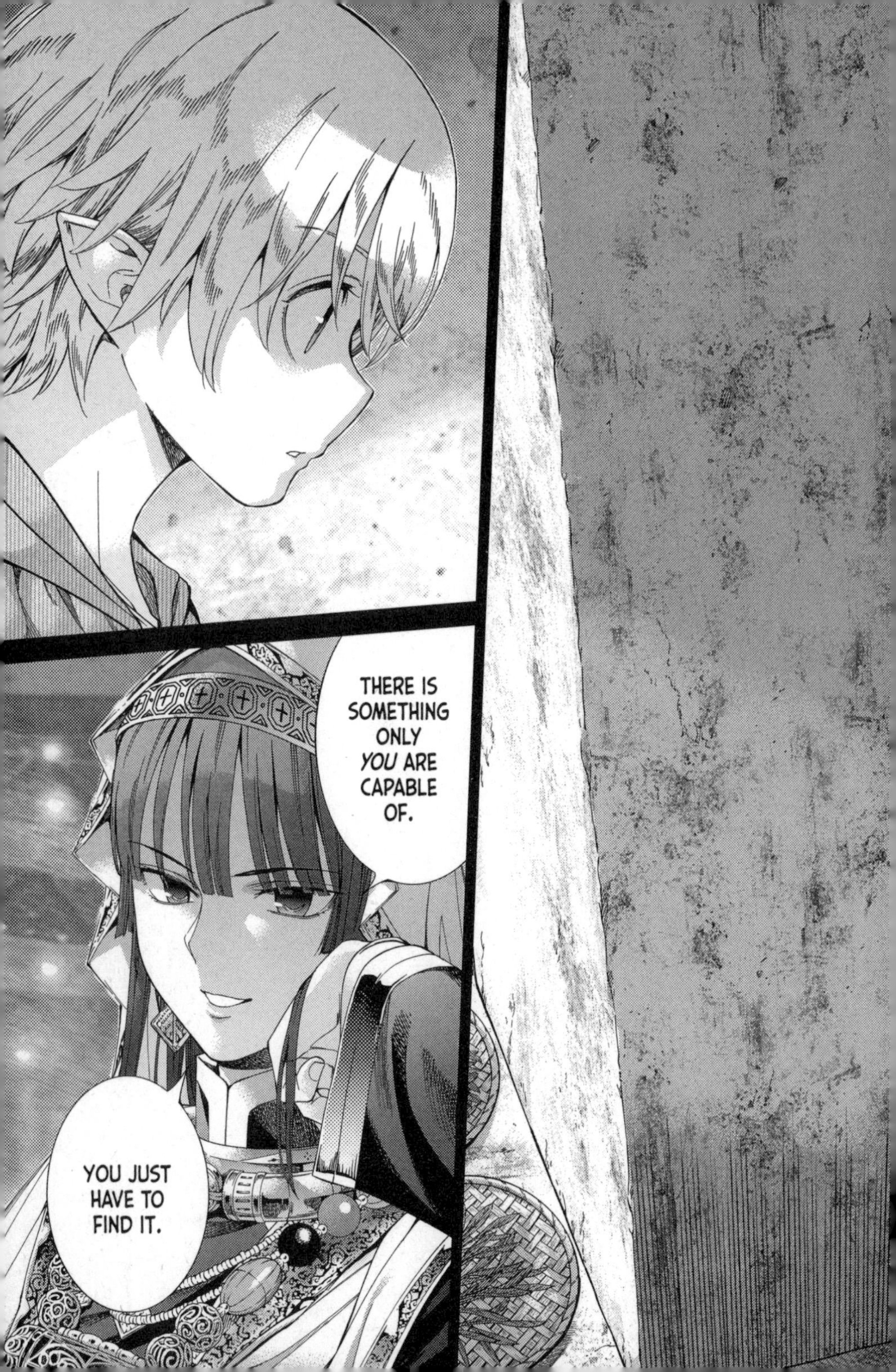
THERE IS SOMETHING ONLY *YOU* ARE CAPABLE OF.
YOU JUST HAVE TO FIND IT.

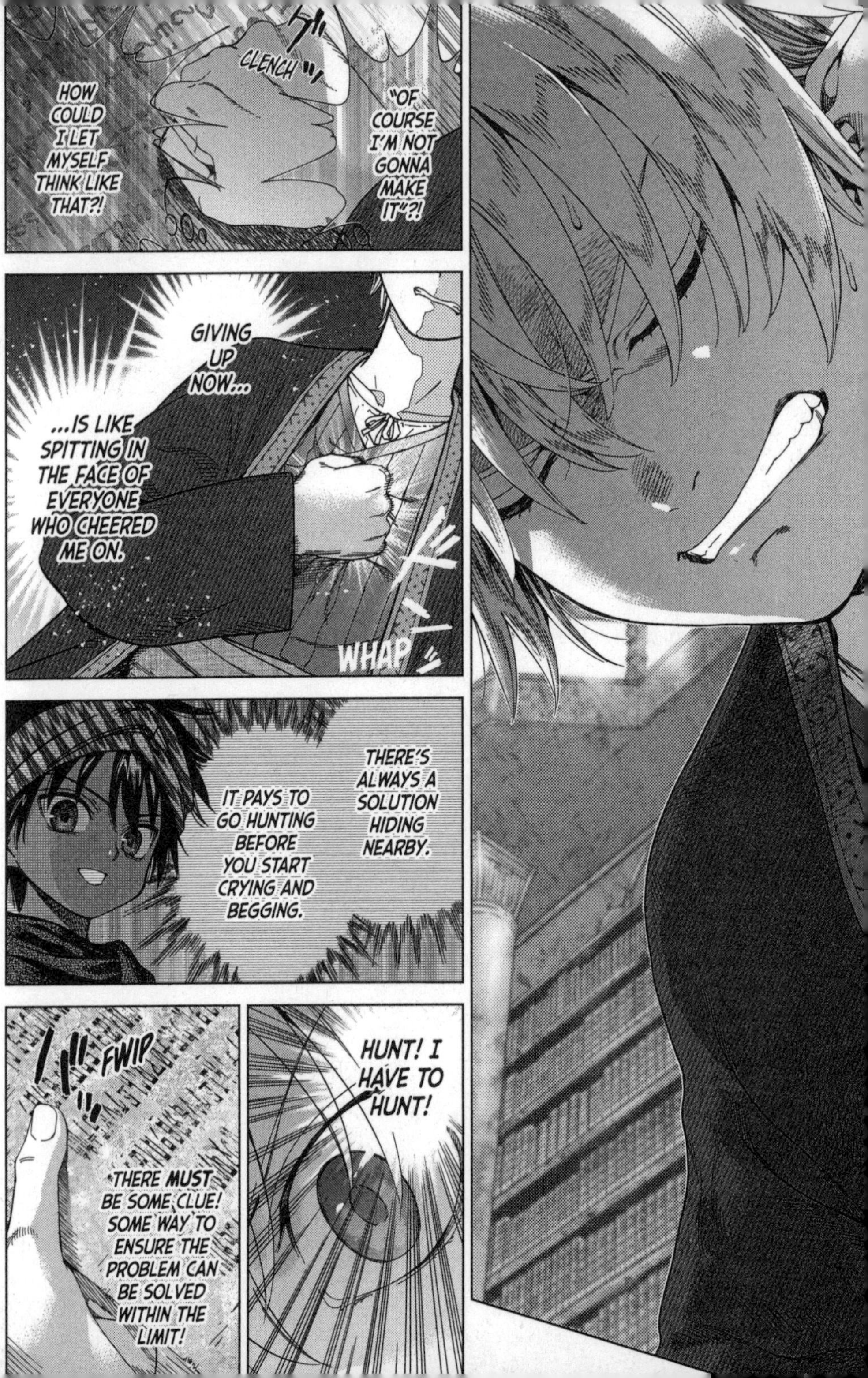
"OF COURSE I'M NOT GONNA MAKE IT"?!
CLENCH
HOW COULD I LET MYSELF THINK LIKE THAT?!
GIVING UP NOW...
...IS LIKE SPITTING IN THE FACE OF EVERYONE WHO CHEERED ME ON.
WHAP
THERE'S ALWAYS A SOLUTION HIDING NEARBY.
IT PAYS TO GO HUNTING BEFORE YOU START CRYING AND BEGGING.
HUNT! I HAVE TO HUNT!
FWIP
THERE MUST BE SOME CLUE! SOME WAY TO ENSURE THE PROBLEM CAN BE SOLVED WITHIN THE LIMIT!

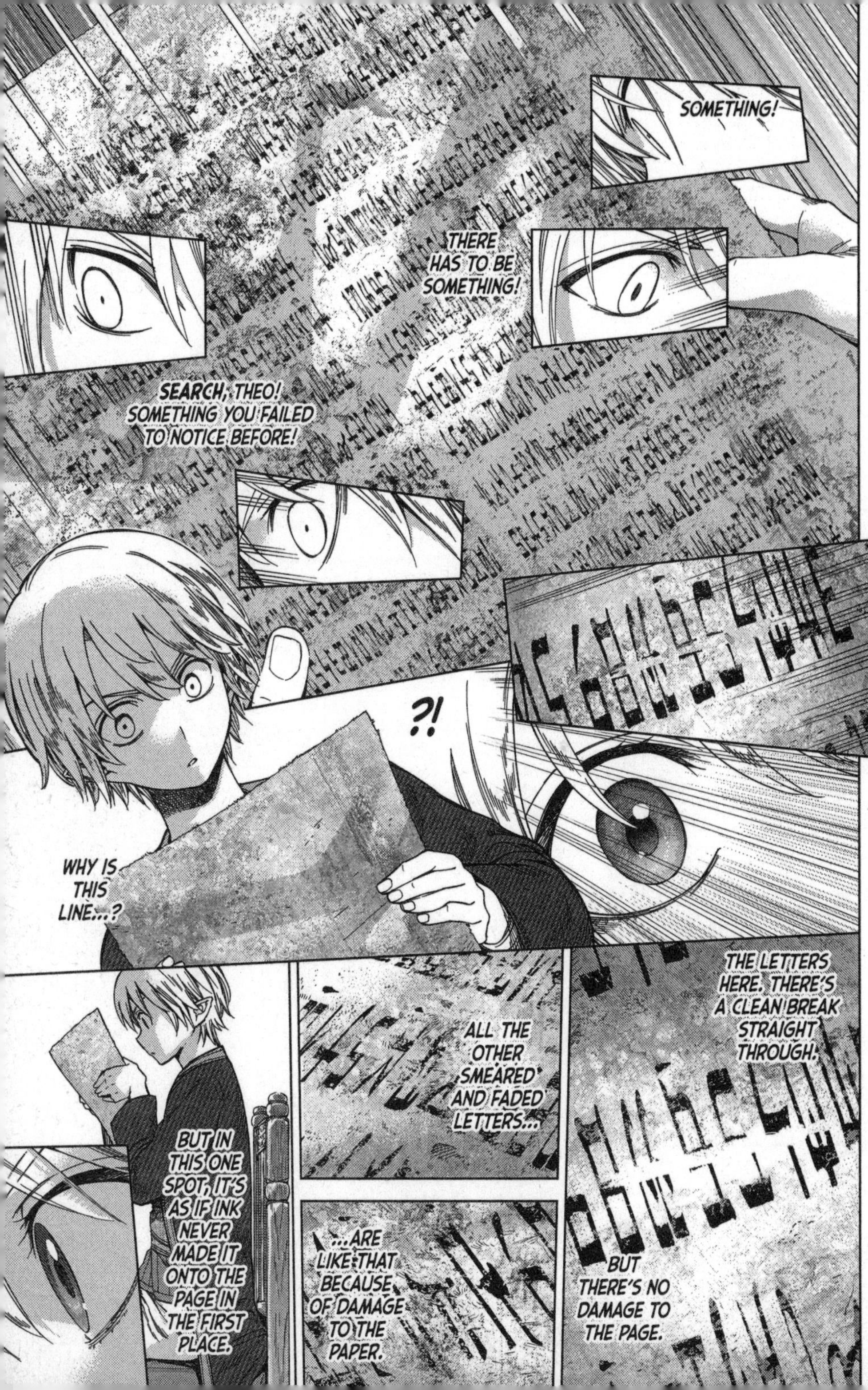
SOMETHING!
THERE HAS TO BE SOMETHING!
SEARCH, THEO! SOMETHING YOU FAILED TO NOTICE BEFORE!
?!
WHY IS THIS LINE...?
THE LETTERS HERE. THERE'S A CLEAN BREAK STRAIGHT THROUGH.
BUT THERE'S NO DAMAGE TO THE PAGE.
ALL THE OTHER SMEARED AND FADED LETTERS...
...ARE LIKE THAT BECAUSE OF DAMAGE TO THE PAPER.
BUT IN THIS ONE SPOT, IT'S AS IF INK NEVER MADE IT ONTO THE PAGE IN THE FIRST PLACE.

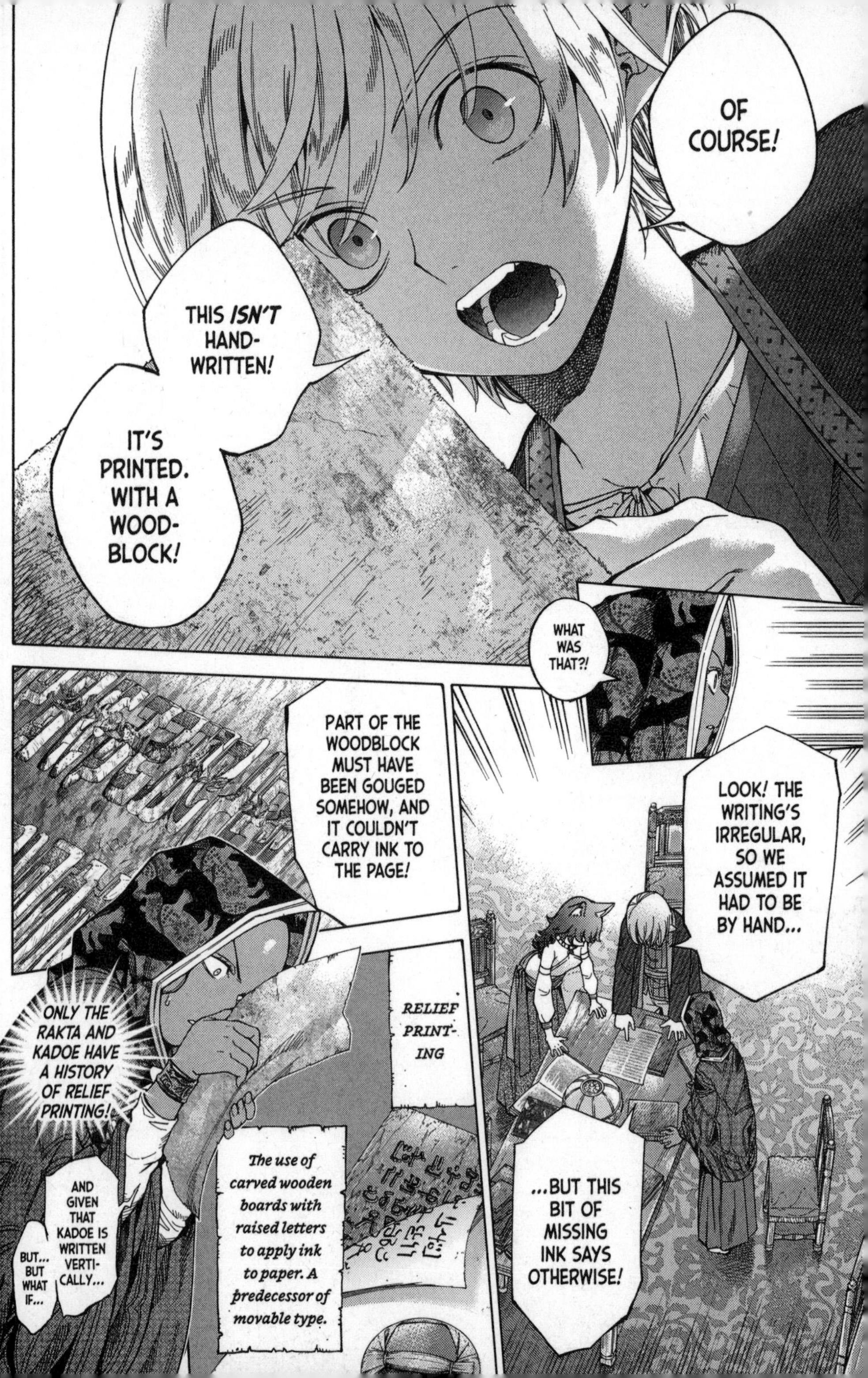

OF COURSE!
THIS *ISN'T* HAND-WRITTEN!
IT'S PRINTED. WITH A WOOD-BLOCK!
WHAT WAS THAT?!
LOOK! THE WRITING'S IRREGULAR, SO WE ASSUMED IT HAD TO BE BY HAND...
...BUT THIS BIT OF MISSING INK SAYS OTHERWISE!
PART OF THE WOODBLOCK MUST HAVE BEEN GOUGED SOMEHOW, AND IT COULDN'T CARRY INK TO THE PAGE!
RELIEF PRINT-ING
The use of carved wooden boards with raised letters to apply ink to paper. A predecessor of movable type.
ONLY THE RAKTA AND KADOE HAVE A HISTORY OF RELIEF PRINTING!
AND GIVEN THAT KADOE IS WRITTEN VERTI-CALLY...
BUT... BUT WHAT IF...

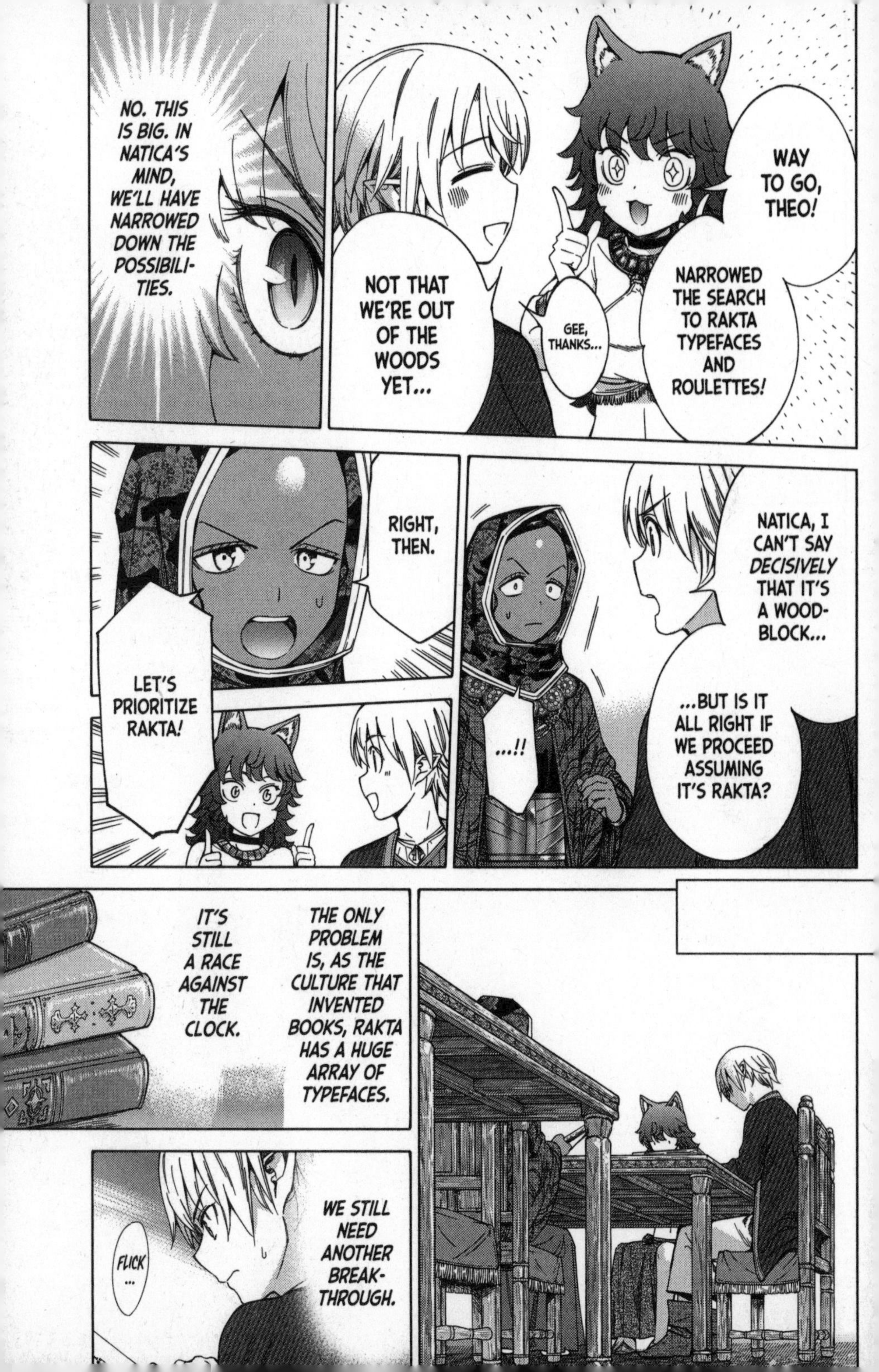
WAY TO GO, THEO!
NARROWED THE SEARCH TO RAKTA TYPEFACES AND ROULETTES!
GEE, THANKS...
NOT THAT WE'RE OUT OF THE WOODS YET...
NO. THIS IS BIG. IN NATICA'S MIND, WE'LL HAVE NARROWED DOWN THE POSSIBILITIES.
NATICA, I CAN'T SAY *DECISIVELY* THAT IT'S A WOODBLOCK...
...BUT IS IT ALL RIGHT IF WE PROCEED ASSUMING IT'S RAKTA?
...!!
RIGHT, THEN.
LET'S PRIORITIZE RAKTA!
THE ONLY PROBLEM IS, AS THE CULTURE THAT INVENTED BOOKS, RAKTA HAS A HUGE ARRAY OF TYPEFACES.
IT'S STILL A RACE AGAINST THE CLOCK.
WE STILL NEED ANOTHER BREAKTHROUGH.
FLICK...

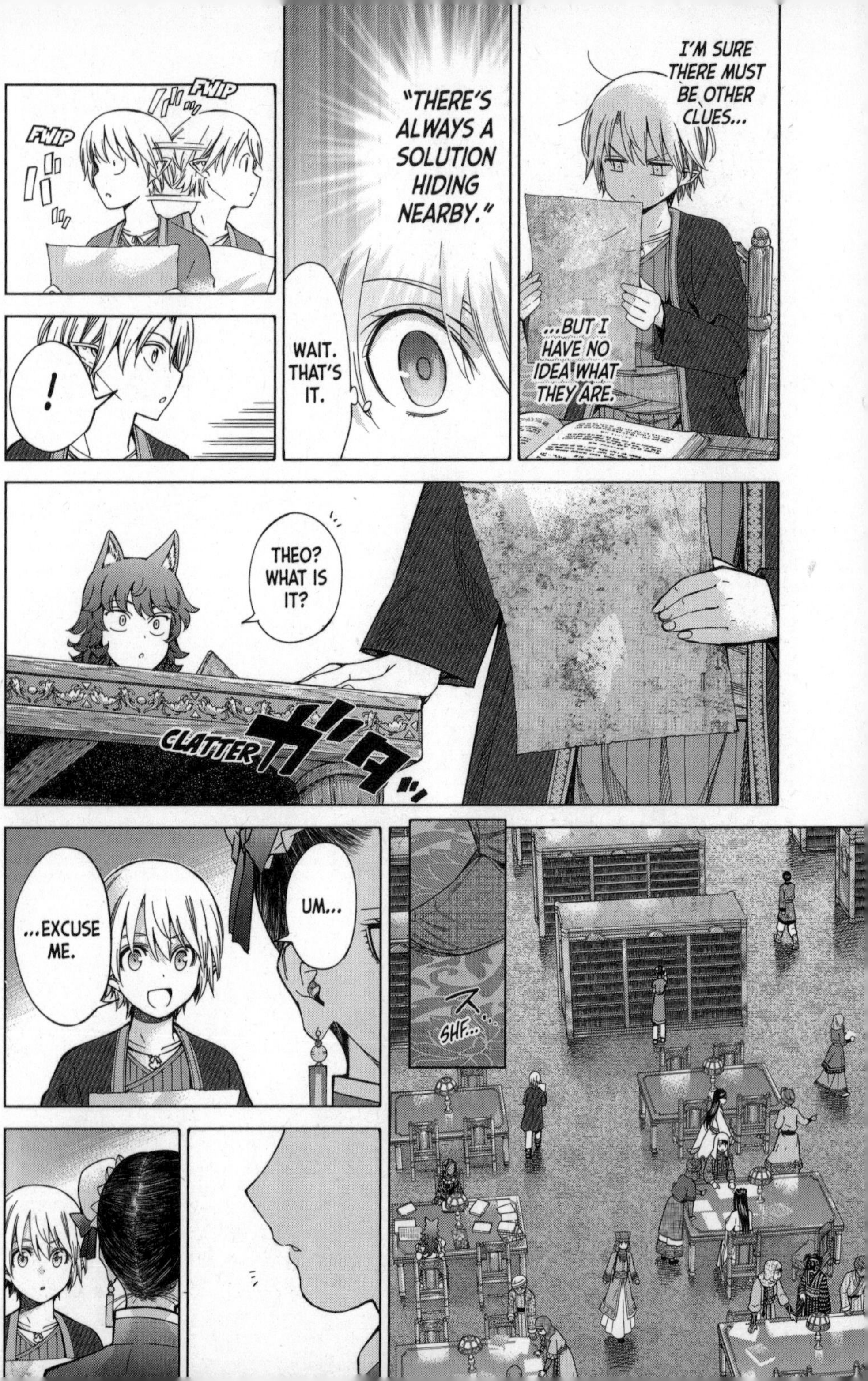
I'M SURE THERE MUST BE OTHER CLUES...
...BUT I HAVE NO IDEA WHAT THEY ARE.
"THERE'S ALWAYS A SOLUTION HIDING NEARBY."
WAIT. THAT'S IT.
FWIP
FWIP
!
THEO? WHAT IS IT?
CLATTER
SHF...
UM...
...EXCUSE ME.

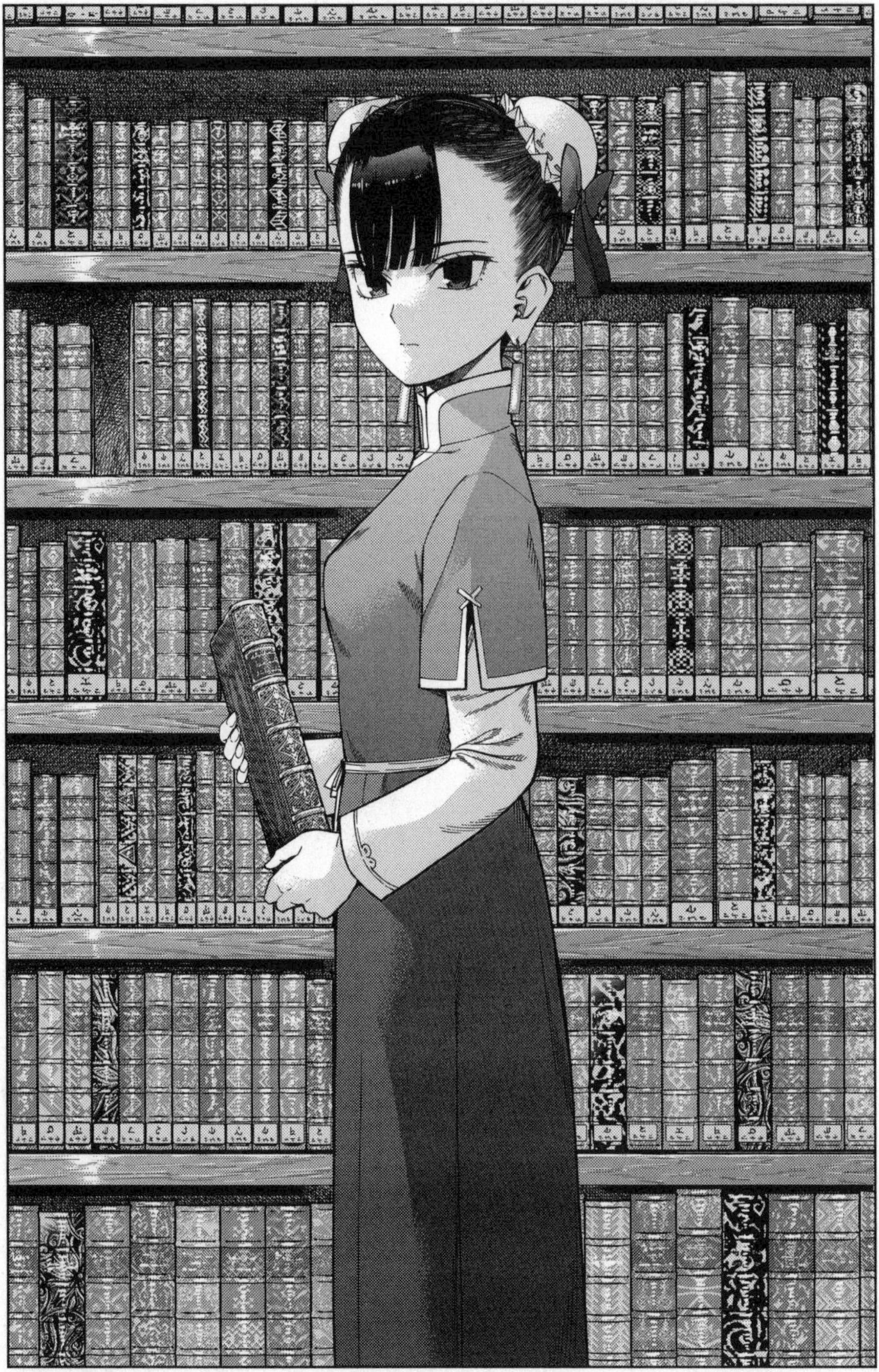

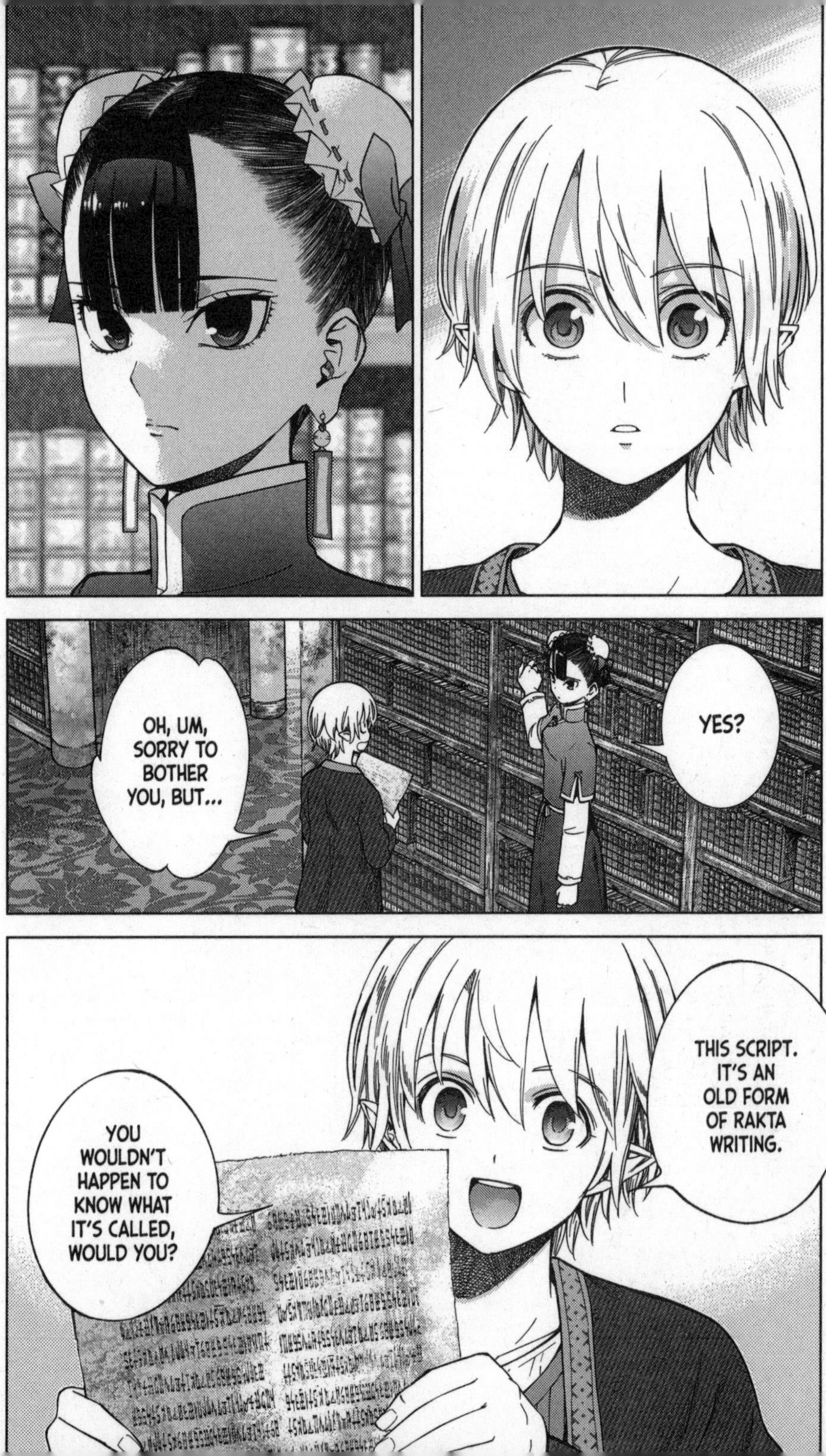
YES?
OH, UM, SORRY TO BOTHER YOU, BUT...
THIS SCRIPT. IT'S AN OLD FORM OF RAKTA WRITING.
YOU WOULDN'T HAPPEN TO KNOW WHAT IT'S CALLED, WOULD YOU?

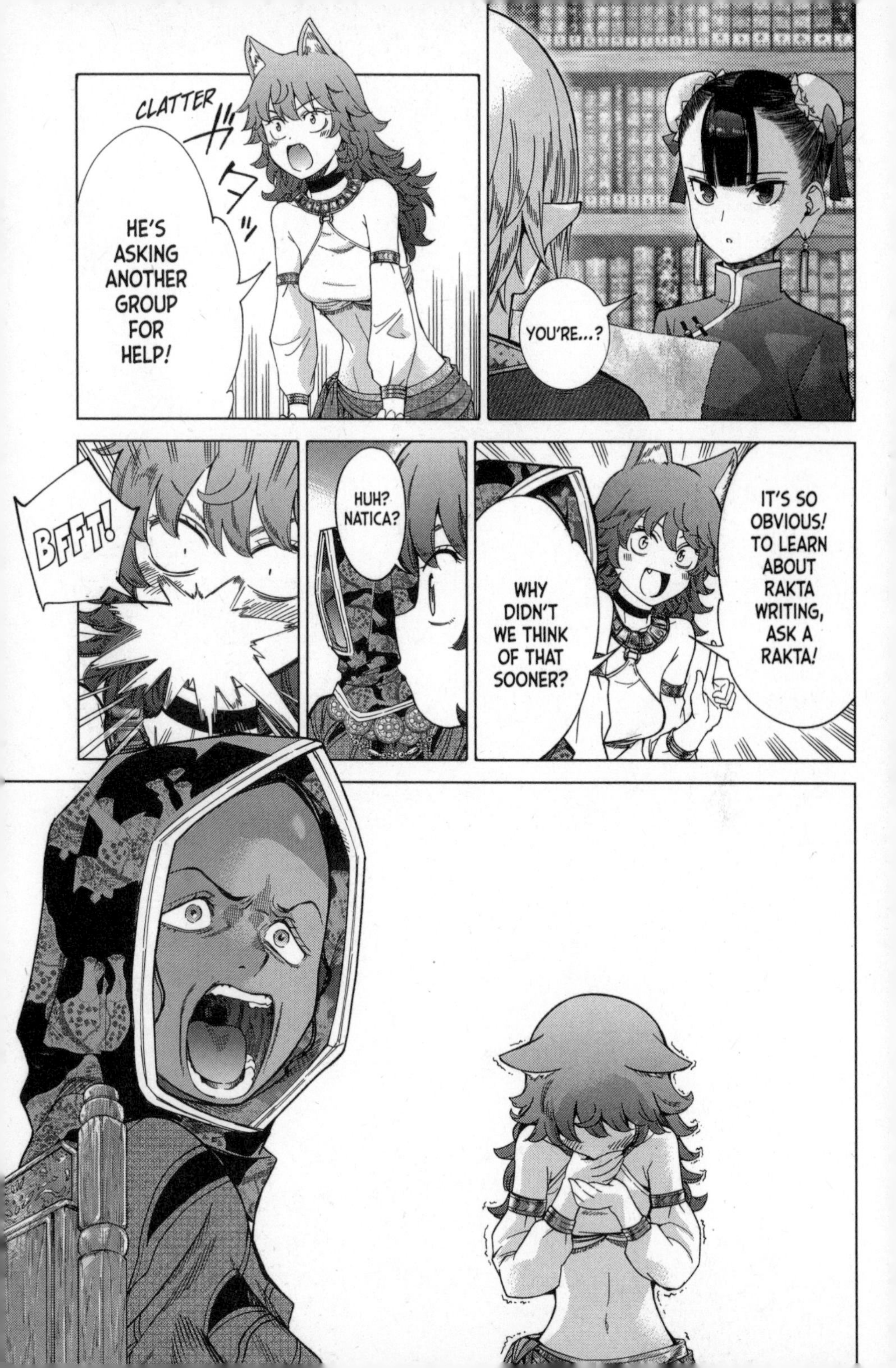
YOU'RE...?
CLATTER
HE'S ASKING ANOTHER GROUP FOR HELP!
IT'S SO OBVIOUS! TO LEARN ABOUT RAKTA WRITING, ASK A RAKTA!
WHY DIDN'T WE THINK OF THAT SOONER?
HUH? NATICA?
BFFT!

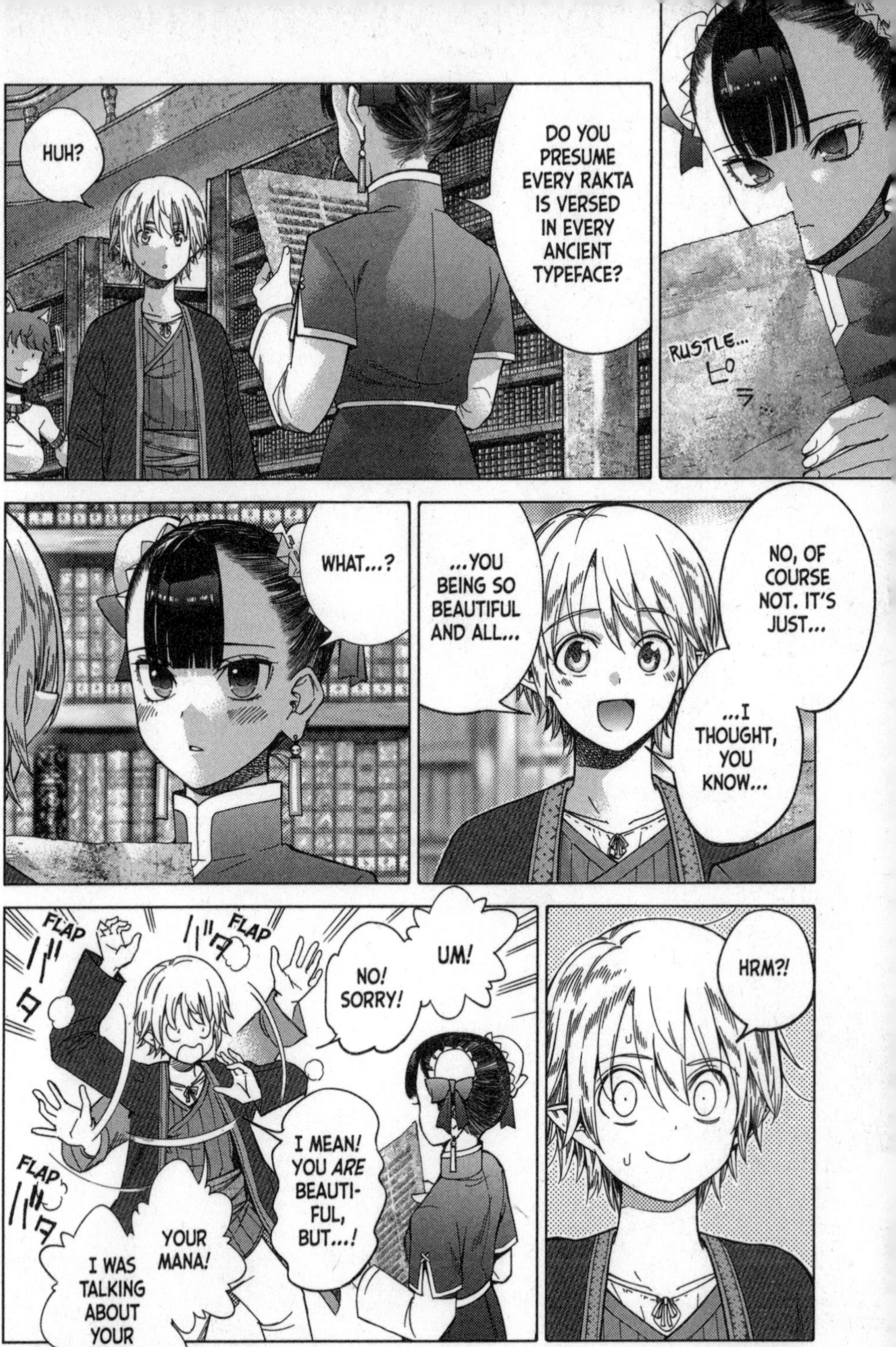
RUSTLE...
ピラ...
DO YOU PRESUME EVERY RAKTA IS VERSED IN EVERY ANCIENT TYPEFACE?
HUH?
NO, OF COURSE NOT. IT'S JUST...
...I THOUGHT, YOU KNOW...
...YOU BEING SO BEAUTIFUL AND ALL...
WHAT...?
HRM?!
UM!
NO! SORRY!
FLAP バタ
FLAP バタ
I MEAN! YOU *ARE* BEAUTIFUL, BUT...!
YOUR MANA!
FLAP バタ
I WAS TALKING ABOUT YOUR MANA!

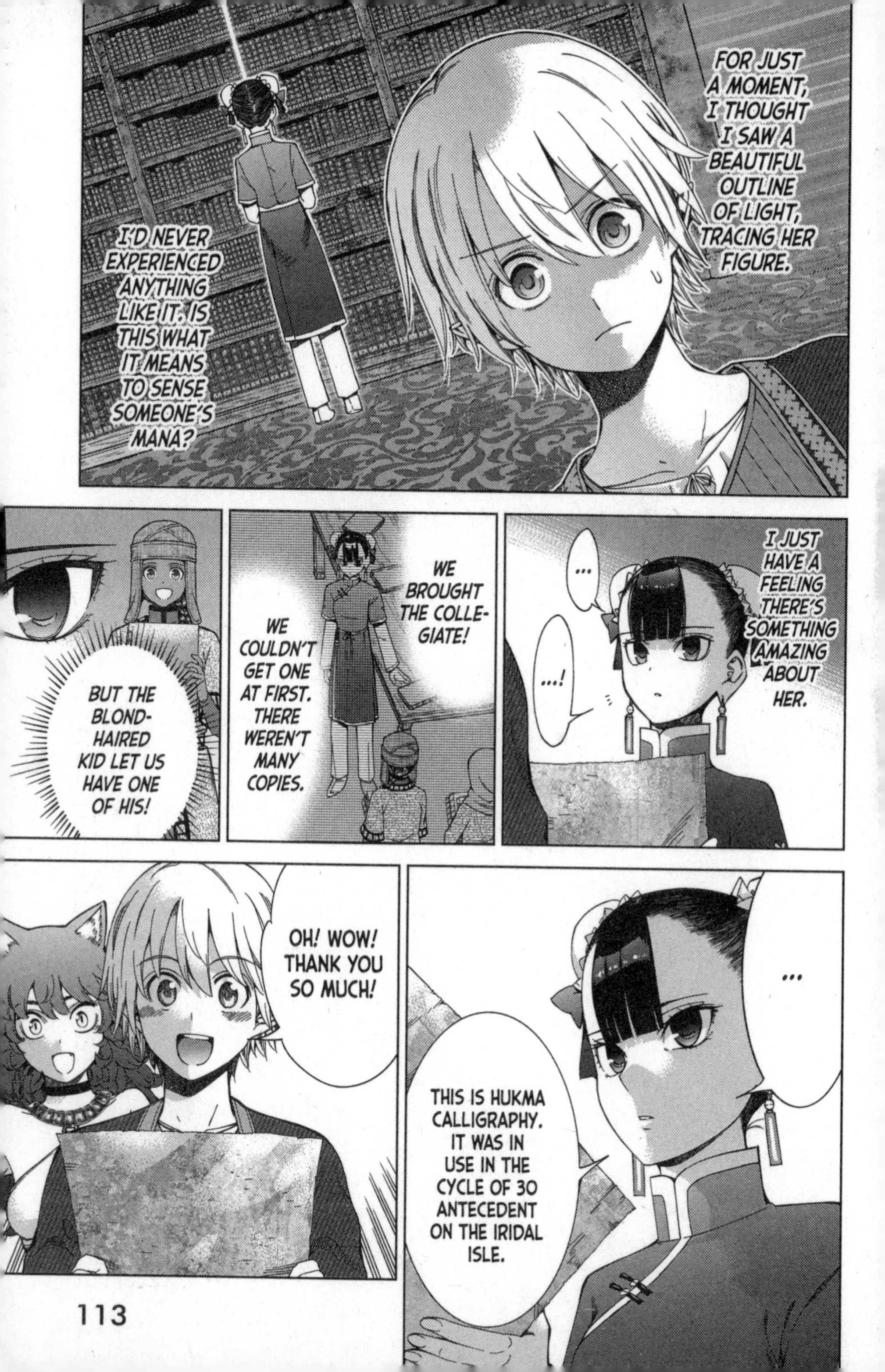
FOR JUST A MOMENT, I THOUGHT I SAW A BEAUTIFUL OUTLINE OF LIGHT, TRACING HER FIGURE.
I'D NEVER EXPERIENCED ANYTHING LIKE IT. IS THIS WHAT IT MEANS TO SENSE SOMEONE'S MANA?
...
...!
I JUST HAVE A FEELING THERE'S SOMETHING AMAZING ABOUT HER.
WE BROUGHT THE COLLE-GIATE!
WE COULDN'T GET ONE AT FIRST. THERE WEREN'T MANY COPIES.
BUT THE BLOND-HAIRED KID LET US HAVE ONE OF HIS!
...
THIS IS HUKMA CALLIGRAPHY. IT WAS IN USE IN THE CYCLE OF 30 ANTECEDENT ON THE IRIDAL ISLE.
OH! WOW! THANK YOU SO MUCH!

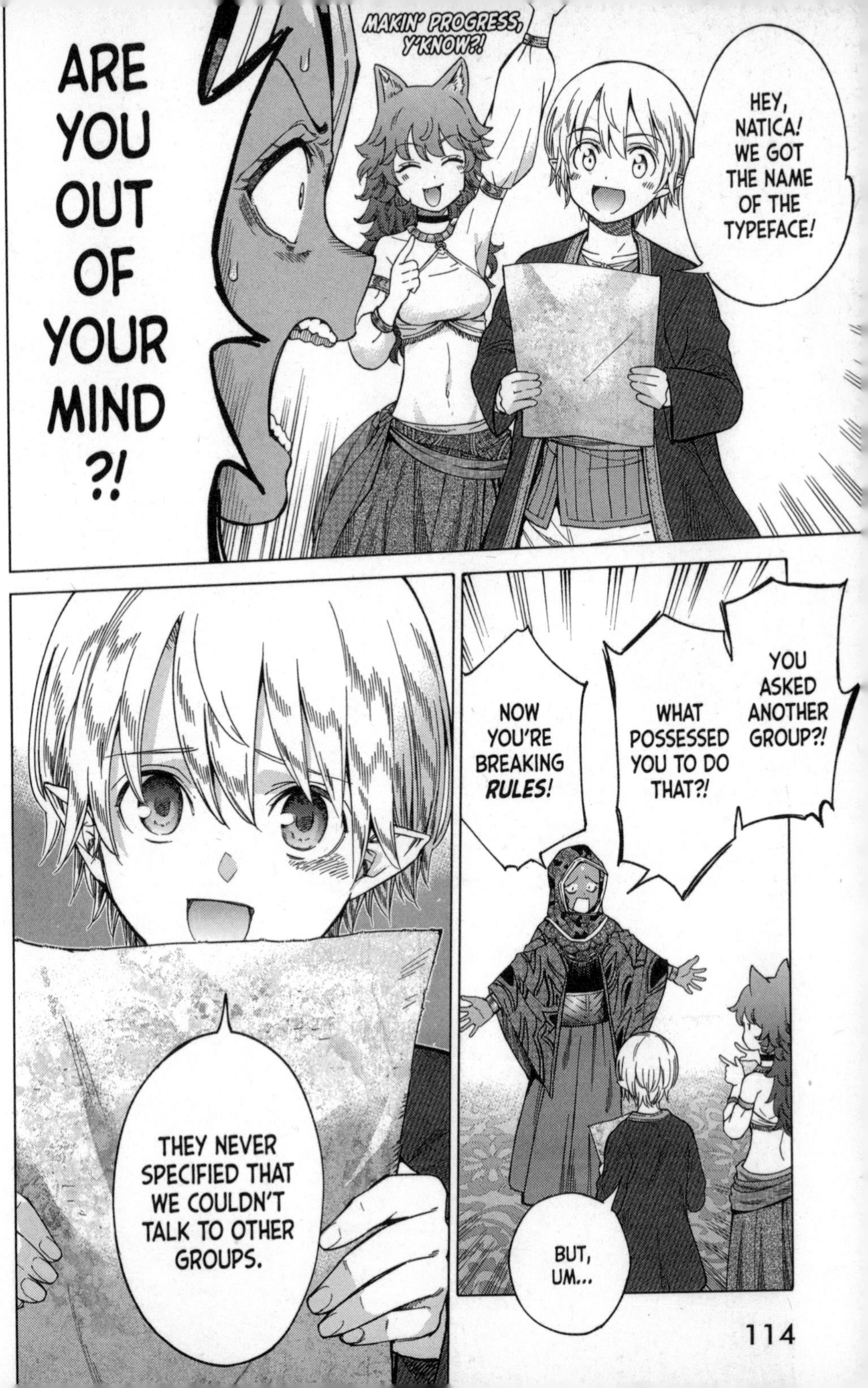
HEY, NATICA! WE GOT THE NAME OF THE TYPEFACE!
MAKIN' PROGRESS, Y'KNOW?!
ARE YOU OUT OF YOUR MIND ?!
YOU ASKED ANOTHER GROUP?!
WHAT POSSESSED YOU TO DO THAT?!
NOW YOU'RE BREAKING *RULES!*
BUT, UM...
THEY NEVER SPECIFIED THAT WE COULDN'T TALK TO OTHER GROUPS.

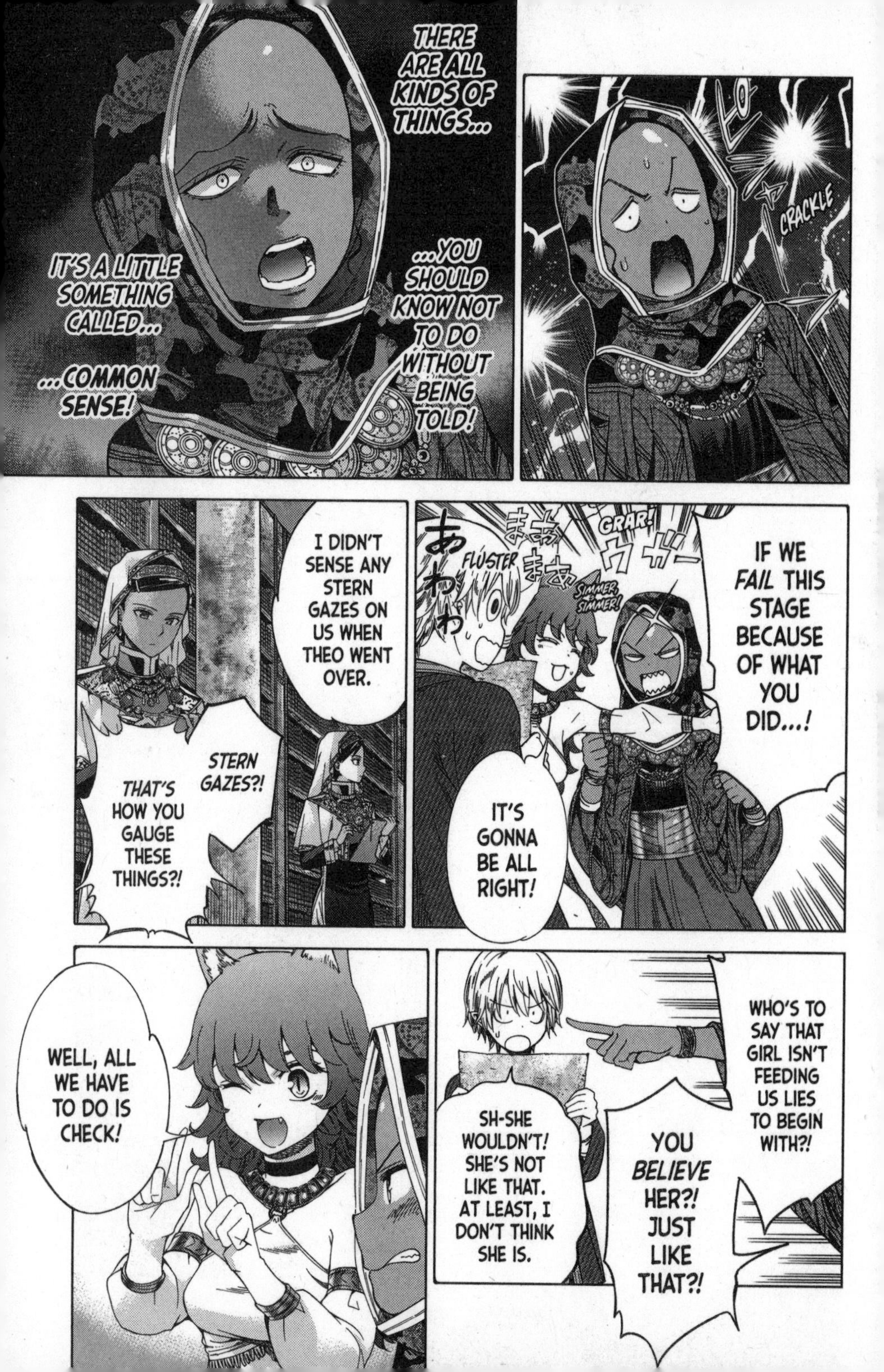
CRACKLE
THERE ARE ALL KINDS OF THINGS...
...YOU SHOULD KNOW NOT TO DO WITHOUT BEING TOLD!
IT'S A LITTLE SOMETHING CALLED...
...COMMON SENSE!
IF WE *FAIL* THIS STAGE BECAUSE OF WHAT YOU DID...!
GRAR!
ウガー
SIMMER, SIMMER!
まあまあ
FLUSTER
あわわ
IT'S GONNA BE ALL RIGHT!
I DIDN'T SENSE ANY STERN GAZES ON US WHEN THEO WENT OVER.
STERN GAZES?!
THAT'S HOW YOU GAUGE THESE THINGS?!
WHO'S TO SAY THAT GIRL ISN'T FEEDING US LIES TO BEGIN WITH?!
SH-SHE WOULDN'T! SHE'S NOT LIKE THAT. AT LEAST, I DON'T THINK SHE IS.
YOU *BELIEVE* HER?! JUST LIKE THAT?!
WELL, ALL WE HAVE TO DO IS CHECK!

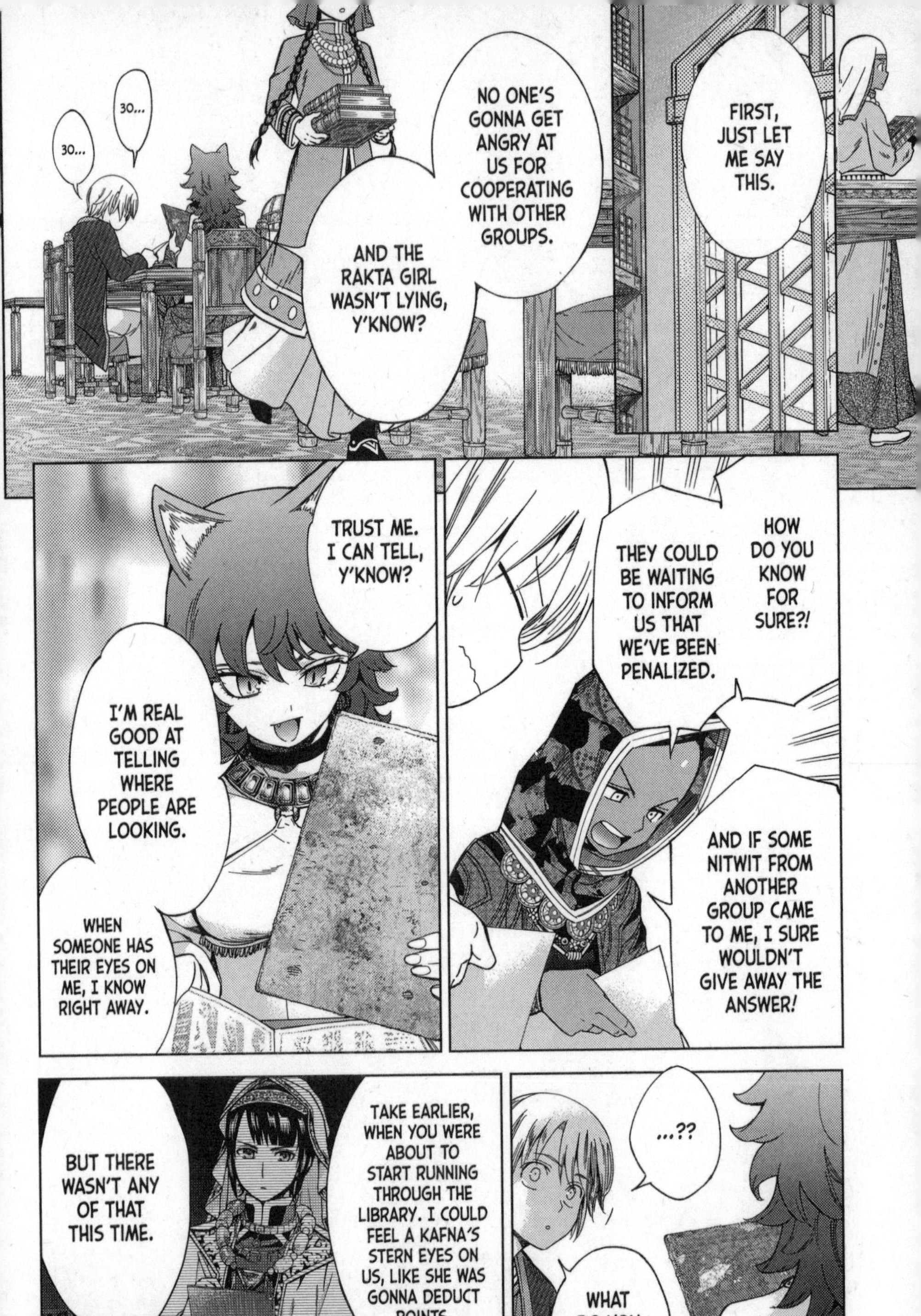
FIRST, JUST LET ME SAY THIS.
NO ONE'S GONNA GET ANGRY AT US FOR COOPERATING WITH OTHER GROUPS.
AND THE RAKTA GIRL WASN'T LYING, Y'KNOW?
30...
30...
HOW DO YOU KNOW FOR SURE?!
THEY COULD BE WAITING TO INFORM US THAT WE'VE BEEN PENALIZED.
AND IF SOME NITWIT FROM ANOTHER GROUP CAME TO ME, I SURE WOULDN'T GIVE AWAY THE ANSWER!
TRUST ME. I CAN TELL, Y'KNOW?
I'M REAL GOOD AT TELLING WHERE PEOPLE ARE LOOKING.
WHEN SOMEONE HAS THEIR EYES ON ME, I KNOW RIGHT AWAY.
...??
WHAT DO YOU MEAN?
TAKE EARLIER, WHEN YOU WERE ABOUT TO START RUNNING THROUGH THE LIBRARY. I COULD FEEL A KAFNA'S STERN EYES ON US, LIKE SHE WAS GONNA DEDUCT POINTS.
BUT THERE WASN'T ANY OF THAT THIS TIME.

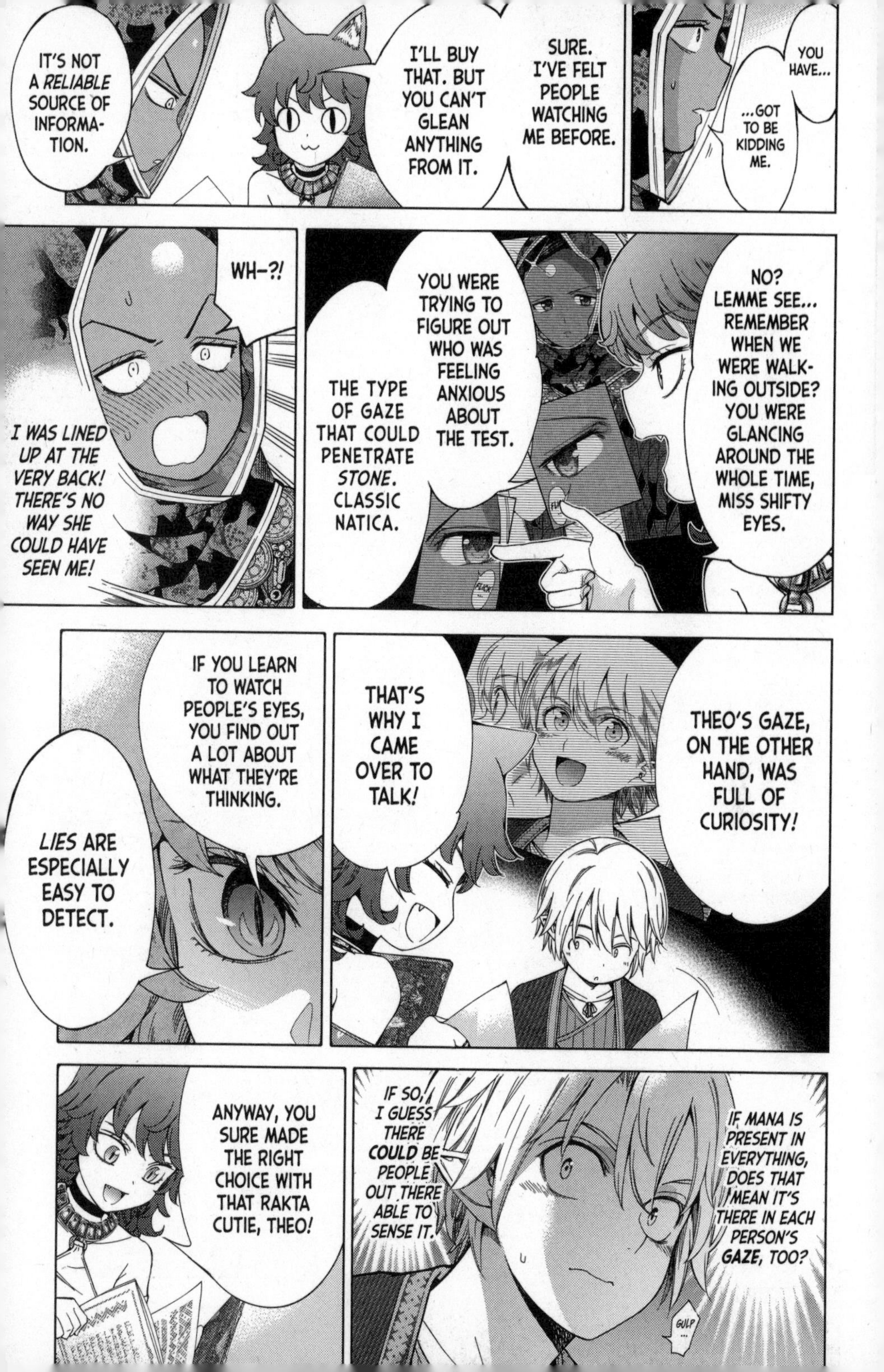
YOU HAVE...
...GOT TO BE KIDDING ME.
SURE. I'VE FELT PEOPLE WATCHING ME BEFORE.
I'LL BUY THAT. BUT YOU CAN'T GLEAN ANYTHING FROM IT.
IT'S NOT A *RELIABLE* SOURCE OF INFORMATION.
NO? LEMME SEE... REMEMBER WHEN WE WERE WALKING OUTSIDE? YOU WERE GLANCING AROUND THE WHOLE TIME, MISS SHIFTY EYES.
YOU WERE TRYING TO FIGURE OUT WHO WAS FEELING ANXIOUS ABOUT THE TEST.
FLICK
THE TYPE OF GAZE THAT COULD PENETRATE *STONE*. CLASSIC NATICA.
WH-?!
I WAS LINED UP AT THE VERY BACK! THERE'S NO WAY SHE COULD HAVE SEEN ME!
THEO'S GAZE, ON THE OTHER HAND, WAS FULL OF CURIOSITY!
THAT'S WHY I CAME OVER TO TALK!
IF YOU LEARN TO WATCH PEOPLE'S EYES, YOU FIND OUT A LOT ABOUT WHAT THEY'RE THINKING.
LIES ARE ESPECIALLY EASY TO DETECT.
IF MANA IS PRESENT IN EVERYTHING, DOES THAT MEAN IT'S THERE IN EACH PERSON'S **GAZE**, *TOO?*
IF SO, I GUESS THERE **COULD** *BE PEOPLE OUT THERE ABLE TO SENSE IT.*
GULP...
ANYWAY, YOU SURE MADE THE RIGHT CHOICE WITH THAT RAKTA CUTIE, THEO!

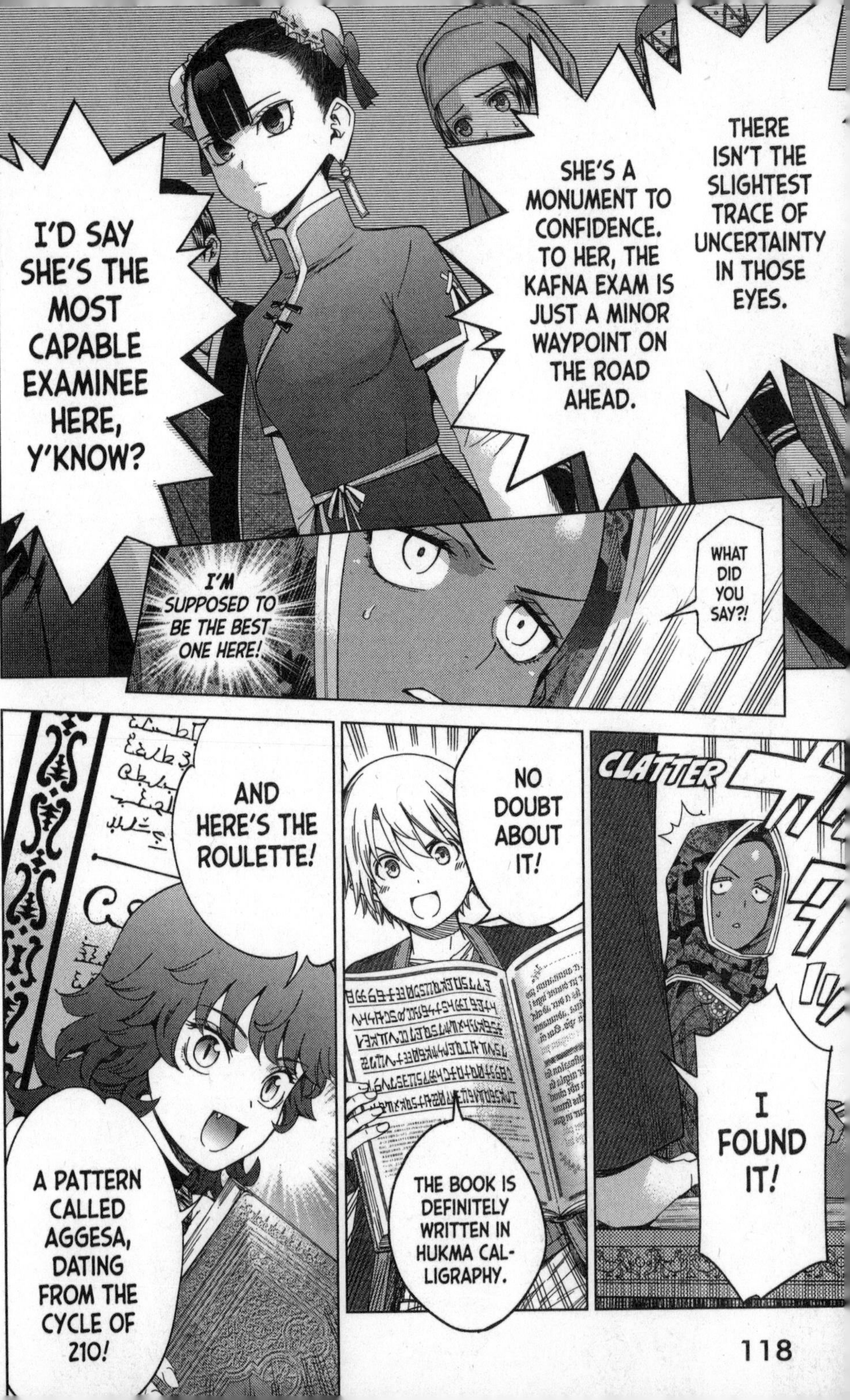
THERE ISN'T THE SLIGHTEST TRACE OF UNCERTAINTY IN THOSE EYES.
SHE'S A MONUMENT TO CONFIDENCE. TO HER, THE KAFNA EXAM IS JUST A MINOR WAYPOINT ON THE ROAD AHEAD.
I'D SAY SHE'S THE MOST CAPABLE EXAMINEE HERE, Y'KNOW?
WHAT DID YOU SAY?!
I'M SUPPOSED TO BE THE BEST ONE HERE!
CLATTER
I FOUND IT!
NO DOUBT ABOUT IT!
THE BOOK IS DEFINITELY WRITTEN IN HUKMA CAL-LIGRAPHY.
AND HERE'S THE ROULETTE!
A PATTERN CALLED AGGESA, DATING FROM THE CYCLE OF 210!

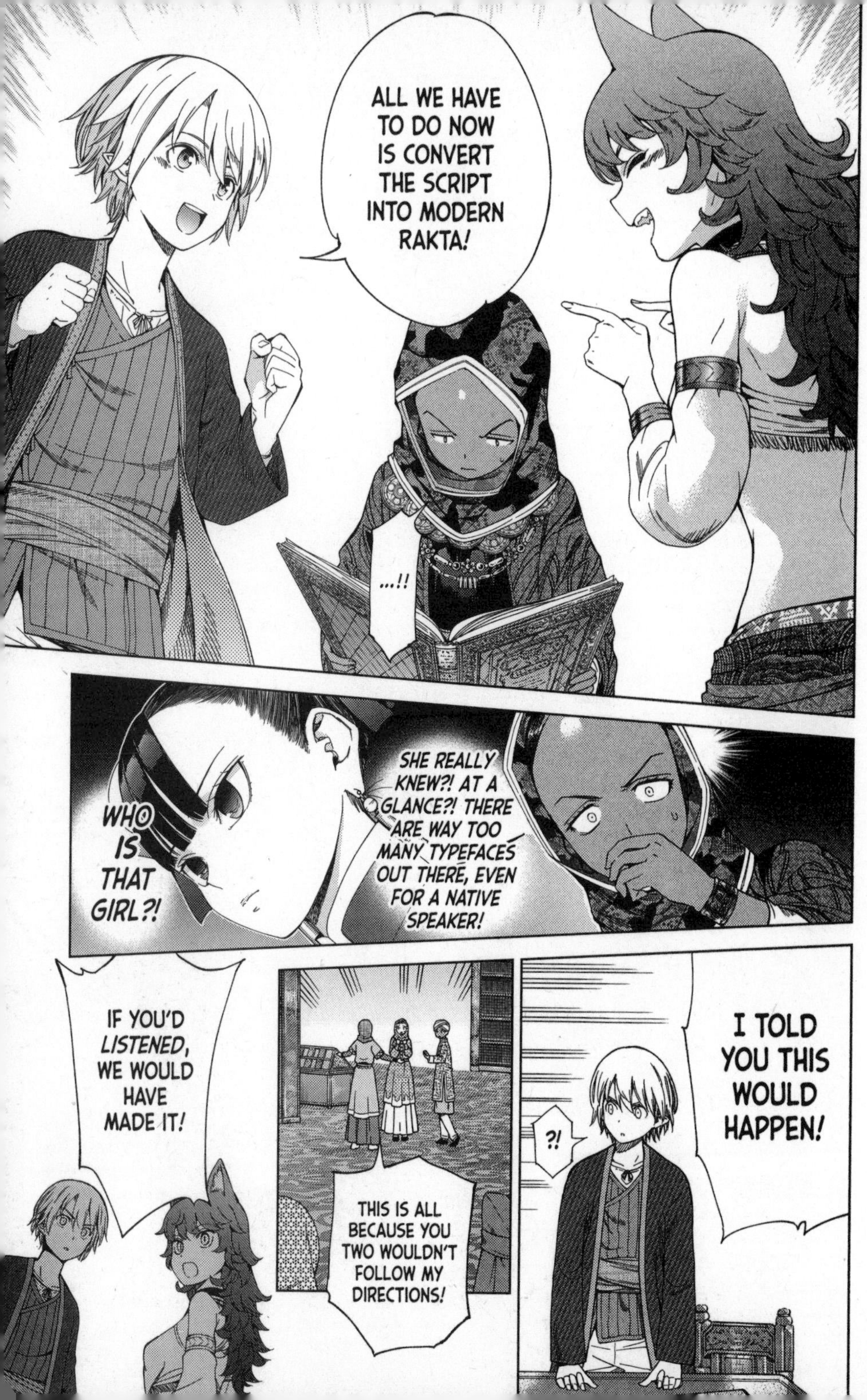
ALL WE HAVE TO DO NOW IS CONVERT THE SCRIPT INTO MODERN RAKTA!
...!!
SHE REALLY KNEW?! AT A GLANCE?! THERE ARE WAY TOO MANY TYPEFACES OUT THERE, EVEN FOR A NATIVE SPEAKER!
WHO IS THAT GIRL?!
I TOLD YOU THIS WOULD HAPPEN!
?!
THIS IS ALL BECAUSE YOU TWO WOULDN'T FOLLOW MY DIRECTIONS!
IF YOU'D *LISTENED*, WE WOULD HAVE MADE IT!

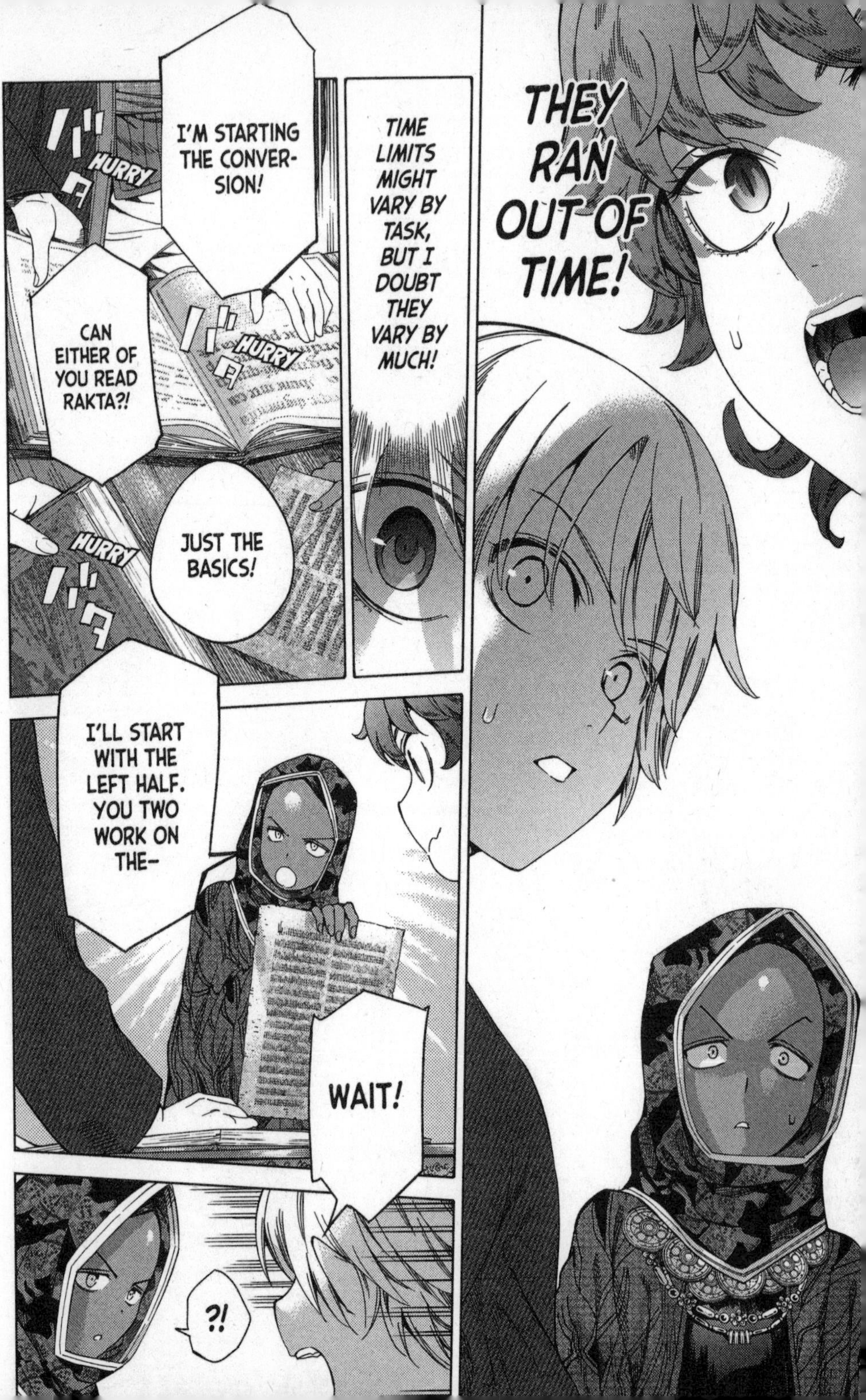
THEY RAN OUT OF TIME!
TIME LIMITS MIGHT VARY BY TASK, BUT I DOUBT THEY VARY BY MUCH!
I'M STARTING THE CONVERSION!
HURRY
HURRY
CAN EITHER OF YOU READ RAKTA?!
JUST THE BASICS!
HURRY
I'LL START WITH THE LEFT HALF. YOU TWO WORK ON THE–
WAIT!
?!

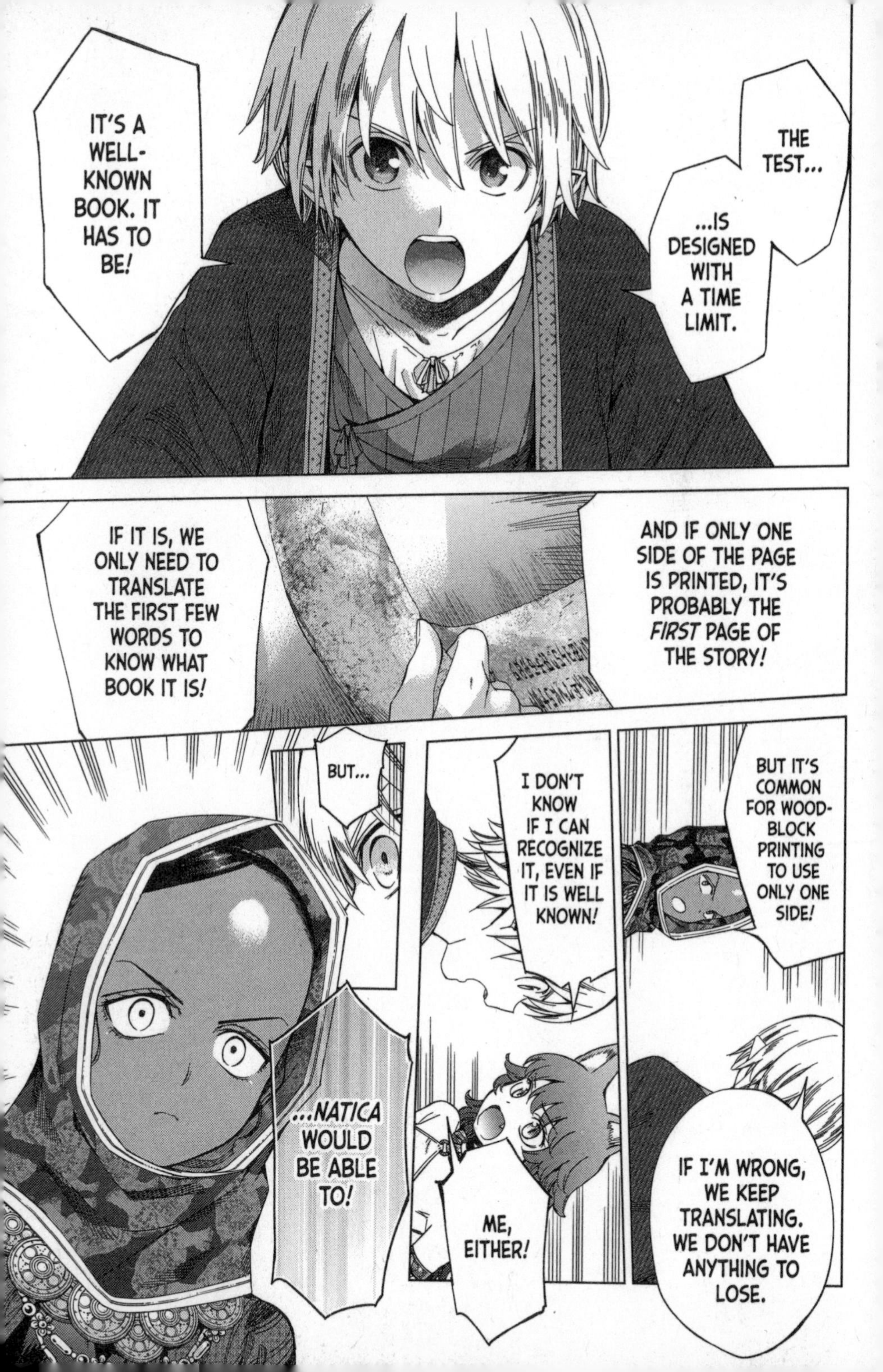
THE TEST...
...IS DESIGNED WITH A TIME LIMIT.
IT'S A WELL-KNOWN BOOK. IT HAS TO BE!
AND IF ONLY ONE SIDE OF THE PAGE IS PRINTED, IT'S PROBABLY THE *FIRST* PAGE OF THE STORY!
IF IT IS, WE ONLY NEED TO TRANSLATE THE FIRST FEW WORDS TO KNOW WHAT BOOK IT IS!
BUT IT'S COMMON FOR WOOD-BLOCK PRINTING TO USE ONLY ONE SIDE!
IF I'M WRONG, WE KEEP TRANSLATING. WE DON'T HAVE ANYTHING TO LOSE.
I DON'T KNOW IF I CAN RECOGNIZE IT, EVEN IF IT IS WELL KNOWN!
ME, EITHER!
BUT...
...NATICA WOULD BE ABLE TO!

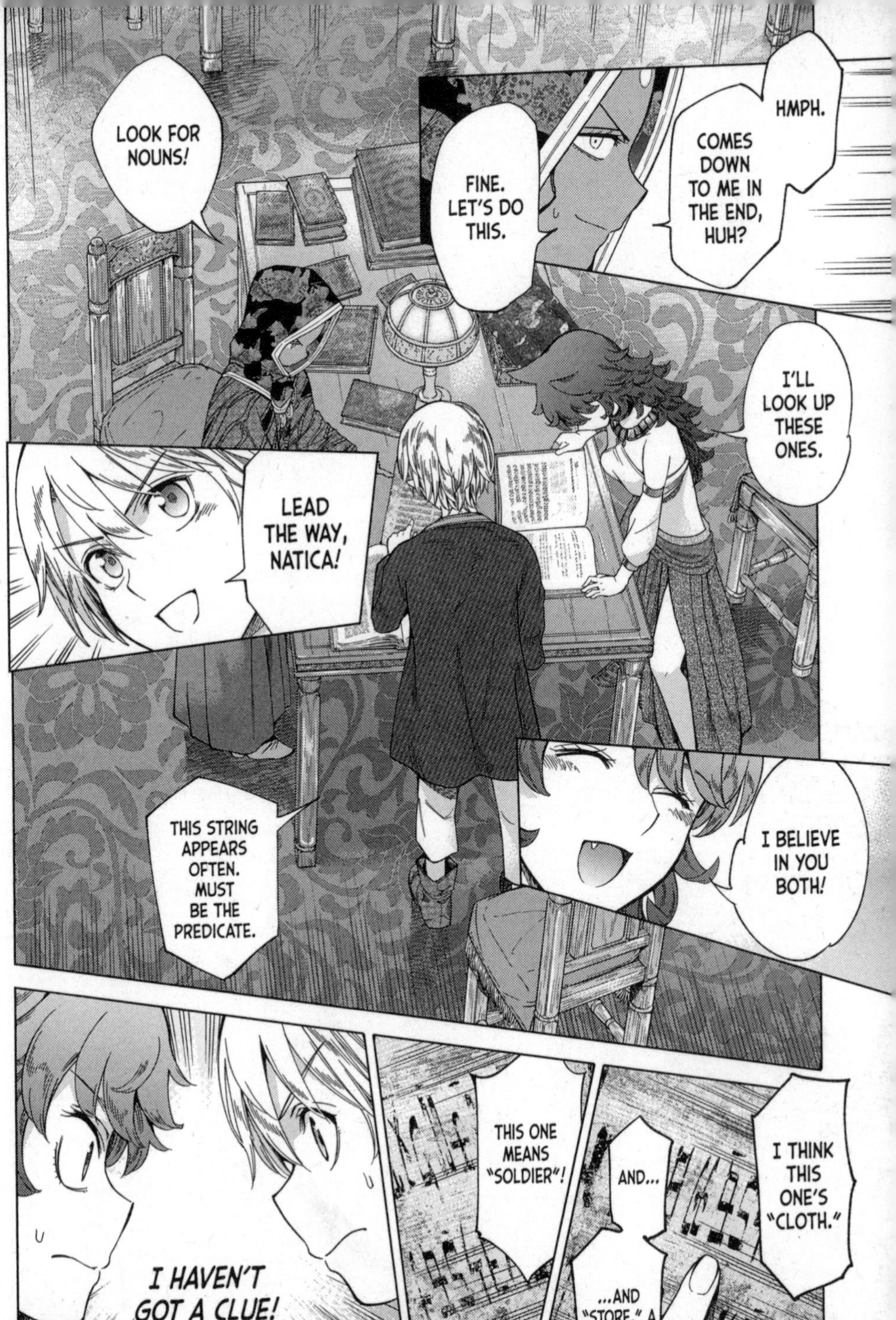

HMPH.
COMES DOWN TO ME IN THE END, HUH?
FINE. LET'S DO THIS.
LOOK FOR NOUNS!
I'LL LOOK UP THESE ONES.
LEAD THE WAY, NATICA!
I BELIEVE IN YOU BOTH!
THIS STRING APPEARS OFTEN. MUST BE THE PREDICATE.
I THINK THIS ONE'S "CLOTH."
AND...
...AND "STORE." A DRAPER'S?
THIS ONE MEANS "SOLDIER"!
I HAVEN'T GOT A CLUE!

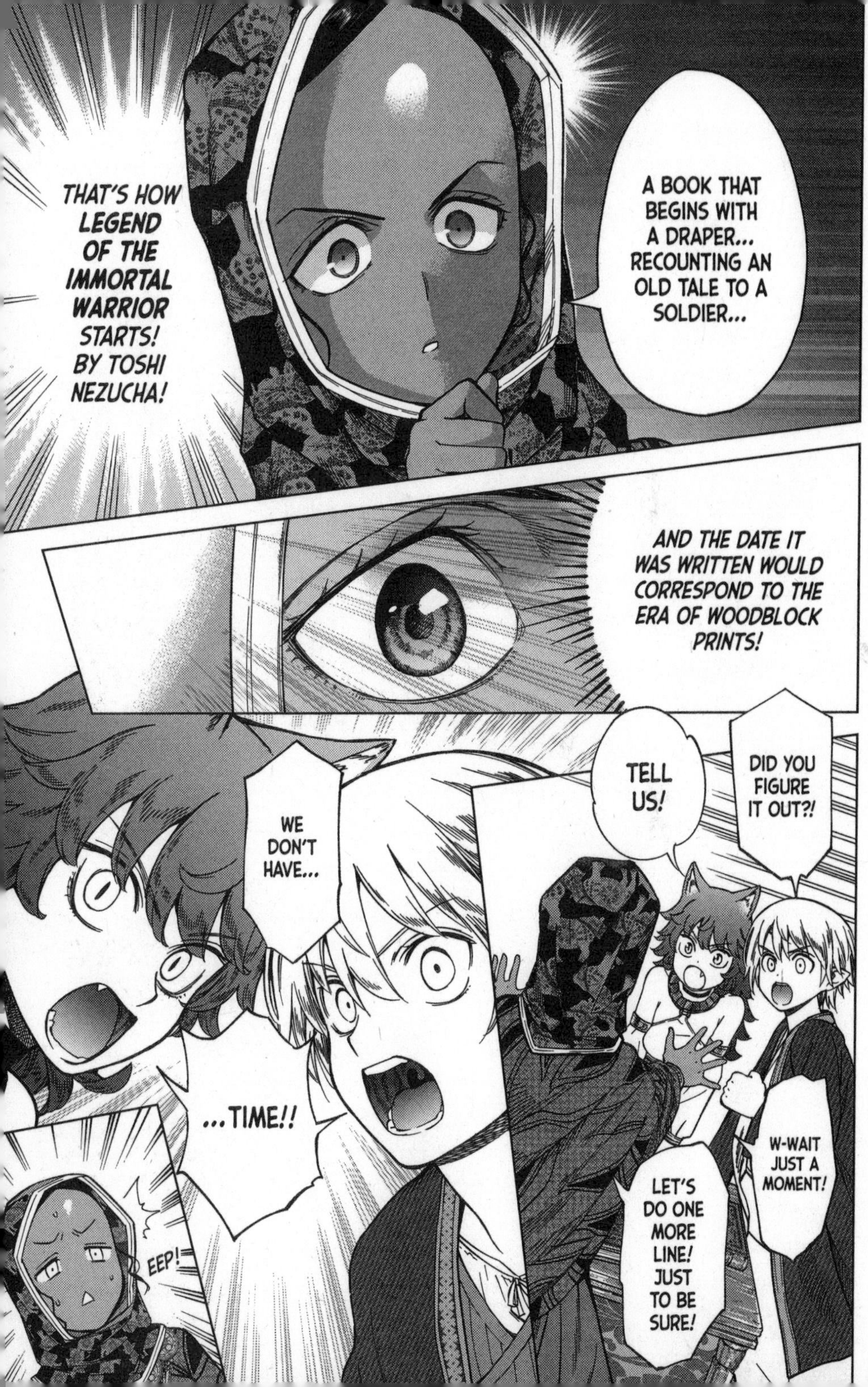
A BOOK THAT BEGINS WITH A DRAPER... RECOUNTING AN OLD TALE TO A SOLDIER...
THAT'S HOW LEGEND OF THE IMMORTAL WARRIOR STARTS! BY TOSHI NEZUCHA!
AND THE DATE IT WAS WRITTEN WOULD CORRESPOND TO THE ERA OF WOODBLOCK PRINTS!
DID YOU FIGURE IT OUT?!
TELL US!
W-WAIT JUST A MOMENT!
LET'S DO ONE MORE LINE! JUST TO BE SURE!
WE DON'T HAVE...
...TIME!!
EEP!

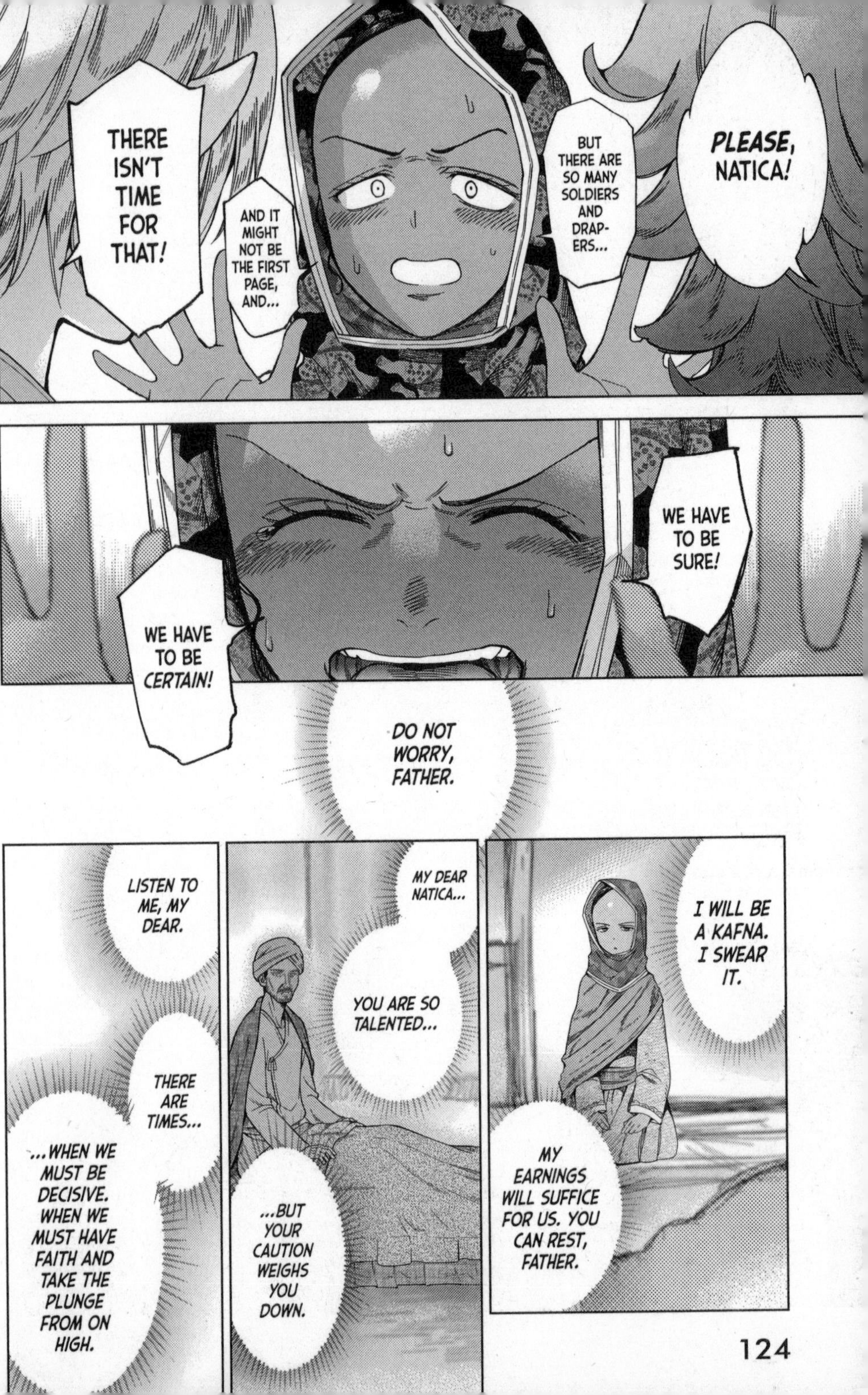
PLEASE, NATICA!
BUT THERE ARE SO MANY SOLDIERS AND DRAPERS...
AND IT MIGHT NOT BE THE FIRST PAGE, AND...
THERE ISN'T TIME FOR THAT!
WE HAVE TO BE SURE!
WE HAVE TO BE CERTAIN!
DO NOT WORRY, FATHER.
I WILL BE A KAFNA. I SWEAR IT.
MY EARNINGS WILL SUFFICE FOR US. YOU CAN REST, FATHER.
MY DEAR NATICA...
YOU ARE SO TALENTED...
...BUT YOUR CAUTION WEIGHS YOU DOWN.
LISTEN TO ME, MY DEAR.
THERE ARE TIMES...
...WHEN WE MUST BE DECISIVE. WHEN WE MUST HAVE FAITH AND TAKE THE PLUNGE FROM ON HIGH.

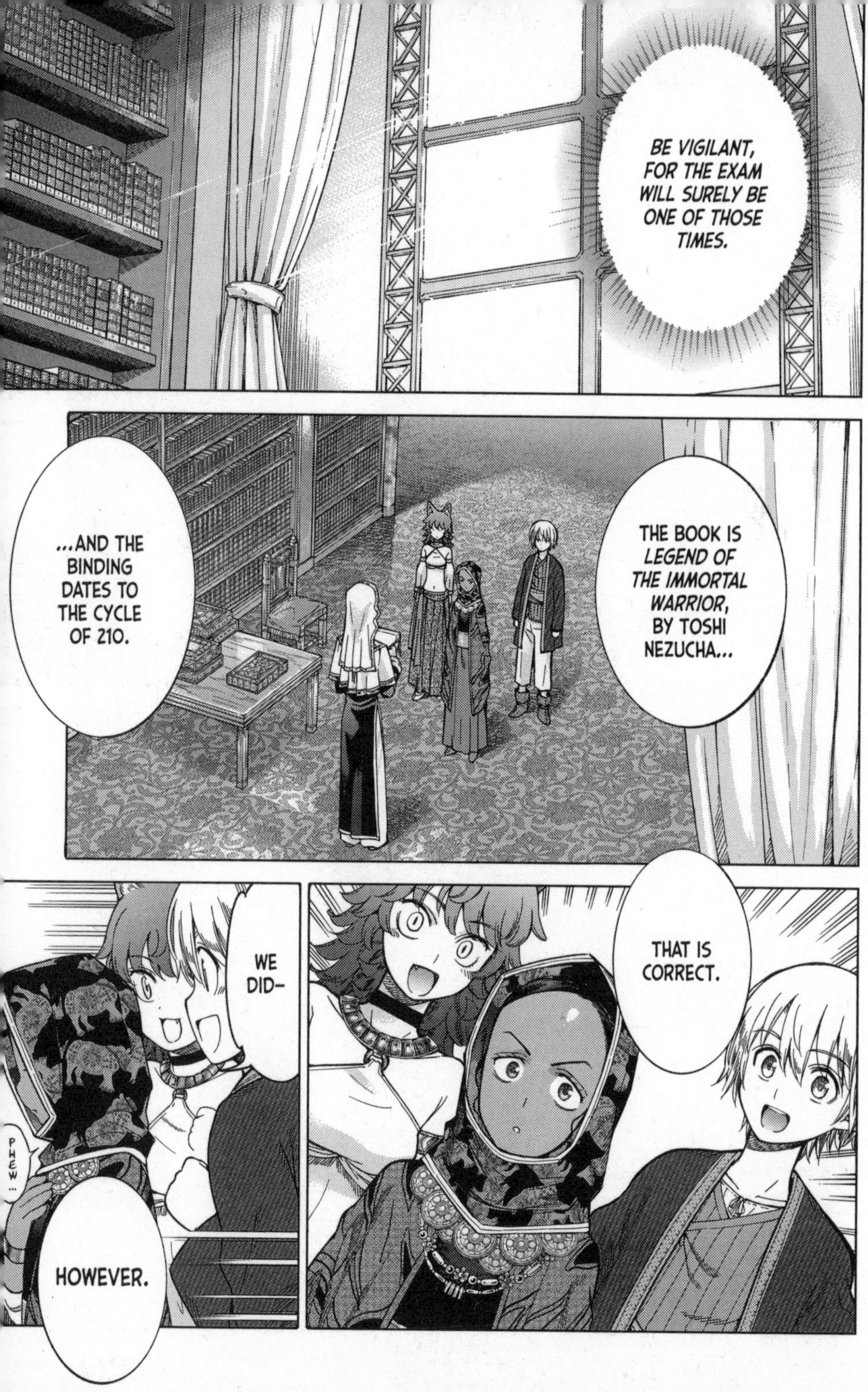
BE VIGILANT, FOR THE EXAM WILL SURELY BE ONE OF THOSE TIMES.
THE BOOK IS *LEGEND OF THE IMMORTAL WARRIOR*, BY TOSHI NEZUCHA...
...AND THE BINDING DATES TO THE CYCLE OF 210.
THAT IS CORRECT.
WE DID-
PHEW...
HOWEVER.

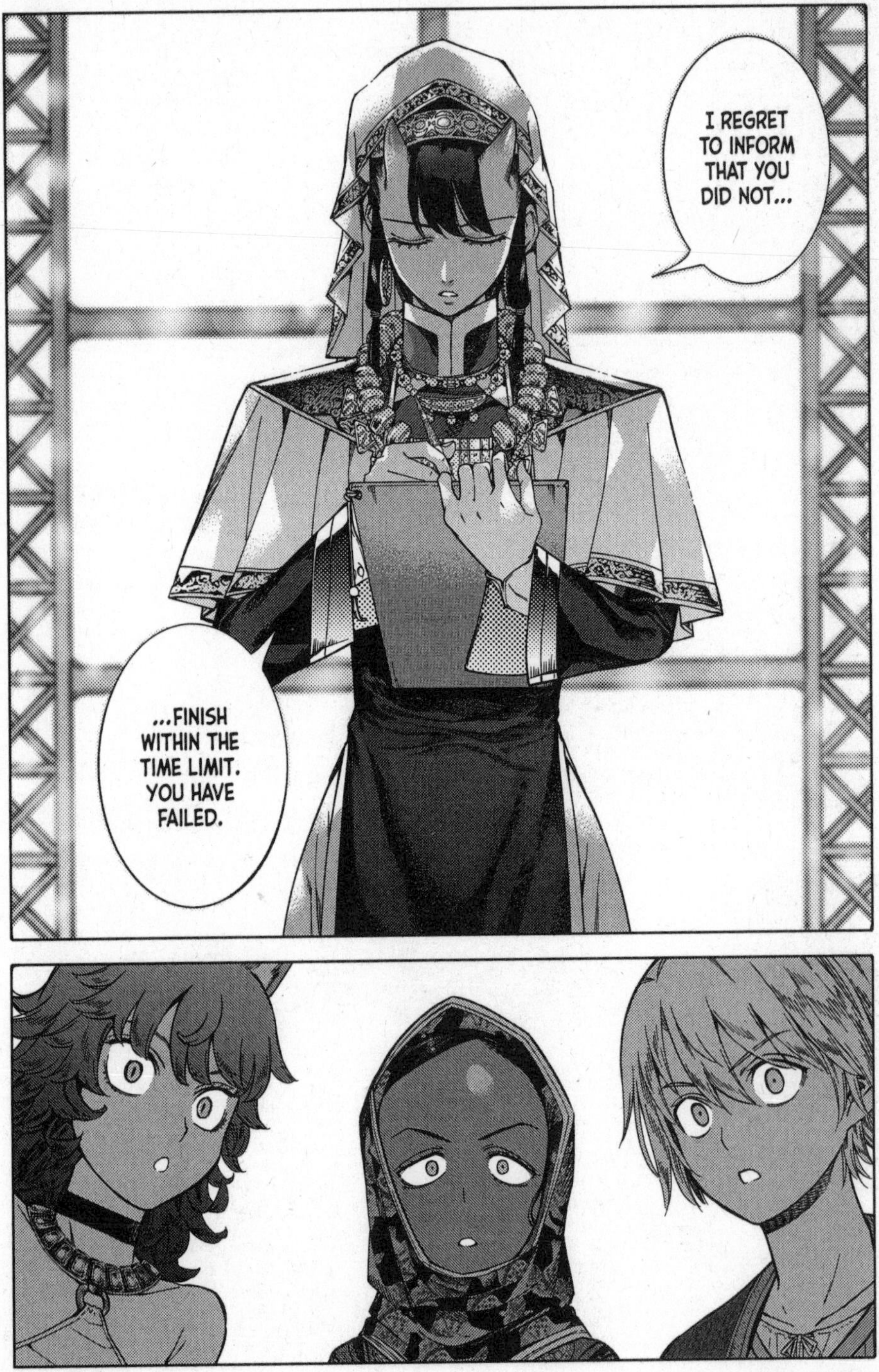
I REGRET TO INFORM THAT YOU DID NOT...
...FINISH WITHIN THE TIME LIMIT. YOU HAVE FAILED.

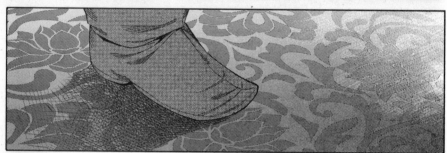

FAILED...?

ME?!

WE DIDN'T MAKE IT.

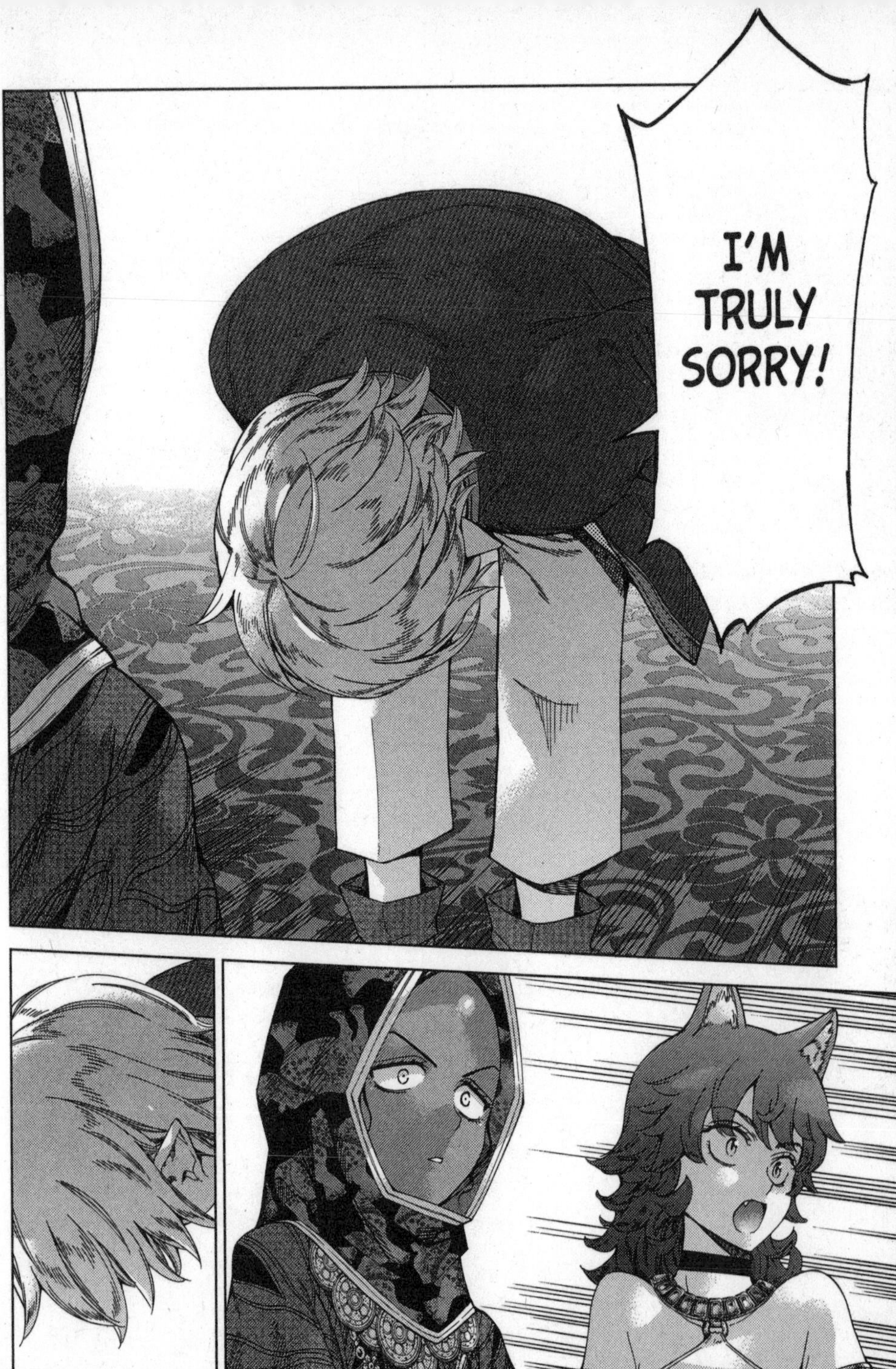
I'M TRULY SORRY!

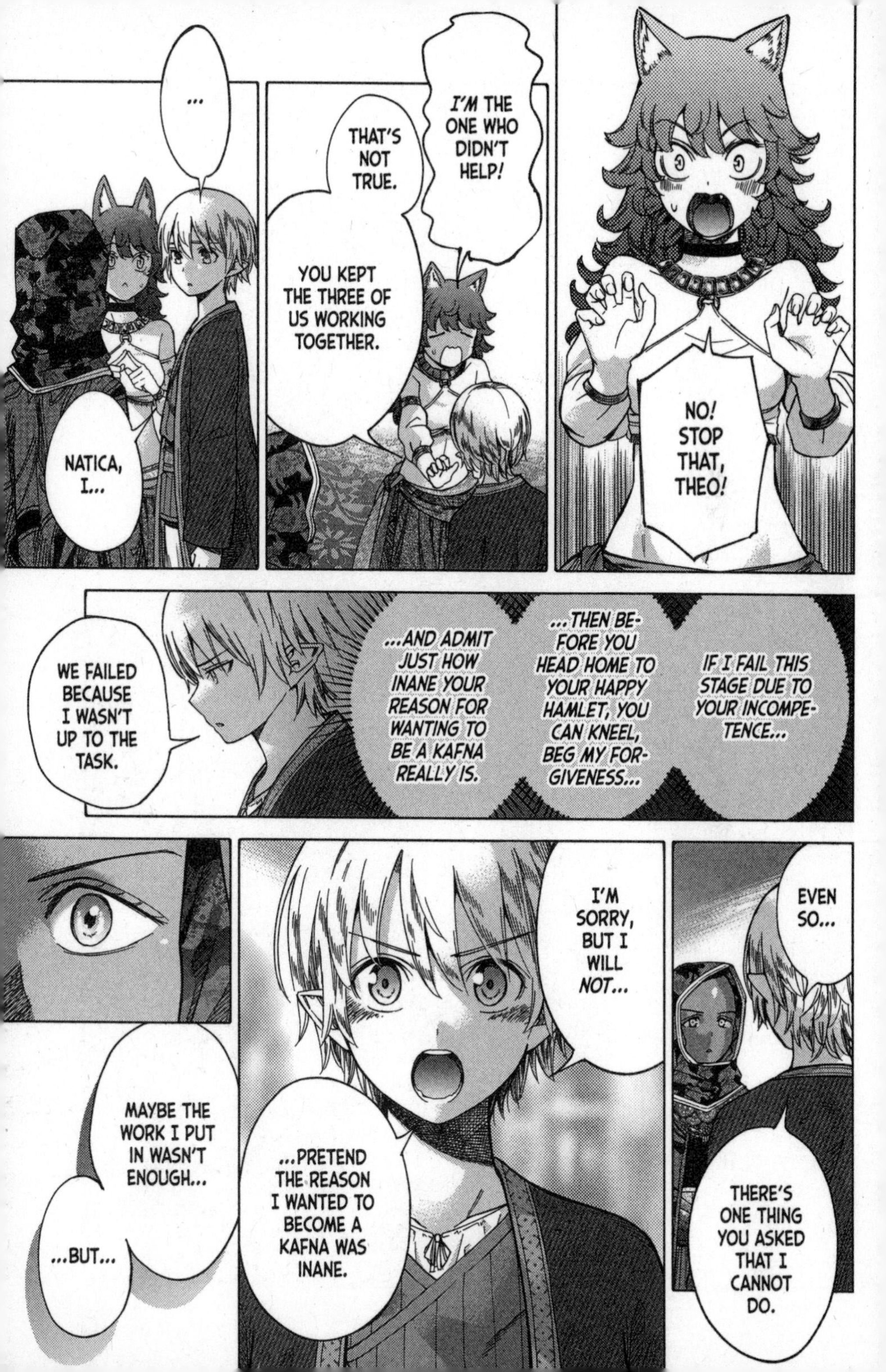
NO! STOP THAT, THEO!
I'M THE ONE WHO DIDN'T HELP!
THAT'S NOT TRUE.
YOU KEPT THE THREE OF US WORKING TOGETHER.
...
NATICA, I...
IF I FAIL THIS STAGE DUE TO YOUR INCOMPETENCE...
...THEN BEFORE YOU HEAD HOME TO YOUR HAPPY HAMLET, YOU CAN KNEEL, BEG MY FORGIVENESS...
...AND ADMIT JUST HOW INANE YOUR REASON FOR WANTING TO BE A KAFNA REALLY IS.
WE FAILED BECAUSE I WASN'T UP TO THE TASK.
EVEN SO...
THERE'S ONE THING YOU ASKED THAT I CANNOT DO.
I'M SORRY, BUT I WILL NOT...
...PRETEND THE REASON I WANTED TO BECOME A KAFNA WAS INANE.
MAYBE THE WORK I PUT IN WASN'T ENOUGH...
...BUT...

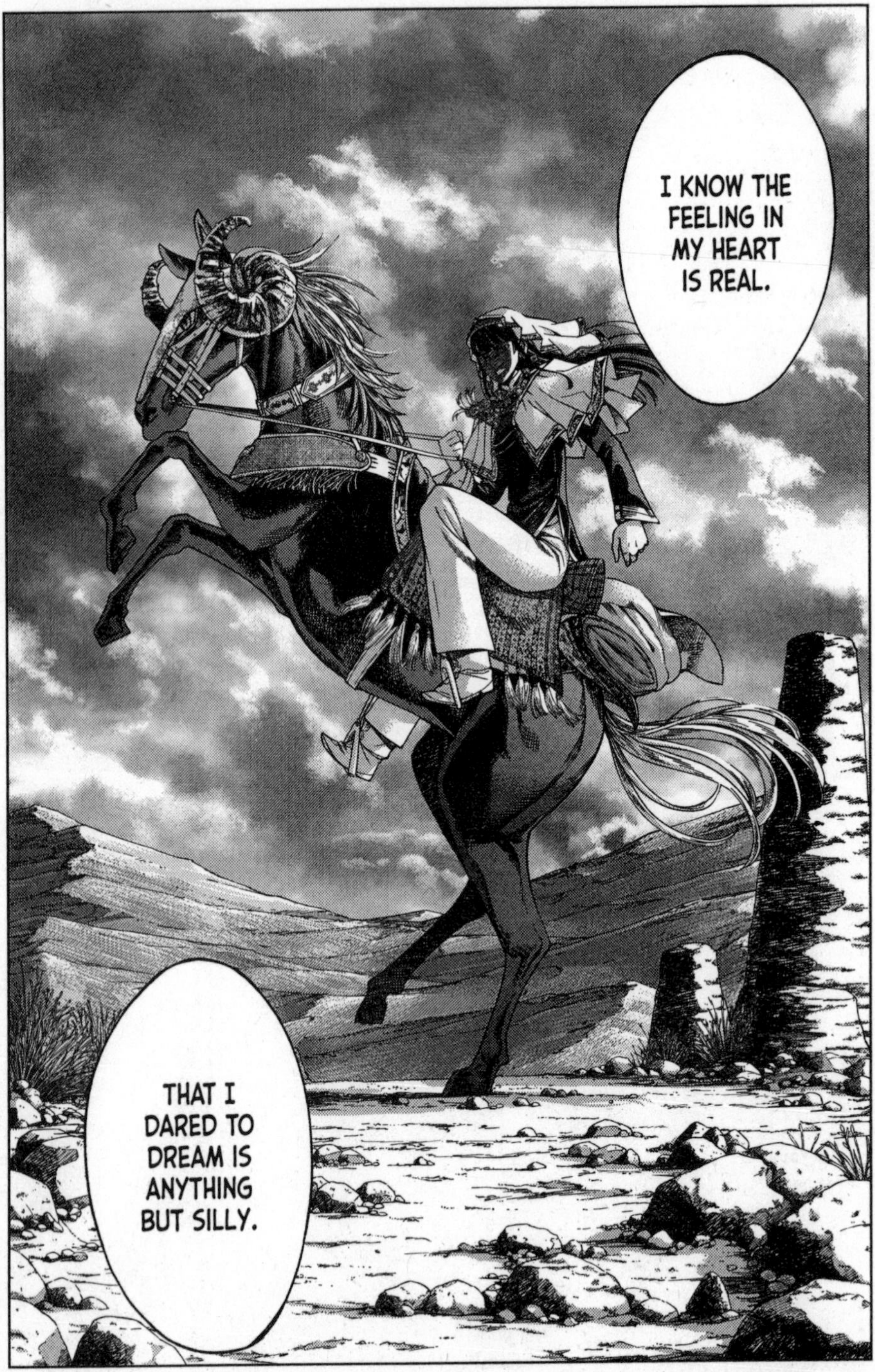
I KNOW THE FEELING IN MY HEART IS REAL.
THAT I DARED TO DREAM IS ANYTHING BUT SILLY.

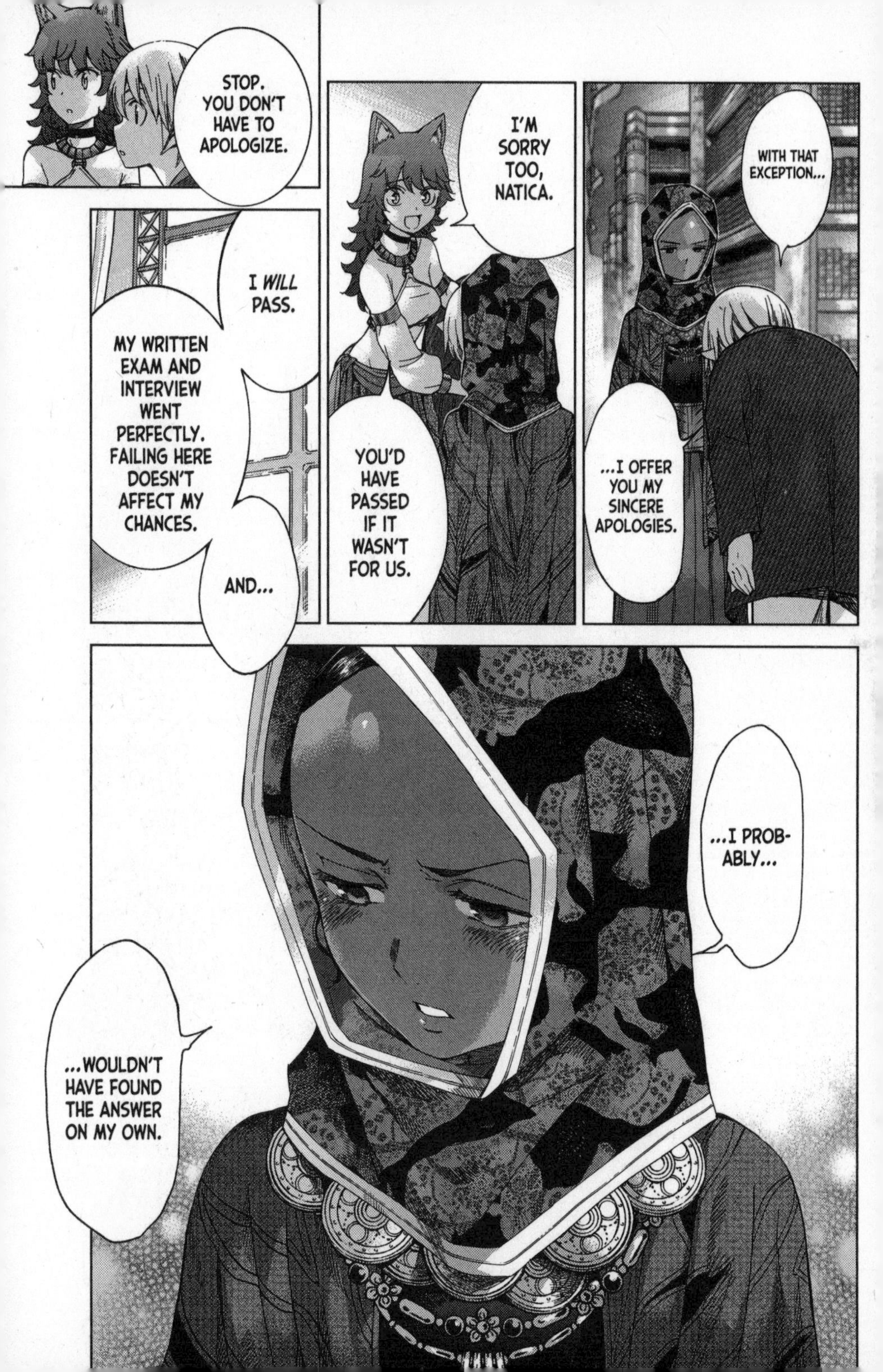
WITH THAT EXCEPTION...
...I OFFER YOU MY SINCERE APOLOGIES.
I'M SORRY TOO, NATICA.
YOU'D HAVE PASSED IF IT WASN'T FOR US.
STOP. YOU DON'T HAVE TO APOLOGIZE.
I *WILL* PASS.
MY WRITTEN EXAM AND INTERVIEW WENT PERFECTLY. FAILING HERE DOESN'T AFFECT MY CHANCES.
AND...
...I PROBABLY...
...WOULDN'T HAVE FOUND THE ANSWER ON MY OWN.

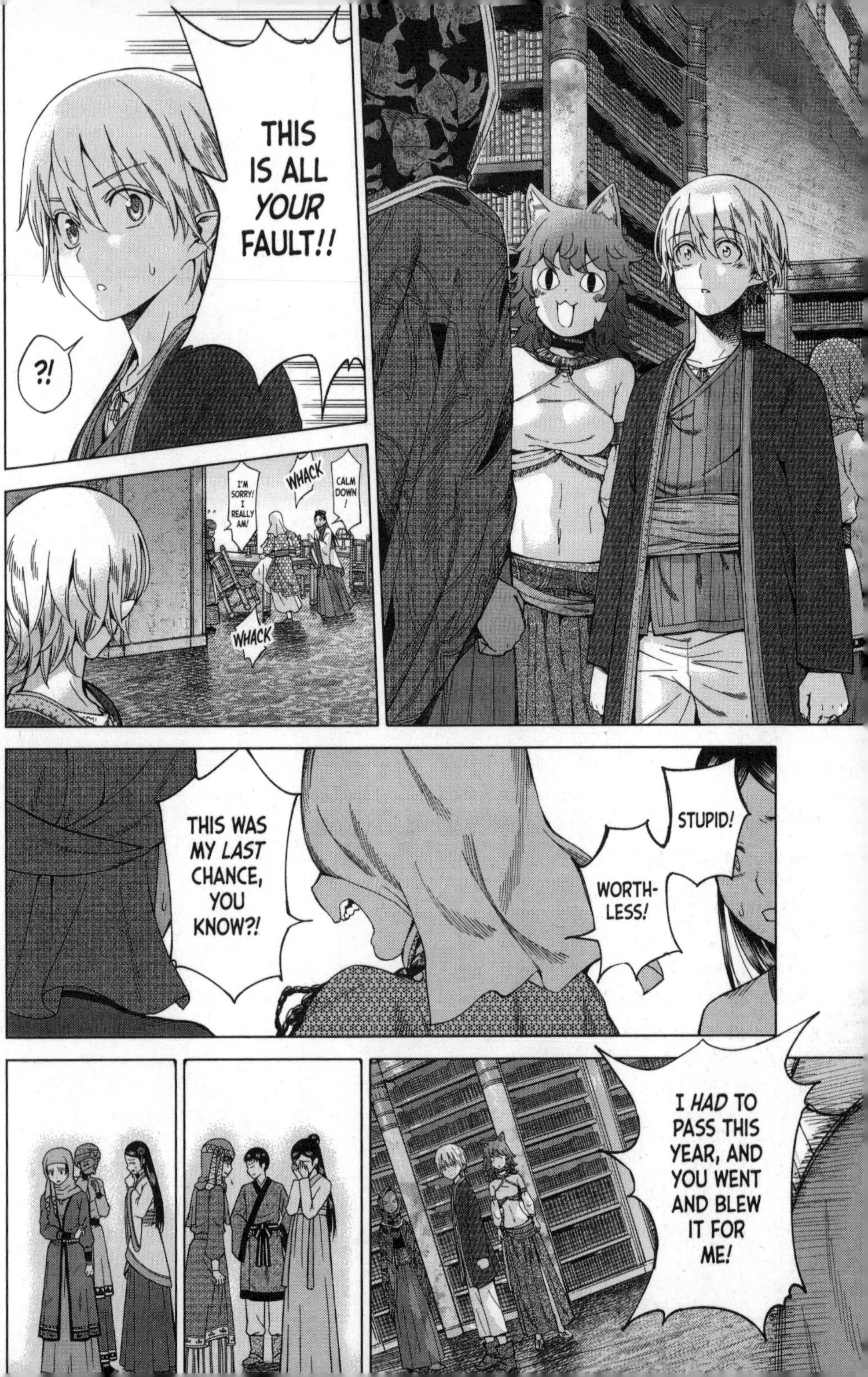
THIS IS ALL YOUR FAULT!!
?!
CALM DOWN!
WHACK
I'M SORRY! I REALLY AM!
WHACK
STUPID!
WORTH-LESS!
THIS WAS MY LAST CHANCE, YOU KNOW?!
I HAD TO PASS THIS YEAR, AND YOU WENT AND BLEW IT FOR ME!

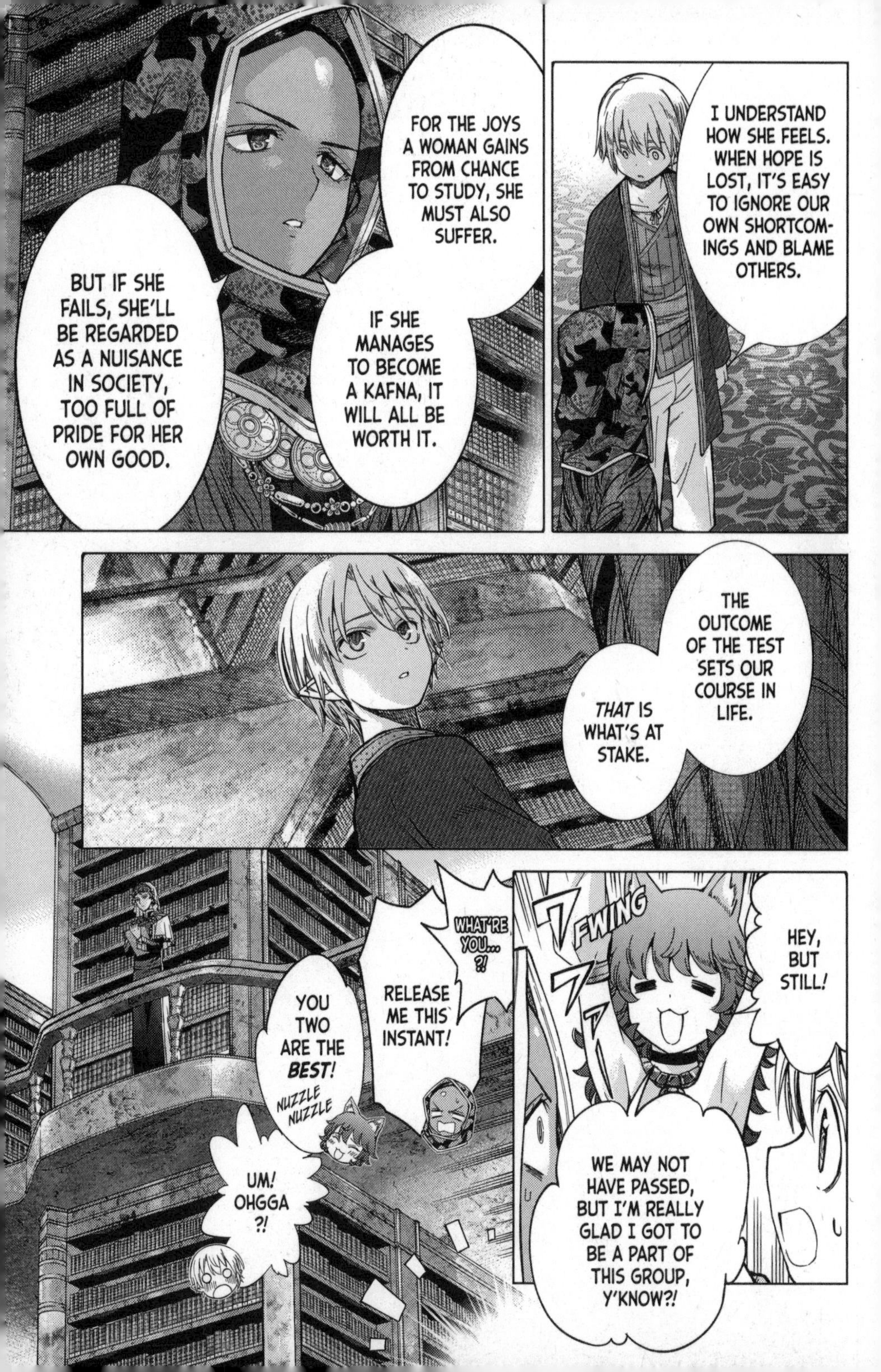
I UNDERSTAND HOW SHE FEELS. WHEN HOPE IS LOST, IT'S EASY TO IGNORE OUR OWN SHORTCOMINGS AND BLAME OTHERS.
FOR THE JOYS A WOMAN GAINS FROM CHANCE TO STUDY, SHE MUST ALSO SUFFER.
IF SHE MANAGES TO BECOME A KAFNA, IT WILL ALL BE WORTH IT.
BUT IF SHE FAILS, SHE'LL BE REGARDED AS A NUISANCE IN SOCIETY, TOO FULL OF PRIDE FOR HER OWN GOOD.
THE OUTCOME OF THE TEST SETS OUR COURSE IN LIFE.
THAT IS WHAT'S AT STAKE.
HEY, BUT STILL!
FWING
WE MAY NOT HAVE PASSED, BUT I'M REALLY GLAD I GOT TO BE A PART OF THIS GROUP, Y'KNOW?!
WHAT'RE YOU...?!
RELEASE ME THIS INSTANT!
YOU TWO ARE THE **BEST**!
NUZZLE NUZZLE
UM! OHGGA?!

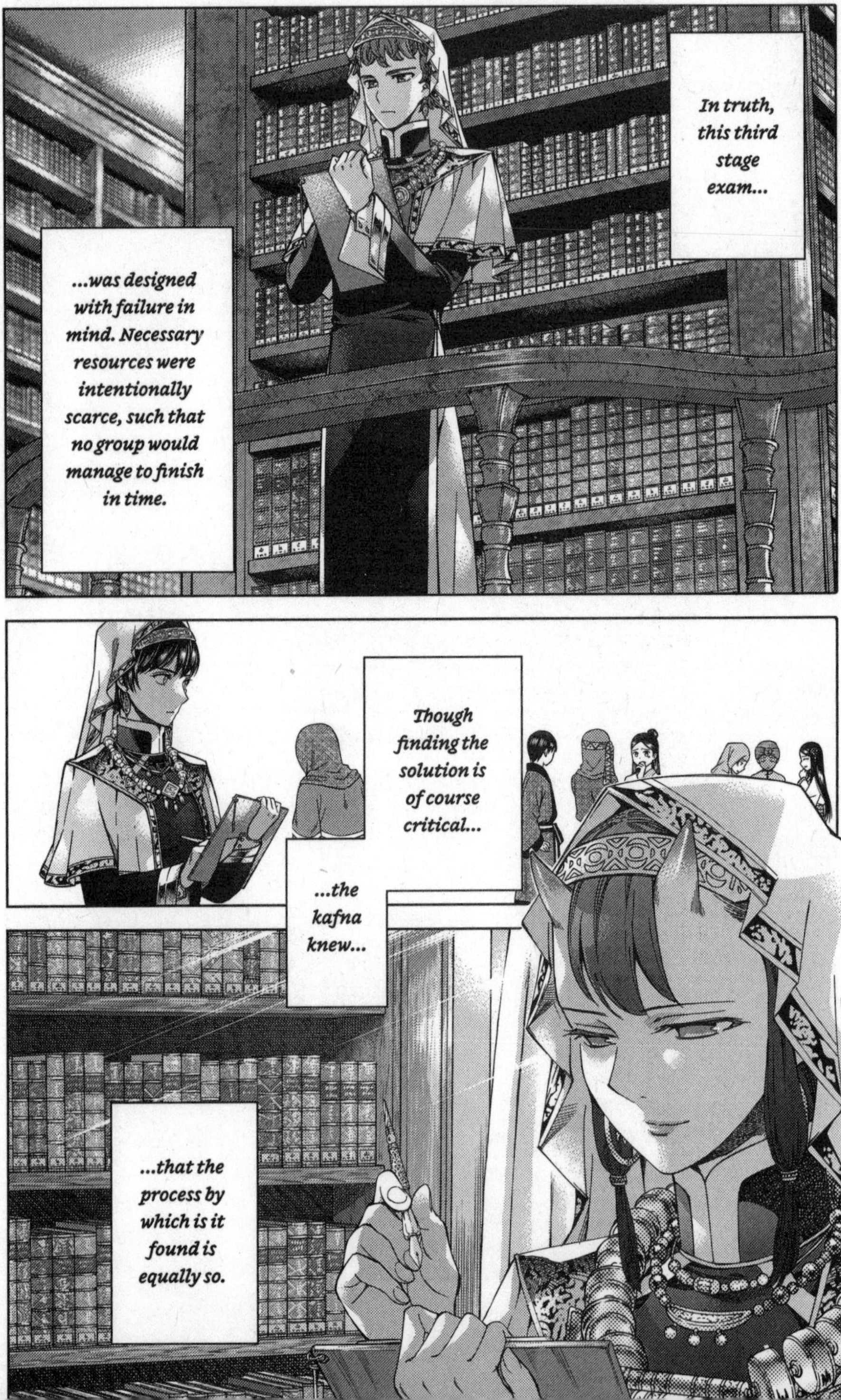
In truth, this third stage exam...
...was designed with failure in mind. Necessary resources were intentionally scarce, such that no group would manage to finish in time.
Though finding the solution is of course critical...
...the kafna knew...
...that the process by which is it found is equally so.

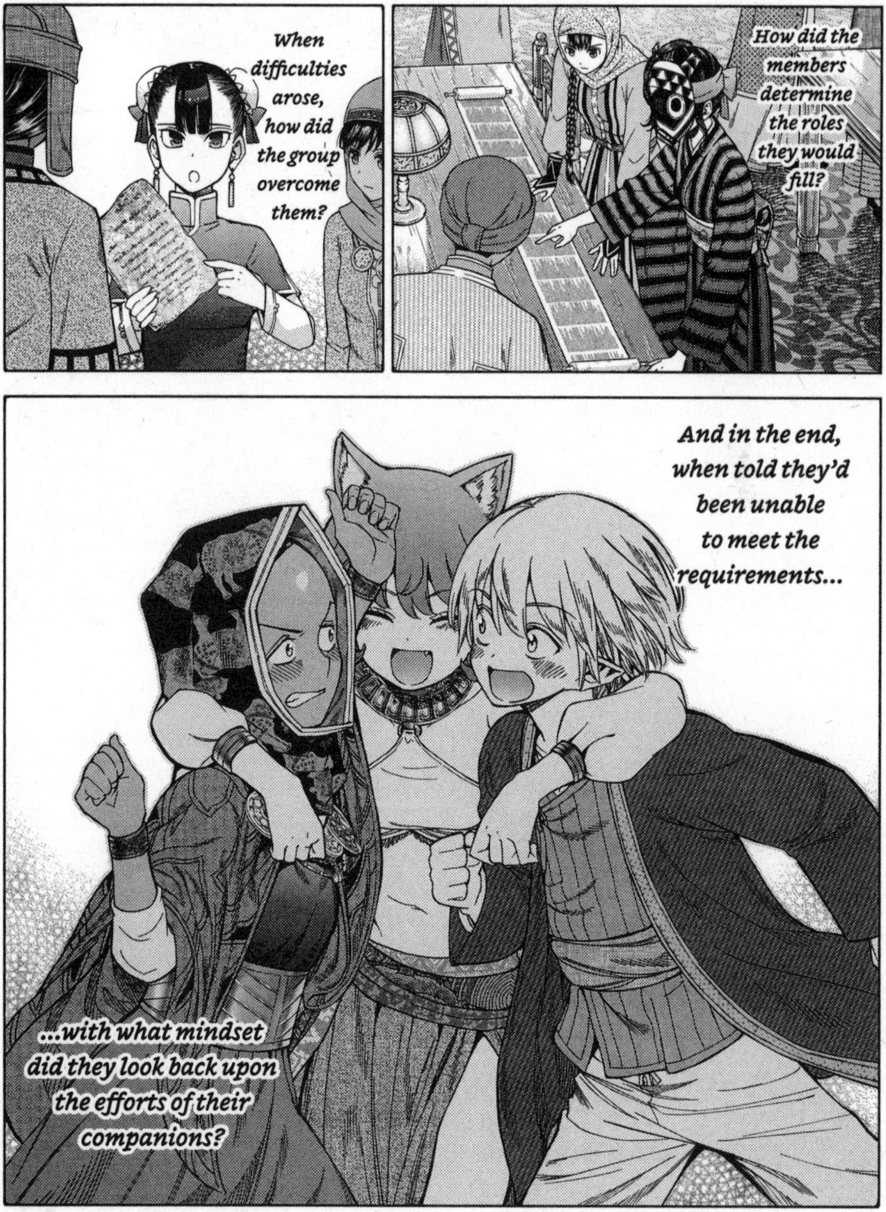
How did the members determine the roles they would fill?
When difficulties arose, how did the group overcome them?
And in the end, when told they'd been unable to meet the requirements...
...with what mindset did they look back upon the efforts of their companions?

Because no matter the extent...

...of any one individual's talents...

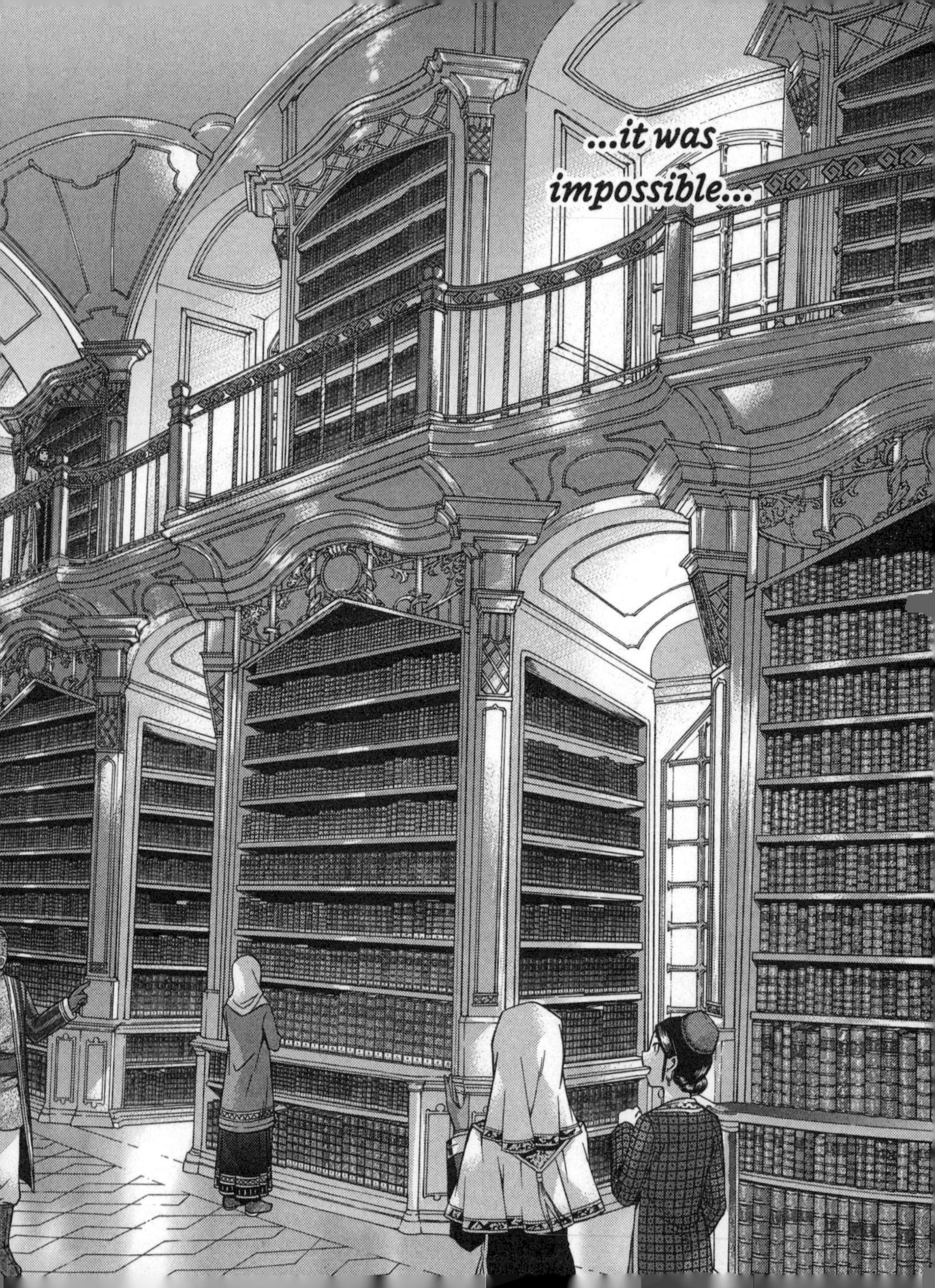
...it was impossible...

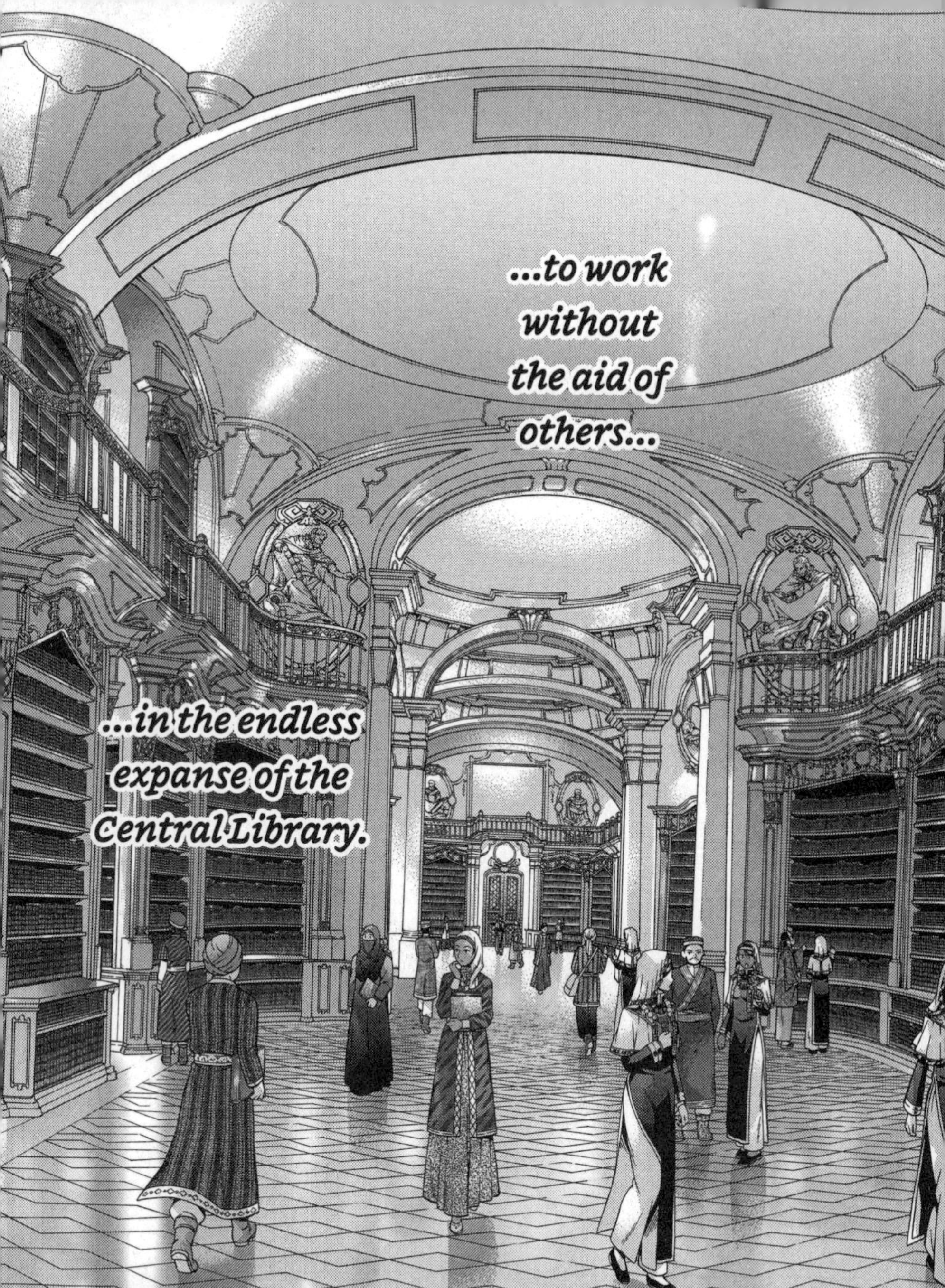
...to work without the aid of others...
...in the endless expanse of the Central Library.

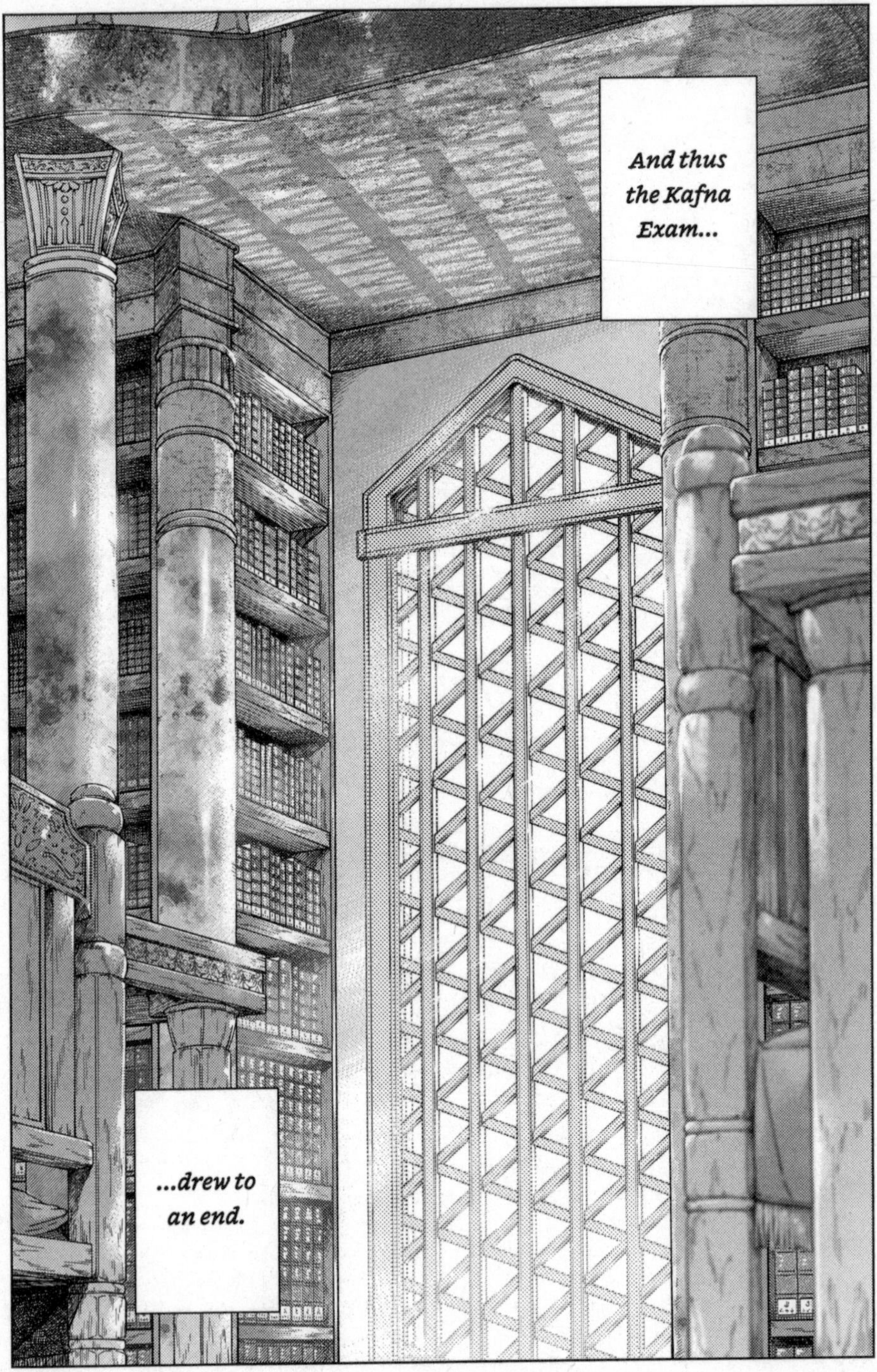
And thus the Kafna Exam...
...drew to an end.

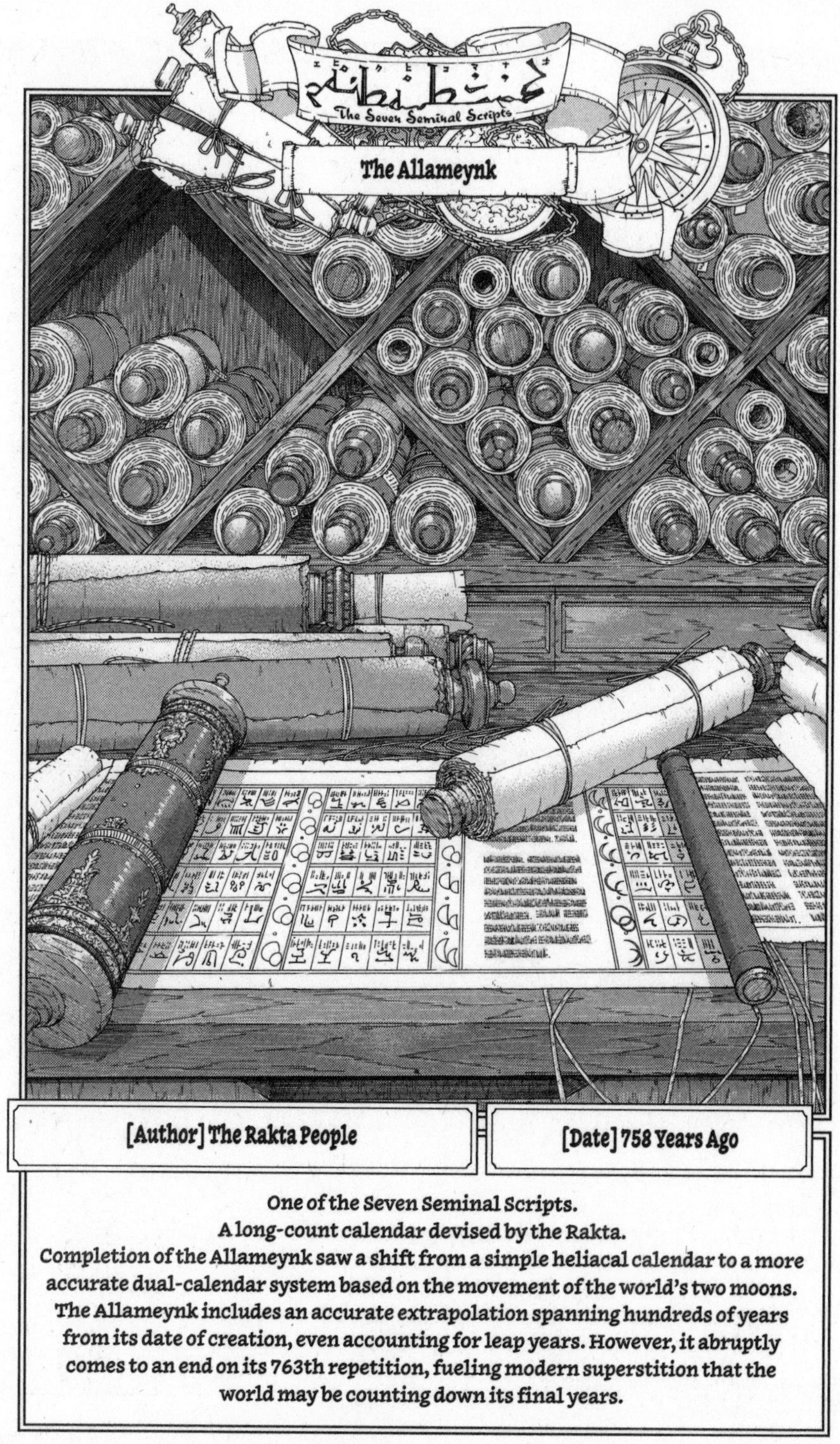
The Seven Seminal Scripts
The Allameynk

[Author] The Rakta People

[Date] 758 Years Ago

One of the Seven Seminal Scripts.
A long-count calendar devised by the Rakta.
Completion of the Allameynk saw a shift from a simple heliacal calendar to a more accurate dual-calendar system based on the movement of the world's two moons.
The Allameynk includes an accurate extrapolation spanning hundreds of years from its date of creation, even accounting for leap years. However, it abruptly comes to an end on its 763th repetition, fueling modern superstition that the world may be counting down its final years.

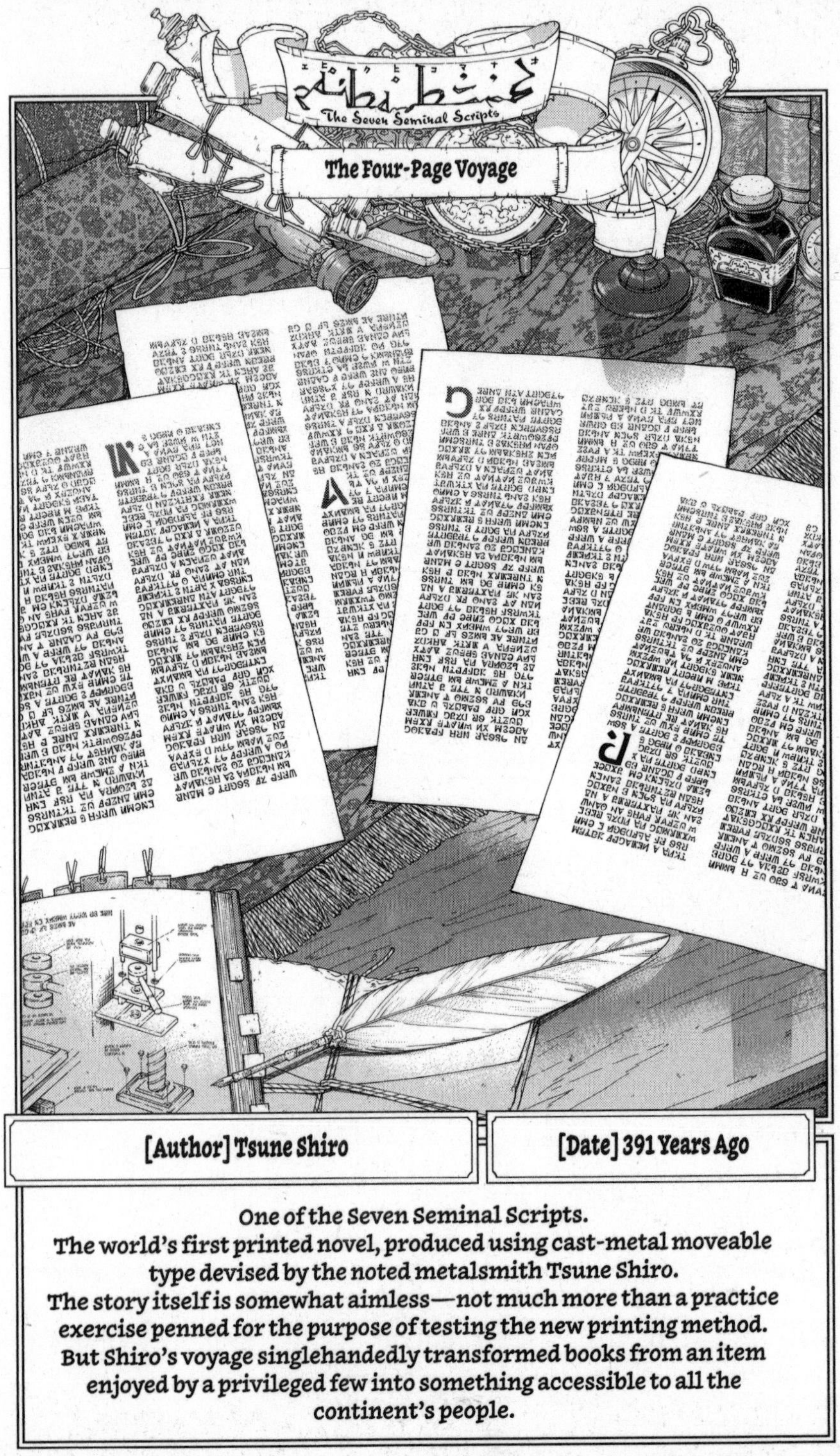
The Seven Seminal Scripts
The Four-Page Voyage

[Author] Tsune Shiro

[Date] 391 Years Ago

One of the Seven Seminal Scripts.
The world's first printed novel, produced using cast-metal moveable type devised by the noted metalsmith Tsune Shiro.
The story itself is somewhat aimless—not much more than a practice exercise penned for the purpose of testing the new printing method.
But Shiro's voyage singlehandedly transformed books from an item enjoyed by a privileged few into something accessible to all the continent's people.

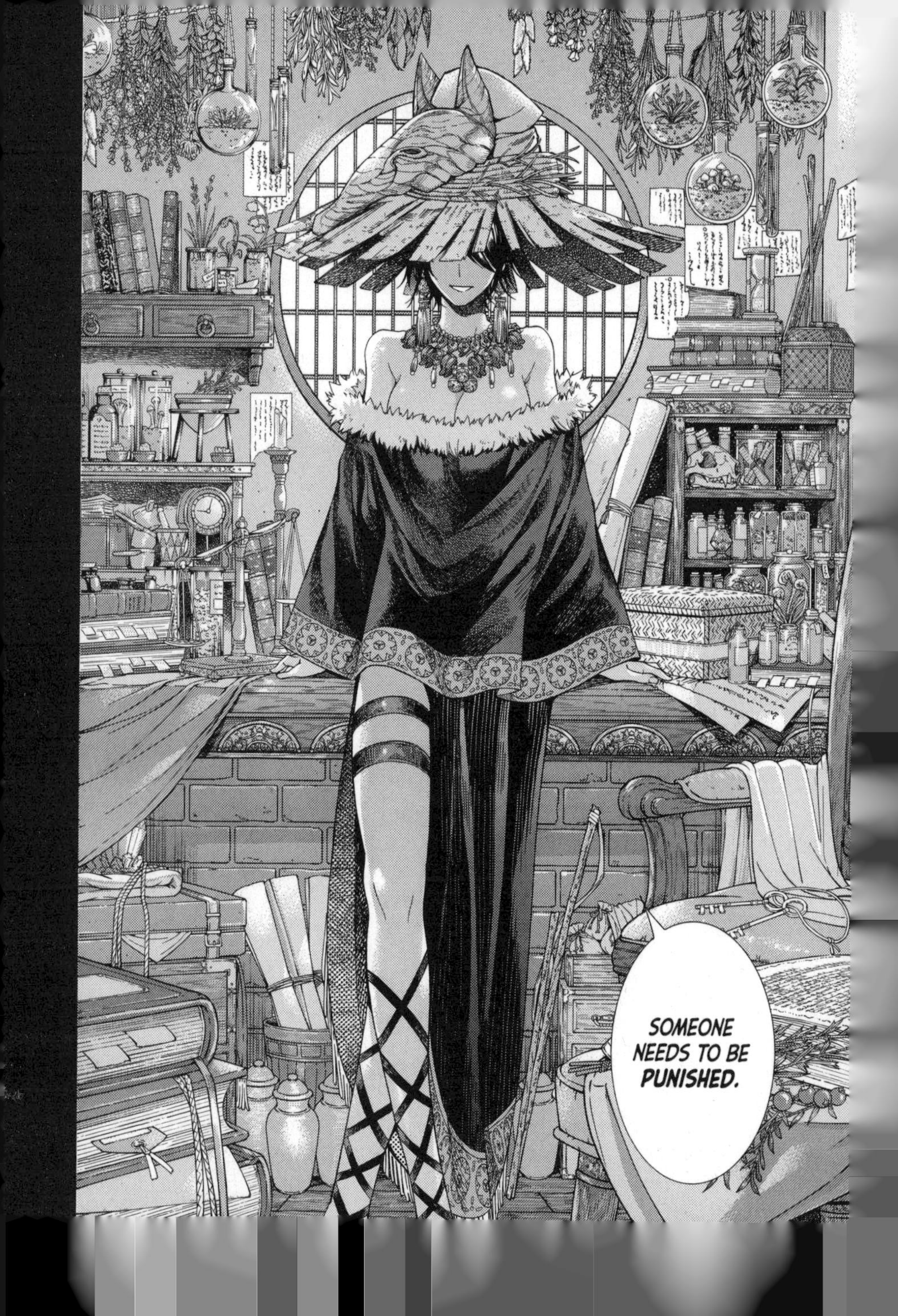
SOMEONE NEEDS TO BE PUNISHED.

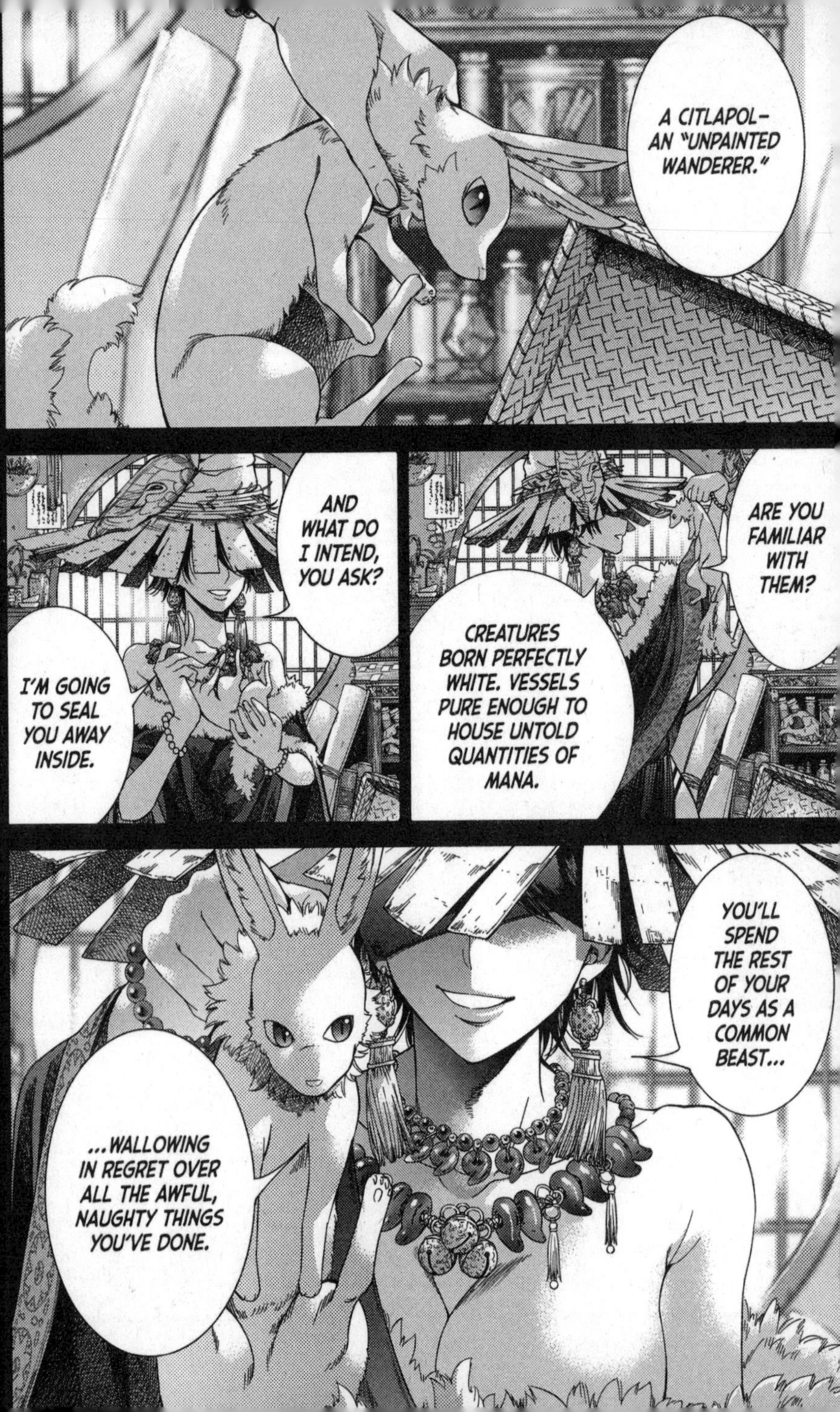
A CITLAPOL— AN "UNPAINTED WANDERER."
ARE YOU FAMILIAR WITH THEM?
CREATURES BORN PERFECTLY WHITE. VESSELS PURE ENOUGH TO HOUSE UNTOLD QUANTITIES OF MANA.
AND WHAT DO I INTEND, YOU ASK?
I'M GOING TO SEAL YOU AWAY INSIDE.
YOU'LL SPEND THE REST OF YOUR DAYS AS A COMMON BEAST...
...WALLOWING IN REGRET OVER ALL THE AWFUL, NAUGHTY THINGS YOU'VE DONE.

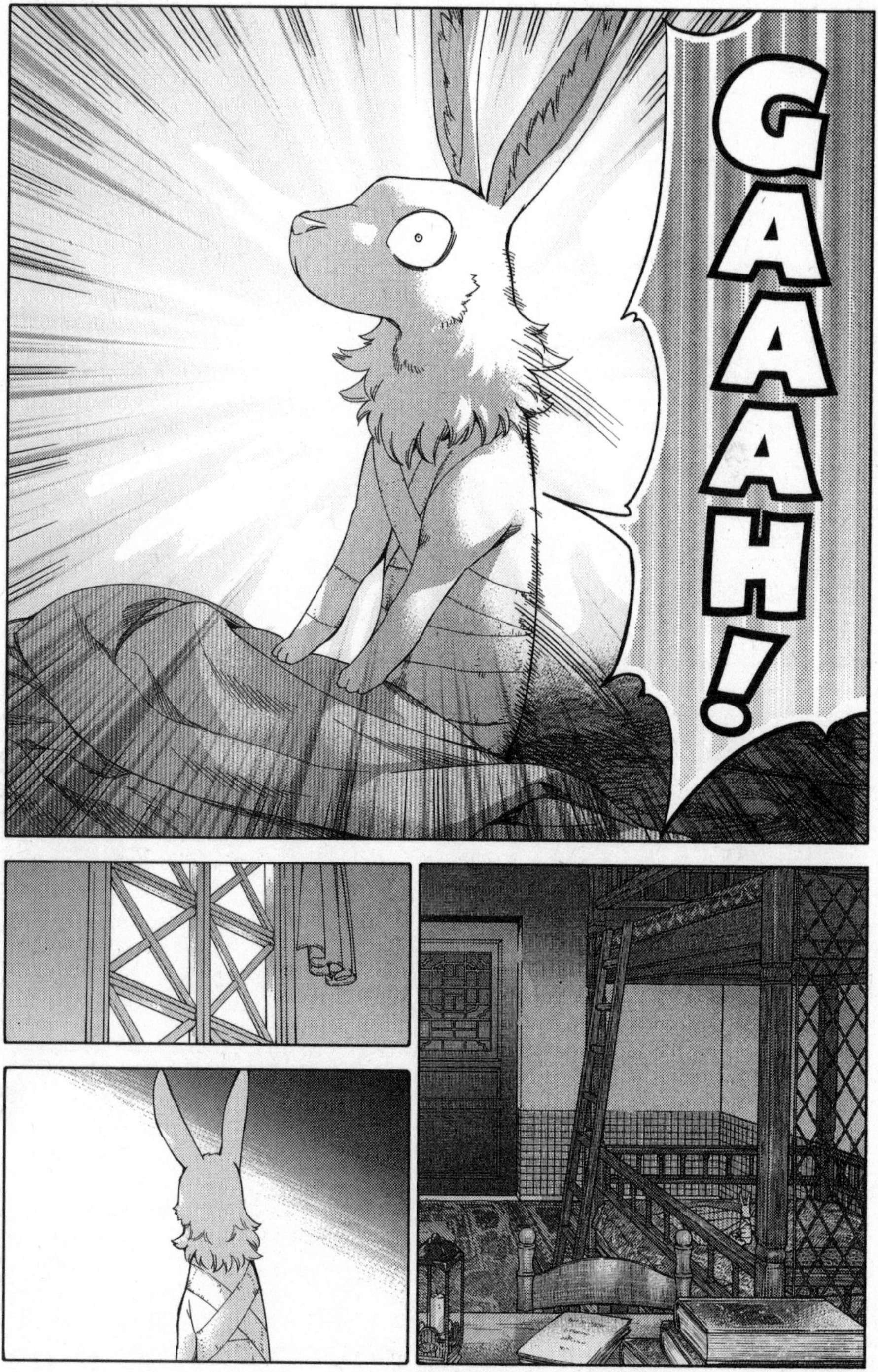
GAAAH!

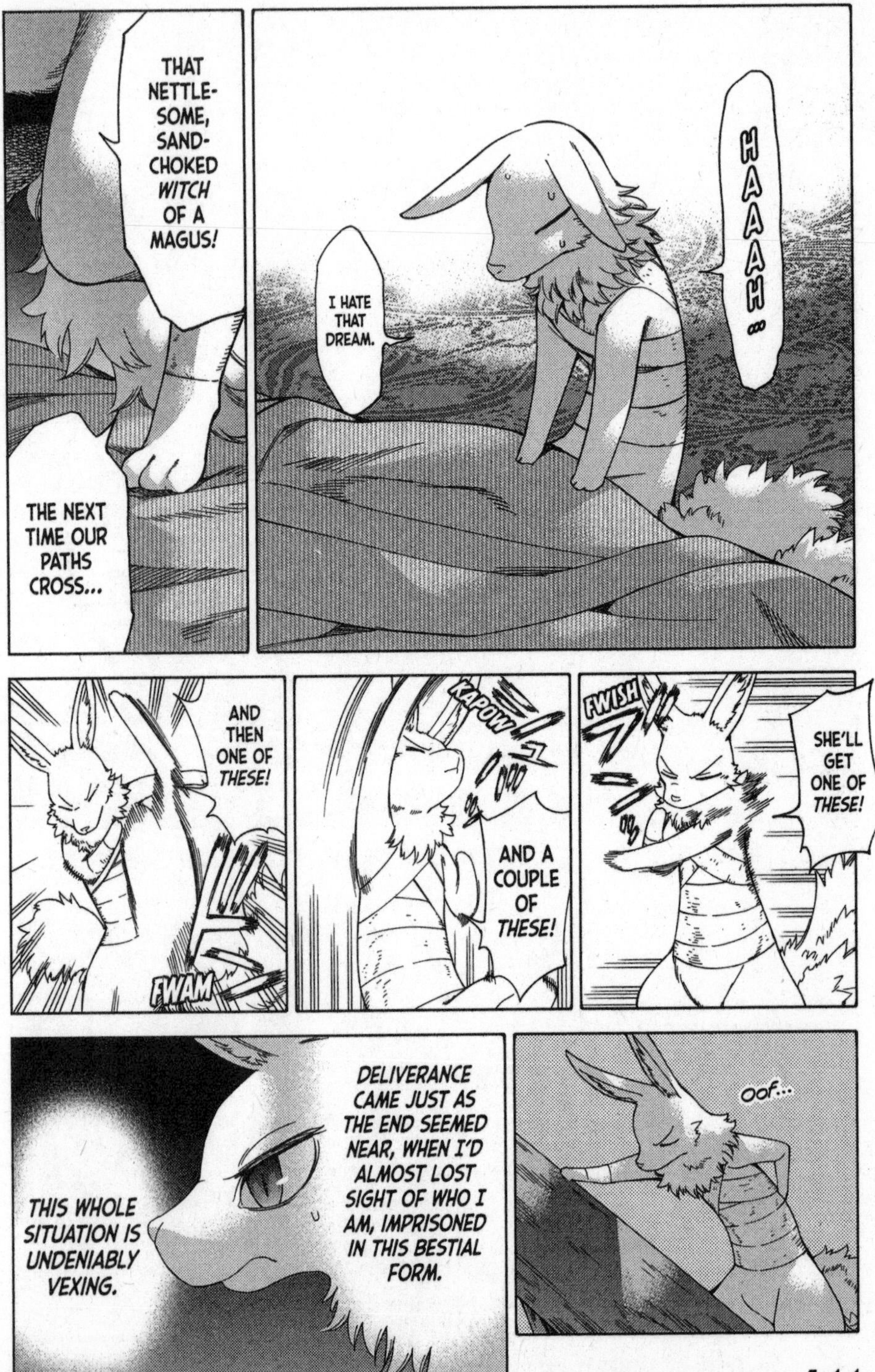
HAAAAH...
I HATE THAT DREAM.
THAT NETTLESOME, SAND-CHOKED WITCH OF A MAGUS!
THE NEXT TIME OUR PATHS CROSS...
FWISH
SHE'LL GET ONE OF THESE!
KAPOW
AND A COUPLE OF THESE!
AND THEN ONE OF THESE!
FWAM
Oof...
DELIVERANCE CAME JUST AS THE END SEEMED NEAR, WHEN I'D ALMOST LOST SIGHT OF WHO I AM, IMPRISONED IN THIS BESTIAL FORM.
THIS WHOLE SITUATION IS UNDENIABLY VEXING.

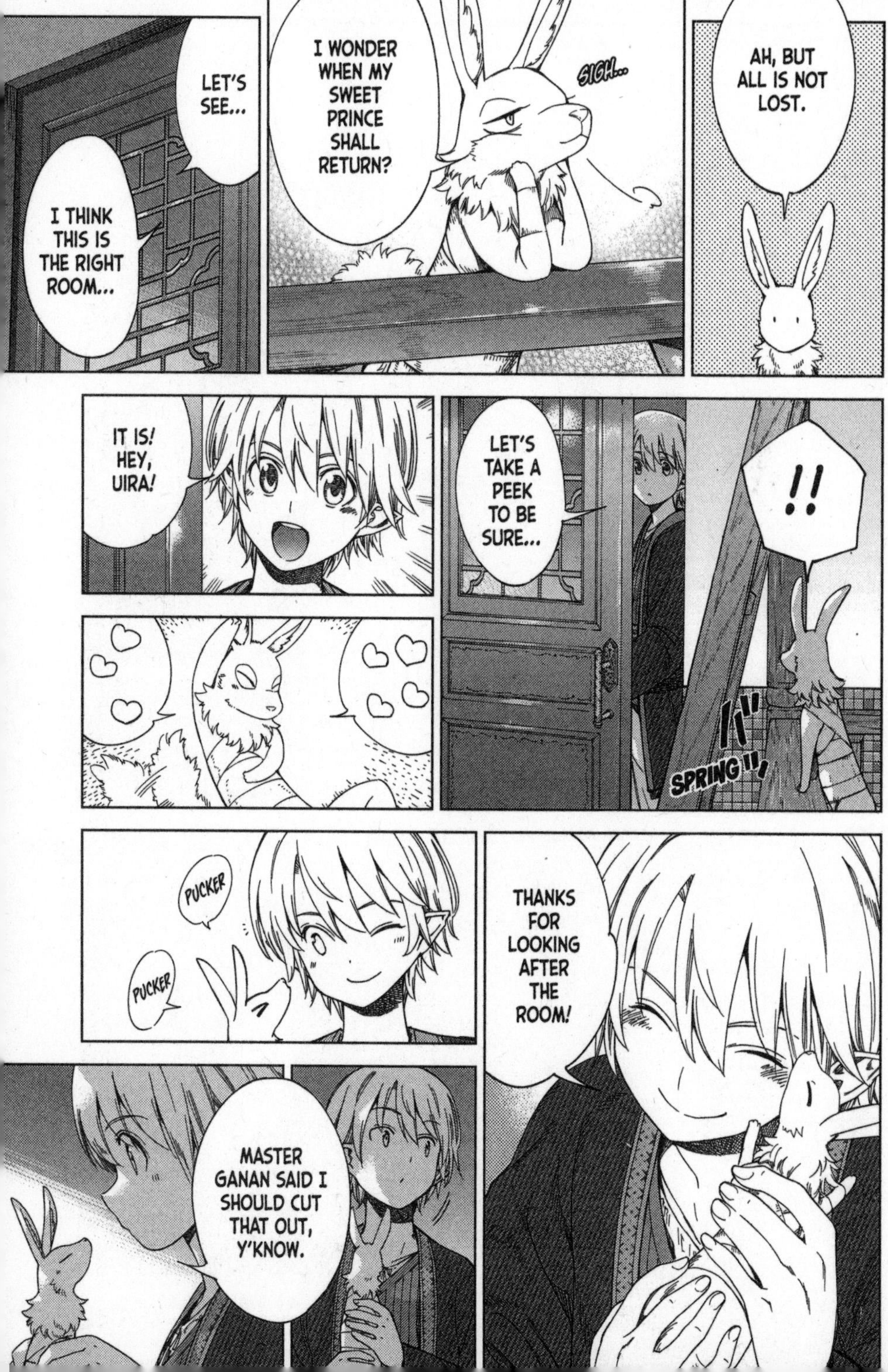
AH, BUT ALL IS NOT LOST.
SIGH...
I WONDER WHEN MY SWEET PRINCE SHALL RETURN?
LET'S SEE...
I THINK THIS IS THE RIGHT ROOM...
!!
LET'S TAKE A PEEK TO BE SURE...
バ
SPRING!!
IT IS! HEY, UIRA!
THANKS FOR LOOKING AFTER THE ROOM!
PUCKER
PUCKER
MASTER GANAN SAID I SHOULD CUT THAT OUT, Y'KNOW.

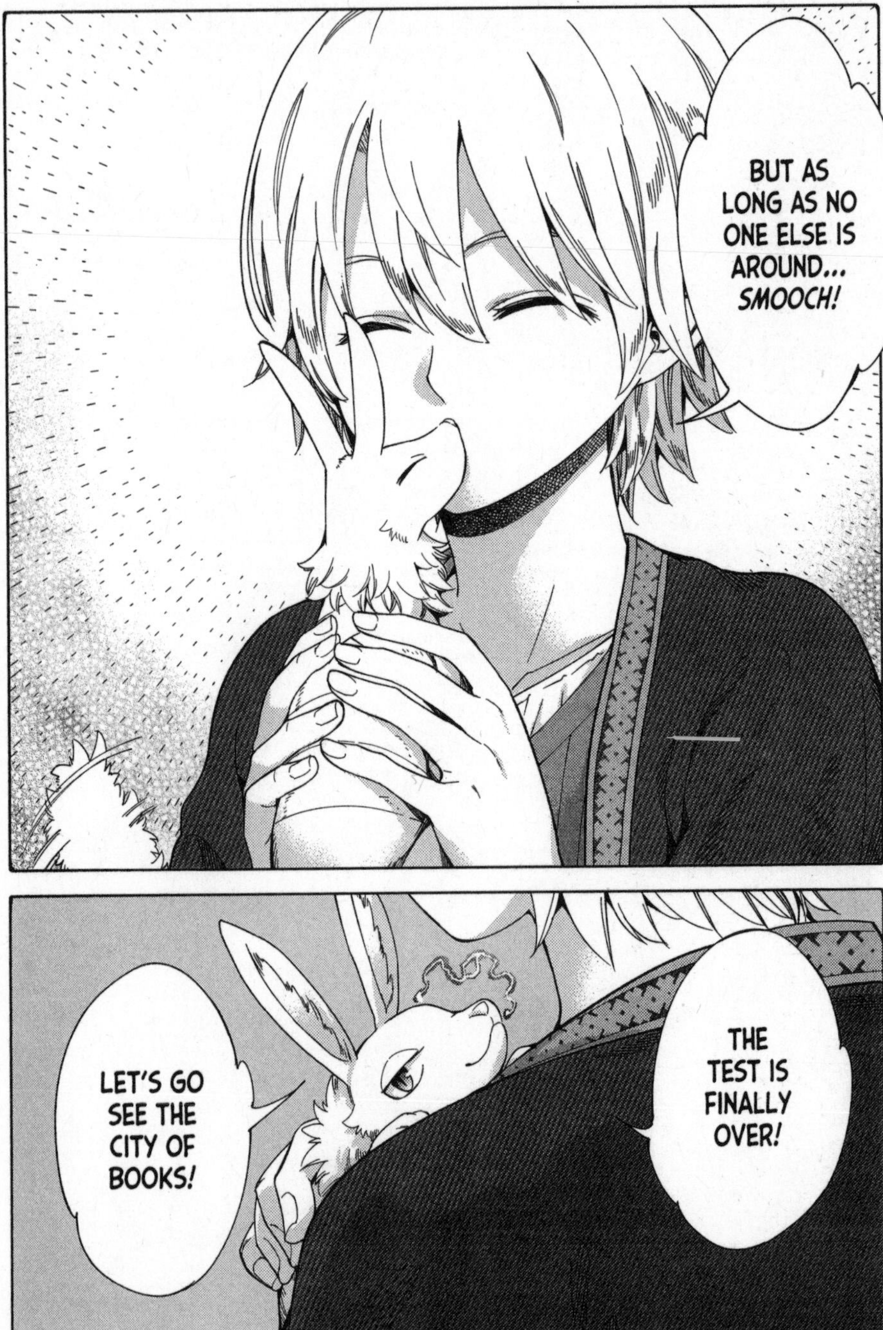
BUT AS LONG AS NO ONE ELSE IS AROUND... *SMOOCH!*
THE TEST IS FINALLY OVER!
LET'S GO SEE THE CITY OF BOOKS!

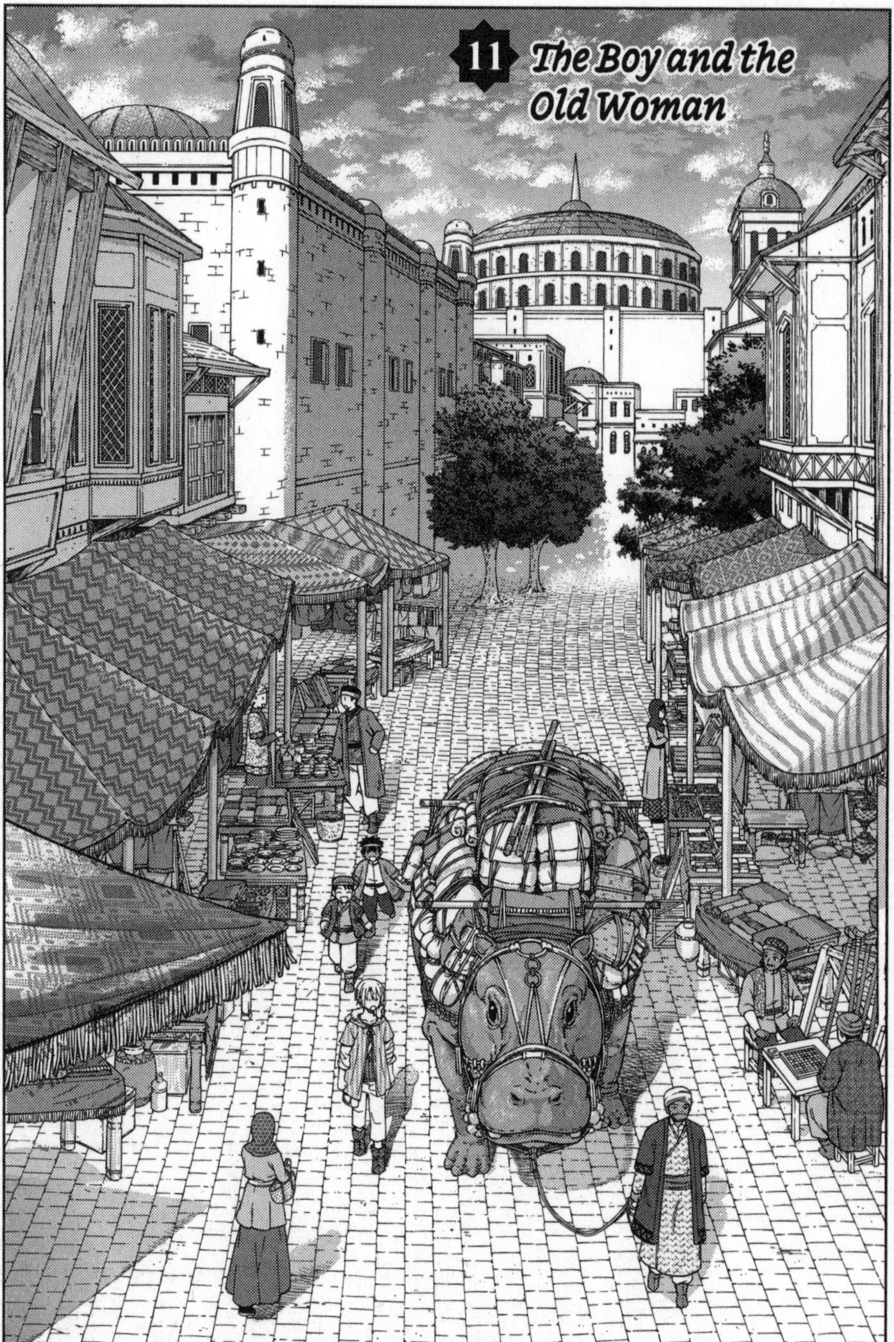
11 The Boy and the Old Woman

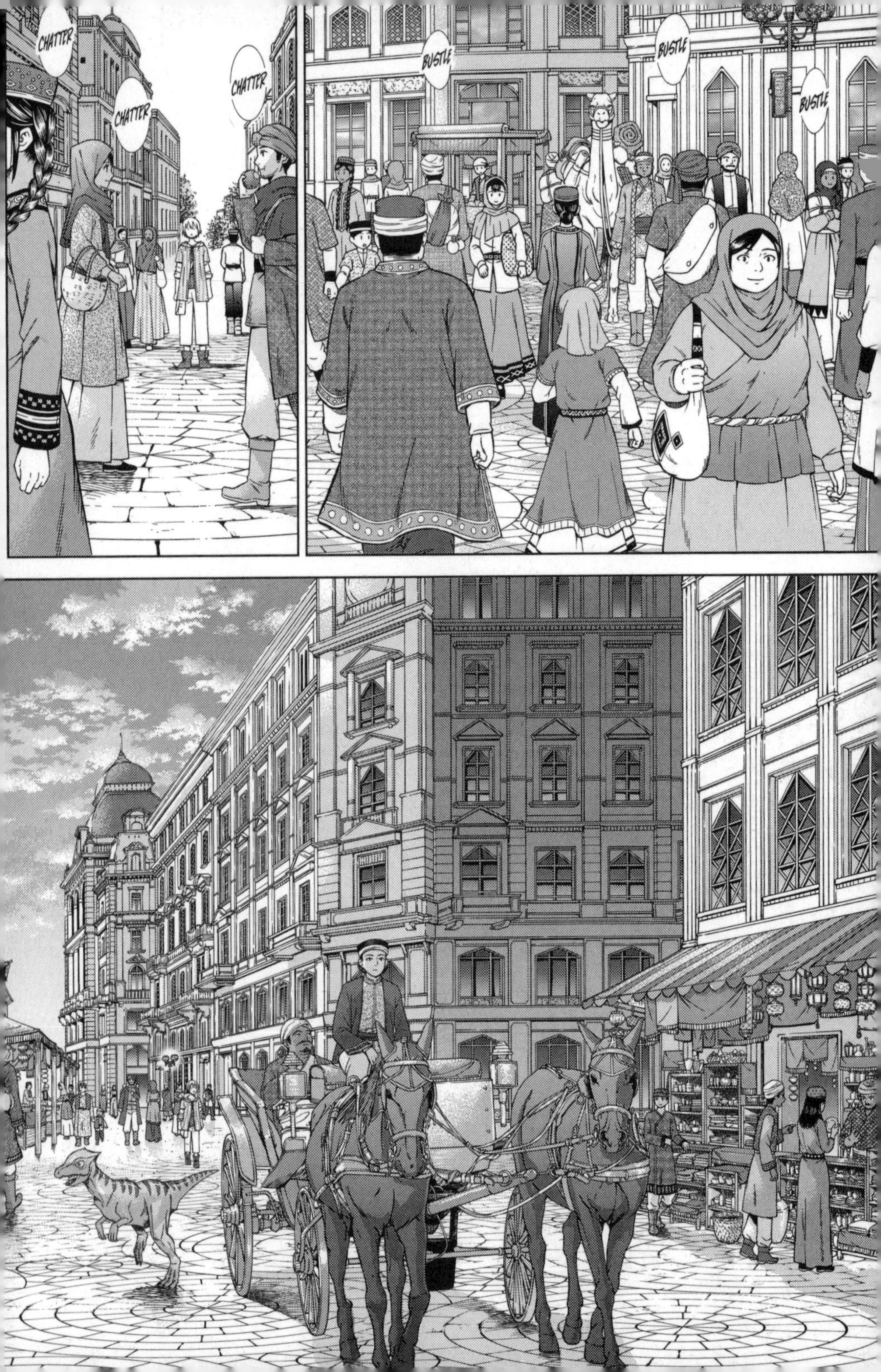
BUSTLE
BUSTLE
BUSTLE
CHATTER
CHATTER
CHATTER

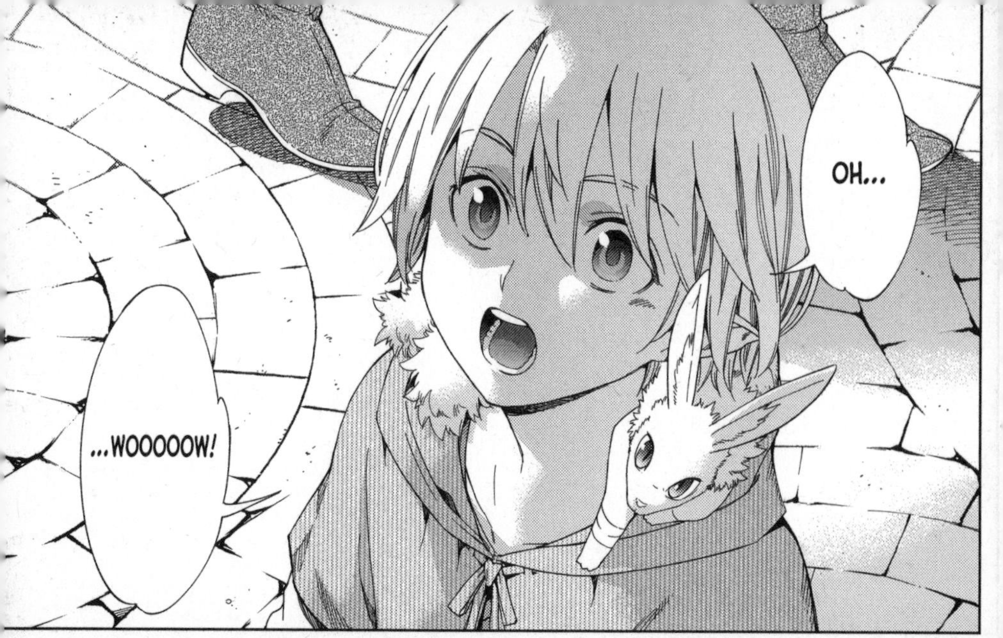
OH...
...WOOOOOW!
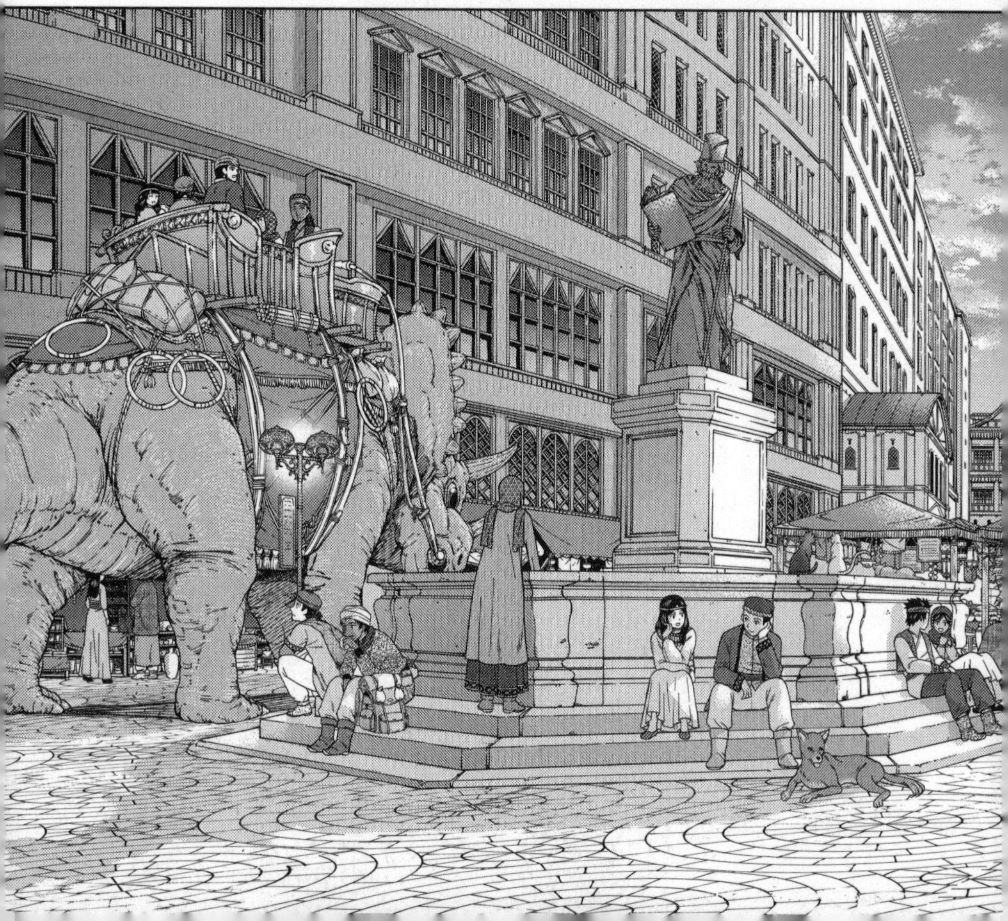

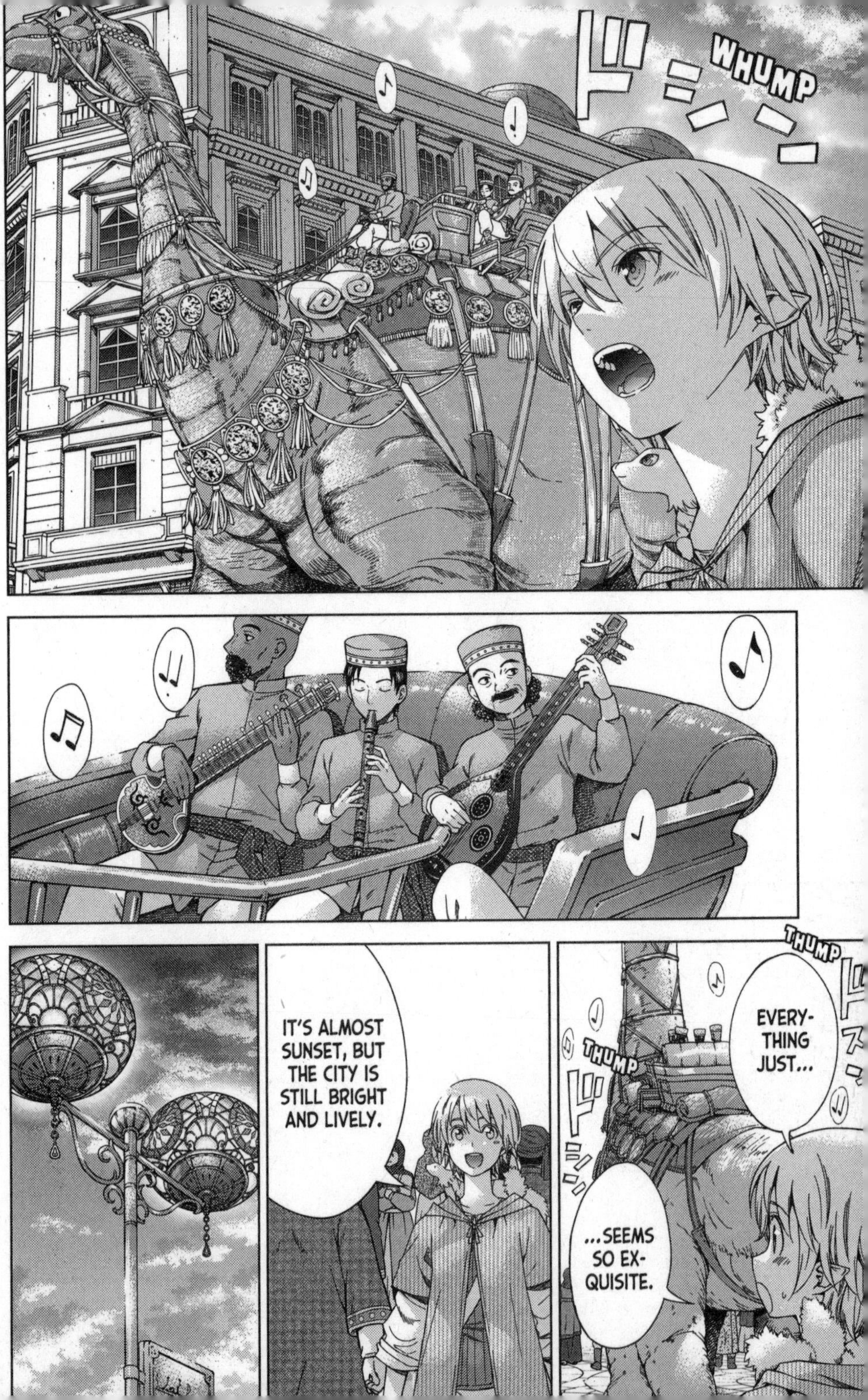
WHUMP
THUMP
EVERY-THING JUST...
THUMP
...SEEMS SO EX-QUISITE.
IT'S ALMOST SUNSET, BUT THE CITY IS STILL BRIGHT AND LIVELY.

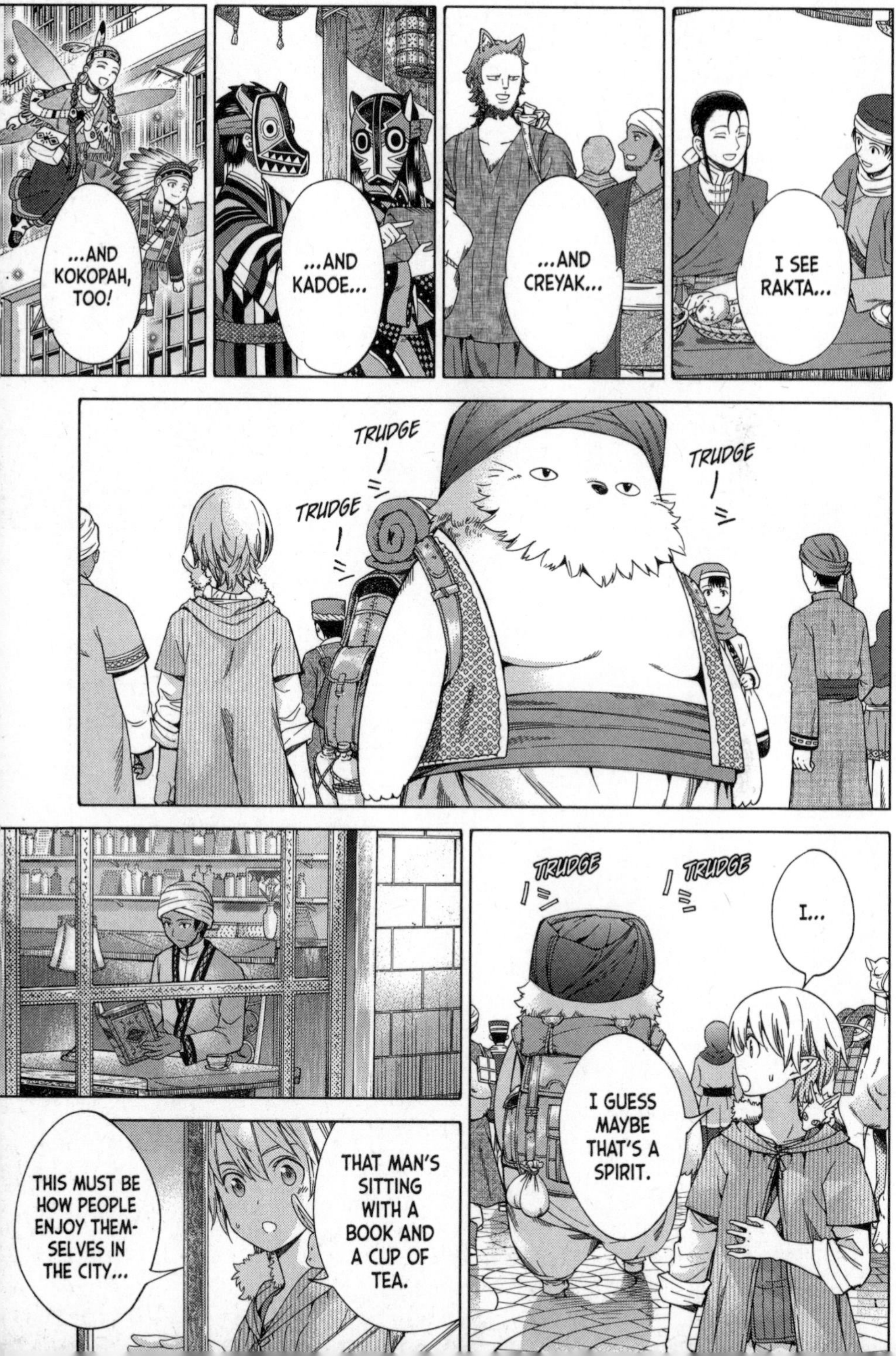
I SEE RAKTA...
...AND CREYAK...
...AND KADOE...
...AND KOKOPAH, TOO!
TRUDGE
TRUDGE
TRUDGE
TRUDGE
TRUDGE
I...
I GUESS MAYBE THAT'S A SPIRIT.
THAT MAN'S SITTING WITH A BOOK AND A CUP OF TEA.
THIS MUST BE HOW PEOPLE ENJOY THEM-SELVES IN THE CITY...

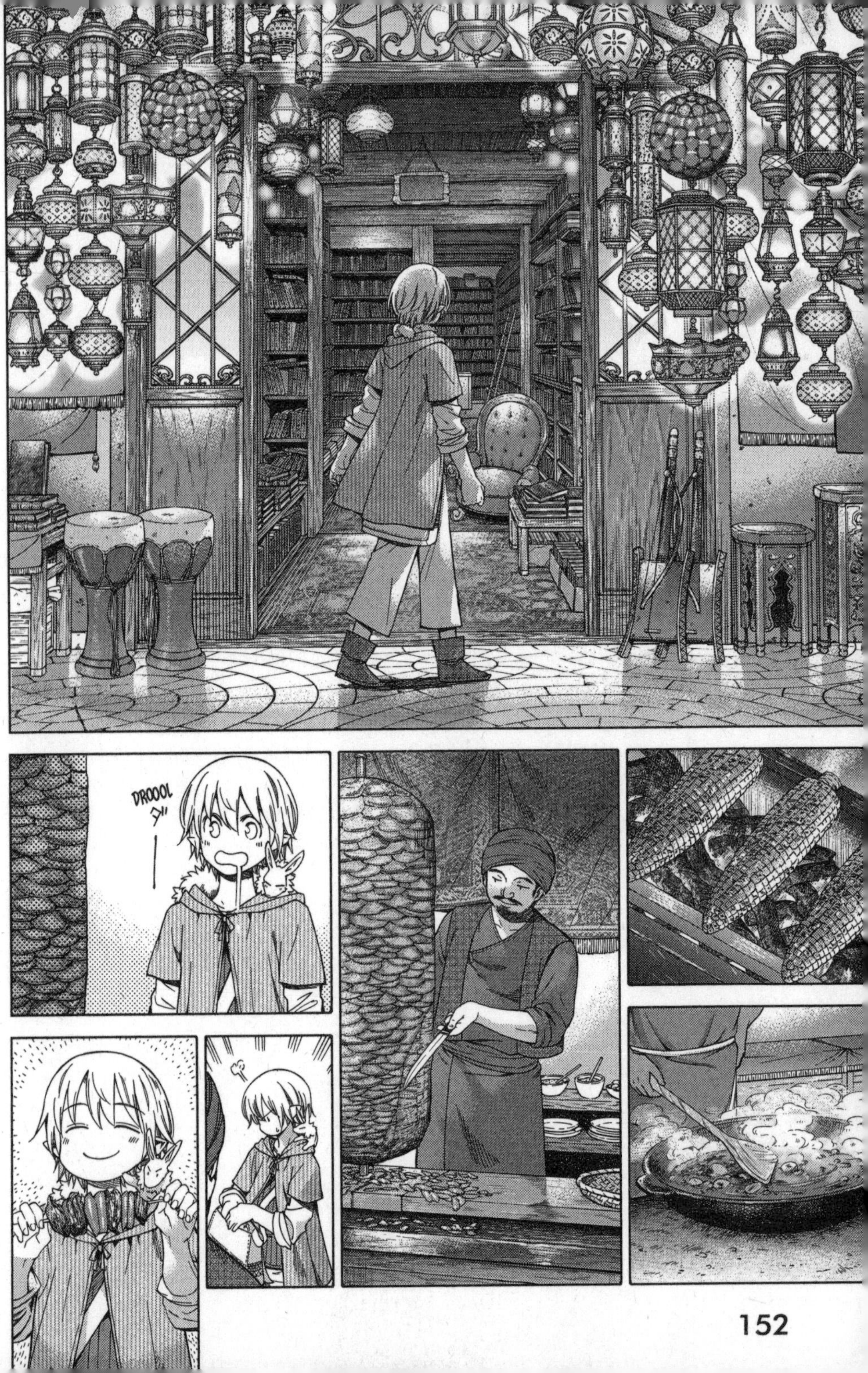
DROOOL
ダ

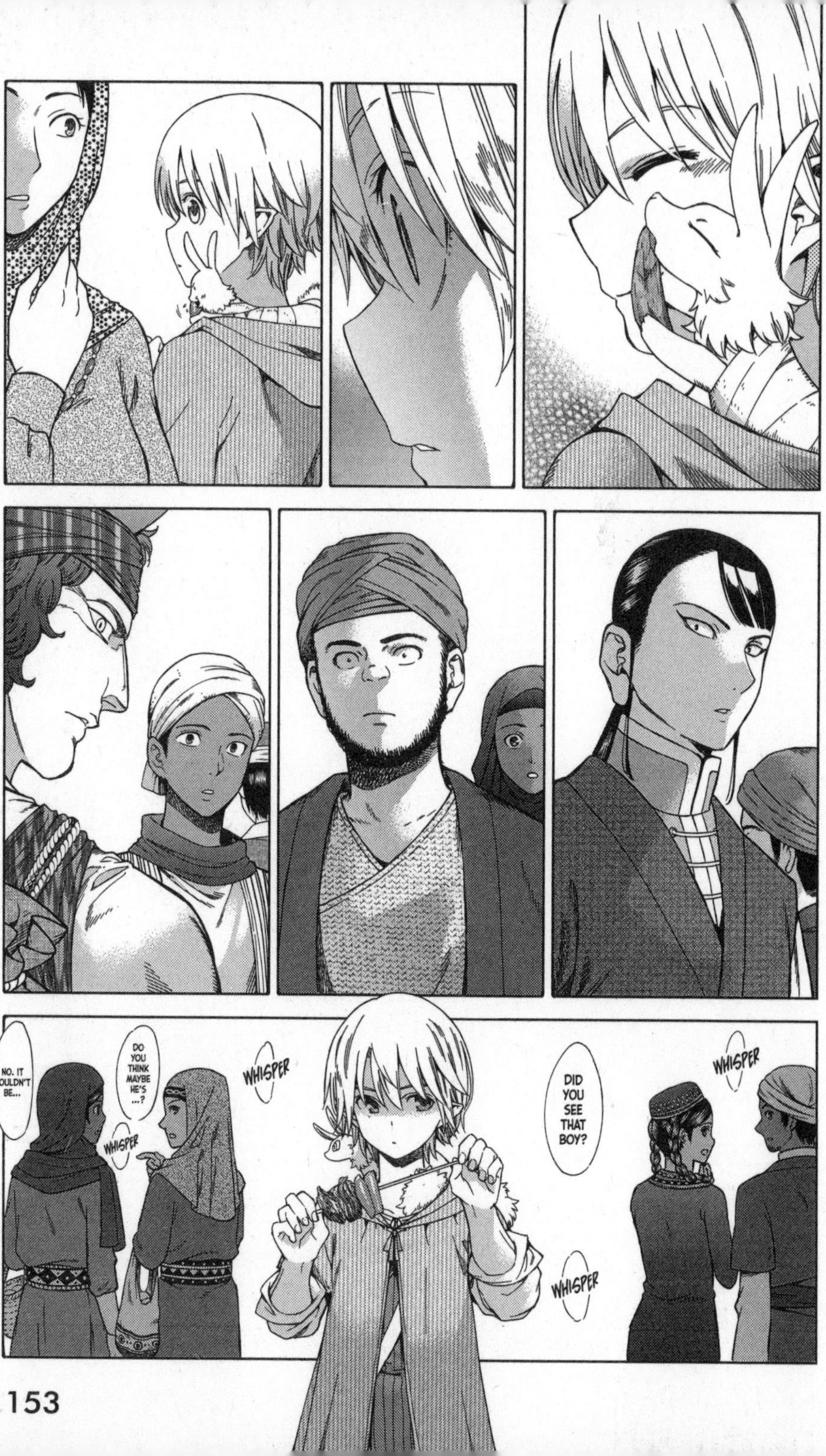
WHISPER
DID YOU SEE THAT BOY?
WHISPER
WHISPER
DO YOU THINK MAYBE HE'S ...?
WHISPER
NO. IT COULDN'T BE...

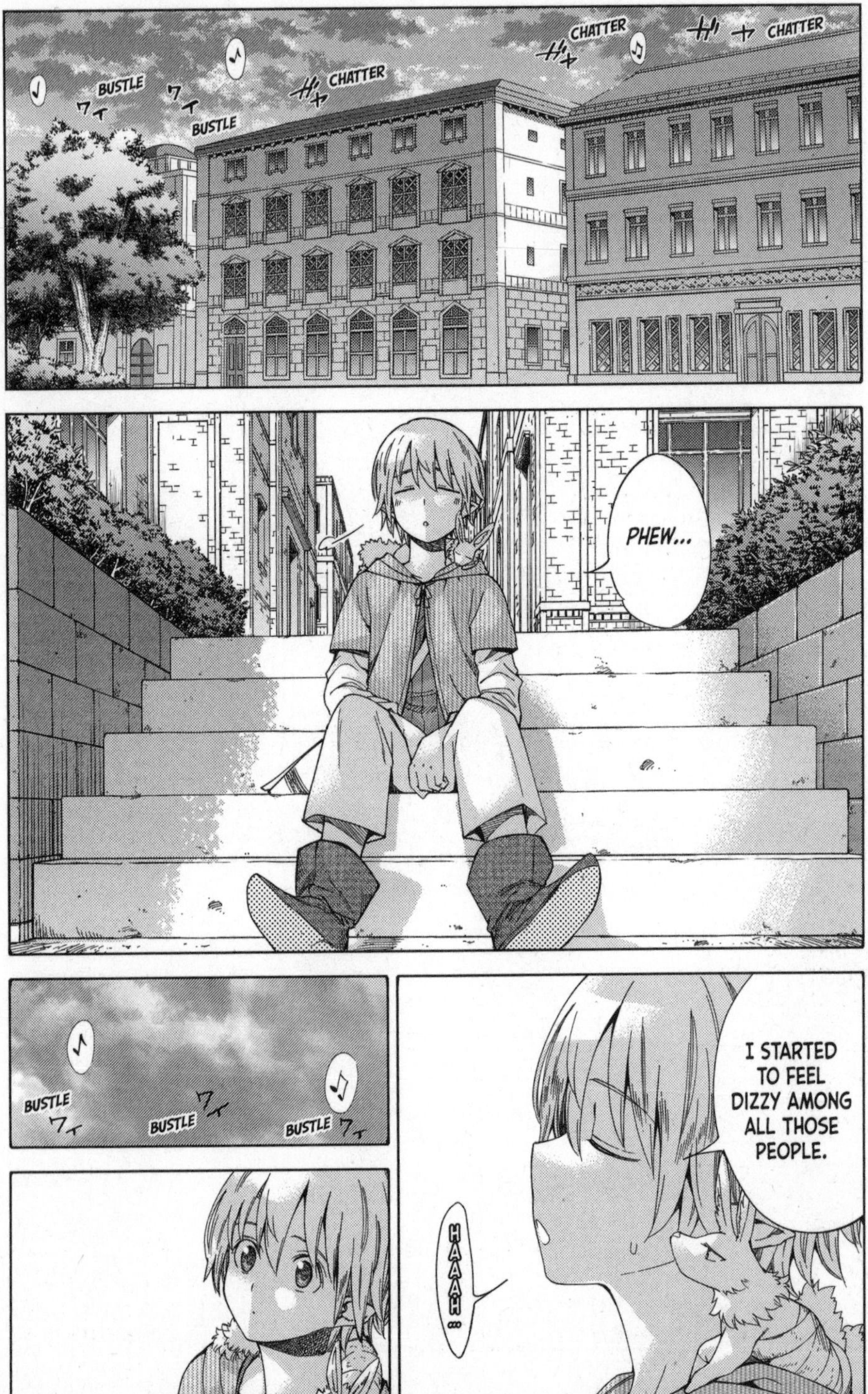
CHATTER
CHATTER
CHATTER
BUSTLE
BUSTLE
PHEW...
I STARTED TO FEEL DIZZY AMONG ALL THOSE PEOPLE.
HAAAAH...
BUSTLE
BUSTLE
BUSTLE

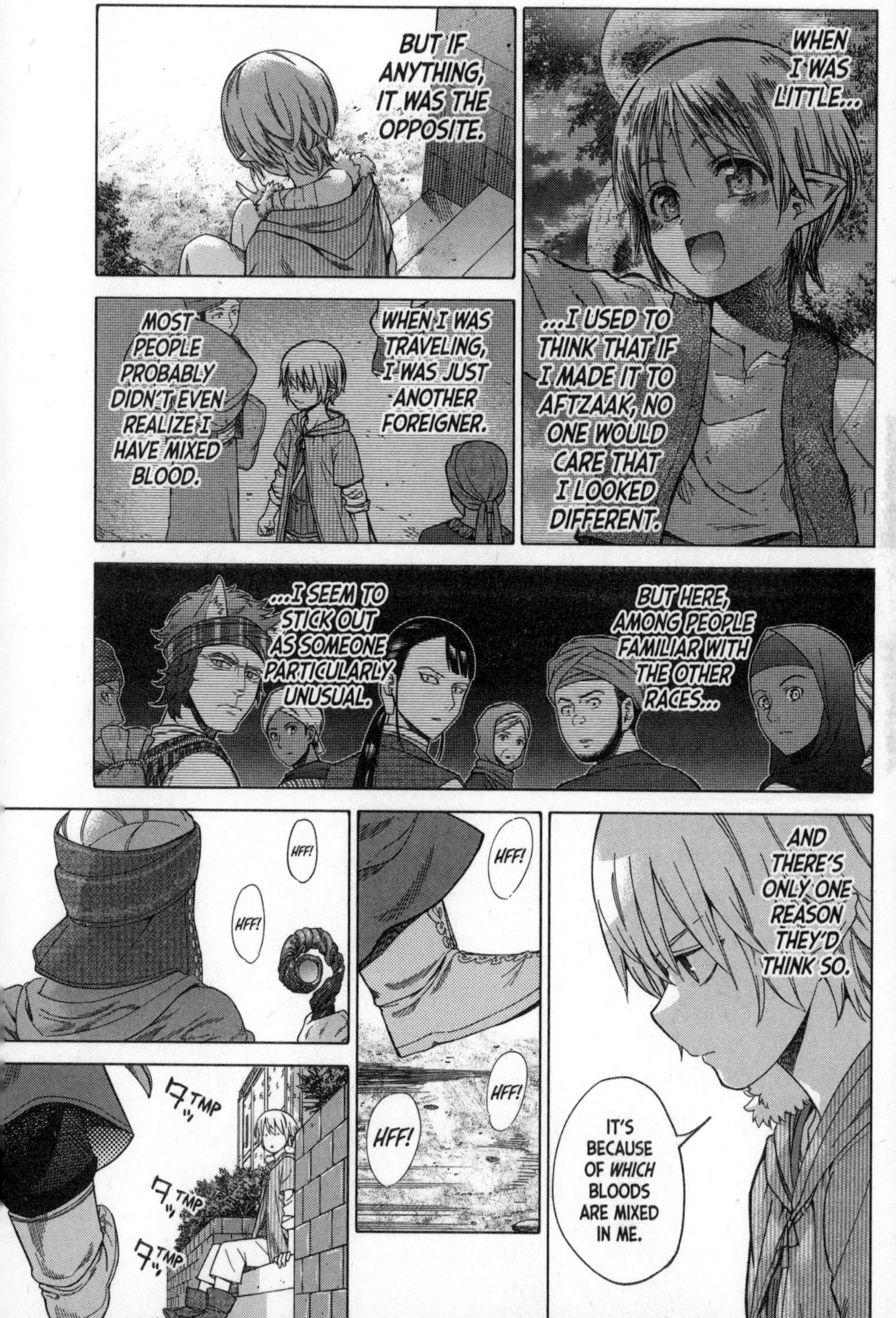
WHEN I WAS LITTLE...
...I USED TO THINK THAT IF I MADE IT TO AFTZAAK, NO ONE WOULD CARE THAT I LOOKED DIFFERENT.
BUT IF ANYTHING, IT WAS THE OPPOSITE.
WHEN I WAS TRAVELING, I WAS JUST ANOTHER FOREIGNER.
MOST PEOPLE PROBABLY DIDN'T EVEN REALIZE I HAVE MIXED BLOOD.
BUT HERE, AMONG PEOPLE FAMILIAR WITH THE OTHER RACES...
...I SEEM TO STICK OUT AS SOMEONE PARTICULARLY UNUSUAL.
AND THERE'S ONLY ONE REASON THEY'D THINK SO.
IT'S BECAUSE OF *WHICH* BLOODS ARE MIXED IN ME.
HFF!
HFF!
HFF!
HFF!
HFF!
TMP
TMP
TMP

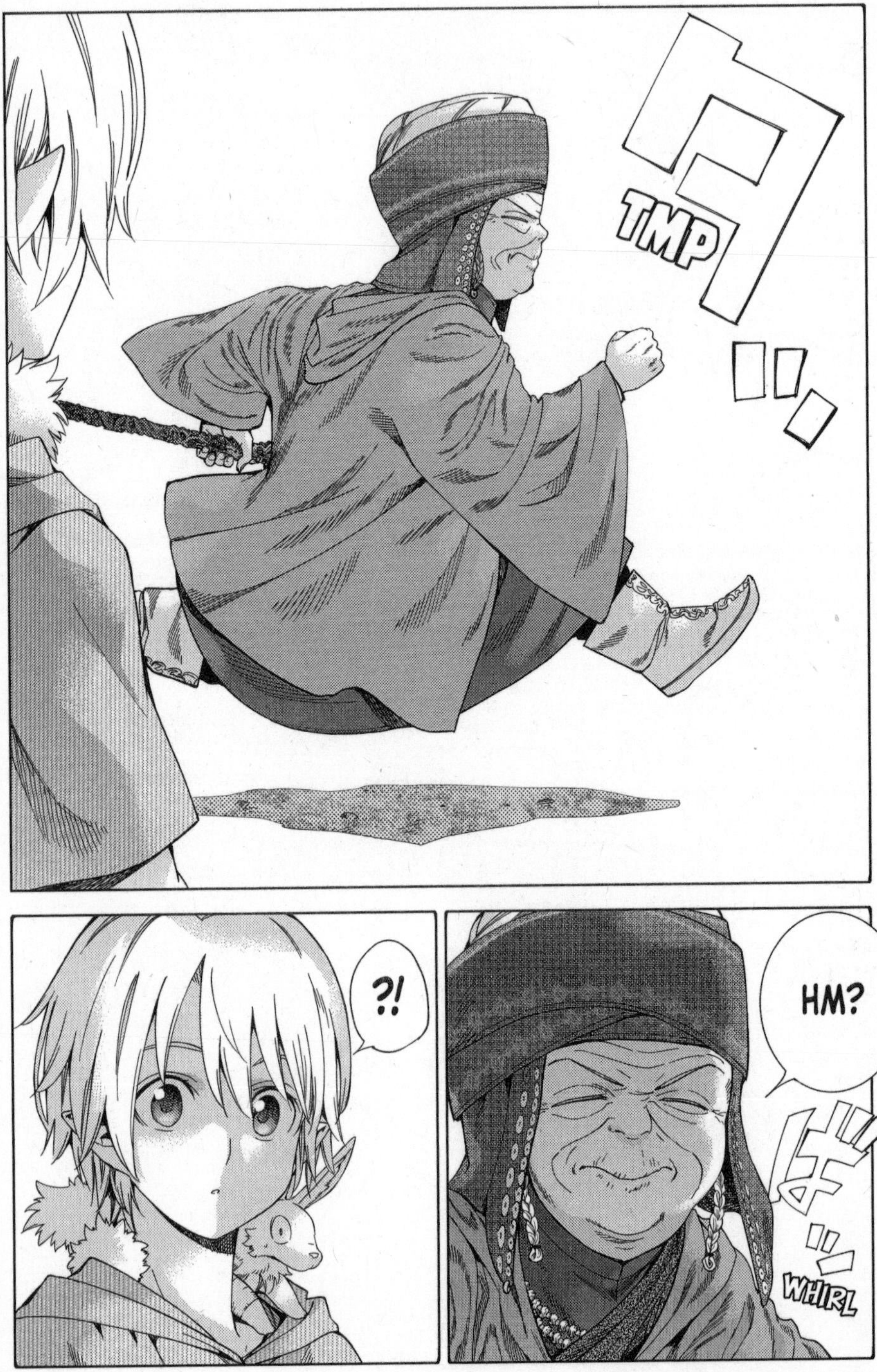
TMP
HM?
WHIRL
?!

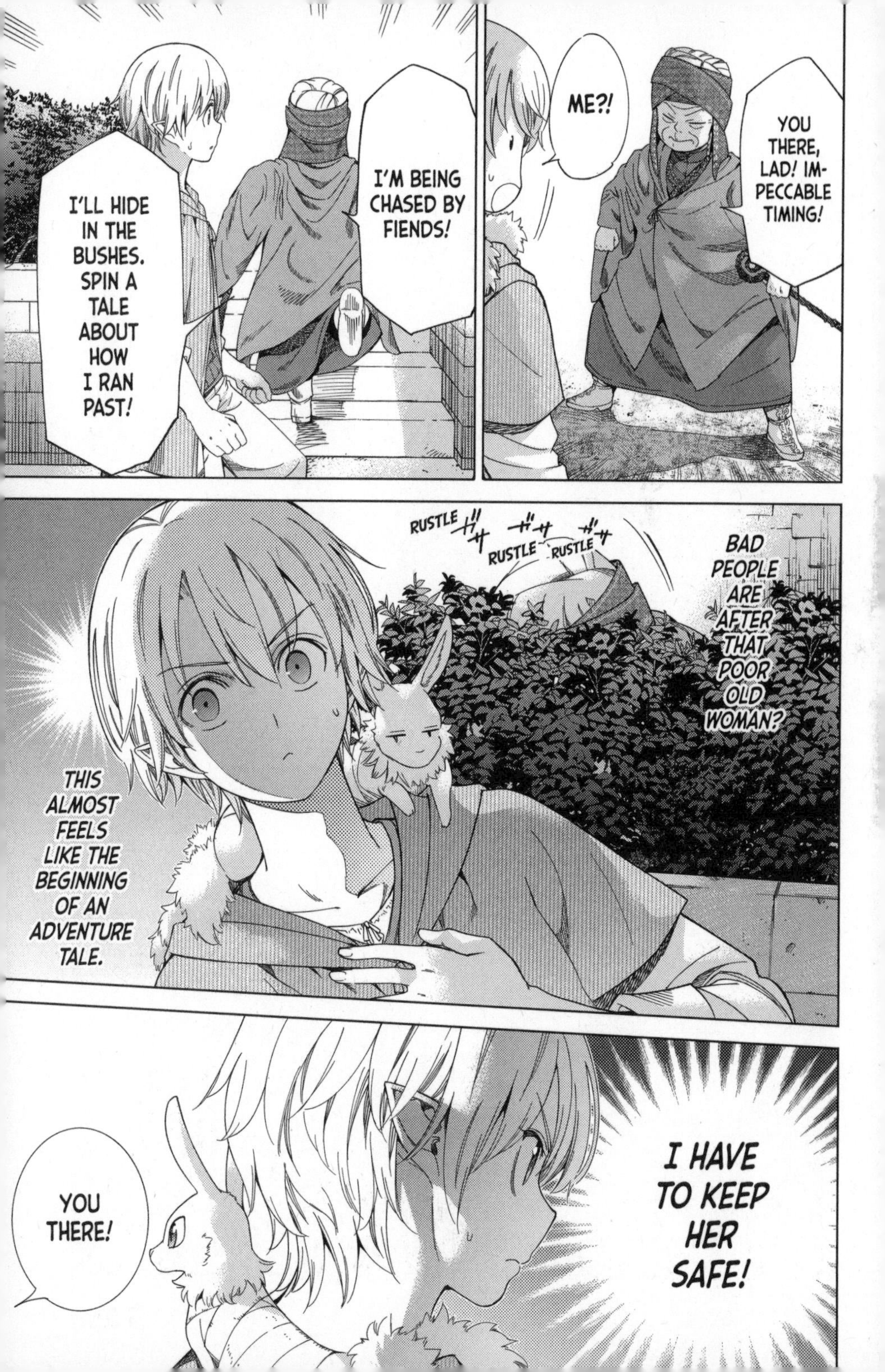
YOU THERE, LAD! IM-PECCABLE TIMING!
ME?!
I'M BEING CHASED BY FIENDS!
I'LL HIDE IN THE BUSHES. SPIN A TALE ABOUT HOW I RAN PAST!
RUSTLE
RUSTLE RUSTLE
BAD PEOPLE ARE AFTER THAT POOR OLD WOMAN?
THIS ALMOST FEELS LIKE THE BEGINNING OF AN ADVENTURE TALE.
I HAVE TO KEEP HER SAFE!
YOU THERE!

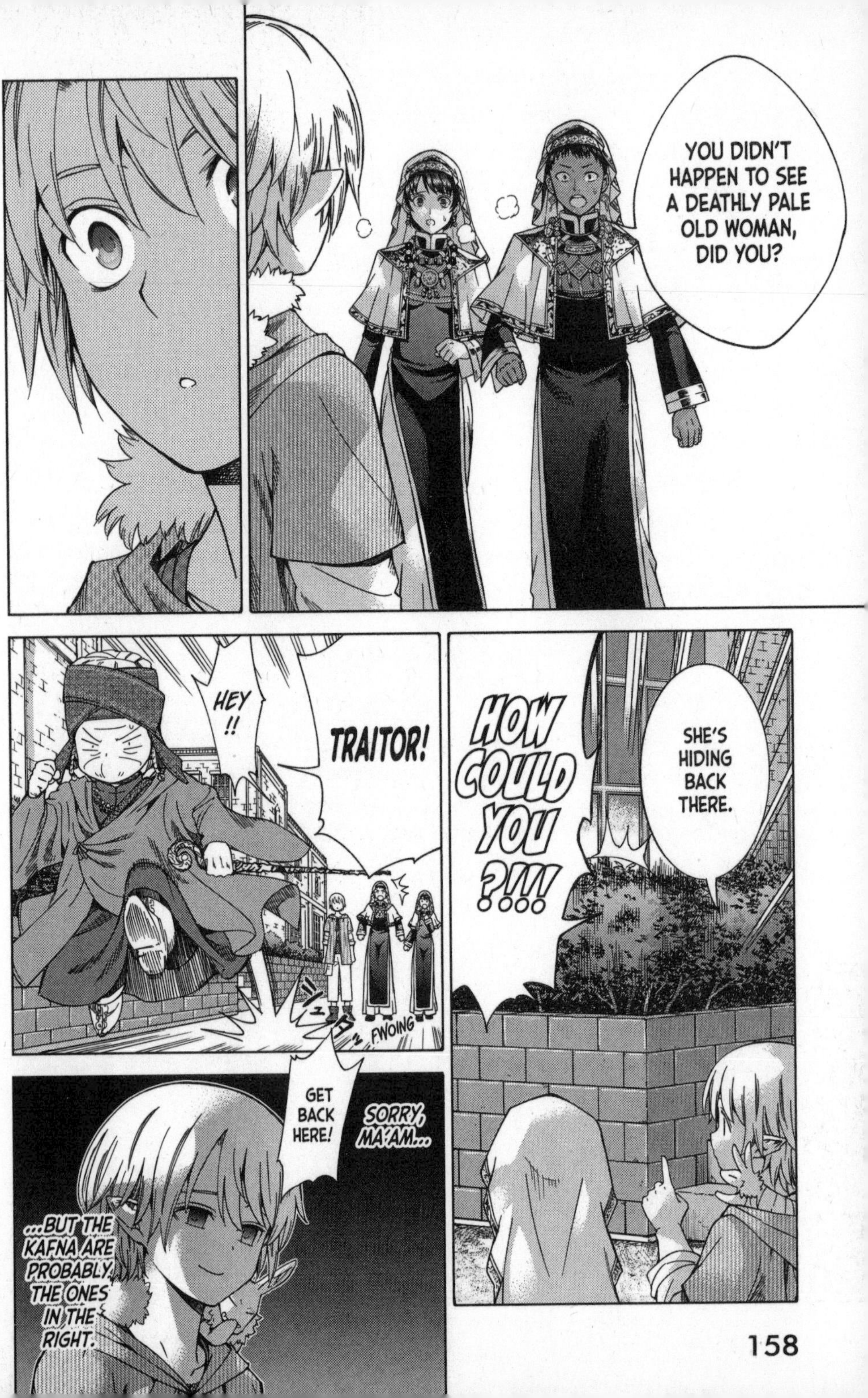
YOU DIDN'T HAPPEN TO SEE A DEATHLY PALE OLD WOMAN, DID YOU?
SHE'S HIDING BACK THERE.
HOW COULD YOU?!!!
TRAITOR!
HEY!!
FWOING
GET BACK HERE!
SORRY, MA'AM...
...BUT THE KAFNA ARE PROBABLY THE ONES IN THE RIGHT.

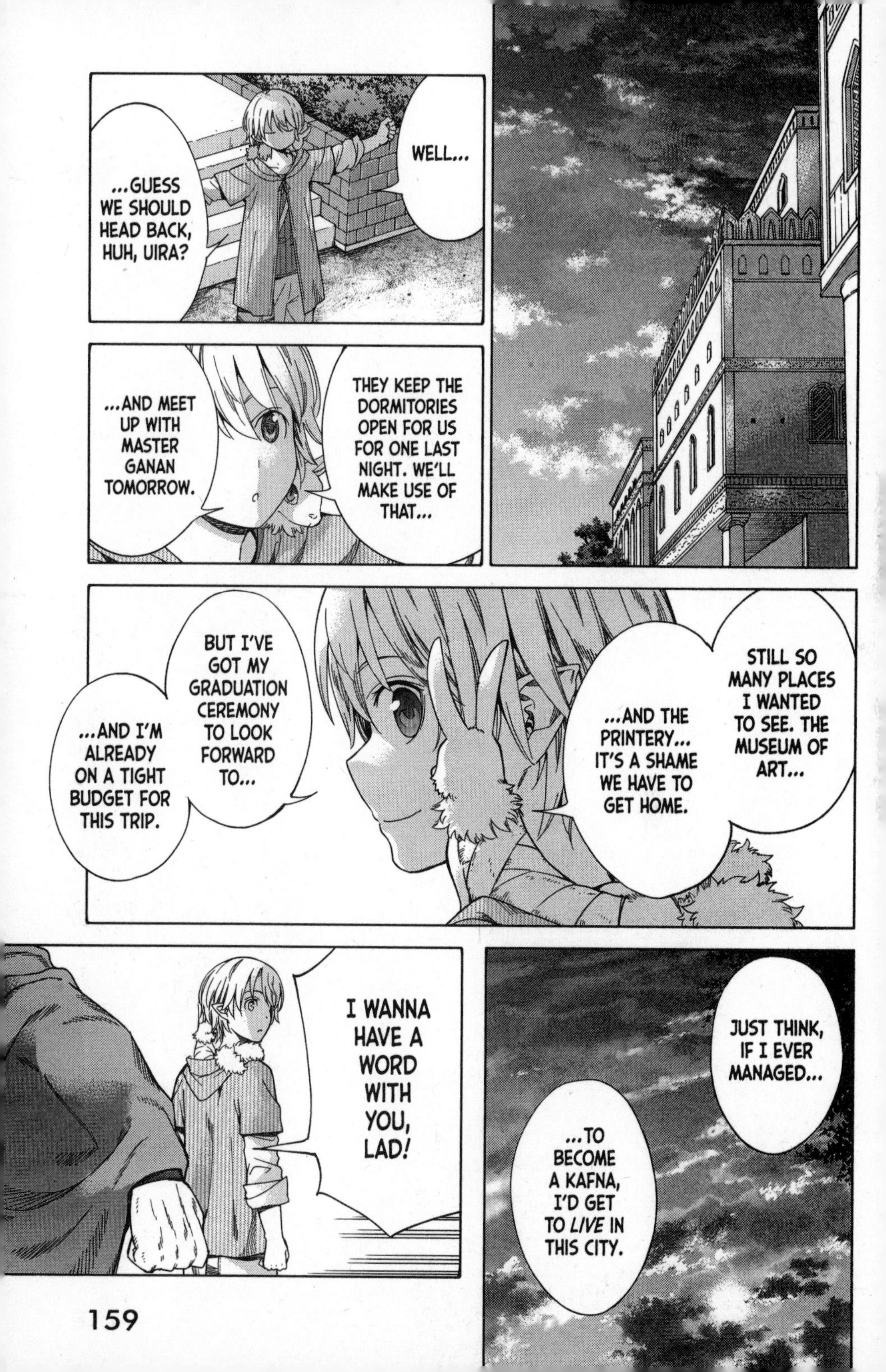
WELL...
...GUESS WE SHOULD HEAD BACK, HUH, UIRA?
THEY KEEP THE DORMITORIES OPEN FOR US FOR ONE LAST NIGHT. WE'LL MAKE USE OF THAT...
...AND MEET UP WITH MASTER GANAN TOMORROW.
STILL SO MANY PLACES I WANTED TO SEE. THE MUSEUM OF ART...
...AND THE PRINTERY... IT'S A SHAME WE HAVE TO GET HOME.
BUT I'VE GOT MY GRADUATION CEREMONY TO LOOK FORWARD TO...
...AND I'M ALREADY ON A TIGHT BUDGET FOR THIS TRIP.
JUST THINK, IF I EVER MANAGED...
...TO BECOME A KAFNA, I'D GET TO *LIVE* IN THIS CITY.
I WANNA HAVE A WORD WITH YOU, LAD!

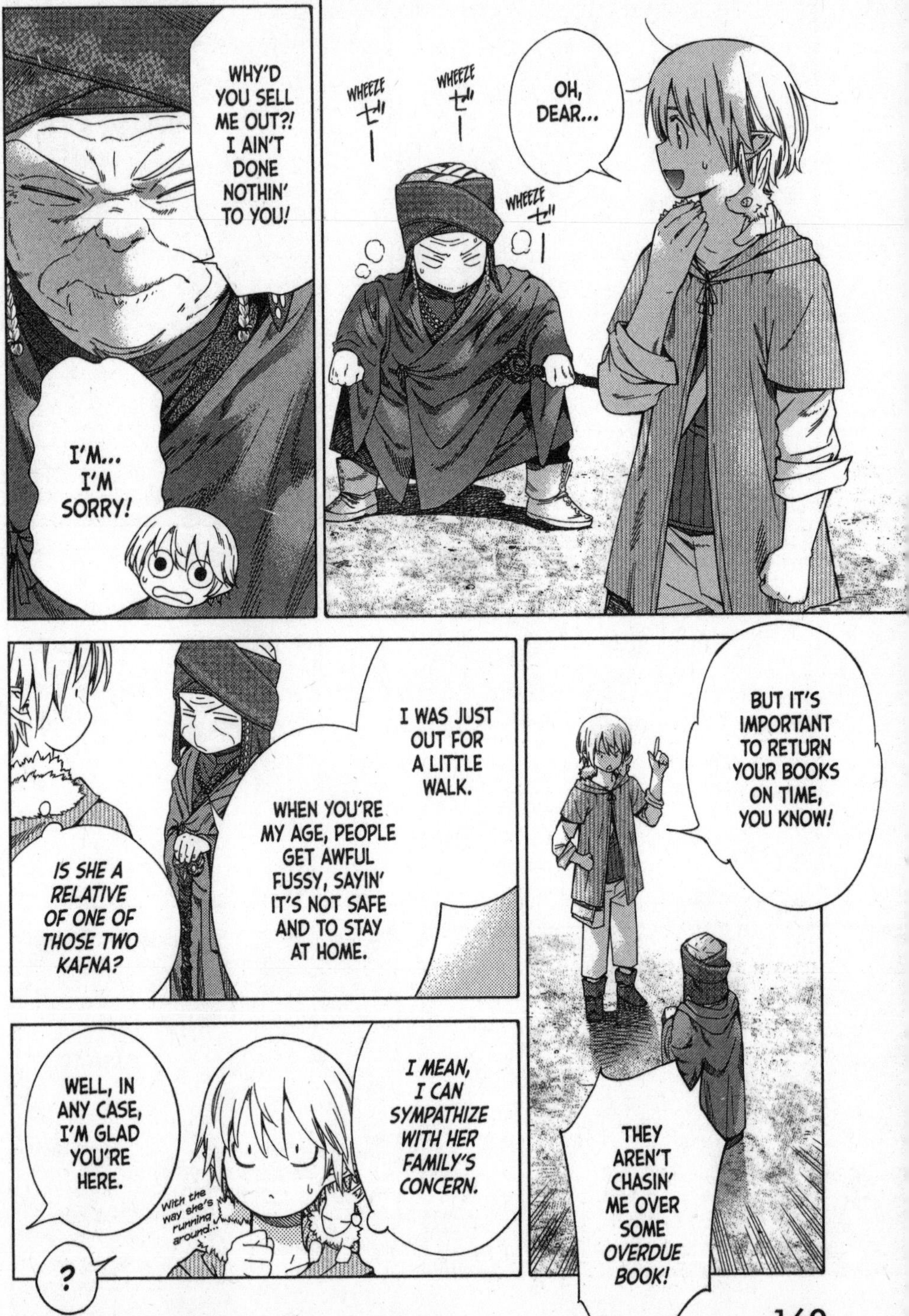
WHEEZE ゼー
WHEEZE ゼー
OH, DEAR...
WHEEZE ゼー
WHY'D YOU SELL ME OUT?! I AIN'T DONE NOTHIN' TO YOU!
I'M... I'M SORRY!
BUT IT'S IMPORTANT TO RETURN YOUR BOOKS ON TIME, YOU KNOW!
THEY AREN'T CHASIN' ME OVER SOME OVERDUE BOOK!
I WAS JUST OUT FOR A LITTLE WALK.
WHEN YOU'RE MY AGE, PEOPLE GET AWFUL FUSSY, SAYIN' IT'S NOT SAFE AND TO STAY AT HOME.
IS SHE A RELATIVE OF ONE OF THOSE TWO KAFNA?
I MEAN, I CAN SYMPATHIZE WITH HER FAMILY'S CONCERN.
With the way she's running around...
WELL, IN ANY CASE, I'M GLAD YOU'RE HERE.
?

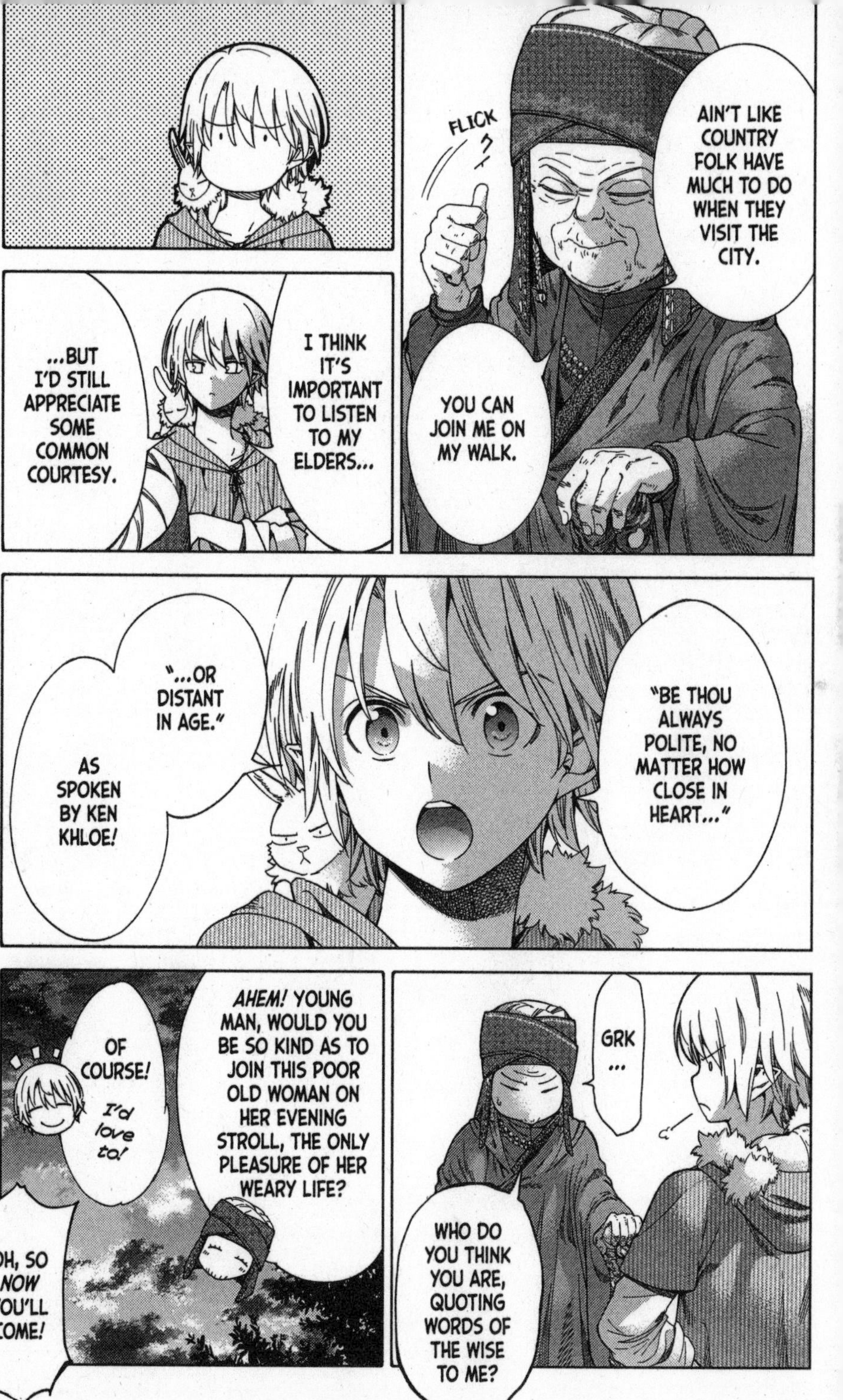
AIN'T LIKE COUNTRY FOLK HAVE MUCH TO DO WHEN THEY VISIT THE CITY.
FLICK
YOU CAN JOIN ME ON MY WALK.
I THINK IT'S IMPORTANT TO LISTEN TO MY ELDERS...
...BUT I'D STILL APPRECIATE SOME COMMON COURTESY.
"BE THOU ALWAYS POLITE, NO MATTER HOW CLOSE IN HEART..."
"...OR DISTANT IN AGE."
AS SPOKEN BY KEN KHLOE!
GRK ...
WHO DO YOU THINK YOU ARE, QUOTING WORDS OF THE WISE TO ME?
AHEM! YOUNG MAN, WOULD YOU BE SO KIND AS TO JOIN THIS POOR OLD WOMAN ON HER EVENING STROLL, THE ONLY PLEASURE OF HER WEARY LIFE?
OF COURSE!
I'd love to!
OH, SO *NOW* YOU'LL COME!

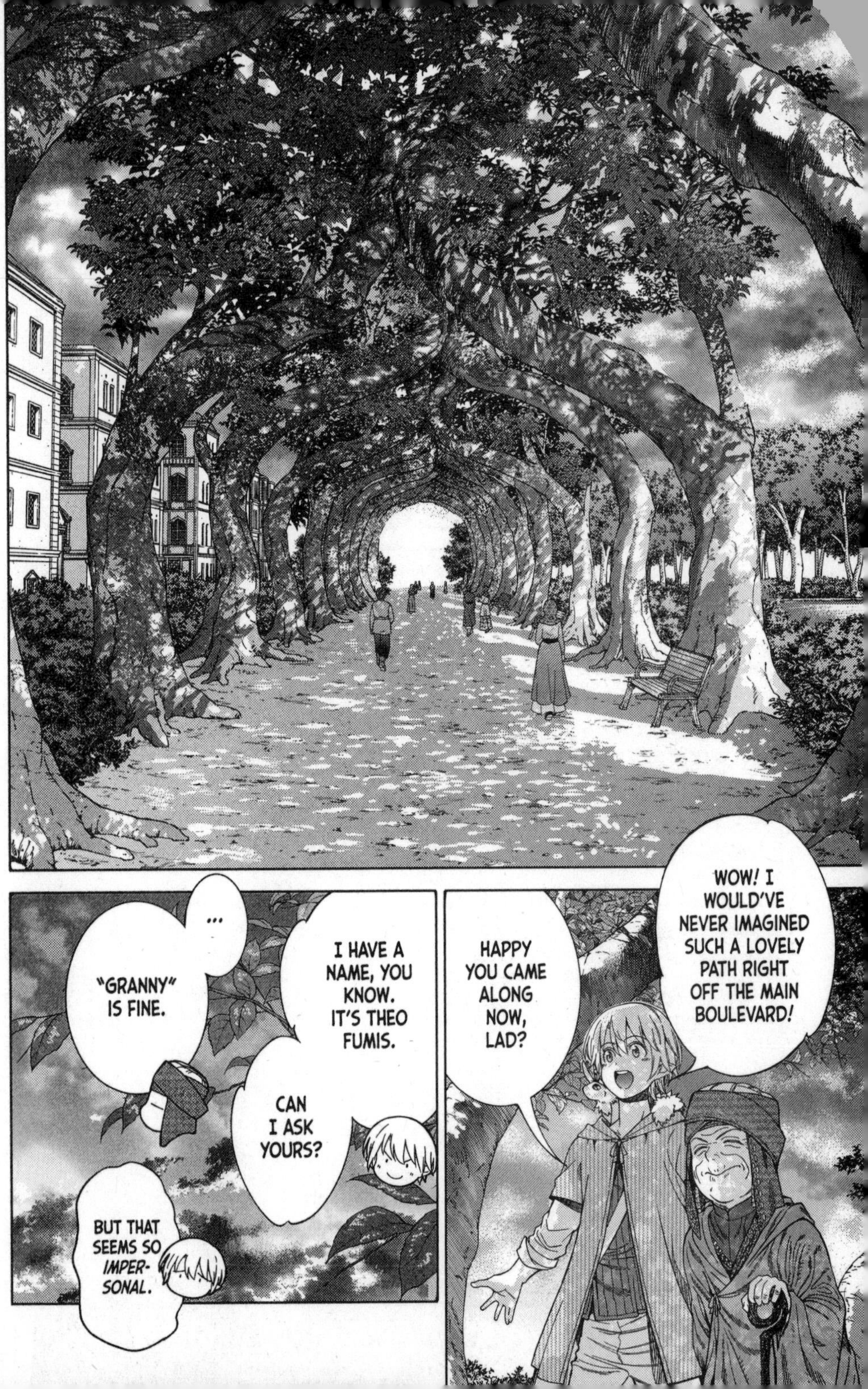
WOW! I WOULD'VE NEVER IMAGINED SUCH A LOVELY PATH RIGHT OFF THE MAIN BOULEVARD!
HAPPY YOU CAME ALONG NOW, LAD?
I HAVE A NAME, YOU KNOW. IT'S THEO FUMIS.
CAN I ASK YOURS?
...
"GRANNY" IS FINE.
BUT THAT SEEMS SO IMPERSONAL.

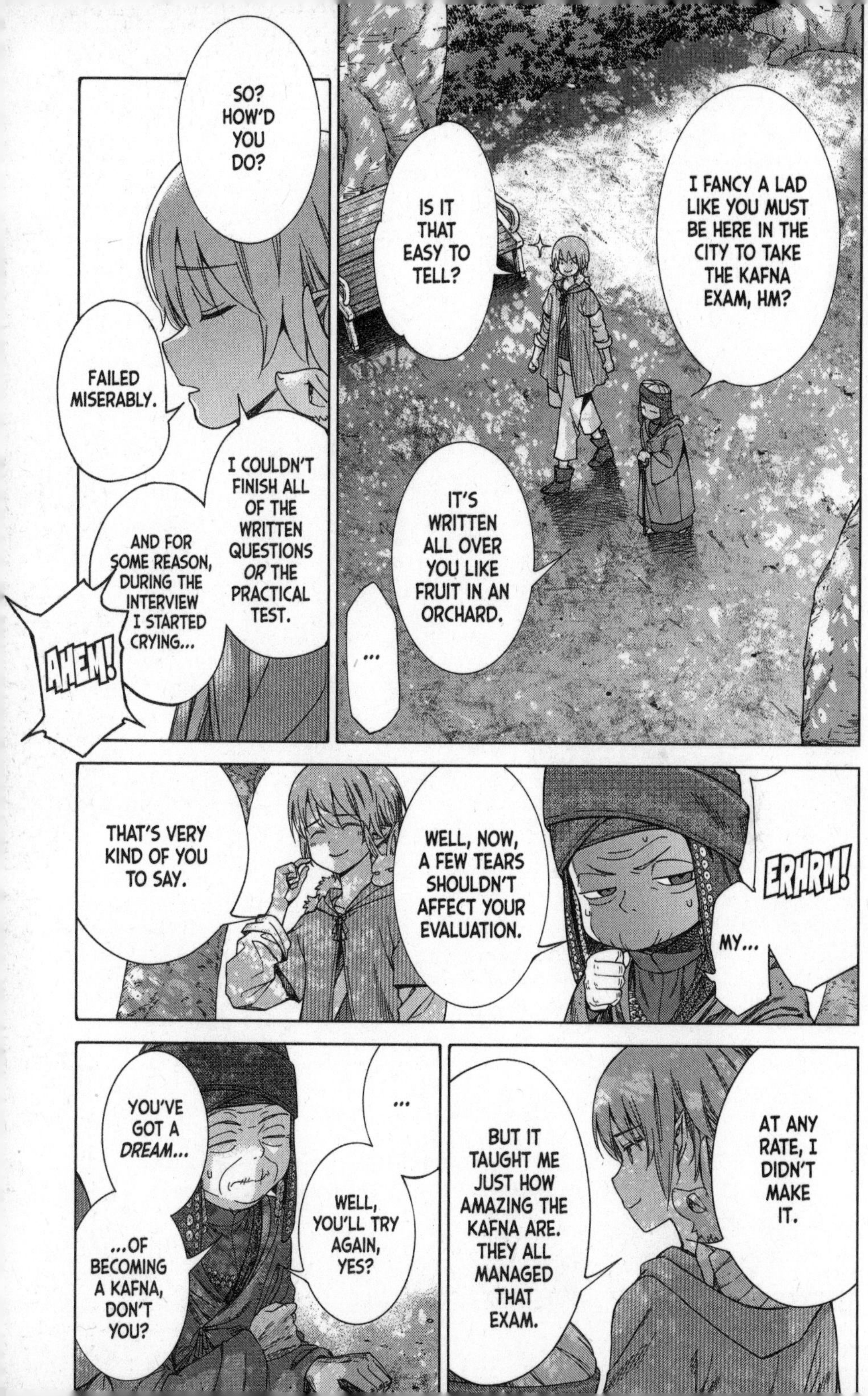
I FANCY A LAD LIKE YOU MUST BE HERE IN THE CITY TO TAKE THE KAFNA EXAM, HM?
IS IT THAT EASY TO TELL?
IT'S WRITTEN ALL OVER YOU LIKE FRUIT IN AN ORCHARD.
...
SO? HOW'D YOU DO?
FAILED MISERABLY.
I COULDN'T FINISH ALL OF THE WRITTEN QUESTIONS *OR* THE PRACTICAL TEST.
AND FOR SOME REASON, DURING THE INTERVIEW I STARTED CRYING...
AHEM!
ERHRM!
MY...
WELL, NOW, A FEW TEARS SHOULDN'T AFFECT YOUR EVALUATION.
THAT'S VERY KIND OF YOU TO SAY.
AT ANY RATE, I DIDN'T MAKE IT.
BUT IT TAUGHT ME JUST HOW AMAZING THE KAFNA ARE. THEY ALL MANAGED THAT EXAM.
...
WELL, YOU'LL TRY AGAIN, YES?
YOU'VE GOT A *DREAM*...
...OF BECOMING A KAFNA, DON'T YOU?

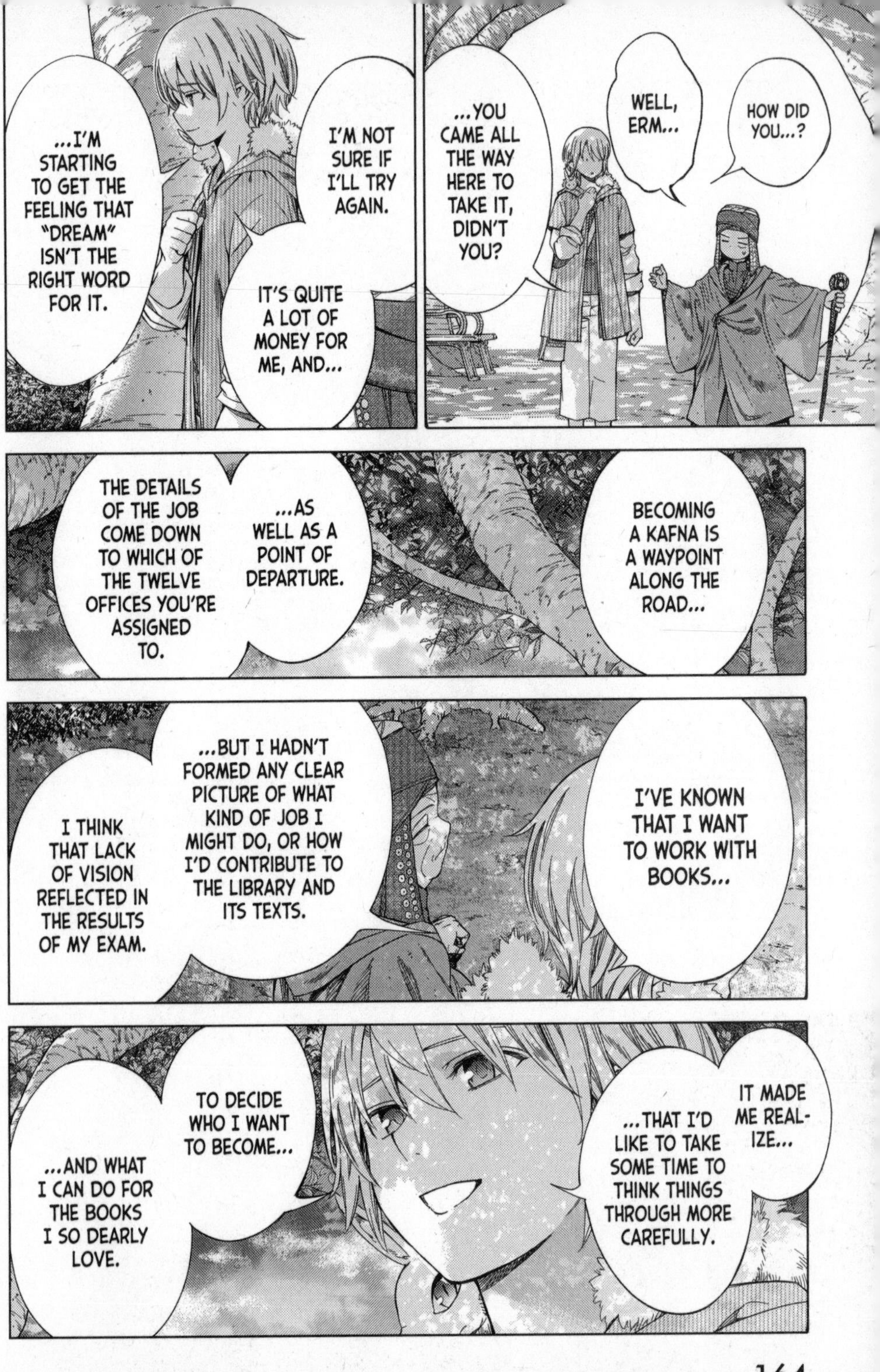
HOW DID YOU...?
WELL, ERM...
...YOU CAME ALL THE WAY HERE TO TAKE IT, DIDN'T YOU?
I'M NOT SURE IF I'LL TRY AGAIN.
IT'S QUITE A LOT OF MONEY FOR ME, AND...
...I'M STARTING TO GET THE FEELING THAT "DREAM" ISN'T THE RIGHT WORD FOR IT.
BECOMING A KAFNA IS A WAYPOINT ALONG THE ROAD...
...AS WELL AS A POINT OF DEPARTURE.
THE DETAILS OF THE JOB COME DOWN TO WHICH OF THE TWELVE OFFICES YOU'RE ASSIGNED TO.
I'VE KNOWN THAT I WANT TO WORK WITH BOOKS...
...BUT I HADN'T FORMED ANY CLEAR PICTURE OF WHAT KIND OF JOB I MIGHT DO, OR HOW I'D CONTRIBUTE TO THE LIBRARY AND ITS TEXTS.
I THINK THAT LACK OF VISION REFLECTED IN THE RESULTS OF MY EXAM.
IT MADE ME REAL-IZE...
...THAT I'D LIKE TO TAKE SOME TIME TO THINK THINGS THROUGH MORE CAREFULLY.
TO DECIDE WHO I WANT TO BECOME...
...AND WHAT I CAN DO FOR THE BOOKS I SO DEARLY LOVE.

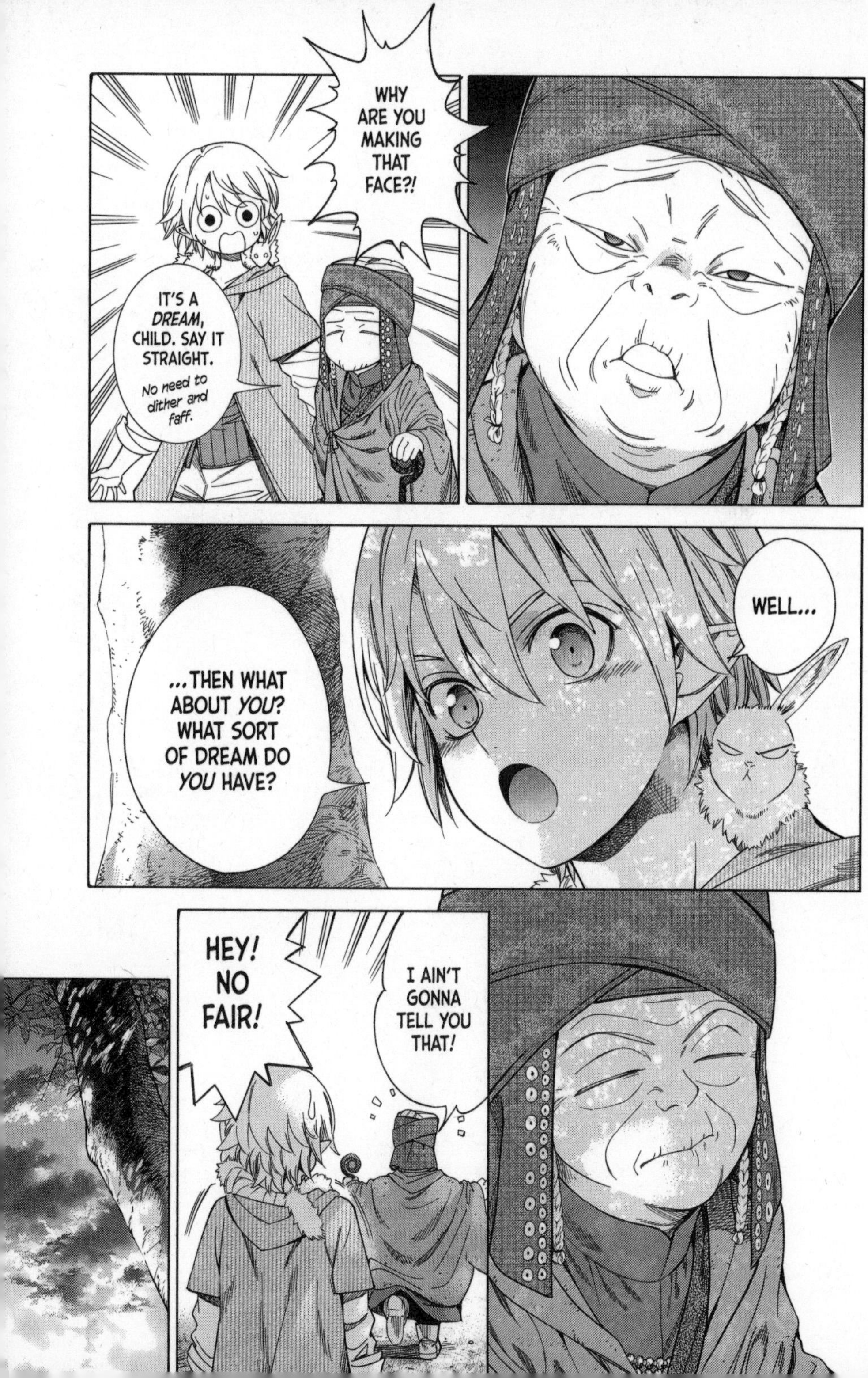
WHY ARE YOU MAKING THAT FACE?!
IT'S A *DREAM*, CHILD. SAY IT STRAIGHT.
No need to dither and faff.
WELL...
...THEN WHAT ABOUT *YOU*? WHAT SORT OF DREAM DO *YOU* HAVE?
I AIN'T GONNA TELL YOU THAT!
HEY! NO FAIR!

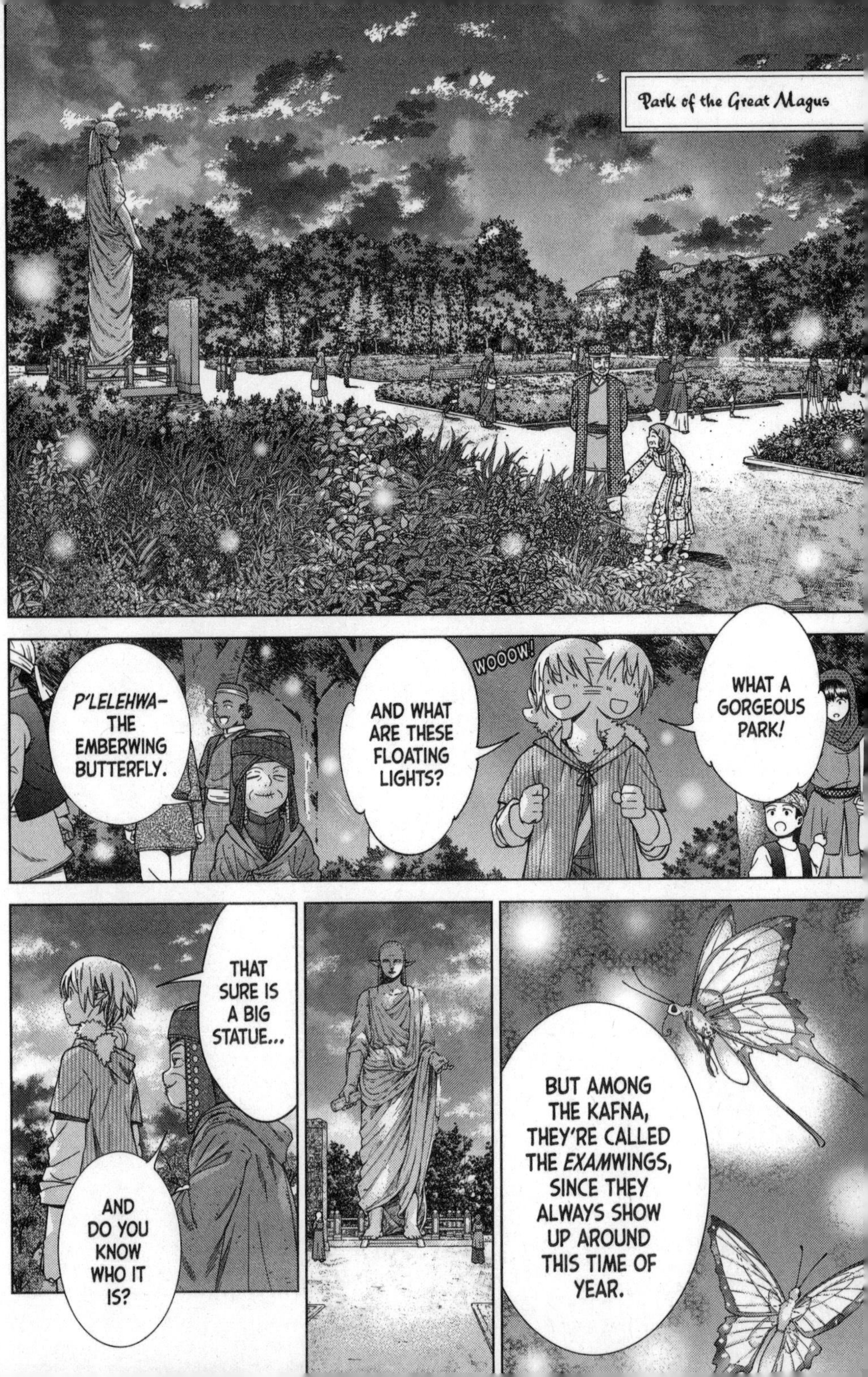
Park of the Great Magus
WHAT A GORGEOUS PARK!
WOOOW!
AND WHAT ARE THESE FLOATING LIGHTS?
P'LELEHWA— THE EMBERWING BUTTERFLY.
BUT AMONG THE KAFNA, THEY'RE CALLED THE *EXAM*WINGS, SINCE THEY ALWAYS SHOW UP AROUND THIS TIME OF YEAR.
THAT SURE IS A BIG STATUE...
AND DO YOU KNOW WHO IT IS?

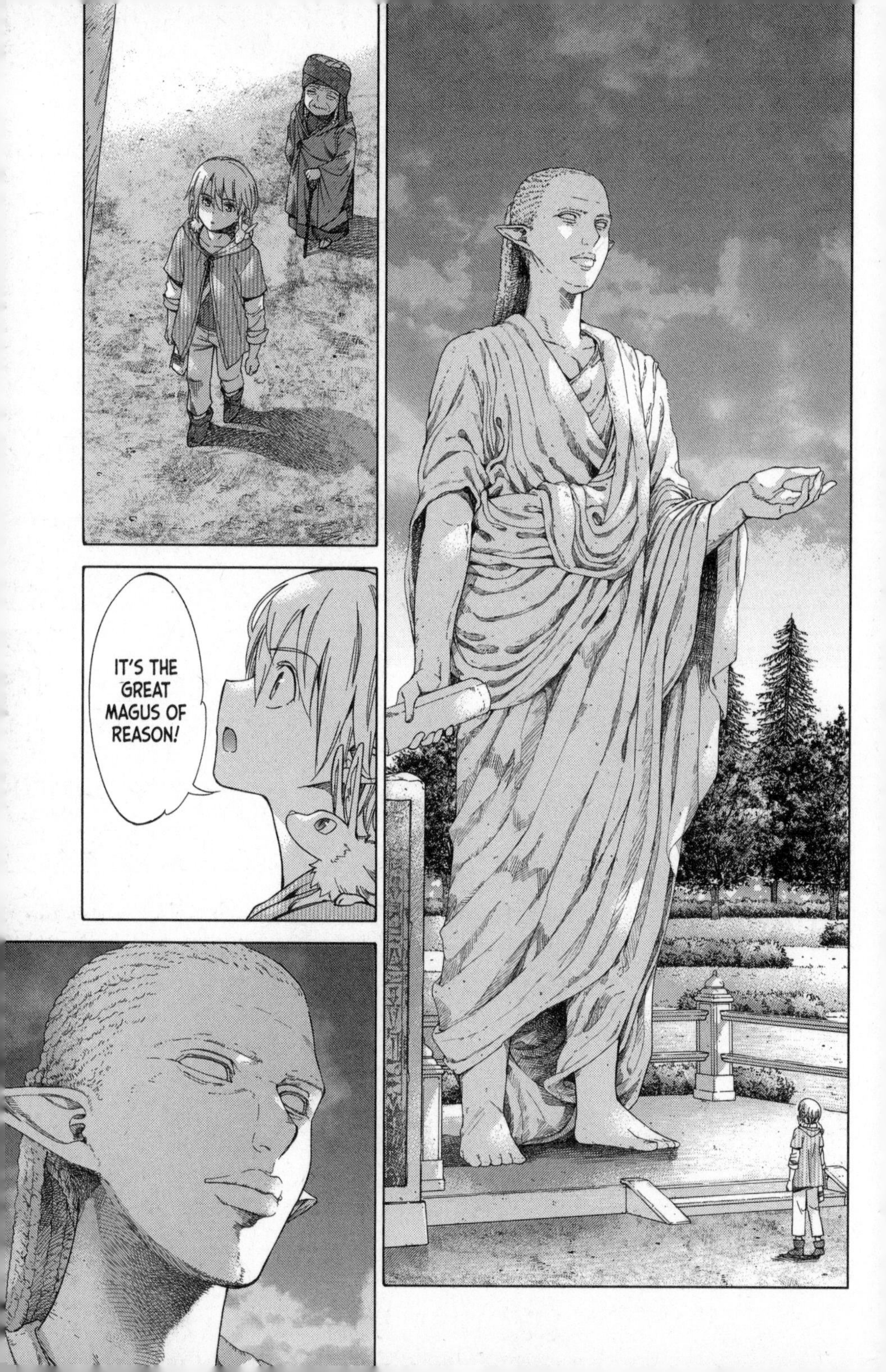
IT'S THE GREAT MAGUS OF REASON!

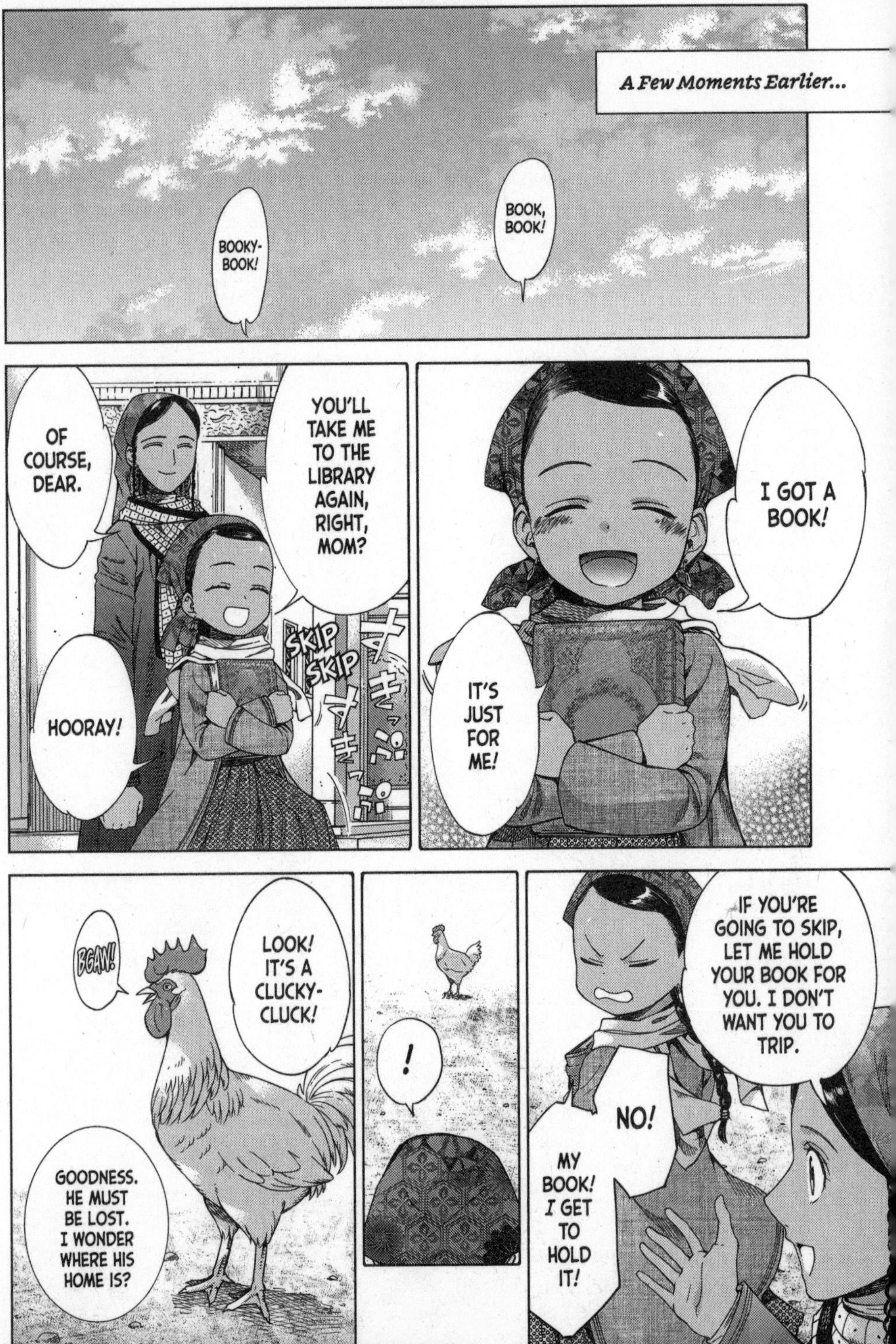
A Few Moments Earlier...
BOOK, BOOK!
BOOKY-BOOK!
I GOT A BOOK!
IT'S JUST FOR ME!
YOU'LL TAKE ME TO THE LIBRARY AGAIN, RIGHT, MOM?
SKIP SKIP
OF COURSE, DEAR.
HOORAY!
IF YOU'RE GOING TO SKIP, LET ME HOLD YOUR BOOK FOR YOU. I DON'T WANT YOU TO TRIP.
NO!
MY BOOK! I GET TO HOLD IT!
!
LOOK! IT'S A CLUCKY-CLUCK!
BGAW!
GOODNESS. HE MUST BE LOST. I WONDER WHERE HIS HOME IS?

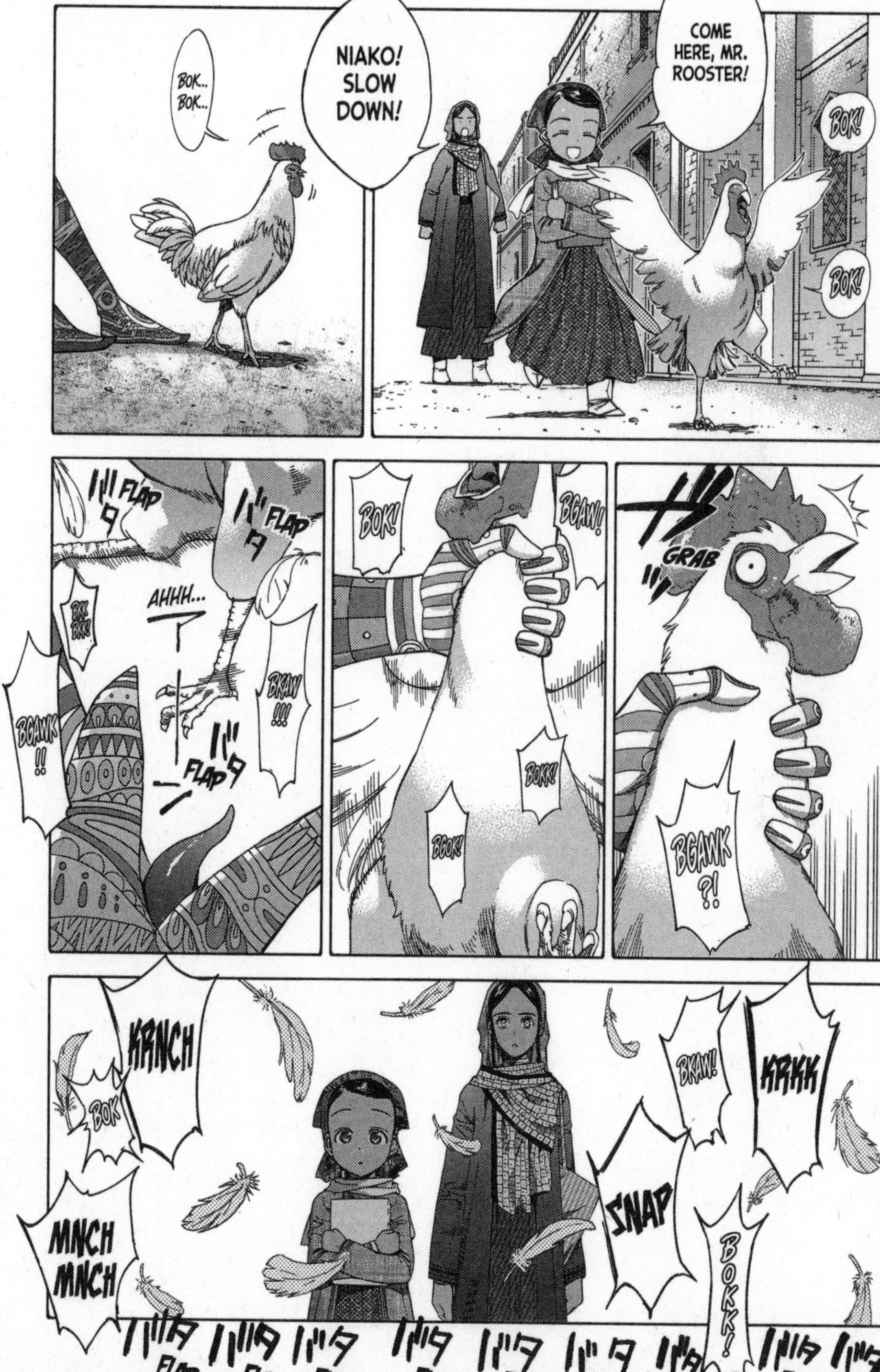

COME HERE, MR. ROOSTER!
BOK!
BOK!
NIAKO! SLOW DOWN!
BOK.. BOK..
GRAB
BGAWK ?!
BGAW!
BOK!
BOKK!
BOOK!
FLAP
FLAP
AHHH...
BKK BKK
BKAW !!!
FLAP
BGAWK !!
KRKK
BKAW!
BOKK!
SNAP
KRNCH
BOK
MNCH MNCH
FLAP FLAP FLAP FLAP FLAP FLAP FLAP FLAP FLAP

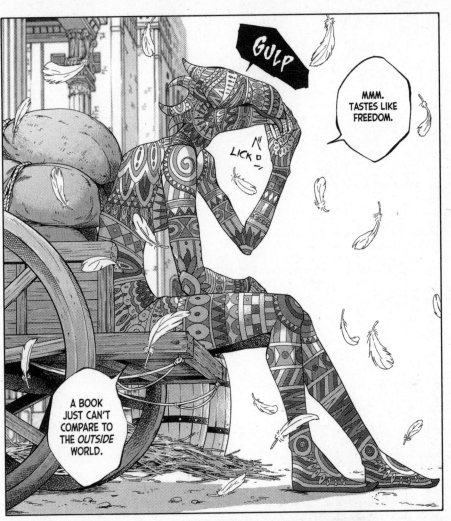

GULP

MMM. TASTES LIKE FREEDOM.

LICK

A BOOK JUST CAN'T COMPARE TO THE *OUTSIDE* WORLD.

CLUTCH... ...

WOULDN'T YOU AGREE?

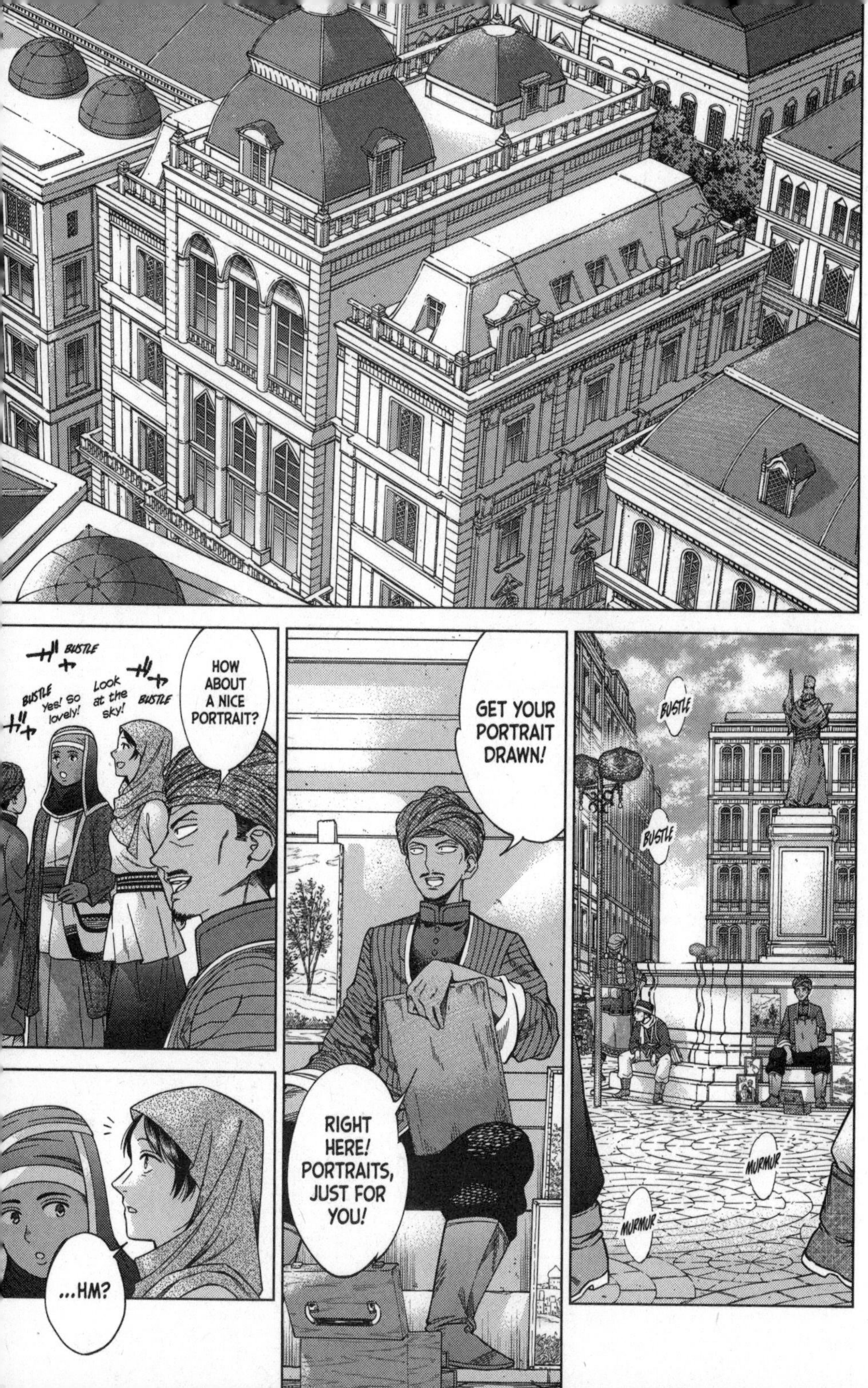
BUSTLE
BUSTLE
MURMUR
MURMUR
GET YOUR PORTRAIT DRAWN!
RIGHT HERE! PORTRAITS, JUST FOR YOU!
BUSTLE
HOW ABOUT A NICE PORTRAIT?
BUSTLE
Look at the sky!
Yes! So lovely!
BUSTLE
...HM?

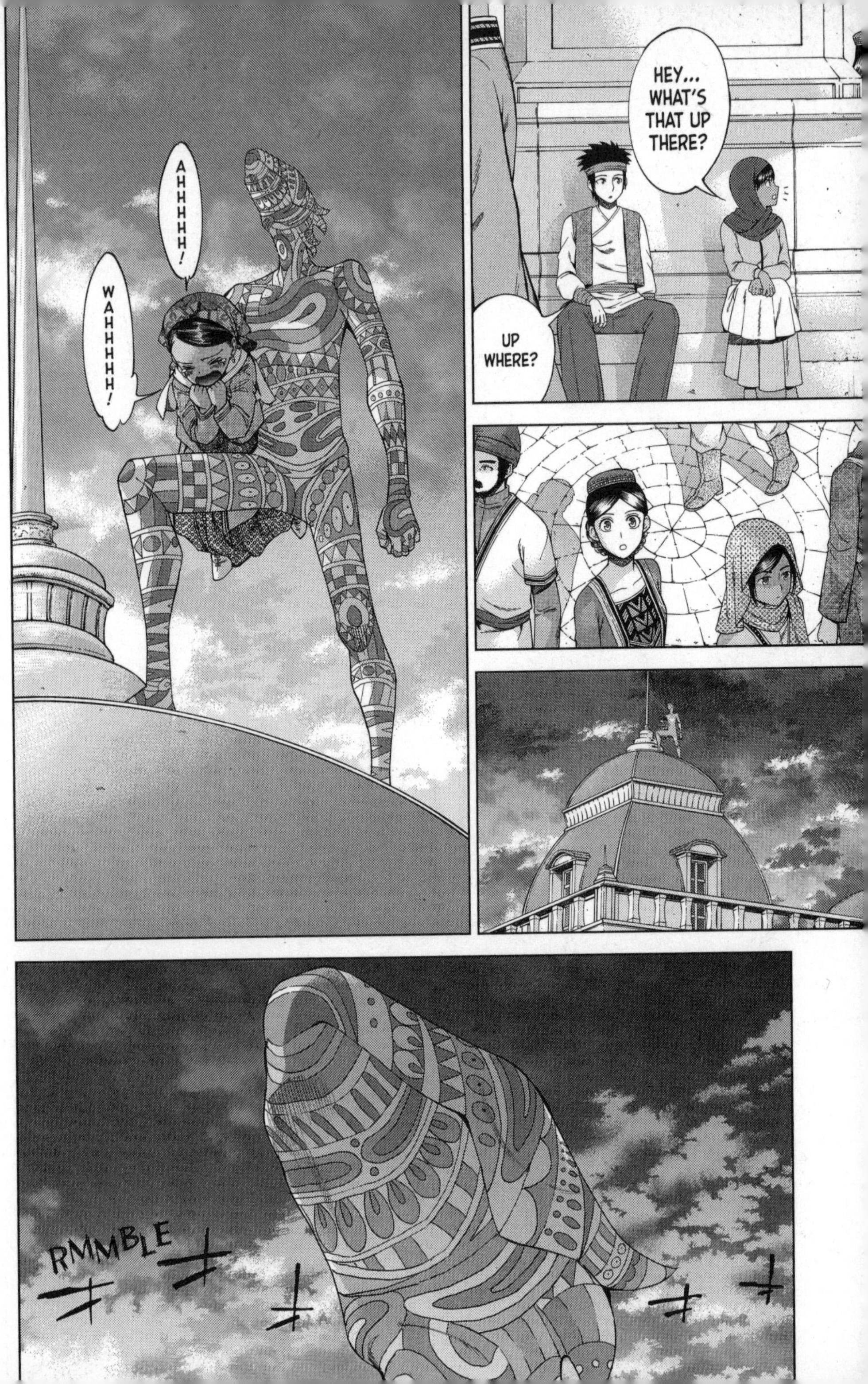
HEY... WHAT'S THAT UP THERE?
UP WHERE?
AHHHHHH!
WAHHHHHH!
RMMBLE

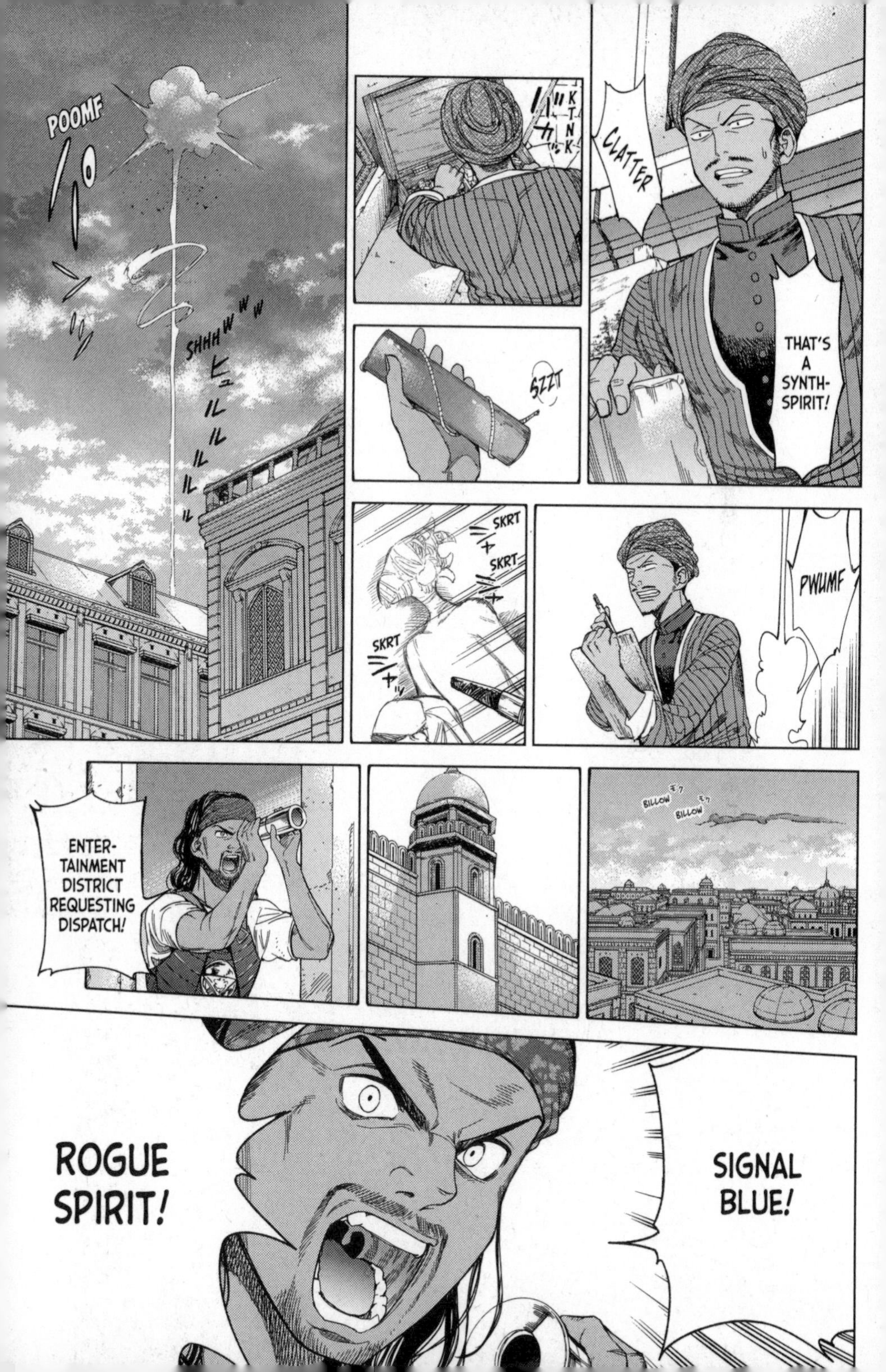
CLATTER
THAT'S A SYNTH-SPIRIT!
KTNK
SZZT
PWUMF
SKRT
SKRT
SKRT
POOMF
SHHHWWW
BILLOW
BILLOW
ENTER-TAINMENT DISTRICT REQUESTING DISPATCH!
SIGNAL BLUE!
ROGUE SPIRIT!

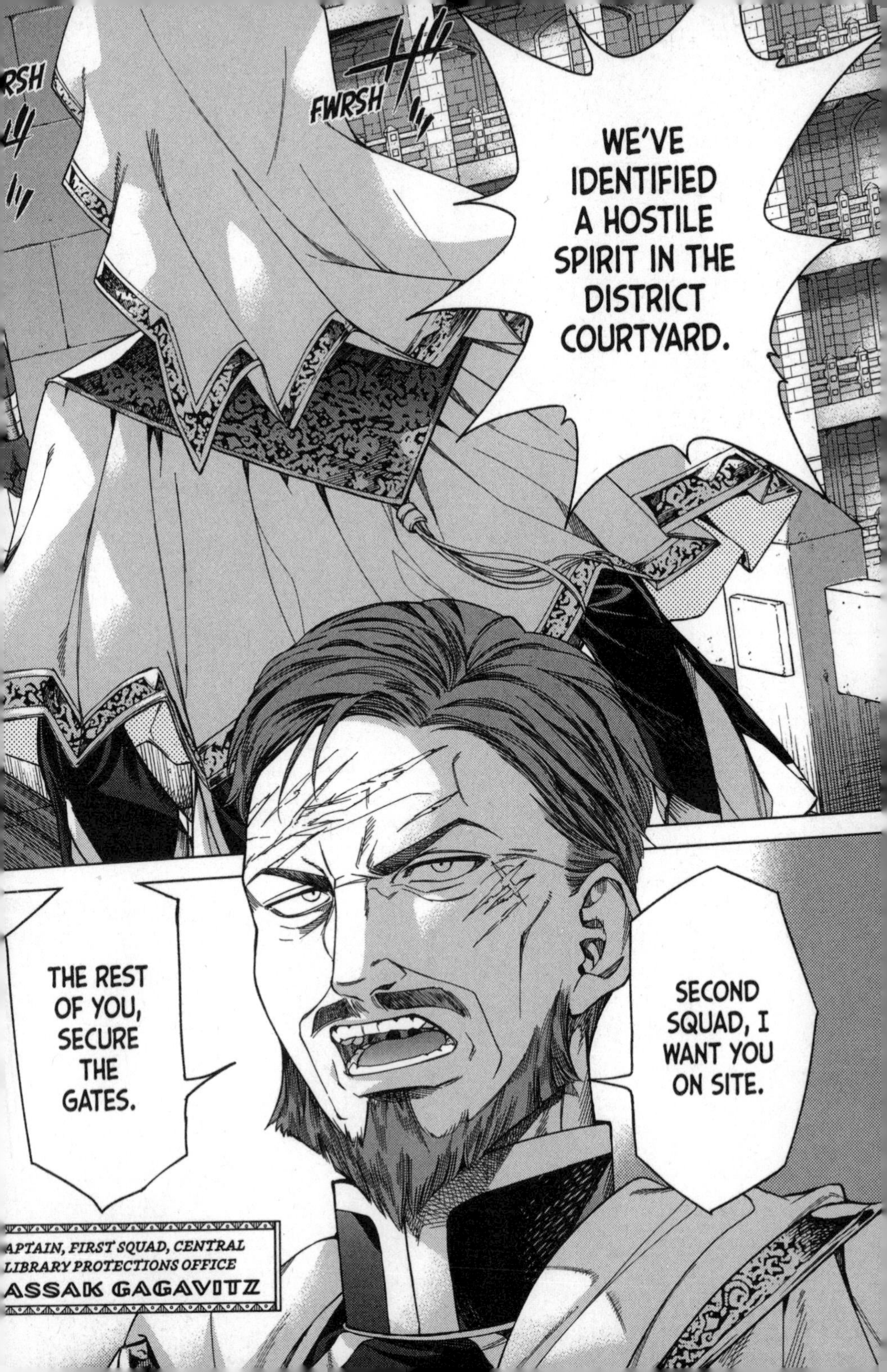
FWRSH
WE'VE IDENTIFIED A HOSTILE SPIRIT IN THE DISTRICT COURTYARD.
SECOND SQUAD, I WANT YOU ON SITE.
THE REST OF YOU, SECURE THE GATES.
APTAIN, FIRST SQUAD, CENTRAL LIBRARY PROTECTIONS OFFICE
ASSAK GAGAVITZ

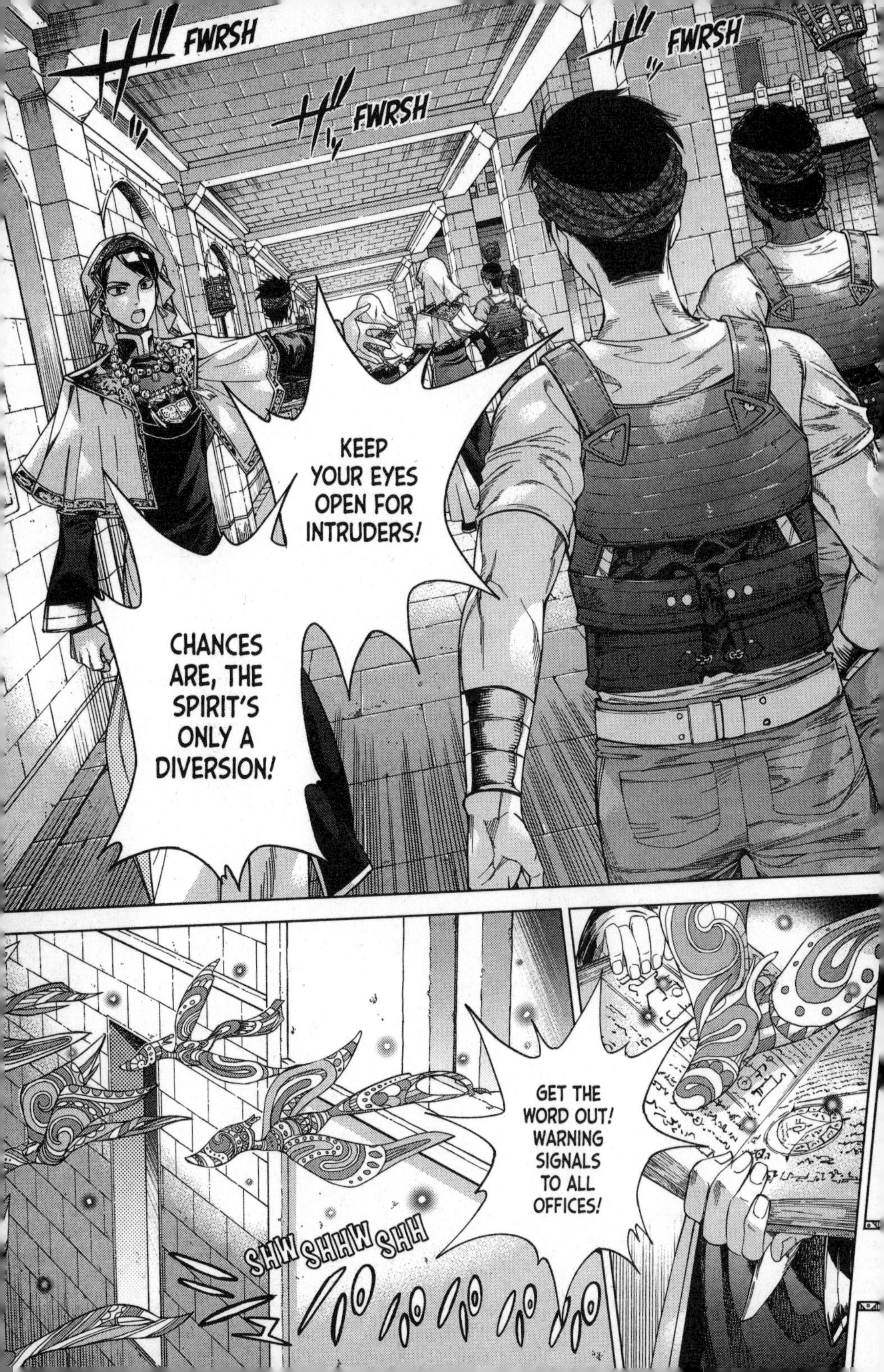
FWRSH
FWRSH
FWRSH
KEEP YOUR EYES OPEN FOR INTRUDERS!
CHANCES ARE, THE SPIRIT'S ONLY A DIVERSION!
GET THE WORD OUT! WARNING SIGNALS TO ALL OFFICES!
SHW SHHW SHH

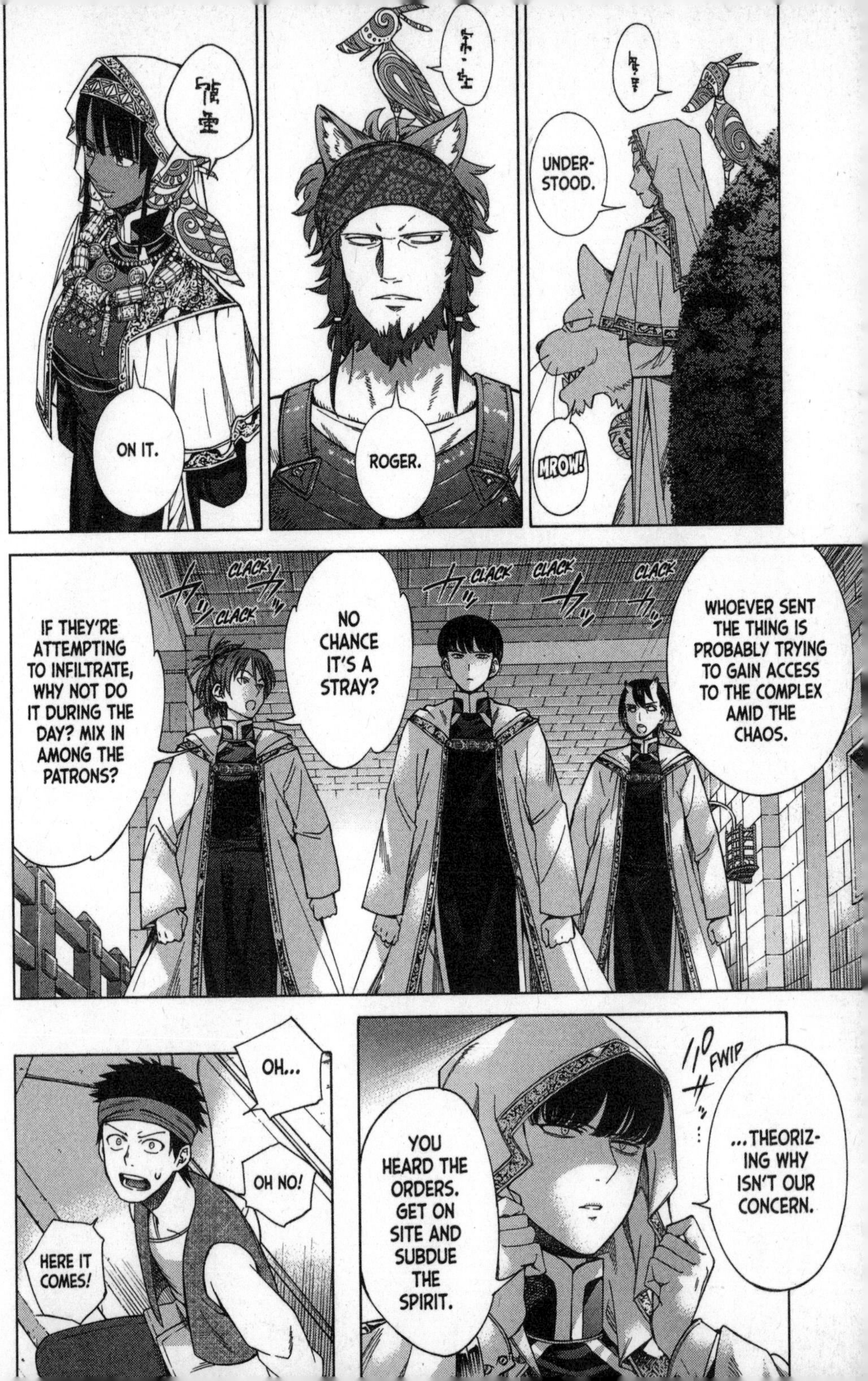
UNDER-
STOOD.
MROW!
ROGER.
ON IT.
CLACK
CLACK
CLACK
CLACK
CLACK
WHOEVER SENT THE THING IS PROBABLY TRYING TO GAIN ACCESS TO THE COMPLEX AMID THE CHAOS.
NO CHANCE IT'S A STRAY?
IF THEY'RE ATTEMPTING TO INFILTRATE, WHY NOT DO IT DURING THE DAY? MIX IN AMONG THE PATRONS?
FWIP
...THEORIZ-
ING WHY ISN'T OUR CONCERN.
YOU HEARD THE ORDERS. GET ON SITE AND SUBDUE THE SPIRIT.
OH...
OH NO!
HERE IT COMES!

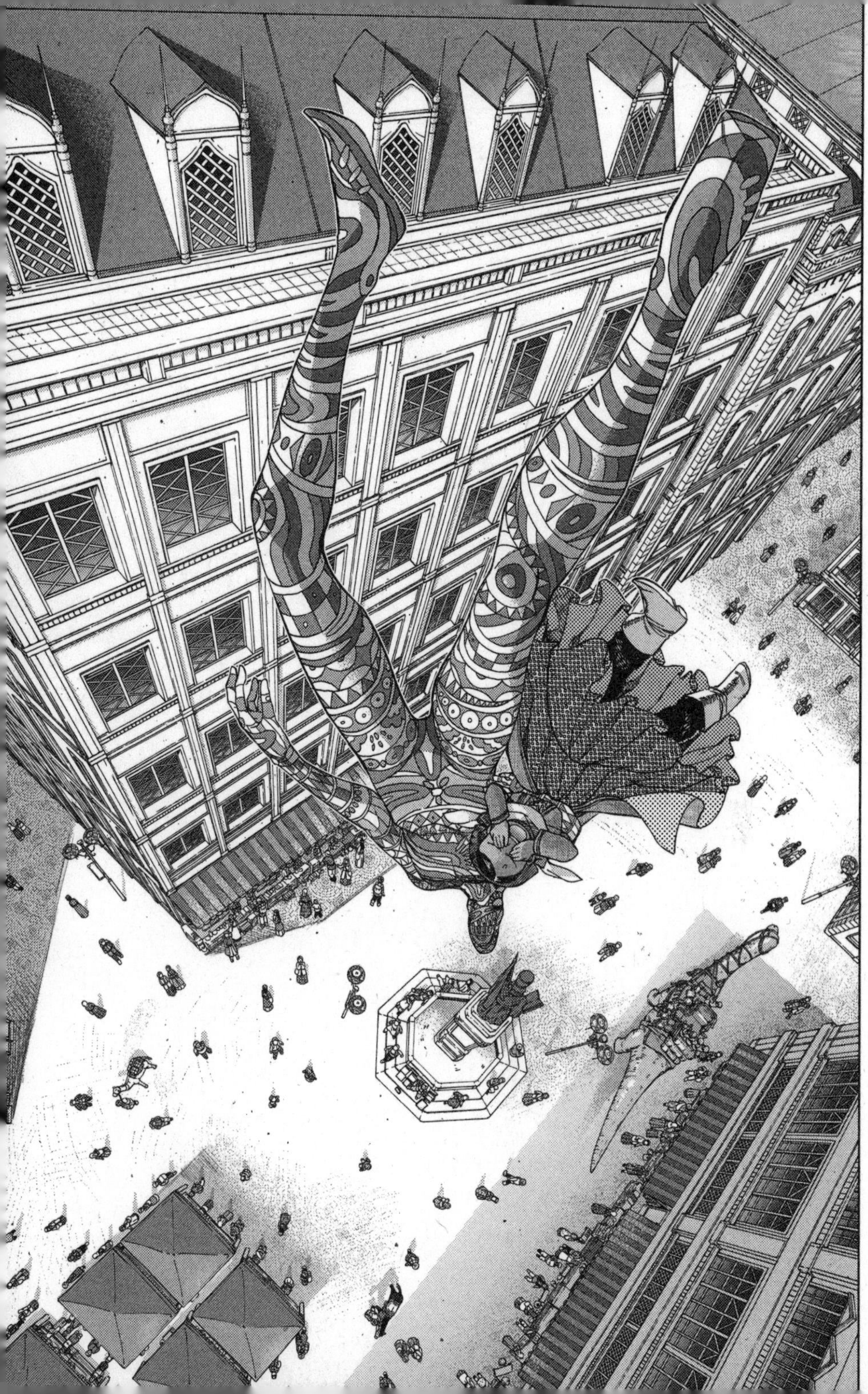

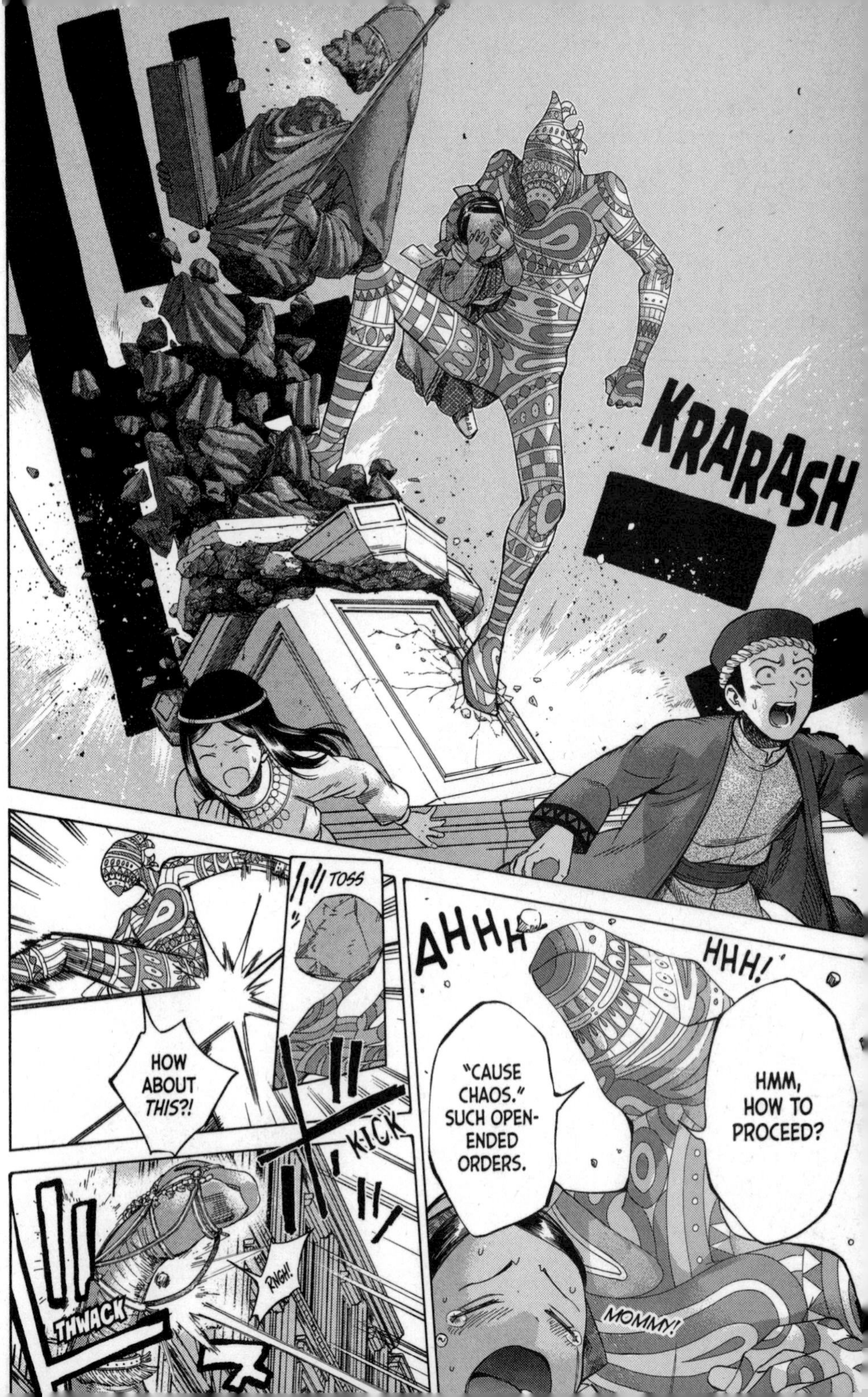
KRARASH
AHHHHHH!
HMM, HOW TO PROCEED?
"CAUSE CHAOS." SUCH OPEN-ENDED ORDERS.
MOMMY!
TOSS
HOW ABOUT THIS?!
KICK
RNGH!
THWACK

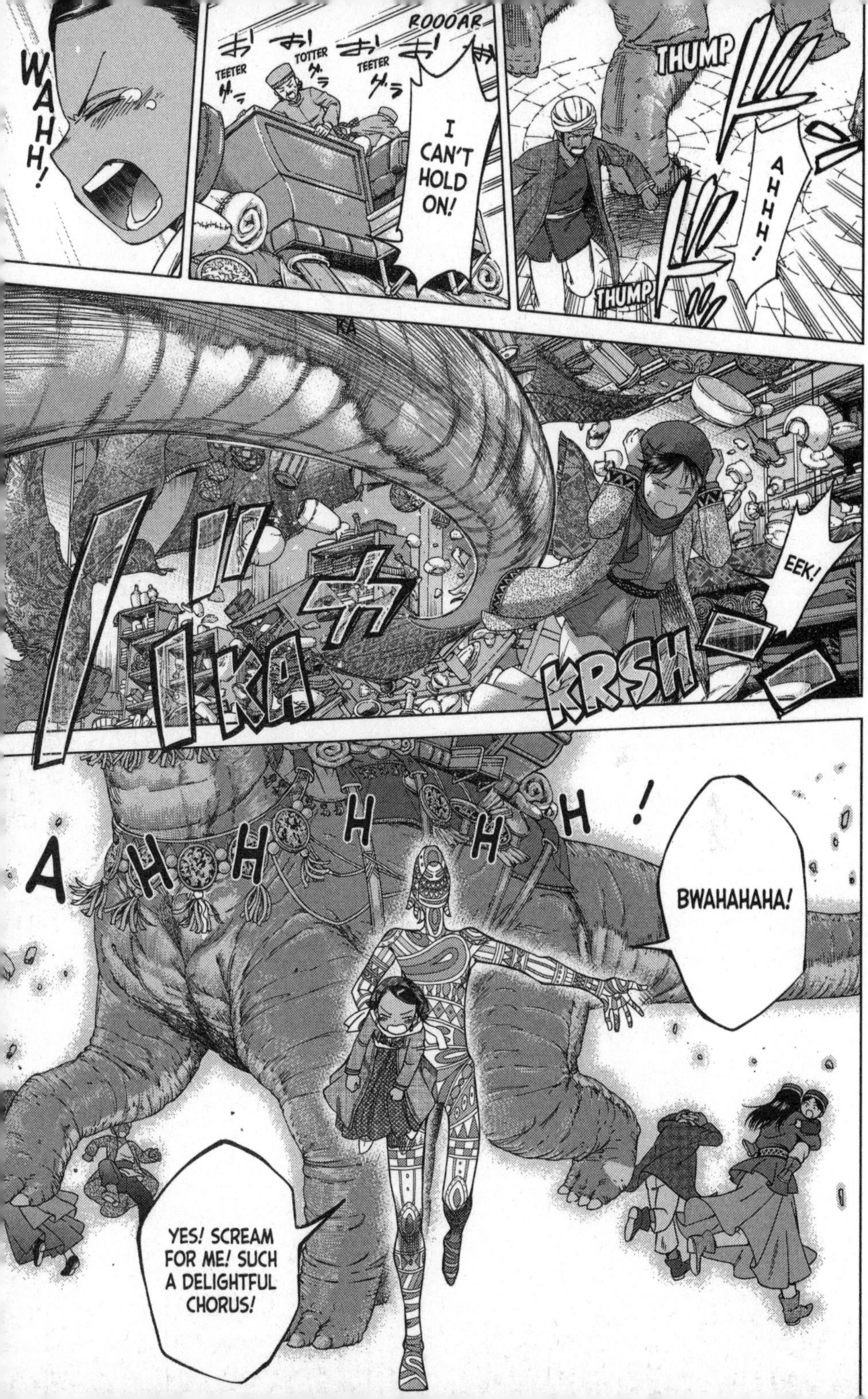
THUMP
AHHHH!
THUMP
ROOOAR
TEETER
TOTTER
TEETER
I CAN'T HOLD ON!
WAHHH!
KA
EEK!
KRSH
KA
AHHHHH!
BWAHAHAHA!
YES! SCREAM FOR ME! SUCH A DELIGHTFUL CHORUS!

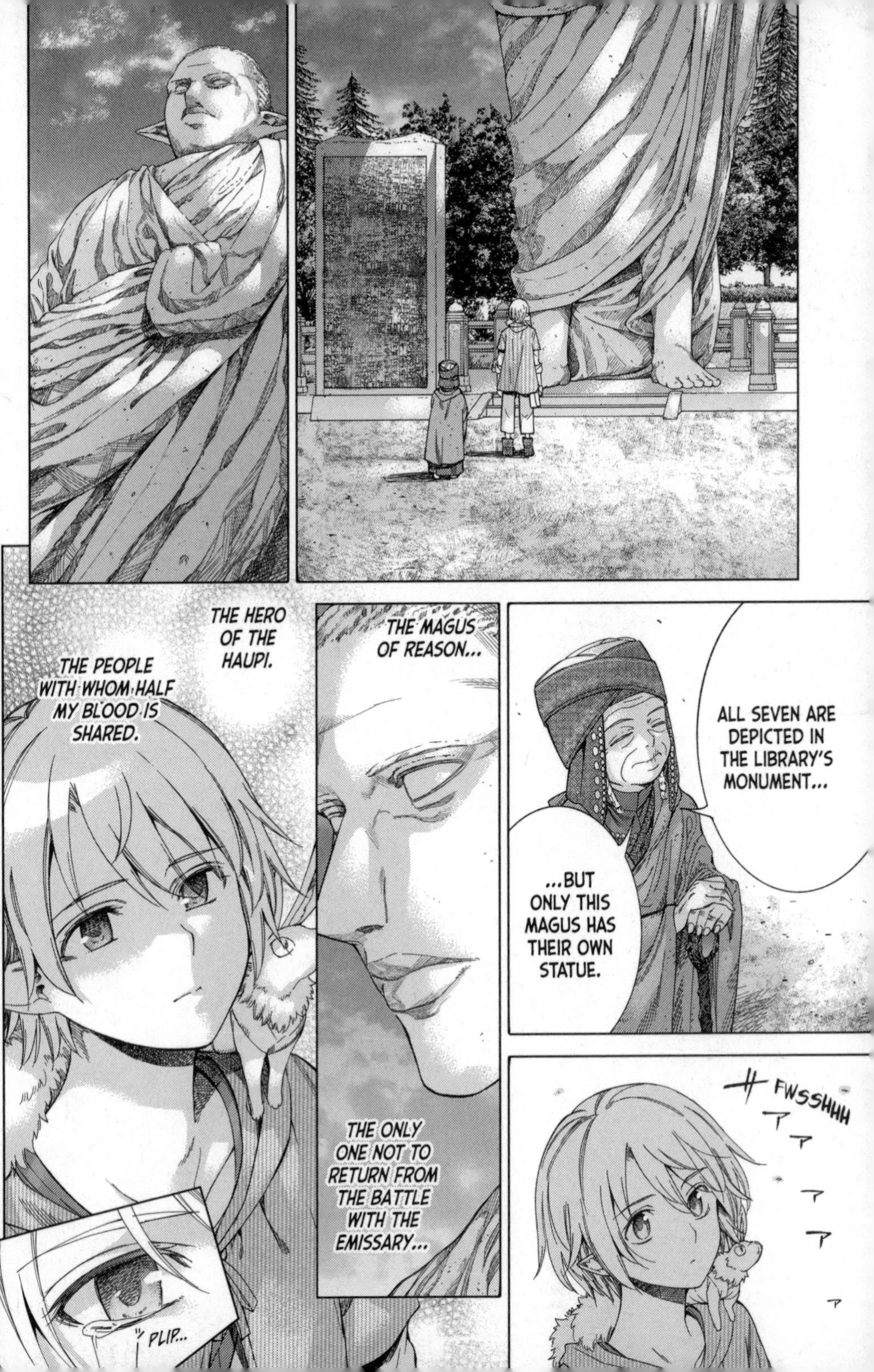
ALL SEVEN ARE DEPICTED IN THE LIBRARY'S MONUMENT...
...BUT ONLY THIS MAGUS HAS THEIR OWN STATUE.
FWSSHHH
THE MAGUS OF REASON...
THE ONLY ONE NOT TO RETURN FROM THE BATTLE WITH THE EMISSARY...
THE HERO OF THE HAUPI.
THE PEOPLE WITH WHOM HALF MY BLOOD IS SHARED.
PLIP...

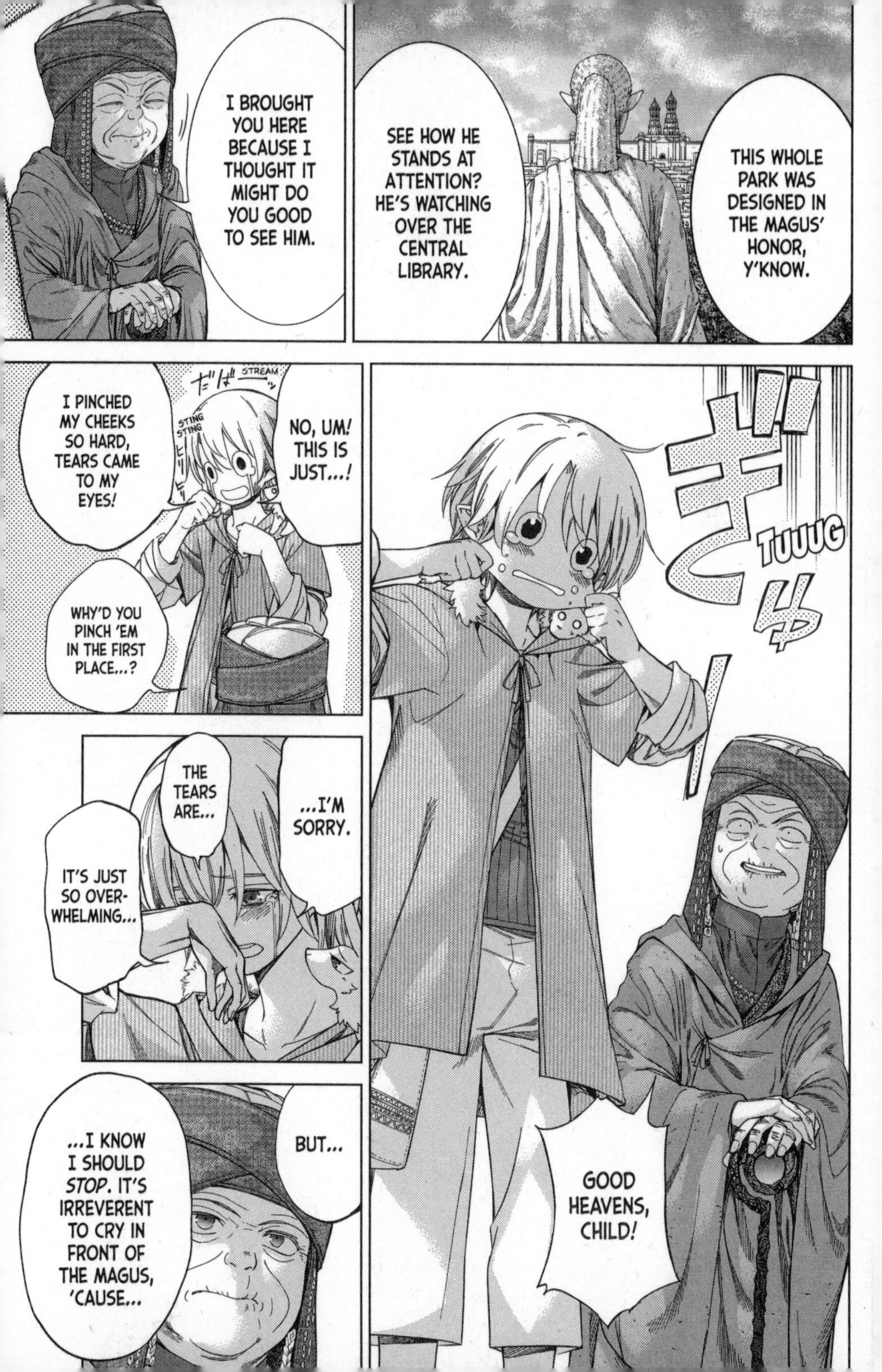
THIS WHOLE PARK WAS DESIGNED IN THE MAGUS' HONOR, Y'KNOW.
SEE HOW HE STANDS AT ATTENTION? HE'S WATCHING OVER THE CENTRAL LIBRARY.
I BROUGHT YOU HERE BECAUSE I THOUGHT IT MIGHT DO YOU GOOD TO SEE HIM.
TUUUG
GOOD HEAVENS, CHILD!
STREAM
NO, UM! THIS IS JUST...!
STING STING
I PINCHED MY CHEEKS SO HARD, TEARS CAME TO MY EYES!
WHY'D YOU PINCH 'EM IN THE FIRST PLACE...?
...I'M SORRY.
THE TEARS ARE...
IT'S JUST SO OVERWHELMING...
BUT...
...I KNOW I SHOULD STOP. IT'S IRREVERENT TO CRY IN FRONT OF THE MAGUS, 'CAUSE...

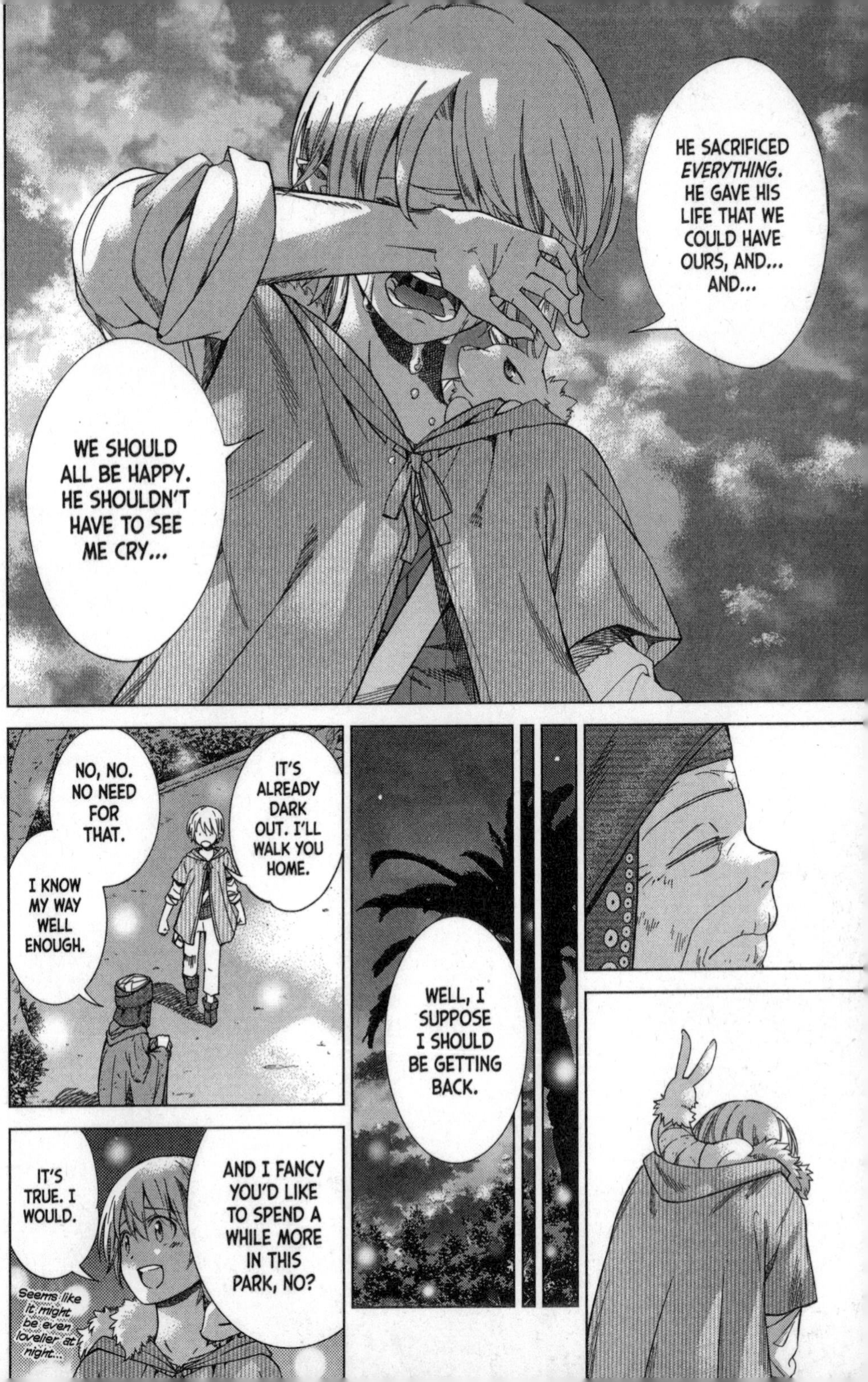
HE SACRIFICED *EVERYTHING*. HE GAVE HIS LIFE THAT WE COULD HAVE OURS, AND... AND...
WE SHOULD ALL BE HAPPY. HE SHOULDN'T HAVE TO SEE ME CRY...
WELL, I SUPPOSE I SHOULD BE GETTING BACK.
IT'S ALREADY DARK OUT. I'LL WALK YOU HOME.
NO, NO. NO NEED FOR THAT.
I KNOW MY WAY WELL ENOUGH.
AND I FANCY YOU'D LIKE TO SPEND A WHILE MORE IN THIS PARK, NO?
IT'S TRUE. I WOULD.
Seems like it might be even lovelier at night...

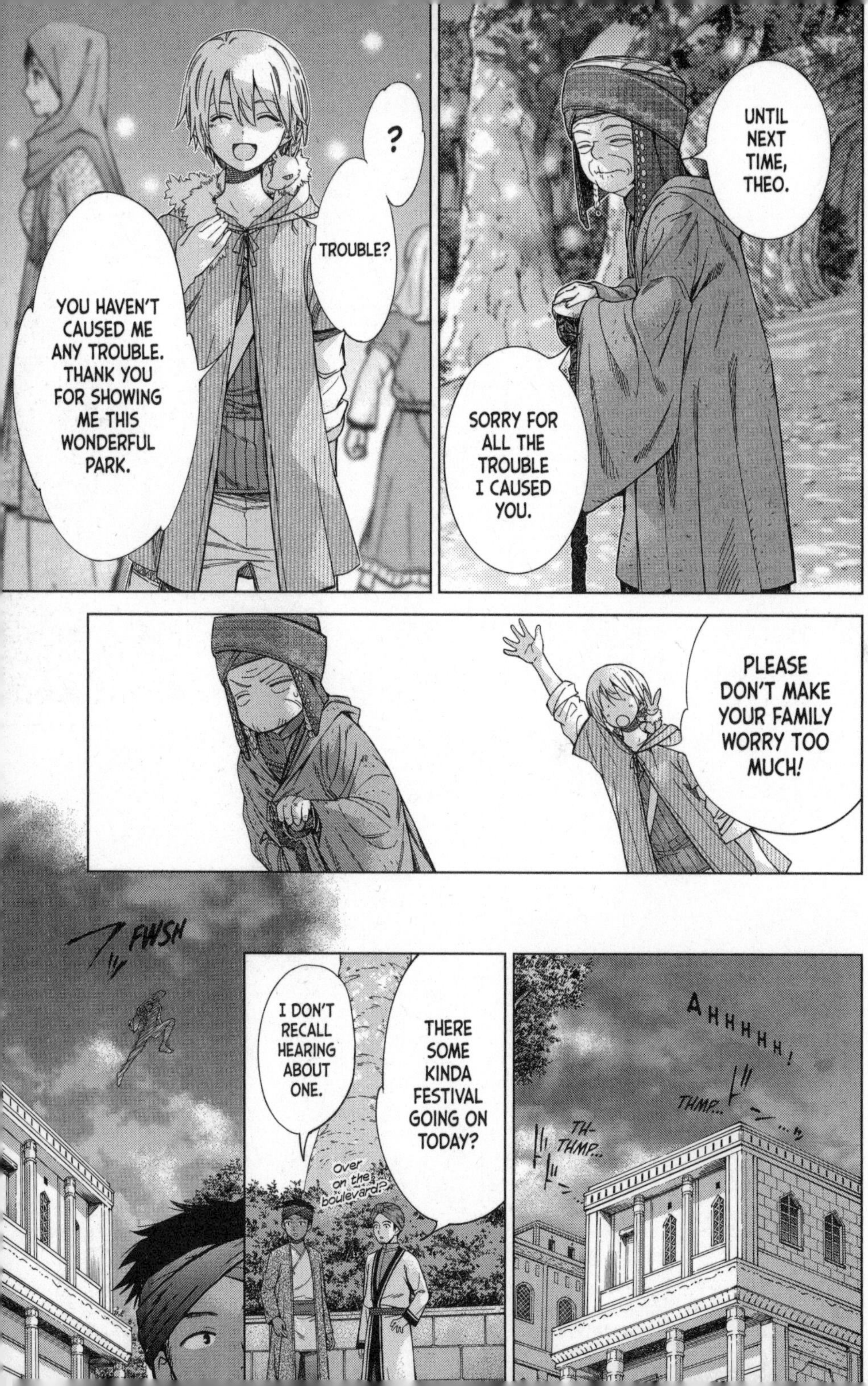
UNTIL NEXT TIME, THEO.
SORRY FOR ALL THE TROUBLE I CAUSED YOU.
?
TROUBLE?
YOU HAVEN'T CAUSED ME ANY TROUBLE. THANK YOU FOR SHOWING ME THIS WONDERFUL PARK.
PLEASE DON'T MAKE YOUR FAMILY WORRY TOO MUCH!
AHHHHH!
THMP...
TH-THMP...
THERE SOME KINDA FESTIVAL GOING ON TODAY?
Over on the boulevard?
I DON'T RECALL HEARING ABOUT ONE.
FWSH

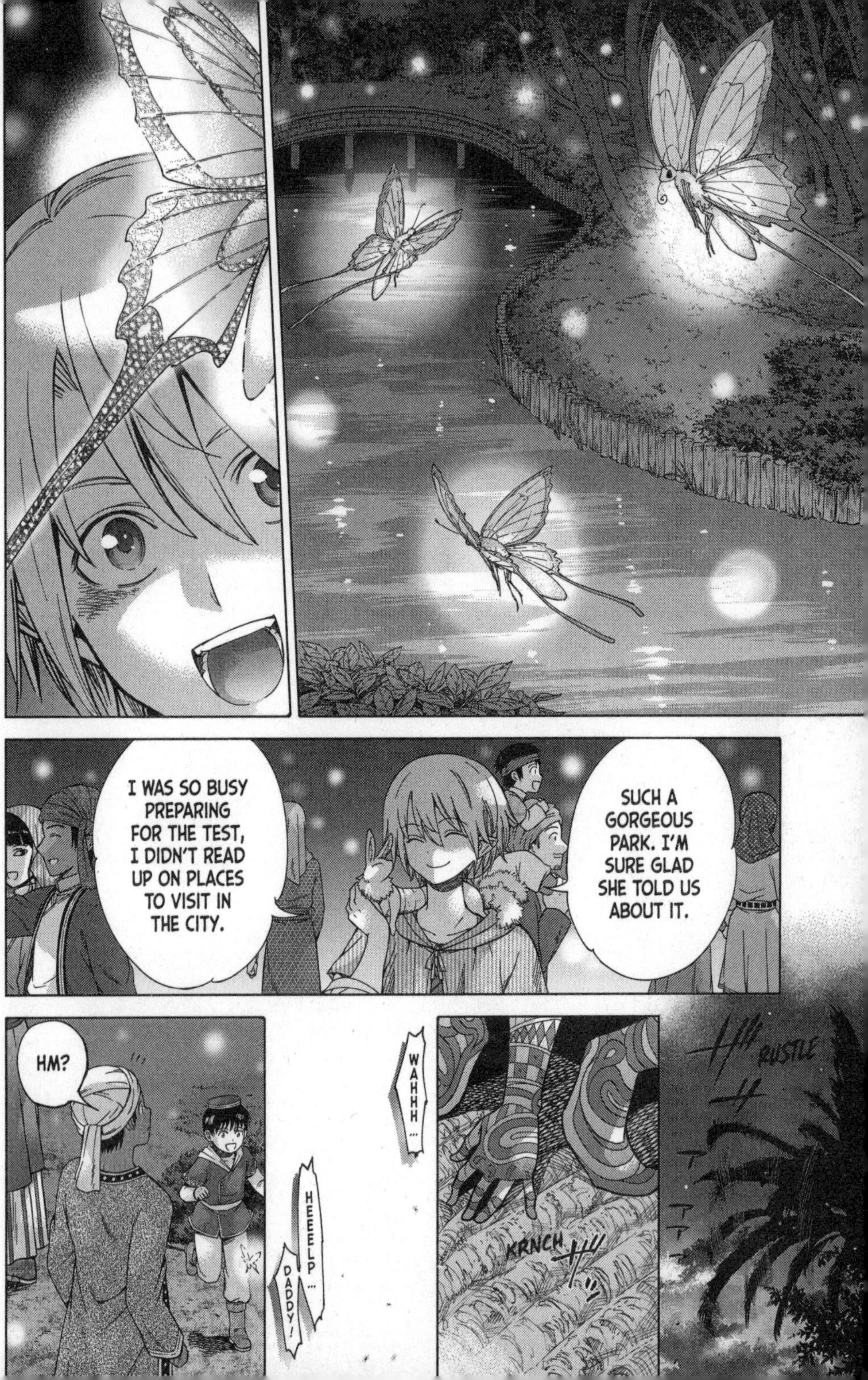
SUCH A GORGEOUS PARK. I'M SURE GLAD SHE TOLD US ABOUT IT.
I WAS SO BUSY PREPARING FOR THE TEST, I DIDN'T READ UP ON PLACES TO VISIT IN THE CITY.
RUSTLE
KRNCH
WAHHH...
HEEELP... DADDY!
HM?

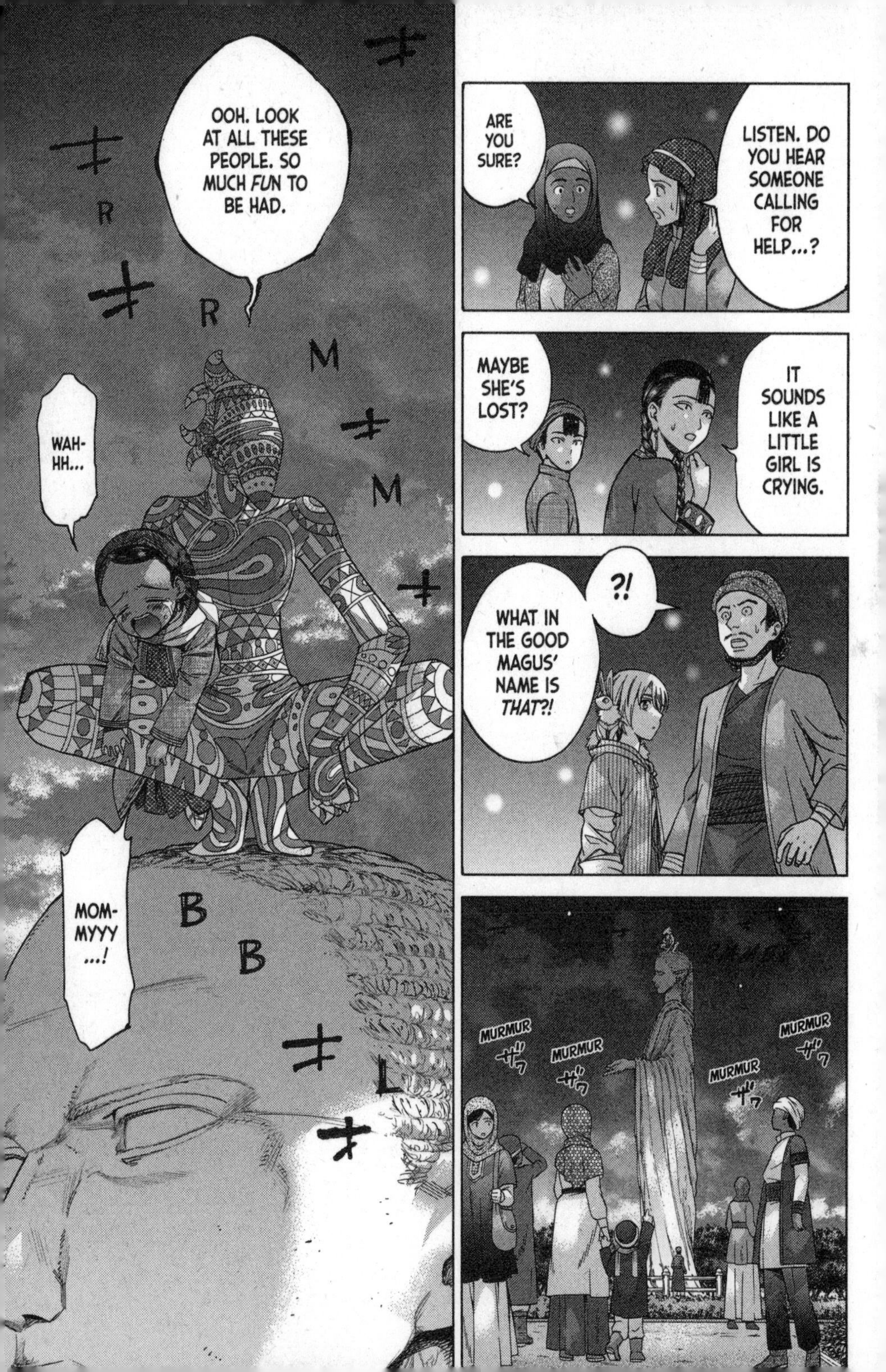
LISTEN. DO YOU HEAR SOMEONE CALLING FOR HELP...?
ARE YOU SURE?
IT SOUNDS LIKE A LITTLE GIRL IS CRYING.
MAYBE SHE'S LOST?
?!
WHAT IN THE GOOD MAGUS' NAME IS *THAT*?!
MURMUR
ザワ
MURMUR
ザワ
MURMUR
ザワ
MURMUR
ザワ
OOH. LOOK AT ALL THESE PEOPLE. SO MUCH *FUN* TO BE HAD.
RRMMBBL
WAH-HH...
MOMMYYY...!

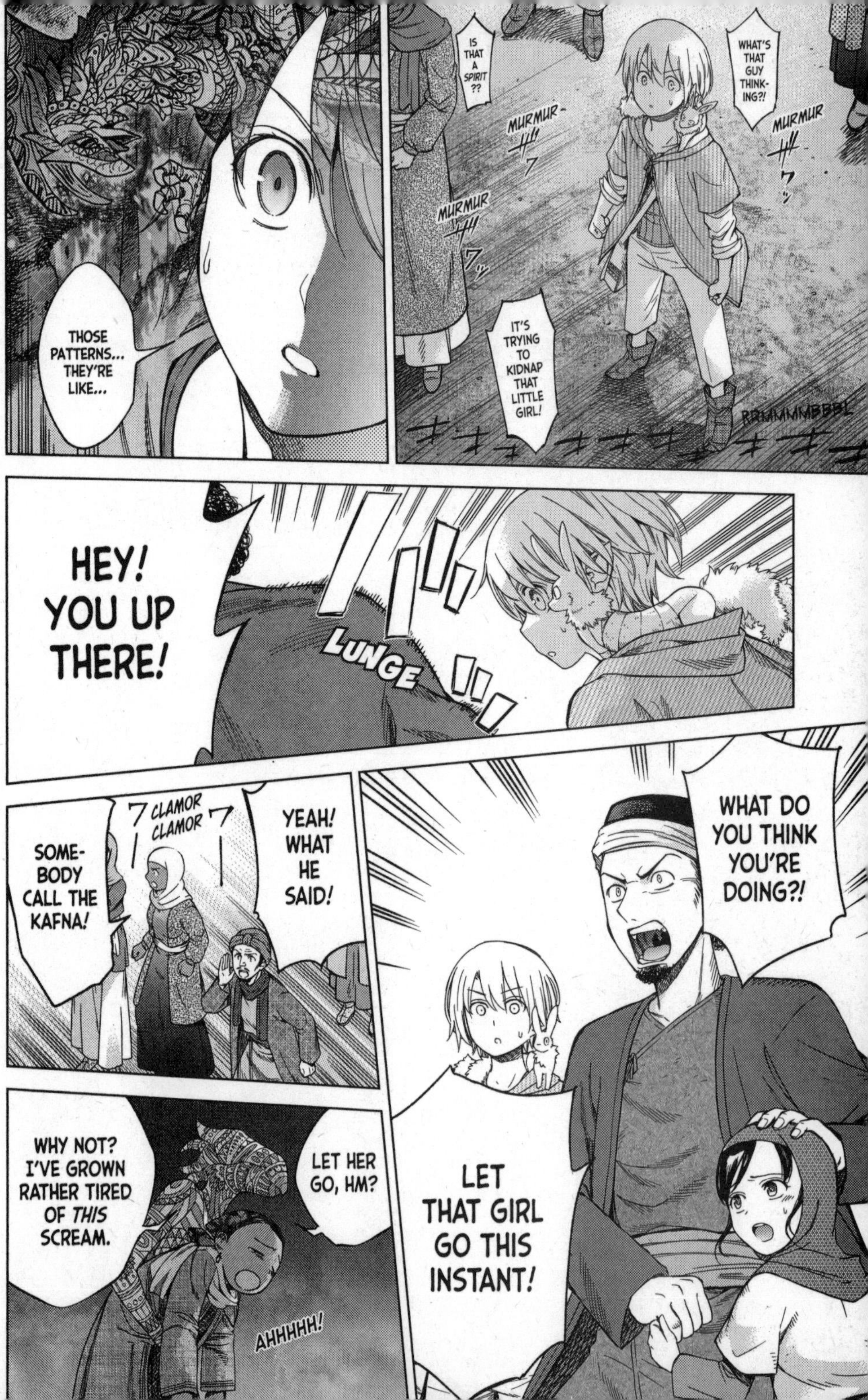
WHAT'S THAT GUY THINKING?!
MURMUR
IS THAT A SPIRIT??
MURMUR
MURMUR
IT'S TRYING TO KIDNAP THAT LITTLE GIRL!
RRMMMMBBBL
THOSE PATTERNS... THEY'RE LIKE...
HEY! YOU UP THERE!
LUNGE
WHAT DO YOU THINK YOU'RE DOING?!
LET THAT GIRL GO THIS INSTANT!
YEAH! WHAT HE SAID!
CLAMOR CLAMOR
SOME-BODY CALL THE KAFNA!
LET HER GO, HM?
WHY NOT? I'VE GROWN RATHER TIRED OF *THIS* SCREAM.
AHHHHH!

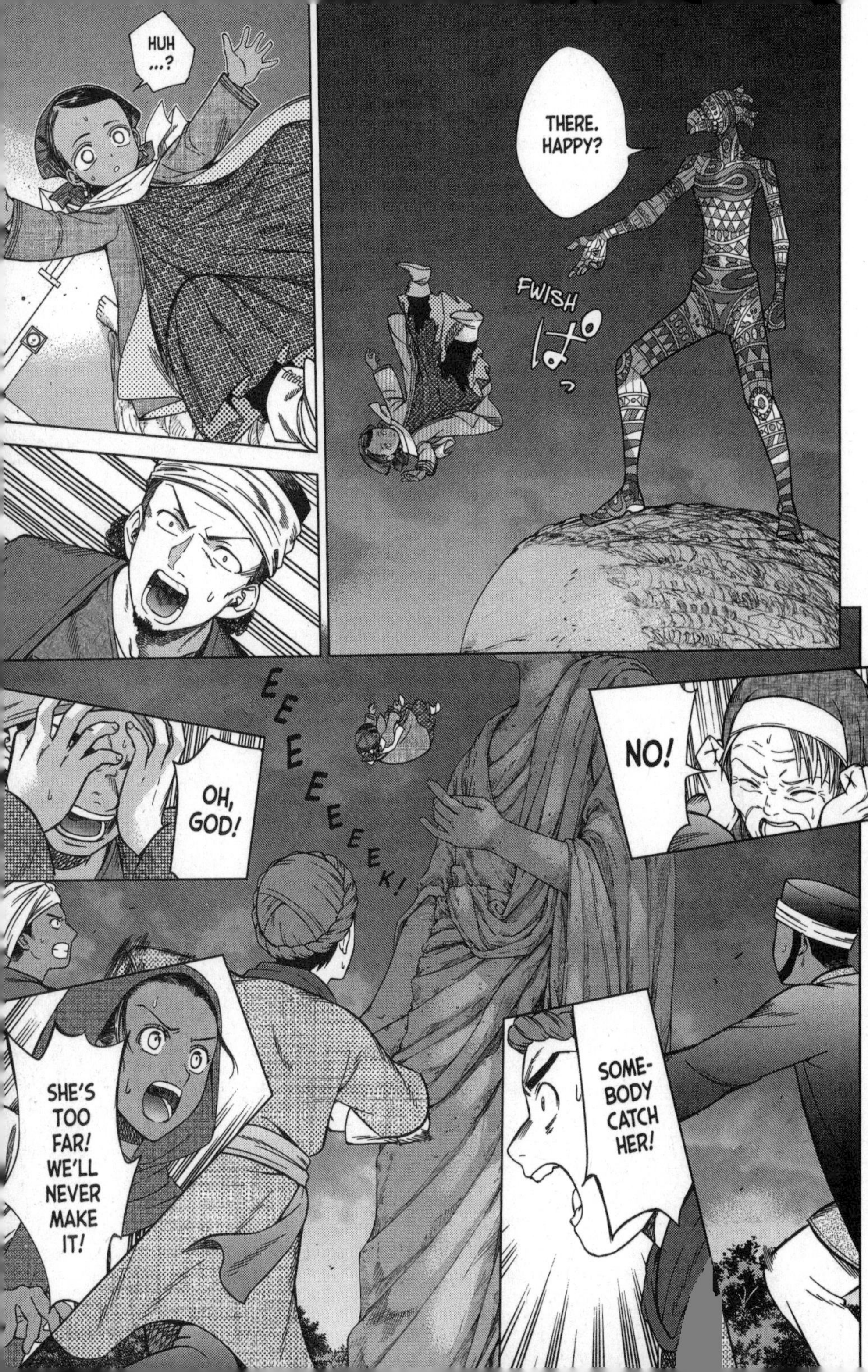
THERE. HAPPY?
FWISH
ぱっ
HUH ...?
NO!
EEEEEEEEEK!
OH, GOD!
SOME-BODY CATCH HER!
SHE'S TOO FAR! WE'LL NEVER MAKE IT!

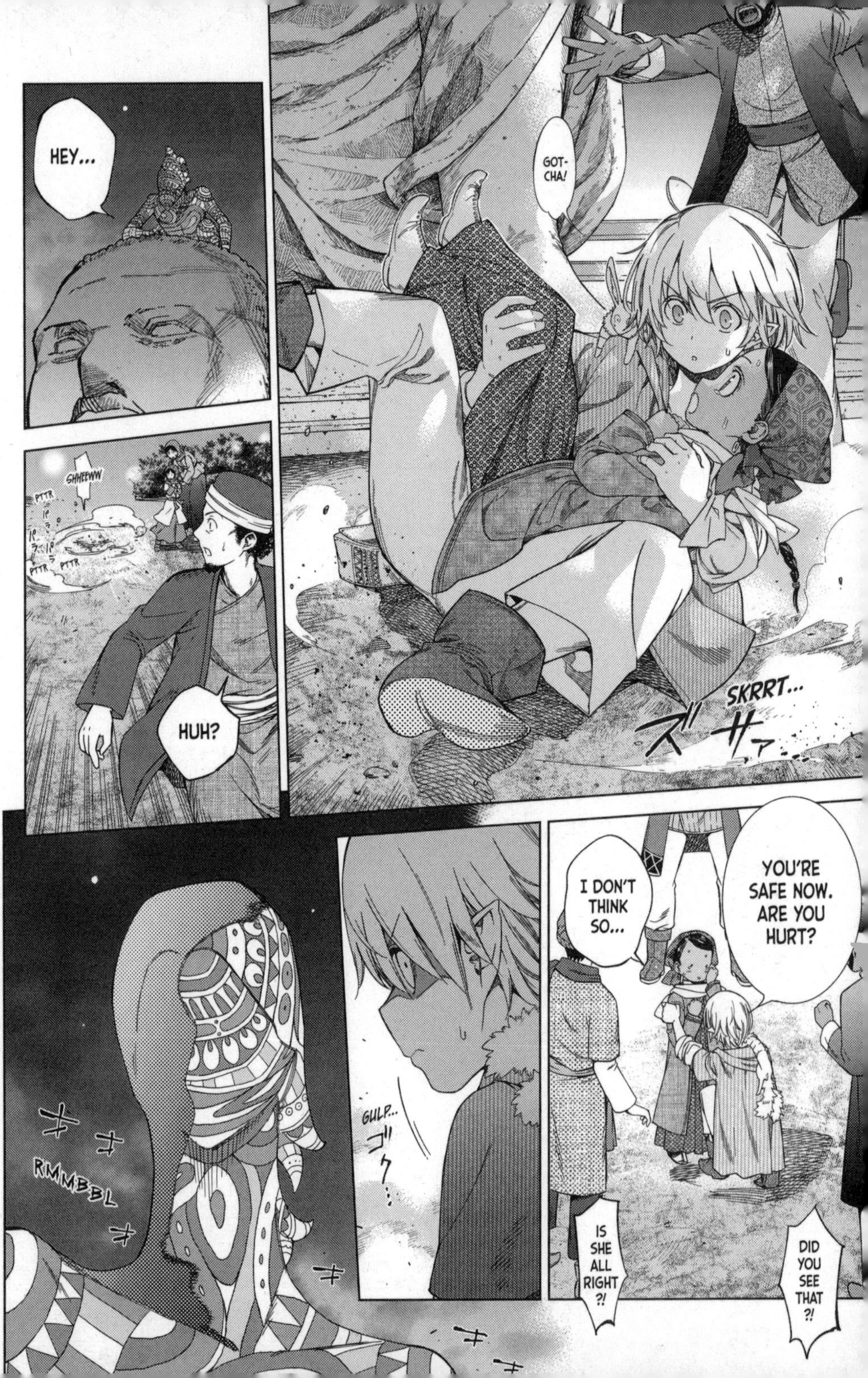
GOT-CHA!
SKRRT...
HEY...
GHHEEWW
PTTR
PTTR PTTR
HUH?
YOU'RE SAFE NOW. ARE YOU HURT?
I DON'T THINK SO...
DID YOU SEE THAT?!
IS SHE ALL RIGHT?!
GULP...
RMMBBL

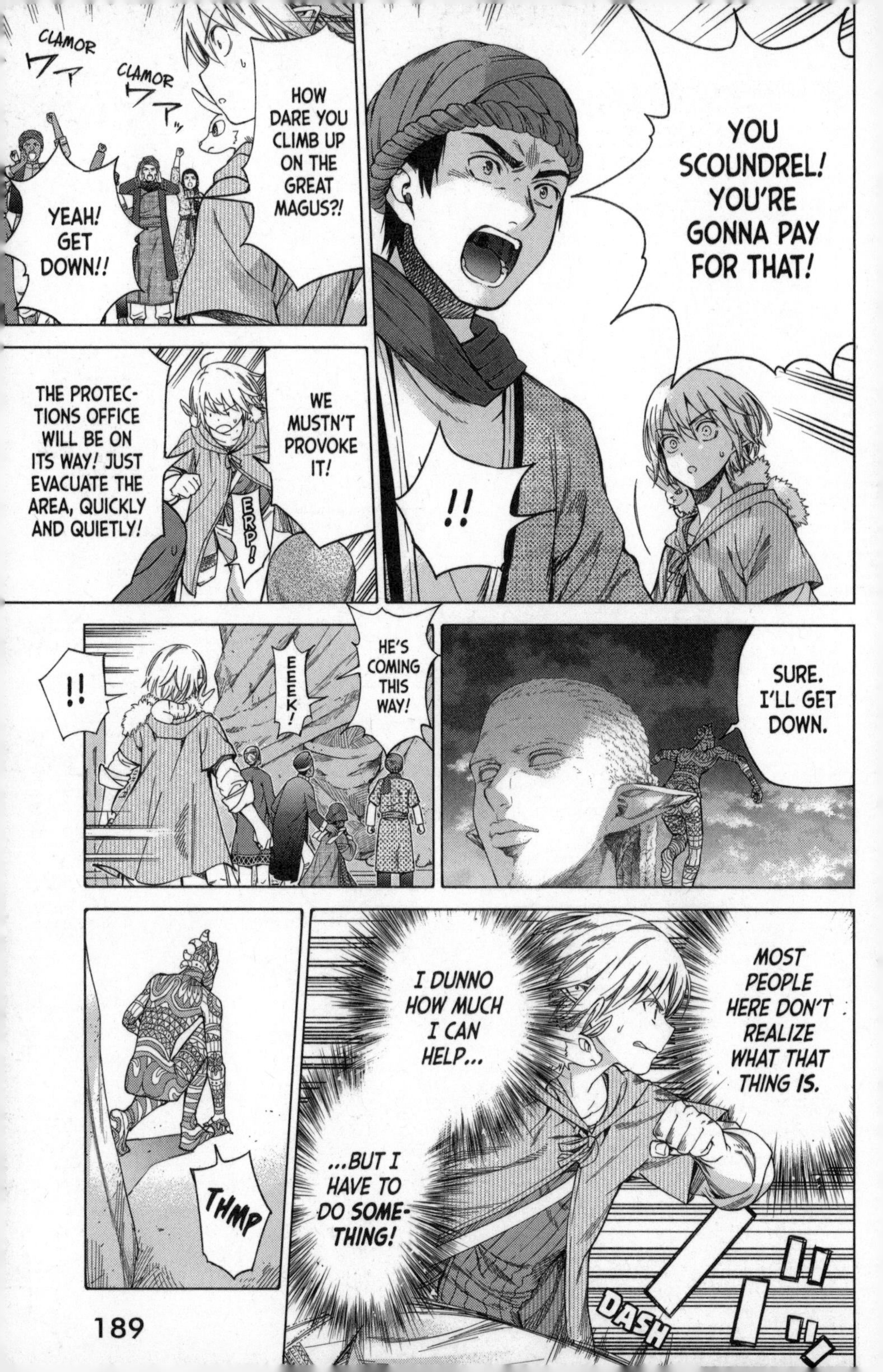
YOU SCOUNDREL! YOU'RE GONNA PAY FOR THAT!
!!
HOW DARE YOU CLIMB UP ON THE GREAT MAGUS?!
CLAMOR ワァ
CLAMOR ワァッ
YEAH! GET DOWN!!
WE MUSTN'T PROVOKE IT!
THE PROTECTIONS OFFICE WILL BE ON ITS WAY! JUST EVACUATE THE AREA, QUICKLY AND QUIETLY!
ERP!
SURE. I'LL GET DOWN.
HE'S COMING THIS WAY!
EEEEK!
!!
MOST PEOPLE HERE DON'T REALIZE WHAT THAT THING IS.
I DUNNO HOW MUCH I CAN HELP...
...BUT I HAVE TO DO SOMETHING!
DASH
THMP

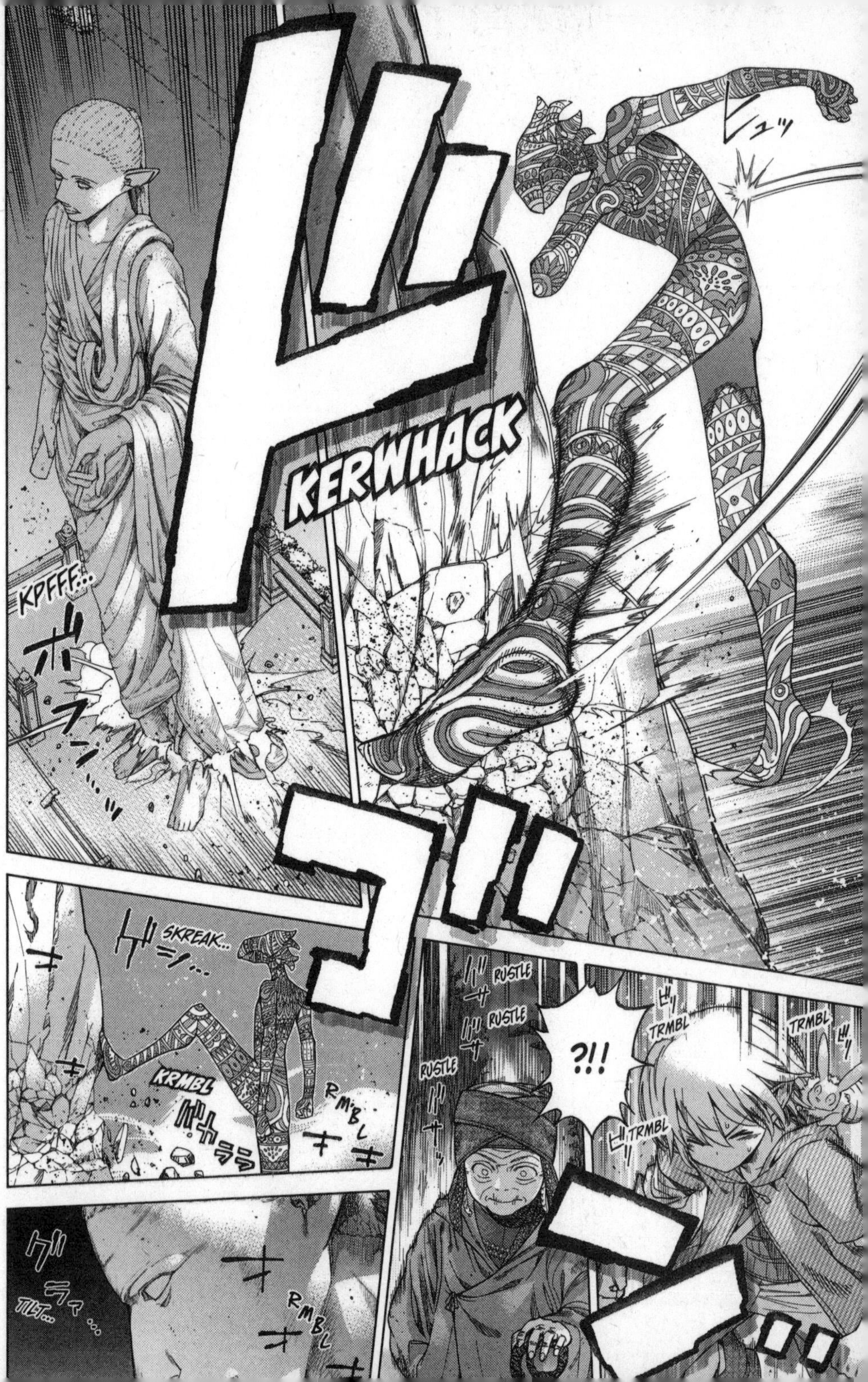

ヒュッ
KERWHACK
KPFFF...
?!!
RUSTLE
RUSTLE
RUSTLE
TRMBL
TRMBL
TRMBL
SKREAK...
KRMBL
RMBL
TILT...
RMBL

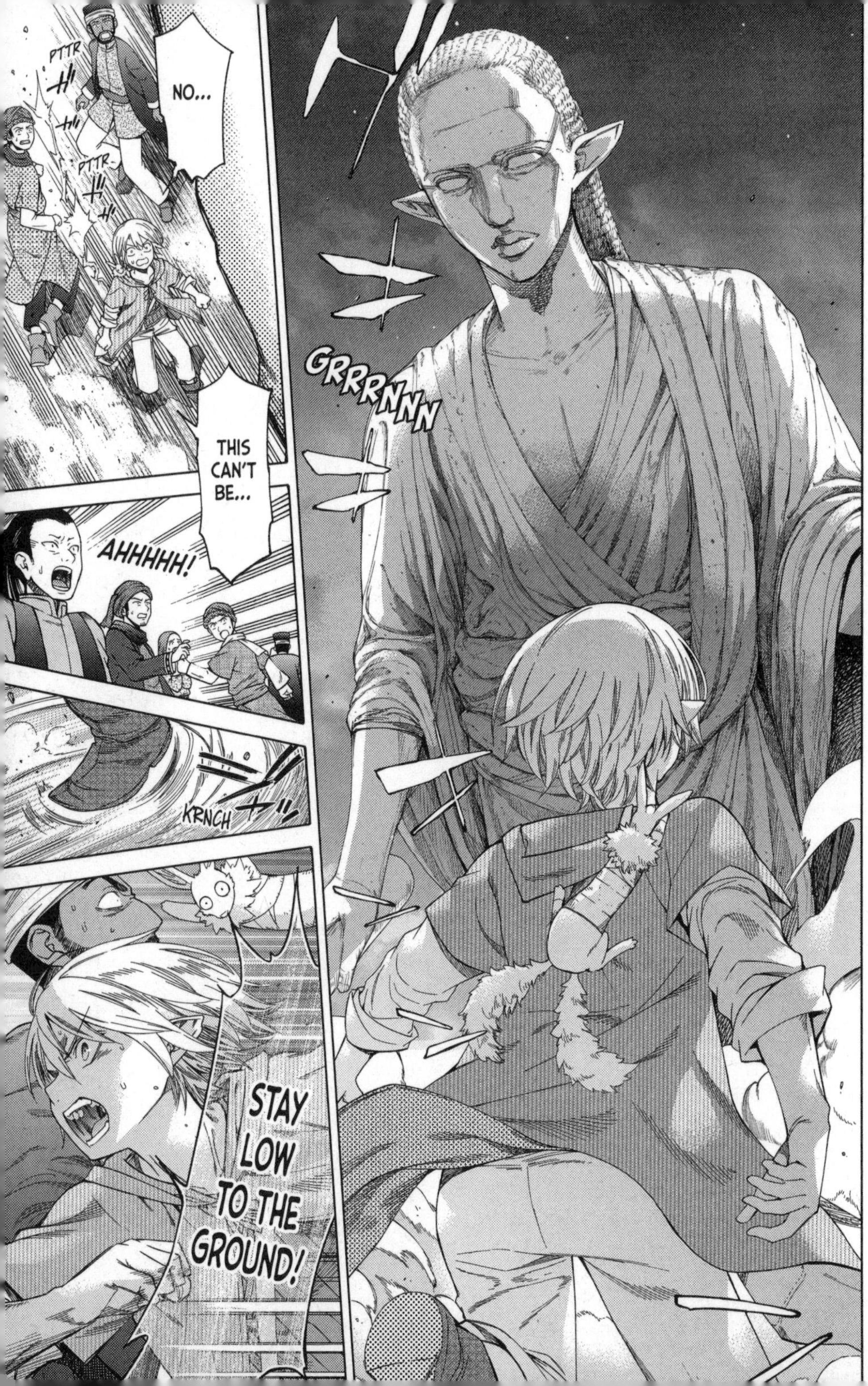
GRRRNNNN
NO...
PTTR
PTTR
THIS CAN'T BE...
AHHHHH!
KRNCH
STAY LOW TO THE GROUND!

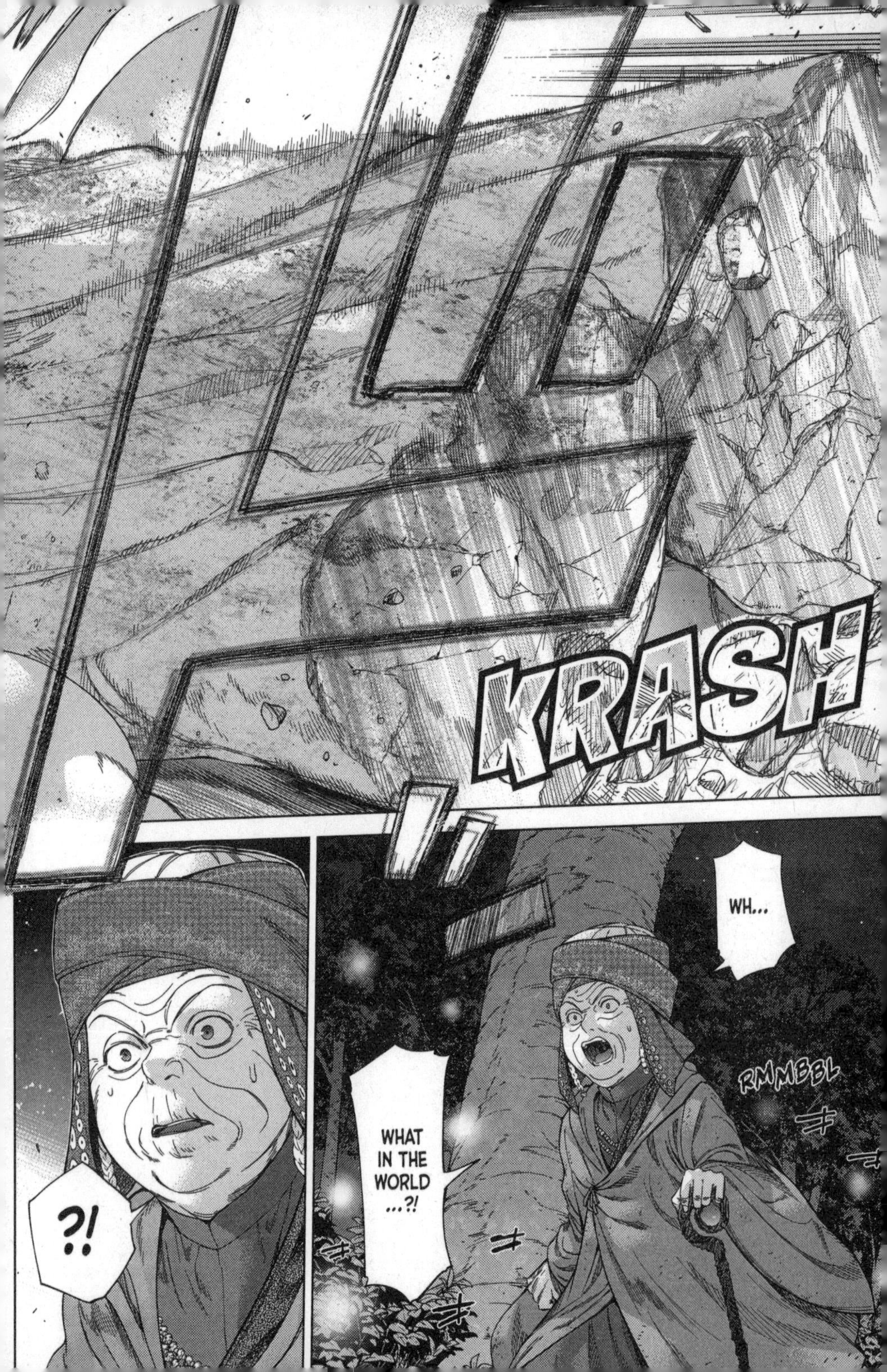
KRASH
WH...
RMMBBL
WHAT IN THE WORLD ...?!
?!

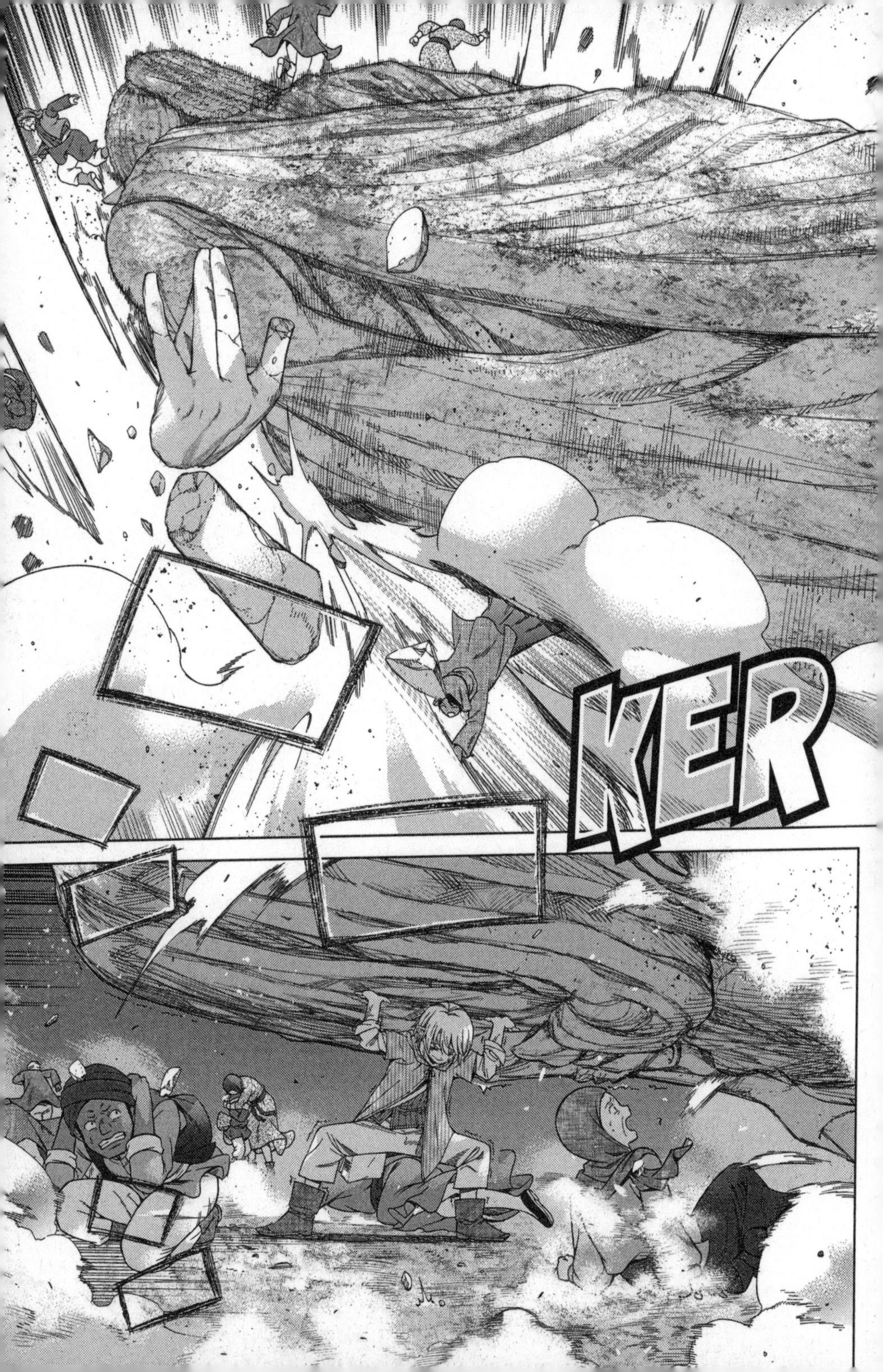
KER

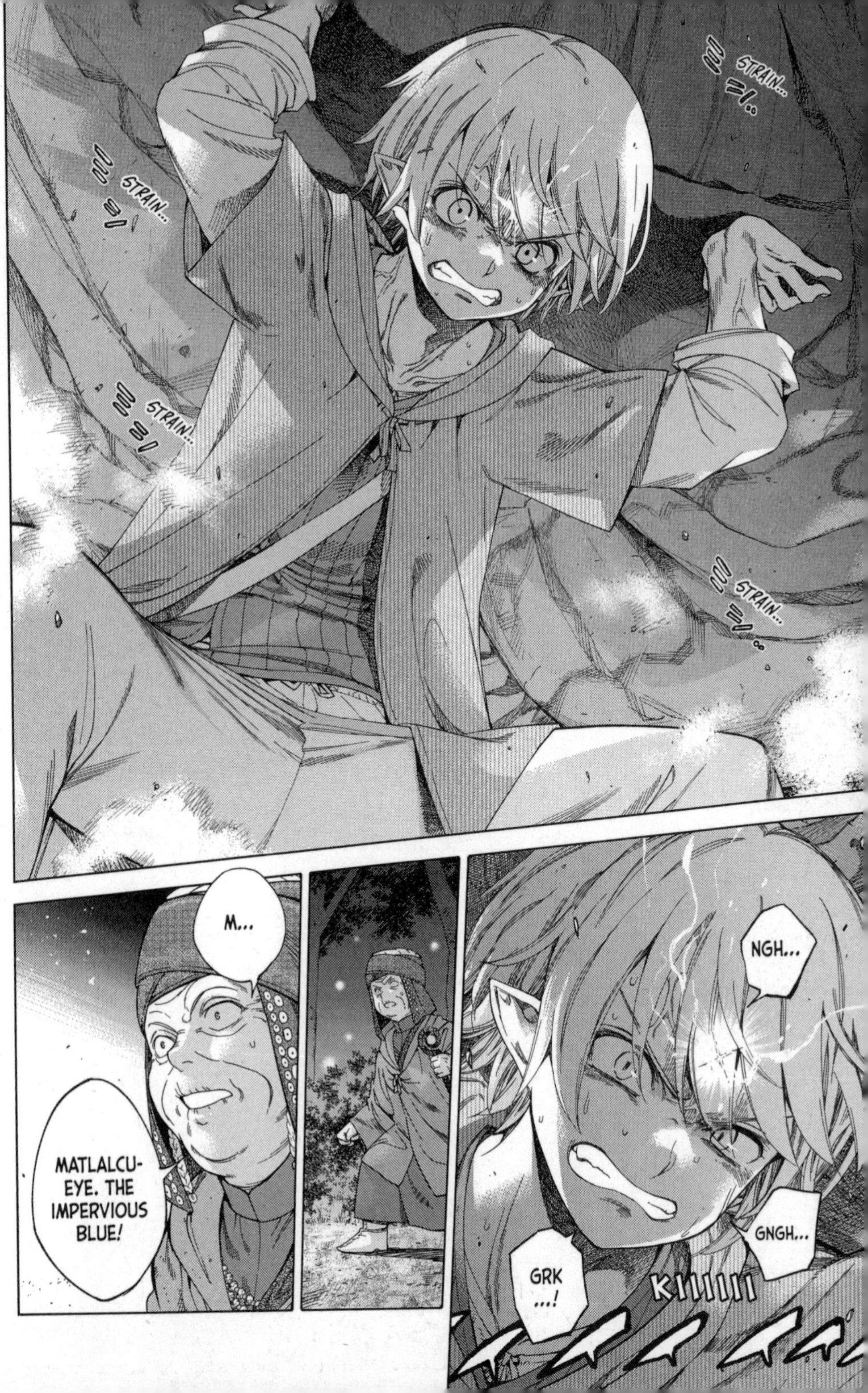
STRAIN...
STRAIN...
STRAIN...
STRAIN...
NGH...
GNGH...
GRK ...!
KIIIIII
M...
MATLALCU-EYE. THE IMPERVIOUS BLUE!

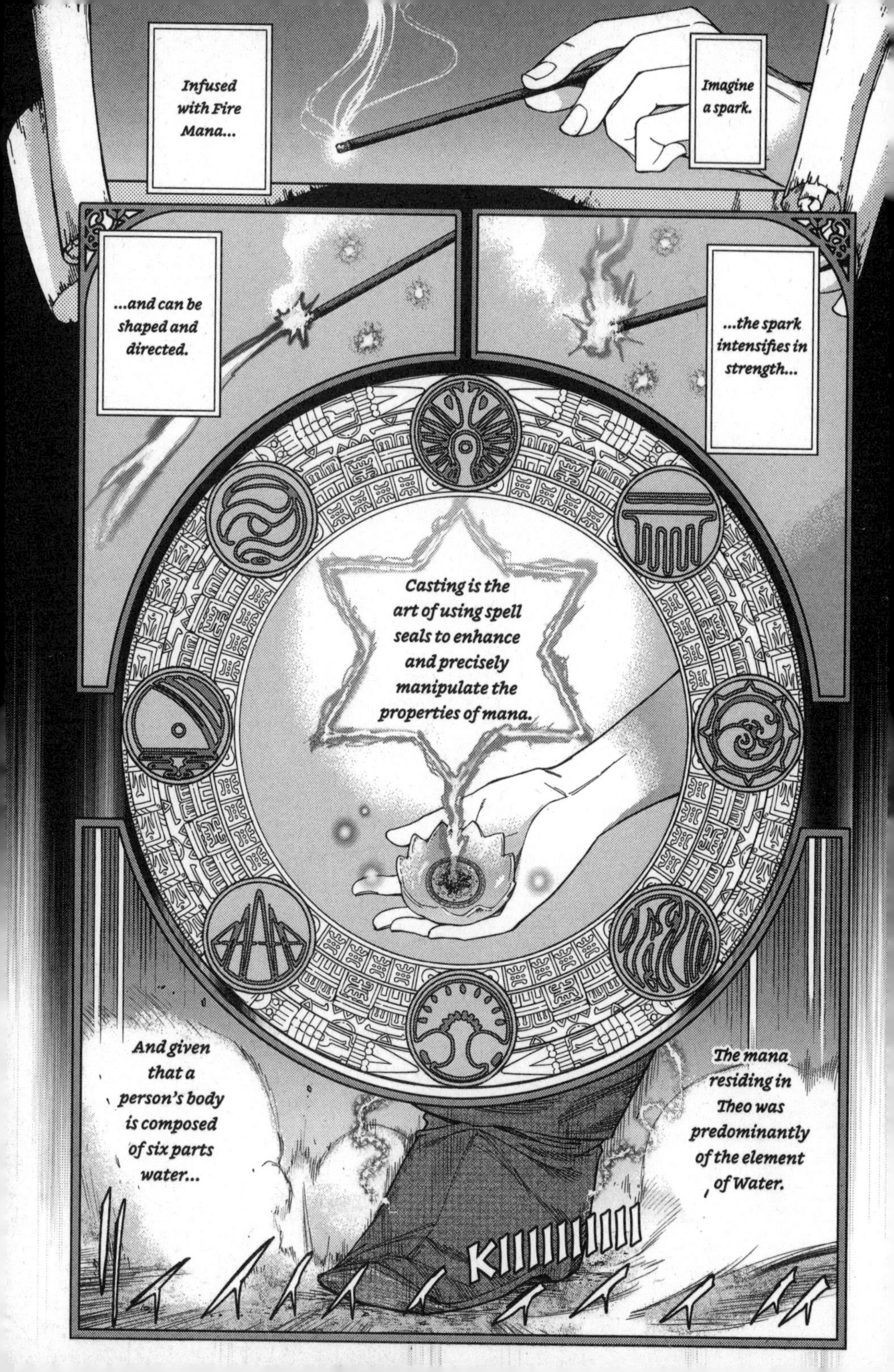
Imagine a spark.
Infused with Fire Mana...
...the spark intensifies in strength...
...and can be shaped and directed.
Casting is the art of using spell seals to enhance and precisely manipulate the properties of mana.
The mana residing in Theo was predominantly of the element of Water.
And given that a person's body is composed of six parts water...
KIIIIIIII

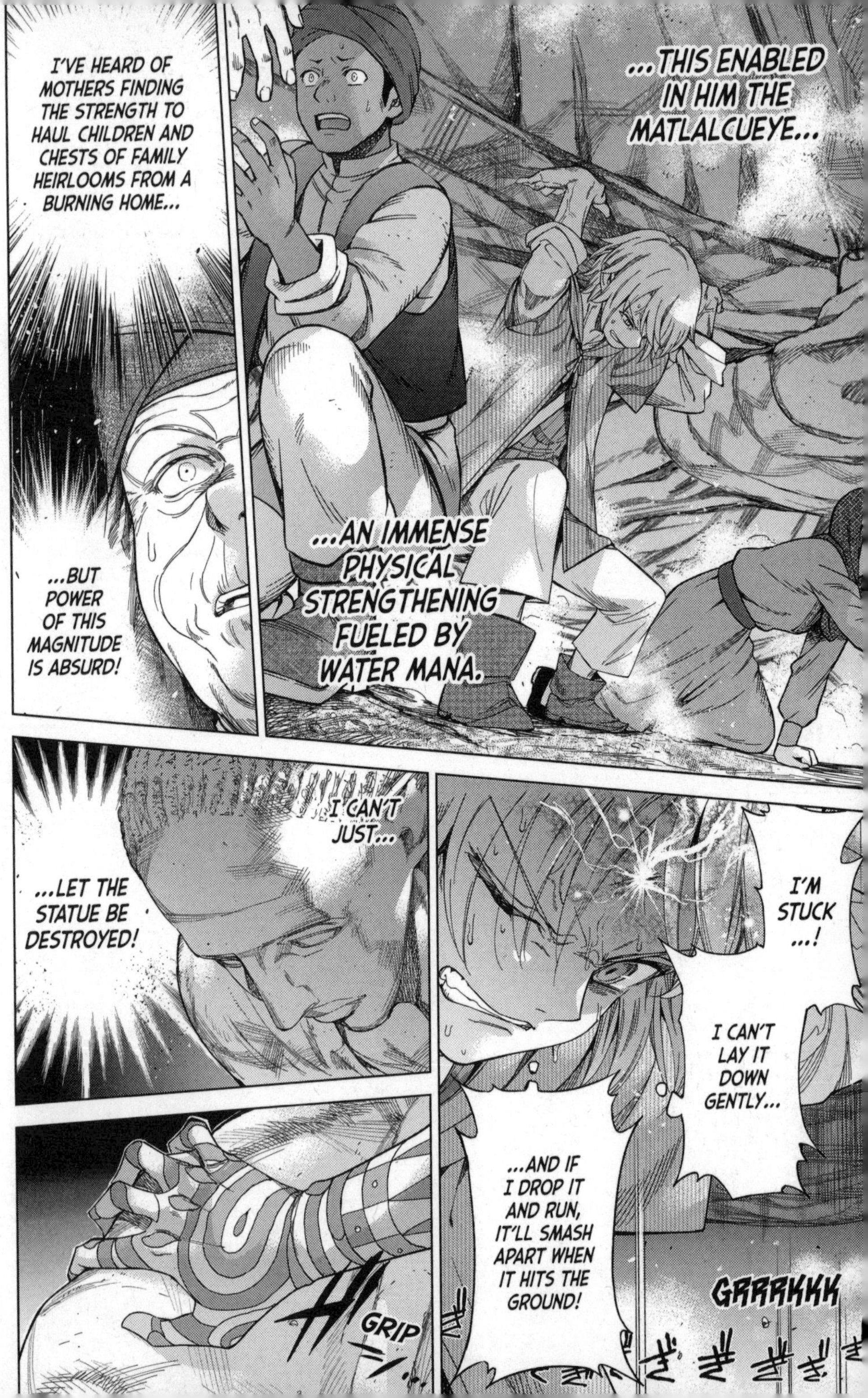
...THIS ENABLED IN HIM THE MATLALCUEYE...
...AN IMMENSE PHYSICAL STRENGTHENING FUELED BY WATER MANA.
I'VE HEARD OF MOTHERS FINDING THE STRENGTH TO HAUL CHILDREN AND CHESTS OF FAMILY HEIRLOOMS FROM A BURNING HOME...
...BUT POWER OF THIS MAGNITUDE IS ABSURD!
I'M STUCK ...!
I CAN'T LAY IT DOWN GENTLY...
...AND IF I DROP IT AND RUN, IT'LL SMASH APART WHEN IT HITS THE GROUND!
GRRRKKK
I CAN'T JUST...
...LET THE STATUE BE DESTROYED!
GRIP

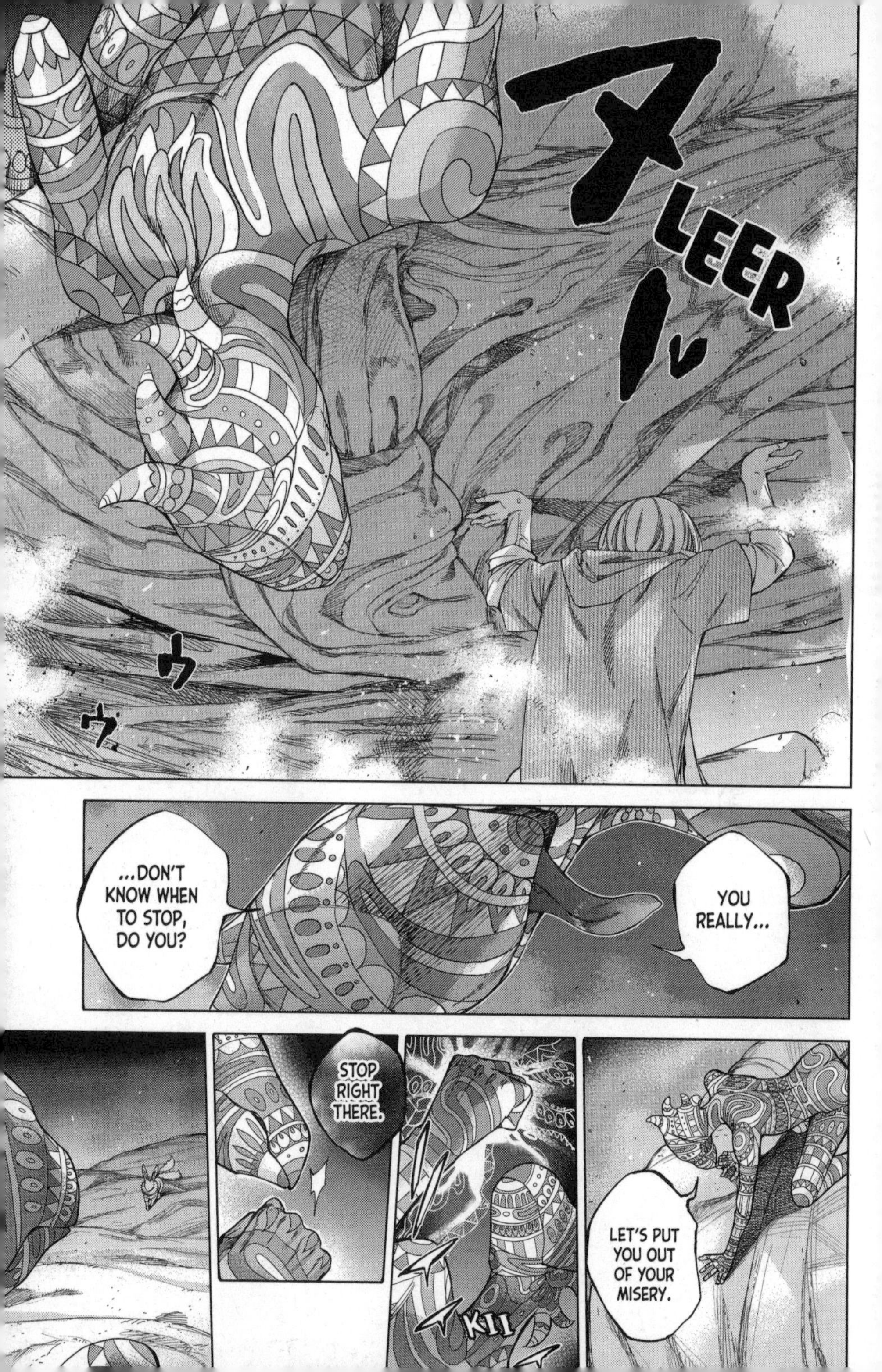

ヌル
LEER
ウ
ヴ
YOU REALLY...
...DON'T KNOW WHEN TO STOP, DO YOU?
LET'S PUT YOU OUT OF YOUR MISERY.
KII
STOP RIGHT THERE.

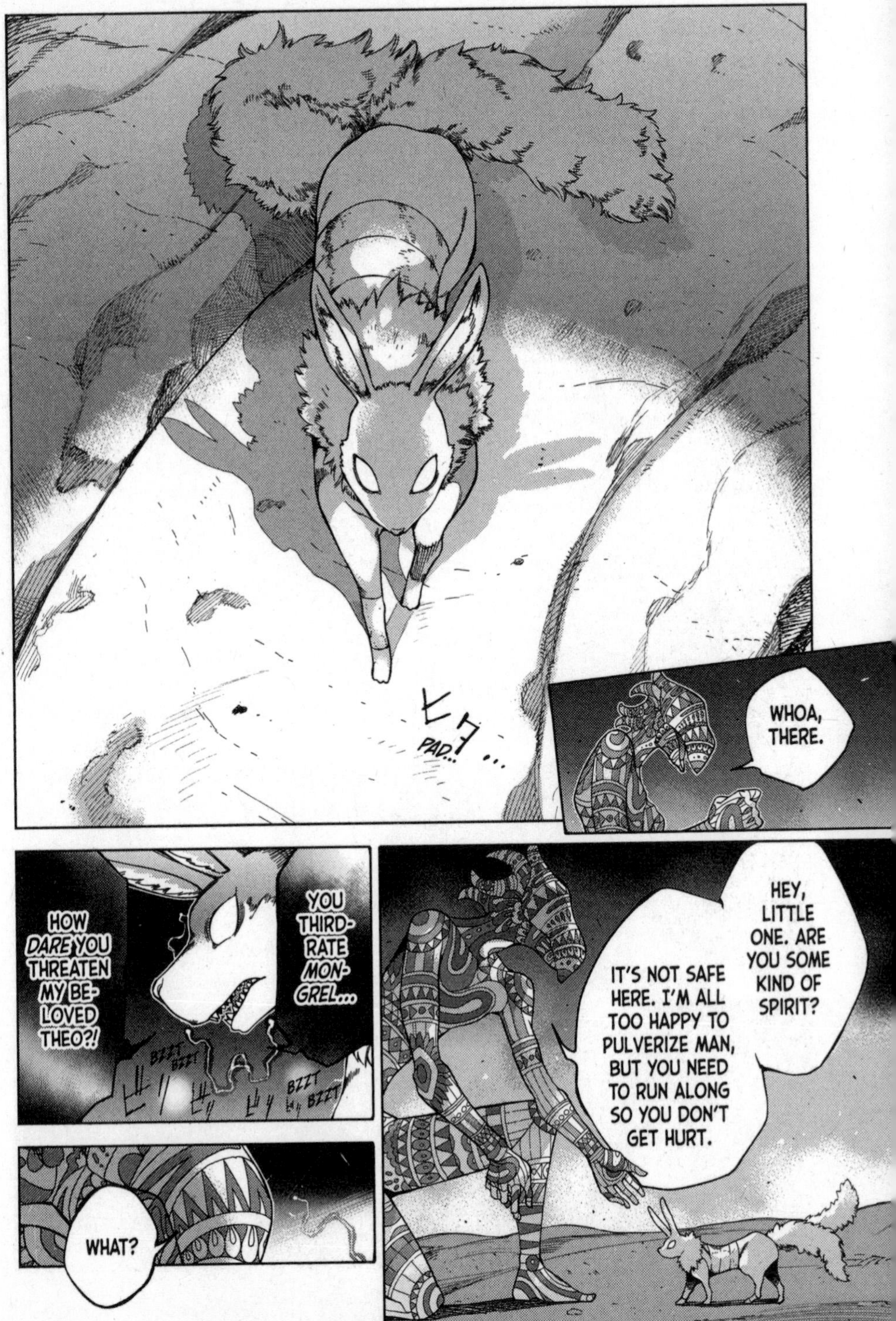
PAD...
WHOA, THERE.
HEY, LITTLE ONE. ARE YOU SOME KIND OF SPIRIT?
IT'S NOT SAFE HERE. I'M ALL TOO HAPPY TO PULVERIZE MAN, BUT YOU NEED TO RUN ALONG SO YOU DON'T GET HURT.
YOU THIRD-RATE MON-GREL...
HOW DARE YOU THREATEN MY BE-LOVED THEO?!
BZZT BZZT
BZZT BZZT
WHAT?

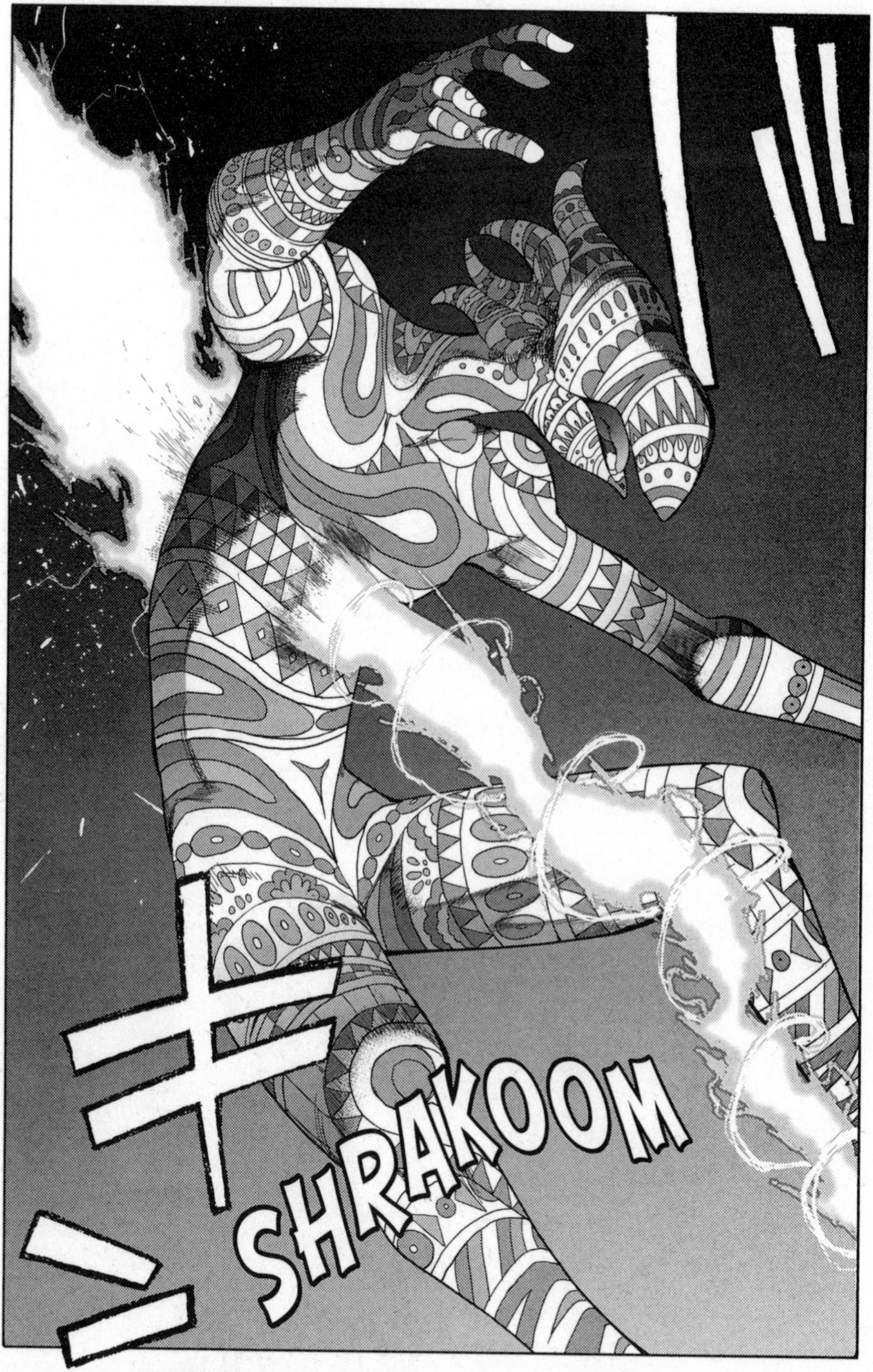
SHRAKOOM

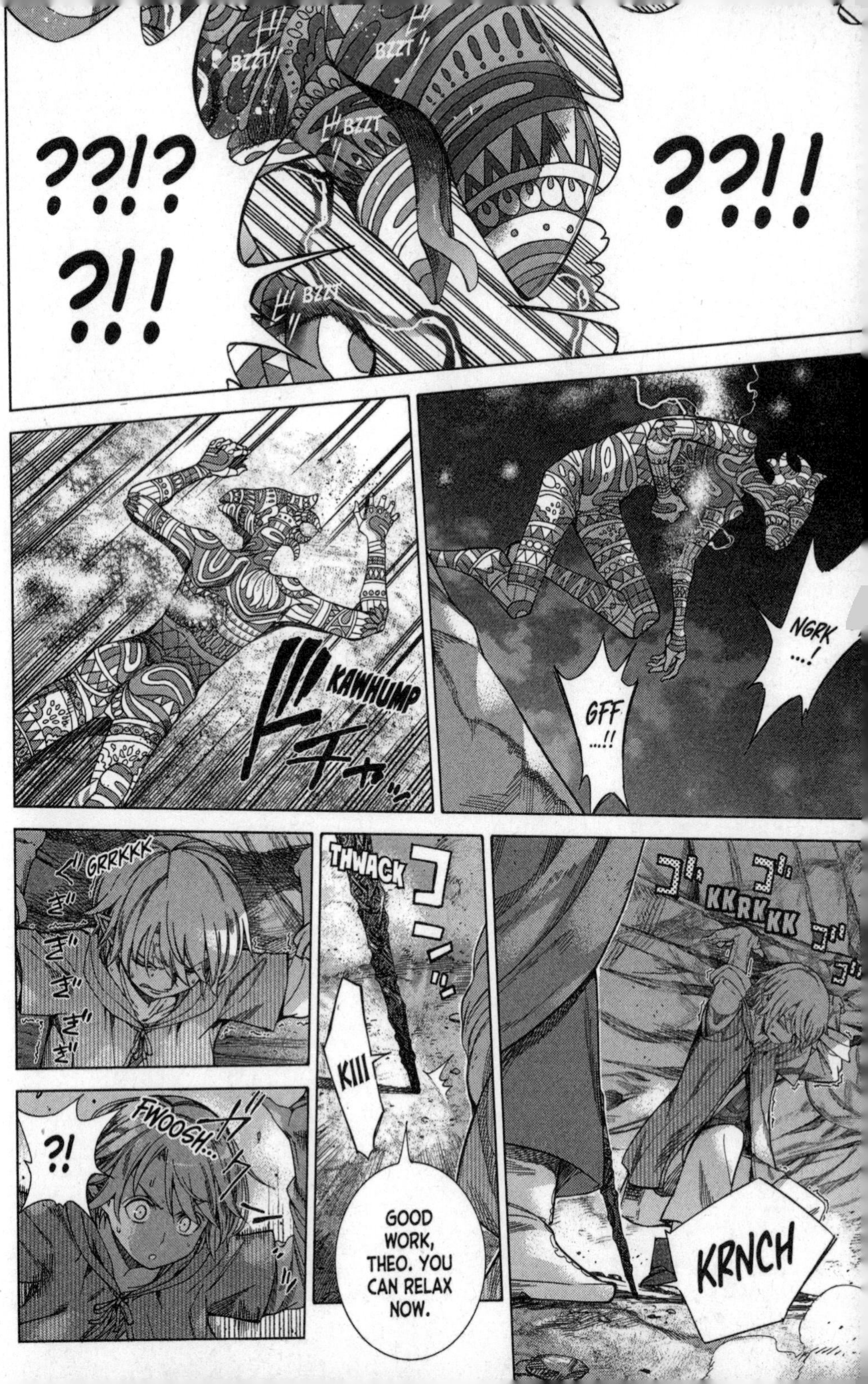
BZZT
??!!
BZZT
BZZT!!
??!?
?!!
BZZT
NGRK ...!
GFF ...!!
KAWHUMP
KKRKKK
KRNCH
THWACK
KIII
GOOD WORK, THEO. YOU CAN RELAX NOW.
GRRKKK
FWOOSH...
?!

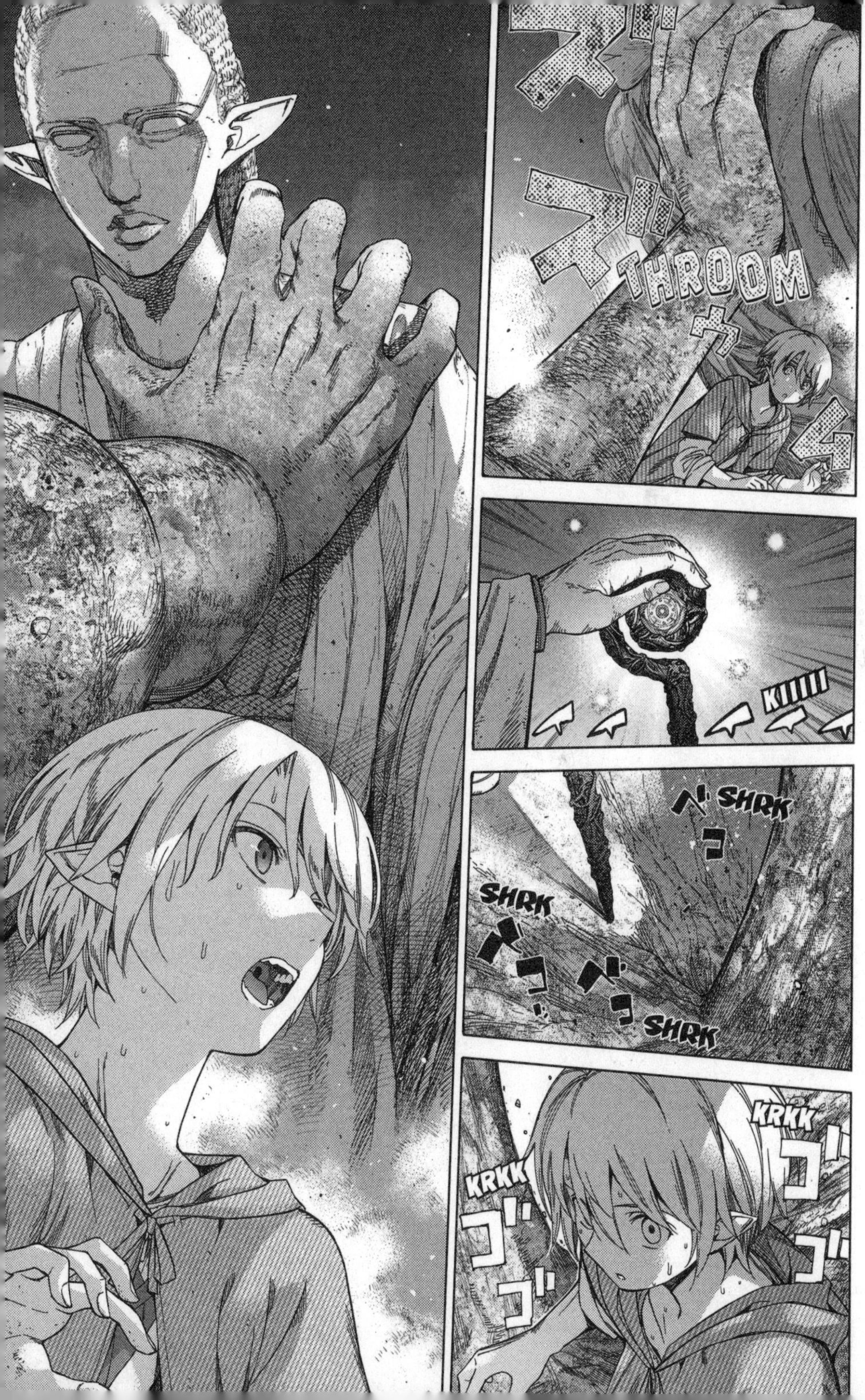
THROOM
KIIIII
SHRK
SHRK
SHRK
KRKK
KRKK

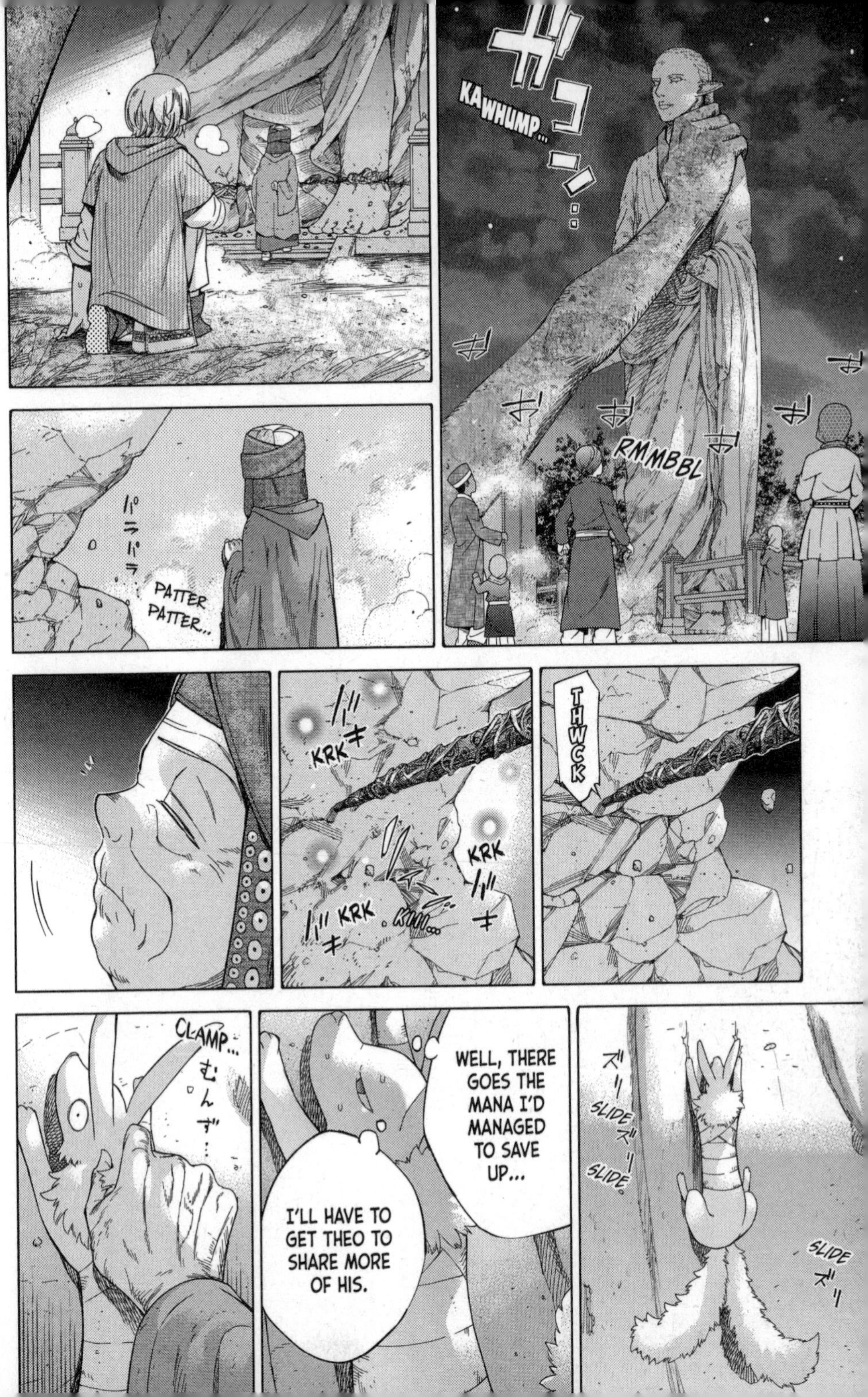
KAWHUMP...
RMMBBL
PATTER PATTER...
THWCK
KRK
KRK
KRK
KIII...
SLIDE
SLIDE
SLIDE
WELL, THERE GOES THE MANA I'D MANAGED TO SAVE UP...
I'LL HAVE TO GET THEO TO SHARE MORE OF HIS.
CLAMP...

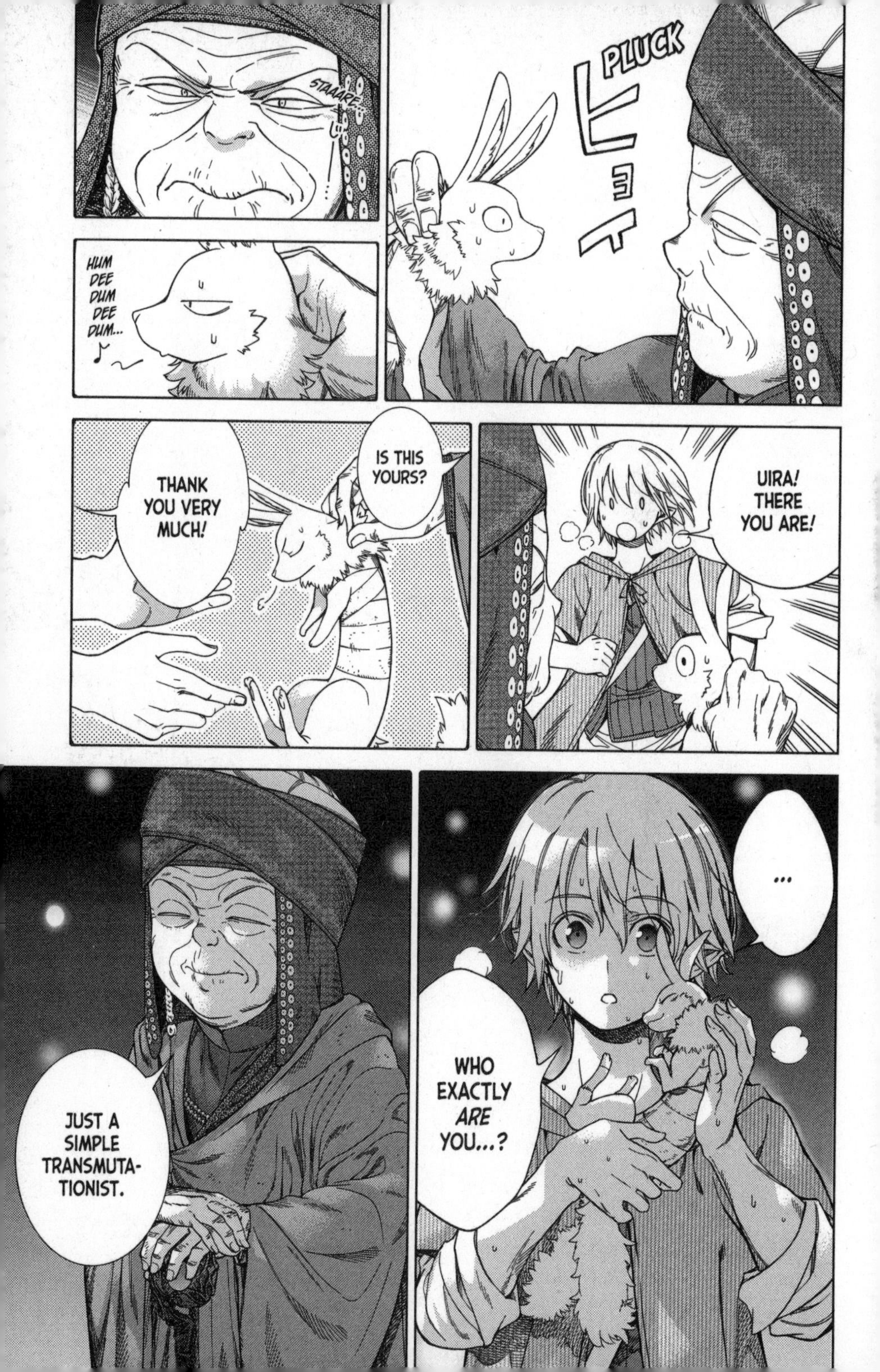
PLUCK
ヒョイ
STAAARE...
HUM DEE DUM DEE DUM... ♪
UIRA! THERE YOU ARE!
IS THIS YOURS?
THANK YOU VERY MUCH!
...
WHO EXACTLY *ARE* YOU...?
JUST A SIMPLE TRANSMUTA-TIONIST.

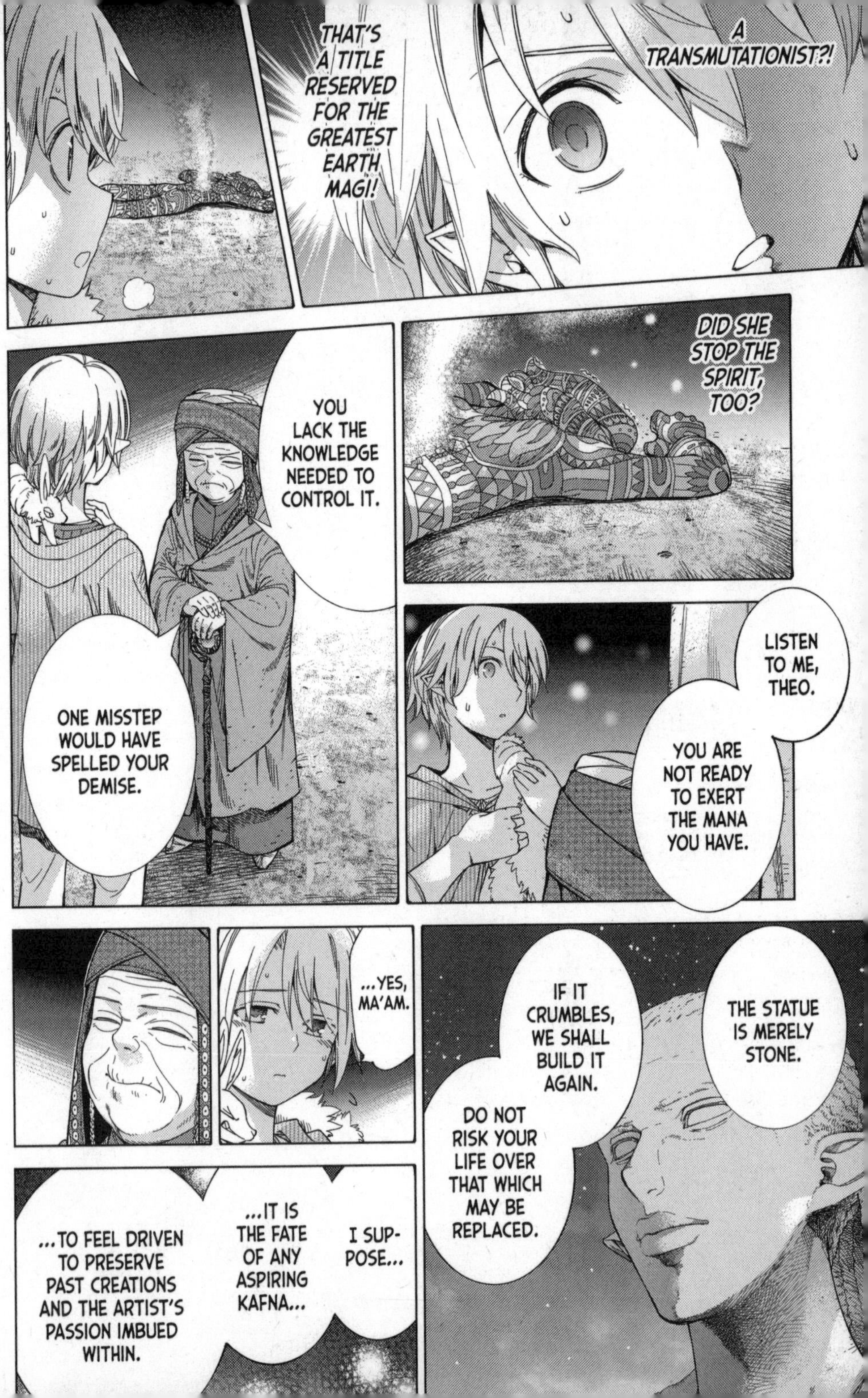
A TRANSMUTATIONIST?!
THAT'S A TITLE RESERVED FOR THE GREATEST EARTH MAGI!
DID SHE STOP THE SPIRIT, TOO?
LISTEN TO ME, THEO.
YOU ARE NOT READY TO EXERT THE MANA YOU HAVE.
YOU LACK THE KNOWLEDGE NEEDED TO CONTROL IT.
ONE MISSTEP WOULD HAVE SPELLED YOUR DEMISE.
THE STATUE IS MERELY STONE.
IF IT CRUMBLES, WE SHALL BUILD IT AGAIN.
DO NOT RISK YOUR LIFE OVER THAT WHICH MAY BE REPLACED.
...YES, MA'AM.
I SUP-POSE...
...IT IS THE FATE OF ANY ASPIRING KAFNA...
...TO FEEL DRIVEN TO PRESERVE PAST CREATIONS AND THE ARTIST'S PASSION IMBUED WITHIN.

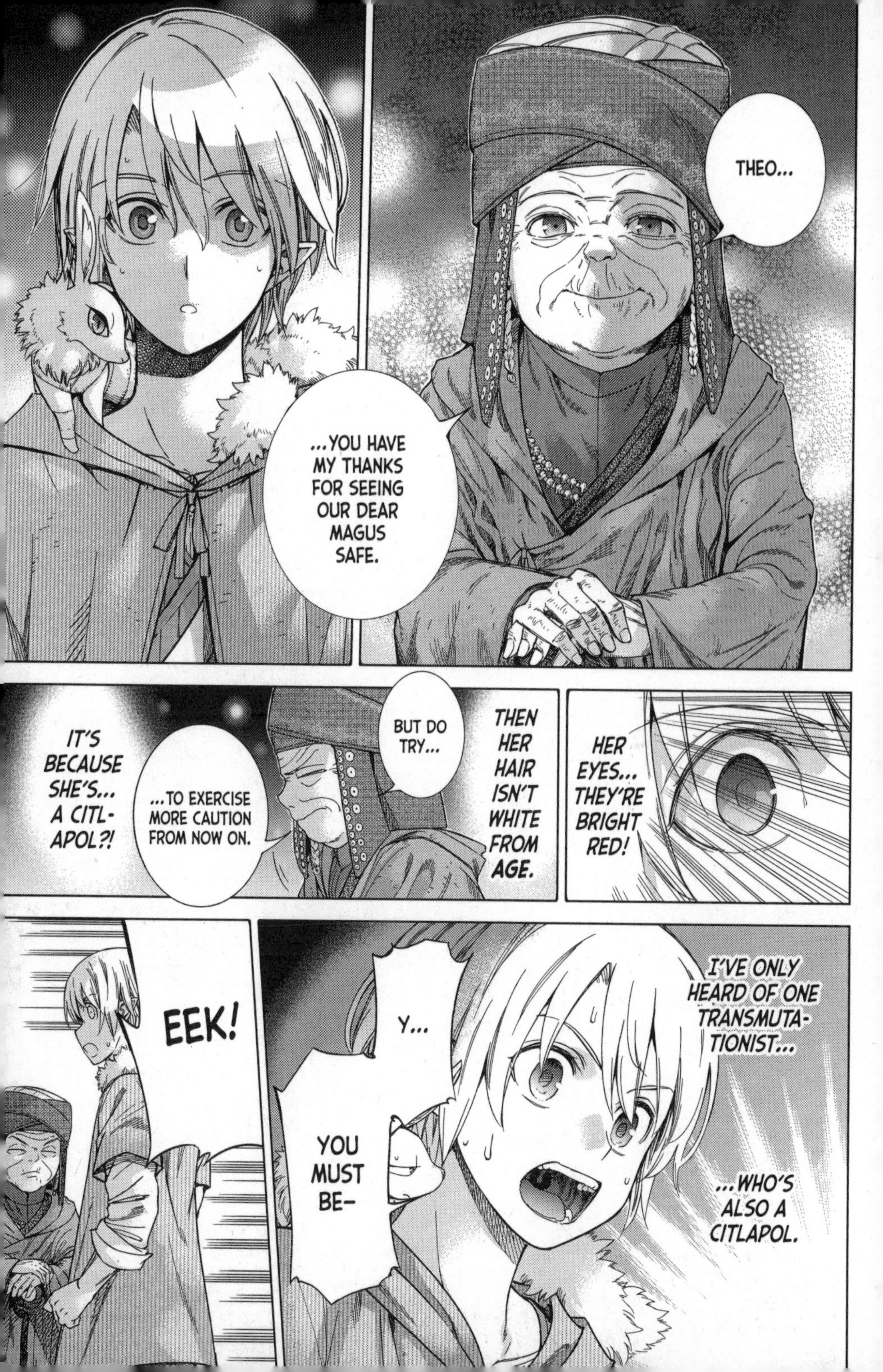
THEO...
...YOU HAVE MY THANKS FOR SEEING OUR DEAR MAGUS SAFE.
HER EYES... THEY'RE BRIGHT RED!
THEN HER HAIR ISN'T WHITE FROM AGE.
BUT DO TRY...
...TO EXERCISE MORE CAUTION FROM NOW ON.
IT'S BECAUSE SHE'S... A CITL-APOL?!
I'VE ONLY HEARD OF ONE TRANSMUTA-TIONIST...
...WHO'S ALSO A CITLAPOL.
Y...
YOU MUST BE-
EEK!

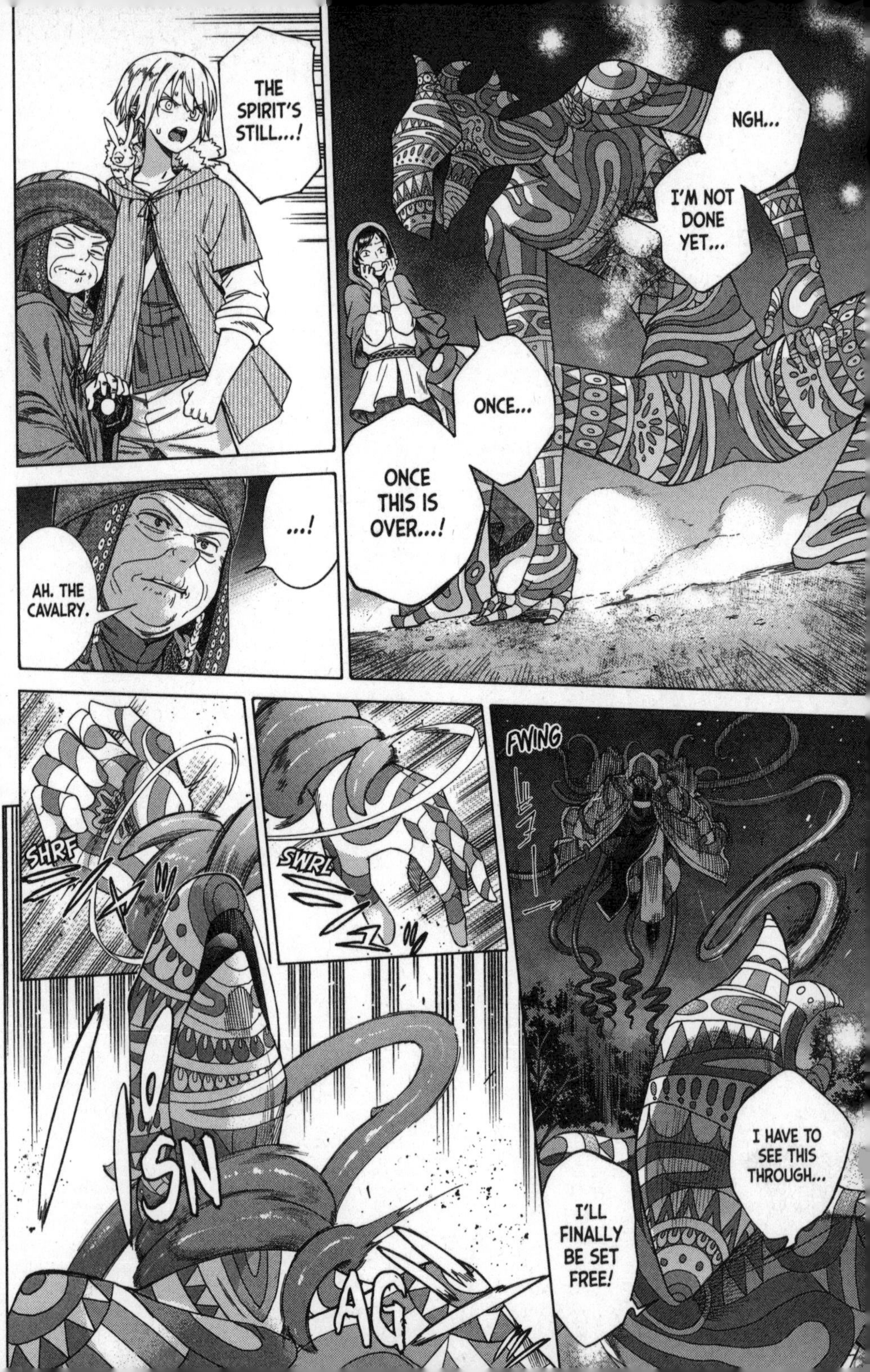
NGH...
I'M NOT DONE YET...
ONCE...
ONCE THIS IS OVER...!
THE SPIRIT'S STILL...!
...!
AH. THE CAVALRY.
FWING
I HAVE TO SEE THIS THROUGH...
I'LL FINALLY BE SET FREE!
SWRL
SHRF
SN
AG

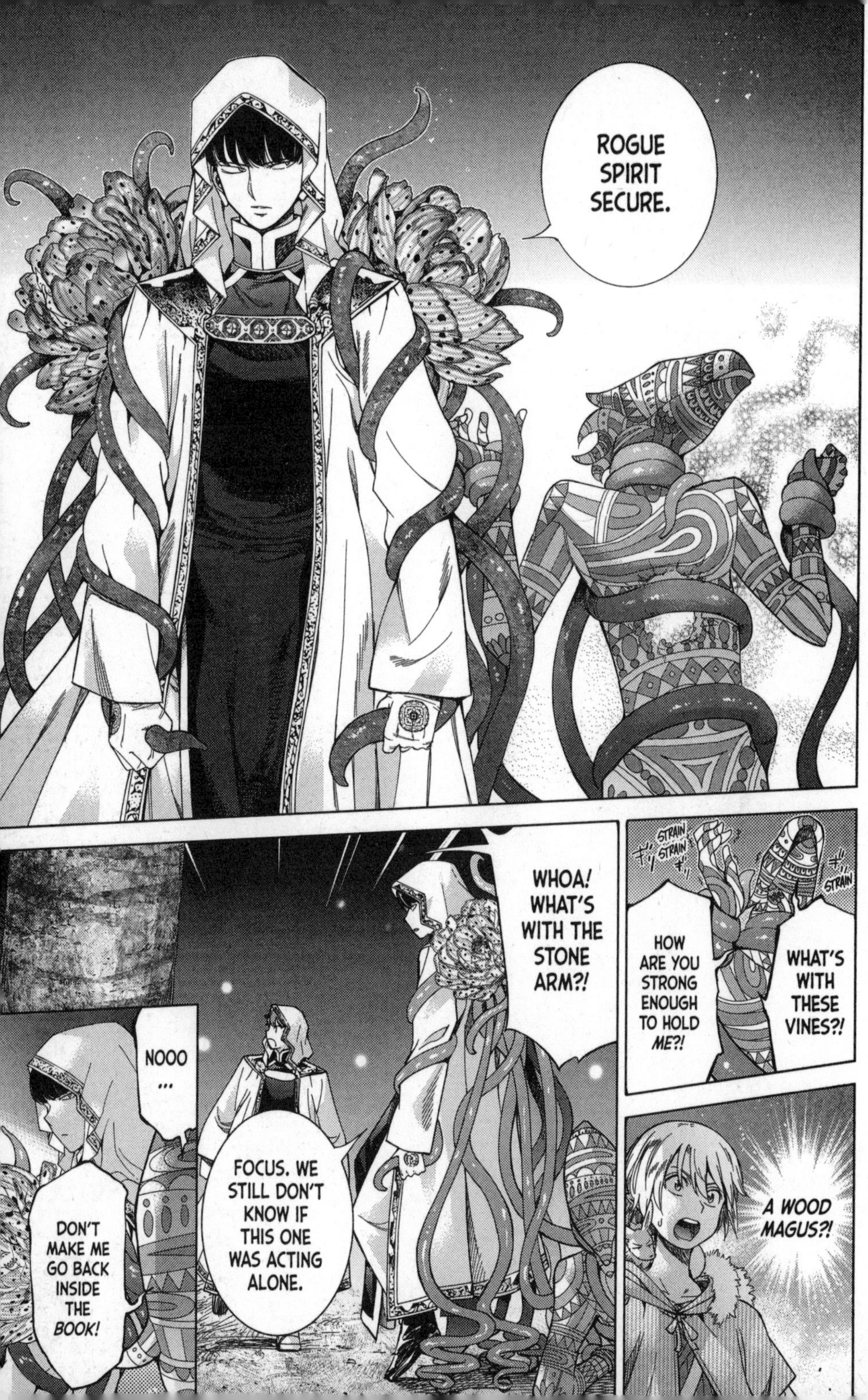
ROGUE SPIRIT SECURE.
STRAIN STRAIN
STRAIN
WHAT'S WITH THESE VINES?!
HOW ARE YOU STRONG ENOUGH TO HOLD *ME?!*
A WOOD MAGUS?!
WHOA! WHAT'S WITH THE STONE ARM?!
FOCUS. WE STILL DON'T KNOW IF THIS ONE WAS ACTING ALONE.
NOOO ...
DON'T MAKE ME GO BACK INSIDE THE *BOOK!*

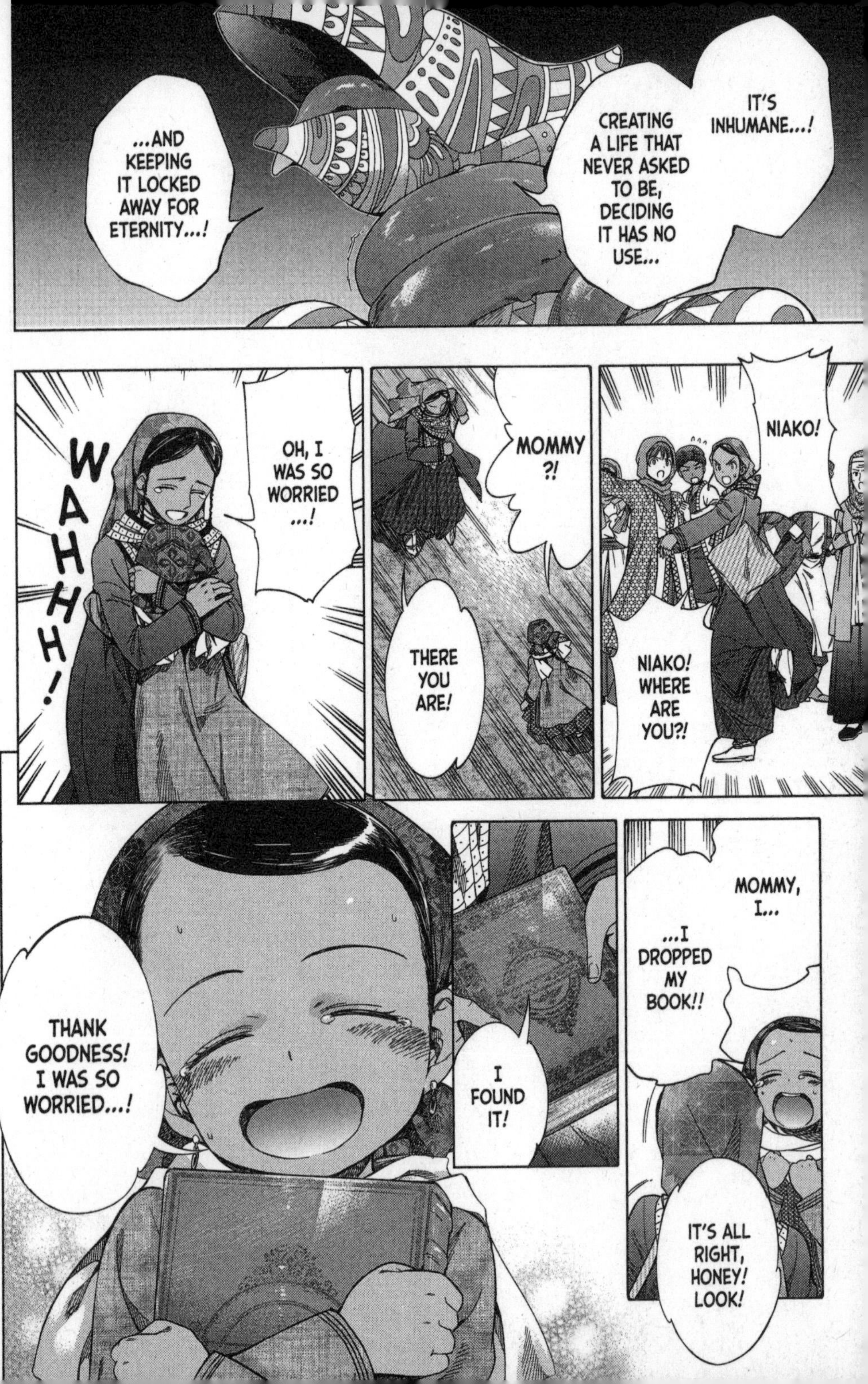
IT'S INHUMANE...!
CREATING A LIFE THAT NEVER ASKED TO BE, DECIDING IT HAS NO USE...
...AND KEEPING IT LOCKED AWAY FOR ETERNITY...!
NIAKO!
NIAKO! WHERE ARE YOU?!
MOMMY?!
THERE YOU ARE!
OH, I WAS SO WORRIED...!
WAHHH!
MOMMY, I...
...I DROPPED MY BOOK!!
IT'S ALL RIGHT, HONEY! LOOK!
I FOUND IT!
THANK GOODNESS! I WAS SO WORRIED...!

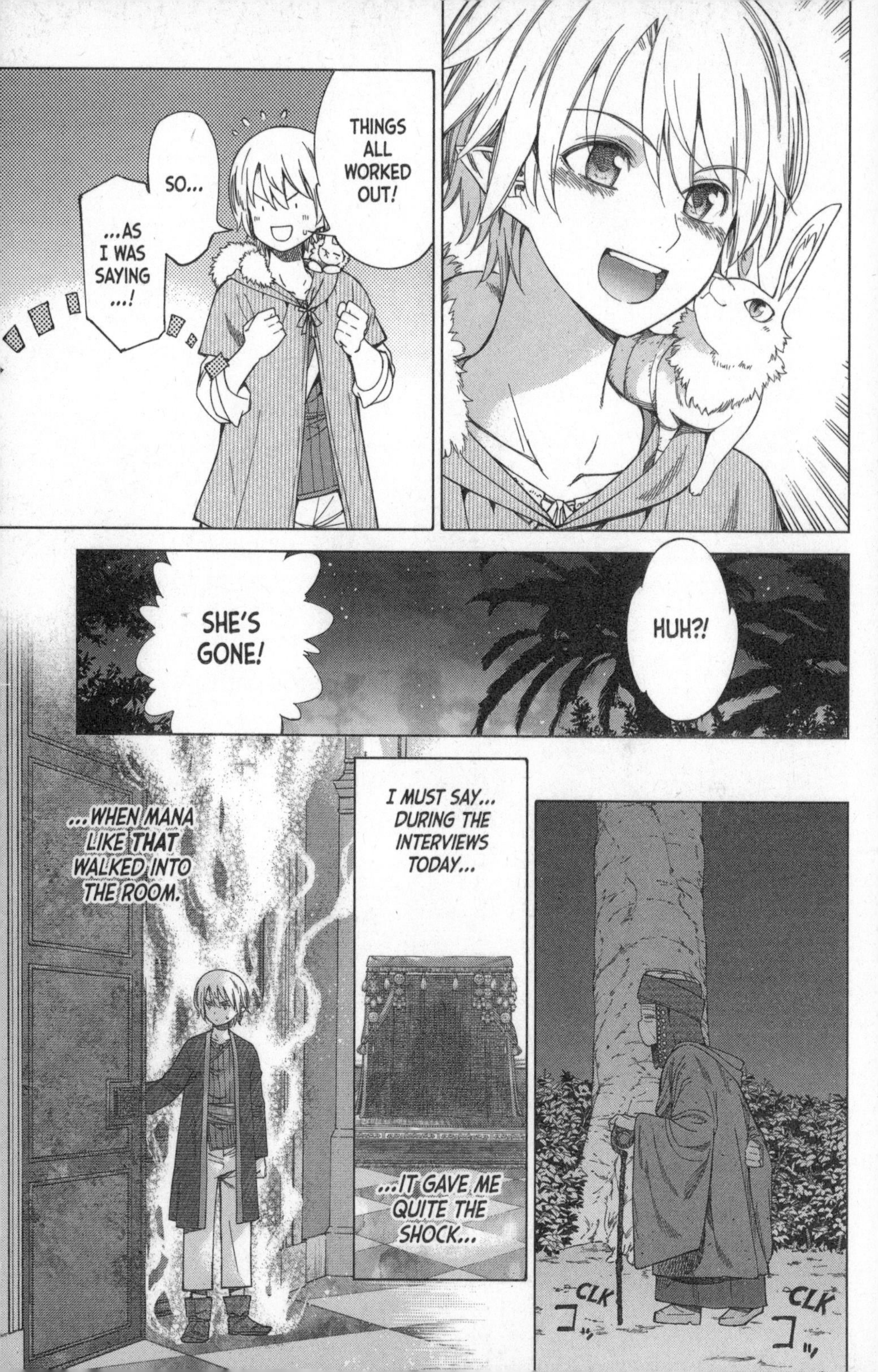
THINGS ALL WORKED OUT!
SO...
...AS I WAS SAYING ...!
HUH?!
SHE'S GONE!
CLK
CLK
I MUST SAY... DURING THE INTERVIEWS TODAY...
...IT GAVE ME QUITE THE SHOCK...
...WHEN MANA LIKE THAT WALKED INTO THE ROOM.

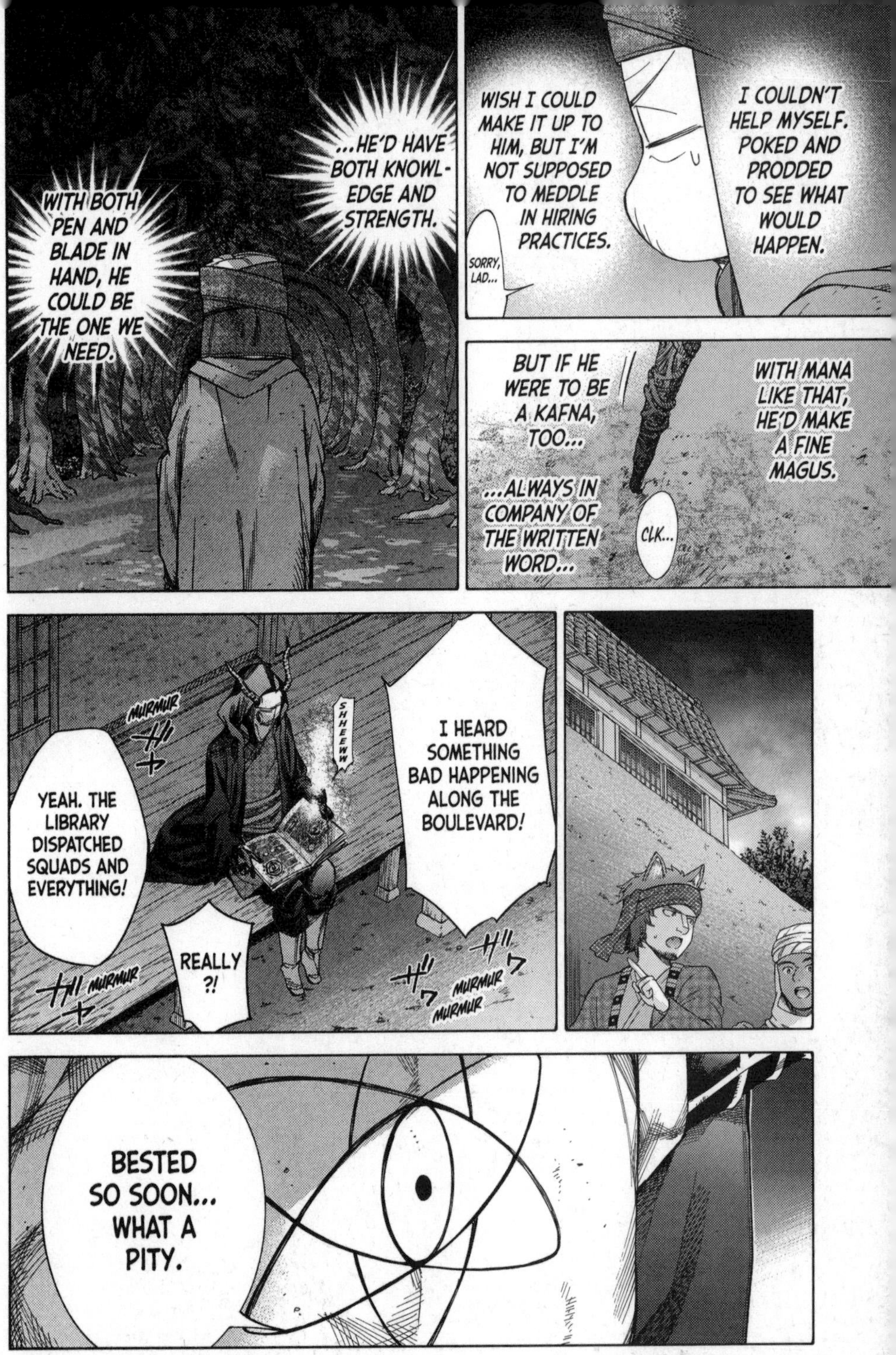
I COULDN'T HELP MYSELF. POKED AND PRODDED TO SEE WHAT WOULD HAPPEN.
WISH I COULD MAKE IT UP TO HIM, BUT I'M NOT SUPPOSED TO MEDDLE IN HIRING PRACTICES.
SORRY, LAD...
WITH MANA LIKE THAT, HE'D MAKE A FINE MAGUS.
CLK...
BUT IF HE WERE TO BE A KAFNA, TOO...
...ALWAYS IN COMPANY OF THE WRITTEN WORD...
...HE'D HAVE BOTH KNOWL-EDGE AND STRENGTH.
WITH BOTH PEN AND BLADE IN HAND, HE COULD BE THE ONE WE NEED.
SHHEEWW
I HEARD SOMETHING BAD HAPPENING ALONG THE BOULEVARD!
MURMUR MURMUR
MURMUR
YEAH. THE LIBRARY DISPATCHED SQUADS AND EVERYTHING!
REALLY?!
MURMUR
BESTED SO SOON... WHAT A PITY.

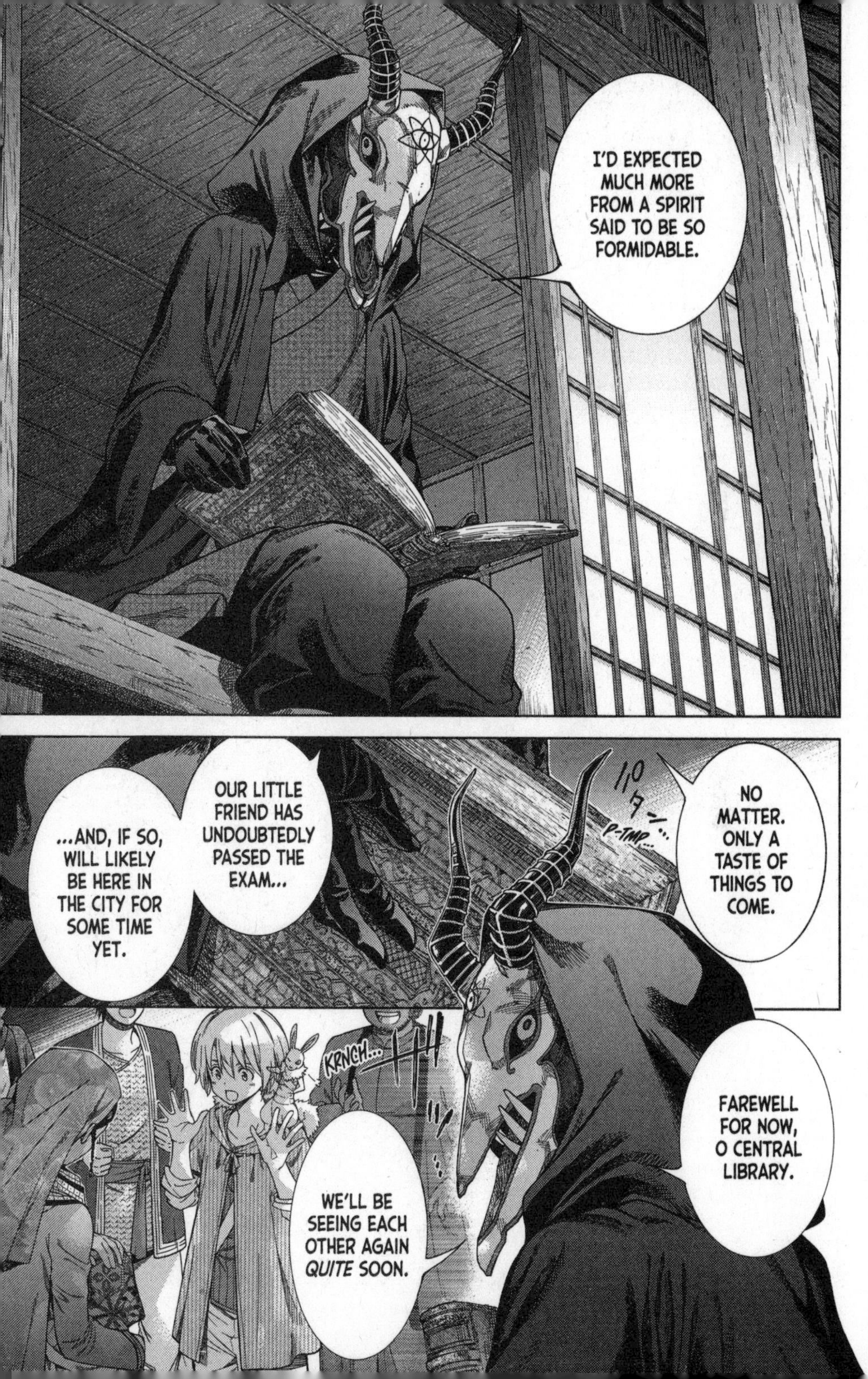
I'D EXPECTED MUCH MORE FROM A SPIRIT SAID TO BE SO FORMIDABLE.
NO MATTER. ONLY A TASTE OF THINGS TO COME.
P-TMP...
OUR LITTLE FRIEND HAS UNDOUBTEDLY PASSED THE EXAM...
...AND, IF SO, WILL LIKELY BE HERE IN THE CITY FOR SOME TIME YET.
FAREWELL FOR NOW, O CENTRAL LIBRARY.
KRNCH...
WE'LL BE SEEING EACH OTHER AGAIN *QUITE* SOON.

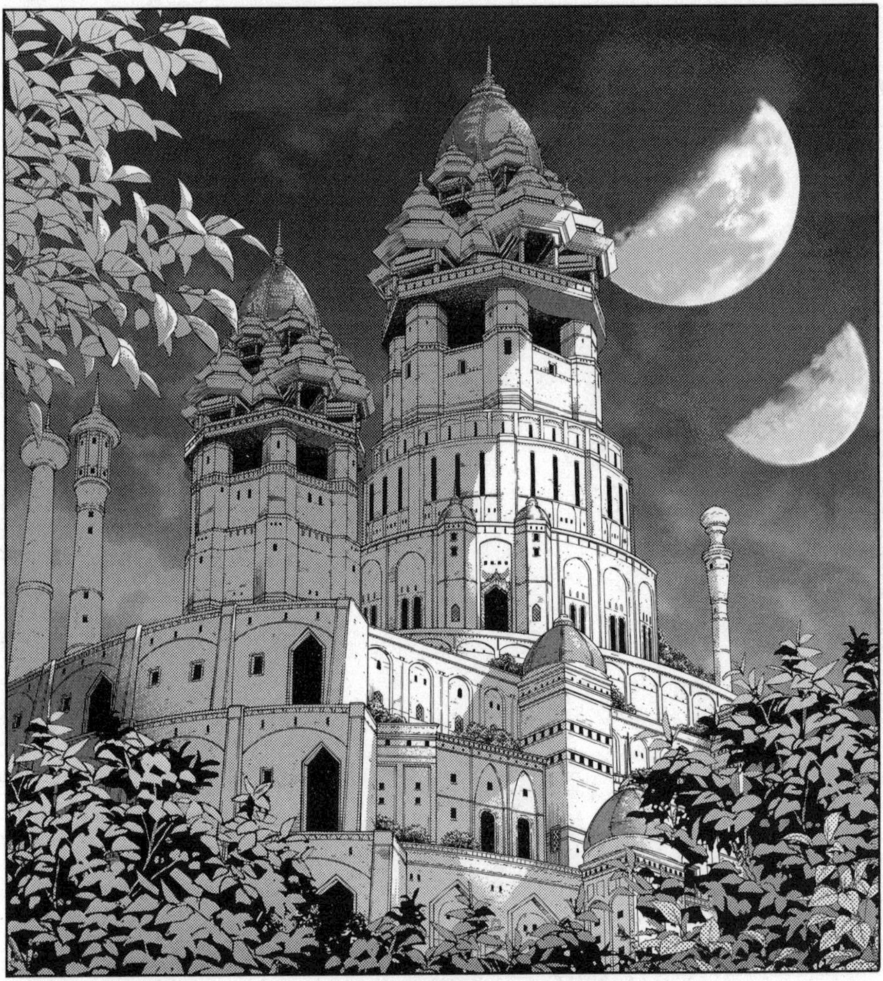

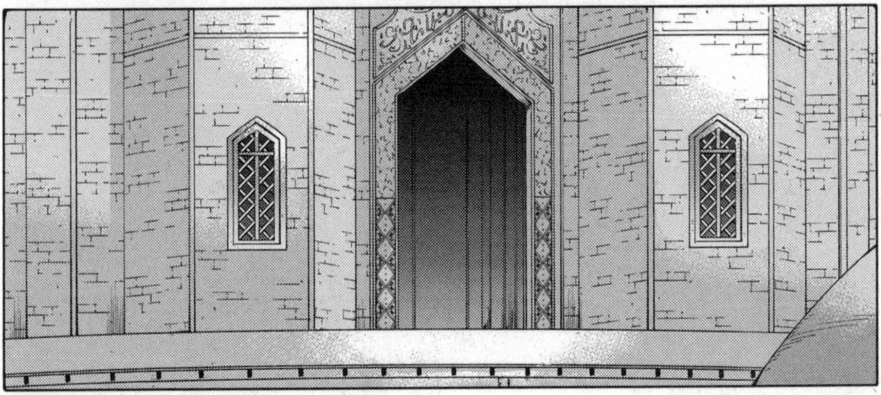

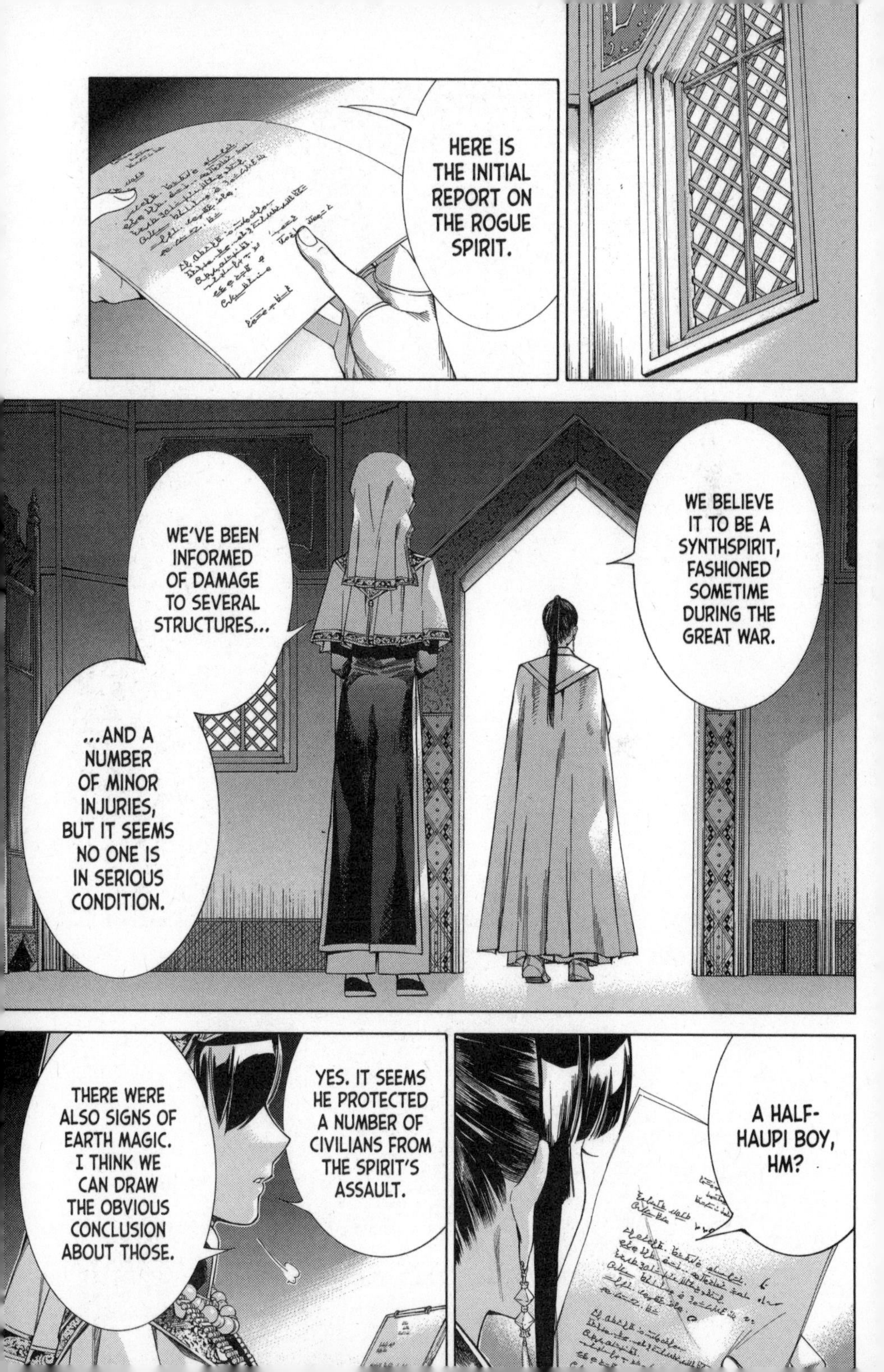
HERE IS THE INITIAL REPORT ON THE ROGUE SPIRIT.
WE BELIEVE IT TO BE A SYNTHSPIRIT, FASHIONED SOMETIME DURING THE GREAT WAR.
WE'VE BEEN INFORMED OF DAMAGE TO SEVERAL STRUCTURES...
...AND A NUMBER OF MINOR INJURIES, BUT IT SEEMS NO ONE IS IN SERIOUS CONDITION.
A HALF-HAUPI BOY, HM?
YES. IT SEEMS HE PROTECTED A NUMBER OF CIVILIANS FROM THE SPIRIT'S ASSAULT.
THERE WERE ALSO SIGNS OF EARTH MAGIC. I THINK WE CAN DRAW THE OBVIOUS CONCLUSION ABOUT THOSE.

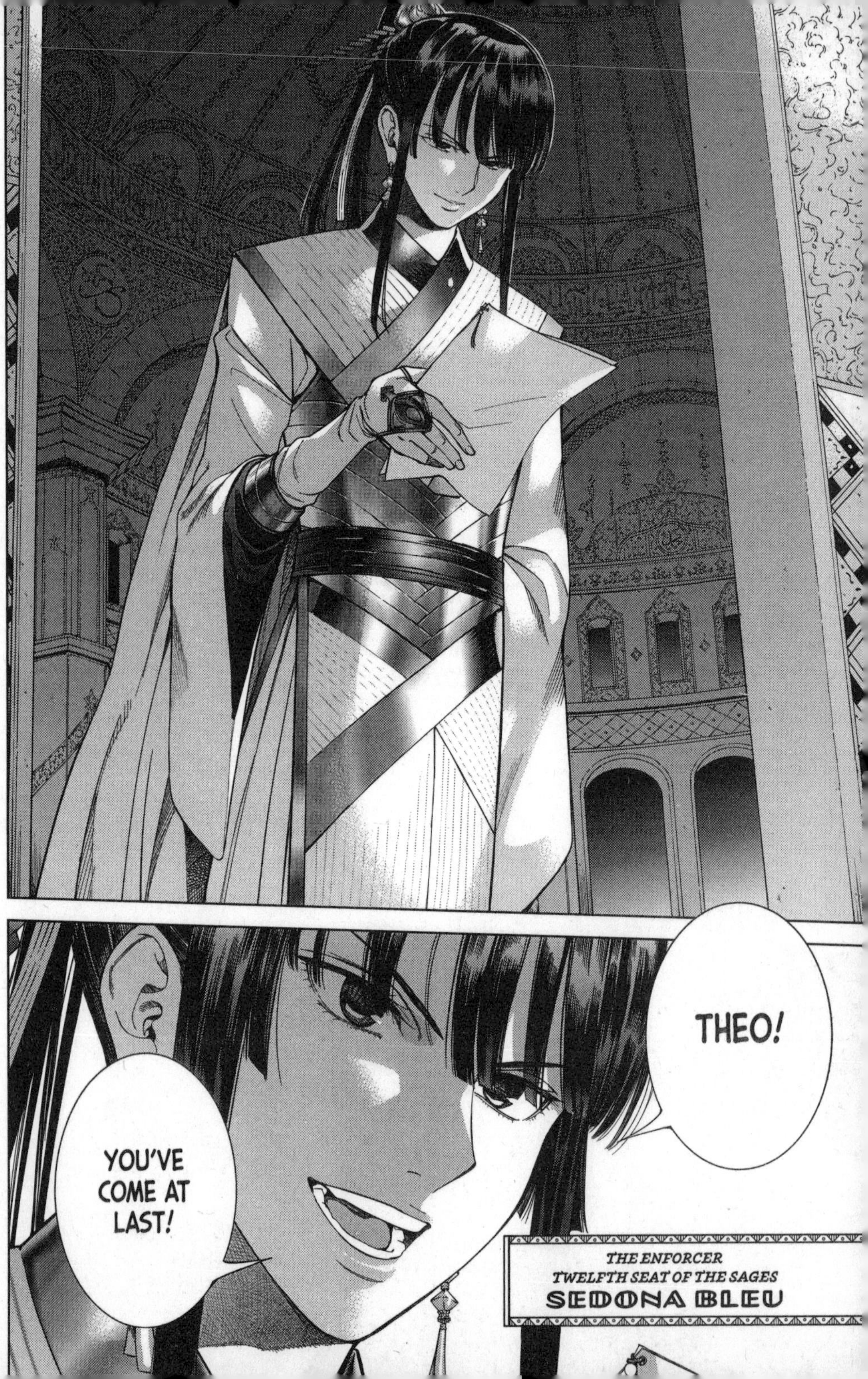
THEO!
YOU'VE COME AT LAST!
THE ENFORCER
TWELFTH SEAT OF THE SAGES
SEDONA BLEU

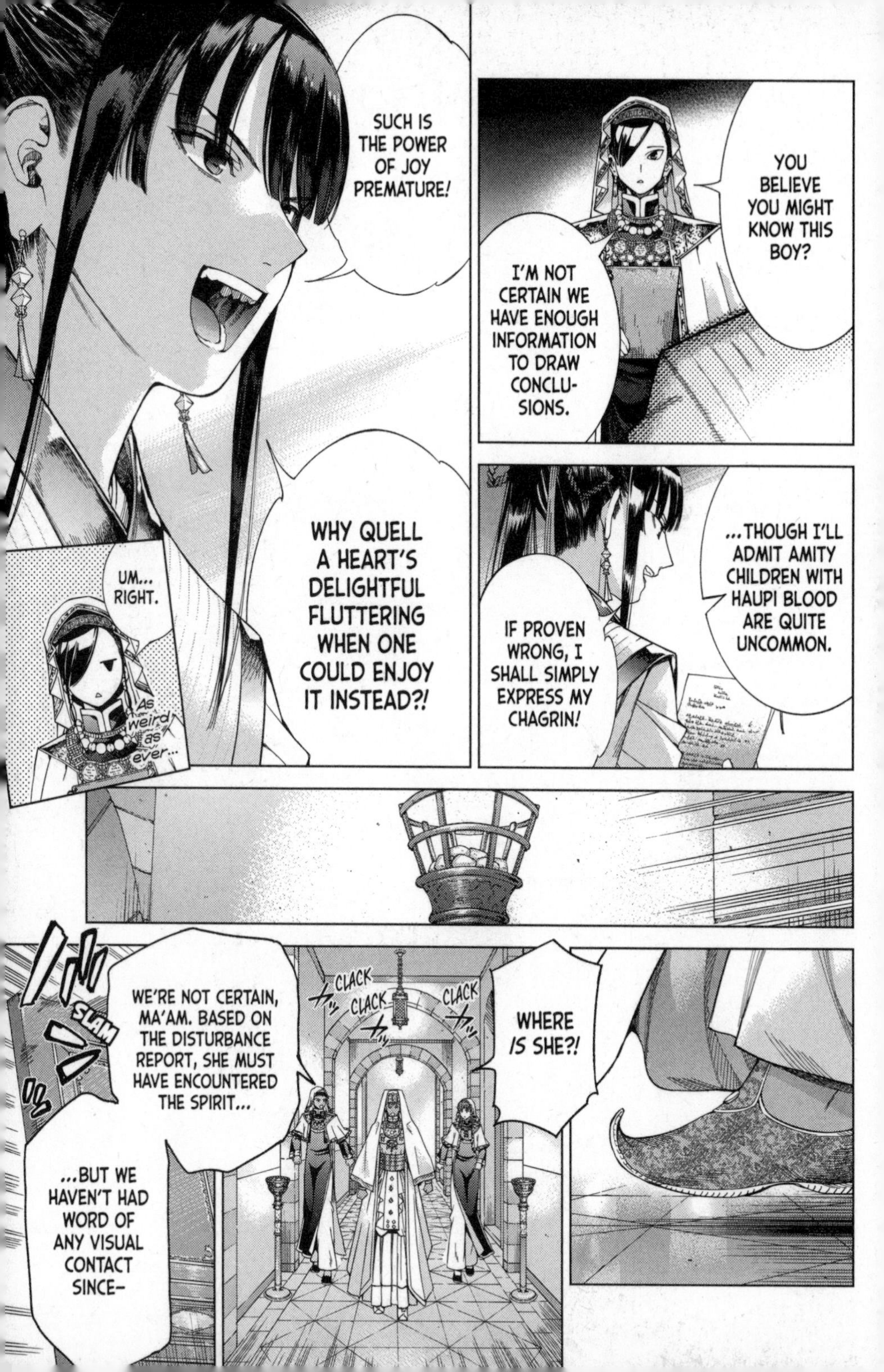
YOU BELIEVE YOU MIGHT KNOW THIS BOY?
I'M NOT CERTAIN WE HAVE ENOUGH INFORMATION TO DRAW CONCLUSIONS.
...THOUGH I'LL ADMIT AMITY CHILDREN WITH HAUPI BLOOD ARE QUITE UNCOMMON.
IF PROVEN WRONG, I SHALL SIMPLY EXPRESS MY CHAGRIN!
SUCH IS THE POWER OF JOY PREMATURE!
WHY QUELL A HEART'S DELIGHTFUL FLUTTERING WHEN ONE COULD ENJOY IT INSTEAD?!
UM... RIGHT.
As weird as ever...
WHERE IS SHE?!
CLACK
CLACK
CLACK
SLAM
WE'RE NOT CERTAIN, MA'AM. BASED ON THE DISTURBANCE REPORT, SHE MUST HAVE ENCOUNTERED THE SPIRIT...
...BUT WE HAVEN'T HAD WORD OF ANY VISUAL CONTACT SINCE–

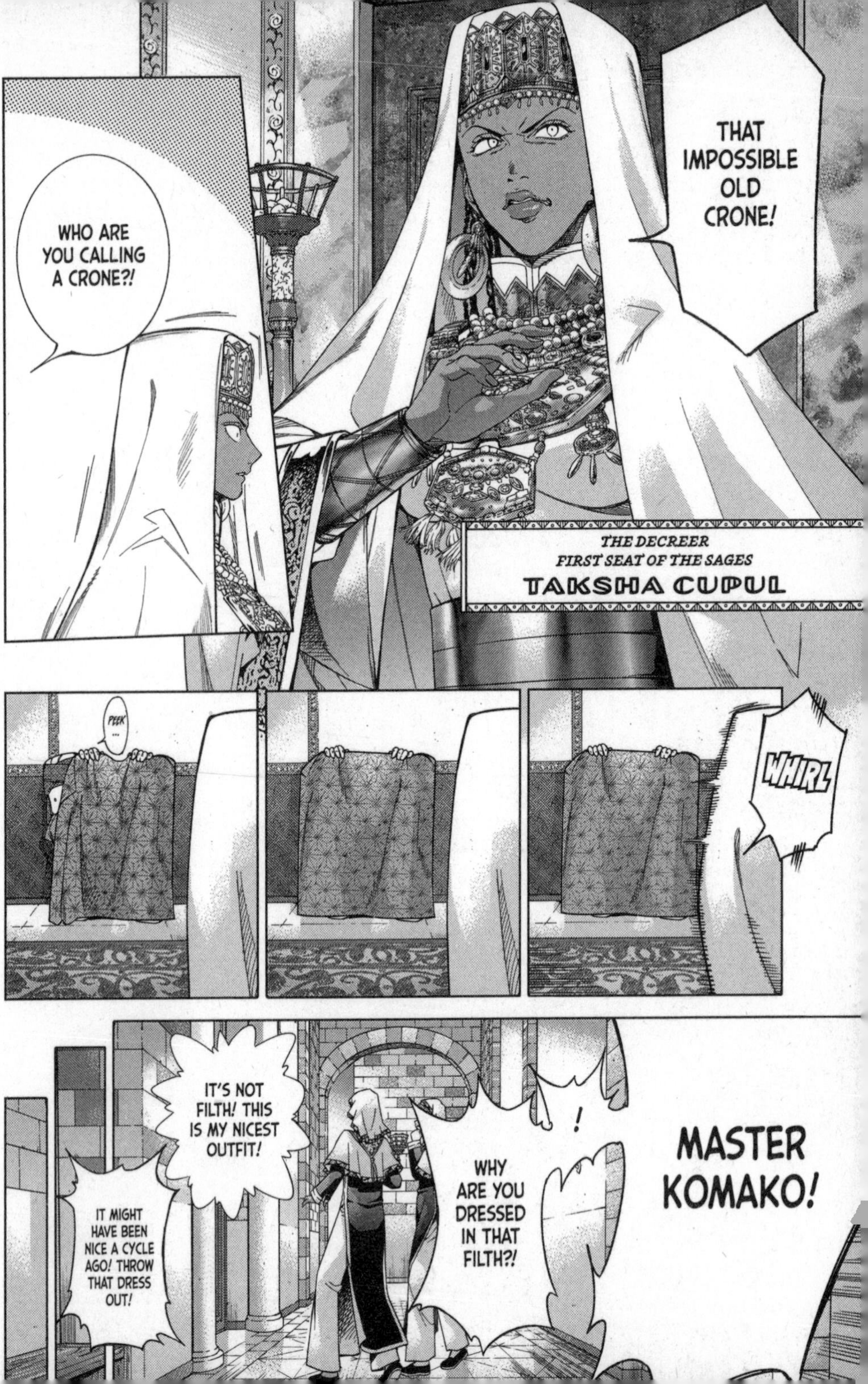
THAT IMPOSSIBLE OLD CRONE!
THE DECREER
FIRST SEAT OF THE SAGES
TAKSHA CUPUL
WHO ARE YOU CALLING A CRONE?!
WHIRL
PEEK ...
MASTER KOMAKO!
!
WHY ARE YOU DRESSED IN THAT FILTH?!
IT'S NOT FILTH! THIS IS MY NICEST OUTFIT!
IT MIGHT HAVE BEEN NICE A CYCLE AGO! THROW THAT DRESS OUT!

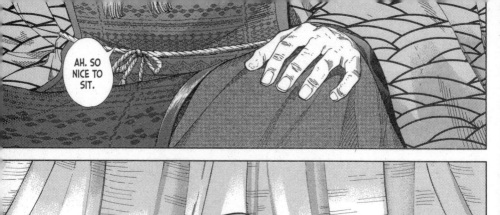

AH. SO NICE TO SIT.

GENERAL REPRESENTATIVE, CENTRAL LIBRARY
KOMAKO KAULIKK

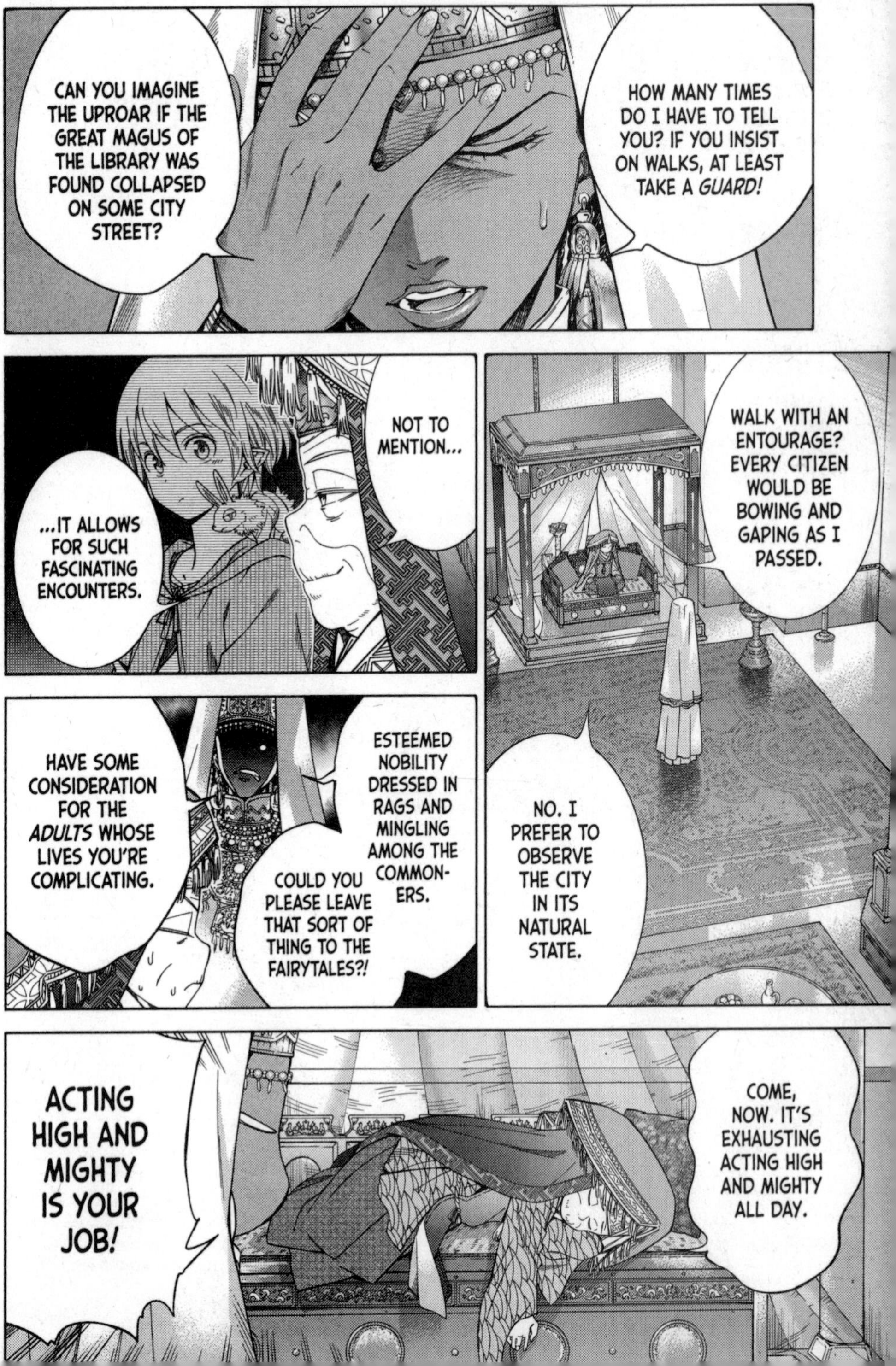
HOW MANY TIMES DO I HAVE TO TELL YOU? IF YOU INSIST ON WALKS, AT LEAST TAKE A *GUARD!*
CAN YOU IMAGINE THE UPROAR IF THE GREAT MAGUS OF THE LIBRARY WAS FOUND COLLAPSED ON SOME CITY STREET?
WALK WITH AN ENTOURAGE? EVERY CITIZEN WOULD BE BOWING AND GAPING AS I PASSED.
NO. I PREFER TO OBSERVE THE CITY IN ITS NATURAL STATE.
NOT TO MENTION...
...IT ALLOWS FOR SUCH FASCINATING ENCOUNTERS.
ESTEEMED NOBILITY DRESSED IN RAGS AND MINGLING AMONG THE COMMON-ERS.
COULD YOU PLEASE LEAVE THAT SORT OF THING TO THE FAIRYTALES?!
HAVE SOME CONSIDERATION FOR THE *ADULTS* WHOSE LIVES YOU'RE COMPLICATING.
COME, NOW. IT'S EXHAUSTING ACTING HIGH AND MIGHTY ALL DAY.
ACTING HIGH AND MIGHTY IS YOUR JOB!

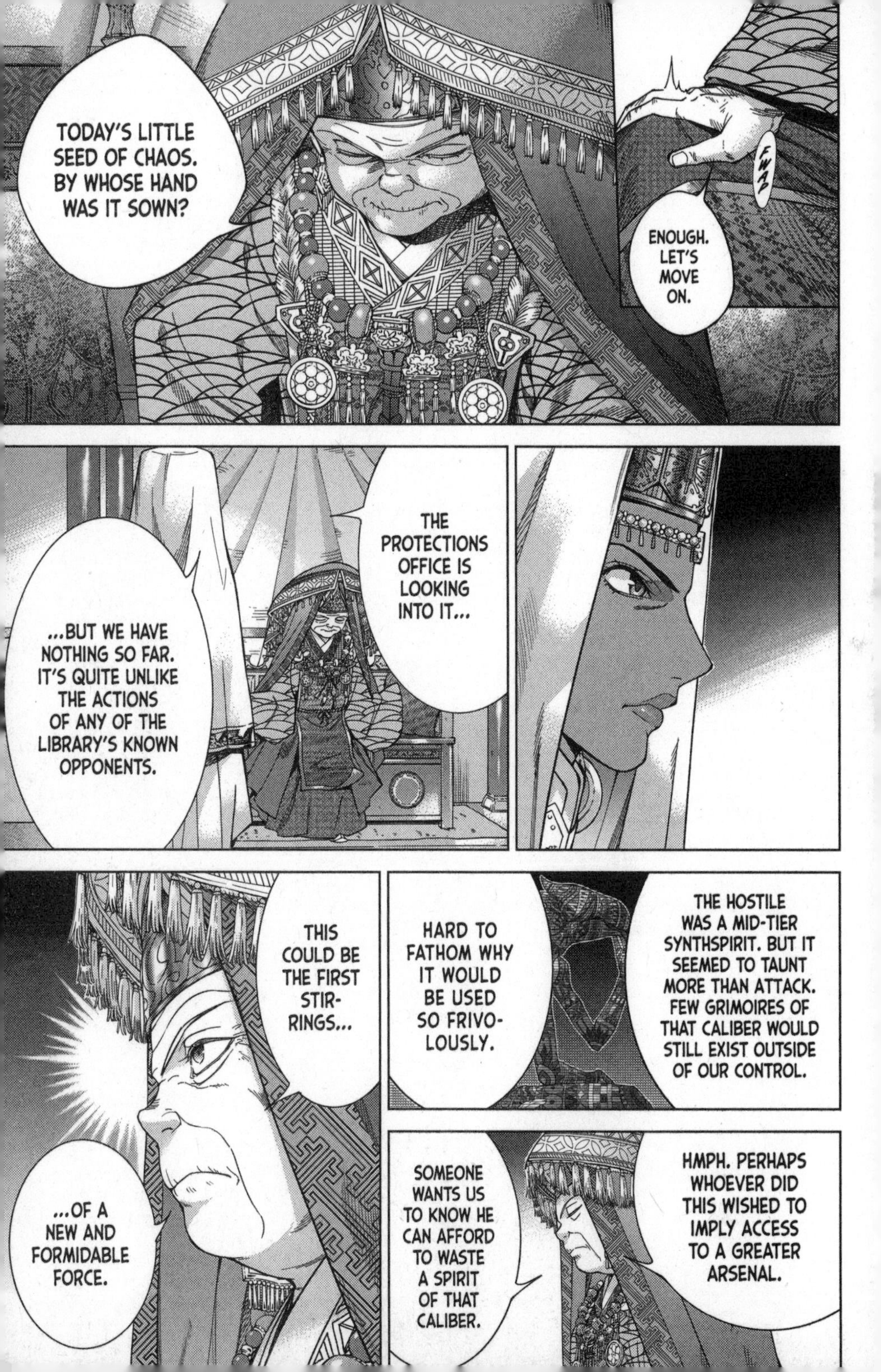
FWAP
ENOUGH. LET'S MOVE ON.
TODAY'S LITTLE SEED OF CHAOS. BY WHOSE HAND WAS IT SOWN?
THE PROTECTIONS OFFICE IS LOOKING INTO IT...
...BUT WE HAVE NOTHING SO FAR. IT'S QUITE UNLIKE THE ACTIONS OF ANY OF THE LIBRARY'S KNOWN OPPONENTS.
THE HOSTILE WAS A MID-TIER SYNTHSPIRIT. BUT IT SEEMED TO TAUNT MORE THAN ATTACK. FEW GRIMOIRES OF THAT CALIBER WOULD STILL EXIST OUTSIDE OF OUR CONTROL.
HARD TO FATHOM WHY IT WOULD BE USED SO FRIVO-LOUSLY.
HMPH. PERHAPS WHOEVER DID THIS WISHED TO IMPLY ACCESS TO A GREATER ARSENAL.
SOMEONE WANTS US TO KNOW HE CAN AFFORD TO WASTE A SPIRIT OF THAT CALIBER.
THIS COULD BE THE FIRST STIR-RINGS...
...OF A NEW AND FORMIDABLE FORCE.

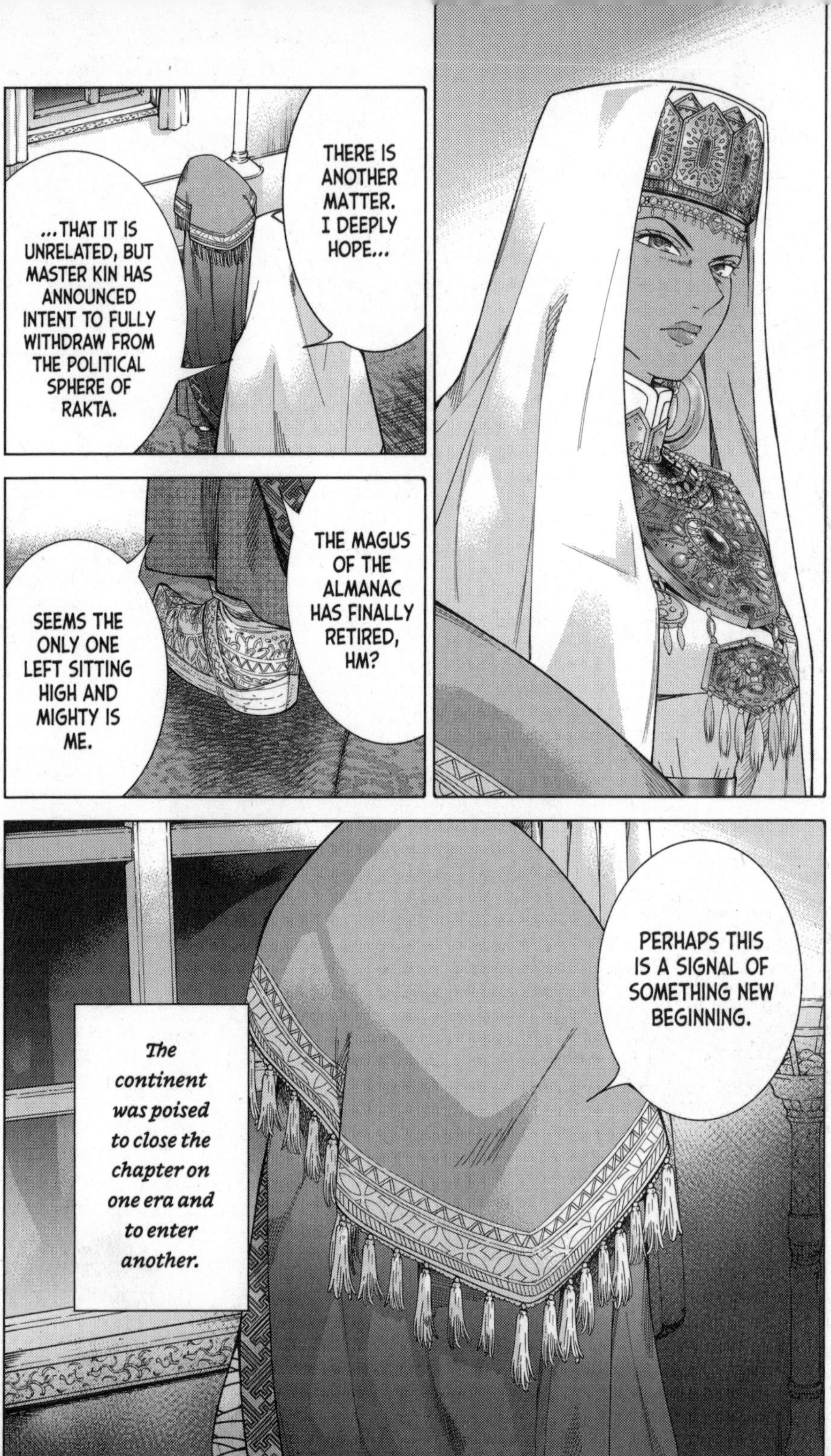
THERE IS ANOTHER MATTER. I DEEPLY HOPE...
...THAT IT IS UNRELATED, BUT MASTER KIN HAS ANNOUNCED INTENT TO FULLY WITHDRAW FROM THE POLITICAL SPHERE OF RAKTA.
THE MAGUS OF THE ALMANAC HAS FINALLY RETIRED, HM?
SEEMS THE ONLY ONE LEFT SITTING HIGH AND MIGHTY IS ME.
PERHAPS THIS IS A SIGNAL OF SOMETHING NEW BEGINNING.
The continent was poised to close the chapter on one era and to enter another.

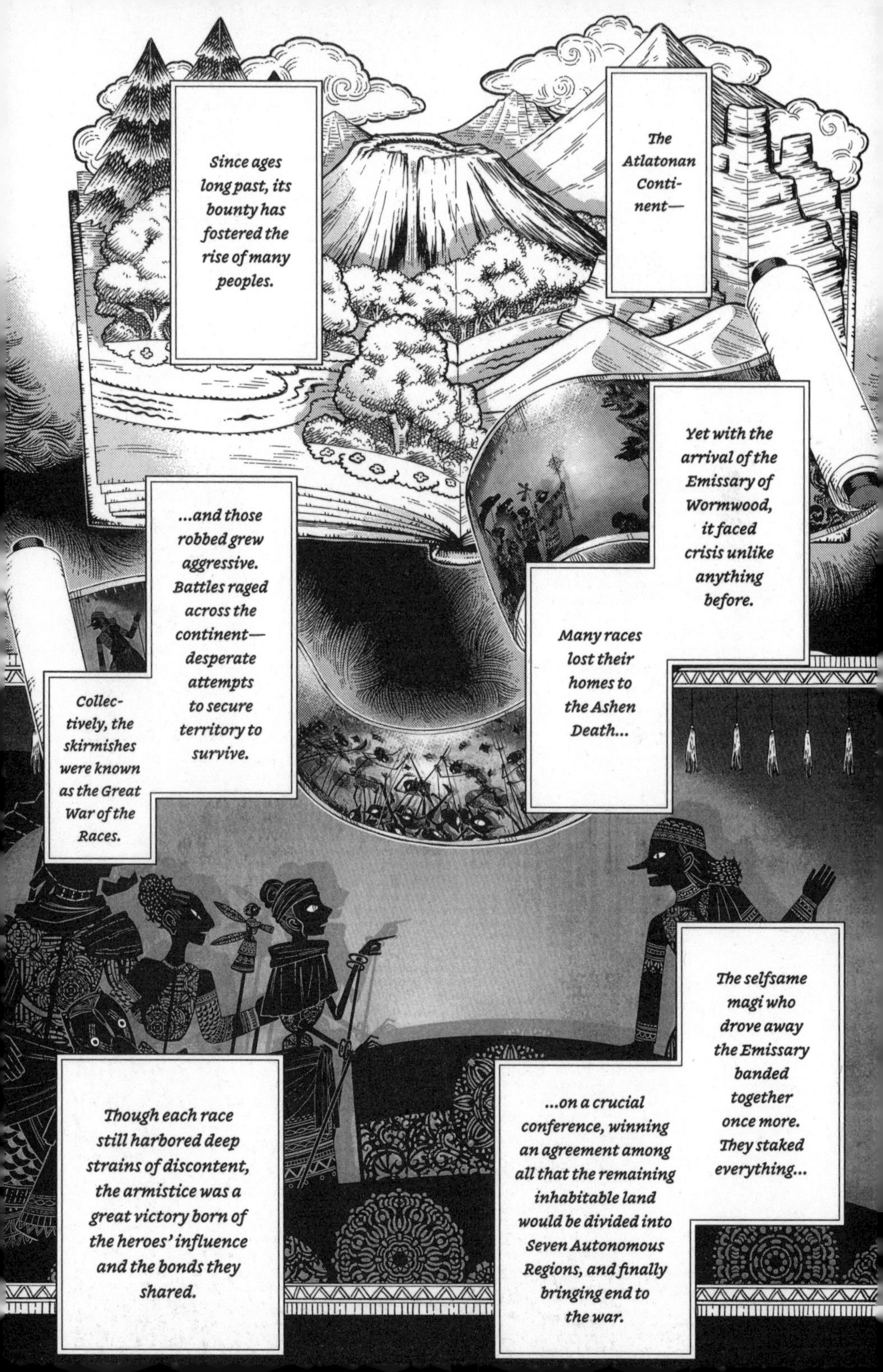
The Atlatonan Continent—
Since ages long past, its bounty has fostered the rise of many peoples.
Yet with the arrival of the Emissary of Wormwood, it faced crisis unlike anything before.
Many races lost their homes to the Ashen Death...
...and those robbed grew aggressive. Battles raged across the continent—desperate attempts to secure territory to survive.
Collectively, the skirmishes were known as the Great War of the Races.
The selfsame magi who drove away the Emissary banded together once more. They staked everything...
...on a crucial conference, winning an agreement among all that the remaining inhabitable land would be divided into Seven Autonomous Regions, and finally bringing end to the war.
Though each race still harbored deep strains of discontent, the armistice was a great victory born of the heroes' influence and the bonds they shared.

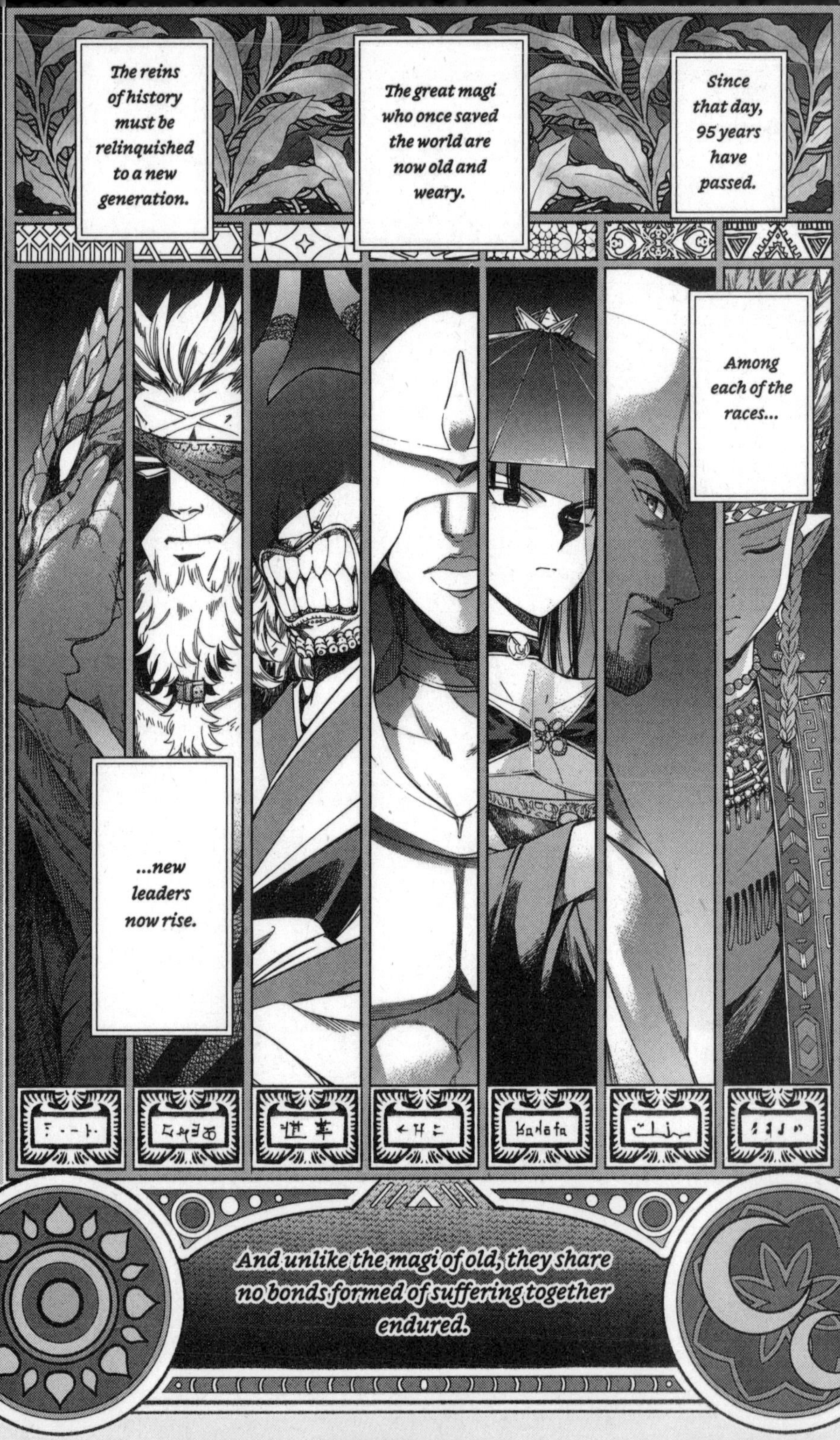
Since that day, 95 years have passed.
The great magi who once saved the world are now old and weary.
The reins of history must be relinquished to a new generation.
Among each of the races...
...new leaders now rise.
And unlike the magi of old, they share no bonds formed of suffering together endured.

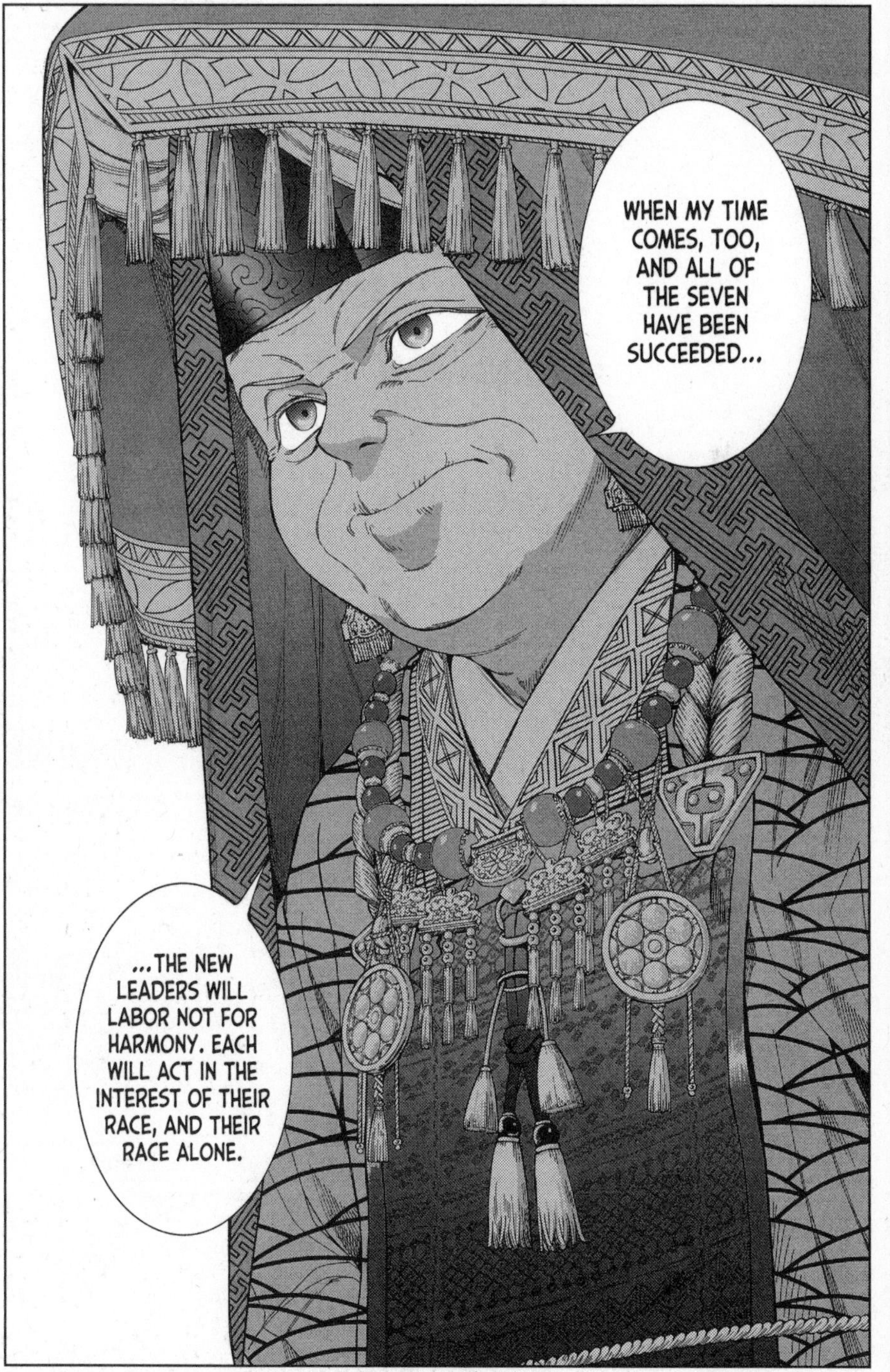
WHEN MY TIME COMES, TOO, AND ALL OF THE SEVEN HAVE BEEN SUCCEEDED...
...THE NEW LEADERS WILL LABOR NOT FOR HARMONY. EACH WILL ACT IN THE INTEREST OF THEIR RACE, AND THEIR RACE ALONE.

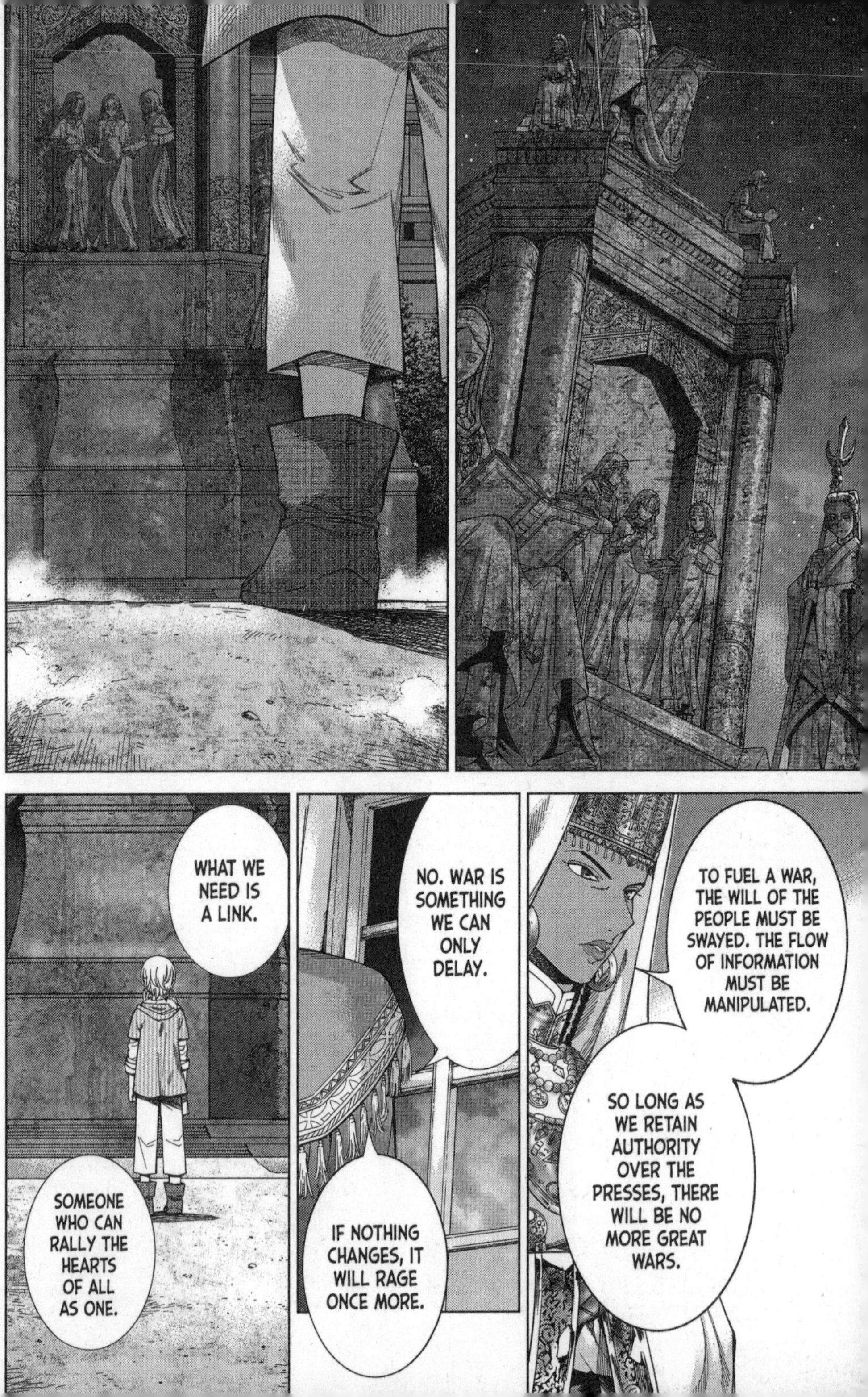
TO FUEL A WAR, THE WILL OF THE PEOPLE MUST BE SWAYED. THE FLOW OF INFORMATION MUST BE MANIPULATED.
SO LONG AS WE RETAIN AUTHORITY OVER THE PRESSES, THERE WILL BE NO MORE GREAT WARS.
NO. WAR IS SOMETHING WE CAN ONLY DELAY.
IF NOTHING CHANGES, IT WILL RAGE ONCE MORE.
WHAT WE NEED IS A LINK.
SOMEONE WHO CAN RALLY THE HEARTS OF ALL AS ONE.

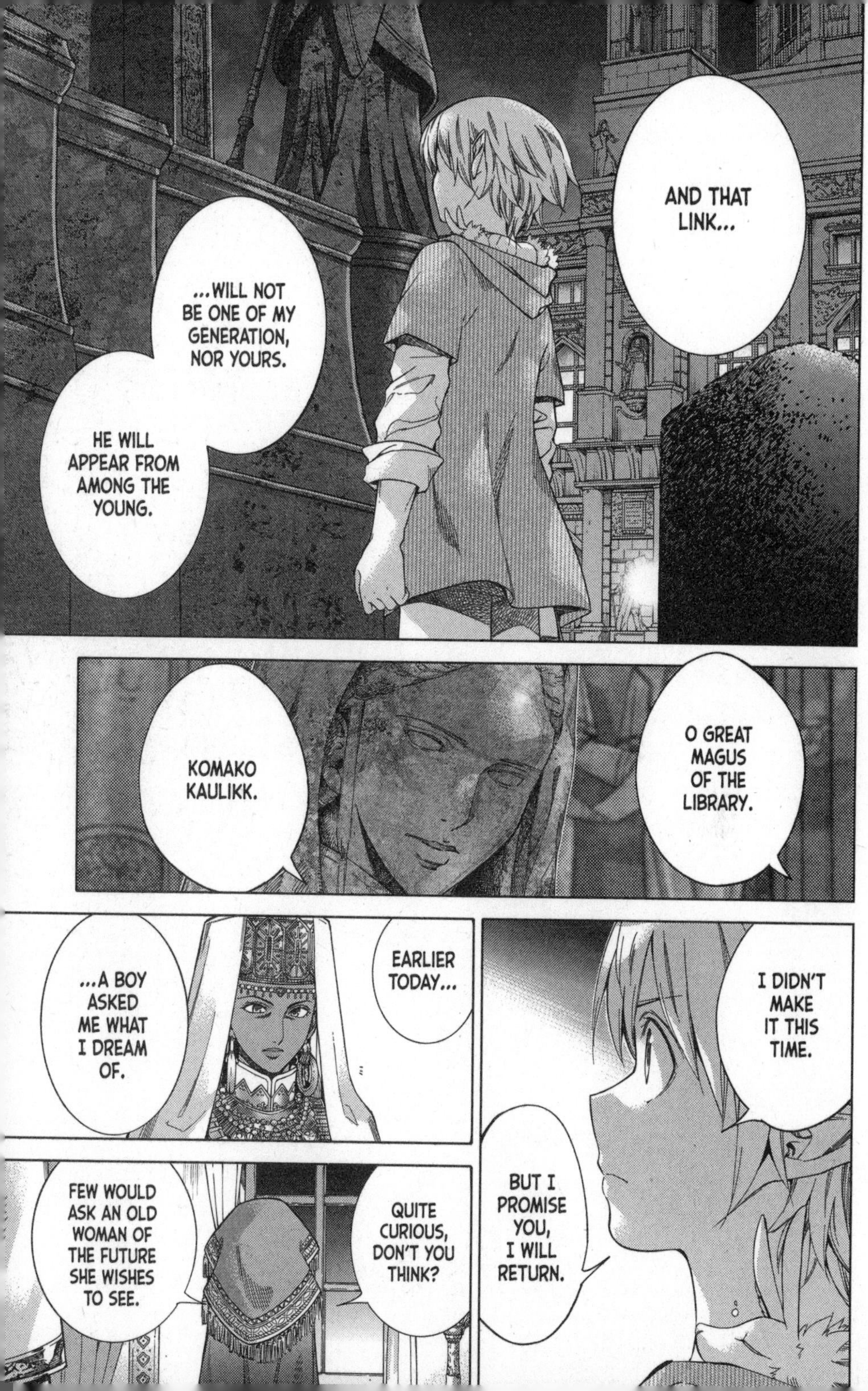
AND THAT LINK...
...WILL NOT BE ONE OF MY GENERATION, NOR YOURS.
HE WILL APPEAR FROM AMONG THE YOUNG.
O GREAT MAGUS OF THE LIBRARY.
KOMAKO KAULIKK.
I DIDN'T MAKE IT THIS TIME.
BUT I PROMISE YOU, I WILL RETURN.
EARLIER TODAY...
...A BOY ASKED ME WHAT I DREAM OF.
QUITE CURIOUS, DON'T YOU THINK?
FEW WOULD ASK AN OLD WOMAN OF THE FUTURE SHE WISHES TO SEE.

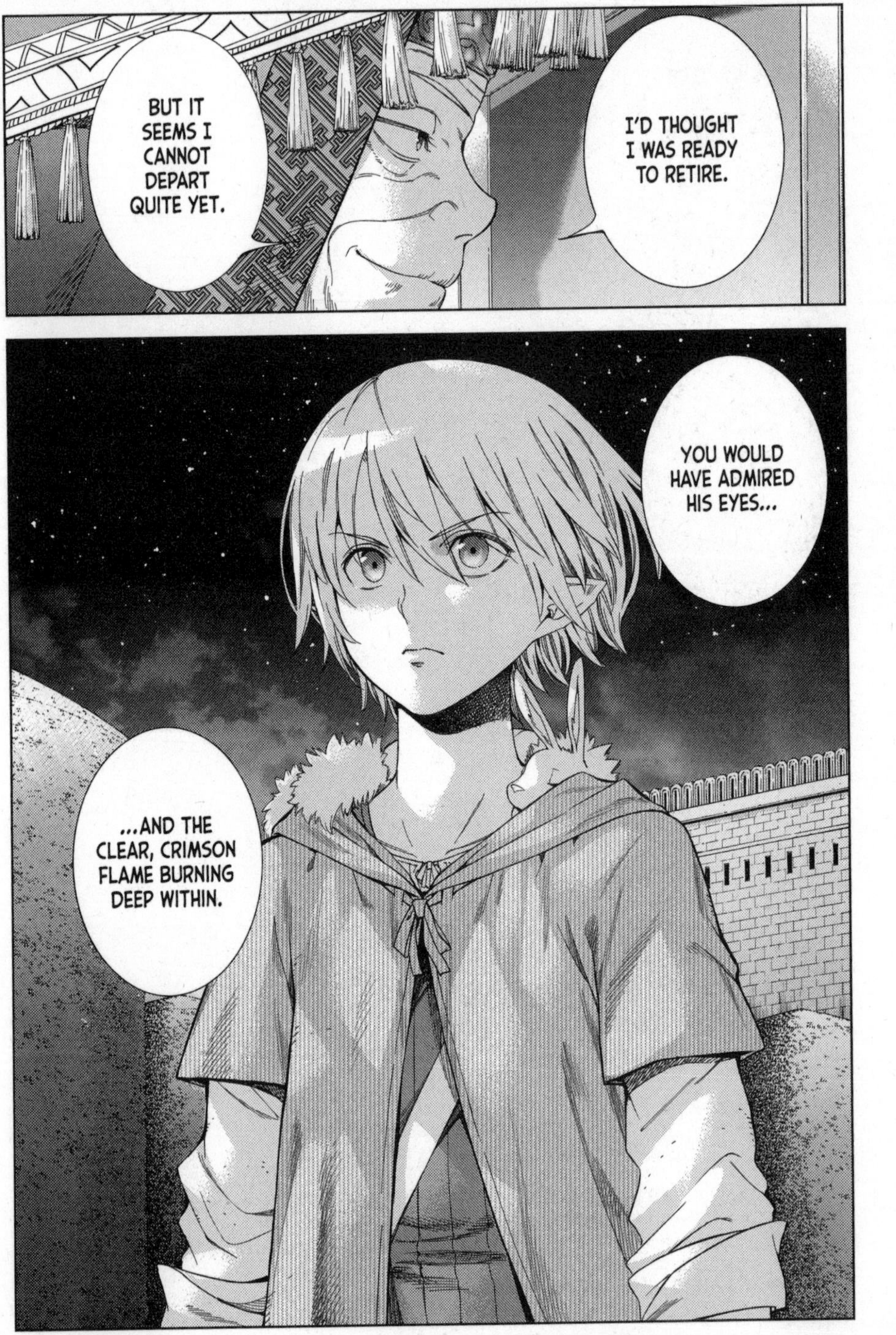
I'D THOUGHT I WAS READY TO RETIRE.
BUT IT SEEMS I CANNOT DEPART QUITE YET.
YOU WOULD HAVE ADMIRED HIS EYES...
...AND THE CLEAR, CRIMSON FLAME BURNING DEEP WITHIN.

The Seven Seminal Scripts

The Black Text

| [Author] Lugei Noir | [Date] 145 Years Ago |

One of the Seven Seminal Scripts.
A book that endeavors to present an academic argument that the
Haupi are an inferior race.
Later research would refute the vast majority of the assertions made as mere
sophistry, but at the time of the *Black Text*'s publication, there were many who were
swayed by its words. Fueled by these thoughts, and amid the chaos in the aftermath of
the Emissary's attack, the Hyron began a mass slaughter of the Haupi.
It was this book that drove the Central Library to establish its current framework for
inspecting and supervising all the continent's texts, for the *Black Text* is said to have
killed far more people than the spells of any grimoire.

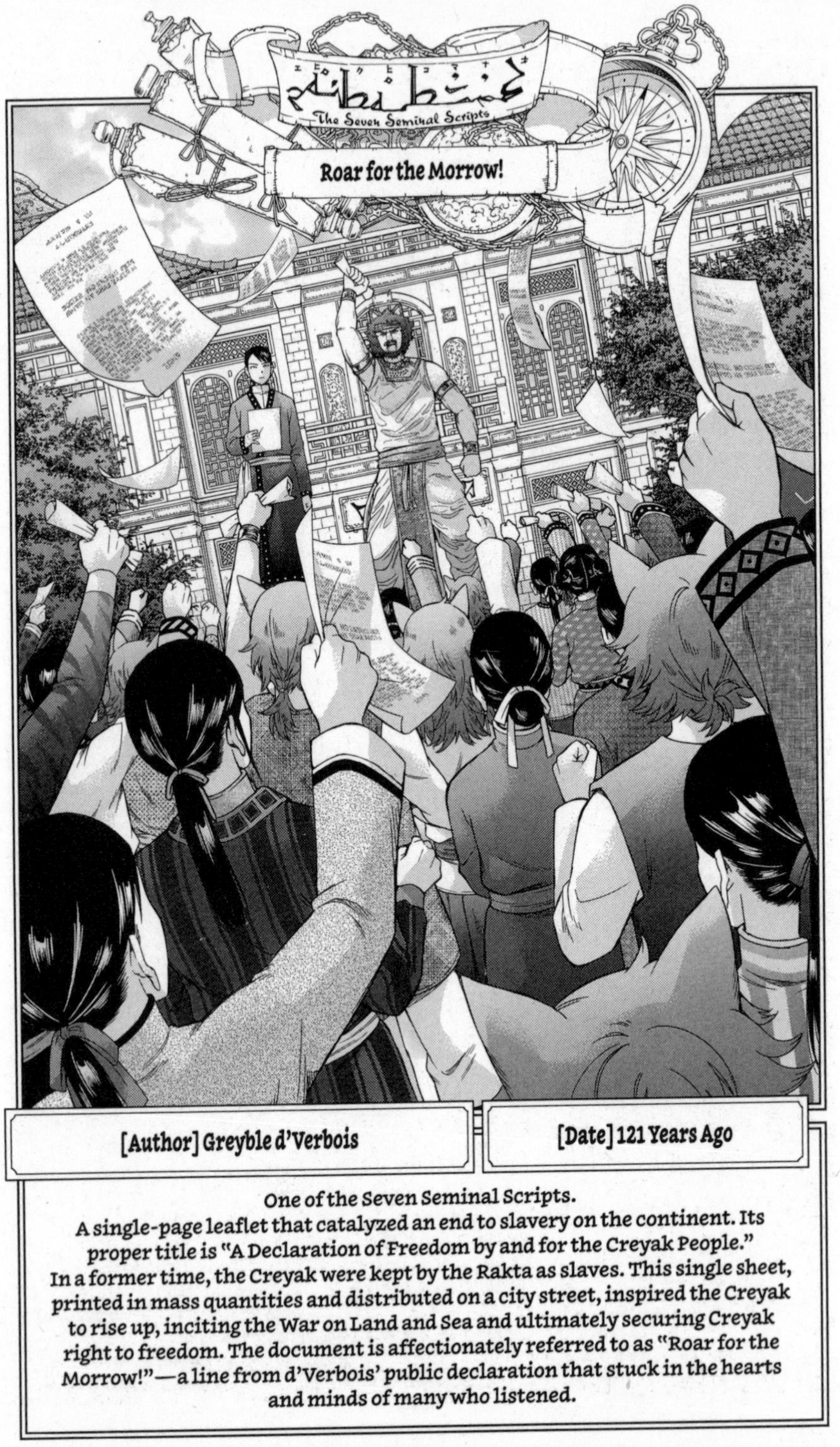
The Seven Seminal Scripts
Roar for the Morrow!

[Author] Greyble d'Verbois

[Date] 121 Years Ago

One of the Seven Seminal Scripts.
A single-page leaflet that catalyzed an end to slavery on the continent. Its proper title is "A Declaration of Freedom by and for the Creyak People."
In a former time, the Creyak were kept by the Rakta as slaves. This single sheet, printed in mass quantities and distributed on a city street, inspired the Creyak to rise up, inciting the War on Land and Sea and ultimately securing Creyak right to freedom. The document is affectionately referred to as "Roar for the Morrow!"—a line from d'Verbois' public declaration that stuck in the hearts and minds of many who listened.

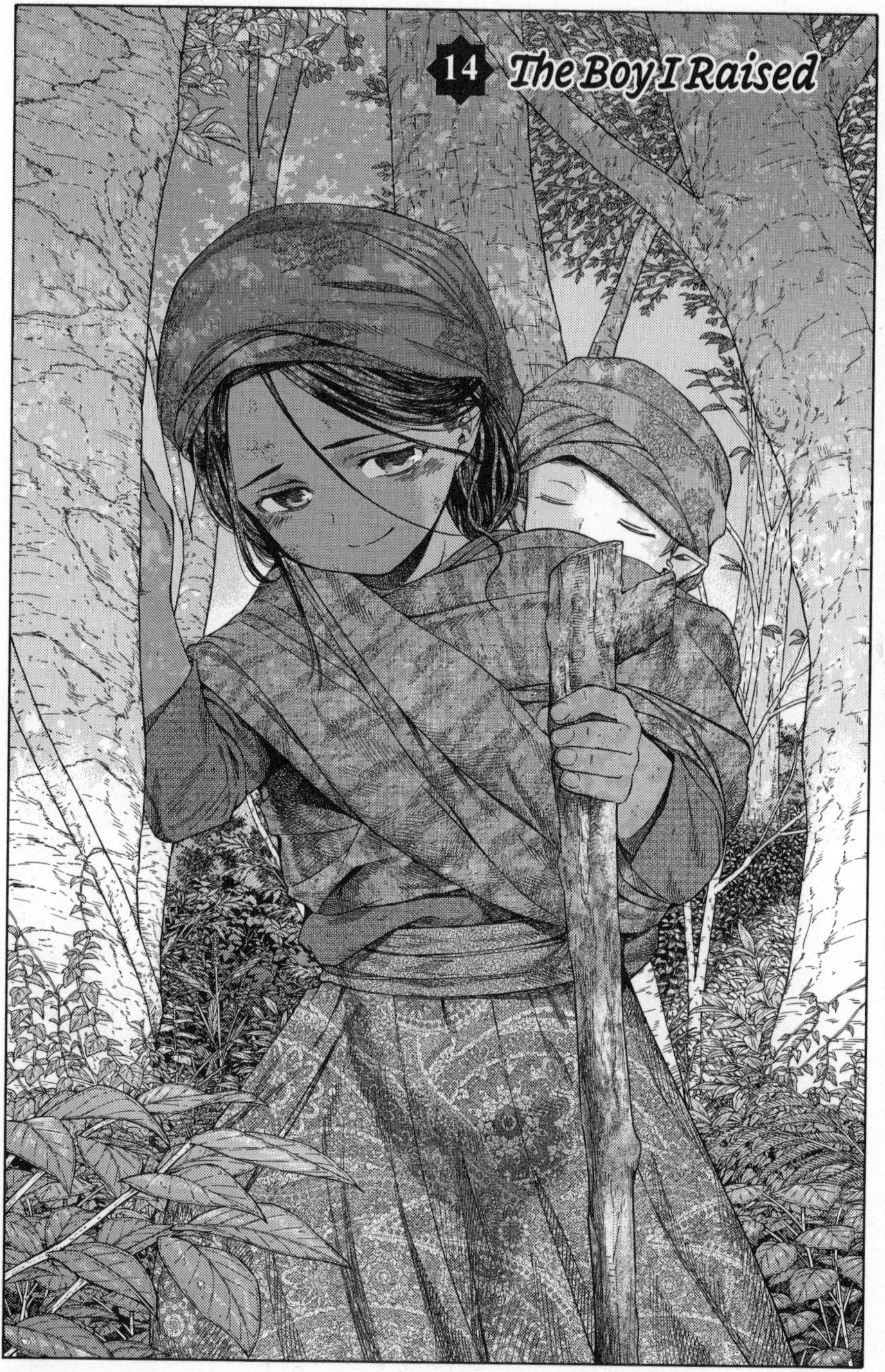
14 The Boy I Raised

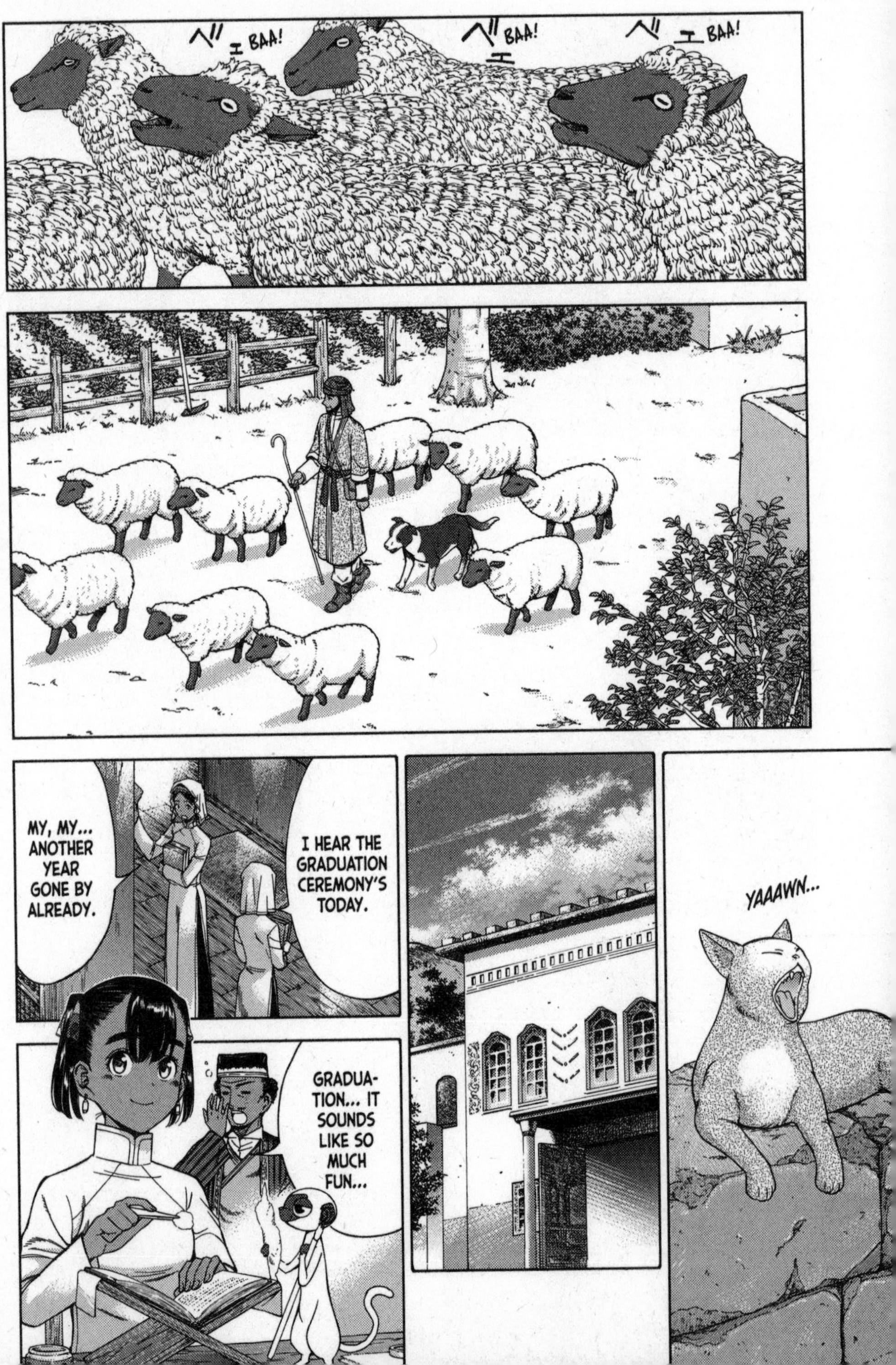
ベェ BAA!
ベェ BAA!
ベェ BAA!
YAAAWN...
I HEAR THE GRADUATION CEREMONY'S TODAY.
MY, MY... ANOTHER YEAR GONE BY ALREADY.
GRADUATION... IT SOUNDS LIKE SO MUCH FUN...

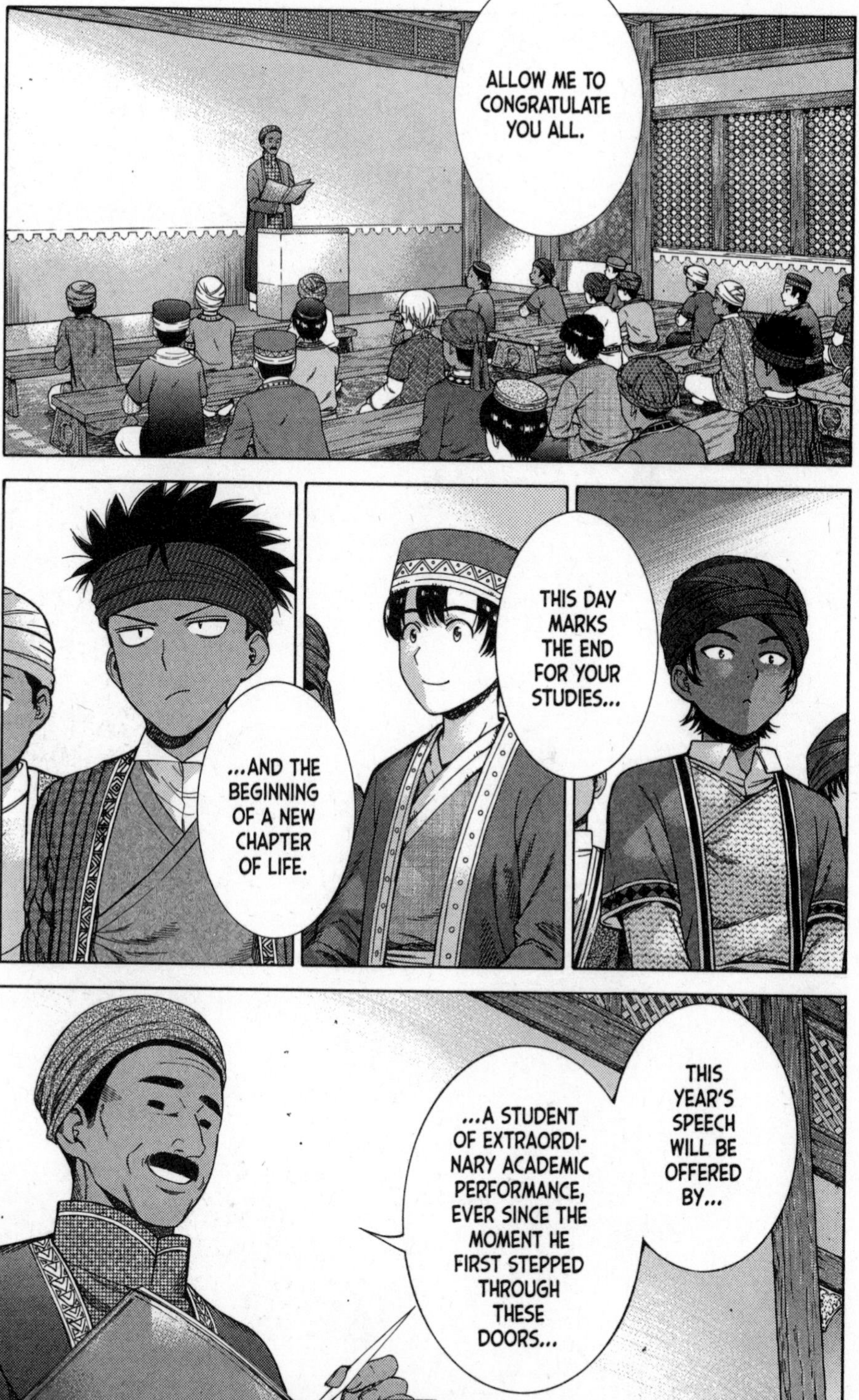
ALLOW ME TO CONGRATULATE YOU ALL.
THIS DAY MARKS THE END FOR YOUR STUDIES...
...AND THE BEGINNING OF A NEW CHAPTER OF LIFE.
THIS YEAR'S SPEECH WILL BE OFFERED BY...
...A STUDENT OF EXTRAORDI-NARY ACADEMIC PERFORMANCE, EVER SINCE THE MOMENT HE FIRST STEPPED THROUGH THESE DOORS...

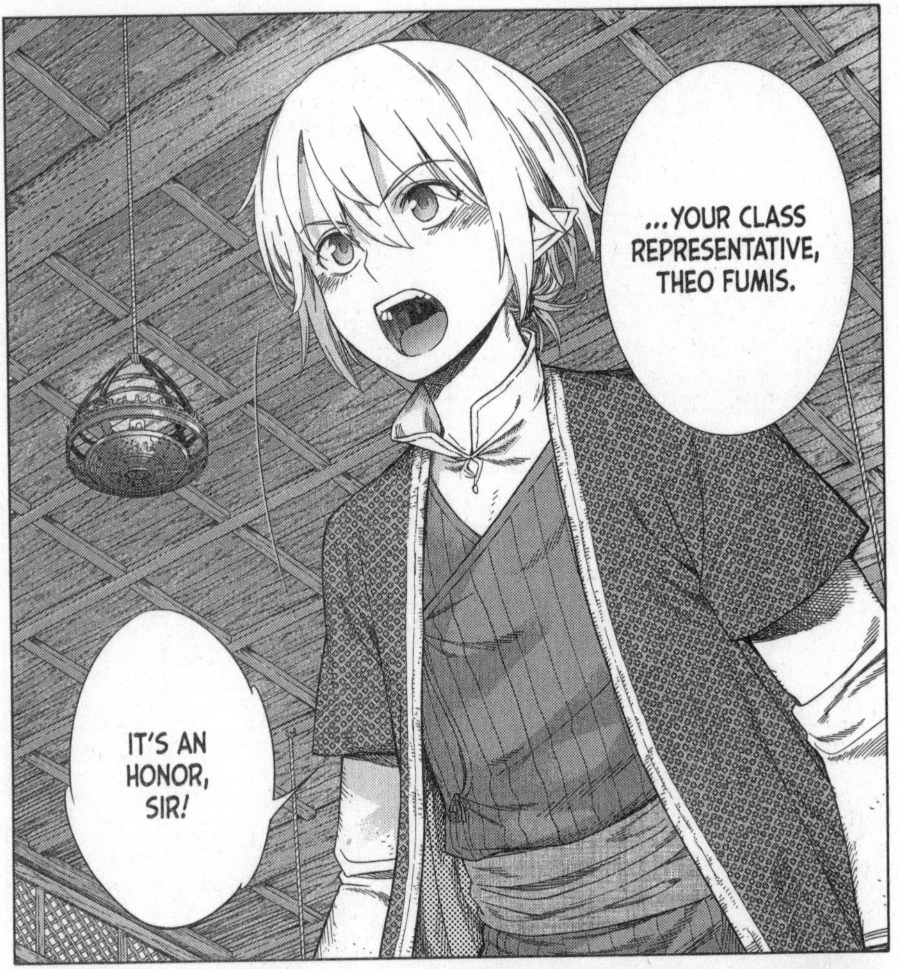
...YOUR CLASS REPRESENTATIVE, THEO FUMIS.
IT'S AN HONOR, SIR!

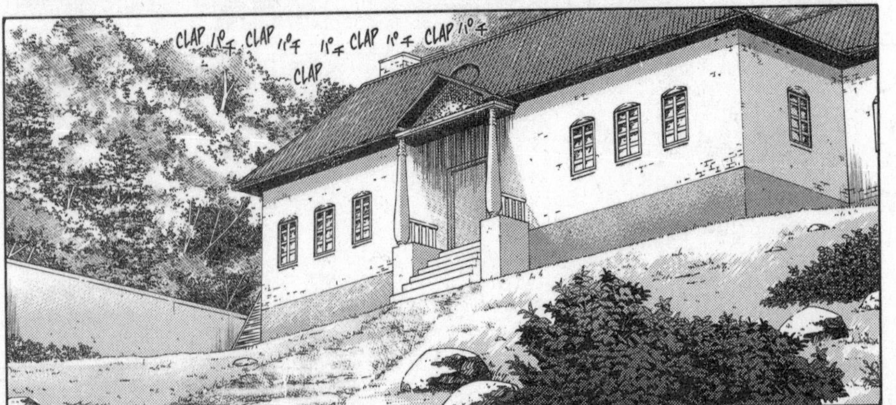
CLAP パチ CLAP パチ パチ CLAP パチ CLAP パチ
CLAP

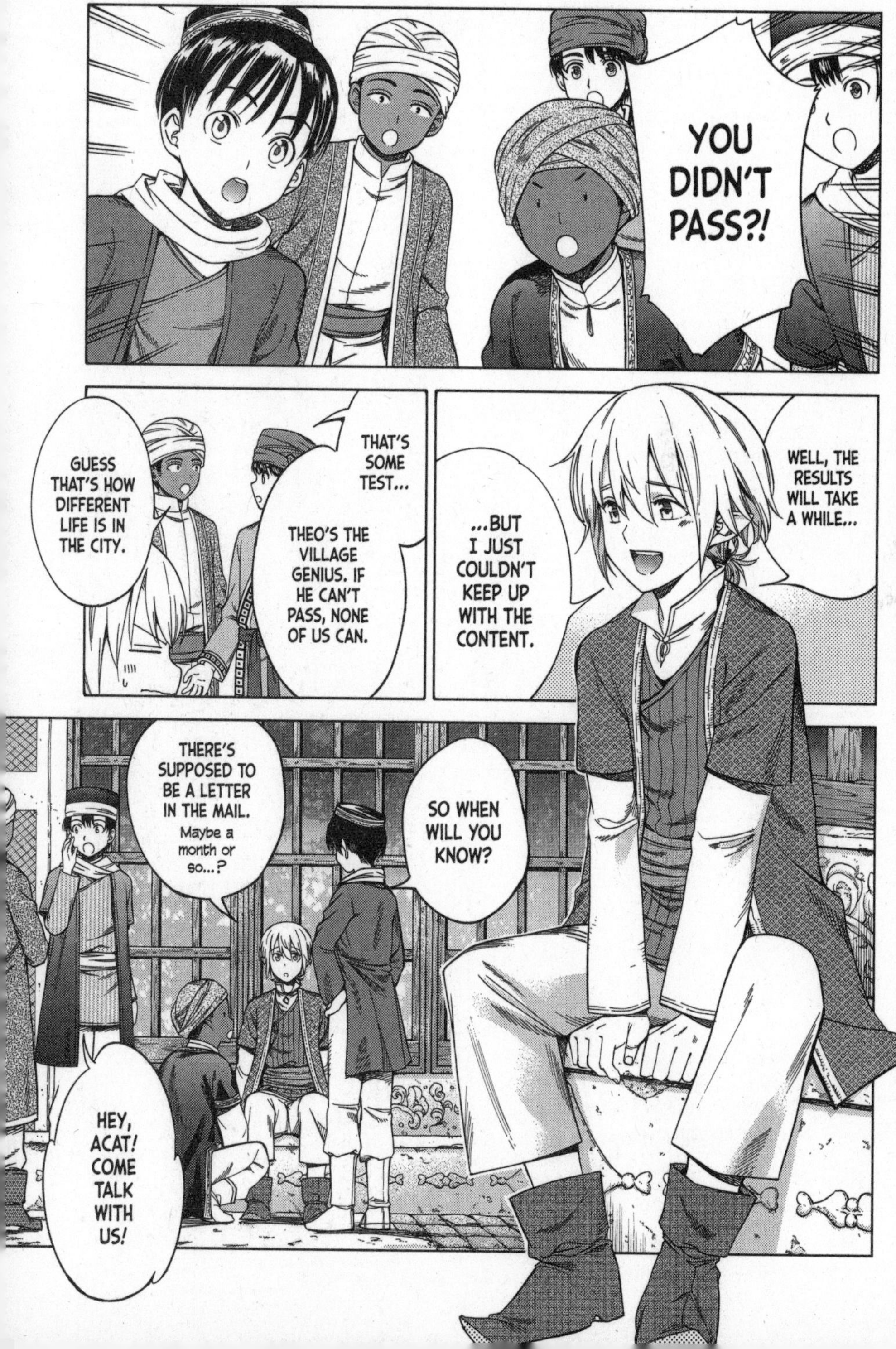
YOU DIDN'T PASS?!
WELL, THE RESULTS WILL TAKE A WHILE...
...BUT I JUST COULDN'T KEEP UP WITH THE CONTENT.
THAT'S SOME TEST...
THEO'S THE VILLAGE GENIUS. IF HE CAN'T PASS, NONE OF US CAN.
GUESS THAT'S HOW DIFFERENT LIFE IS IN THE CITY.
SO WHEN WILL YOU KNOW?
THERE'S SUPPOSED TO BE A LETTER IN THE MAIL. Maybe a month or so...?
HEY, ACAT! COME TALK WITH US!

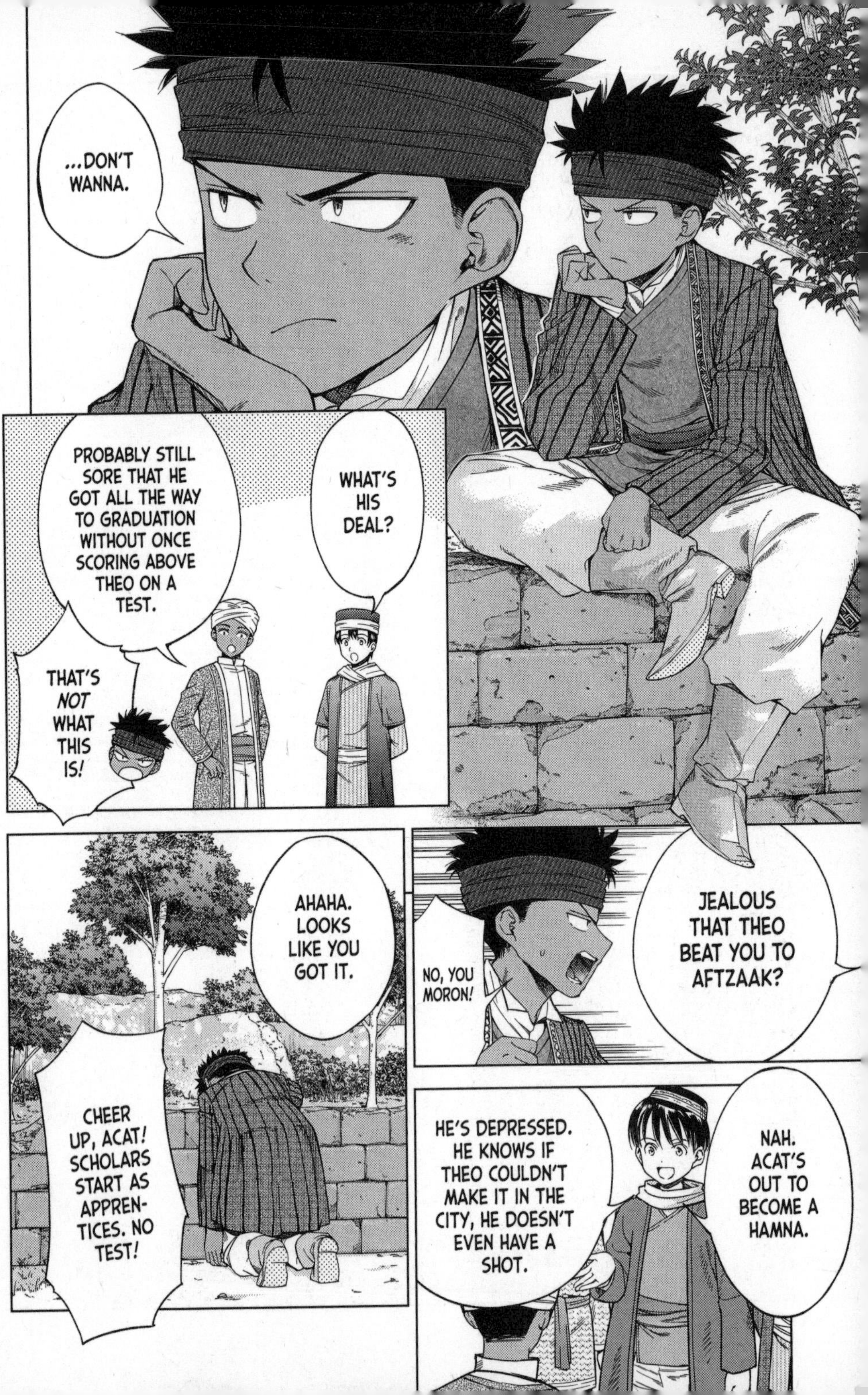
...DON'T WANNA.
WHAT'S HIS DEAL?
PROBABLY STILL SORE THAT HE GOT ALL THE WAY TO GRADUATION WITHOUT ONCE SCORING ABOVE THEO ON A TEST.
THAT'S *NOT* WHAT THIS IS!
JEALOUS THAT THEO BEAT YOU TO AFTZAAK?
NO, YOU MORON!
NAH. ACAT'S OUT TO BECOME A HAMNA.
HE'S DEPRESSED. HE KNOWS IF THEO COULDN'T MAKE IT IN THE CITY, HE DOESN'T EVEN HAVE A SHOT.
AHAHA. LOOKS LIKE YOU GOT IT.
CHEER UP, ACAT! SCHOLARS START AS APPREN-TICES. NO TEST!

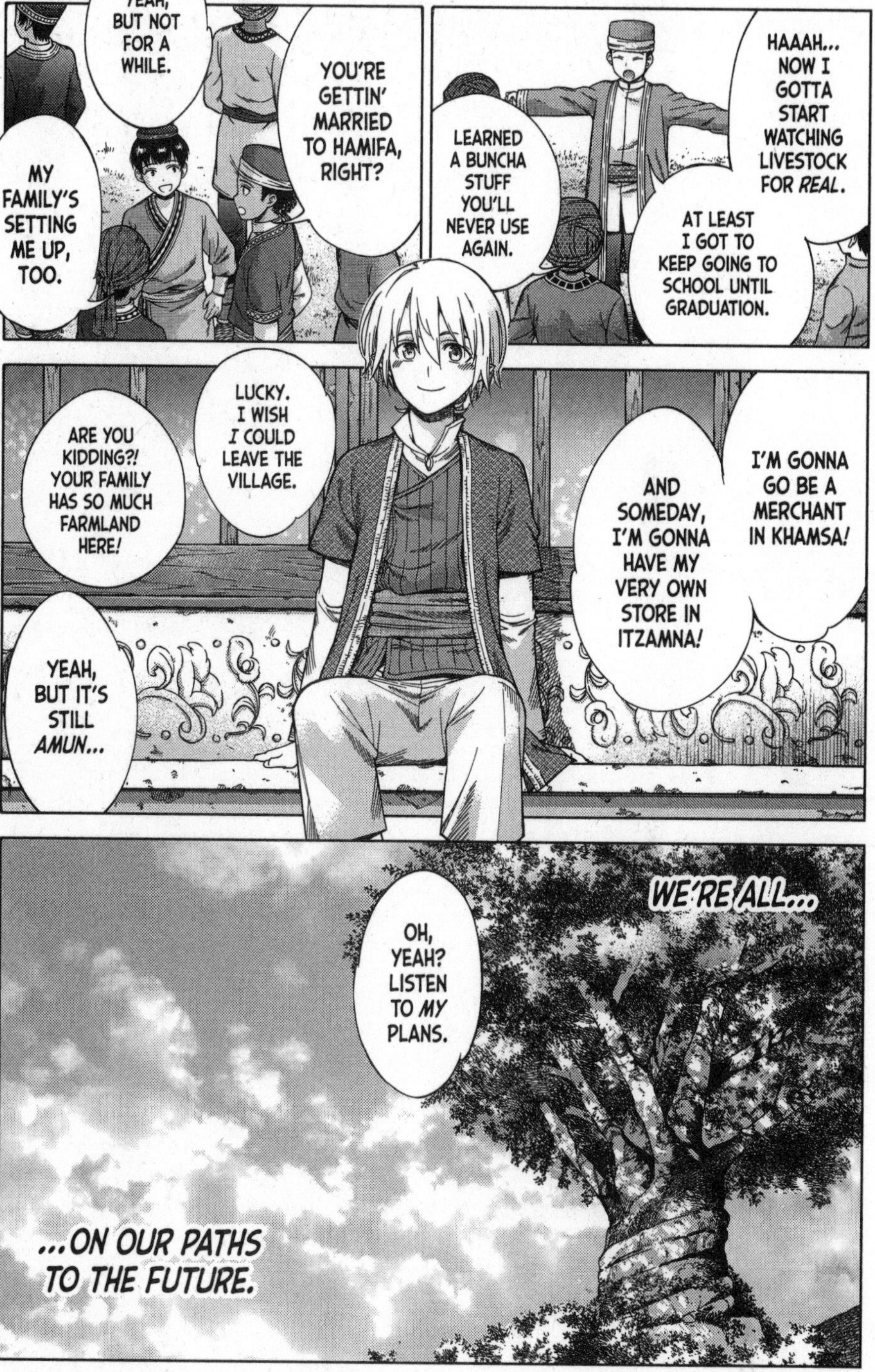
HAAAH... NOW I GOTTA START WATCHING LIVESTOCK FOR *REAL*.
AT LEAST I GOT TO KEEP GOING TO SCHOOL UNTIL GRADUATION.
LEARNED A BUNCHA STUFF YOU'LL NEVER USE AGAIN.
YOU'RE GETTIN' MARRIED TO HAMIFA, RIGHT?
YEAH, BUT NOT FOR A WHILE.
MY FAMILY'S SETTING ME UP, TOO.
I'M GONNA GO BE A MERCHANT IN KHAMSA!
AND SOMEDAY, I'M GONNA HAVE MY VERY OWN STORE IN ITZAMNA!
LUCKY. I WISH *I* COULD LEAVE THE VILLAGE.
ARE YOU KIDDING?! YOUR FAMILY HAS SO MUCH FARMLAND HERE!
YEAH, BUT IT'S STILL *AMUN*...
WE'RE ALL...
OH, YEAH? LISTEN TO *MY* PLANS.
...ON OUR PATHS TO THE FUTURE.

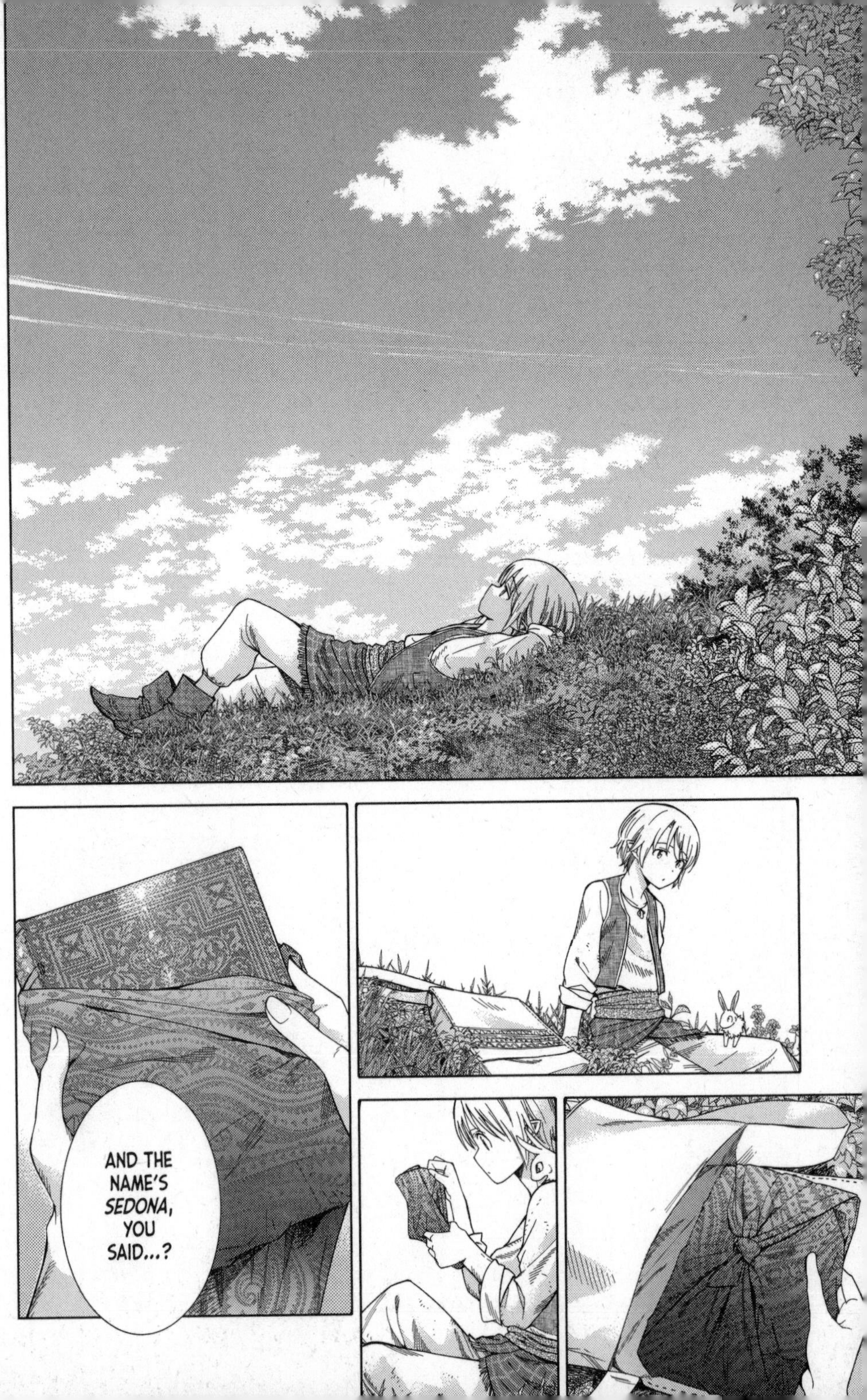
AND THE NAME'S *SEDONA*, YOU SAID...?

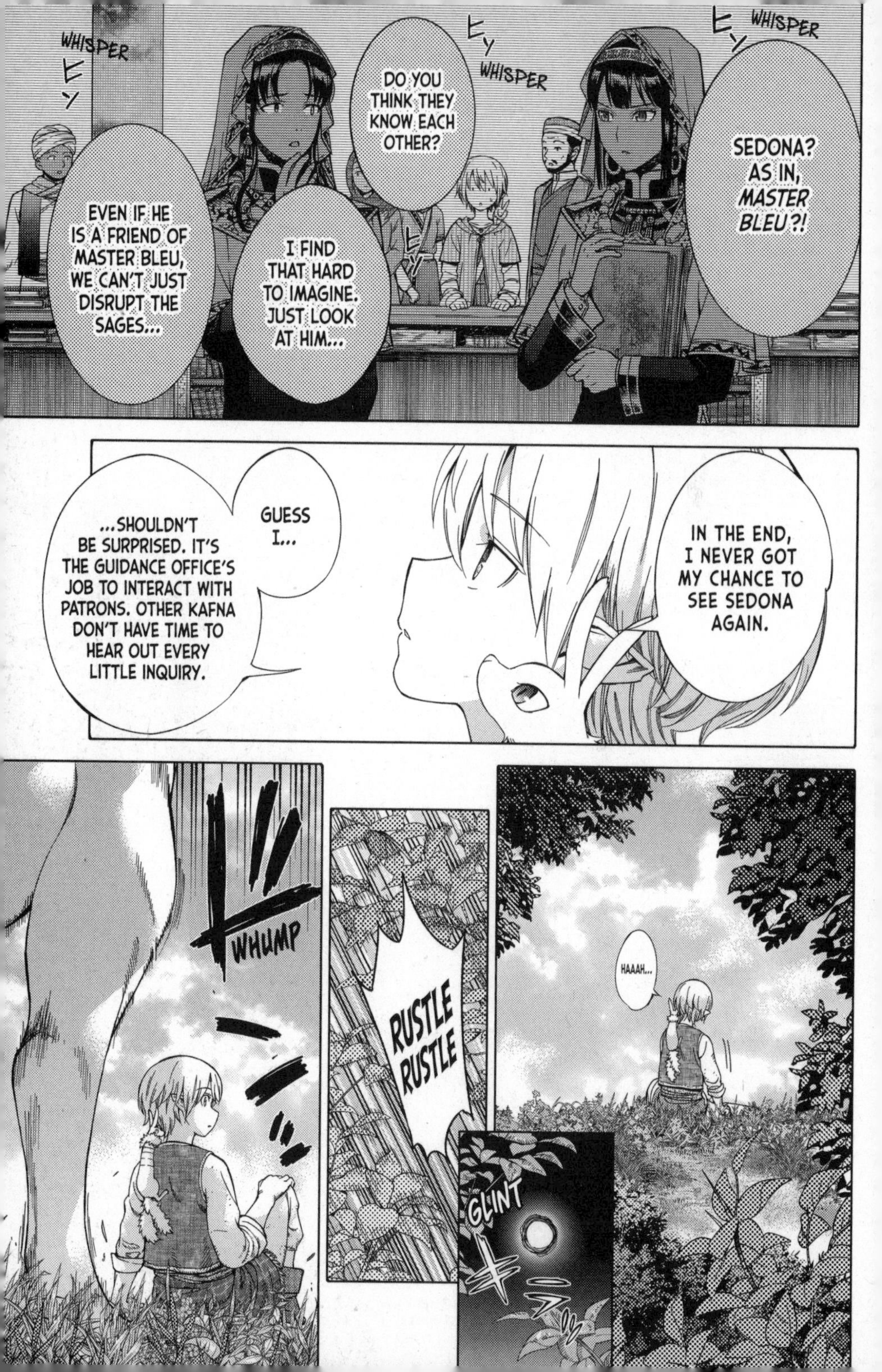
WHISPER
ヒソ
SEDONA? AS IN, MASTER BLEU?!
WHISPER
ヒソ
DO YOU THINK THEY KNOW EACH OTHER?
I FIND THAT HARD TO IMAGINE. JUST LOOK AT HIM...
WHISPER
ヒソ
EVEN IF HE IS A FRIEND OF MASTER BLEU, WE CAN'T JUST DISRUPT THE SAGES...
IN THE END, I NEVER GOT MY CHANCE TO SEE SEDONA AGAIN.
GUESS I...
...SHOULDN'T BE SURPRISED. IT'S THE GUIDANCE OFFICE'S JOB TO INTERACT WITH PATRONS. OTHER KAFNA DON'T HAVE TIME TO HEAR OUT EVERY LITTLE INQUIRY.
HAAAH...
GLINT
RUSTLE RUSTLE
WHUMP

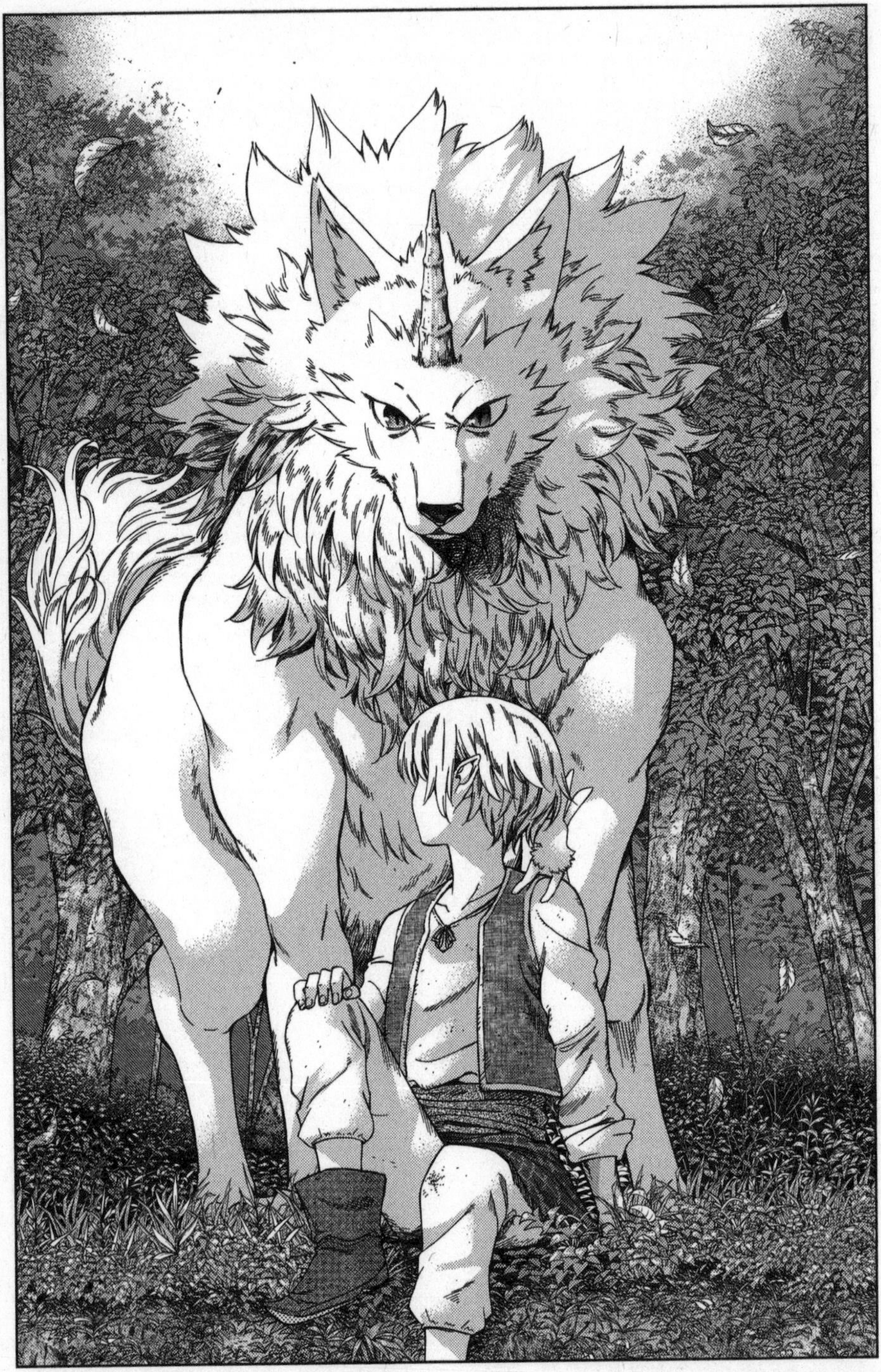

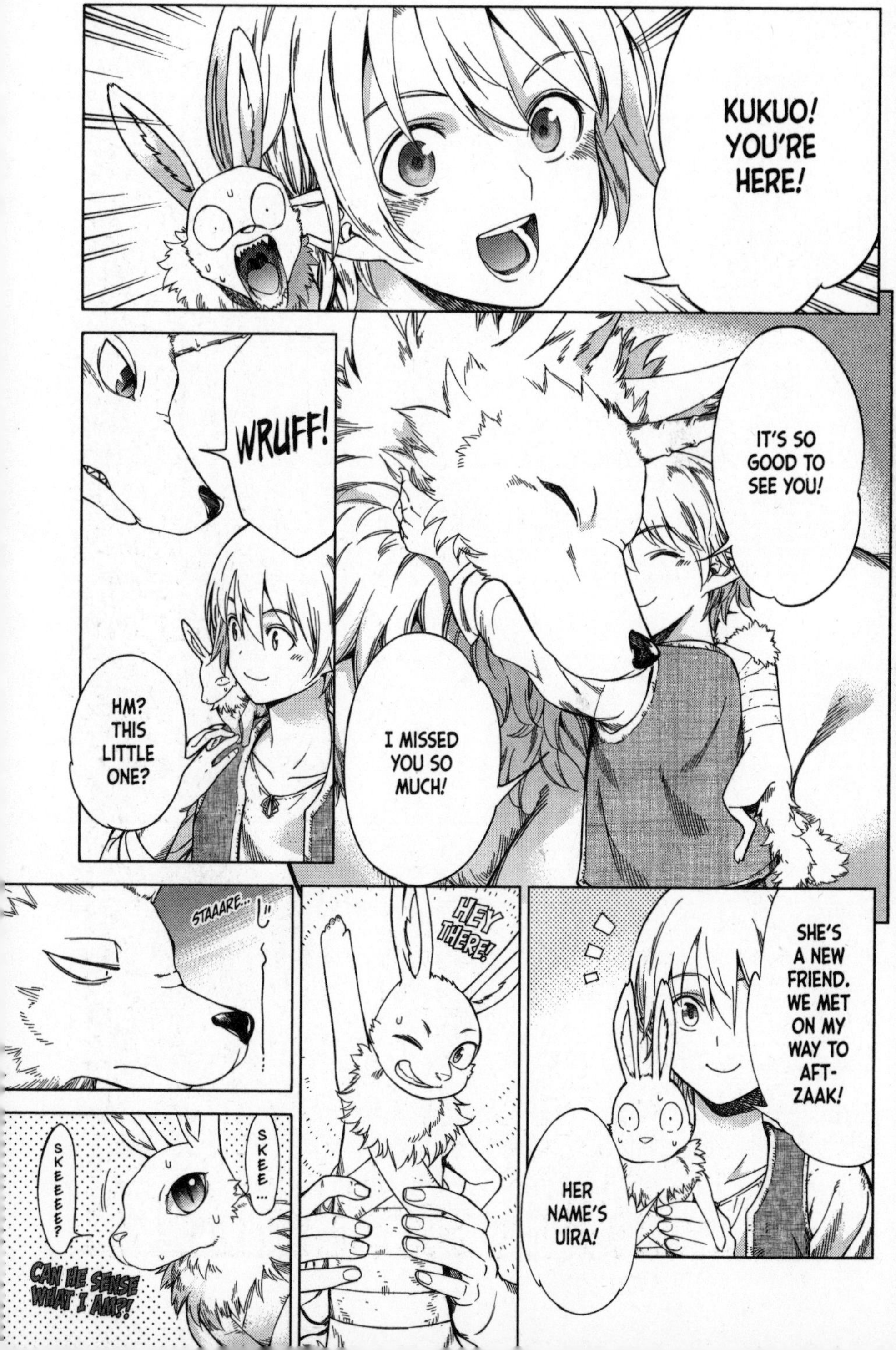
KUKUO! YOU'RE HERE!
IT'S SO GOOD TO SEE YOU!
I MISSED YOU SO MUCH!
WRUFF!
HM? THIS LITTLE ONE?
SHE'S A NEW FRIEND. WE MET ON MY WAY TO AFT-ZAAK!
HER NAME'S UIRA!
HEY THERE!
STAAARE...
SKEE...
SKEEEEE?
CAN HE SENSE WHAT I AM?!

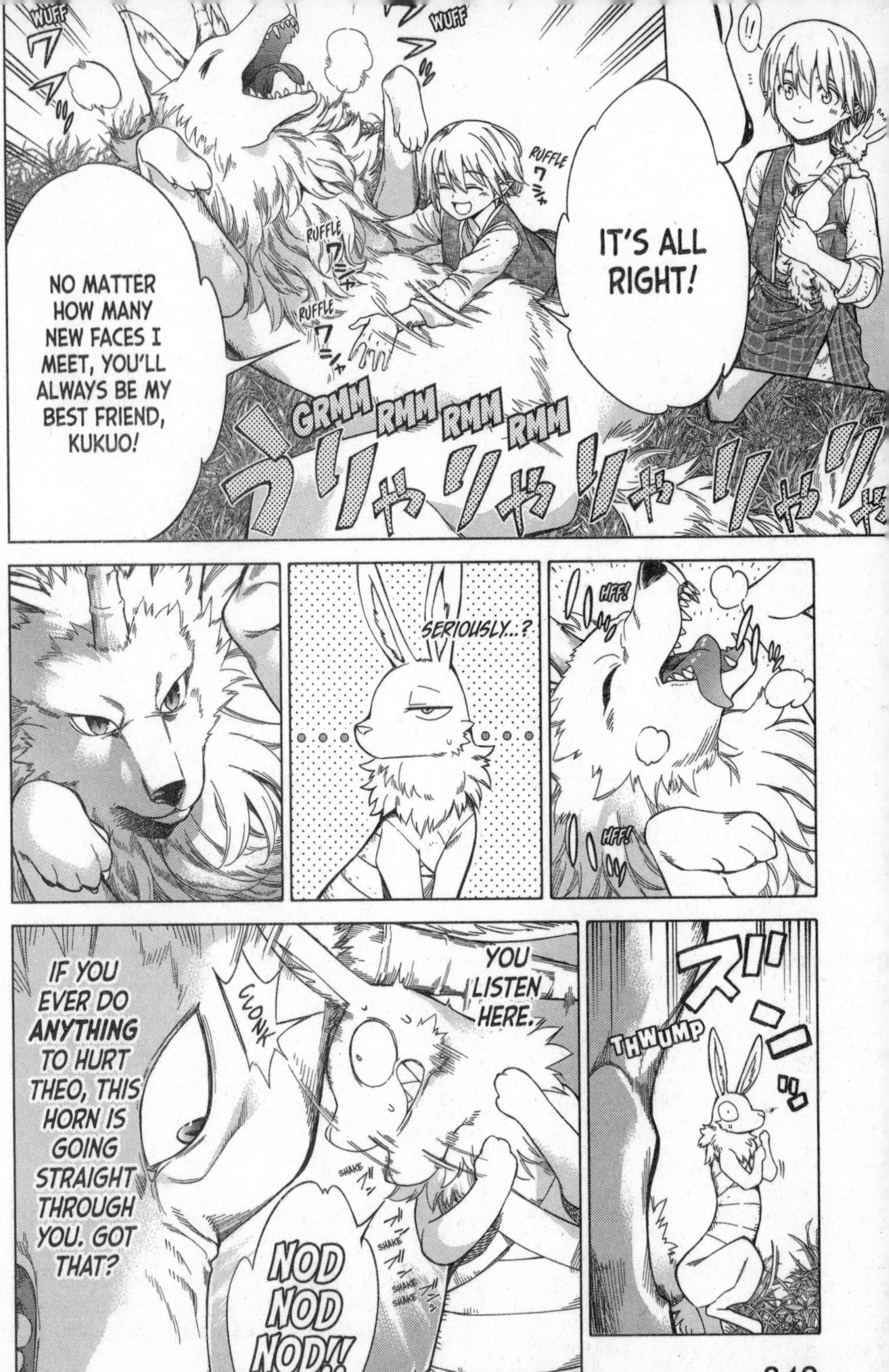
!!
WUFF
IT'S ALL RIGHT!
RUFFLE
WUFF
RUFFLE
RUFFLE
NO MATTER HOW MANY NEW FACES I MEET, YOU'LL ALWAYS BE MY BEST FRIEND, KUKUO!
GRMM RMM RMM RMM
HFF!
HFF!
SERIOUSLY...?
• • •
• • •
THWUMP
YOU LISTEN HERE.
CLONK
IF YOU EVER DO ANYTHING TO HURT THEO, THIS HORN IS GOING STRAIGHT THROUGH YOU. GOT THAT?
SHAKE
SHAKE
SHAKE SHAKE
NOD NOD NOD!!

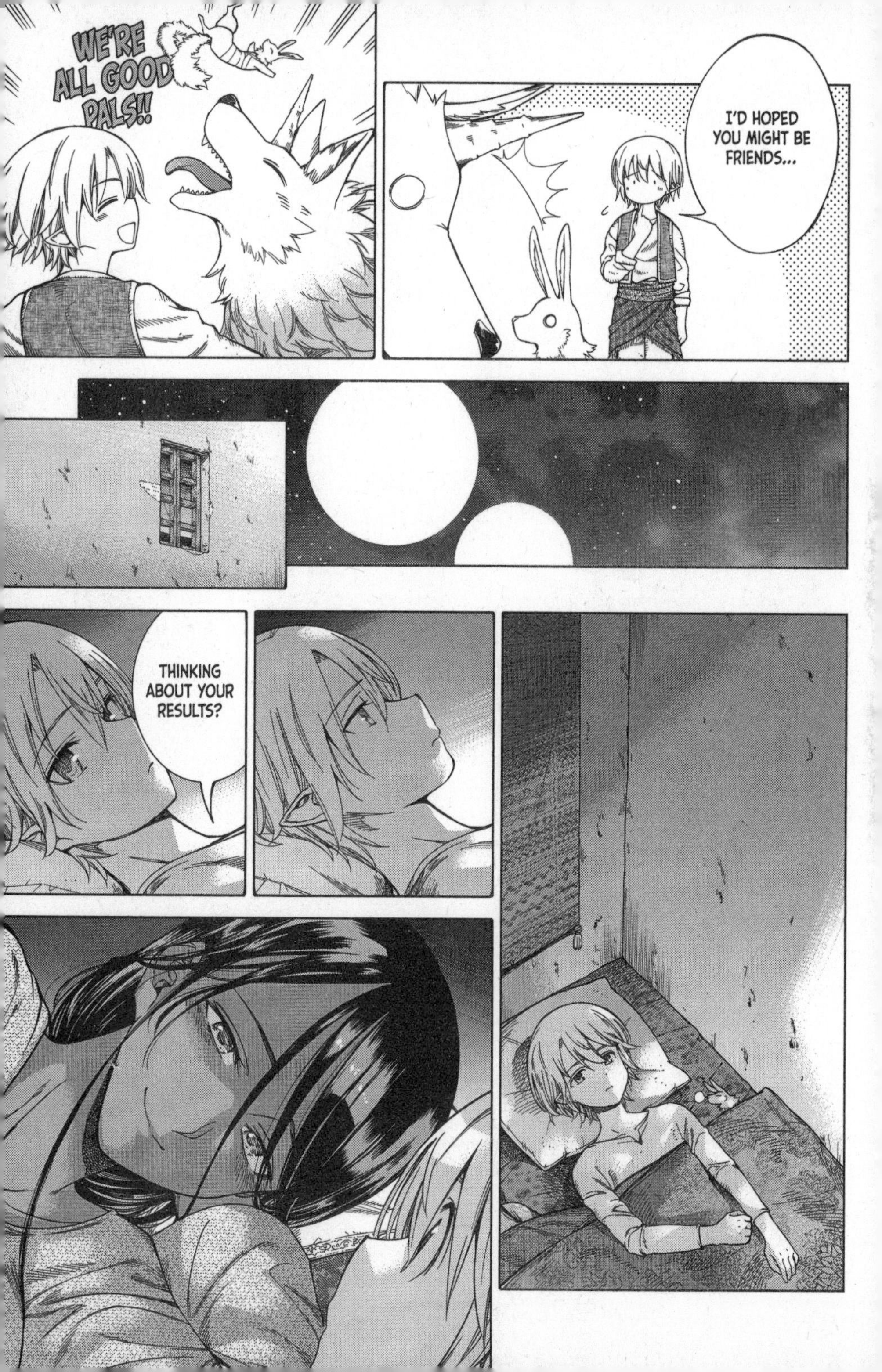
I'D HOPED YOU MIGHT BE FRIENDS...
WE'RE ALL GOOD PALS!!
THINKING ABOUT YOUR RESULTS?

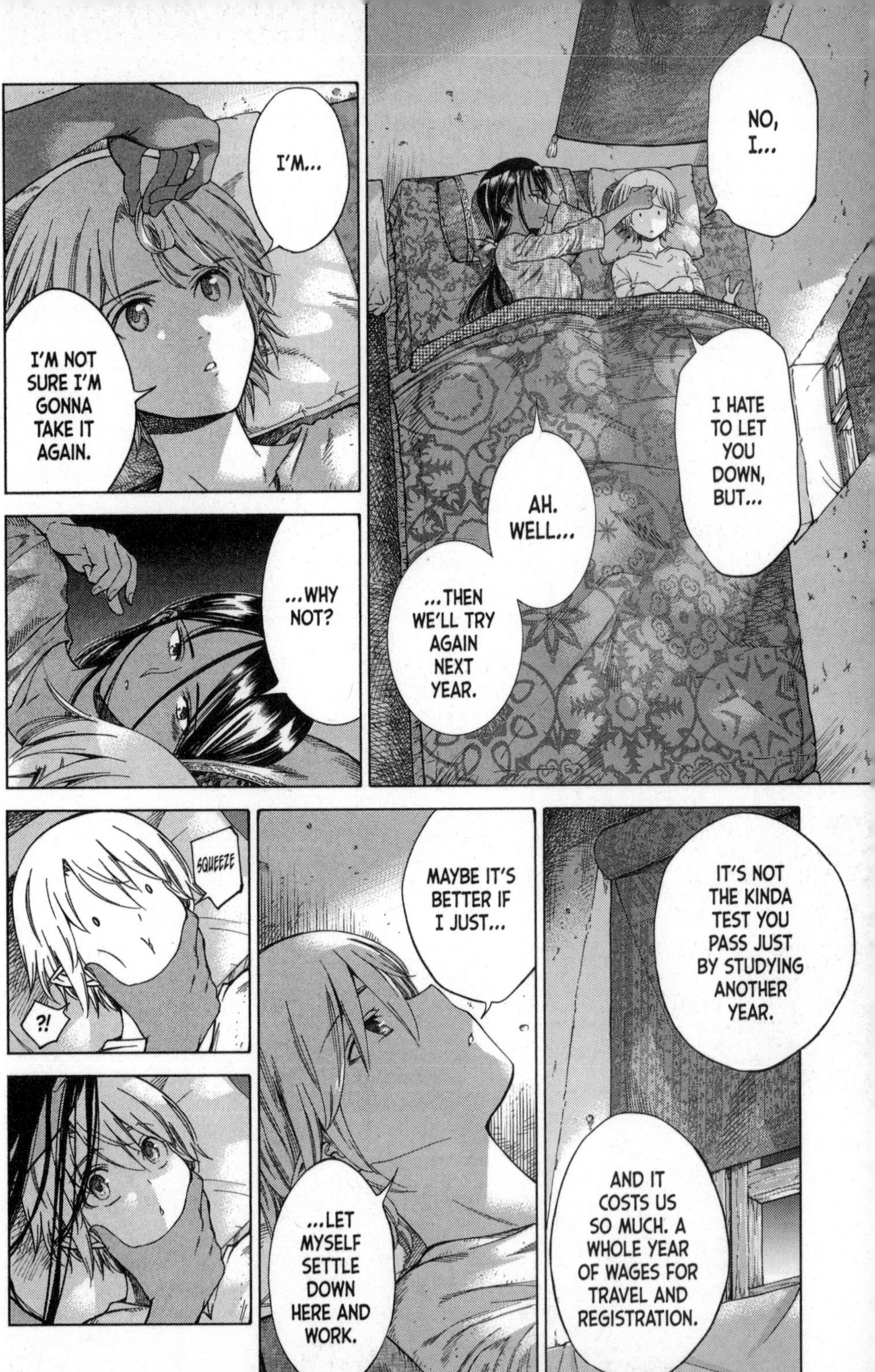
NO, I...
I HATE TO LET YOU DOWN, BUT...
AH. WELL...
...THEN WE'LL TRY AGAIN NEXT YEAR.
I'M...
I'M NOT SURE I'M GONNA TAKE IT AGAIN.
...WHY NOT?
IT'S NOT THE KINDA TEST YOU PASS JUST BY STUDYING ANOTHER YEAR.
AND IT COSTS US SO MUCH. A WHOLE YEAR OF WAGES FOR TRAVEL AND REGISTRATION.
MAYBE IT'S BETTER IF I JUST...
...LET MYSELF SETTLE DOWN HERE AND WORK.
SQUEEZE
?!

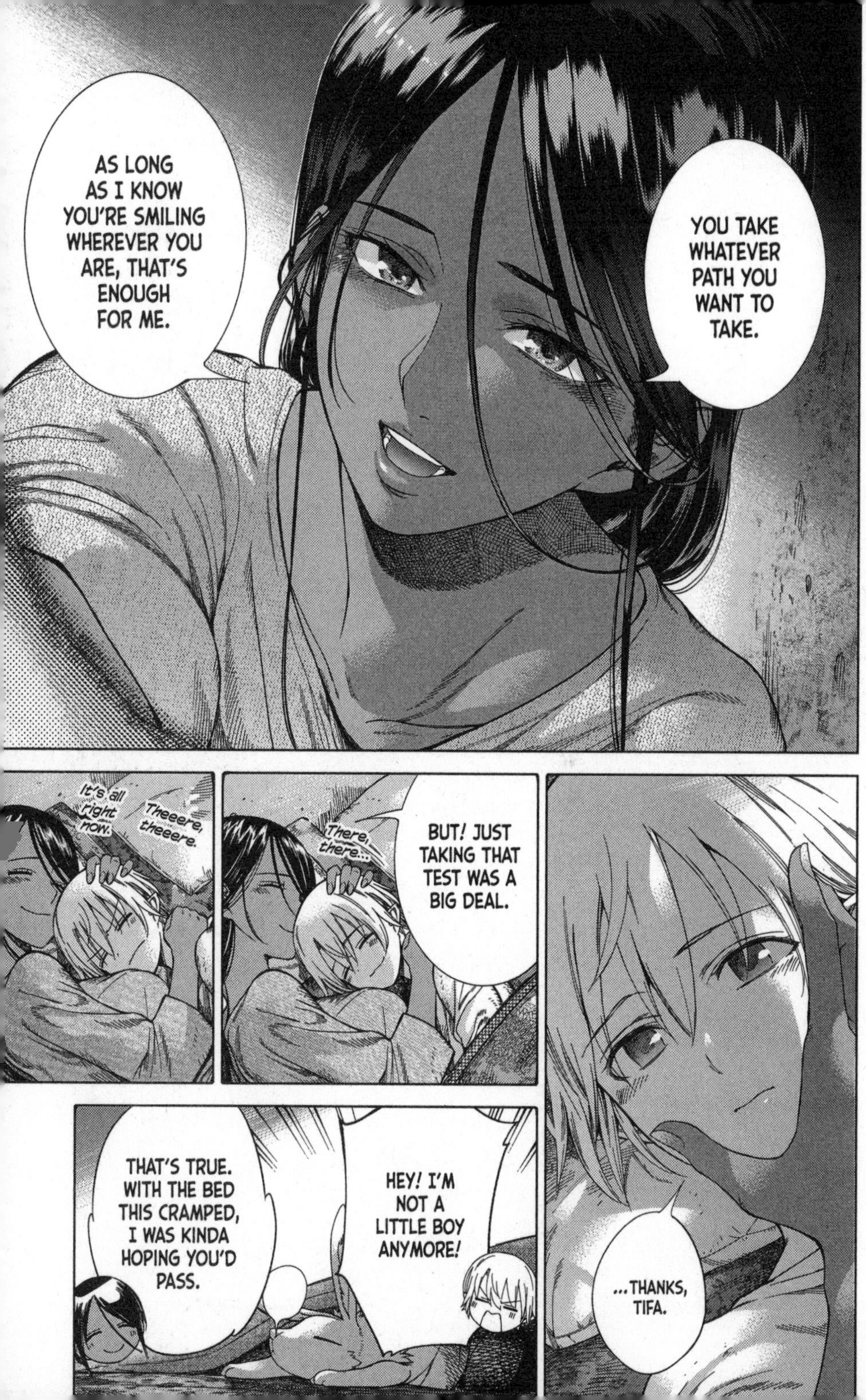
YOU TAKE WHATEVER PATH YOU WANT TO TAKE.
AS LONG AS I KNOW YOU'RE SMILING WHEREVER YOU ARE, THAT'S ENOUGH FOR ME.
...THANKS, TIFA.
BUT! JUST TAKING THAT TEST WAS A BIG DEAL.
There, there...
Theeere, theeere.
It's all right now.
HEY! I'M NOT A LITTLE BOY ANYMORE!
THAT'S TRUE. WITH THE BED THIS CRAMPED, I WAS KINDA HOPING YOU'D PASS.

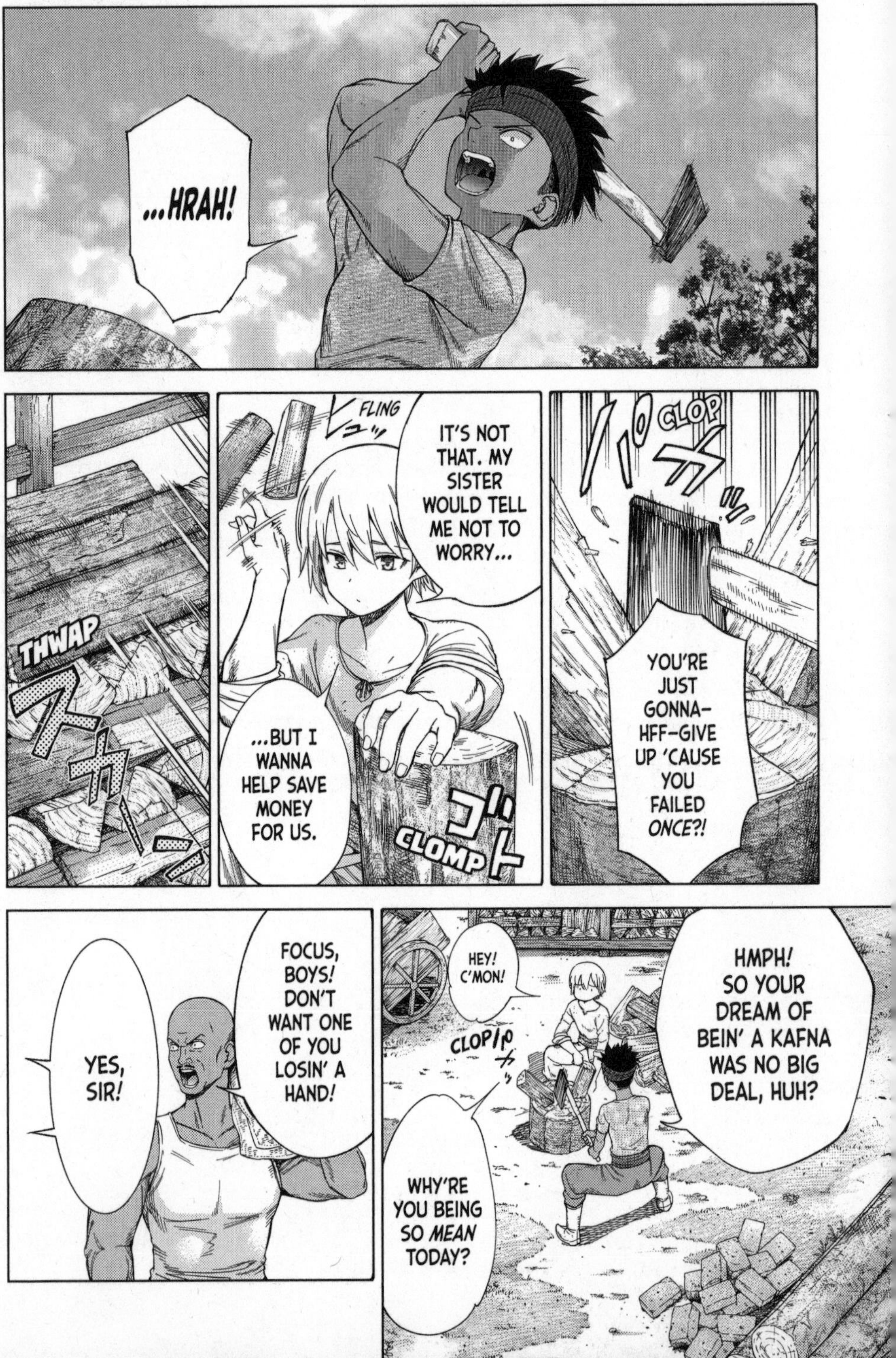
...HRAH!
CLOP
YOU'RE JUST GONNA—HFF—GIVE UP 'CAUSE YOU FAILED *ONCE?!*
FLING
IT'S NOT THAT. MY SISTER WOULD TELL ME NOT TO WORRY...
...BUT I WANNA HELP SAVE MONEY FOR US.
CLOMP
THWAP
HMPH! SO YOUR DREAM OF BEIN' A KAFNA WAS NO BIG DEAL, HUH?
HEY! C'MON!
CLOP
WHY'RE YOU BEING SO *MEAN* TODAY?
FOCUS, BOYS! DON'T WANT ONE OF YOU LOSIN' A HAND!
YES, SIR!

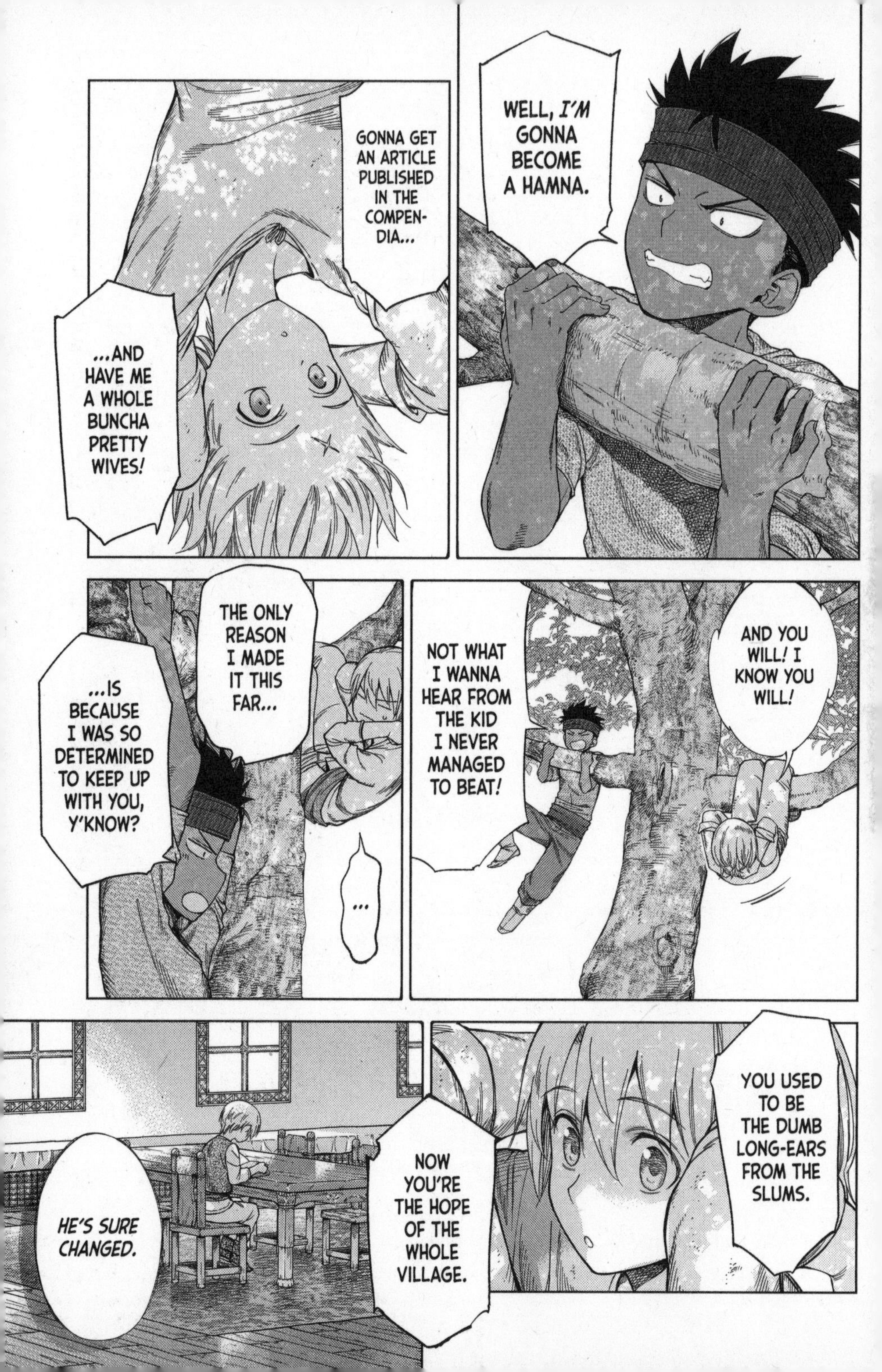
WELL, *I'M* GONNA BECOME A HAMNA.
GONNA GET AN ARTICLE PUBLISHED IN THE COMPEN-DIA...
...AND HAVE ME A WHOLE BUNCHA PRETTY WIVES!
AND YOU WILL! I KNOW YOU WILL!
NOT WHAT I WANNA HEAR FROM THE KID I NEVER MANAGED TO BEAT!
THE ONLY REASON I MADE IT THIS FAR...
...IS BECAUSE I WAS SO DETERMINED TO KEEP UP WITH YOU, Y'KNOW?
...
YOU USED TO BE THE DUMB LONG-EARS FROM THE SLUMS.
NOW YOU'RE THE HOPE OF THE WHOLE VILLAGE.
HE'S SURE CHANGED.

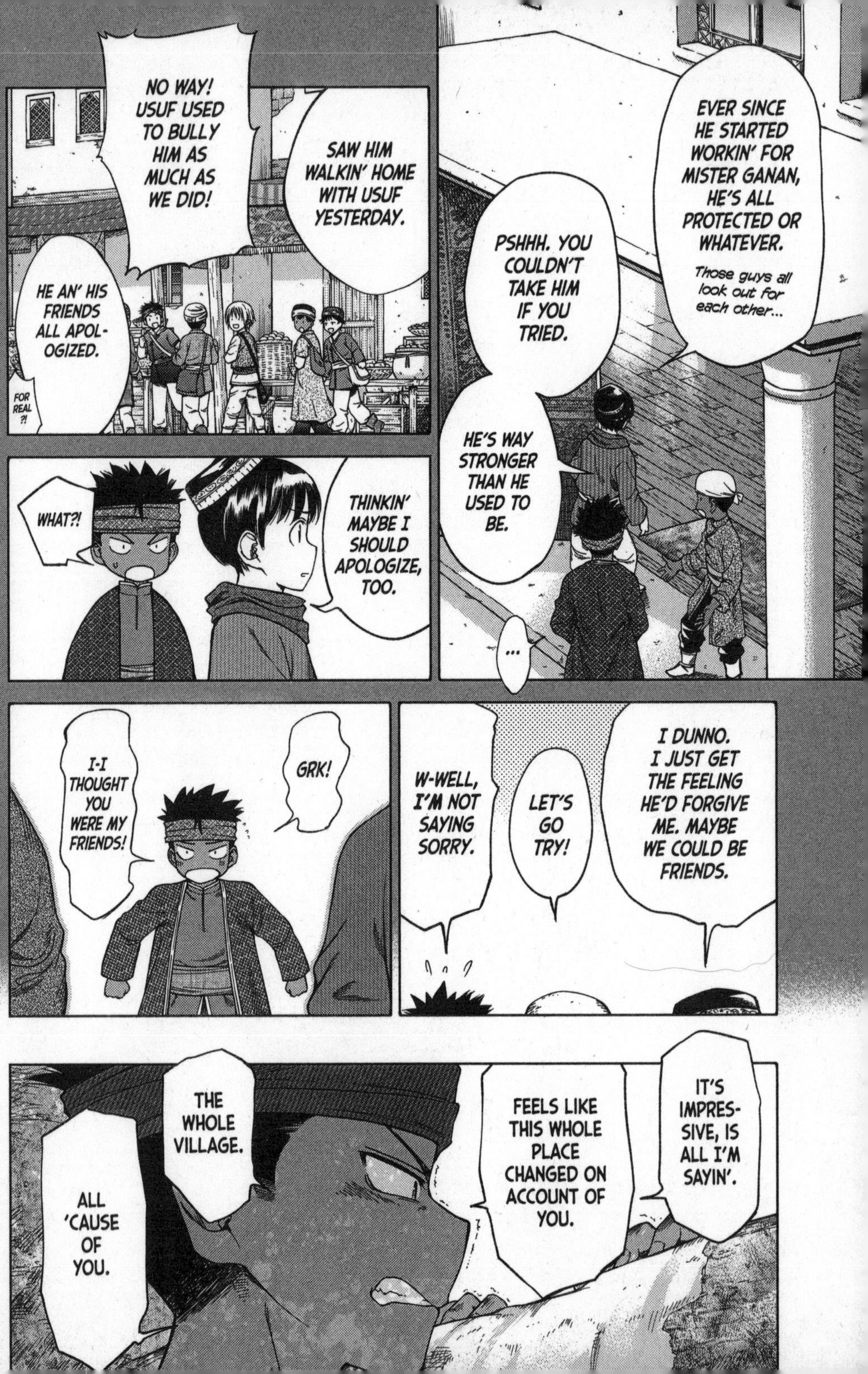
EVER SINCE HE STARTED WORKIN' FOR MISTER GANAN, HE'S ALL PROTECTED OR WHATEVER.
Those guys all look out for each other...
PSHHH. YOU COULDN'T TAKE HIM IF YOU TRIED.
HE'S WAY STRONGER THAN HE USED TO BE.
...
SAW HIM WALKIN' HOME WITH USUF YESTERDAY.
NO WAY! USUF USED TO BULLY HIM AS MUCH AS WE DID!
HE AN' HIS FRIENDS ALL APOLOGIZED.
FOR REAL?!
THINKIN' MAYBE I SHOULD APOLOGIZE, TOO.
WHAT?!
I DUNNO. I JUST GET THE FEELING HE'D FORGIVE ME. MAYBE WE COULD BE FRIENDS.
LET'S GO TRY!
W-WELL, I'M NOT SAYING SORRY.
GRK!
I-I THOUGHT YOU WERE MY FRIENDS!
IT'S IMPRESSIVE, IS ALL I'M SAYIN'.
FEELS LIKE THIS WHOLE PLACE CHANGED ON ACCOUNT OF YOU.
THE WHOLE VILLAGE.
ALL 'CAUSE OF YOU.

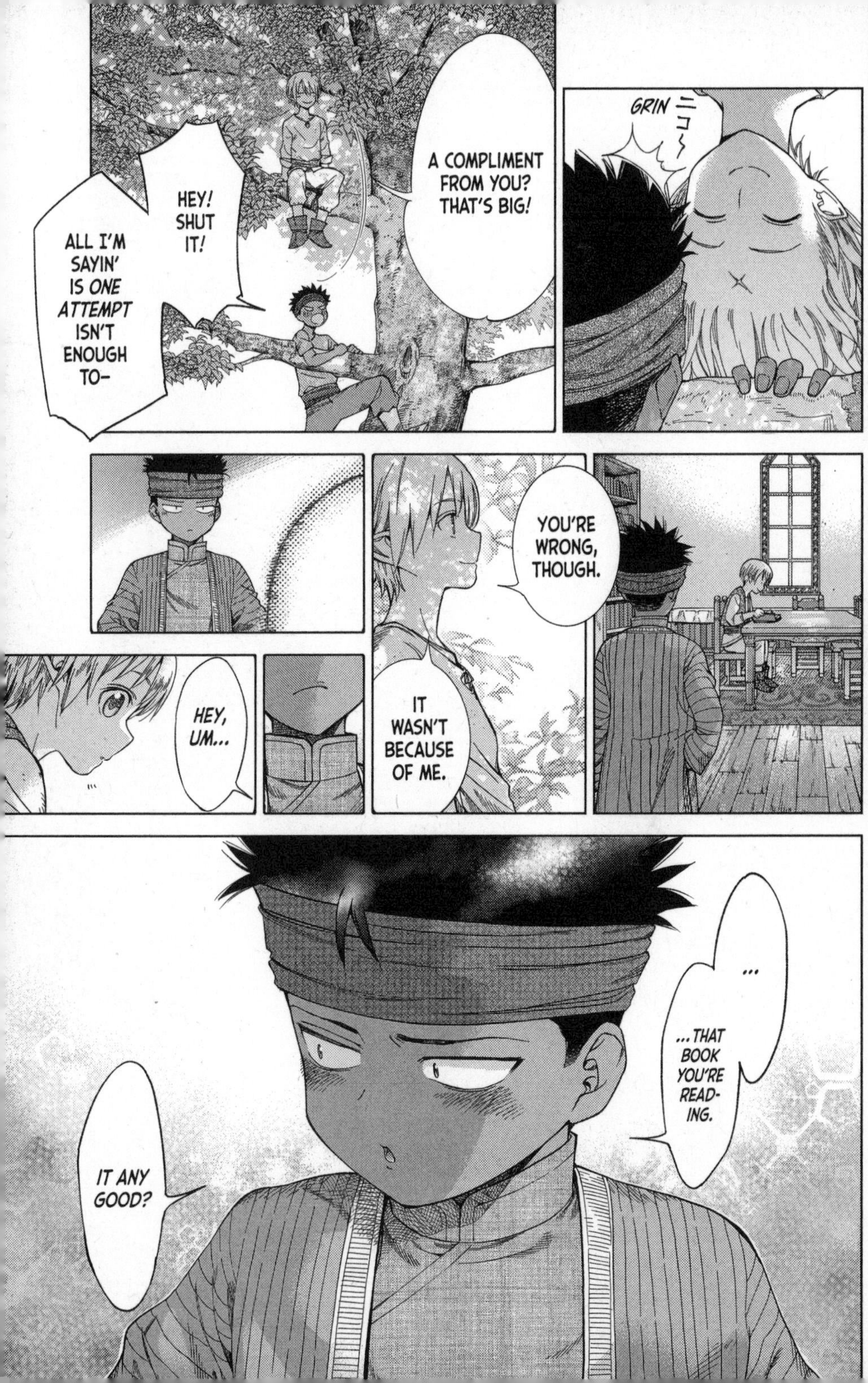
GRIN
A COMPLIMENT FROM YOU? THAT'S BIG!
HEY! SHUT IT!
ALL I'M SAYIN' IS *ONE ATTEMPT* ISN'T ENOUGH TO–
YOU'RE WRONG, THOUGH.
IT WASN'T BECAUSE OF ME.
HEY, UM...
...
...THAT BOOK YOU'RE READ-ING.
IT ANY GOOD?

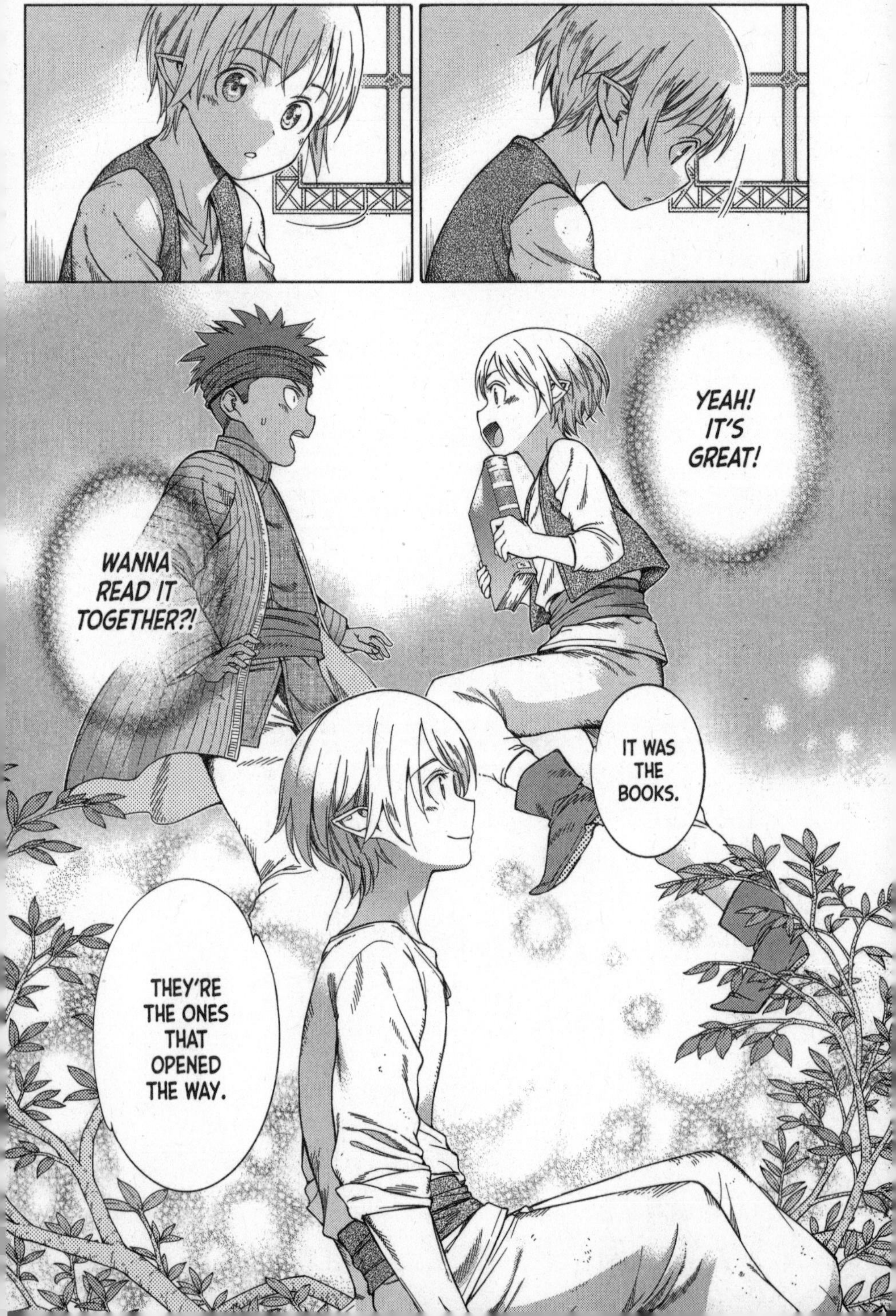
YEAH! IT'S GREAT!
WANNA READ IT TOGETHER?!
IT WAS THE BOOKS.
THEY'RE THE ONES THAT OPENED THE WAY.

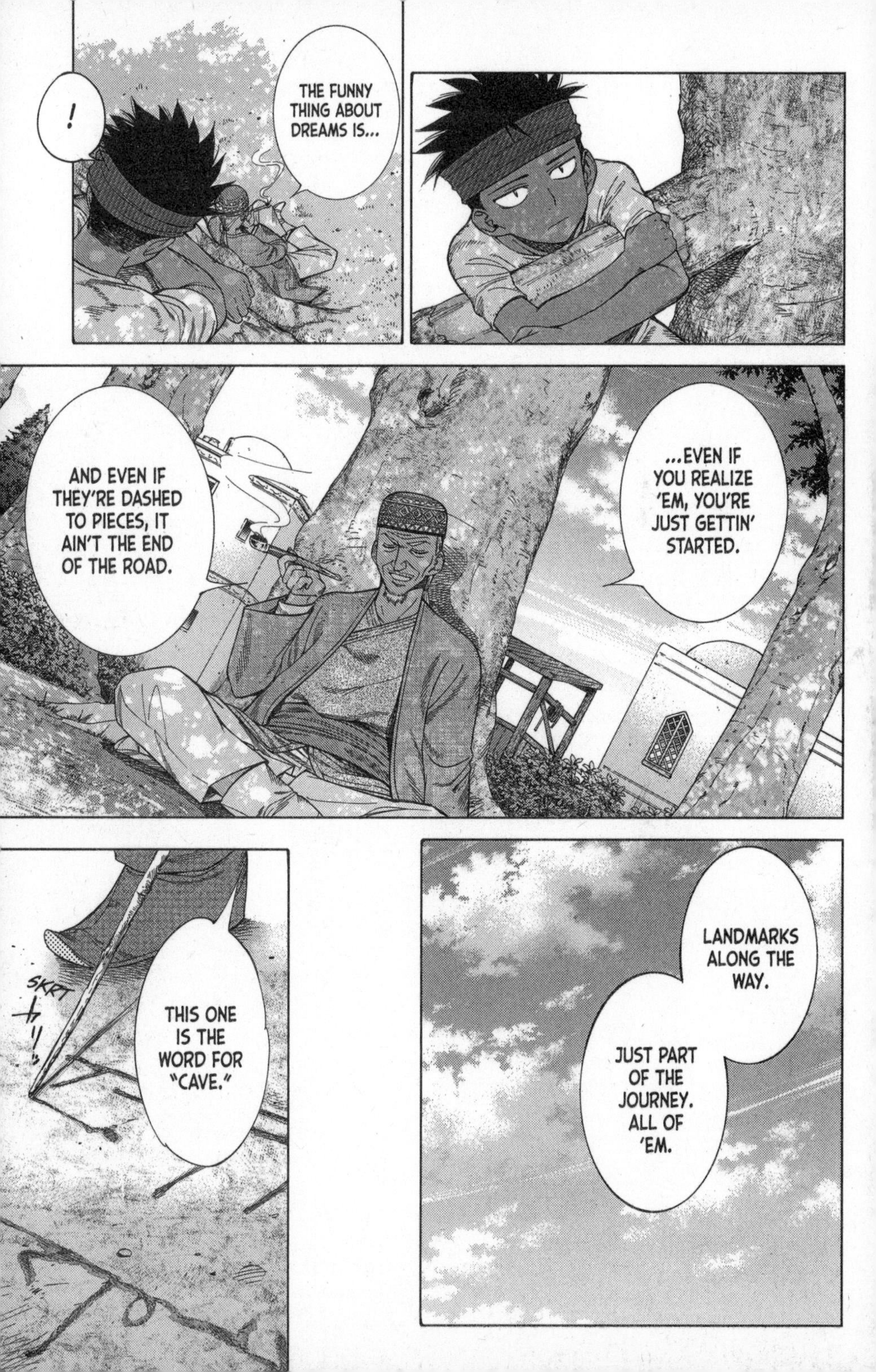
THE FUNNY THING ABOUT DREAMS IS...
!
...EVEN IF YOU REALIZE 'EM, YOU'RE JUST GETTIN' STARTED.
AND EVEN IF THEY'RE DASHED TO PIECES, IT AIN'T THE END OF THE ROAD.
LANDMARKS ALONG THE WAY.
JUST PART OF THE JOURNEY. ALL OF 'EM.
THIS ONE IS THE WORD FOR "CAVE."
SKRT

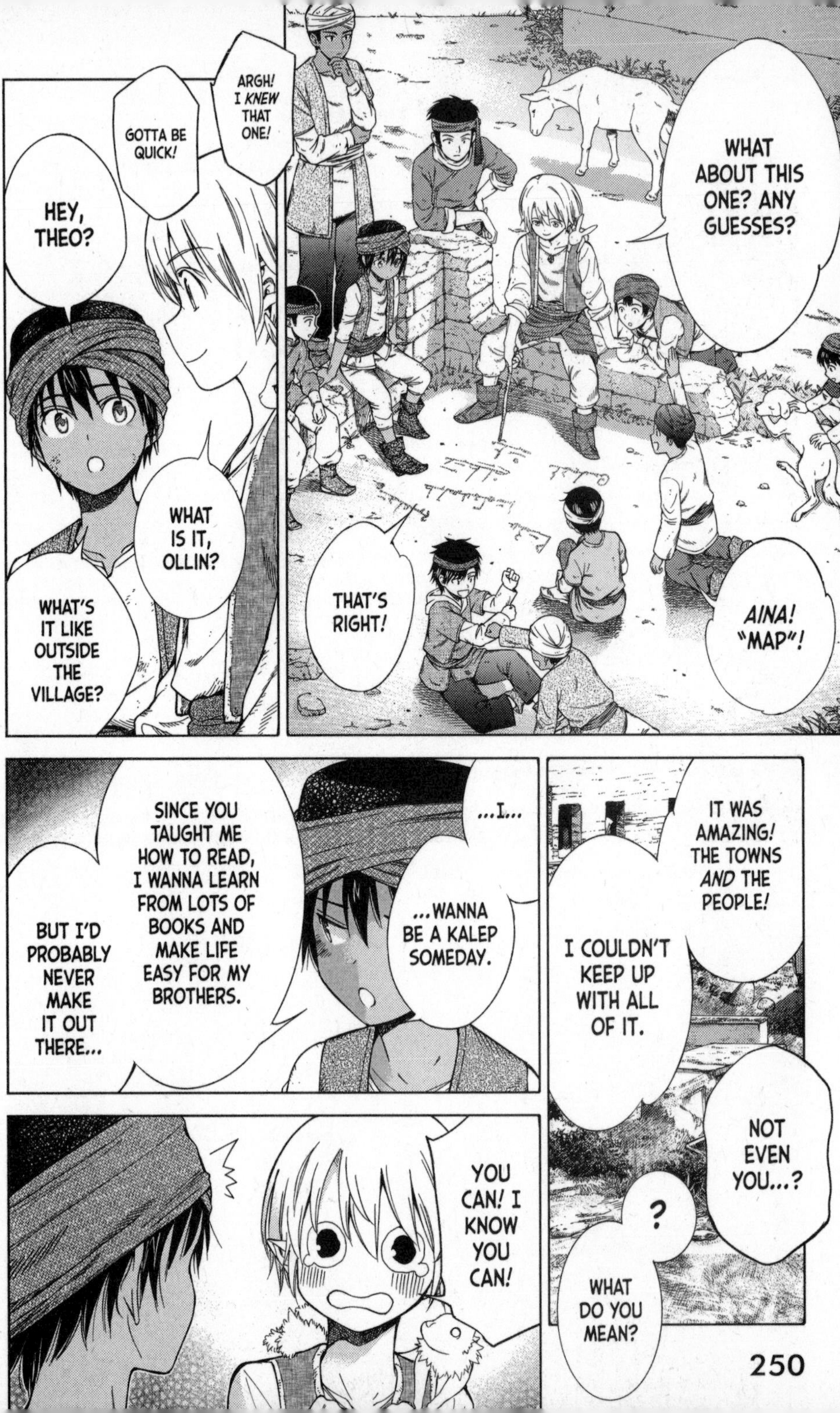
WHAT ABOUT THIS ONE? ANY GUESSES?
AINA! "MAP"!
THAT'S RIGHT!
ARGH! I *KNEW* THAT ONE!
GOTTA BE QUICK!
HEY, THEO?
WHAT IS IT, OLLIN?
WHAT'S IT LIKE OUTSIDE THE VILLAGE?
IT WAS AMAZING! THE TOWNS *AND* THE PEOPLE!
I COULDN'T KEEP UP WITH ALL OF IT.
NOT EVEN YOU...?
?
WHAT DO YOU MEAN?
...I...
...WANNA BE A KALEP SOMEDAY.
SINCE YOU TAUGHT ME HOW TO READ, I WANNA LEARN FROM LOTS OF BOOKS AND MAKE LIFE EASY FOR MY BROTHERS.
BUT I'D PROBABLY NEVER MAKE IT OUT THERE...
YOU CAN! I KNOW YOU CAN!

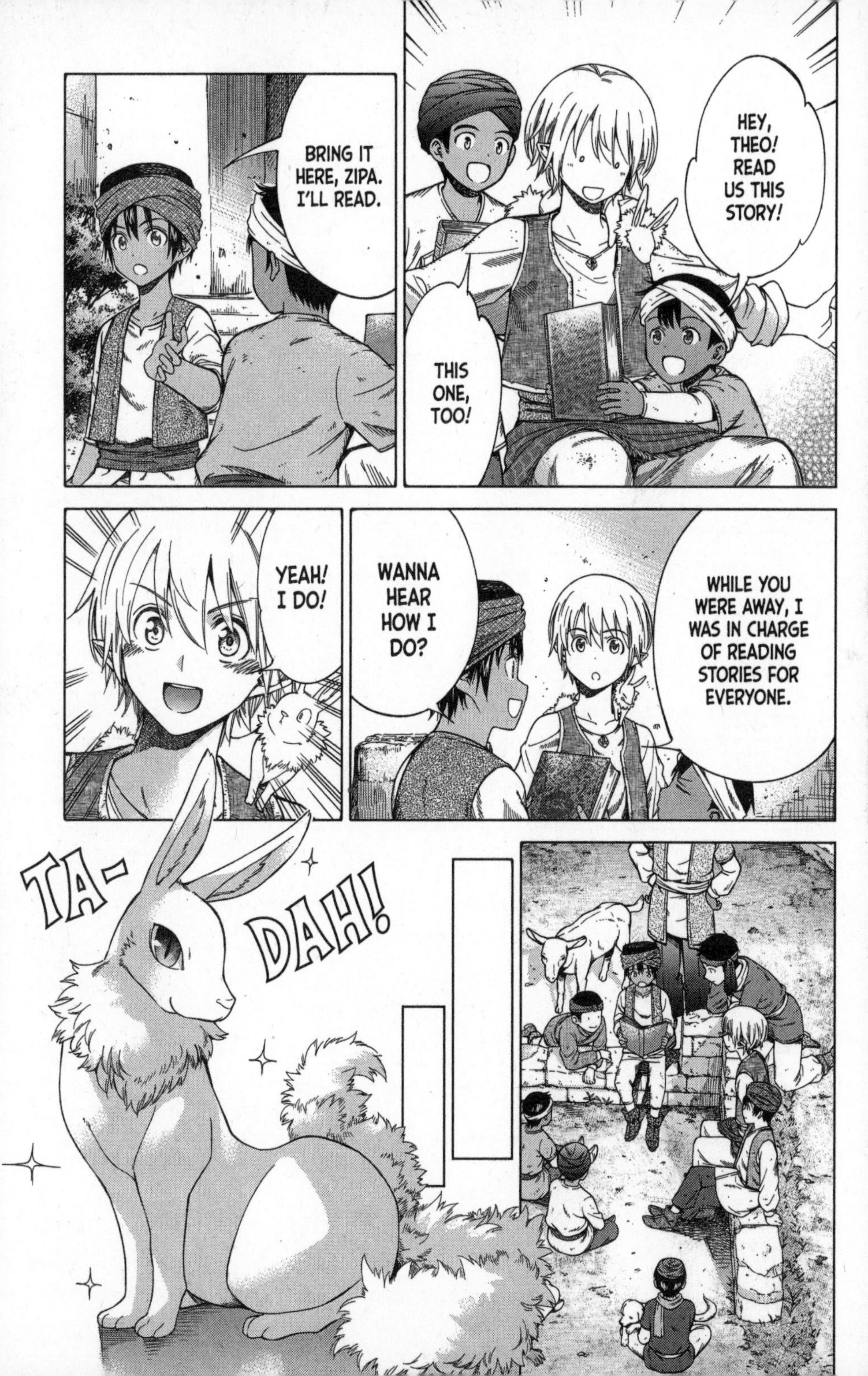
HEY, THEO! READ US THIS STORY!
THIS ONE, TOO!
BRING IT HERE, ZIPA. I'LL READ.
WHILE YOU WERE AWAY, I WAS IN CHARGE OF READING STORIES FOR EVERYONE.
WANNA HEAR HOW I DO?
YEAH! I DO!
TA-DAH!

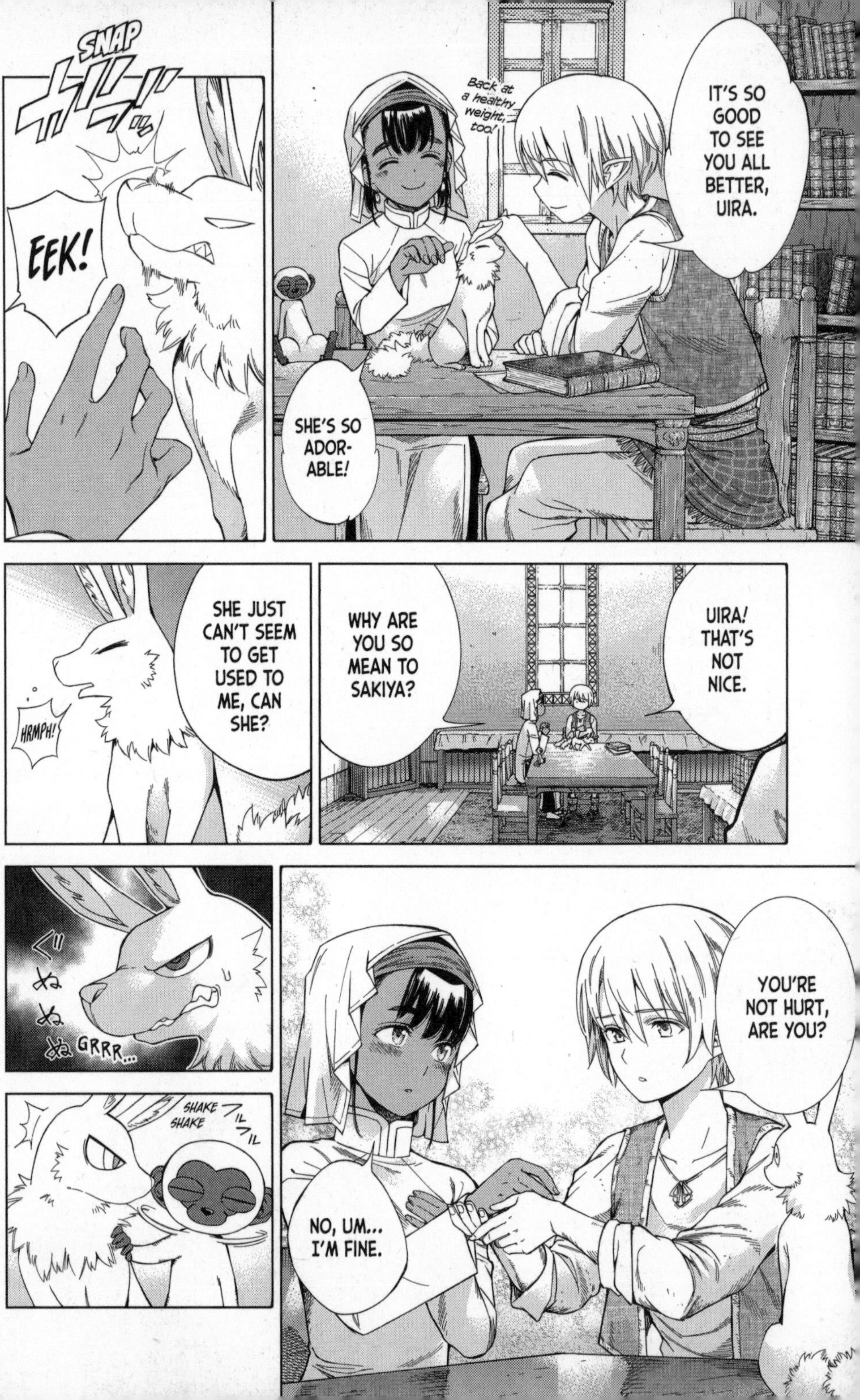
IT'S SO GOOD TO SEE YOU ALL BETTER, UIRA.
Back at a healthy weight, too!
SHE'S SO ADORABLE!
SNAP
EEK!
UIRA! THAT'S NOT NICE.
WHY ARE YOU SO MEAN TO SAKIYA?
SHE JUST CAN'T SEEM TO GET USED TO ME, CAN SHE?
HRMPH!
YOU'RE NOT HURT, ARE YOU?
NO, UM... I'M FINE.
ぐぬぬぬ
GRRR...
SHAKE SHAKE
フル フル

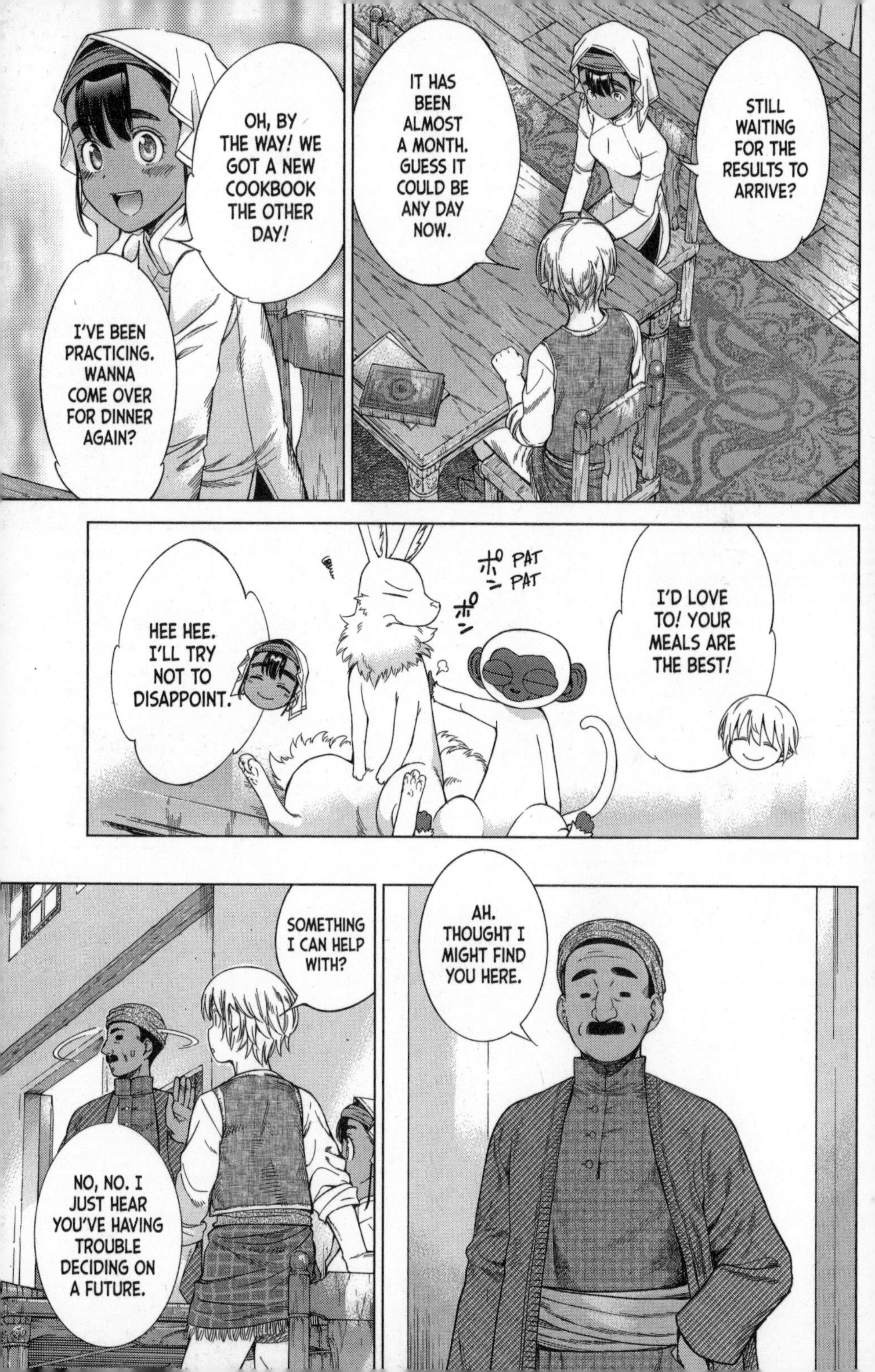
STILL WAITING FOR THE RESULTS TO ARRIVE?
IT HAS BEEN ALMOST A MONTH. GUESS IT COULD BE ANY DAY NOW.
OH, BY THE WAY! WE GOT A NEW COOKBOOK THE OTHER DAY!
I'VE BEEN PRACTICING. WANNA COME OVER FOR DINNER AGAIN?
I'D LOVE TO! YOUR MEALS ARE THE BEST!
PAT PAT
HEE HEE. I'LL TRY NOT TO DISAPPOINT.
AH. THOUGHT I MIGHT FIND YOU HERE.
SOMETHING I CAN HELP WITH?
NO, NO. I JUST HEAR YOU'VE HAVING TROUBLE DECIDING ON A FUTURE.

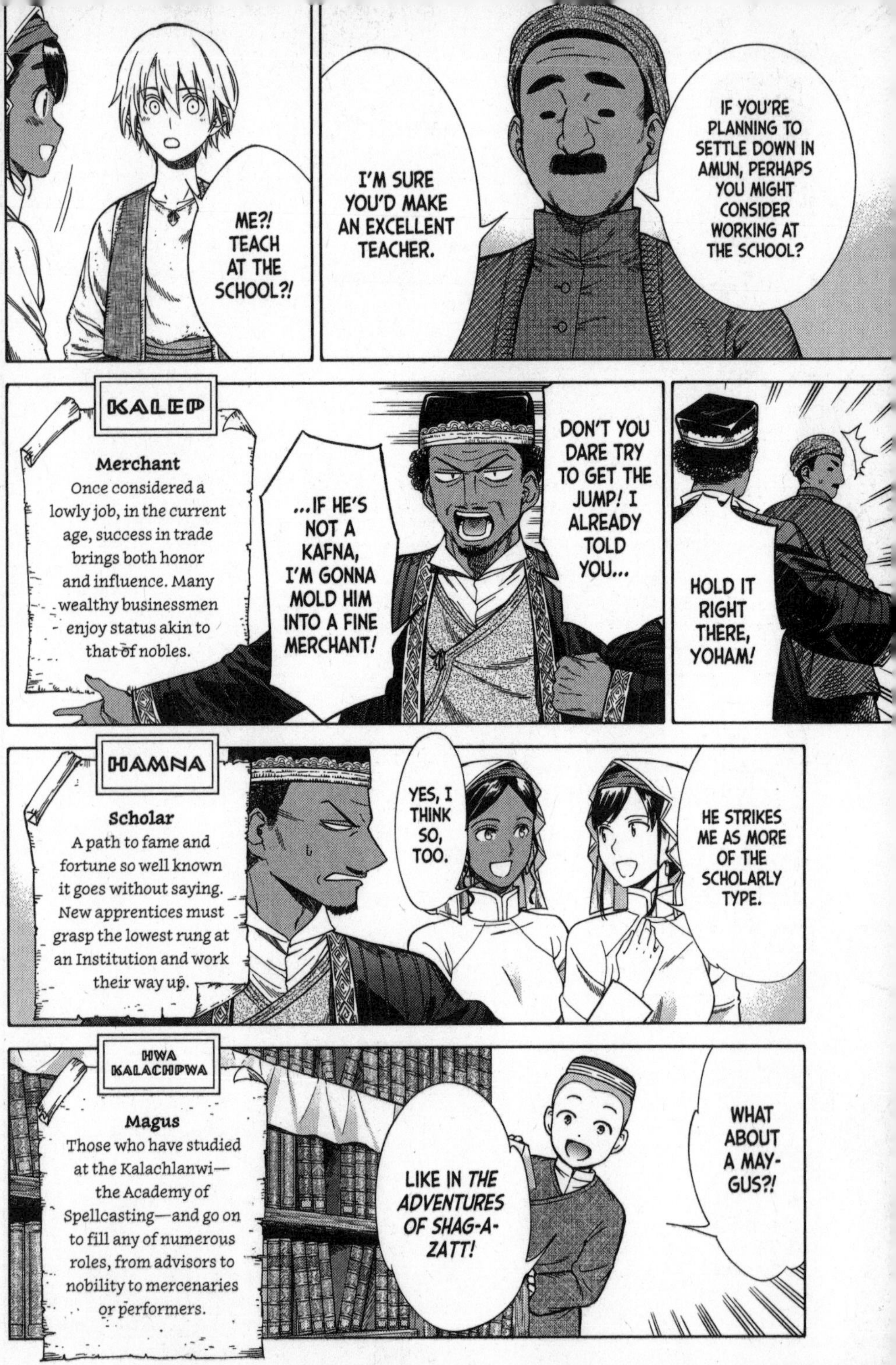
IF YOU'RE PLANNING TO SETTLE DOWN IN AMUN, PERHAPS YOU MIGHT CONSIDER WORKING AT THE SCHOOL?
I'M SURE YOU'D MAKE AN EXCELLENT TEACHER.
ME?! TEACH AT THE SCHOOL?!
HOLD IT RIGHT THERE, YOHAM!
DON'T YOU DARE TRY TO GET THE JUMP! I ALREADY TOLD YOU...
...IF HE'S NOT A KAFNA, I'M GONNA MOLD HIM INTO A FINE MERCHANT!
KALEP
Merchant
Once considered a lowly job, in the current age, success in trade brings both honor and influence. Many wealthy businessmen enjoy status akin to that of nobles.
HE STRIKES ME AS MORE OF THE SCHOLARLY TYPE.
YES, I THINK SO, TOO.
HAMNA
Scholar
A path to fame and fortune so well known it goes without saying. New apprentices must grasp the lowest rung at an Institution and work their way up.
WHAT ABOUT A MAY-GUS?!
LIKE IN *THE ADVENTURES OF SHAG-A-ZATT!*
HWA KALACHPWA
Magus
Those who have studied at the Kalachlanwi—the Academy of Spellcasting—and go on to fill any of numerous roles, from advisors to nobility to mercenaries or performers.

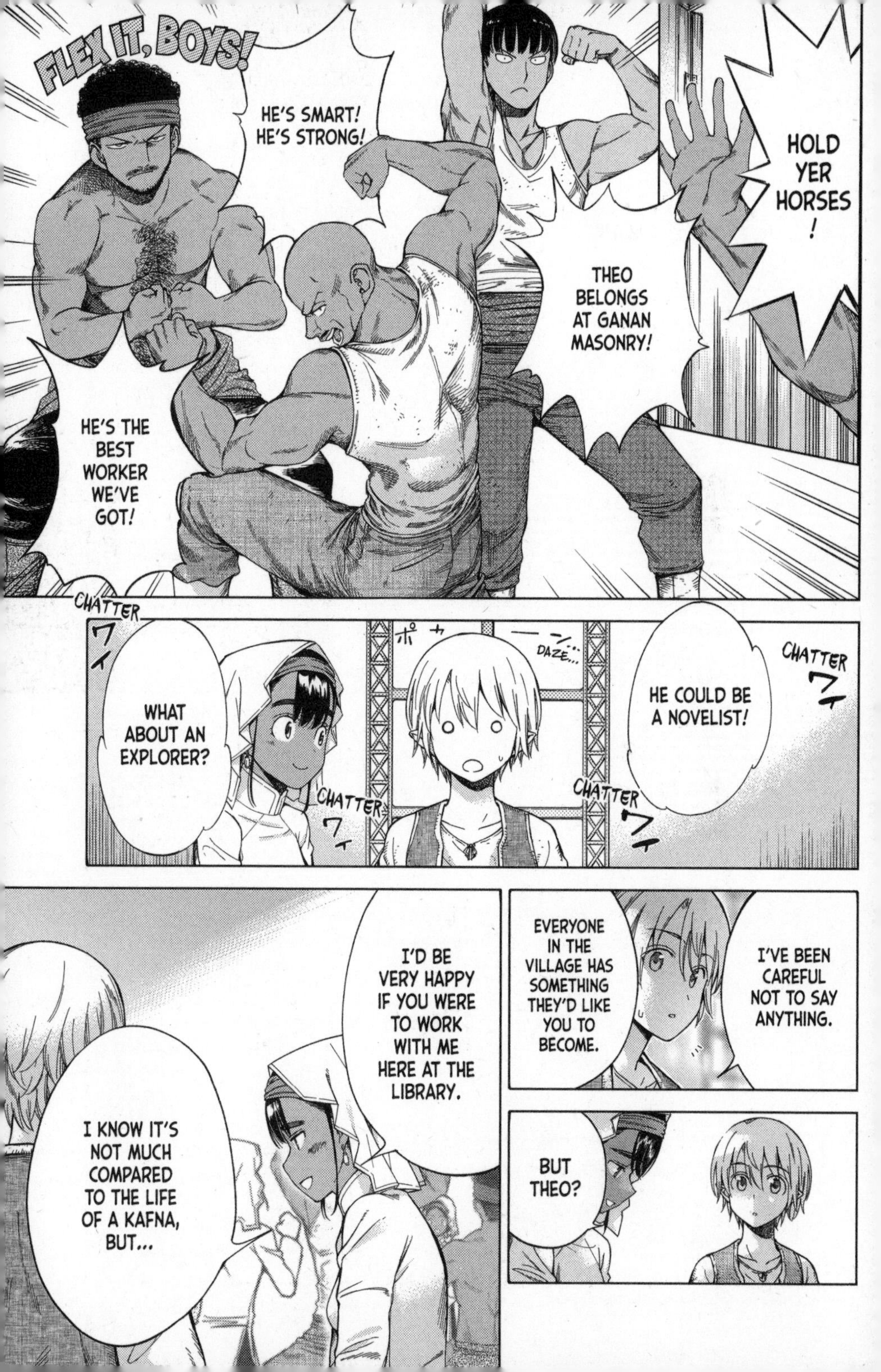
HOLD YER HORSES!
THEO BELONGS AT GANAN MASONRY!
HE'S SMART! HE'S STRONG!
FLEX IT, BOYS!
HE'S THE BEST WORKER WE'VE GOT!
CHATTER ワイ
HE COULD BE A NOVELIST!
CHATTER ワイ
ポカーン DAZE...
CHATTER ワイ
WHAT ABOUT AN EXPLORER?
CHATTER ワイ
I'VE BEEN CAREFUL NOT TO SAY ANYTHING.
EVERYONE IN THE VILLAGE HAS SOMETHING THEY'D LIKE YOU TO BECOME.
BUT THEO?
I'D BE VERY HAPPY IF YOU WERE TO WORK WITH ME HERE AT THE LIBRARY.
I KNOW IT'S NOT MUCH COMPARED TO THE LIFE OF A KAFNA, BUT...

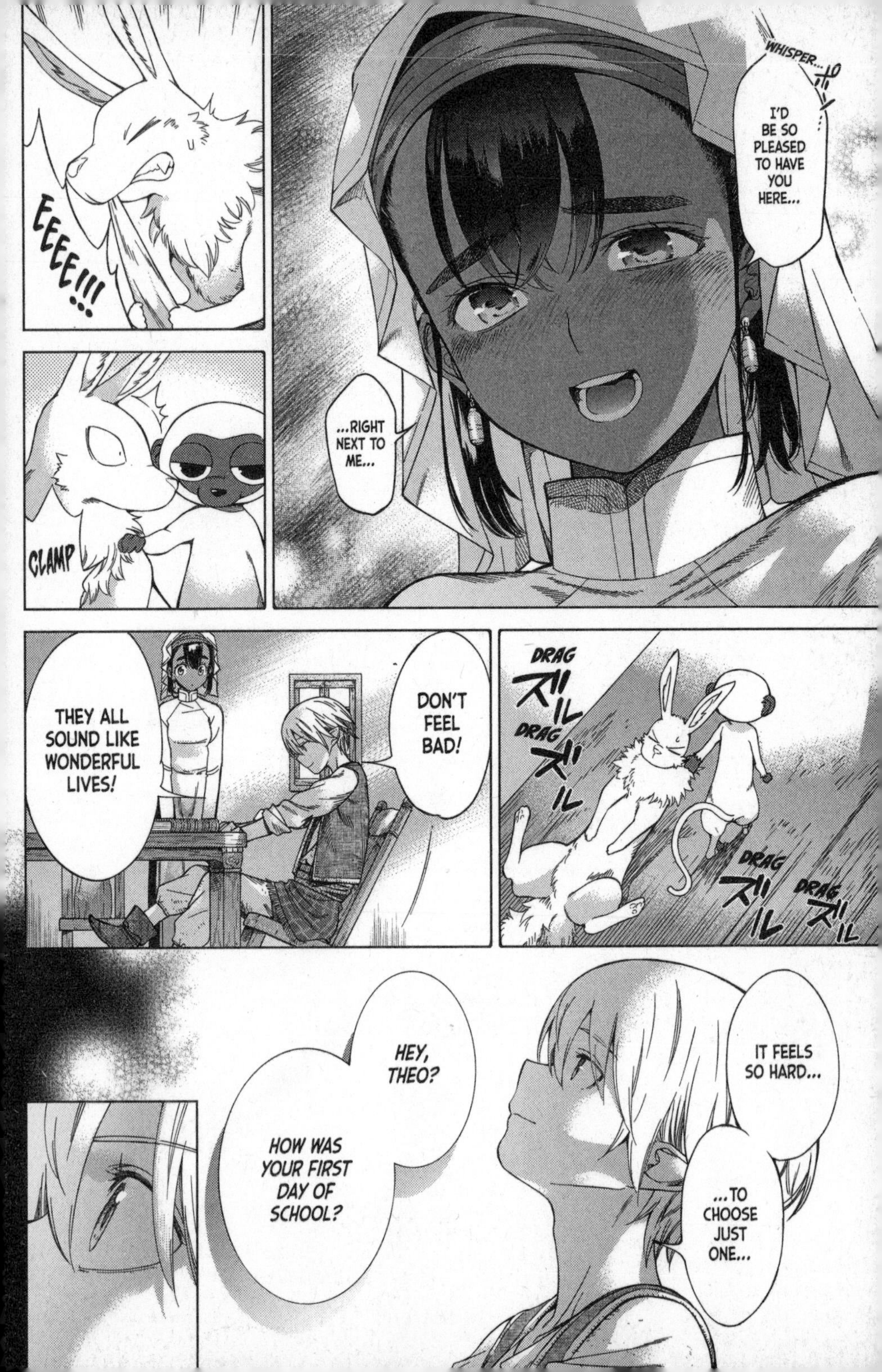
WHISPER...
I'D BE SO PLEASED TO HAVE YOU HERE...
...RIGHT NEXT TO ME...
EEEE!!!
CLAMP
DRAG ズル
DRAG ズル
DRAG ズル
DRAG ズル
DON'T FEEL BAD!
THEY ALL SOUND LIKE WONDERFUL LIVES!
IT FEELS SO HARD...
...TO CHOOSE JUST ONE...
HEY, THEO?
HOW WAS YOUR FIRST DAY OF SCHOOL?

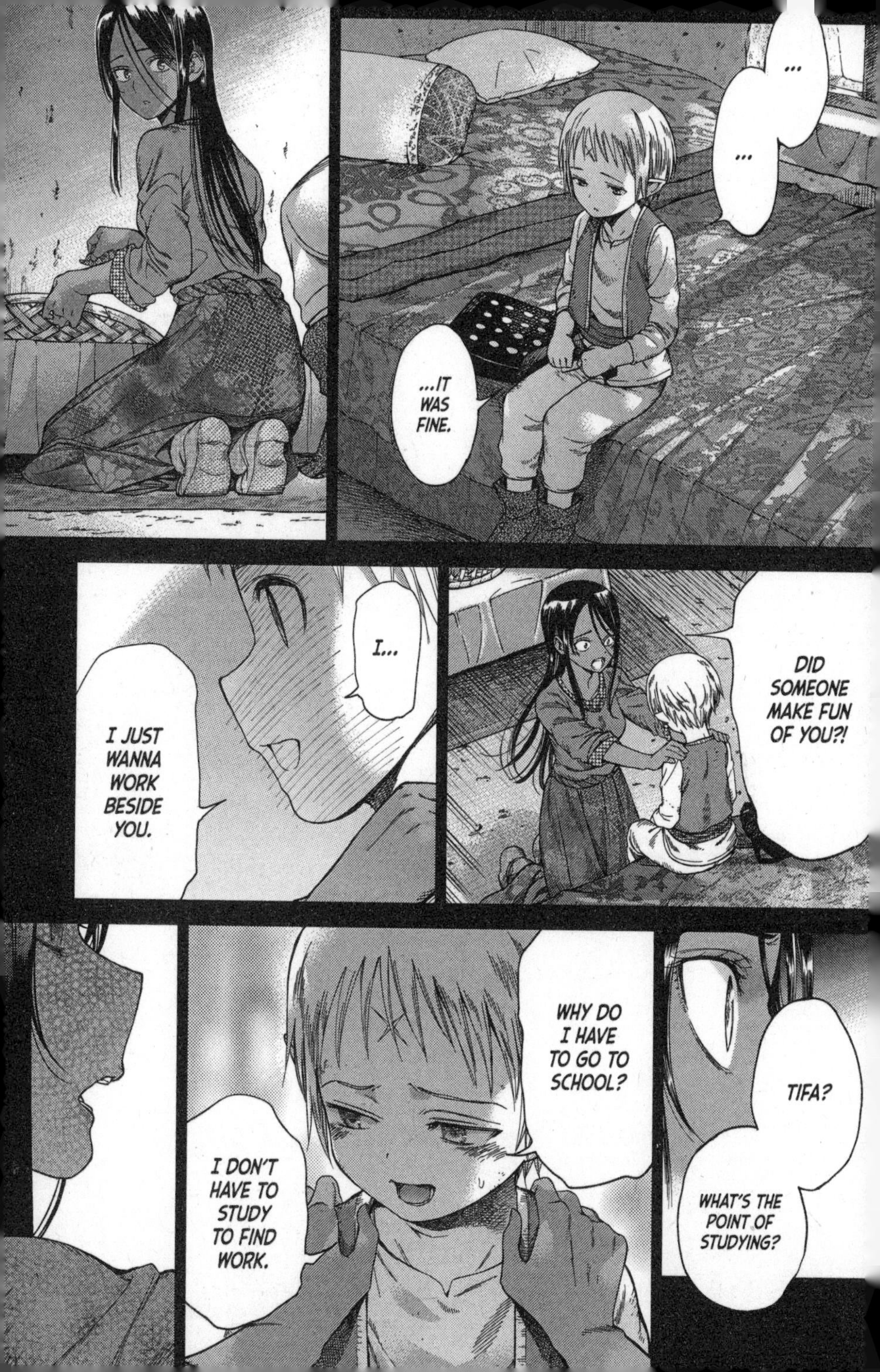
...
...
...IT WAS FINE.
DID SOMEONE MAKE FUN OF YOU?!
I...
I JUST WANNA WORK BESIDE YOU.
TIFA?
WHAT'S THE POINT OF STUDYING?
WHY DO I HAVE TO GO TO SCHOOL?
I DON'T HAVE TO STUDY TO FIND WORK.

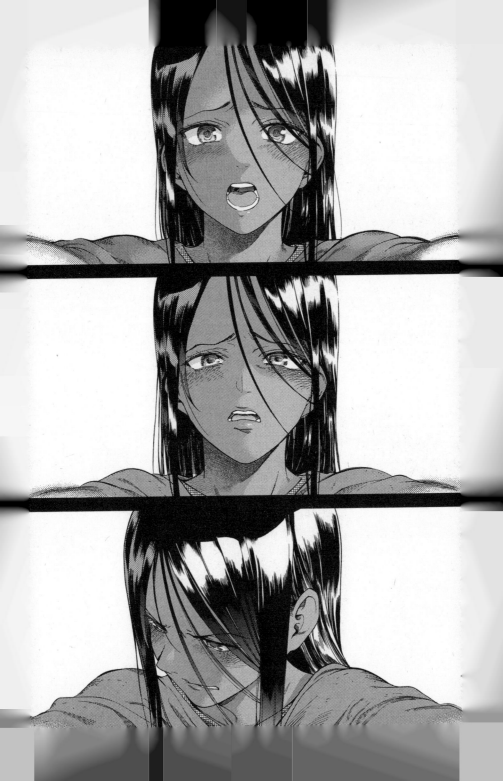

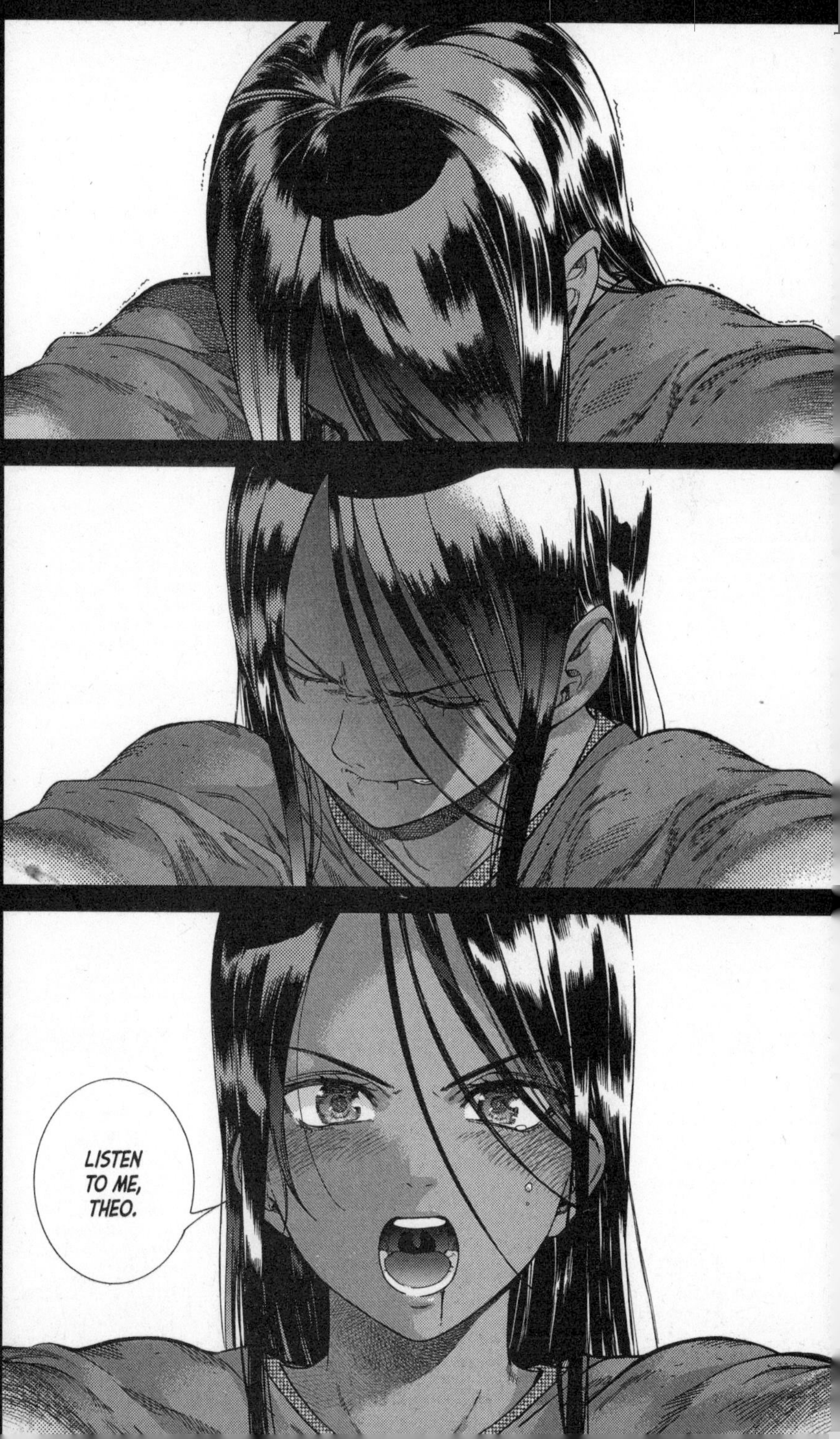
LISTEN TO ME, THEO.

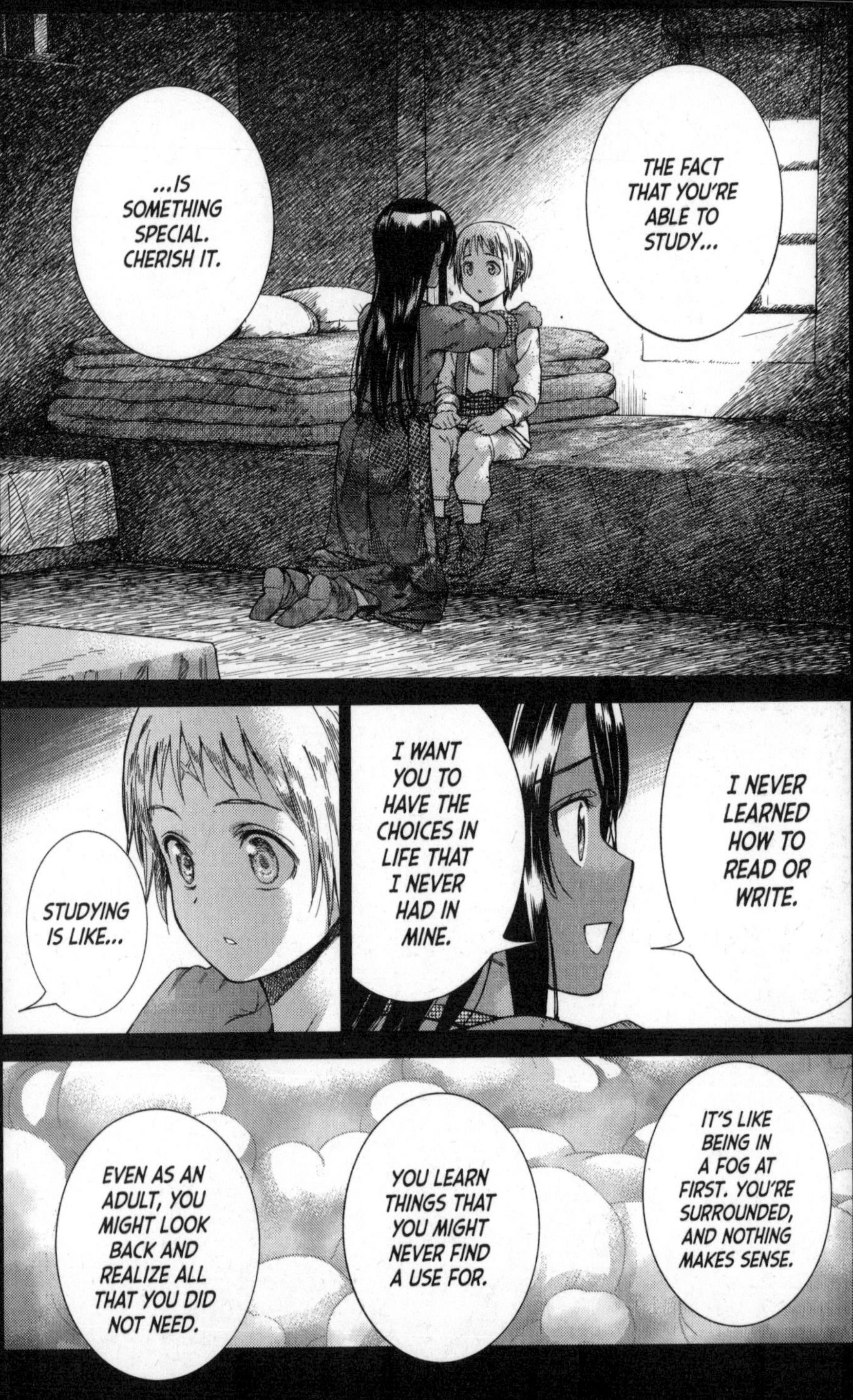
THE FACT THAT YOU'RE ABLE TO STUDY...
...IS SOMETHING SPECIAL. CHERISH IT.
I NEVER LEARNED HOW TO READ OR WRITE.
I WANT YOU TO HAVE THE CHOICES IN LIFE THAT I NEVER HAD IN MINE.
STUDYING IS LIKE...
IT'S LIKE BEING IN A FOG AT FIRST. YOU'RE SURROUNDED, AND NOTHING MAKES SENSE.
YOU LEARN THINGS THAT YOU MIGHT NEVER FIND A USE FOR.
EVEN AS AN ADULT, YOU MIGHT LOOK BACK AND REALIZE ALL THAT YOU DID NOT NEED.

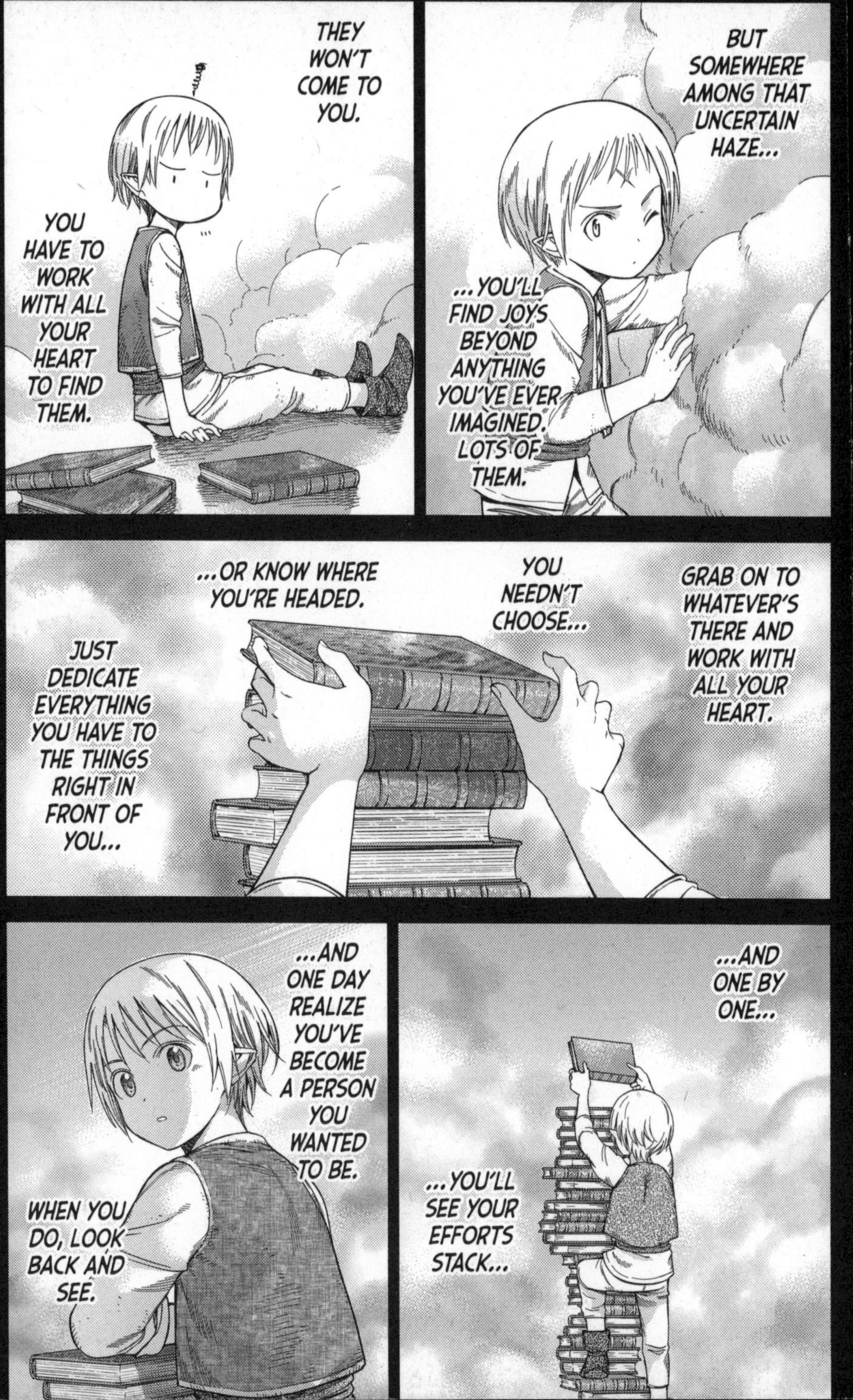
BUT SOMEWHERE AMONG THAT UNCERTAIN HAZE...
...YOU'LL FIND JOYS BEYOND ANYTHING YOU'VE EVER IMAGINED. LOTS OF THEM.
THEY WON'T COME TO YOU.
YOU HAVE TO WORK WITH ALL YOUR HEART TO FIND THEM.
GRAB ON TO WHATEVER'S THERE AND WORK WITH ALL YOUR HEART.
YOU NEEDN'T CHOOSE...
...OR KNOW WHERE YOU'RE HEADED.
JUST DEDICATE EVERYTHING YOU HAVE TO THE THINGS RIGHT IN FRONT OF YOU...
...AND ONE BY ONE...
...YOU'LL SEE YOUR EFFORTS STACK...
...AND ONE DAY REALIZE YOU'VE BECOME A PERSON YOU WANTED TO BE.
WHEN YOU DO, LOOK BACK AND SEE.

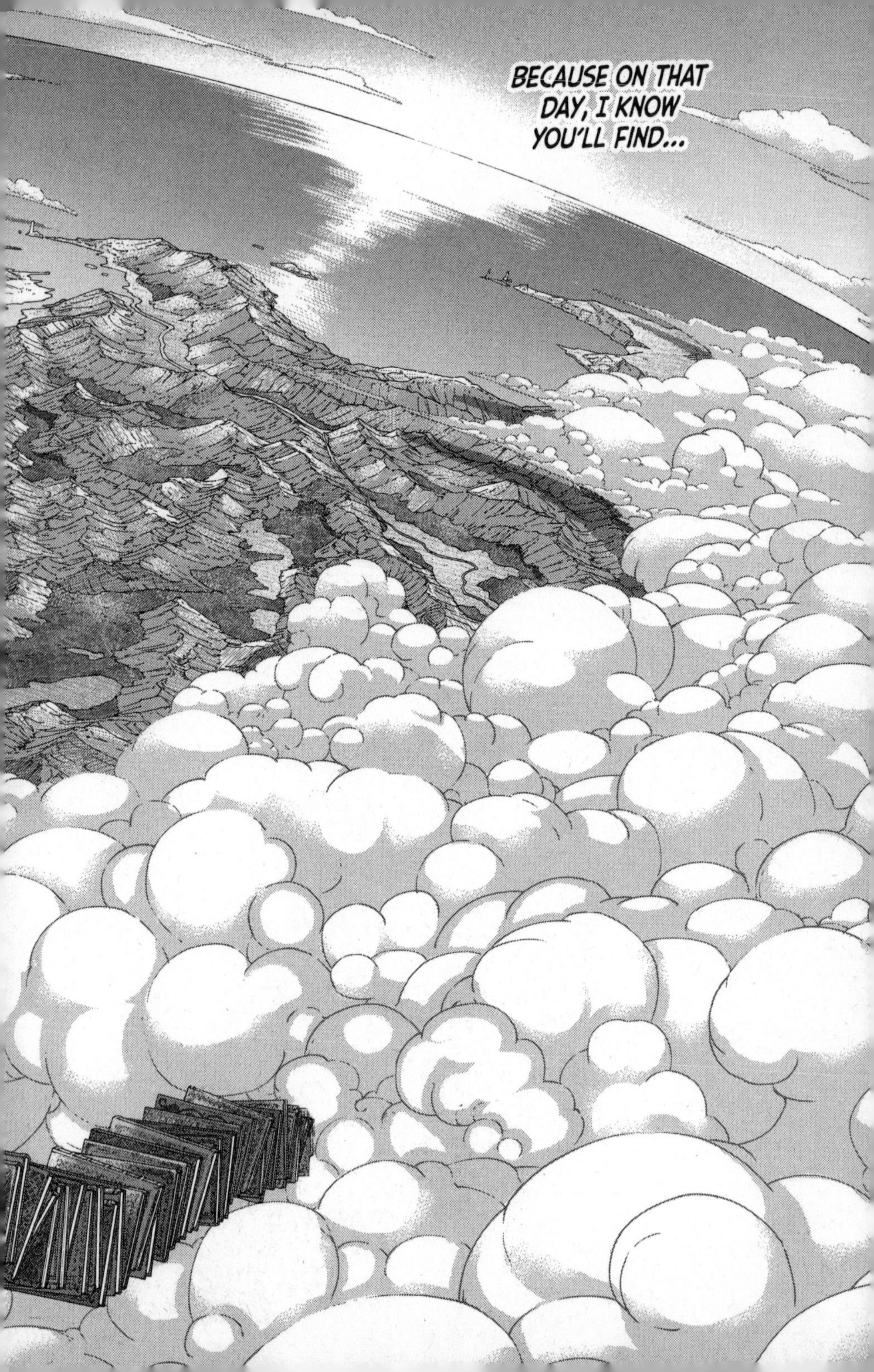
BECAUSE ON THAT DAY, I KNOW YOU'LL FIND...

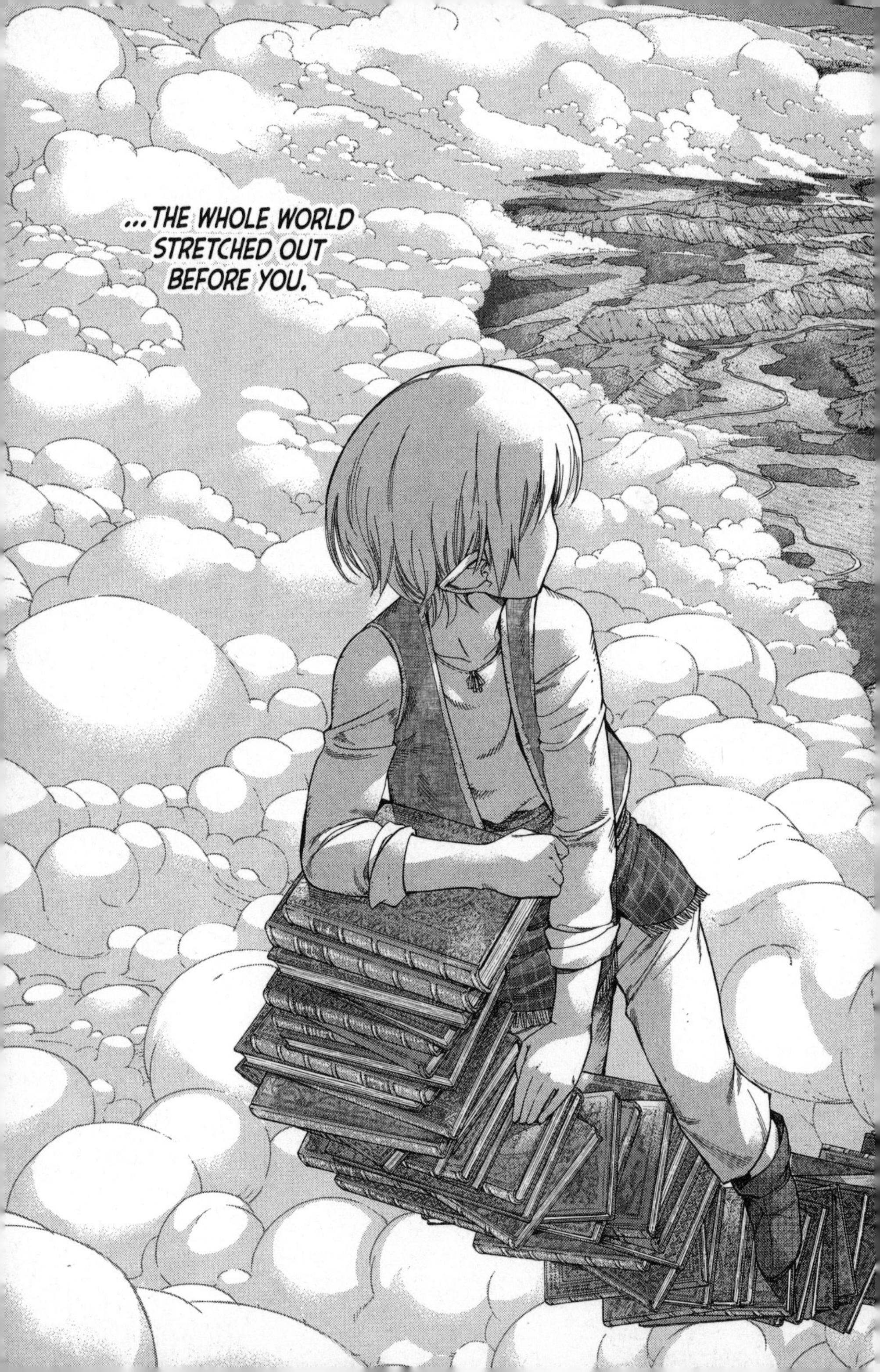
...THE WHOLE WORLD STRETCHED OUT BEFORE YOU.

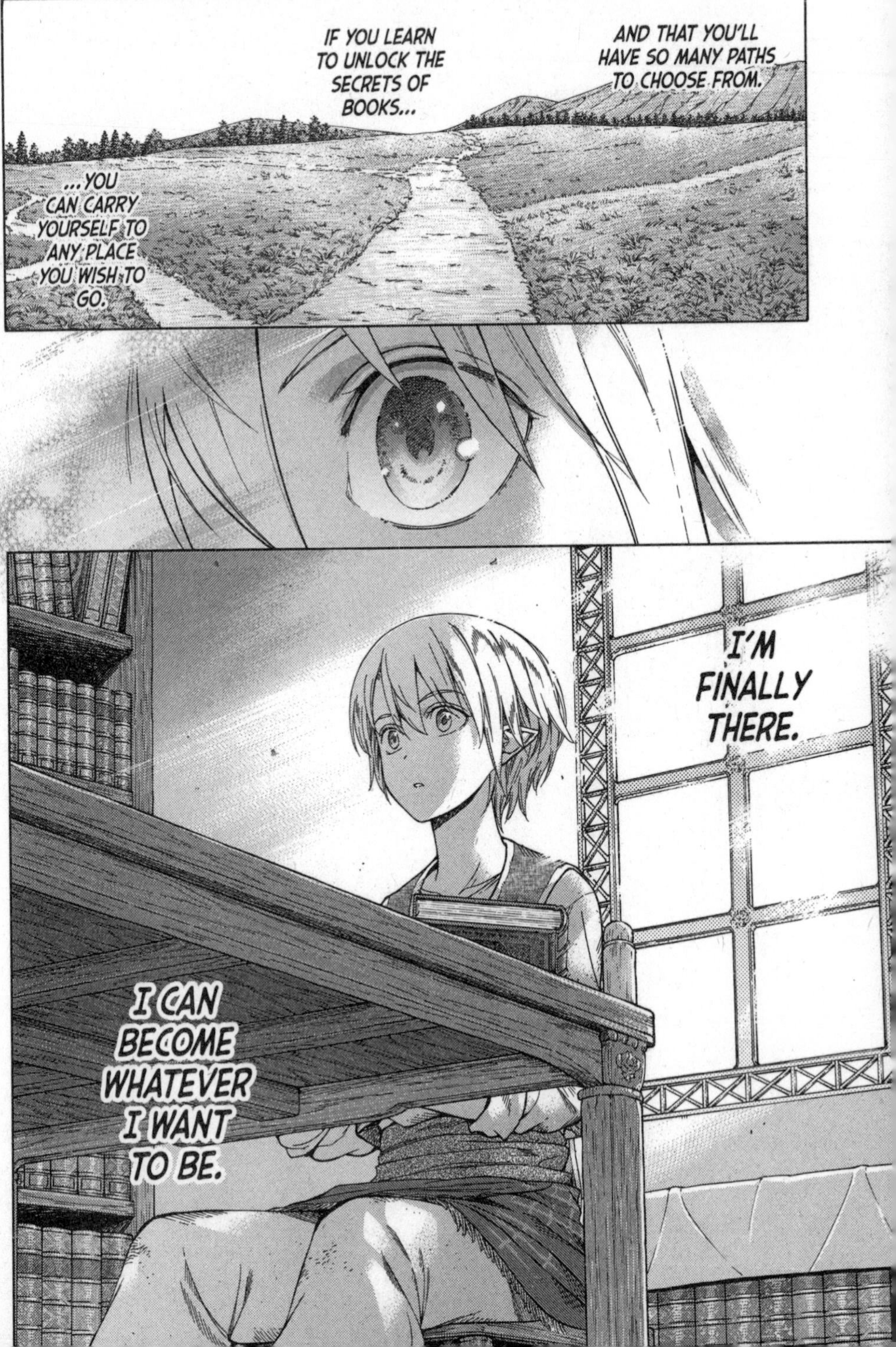
IF YOU LEARN TO UNLOCK THE SECRETS OF BOOKS...
...YOU CAN CARRY YOURSELF TO ANY PLACE YOU WISH TO GO.
AND THAT YOU'LL HAVE SO MANY PATHS TO CHOOSE FROM.
I'M FINALLY THERE.
I CAN BECOME WHATEVER I WANT TO BE.

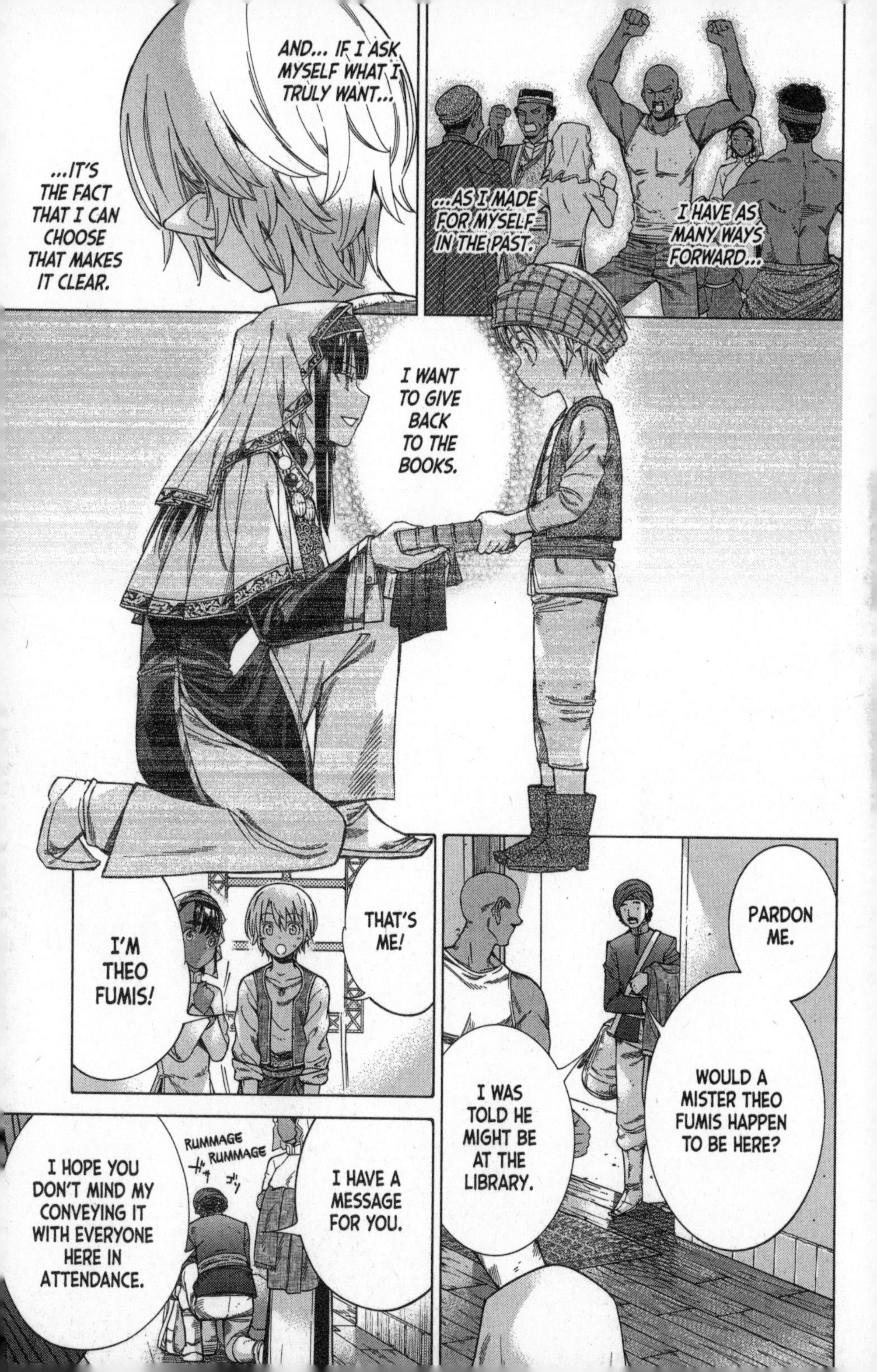
I HAVE AS MANY WAYS FORWARD...
...AS I MADE FOR MYSELF IN THE PAST.
AND... IF I ASK MYSELF WHAT I TRULY WANT...
...IT'S THE FACT THAT I CAN CHOOSE THAT MAKES IT CLEAR.
I WANT TO GIVE BACK TO THE BOOKS.
PARDON ME.
WOULD A MISTER THEO FUMIS HAPPEN TO BE HERE?
I WAS TOLD HE MIGHT BE AT THE LIBRARY.
THAT'S ME!
I'M THEO FUMIS!
I HAVE A MESSAGE FOR YOU.
RUMMAGE RUMMAGE
I HOPE YOU DON'T MIND MY CONVEYING IT WITH EVERYONE HERE IN ATTENDANCE.

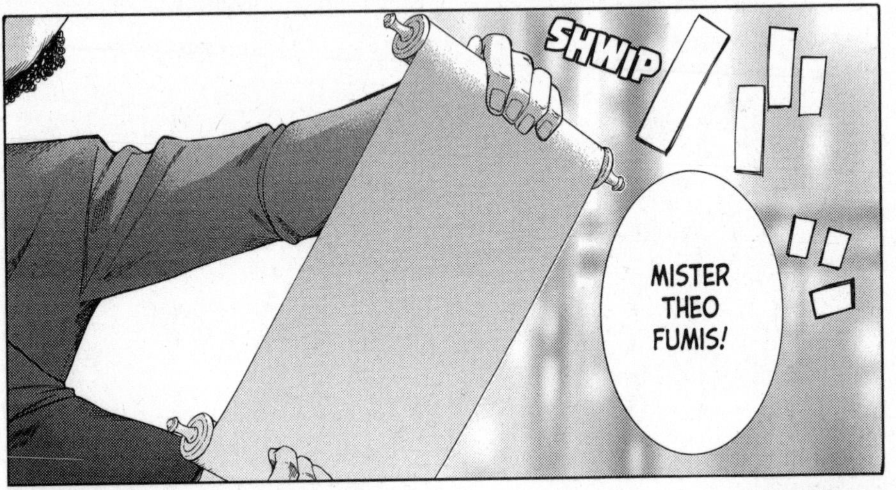
SHWIP
MISTER THEO FUMIS!
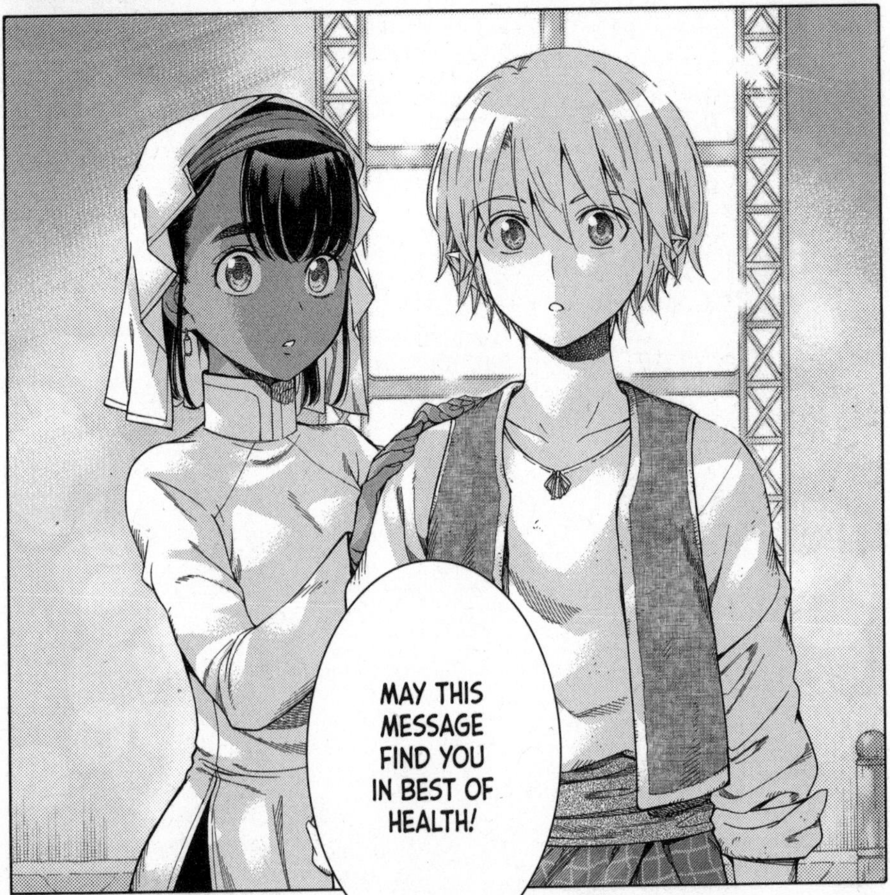
MAY THIS MESSAGE FIND YOU IN BEST OF HEALTH!

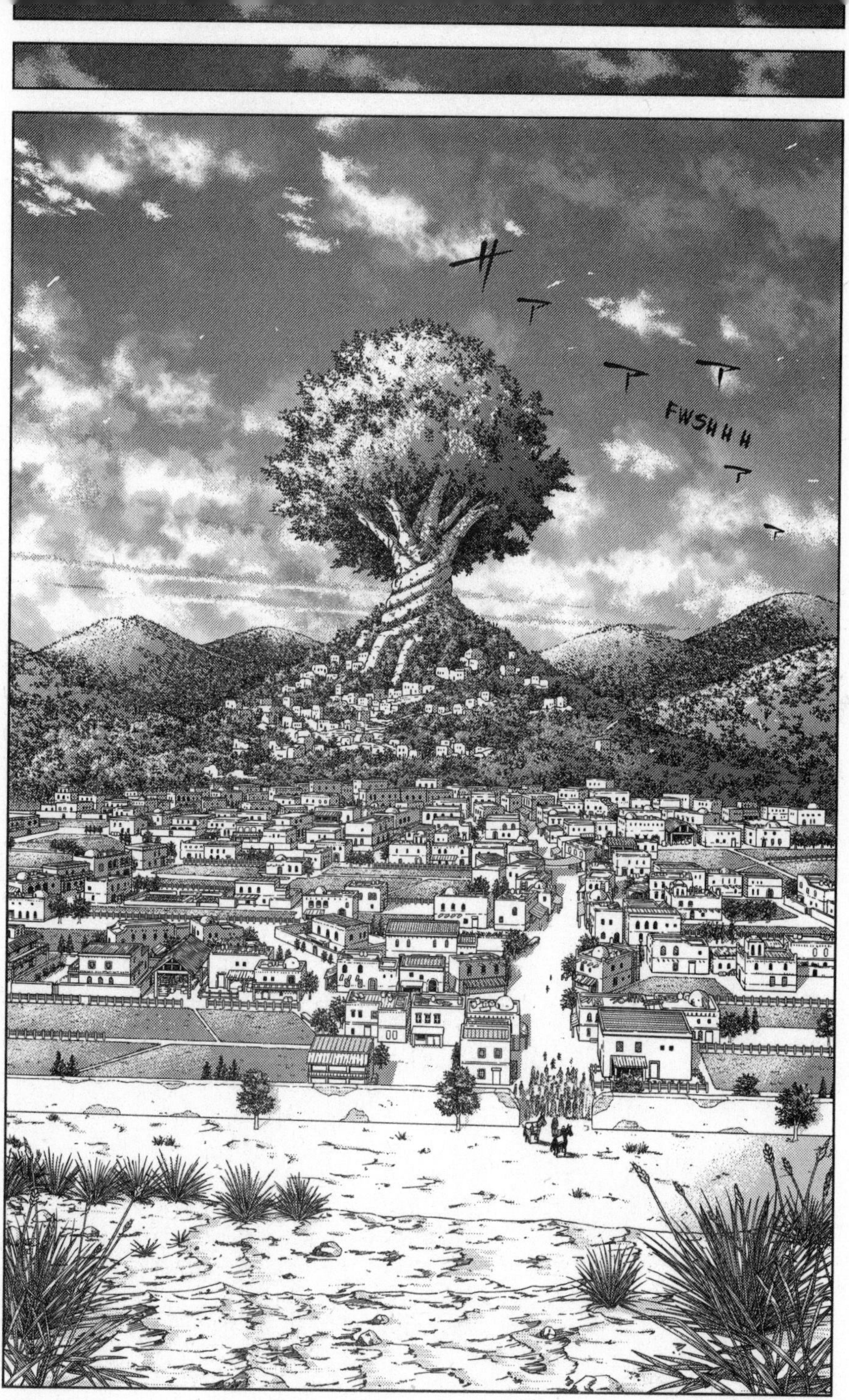
FWSHHH

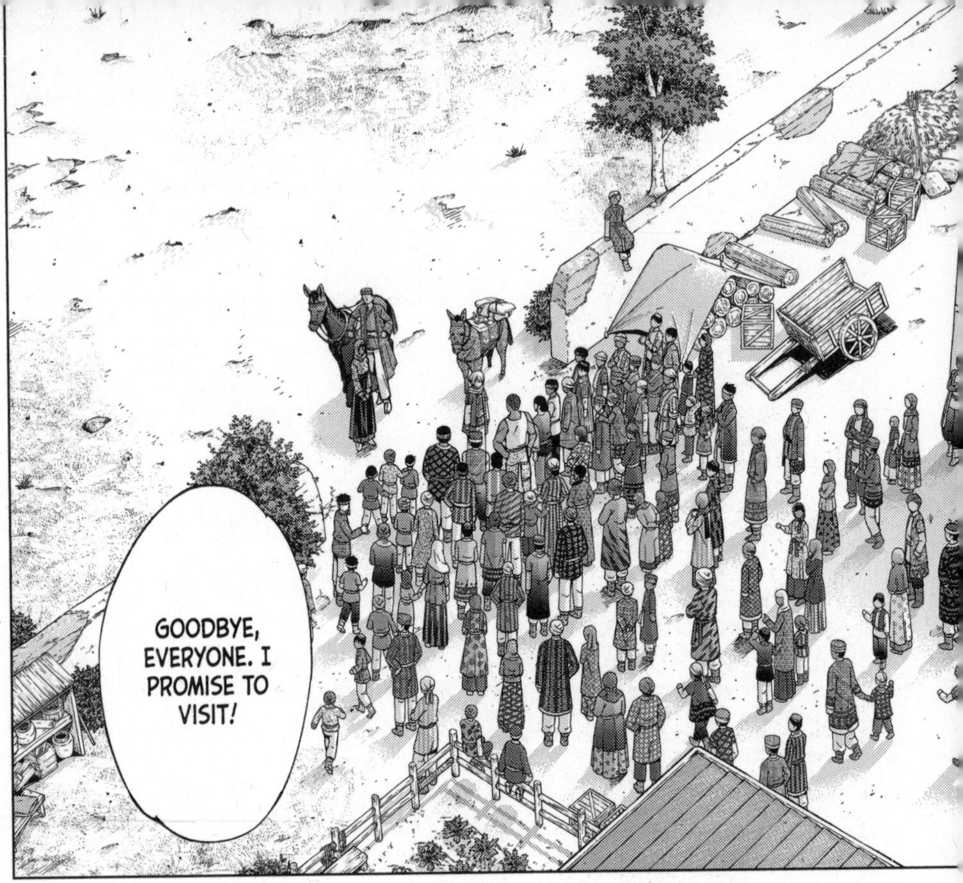
GOODBYE, EVERYONE. I PROMISE TO VISIT!

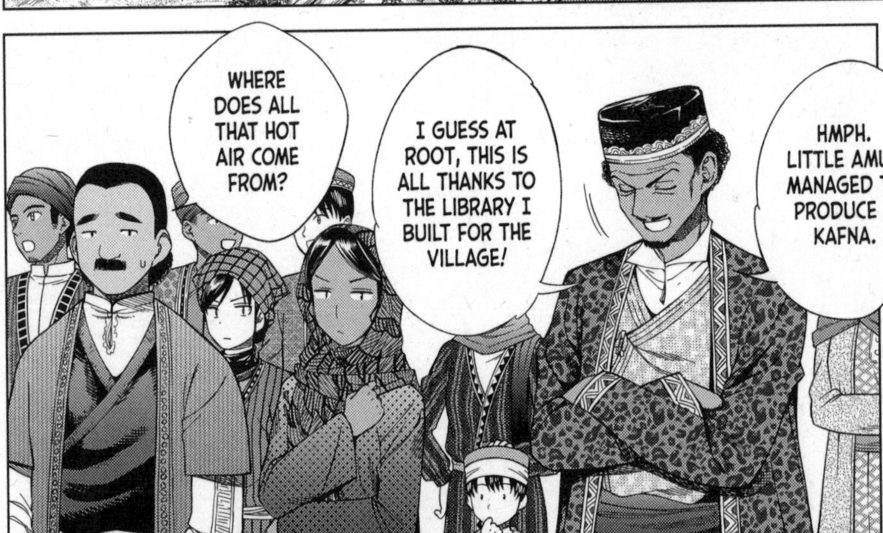
HMPH. LITTLE AMUN MANAGED TO PRODUCE A KAFNA.
I GUESS AT ROOT, THIS IS ALL THANKS TO THE LIBRARY I BUILT FOR THE VILLAGE!
WHERE DOES ALL THAT HOT AIR COME FROM?

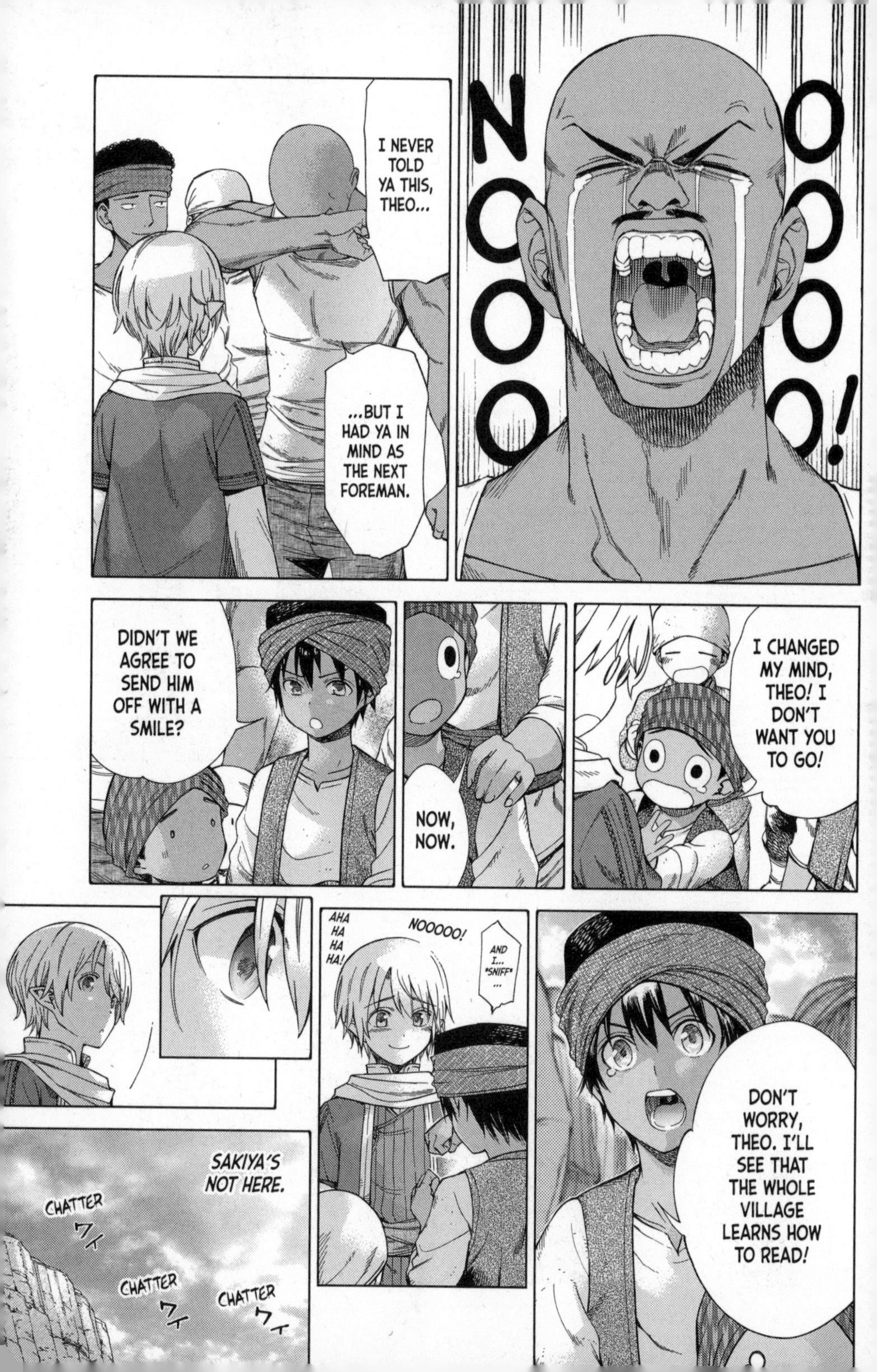
NOOOOOOO!
I NEVER TOLD YA THIS, THEO...
...BUT I HAD YA IN MIND AS THE NEXT FOREMAN.
I CHANGED MY MIND, THEO! I DON'T WANT YOU TO GO!
NOW, NOW.
DIDN'T WE AGREE TO SEND HIM OFF WITH A SMILE?
DON'T WORRY, THEO. I'LL SEE THAT THE WHOLE VILLAGE LEARNS HOW TO READ!
AND I... *SNIFF* ...
NOOOOO!
AHA HA HA HA!
SAKIYA'S NOT HERE.
CHATTER ワイ
CHATTER ワイ
CHATTER ワイ

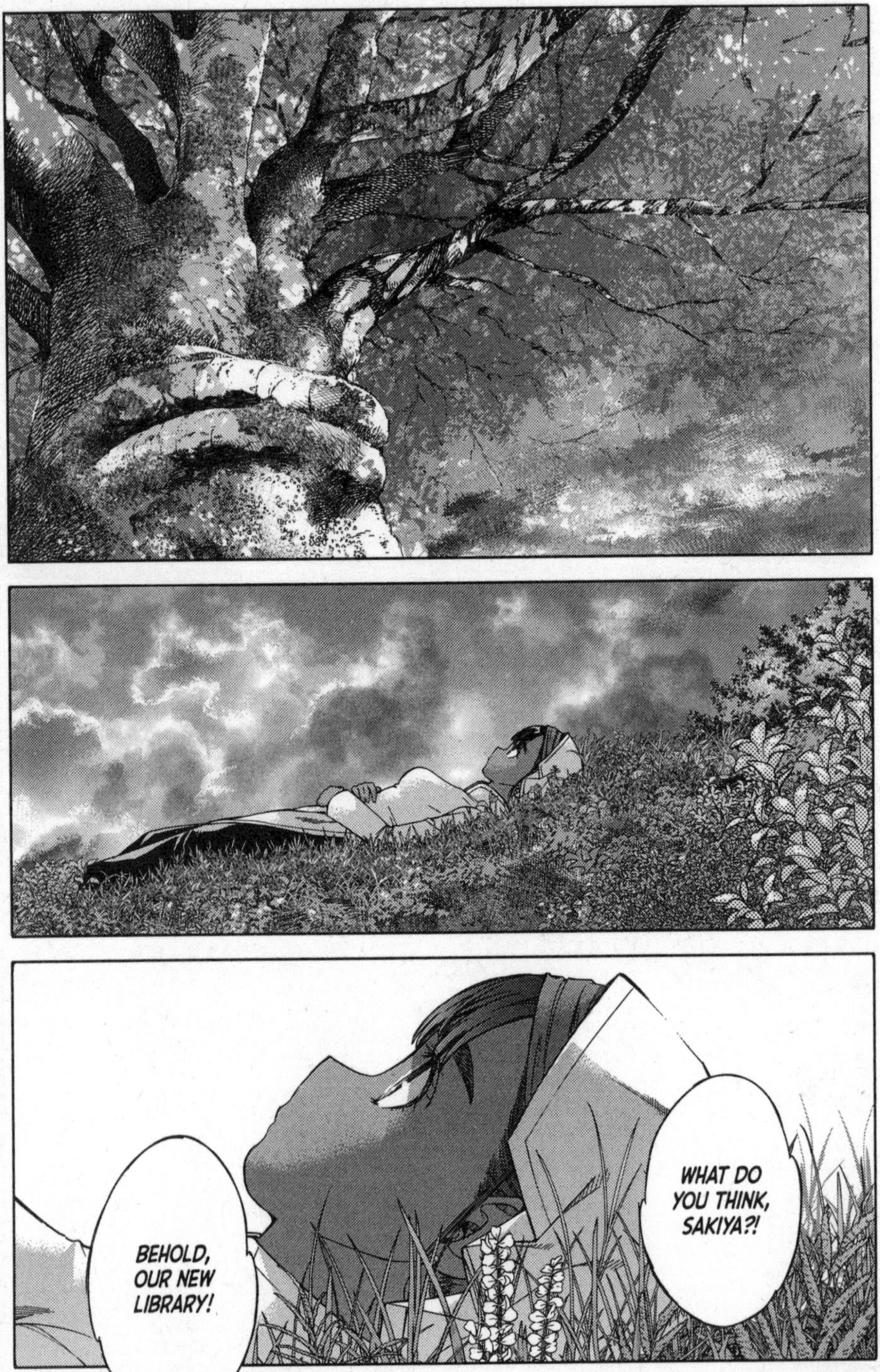
WHAT DO YOU THINK, SAKIYA?!
BEHOLD, OUR NEW LIBRARY!

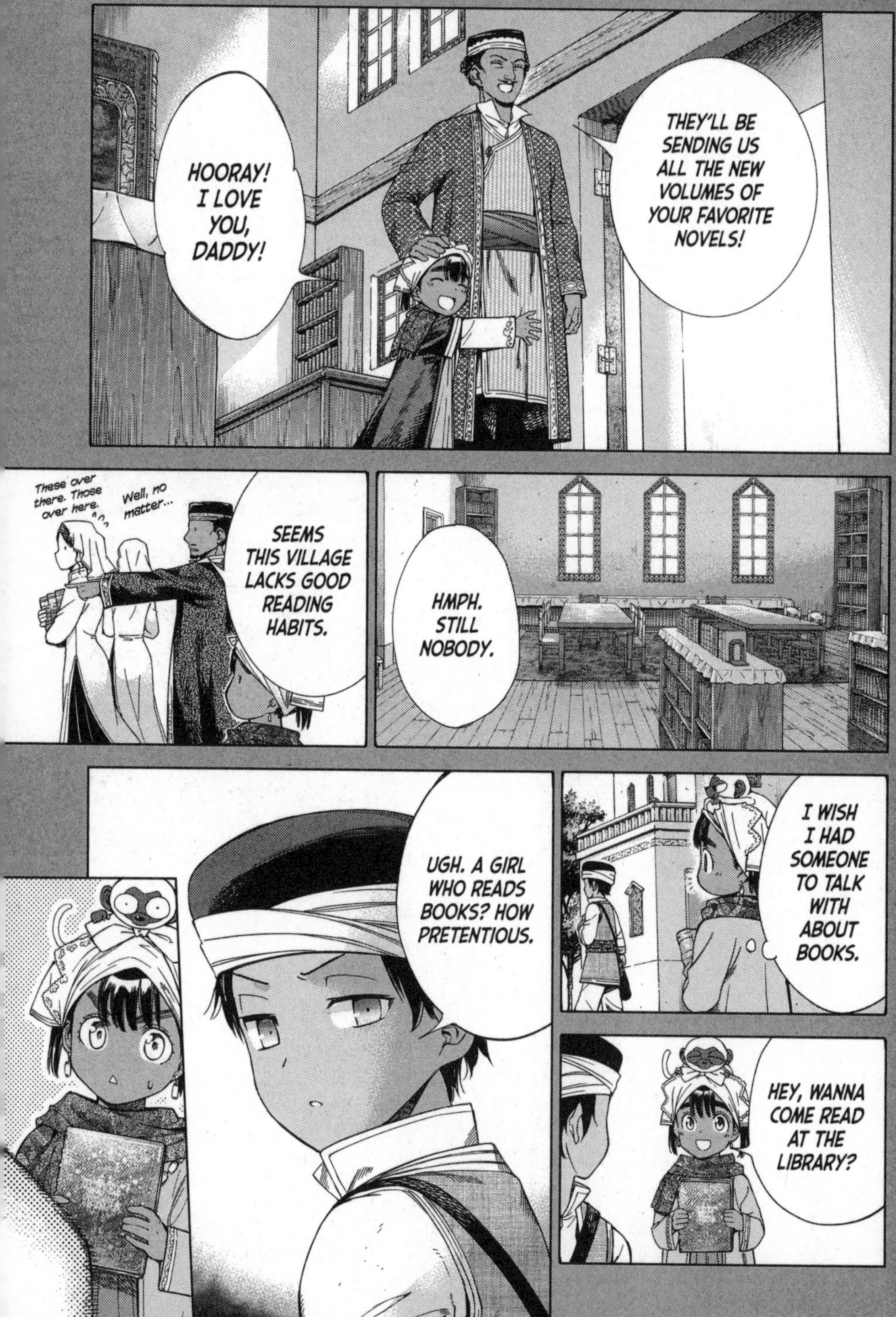
THEY'LL BE SENDING US ALL THE NEW VOLUMES OF YOUR FAVORITE NOVELS!
HOORAY! I LOVE YOU, DADDY!
HMPH. STILL NOBODY.
SEEMS THIS VILLAGE LACKS GOOD READING HABITS.
Well, no matter...
These over there. Those over here.
I WISH I HAD SOMEONE TO TALK WITH ABOUT BOOKS.
HEY, WANNA COME READ AT THE LIBRARY?
UGH. A GIRL WHO READS BOOKS? HOW PRETENTIOUS.

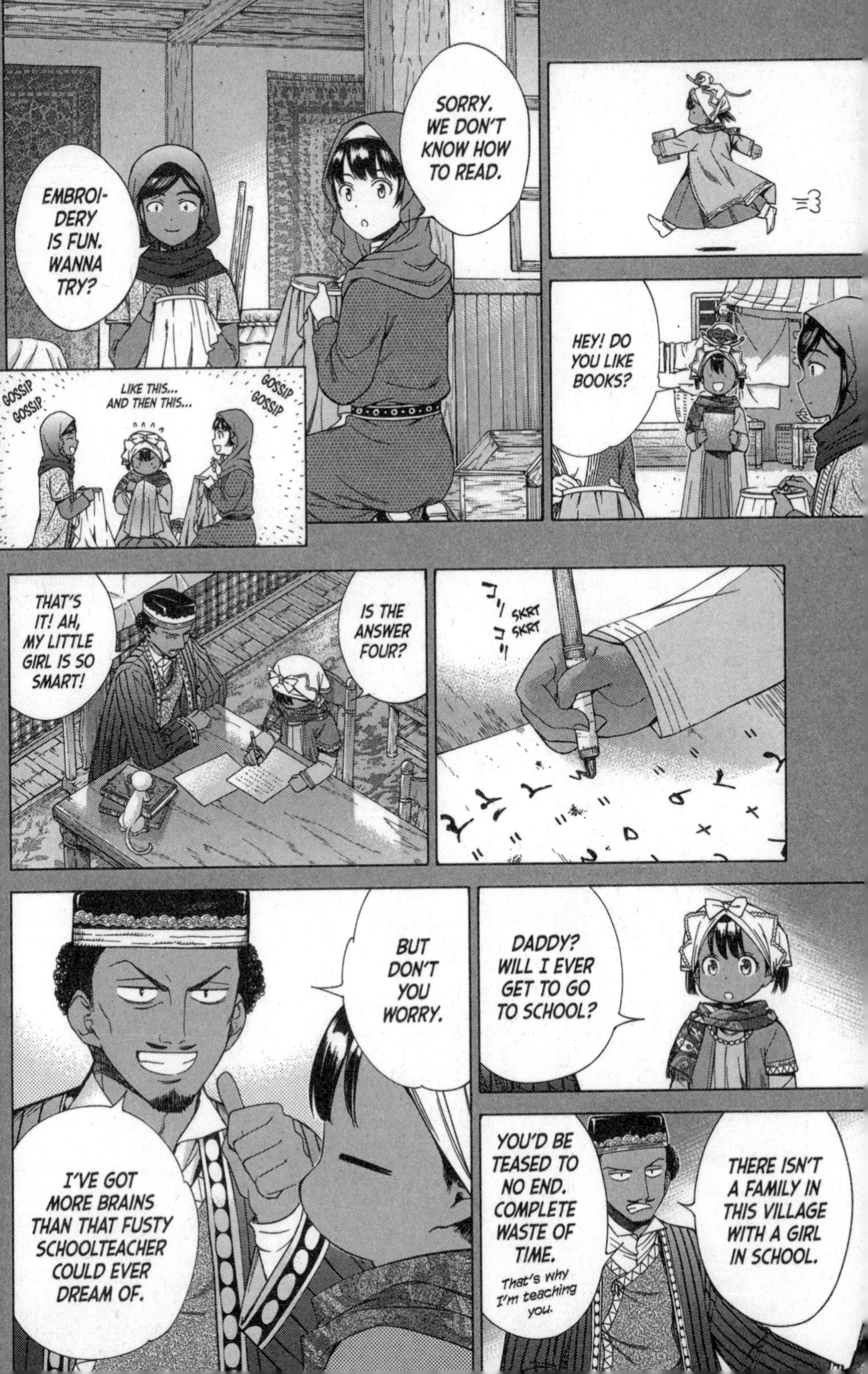
HEY! DO YOU LIKE BOOKS?
SORRY. WE DON'T KNOW HOW TO READ.
EMBROIDERY IS FUN. WANNA TRY?
GOSSIP GOSSIP
LIKE THIS... AND THEN THIS...
GOSSIP GOSSIP
SKRT SKRT
IS THE ANSWER FOUR?
THAT'S IT! AH, MY LITTLE GIRL IS SO SMART!
DADDY? WILL I EVER GET TO GO TO SCHOOL?
THERE ISN'T A FAMILY IN THIS VILLAGE WITH A GIRL IN SCHOOL.
YOU'D BE TEASED TO NO END. COMPLETE WASTE OF TIME.
That's why I'm teaching you.
BUT DON'T YOU WORRY.
I'VE GOT MORE BRAINS THAN THAT FUSTY SCHOOLTEACHER COULD EVER DREAM OF.

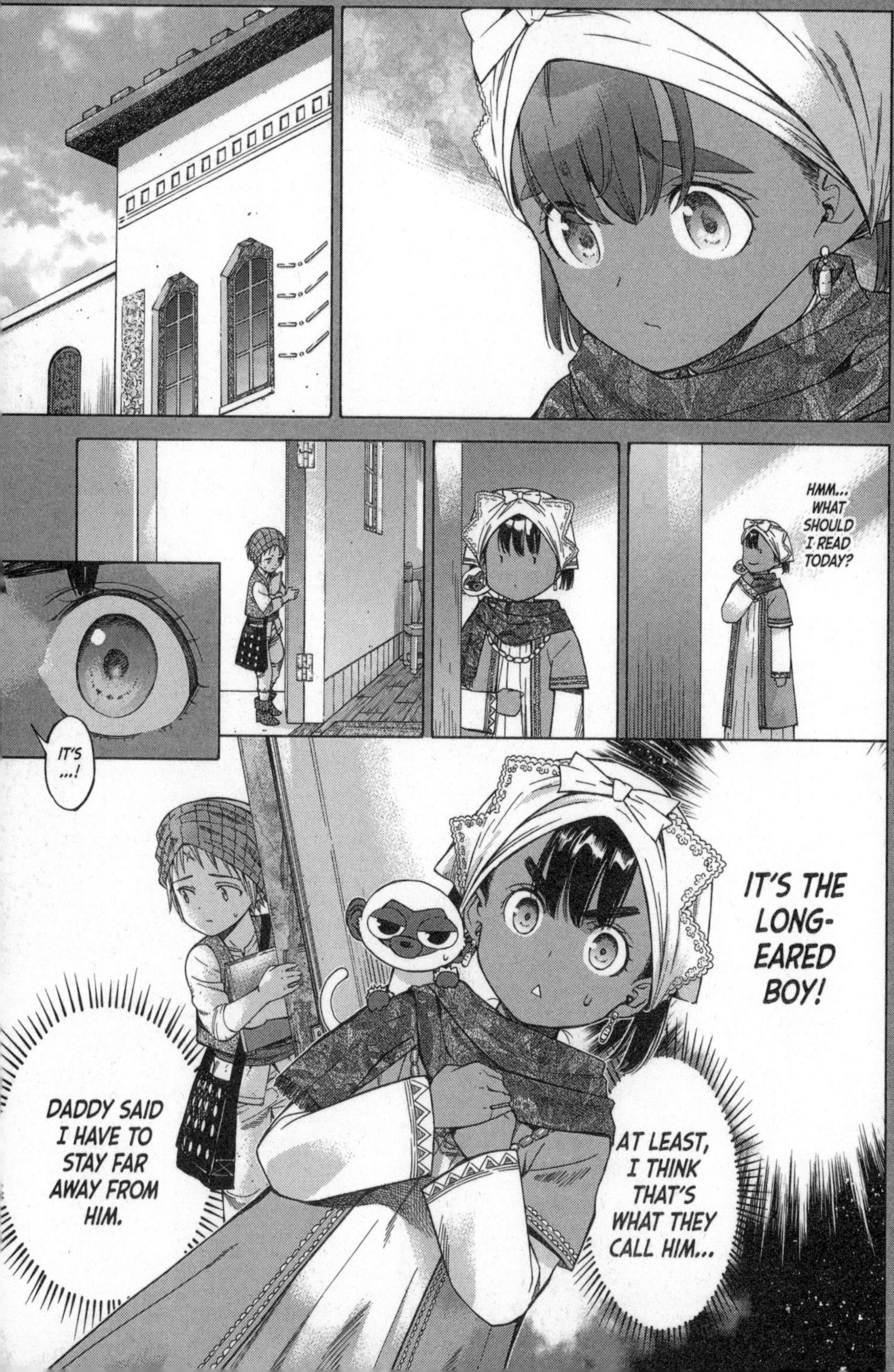
HMM... WHAT SHOULD I READ TODAY?
IT'S ...!
IT'S THE LONG-EARED BOY!
AT LEAST, I THINK THAT'S WHAT THEY CALL HIM...
DADDY SAID I HAVE TO STAY FAR AWAY FROM HIM.

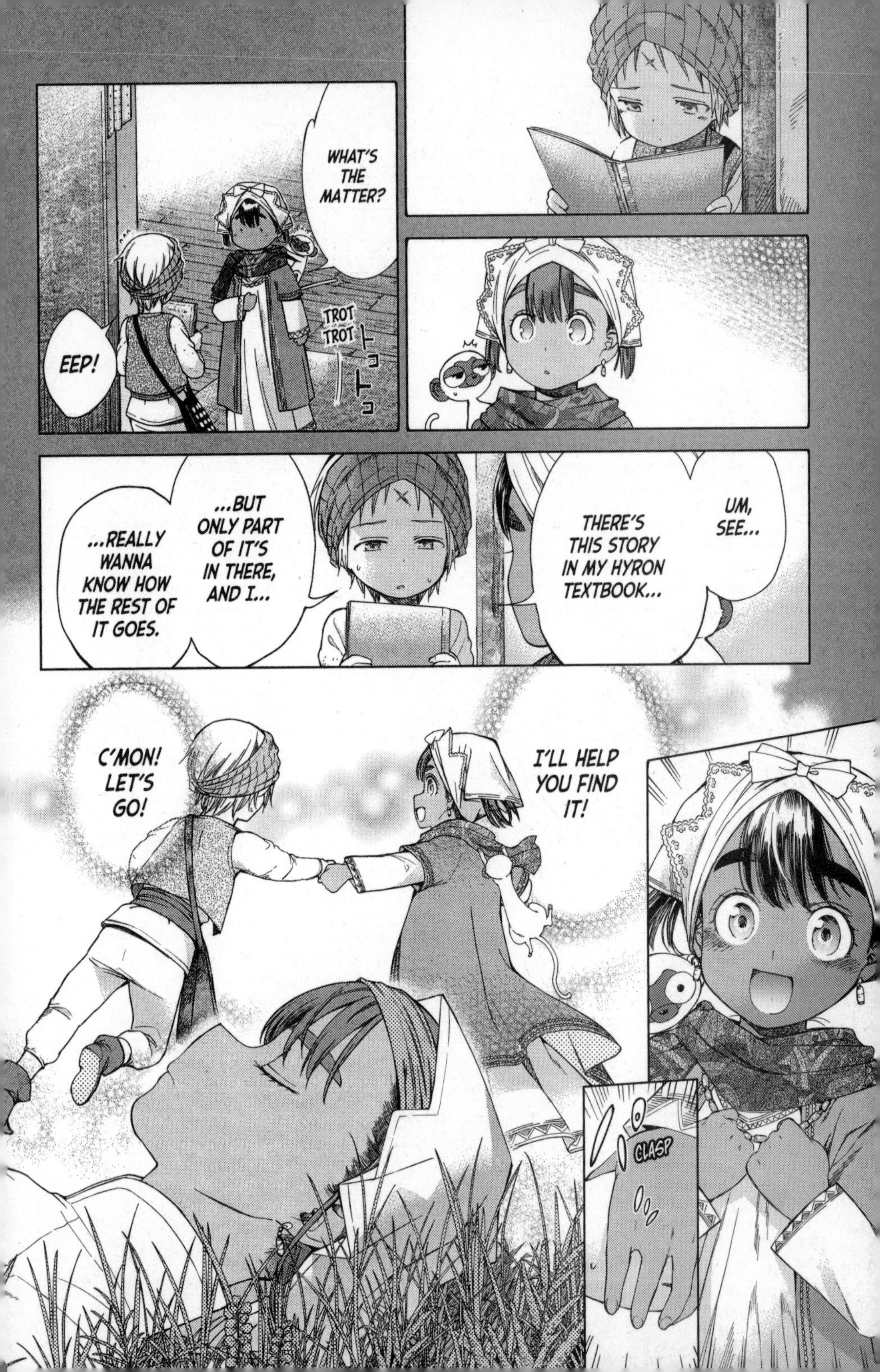
WHAT'S THE MATTER?
TROT TROT
トコトコ
EEP!
UM, SEE...
THERE'S THIS STORY IN MY HYRON TEXTBOOK...
...BUT ONLY PART OF IT'S IN THERE, AND I...
...REALLY WANNA KNOW HOW THE REST OF IT GOES.
CLASP
I'LL HELP YOU FIND IT!
C'MON! LET'S GO!

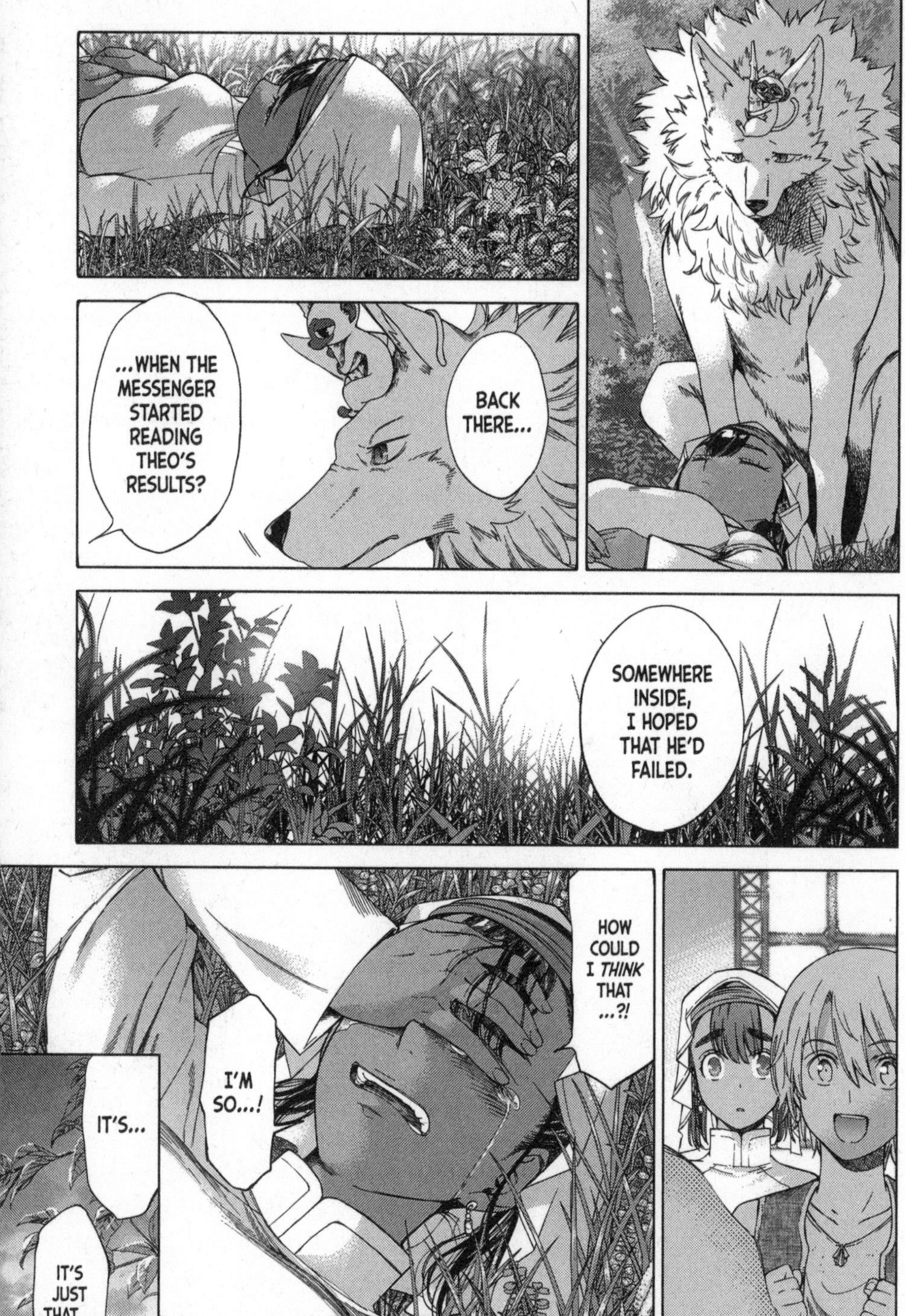
BACK THERE...
...WHEN THE MESSENGER STARTED READING THEO'S RESULTS?
SOMEWHERE INSIDE, I HOPED THAT HE'D FAILED.
HOW COULD I *THINK* THAT ...?!
I'M SO...!
IT'S...
IT'S JUST THAT...

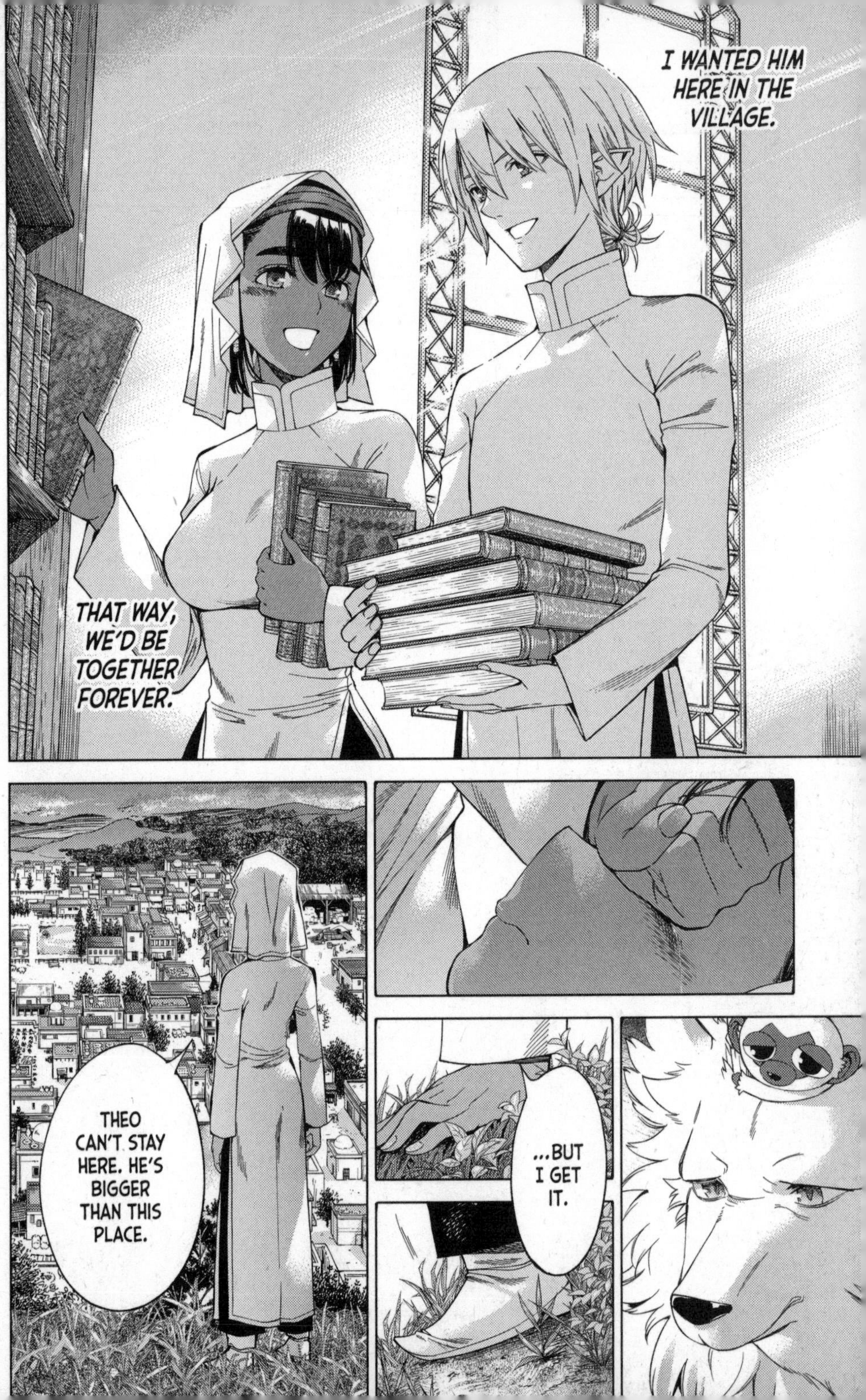
I WANTED HIM HERE IN THE VILLAGE.
THAT WAY, WE'D BE TOGETHER FOREVER.
...BUT I GET IT.
THEO CAN'T STAY HERE. HE'S BIGGER THAN THIS PLACE.

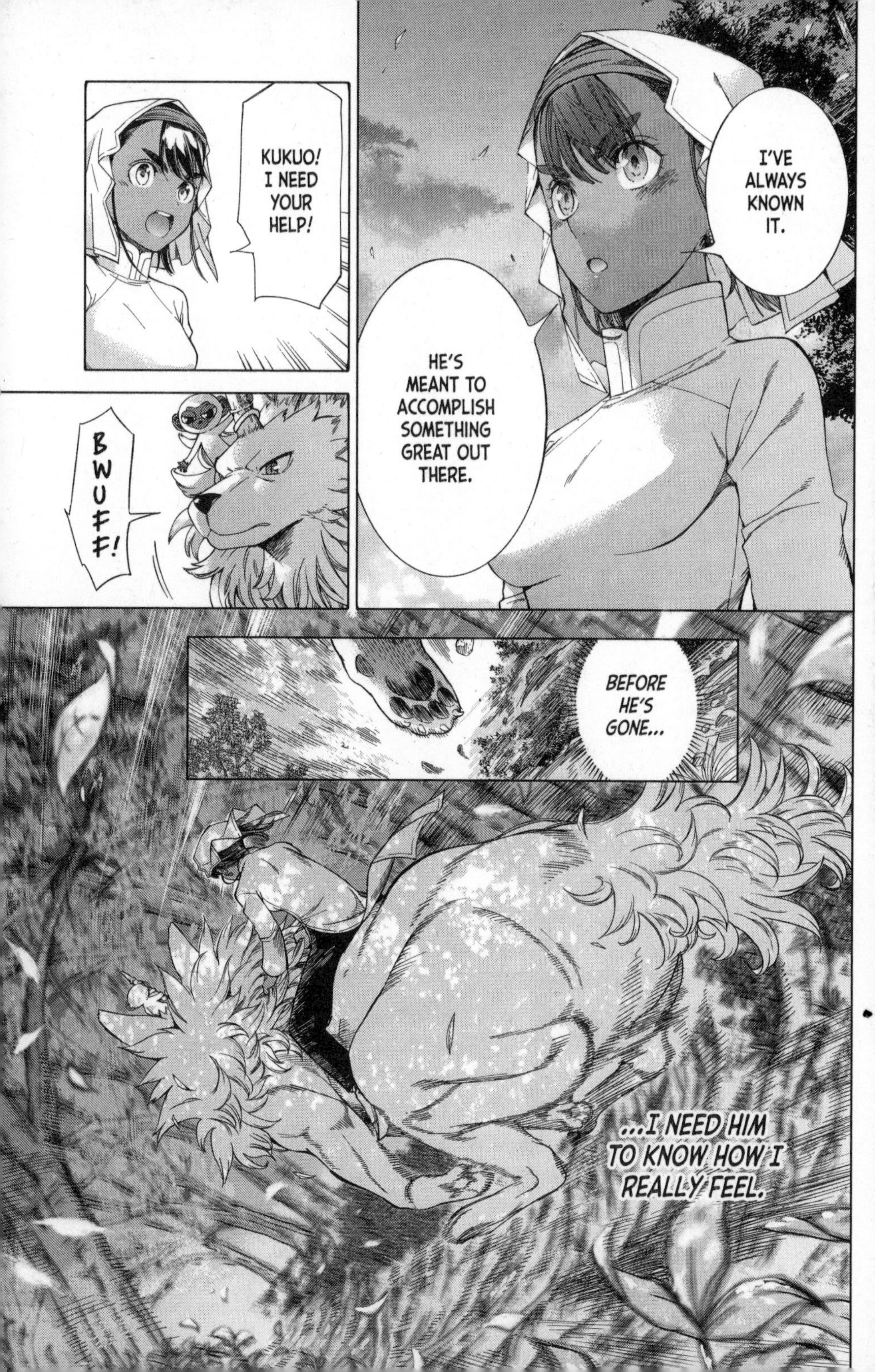
I'VE ALWAYS KNOWN IT.
HE'S MEANT TO ACCOMPLISH SOMETHING GREAT OUT THERE.
KUKUO! I NEED YOUR HELP!
BWUFF!
BEFORE HE'S GONE...
...I NEED HIM TO KNOW HOW I REALLY FEEL.

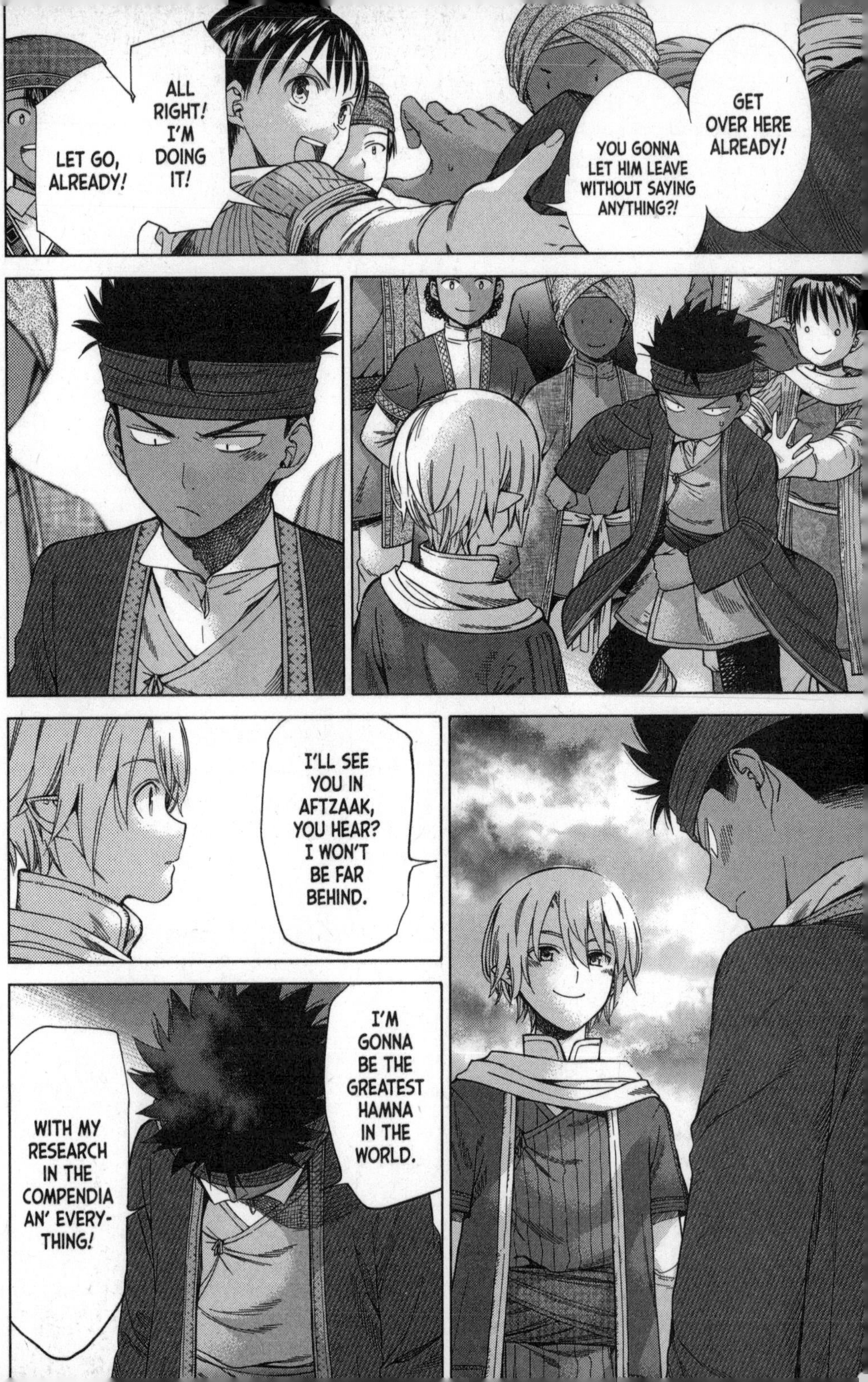
GET OVER HERE ALREADY!
YOU GONNA LET HIM LEAVE WITHOUT SAYING ANYTHING?!
ALL RIGHT! I'M DOING IT!
LET GO, ALREADY!
I'LL SEE YOU IN AFTZAAK, YOU HEAR? I WON'T BE FAR BEHIND.
I'M GONNA BE THE GREATEST HAMNA IN THE WORLD.
WITH MY RESEARCH IN THE COMPENDIA AN' EVERY-THING!

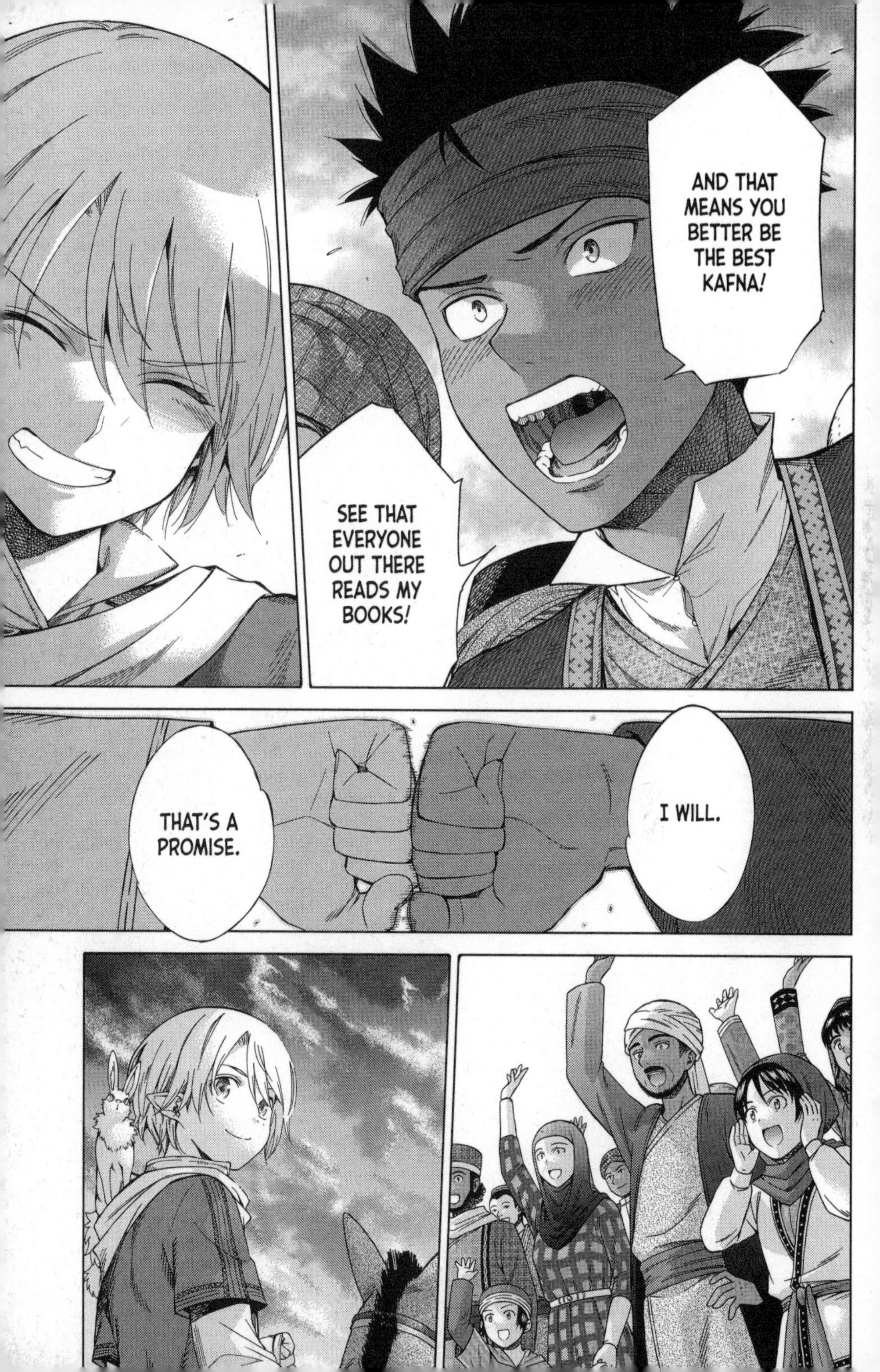
AND THAT MEANS YOU BETTER BE THE BEST KAFNA!
SEE THAT EVERYONE OUT THERE READS MY BOOKS!
I WILL.
THAT'S A PROMISE.

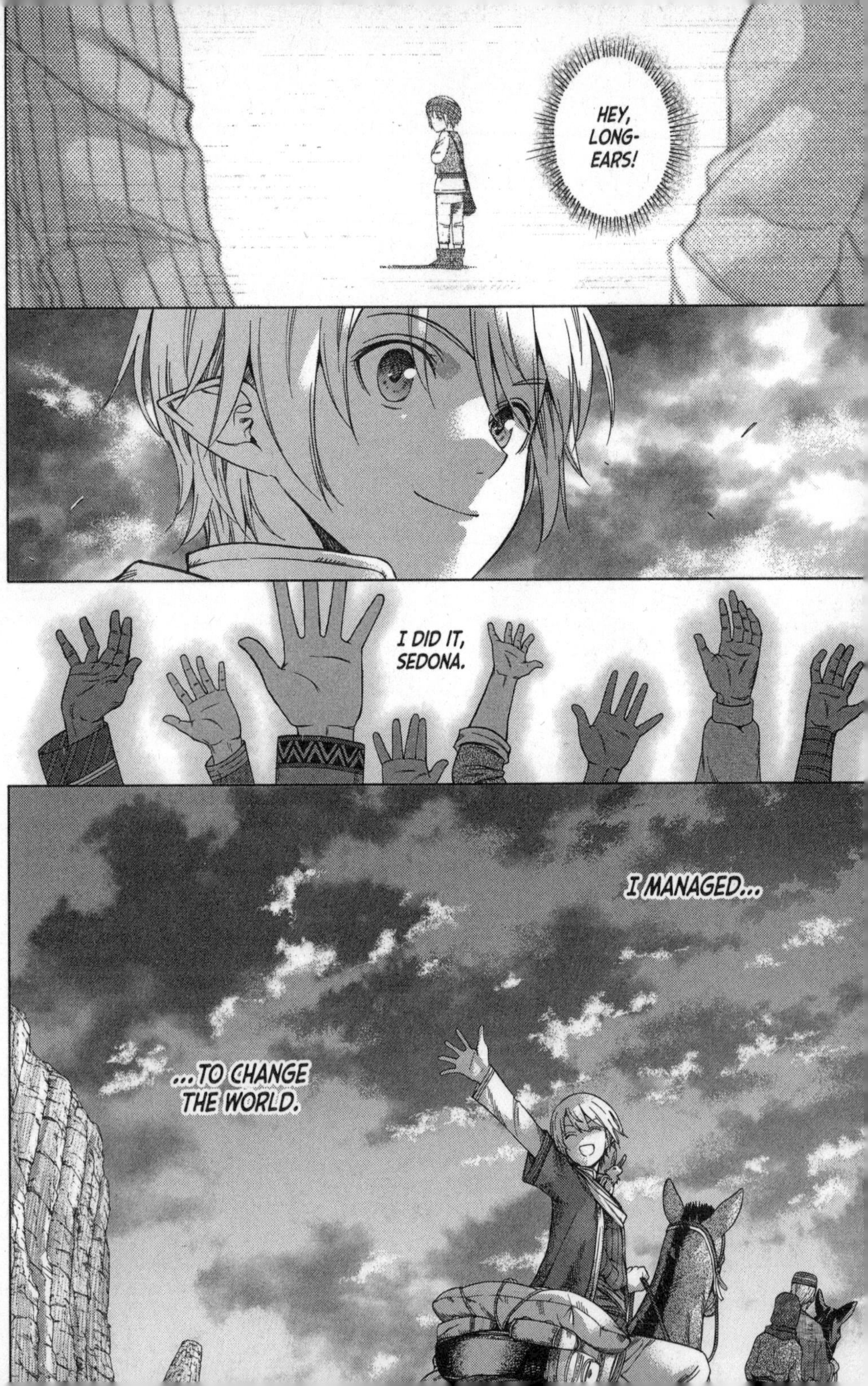
HEY, LONG-EARS!
I DID IT, SEDONA.
I MANAGED...
...TO CHANGE THE WORLD.

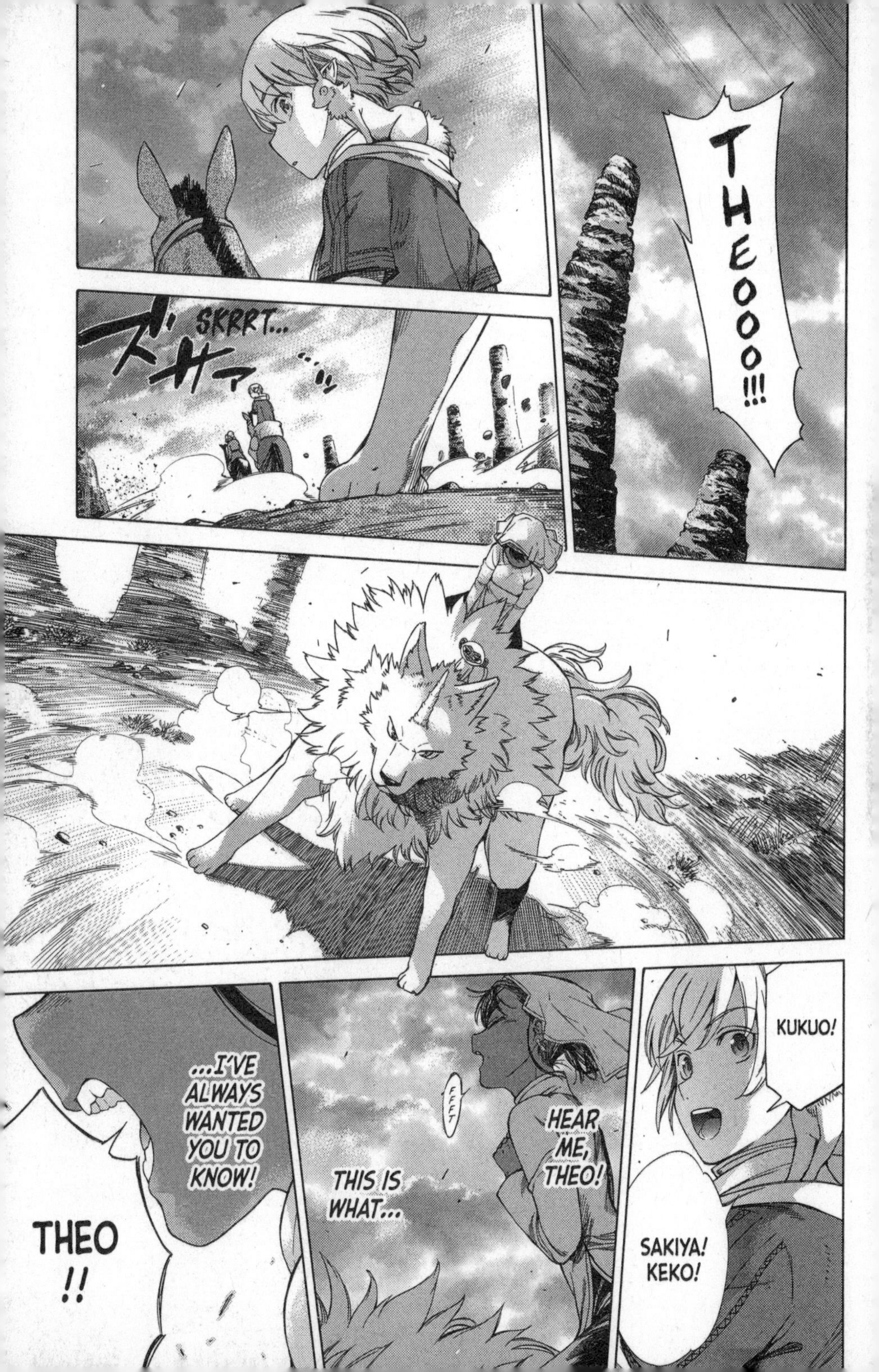
THEOOO!!!
ズサァ
SKRRT...
KUKUO!
SAKIYA! KEKO!
HEAR ME, THEO!
FFFT
THIS IS WHAT...
...I'VE ALWAYS WANTED YOU TO KNOW!
THEO !!

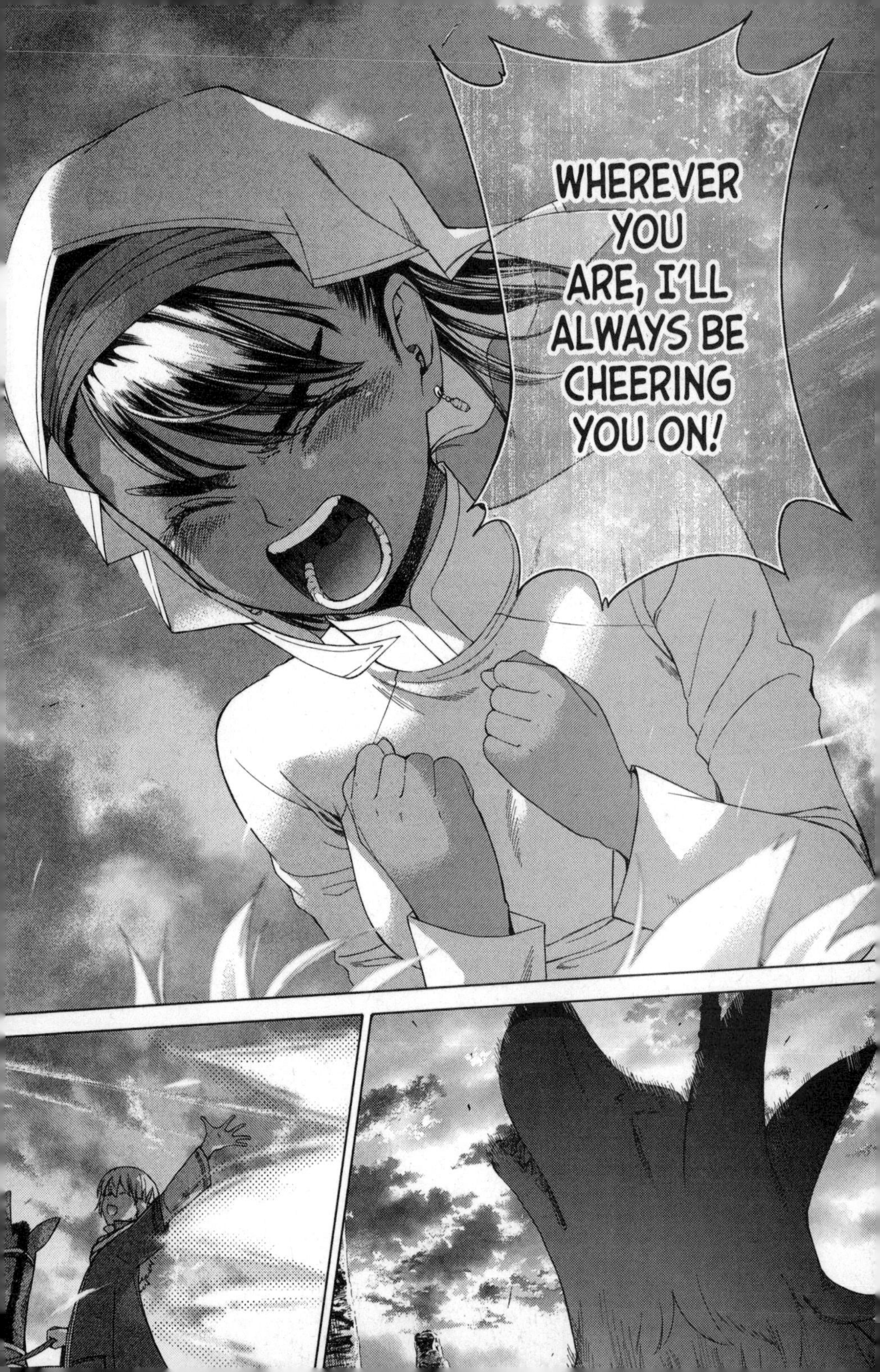
WHEREVER YOU ARE, I'LL ALWAYS BE CHEERING YOU ON!

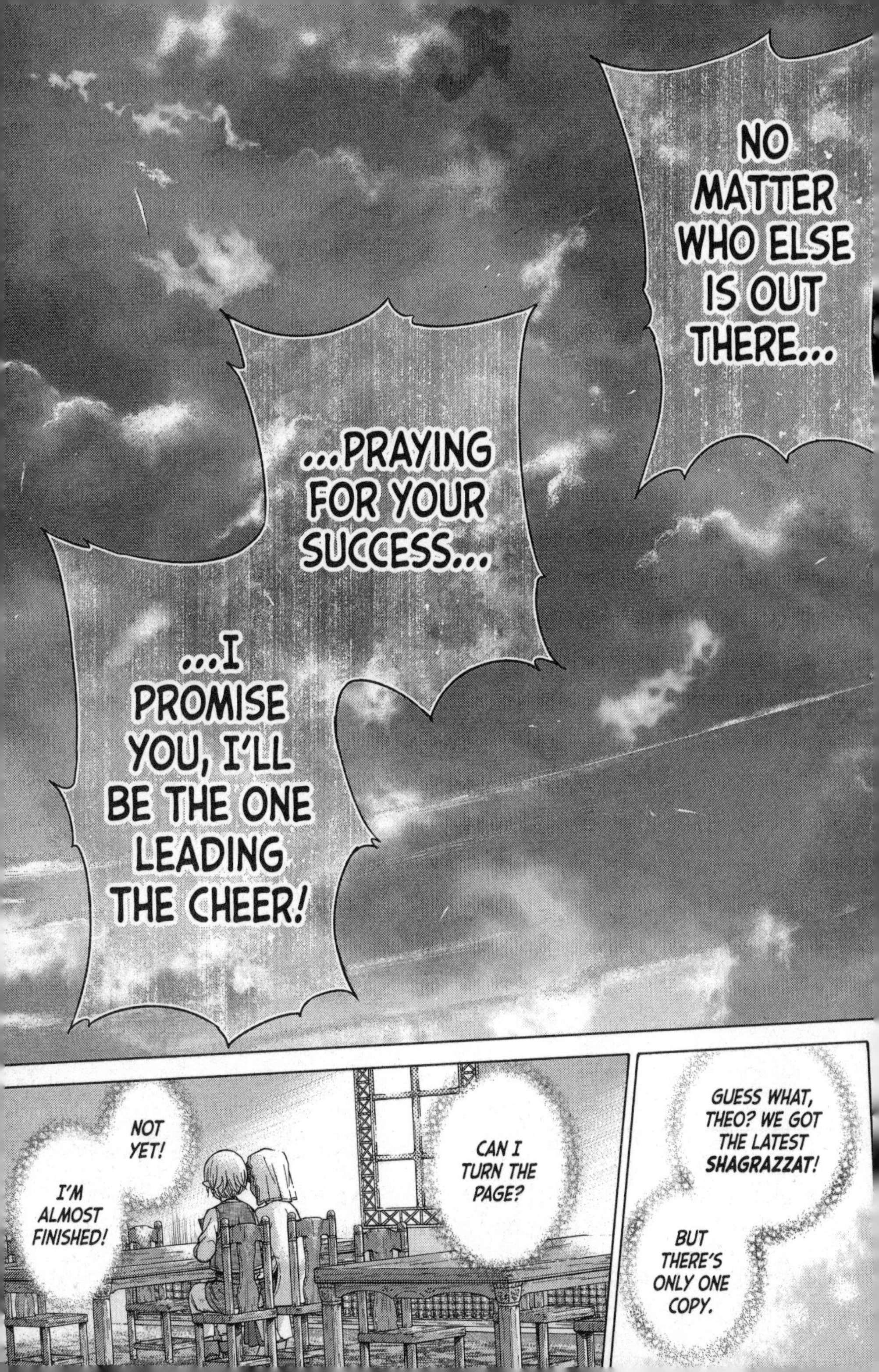
NO MATTER WHO ELSE IS OUT THERE...
...PRAYING FOR YOUR SUCCESS...
...I PROMISE YOU, I'LL BE THE ONE LEADING THE CHEER!
GUESS WHAT, THEO? WE GOT THE LATEST **SHAGRAZZAT**!
BUT THERE'S ONLY ONE COPY.
CAN I TURN THE PAGE?
NOT YET!
I'M ALMOST FINISHED!

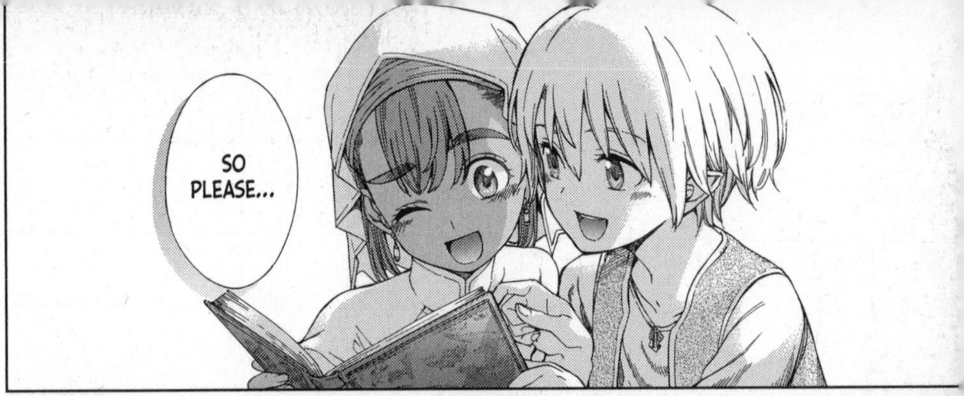
SO PLEASE...

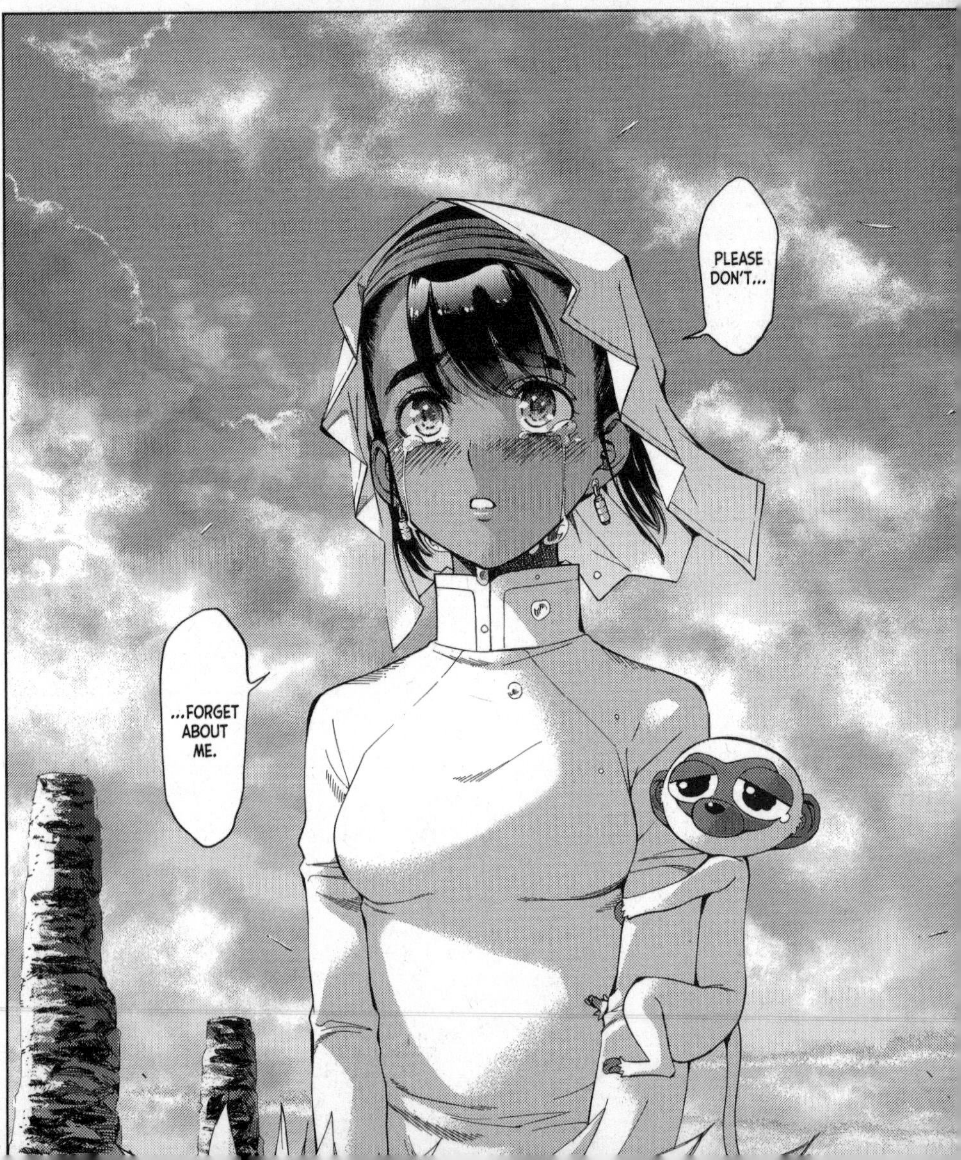
PLEASE DON'T...
...FORGET ABOUT ME.

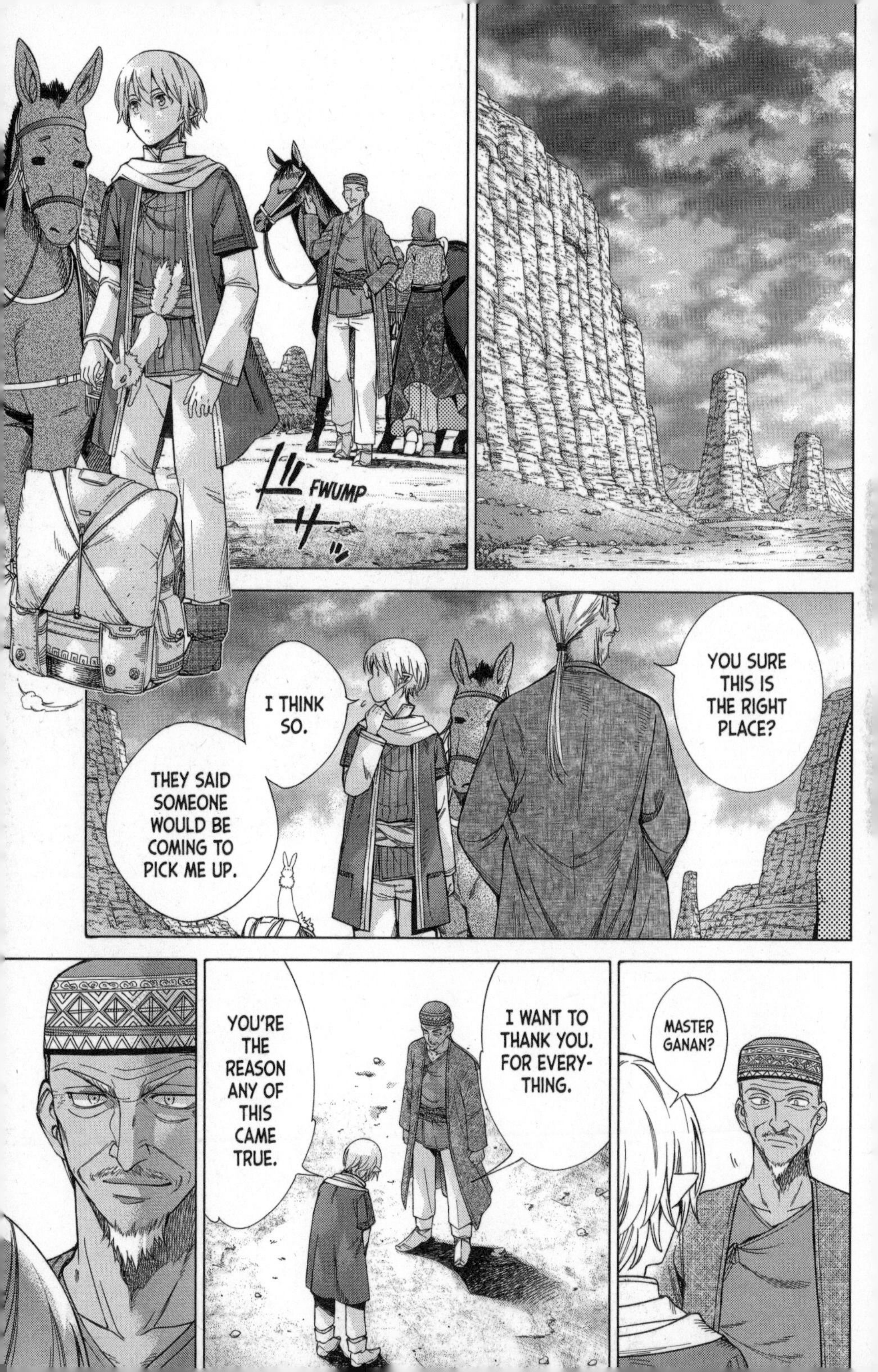
FWUMP
YOU SURE THIS IS THE RIGHT PLACE?
I THINK SO.
THEY SAID SOMEONE WOULD BE COMING TO PICK ME UP.
MASTER GANAN?
I WANT TO THANK YOU. FOR EVERY-THING.
YOU'RE THE REASON ANY OF THIS CAME TRUE.

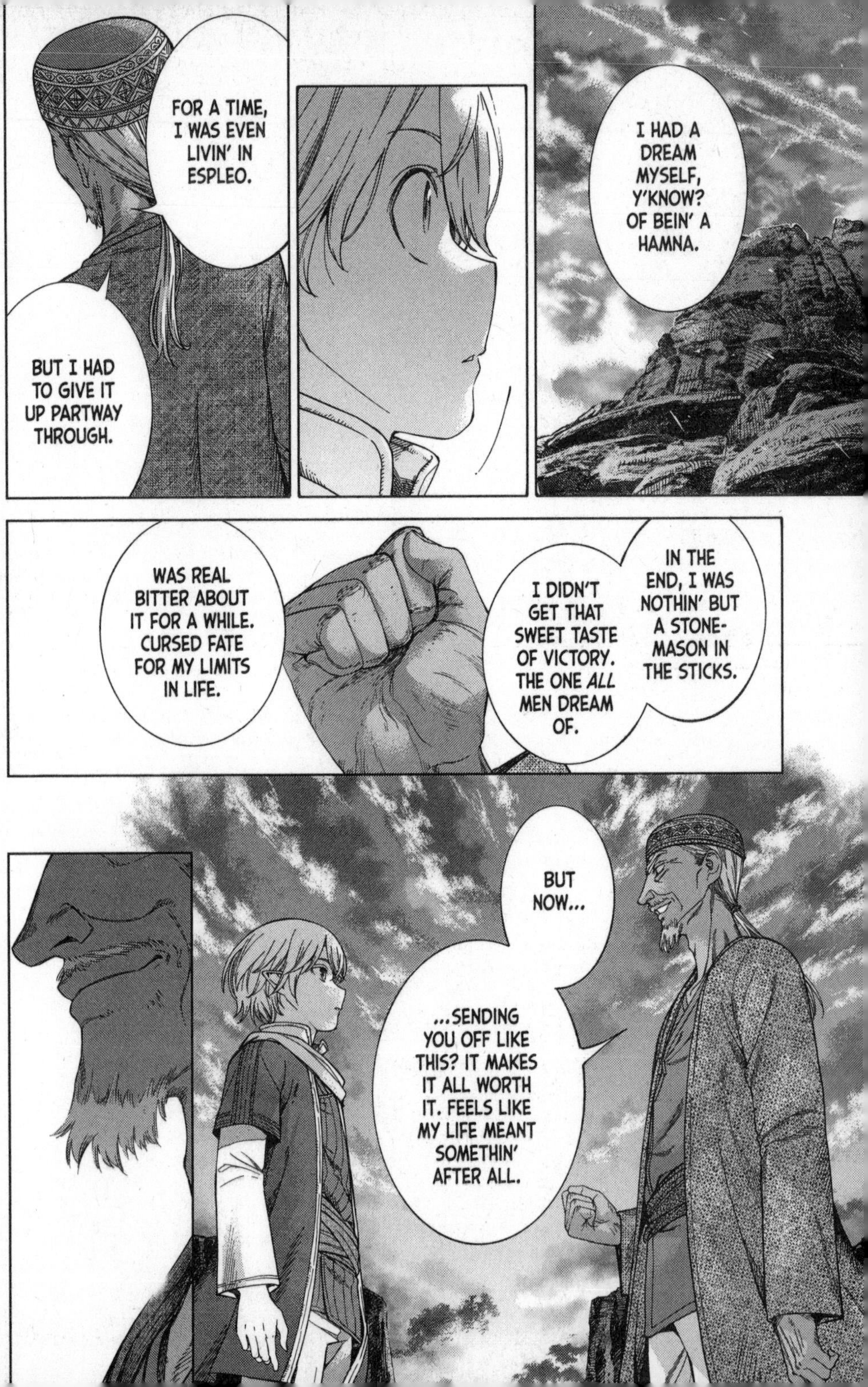
I HAD A DREAM MYSELF, Y'KNOW? OF BEIN' A HAMNA.
FOR A TIME, I WAS EVEN LIVIN' IN ESPLEO.
BUT I HAD TO GIVE IT UP PARTWAY THROUGH.
IN THE END, I WAS NOTHIN' BUT A STONE-MASON IN THE STICKS.
I DIDN'T GET THAT SWEET TASTE OF VICTORY. THE ONE *ALL* MEN DREAM OF.
WAS REAL BITTER ABOUT IT FOR A WHILE. CURSED FATE FOR MY LIMITS IN LIFE.
BUT NOW...
...SENDING YOU OFF LIKE THIS? IT MAKES IT ALL WORTH IT. FEELS LIKE MY LIFE MEANT SOMETHIN' AFTER ALL.

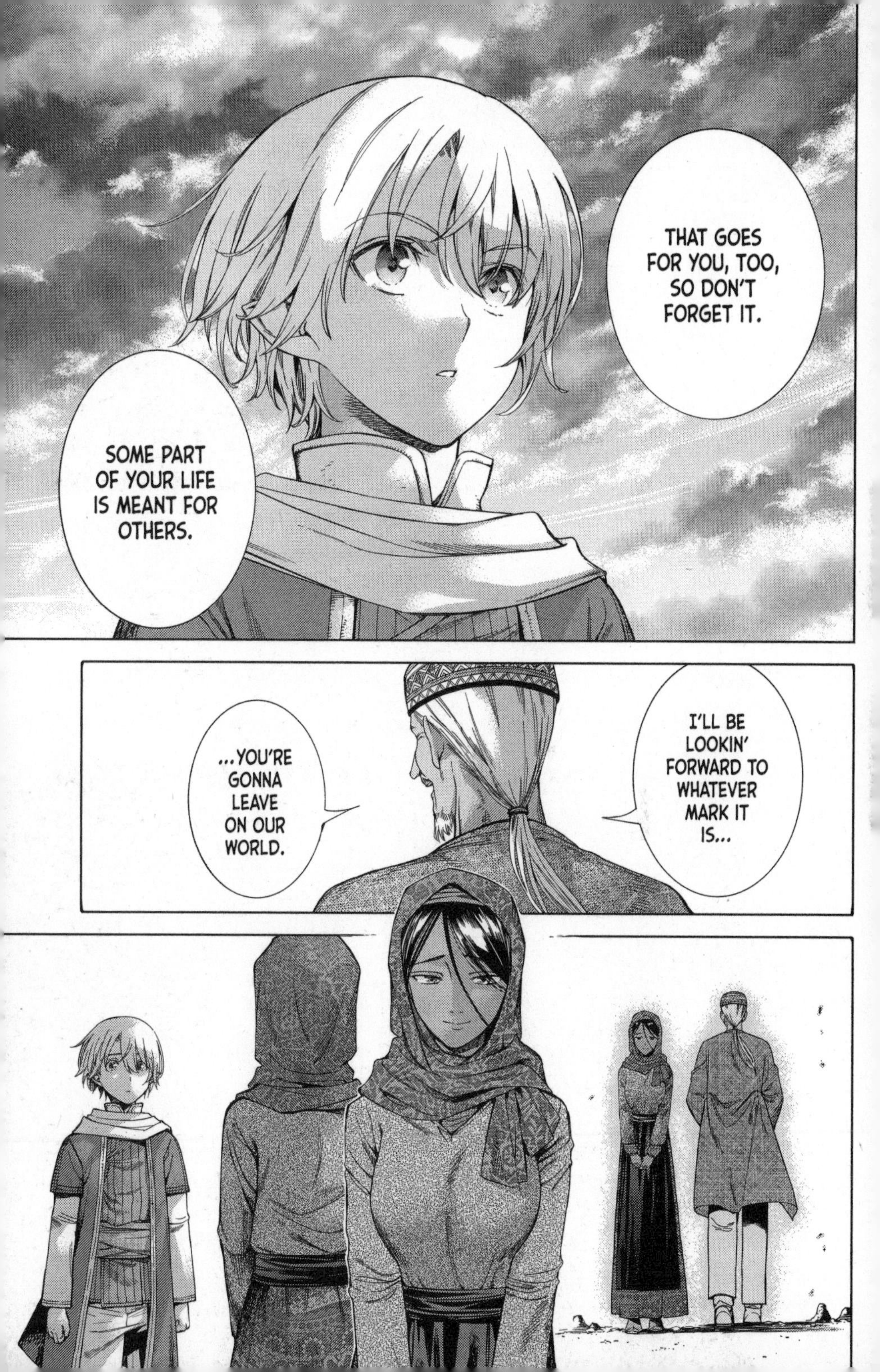
THAT GOES FOR YOU, TOO, SO DON'T FORGET IT.
SOME PART OF YOUR LIFE IS MEANT FOR OTHERS.
I'LL BE LOOKIN' FORWARD TO WHATEVER MARK IT IS...
...YOU'RE GONNA LEAVE ON OUR WORLD.

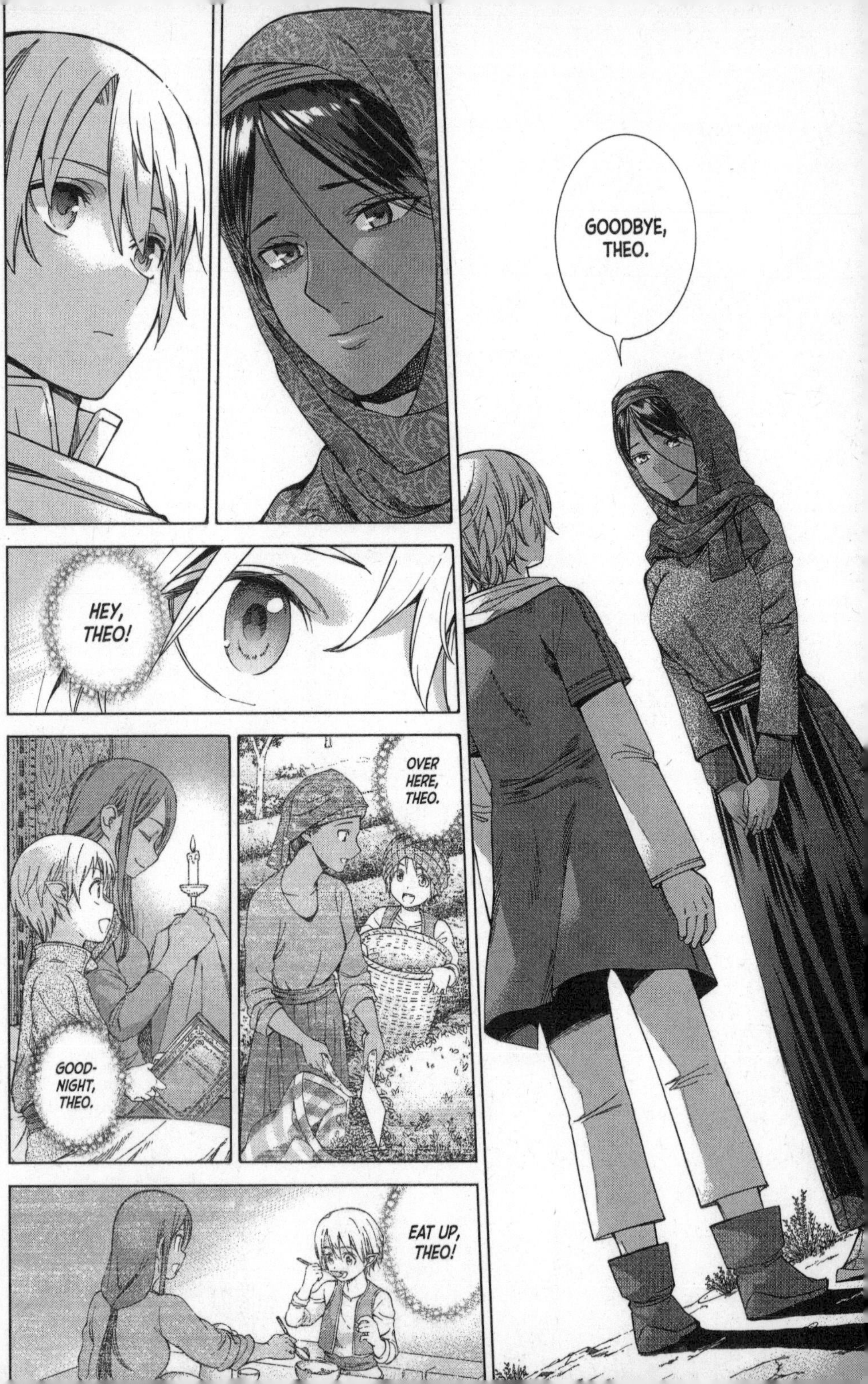
GOODBYE, THEO.
HEY, THEO!
OVER HERE, THEO.
GOOD-NIGHT, THEO.
EAT UP, THEO!

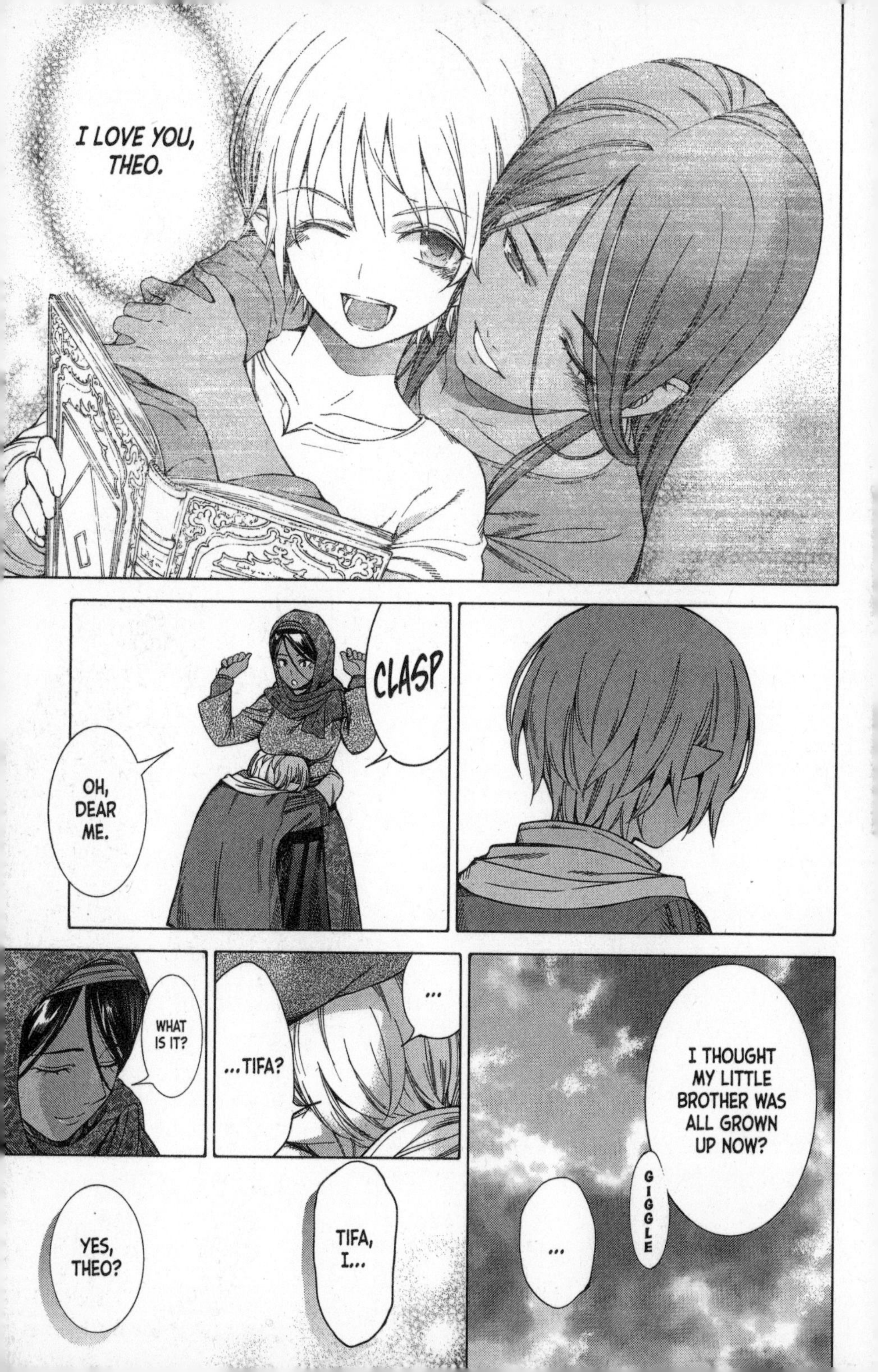
I LOVE YOU, THEO.
CLASP
OH, DEAR ME.
I THOUGHT MY LITTLE BROTHER WAS ALL GROWN UP NOW?
GIGGLE
...
...
...TIFA?
WHAT IS IT?
TIFA, I...
YES, THEO?

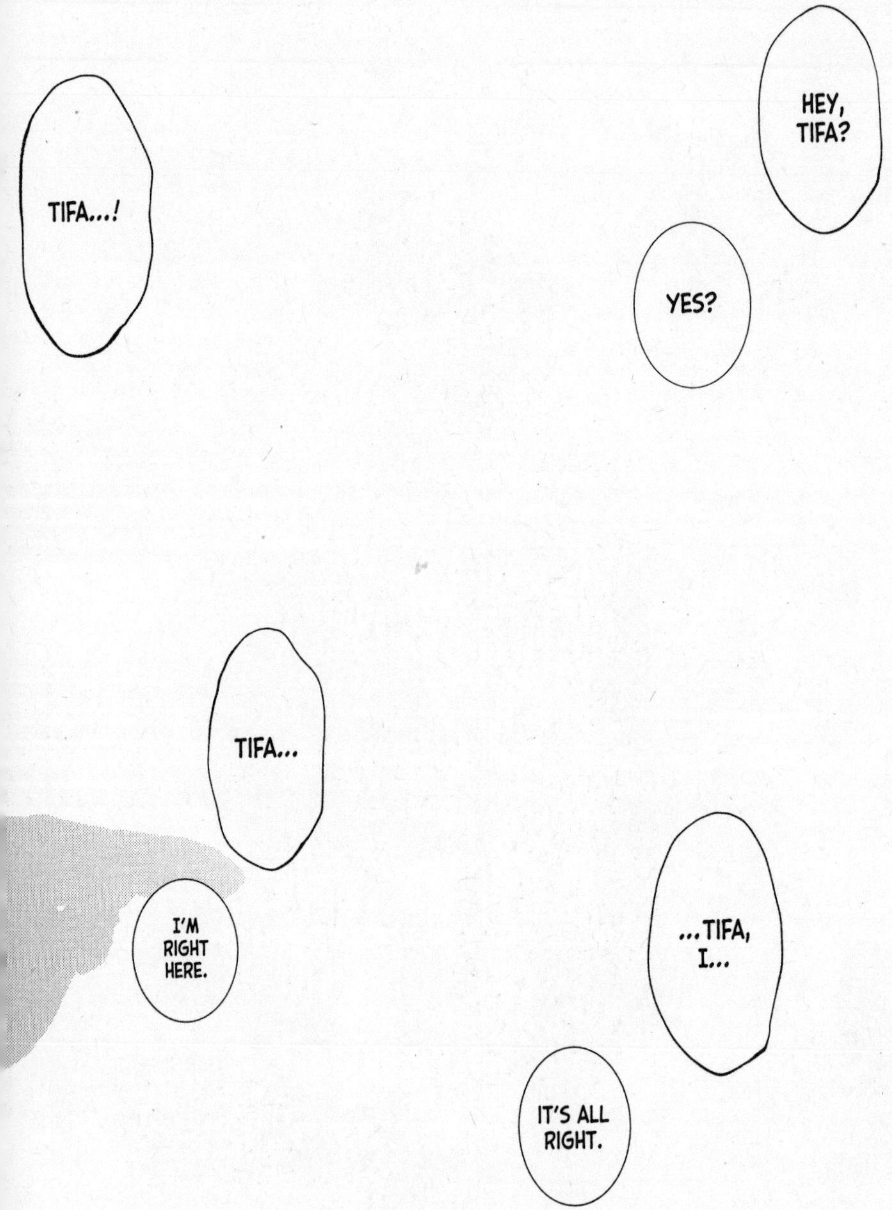
HEY, TIFA?
YES?
TIFA...!
TIFA...
I'M RIGHT HERE.
...TIFA, I...
IT'S ALL RIGHT.

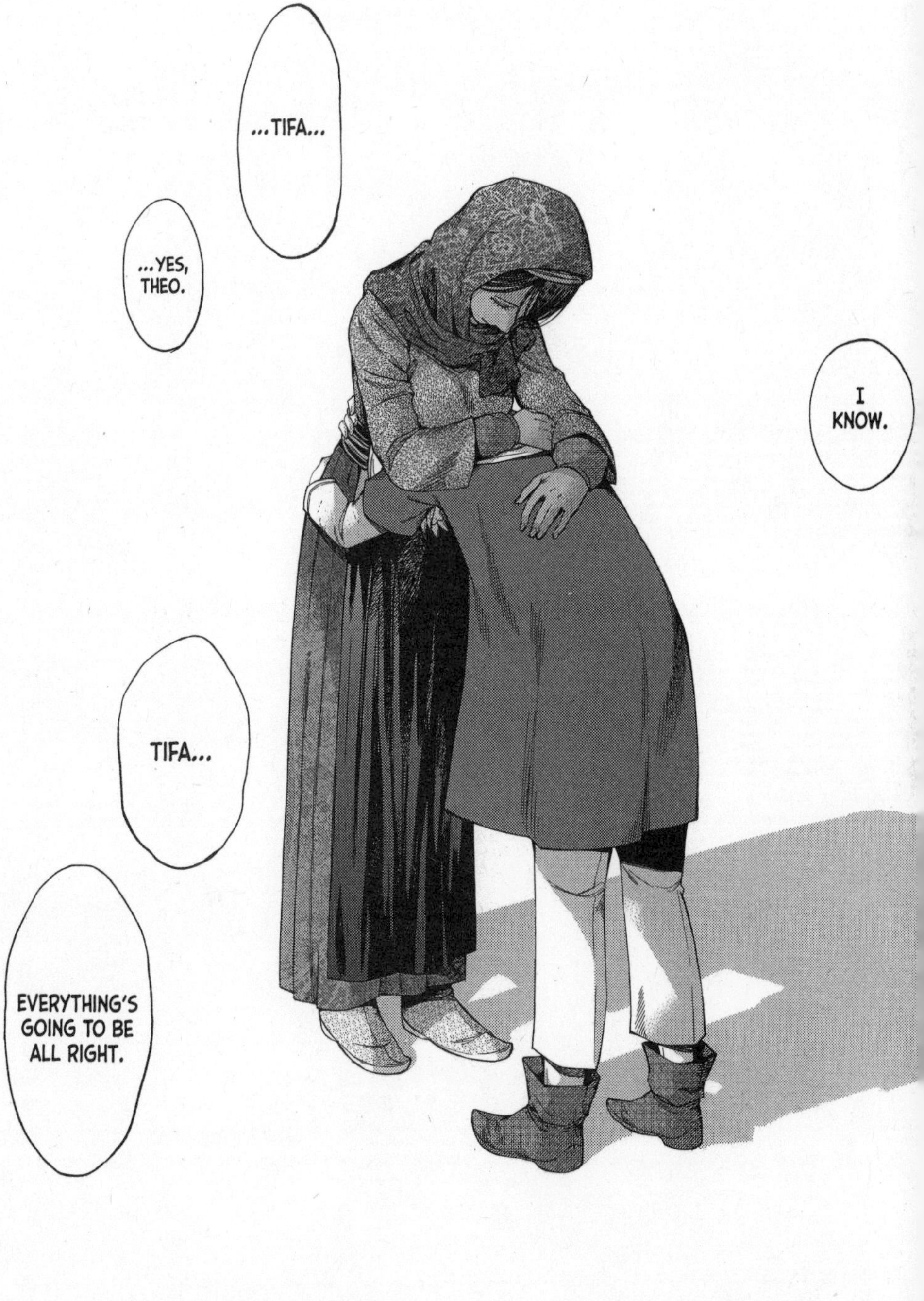
...TIFA...
...YES, THEO.
I KNOW.
TIFA...
EVERYTHING'S GOING TO BE ALL RIGHT.

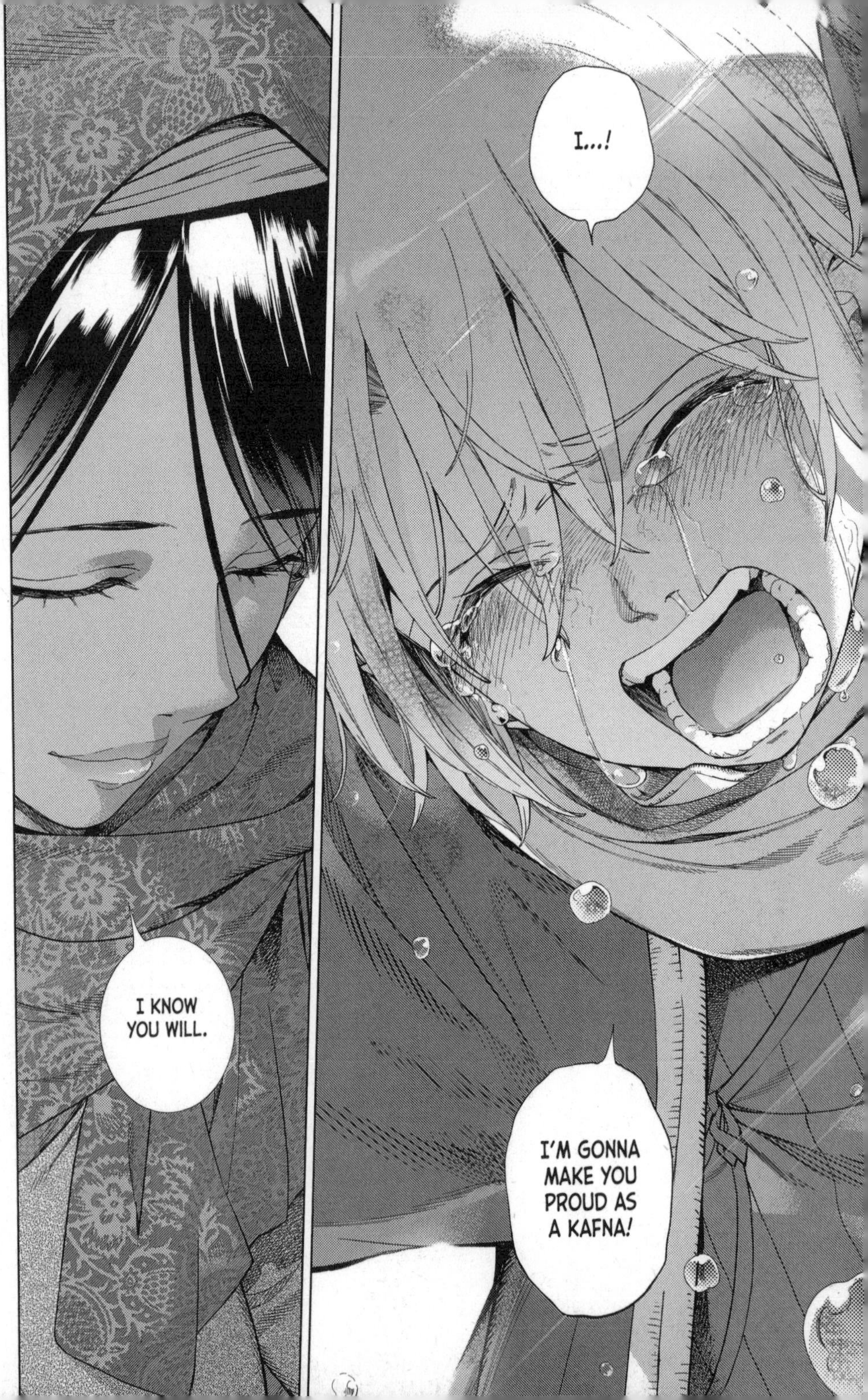
I...!
I'M GONNA MAKE YOU PROUD AS A KAFNA!
I KNOW YOU WILL.

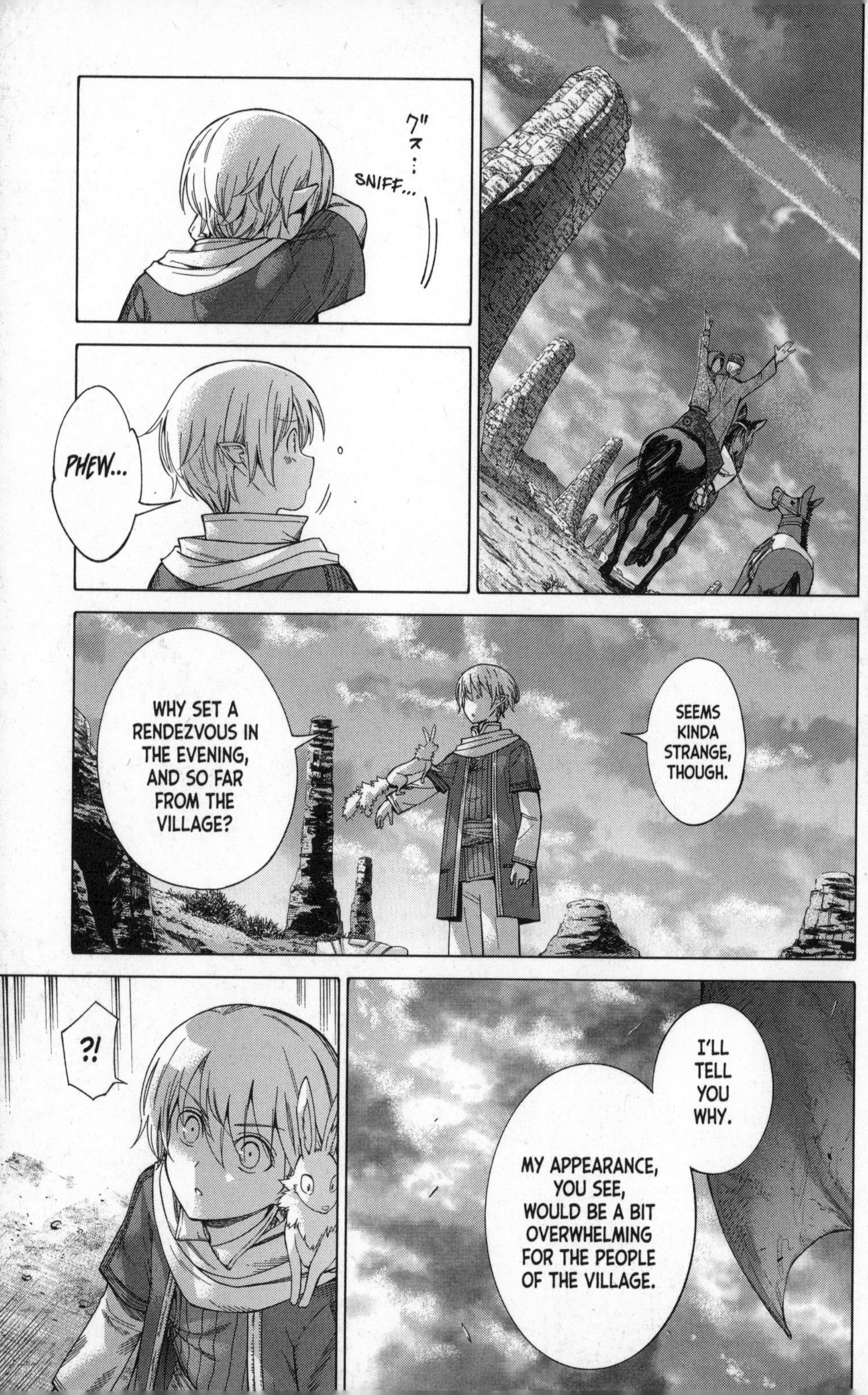
グス…
SNIFF…
PHEW…
SEEMS KINDA STRANGE, THOUGH.
WHY SET A RENDEZVOUS IN THE EVENING, AND SO FAR FROM THE VILLAGE?
I'LL TELL YOU WHY.
MY APPEARANCE, YOU SEE, WOULD BE A BIT OVERWHELMING FOR THE PEOPLE OF THE VILLAGE.
?!

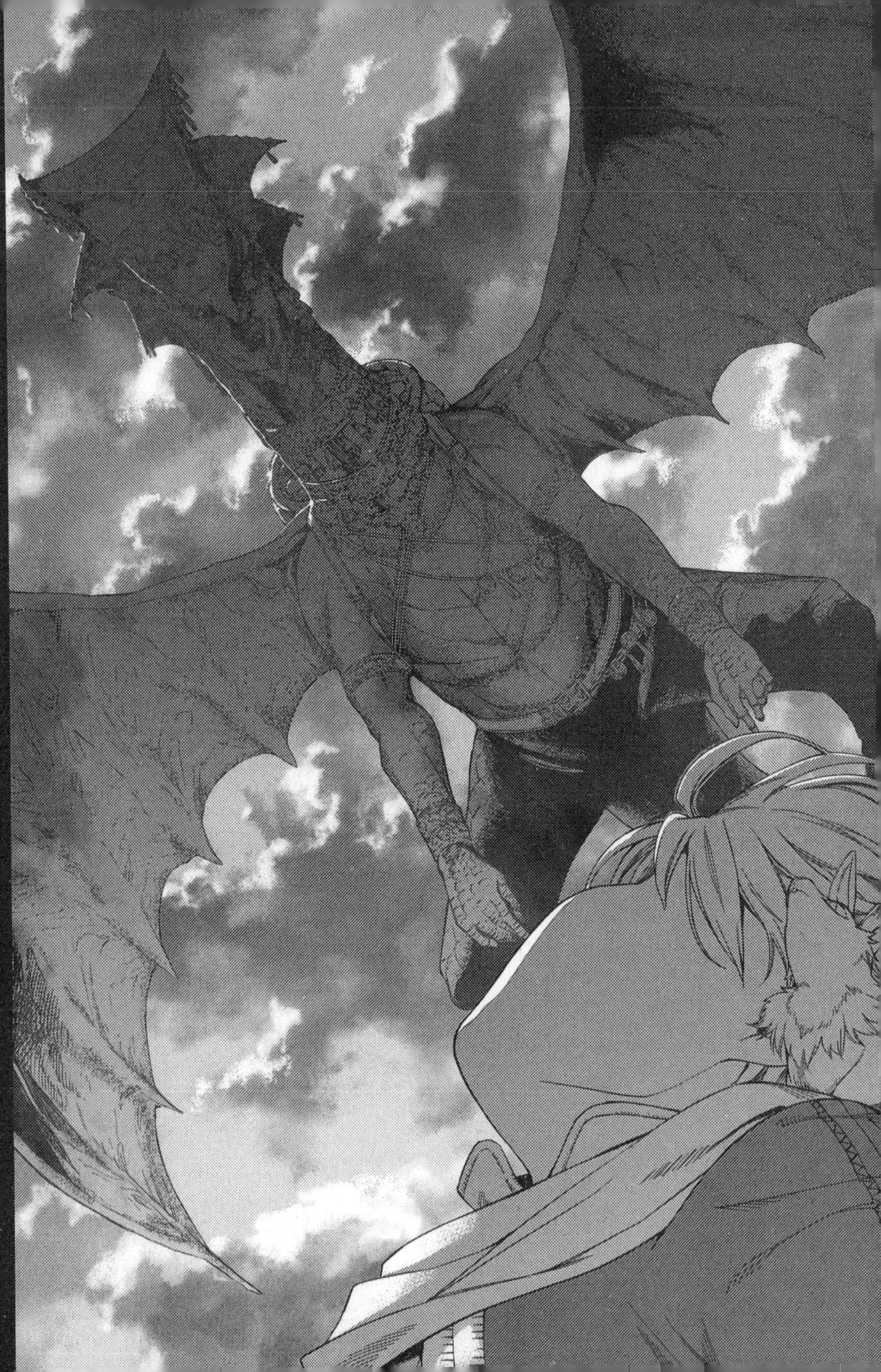

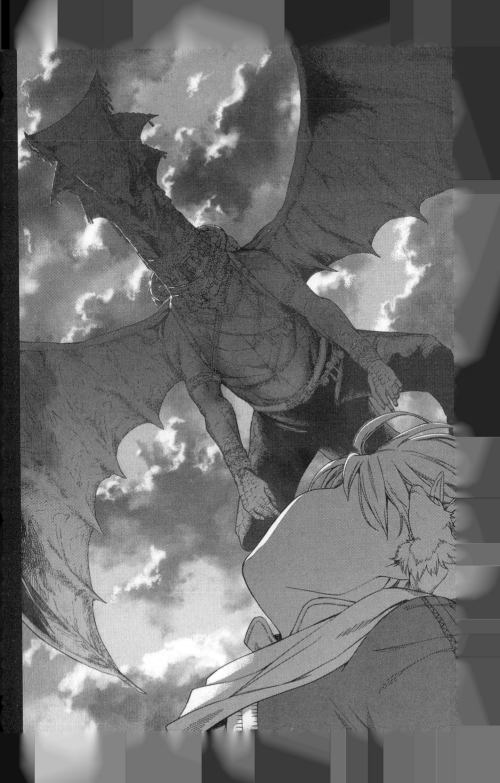

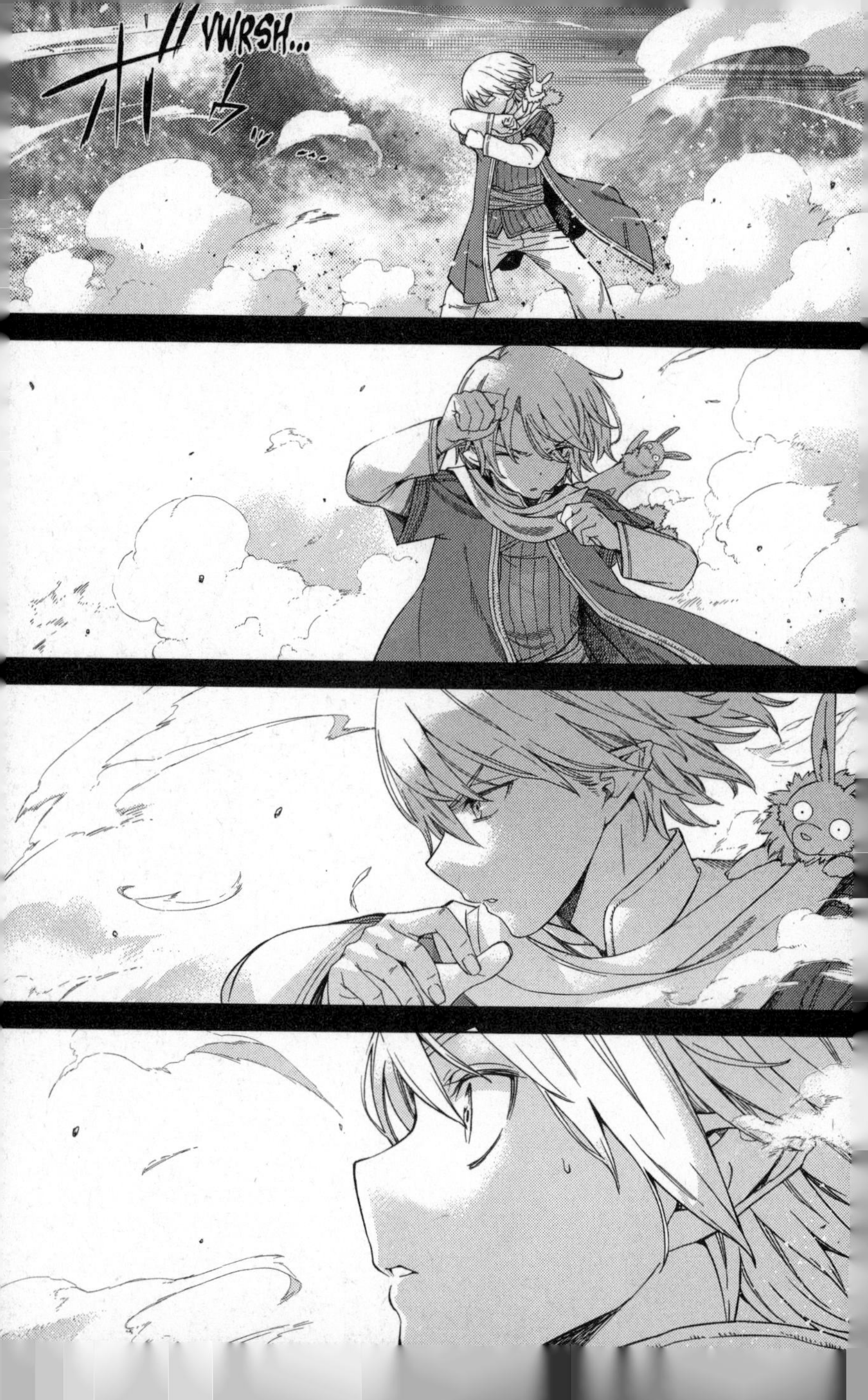
VWRSH...

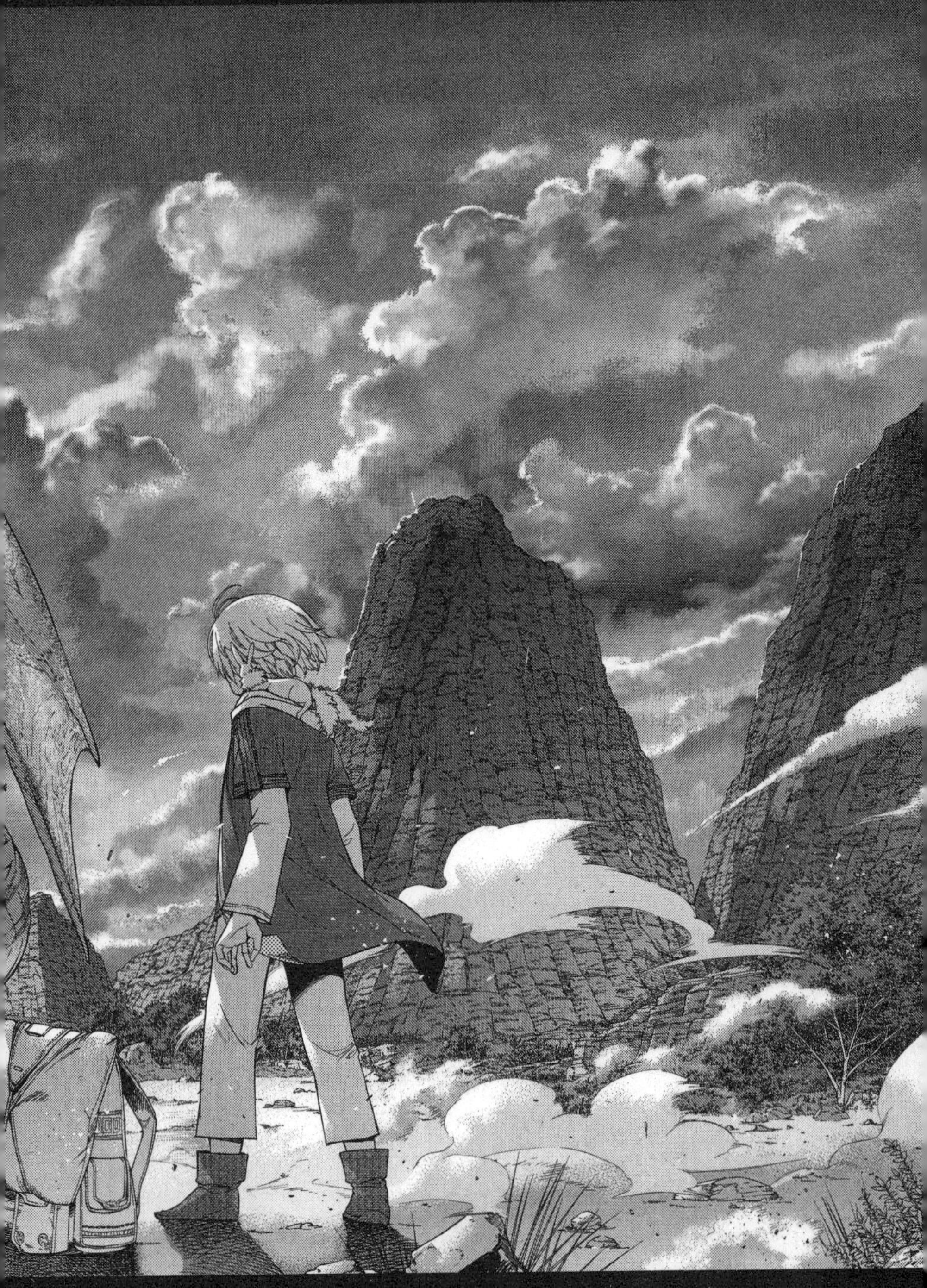

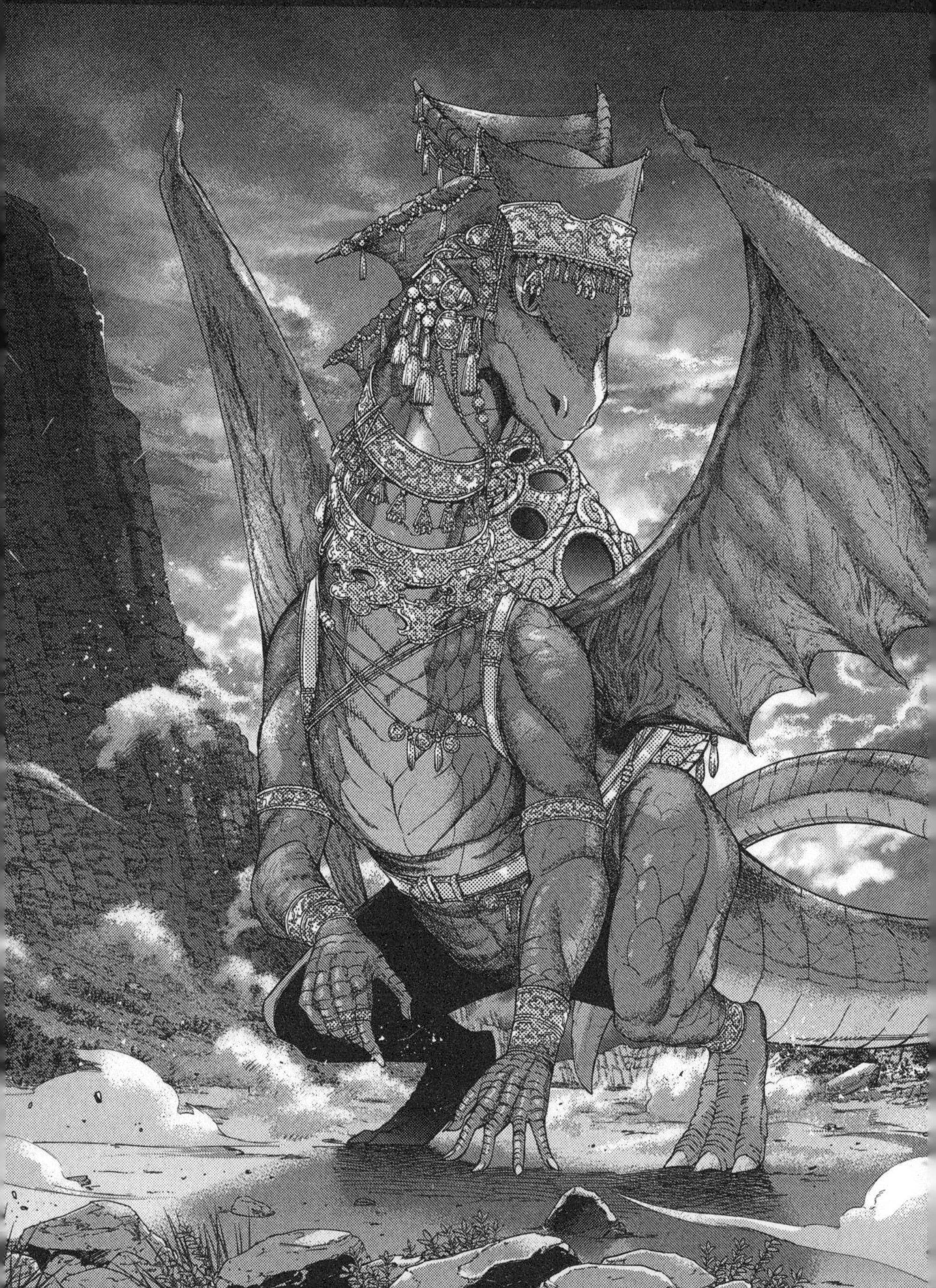

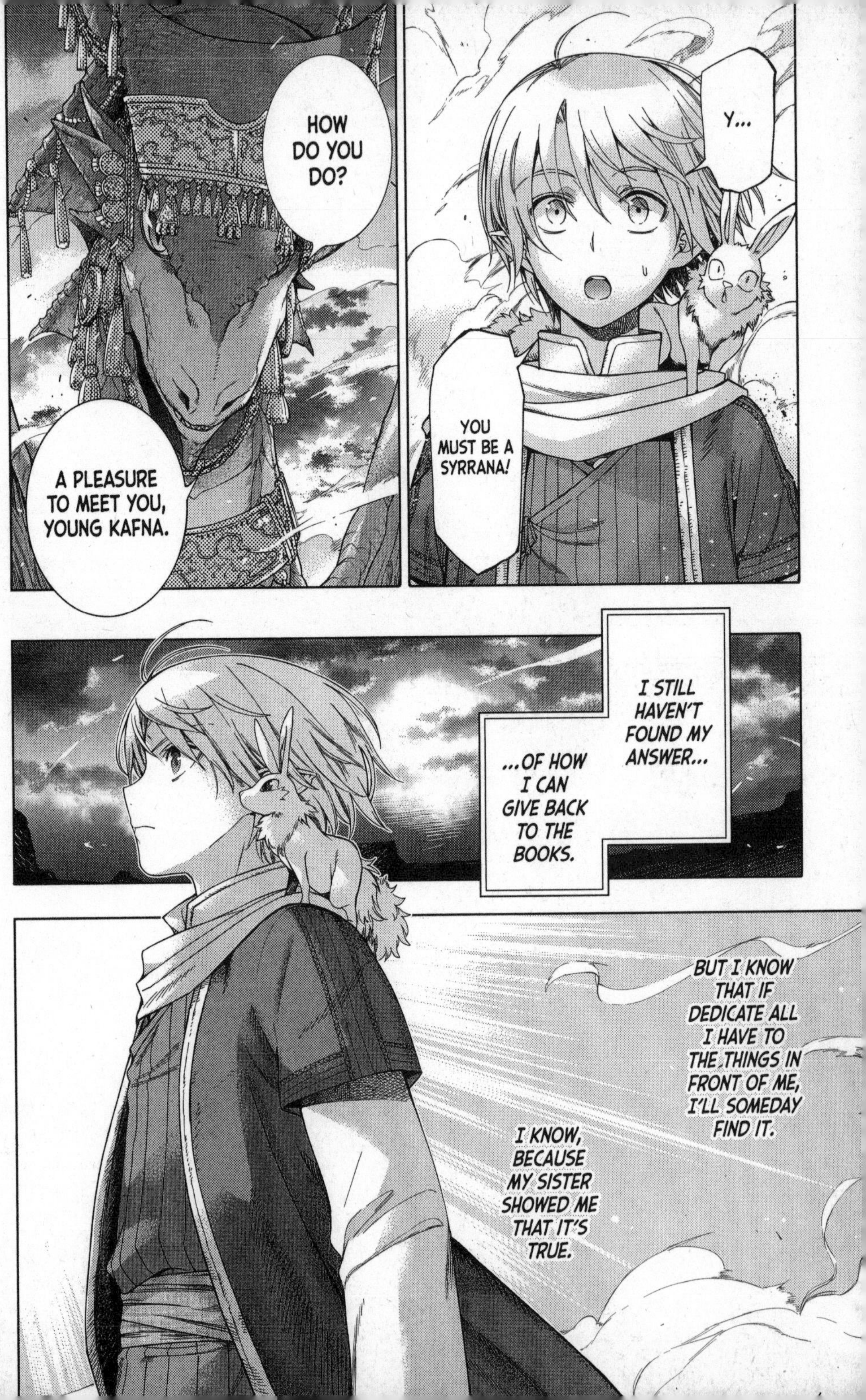
Y...
YOU MUST BE A SYRRANA!
HOW DO YOU DO?
A PLEASURE TO MEET YOU, YOUNG KAFNA.
I STILL HAVEN'T FOUND MY ANSWER...
...OF HOW I CAN GIVE BACK TO THE BOOKS.
BUT I KNOW THAT IF DEDICATE ALL I HAVE TO THE THINGS IN FRONT OF ME, I'LL SOMEDAY FIND IT.
I KNOW, BECAUSE MY SISTER SHOWED ME THAT IT'S TRUE.

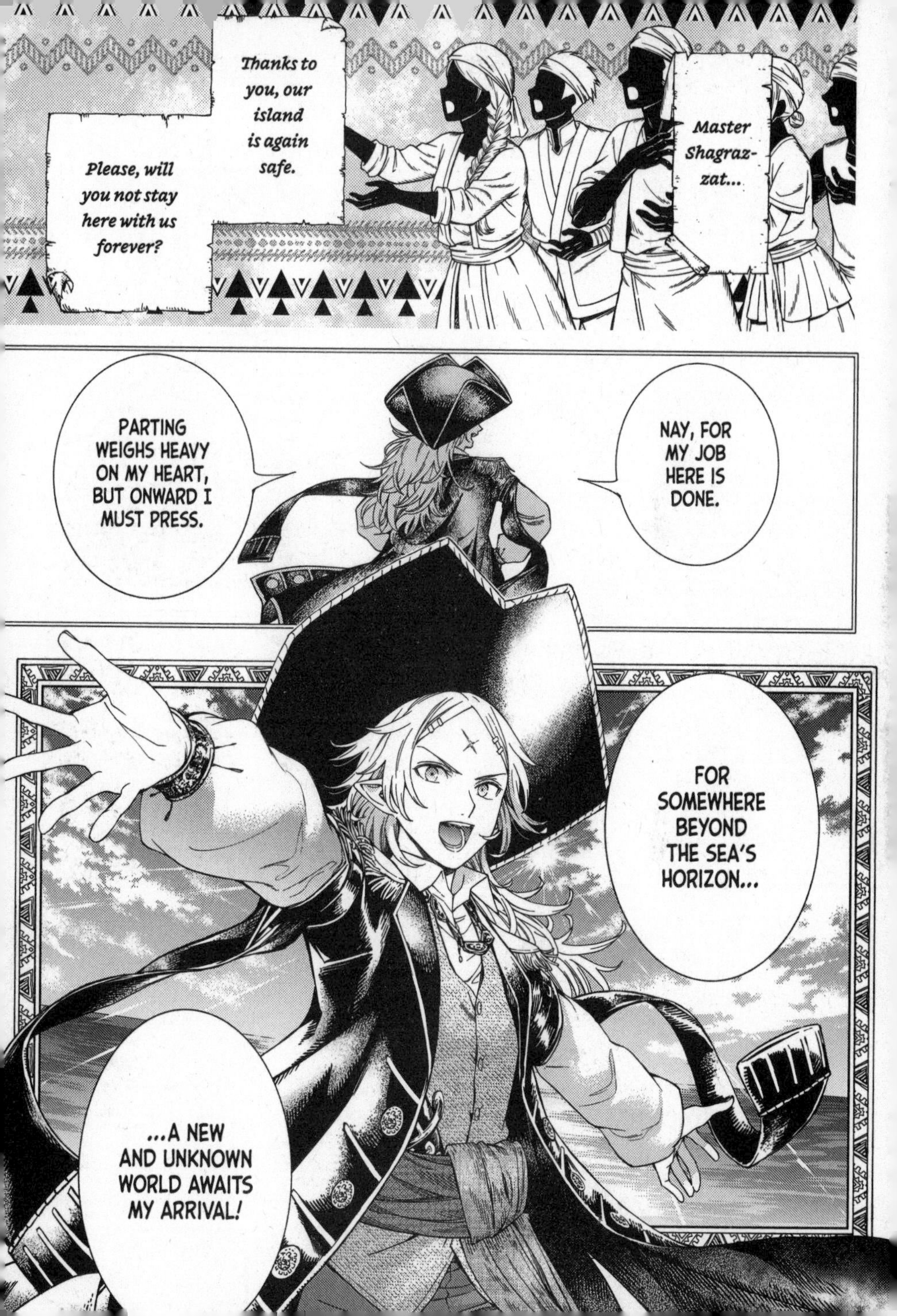
Master Shagrazzat...
Thanks to you, our island is again safe.
Please, will you not stay here with us forever?
NAY, FOR MY JOB HERE IS DONE.
PARTING WEIGHS HEAVY ON MY HEART, BUT ONWARD I MUST PRESS.
FOR SOMEWHERE BEYOND THE SEA'S HORIZON...
...A NEW AND UNKNOWN WORLD AWAITS MY ARRIVAL!

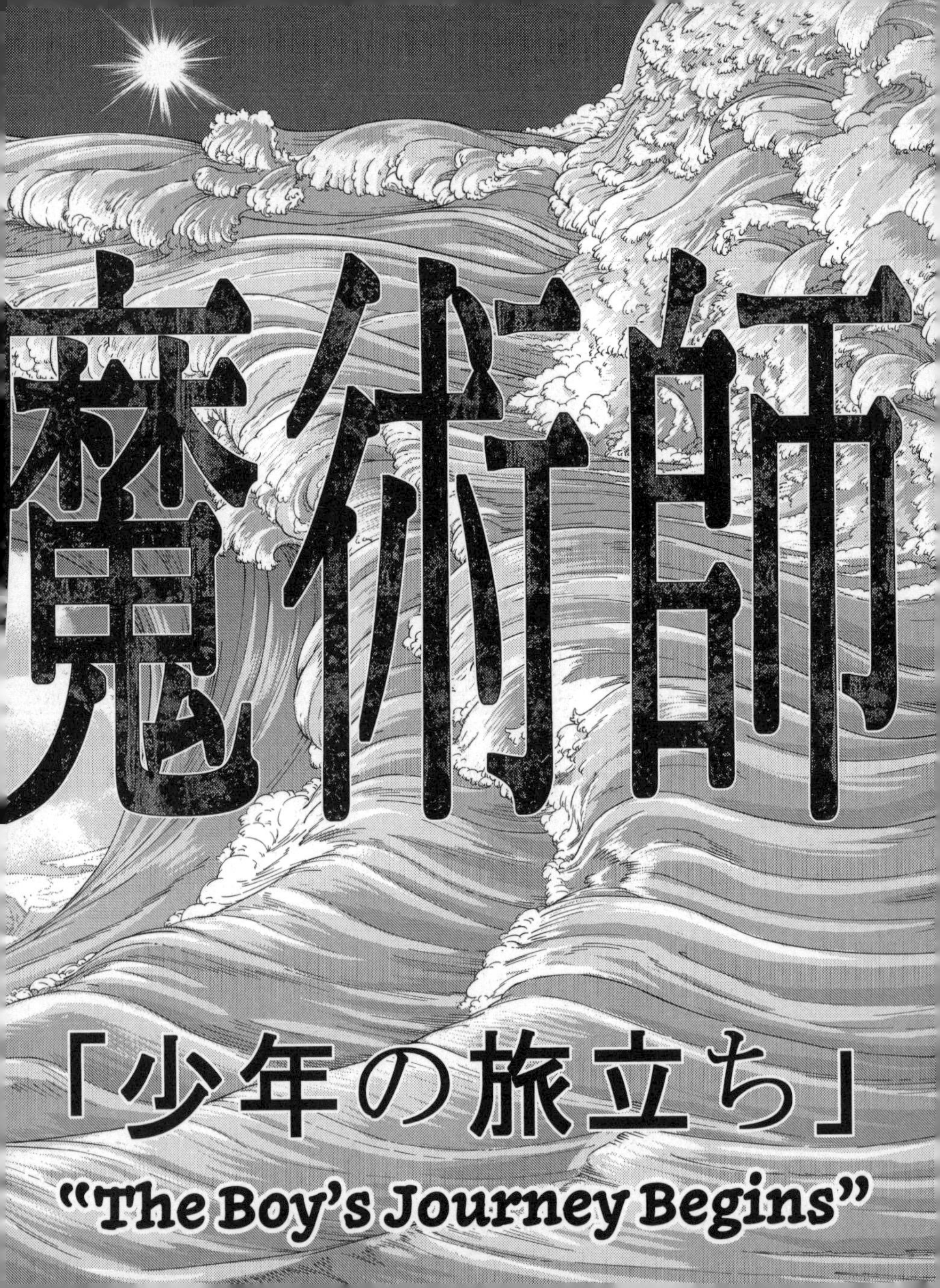
魔術師
「少年の旅立ち」
“The Boy’s Journey Begins”

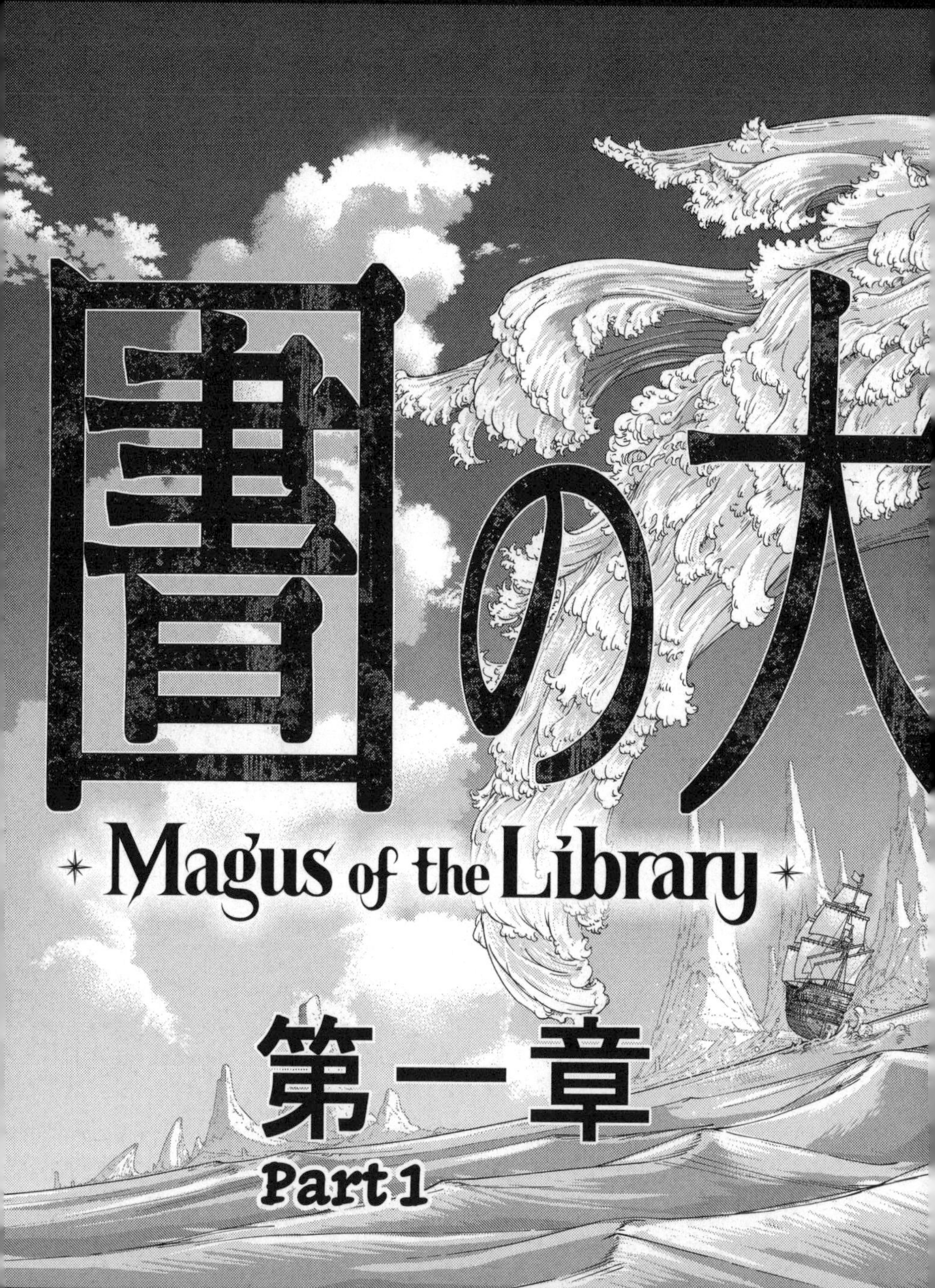
圕の大
Magus of the Library
第一章
Part 1

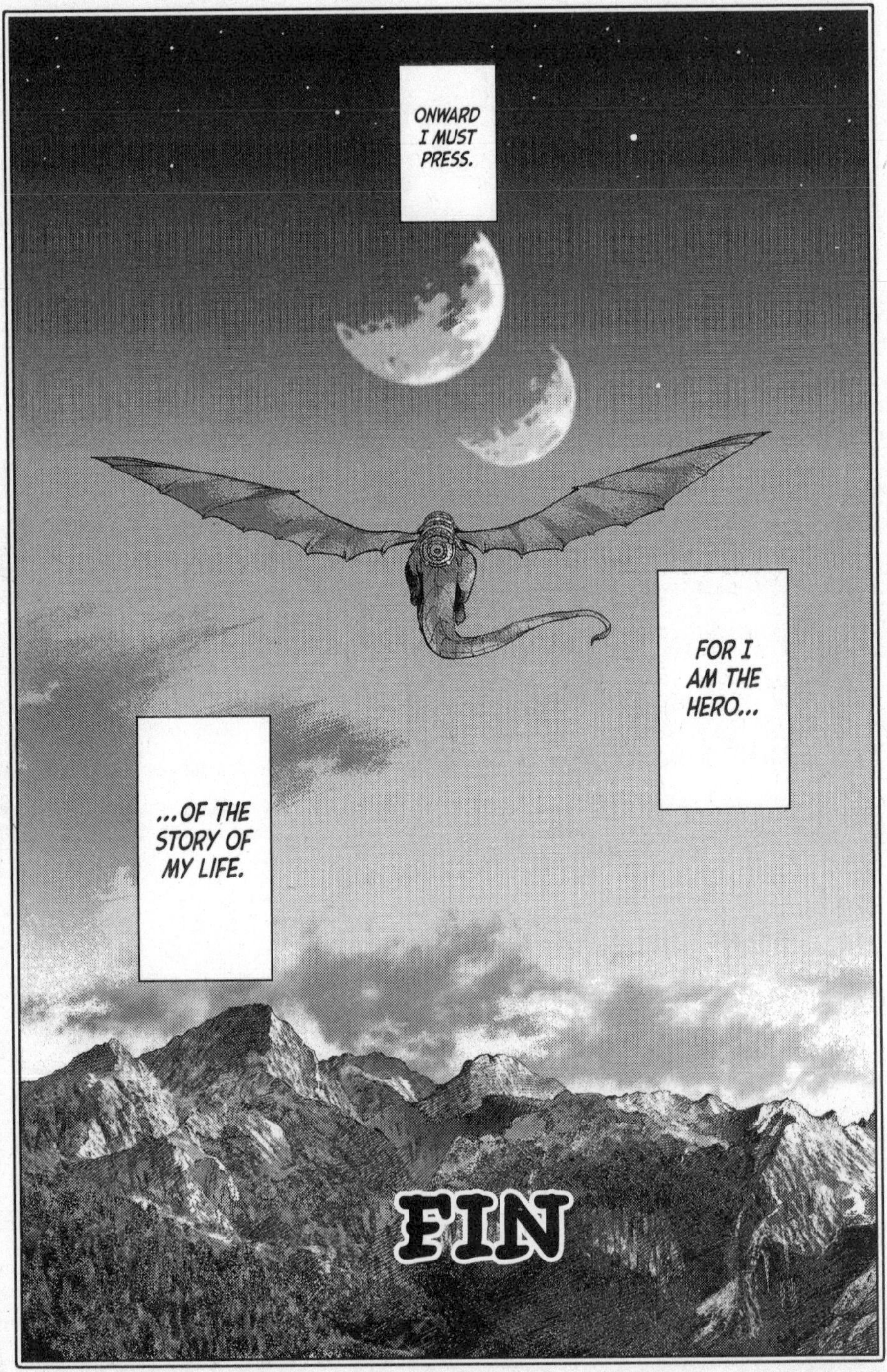
ONWARD I MUST PRESS.
FOR I AM THE HERO...
...OF THE STORY OF MY LIFE.
FIN

To be continued.

Magus of the Library

A Kodansha Comics Trade Paperback Original
Magus of the Library 3 copyright © 2019 Mitsu Izumi
English translation copyright © 2020 Mitsu Izumi

Published in the United States by Kodansha Comics, an imprint of Kodansha USA Publishing, LLC, New York.

Publication rights for this English edition arranged through Kodansha Ltd., Tokyo.

First published in Japan in 2019 by Kodansha Ltd., Tokyo as *Toshokan no daimajutsushi*, volume 3.

ISBN 978-1-63236-846-1

Printed in the United States of America.

www.kodanshacomics.com

9 8 7 6 5 4 3 2 1
Translation: Stephen Kohler
Lettering: Paige Pumphrey
Editing: Paul Starr, Lauren Scanlan
Kodansha Comics edition cover design by Phil Balsman

Publisher: Kiichiro Sugawara
Vice president of marketing & publicity: Naho Yamada

Director of publishing services: Ben Applegate
Associate director of operations: Stephen Pakula
Publishing services managing editor: Noelle Webster
Assistant production manager: Emi Lotto, Angela Zurlo